WHY THE EU]
UNION FA
IN AFGHANISTAN

Transatlantic Relations and the Return of the Taliban

Oz Hassan

BRISTOL
UNIVERSITY
PRESS

First published in Great Britain in 2024 by

Bristol University Press
University of Bristol
1–9 Old Park Hill
Bristol
BS2 8BB
UK
t: +44 (0)117 374 6645
e: bup-info@bristol.ac.uk

Details of international sales and distribution partners are available at bristoluniversitypress.co.uk

© Bristol University Press 2024

British Library Cataloguing in Publication Data
A catalogue record for this book is available from the British Library

ISBN 978-1-5292-4073-3 hardcover
ISBN 978-1-5292-4074-0 paperback
ISBN 978-1-5292-4075-7 ePub
ISBN 978-1-5292-4076-4 ePdf

The right of Oz Hassan to be identified as author of this work has been asserted by him in accordance with the Copyright, Designs and Patents Act 1988.

Cover design: Hayes Design and Advertising
Front cover image: Alamy/Vladislav Mitic
Bristol University Press uses environmentally responsible print partners.
Printed and bound in Great Britain by CPI Group (UK) Ltd, Croydon, CR0 4YY

FSC
www.fsc.org
MIX
Paper | Supporting
responsible forestry
FSC® C013604

Clare, Talisker and Isla.
I cannot express in words what
you mean to me.
Thank you for your love, patience and
encouragement to do hard things.

Contents

List of Figures and Tables

Figures

Tables

Acknowledgements

I never intended to write this book. So, as it makes its way into the world, I hope you see it as a fortunate accident. In 2009 I was lucky enough to have a fellowship on the Seventh framework programme (FP7) Changing Multilateralism: The EU as a Global-regional Actor in Security and Peace (EU:GRASP) project, where I was asked to write a case study on the European Union (EU)'s approach to Afghanistan. Seeing that there was relatively little academic literature on this I took a first stab at putting together a case study that I then proceeded to quietly work on over the next decade. I managed to eventually get this published, after multiple rejections from lots of journals. Through sheer persistence, and the involvement of excellent editors, I found it a home in *European Security*. I had imagined that that would rather be the end of it. However, not long after its publication along with some shorter pieces, I was asked by the European Parliament to write their study into what had gone wrong in Afghanistan. To do that I needed to revisit the nearly 15 years of research I had accumulated on this subject, and was granted access to interview key EU policy makers that participated in developing EU policy in Afghanistan. I was also able to draw on my friends and colleagues in Kabul, and across the Atlantic. To all the people involved in helping me put that study together, I am in your debt, and cannot thank you enough. You not only helped me with the study but demonstrated the need for this book and an academically rigorous account. That is what I hope this volume provides. Yet, knowing who to thank first is a difficult task, given the length of this project and the accidental twists and turns in getting here.

However, I want to particularly acknowledge and thank Ambassador Jean-François Cautain, who was was kind enough to be interviewed on multiple occasions, staff at SIGAR who provided insights that allowed me to pull the international study together, and the many anonymous interviewees cited in this monograph and the study for the European Parliament's Foreign Affairs Committee. In addition Michal Malovec at the Policy Department for External Relations; Sonia Chabane at TEPSA; Caitlyn Scott, and Rachel Cato-Tyson who acted as my undergraduate research assistants at Warwick; and Fahad Al-Marri, Shiyu Lui, Andrew Rizzo, Mingyi Liu and Thais Doria.

I would also like to thank Inderjeet Parmar and Stephen Burman for being amazing role models and mentors over the years; I can't put in words what your support has meant to me.

I also need to especially thank my colleagues on EU:GRASP. Led by Luk Van Langenhove, this book would not have been written without his input in those early years. This is also true of Stuart Croft, George Christou and Richard Youngs at Warwick. At Gothenburg, Fredrik Söderbaum and Michael Schulz. Sonia Lucarelli at Bologna, and Joel Peters at Virginia Tech. I hope this book reflects the intellectual environment you all contributed to and that our paths may cross again someday soon. Straight after this project I was fortunate enough to be invite to the Carnegie Endowment for International Peace in Washington, DC. This was a very formative period, and I would like to thank Thomas Carothers for helping me understand Washington policy making and allowing me to start my junior academic career surrounded by such support and compassionate leadership. Indeed, returning to Warwick, I need to thank Richard Aldrich, Shaun Breslin, Matthew Clayton, Madeleine Fagan, Chris Hughes, Tom Long, Gabrielle Lynch, Chris Moran, Akinyemi Oyawale, Nicola Pratt, Ben Richardson, Nick Vaughan Williams and Matthew Watson. I am lucky to have such a range of amazing colleagues and friends. I would also like to thank Stephen Wenham and Zoe Forbes at Bristol University Press, and Sophia Unger, for helping me though the publication process, and having patience as I juggle competing tasks and deadline.

Finally, but by no means least, there are a range of people in my personal life that need to be thanked publicly. It goes without saying that the burden of a book does not just fall on the author, but those closest to them. So to Clare, Talisker and Isla, I dedicate this book to you for helping me through. To my Mum and Dad, brothers and sister, I thank you for everything you have done over the years. To Michael Lister, we may be older, the wine might be better, the whisky drank less freely, and the off-colour jokes have a more fatherly feel, but I can still think of nobody better to play cards with. And finally, to my neighbours, the Tennants and the Hatherlys, who have had to put up with me talking about this book for too long now – I thank you for your friendship and the bonds we built in the darkest hours. Of course, while making this book took us all, the responsibility of its contents are mine alone. I hope I have done you all proud.

The research leading to these results has received funding from the European Community's Seventh Framework Program (FP7/2007–2013) under grant agreement No. 225722.

Funding was also received from the ESRC Future Research Leaders Award Grant No. ES/K001167/1 Transatlantic Interests and Democratic Possibility in a Transforming Middle East.

Introduction

'We're facing a new and painful reality on the ground in Afghanistan. Let me let me speak clearly and bluntly. This is a catastrophe, a catastrophe for the people, for Western values and credibility, and for international relations. … What has happened raises many questions about the West's twenty years of engagement in the country and what we were able to achieve. … We have been doing a lot in order to build the state in Afghanistan … today twenty years on, we can say that we … failed. We have to ask ourselves some difficult questions to understand why this was possible. And why what has happened has happened.'

Josep Borrell Fontelles,
High Representative of the European Union for
Foreign Affairs and Security Policy

In August 2021 the Taliban, an ultraconservative Islamic fundamentalist group, recaptured the Afghan capital of Kabul after being removed from power 20 years earlier. This was a poignant symbol of the failure of Western powers in Afghanistan. Having been international pariahs when they emerged in the 1990s, the Taliban came to rule Afghanistan and formed a close connection with al Qaeda, the terrorist organization responsible for thousands of deaths in New York, Washington, DC and Pennsylvania on 11 September 2001. Triggering a military response, the Taliban were quickly removed by a United States (US)-led international coalition with the support of many Afghans, who tacitly supported the overthrow of the Taliban regime. Spread across a landmass twice the size of Germany, Afghanistan's population of 35–40 million found themselves under foreign occupation, even if the reach of foreign troops was inhibited by Afghanistan's mixed geographical terrain. What started as a counterterrorism operation soon evolved into a more ambitious plan to rebuild an Afghan state and transform it into a stable functioning democratic system that would eliminate the possibility of the country being used as a sanctuary for terrorists in the future.

As the US, and increasingly the European Union (EU) and its Member States, sought to stabilize Afghanistan through economic development and transformational governance, they found themselves facing a growing insurgency. Afghanistan soon became the longest war in US history, under the mantra *The Forever War*. Over time the Taliban's decades-long insurgency strategy proved successful in corroding the political will of Western powers. Their return to Kabul was not a sudden occurrence, but the culmination of resilience, planning and strategic patience. However, their revival has global, regional and local importance, raising profound questions about the nature of the global order, the effectiveness of international intervention, and the efficacy of power in sustained international efforts to establish and support democratic governance.

Reflecting on the aftermath of Western withdrawal, Afghanistan's descent into further humanitarian crises under Taliban rule underscores the stark disparity between international aspirations and on-the-ground realities. Far from a stable and secure democratic state, the Taliban wasted no time in renewing their campaign of human rights violations, including extrajudicial executions, the imposition of restrictions on women's rights, and the targeting of minority ethnic and religious groups with arbitrary violence. Growing economic hardship and widespread poverty have compounded decades of ongoing humanitarian crises, exacerbating malnutrition, chronic illness and the onset of disease. Moreover, despite pledges to tackle terrorism, Afghanistan has become a renewed haven for terrorist organizations with regional and international aspirations to strike Western partners and targets. Notwithstanding vast quantities of international assistance Afghanistan continues to languish at the bottom of human development indices and remains one of the most fragile and violent states in the world. Twenty years of international support has very little to show for itself in 21st-century Afghanistan.

The Taliban's return should give pause for thought as the international community reflects on what has gone wrong and what lessons can be learned from this experience. Far from Afghanistan moving towards a stable and secure state, many of the same individuals in Taliban leadership positions before 2001 have returned. Having climbed the ranks of the organization, the leadership of the Taliban includes those implicated in terrorism and widespread human rights abuses in the 1990s (Abbas 2023, 83–101).[1] If

---

[1] Mawlawi Hibatullah Akhundzada, for example, returned to power as the Taliban Supreme Leader, having worked his way up the ranks from head of the Taliban's council of religious scholars in 2001. Mohammad Hassan Akhund returned as acting prime minister in 2021, having served as the Taliban foreign minister in the later 1990s. Abdul Ghani Baradar, a

the Taliban needed to be removed in 2001, because of their association and facilitation of terrorism, why in 2021 were the Taliban allowed to seize power? Why did US-led efforts in Afghanistan end so abruptly with the collapse of their allies in the Government of Afghanistan? Are the Taliban capable, or even willing, to combat terrorism and prevent Afghanistan being used as a launch pad for attacks around the globe? Or will Western powers find themselves at war with the Taliban after a fleeting hiatus?

Indubitably, given its status as the principal international actor in Afghanistan, the US must derive the most profound lessons from this misadventure and address these and many more questions. Nevertheless, the academic and policy consensus has overwhelmingly concluded that the longest war in US history ended in failure, even if the cause of that failure will be debated in the decades to come (SIGAR 2021; Brivati 2022; Maley and Jamal 2022; Farhadi and Masya 2023; Gromes 2023; Khosravi and Fayaz 2023; Maley 2023; Murid Partaw 2023; Theros 2023). Given the significance of this failure, it is unavoidable to note that the US should bear the preponderance of accountability for this policy shortfall; notwithstanding its substantial investment of blood and treasure throughout the two decades of conflict. Yet, as Borrell's call for Europe to engage in more profound introspection reveals, European nations and the EU should not evade their burden of responsibility nor avoid scrutiny and accountability. Indeed, as Borrell's comments make clear, the EU was among the myriad of contributors to an ineffectual strategy and overwhelmingly supported the US strategy in and through EU institutions and Member States. As this book will show, European efforts have simply been overshadowed by the US and the dynamics of transatlantic relations. However, the purpose of this book is to cast light on this shadow, contextualizing the EU's involvement and illuminating discussions of why European attempts to support Afghanistan's transition to a secure and democratic state proved so ineffective. This is particularly important if we are to consider the efficacy of European external action in the 21st century and debates around Europe's role in the world.

In many respects, it would be expedient to lay the loss in Afghanistan on the US and its leadership in the North Atlantic Treaty Organization (NATO) alone. This has been the tenuous approach of European governments, who have sought to underplay their own role in the transatlantic alliance now Afghanistan has been lost. Of course, this is in stark contrast to many European powers previously stressing the importance of their contributions

---

founding member of the Taliban, retuned as deputy prime minister. Abdul Kabir returned as political deputy for the prime minister, having served as the acting prime minister of Afghanistan in 2001, before and after the 11 September 2001 terrorist attacks. Nooruddin Turabi returned as director of prisons, having previously served in the Justice Ministry in the 1990s.

during the conflict itself. Yet, laying full responsibility with the US, or the Afghans themselves, would not exonerate EU institutions and Member States. Doing so would be historically inaccurate. It would also serve to obfuscate the importance of the EU's global standing, its internal cohesion and its external relations. This book takes as its central premise that it is crucial to articulate and attribute the complexities of the situation in Afghanistan and not overlook the intricate interplay of history, international relations and the distinctive responsibilities borne by European institutions and Member States. It may be politically useful for European powers to put Afghanistan behind them, but this episode reveals a considerable amount about European external action at the start of the 21st century.

The Afghanistan episode serves as a pivotal case study for understanding the complexities of European integration and foreign policy making, especially in the context of the EU's efforts to balance its transatlantic ties with the US and its geopolitical interests in the broader Turko-Persian region. To oversimplify or overlook the EU's role would require avoiding a critical analysis of Europe's strategic decisions and their long-term consequences. Conversely, by engaging in a thorough examination of the EU's policies and initiatives in Afghanistan, scholars and policy makers can gain invaluable insights into the underlying principles guiding European foreign policy, the challenges of collective action within the EU framework, and the impact of these endeavours on the EU's identity as a global actor. This case study reveals the tensions between national interests and collective European values, the limitations of EU instruments in foreign and security policy, and the strategic recalibrations required to address emerging global challenges.

Moreover, the EU's engagement in Afghanistan is emblematic of the broader dilemmas facing Europe at the dawn of the 21st century. A failure to assess the EU's role in Afghanistan would leave Europe ill-prepared as it navigates its role on the world stage amidst shifting power dynamics and evolving security landscapes. Indeed, a central conclusion of this book is that the EU needs to reflect upon and reassess its approach to external action, and in light of the US proving to be an unreliable long-term partner, enhance EU strategic autonomy while fostering cooperation with international partners. By critically analysing the EU's involvement in Afghanistan, this book contributes to a more nuanced understanding of the intricacies of European integration, the EU's capacity for global leadership, and the implications of its policies for regional stability and international relations. The examination of the EU's involvement in Afghanistan is not merely an academic exercise but a vital endeavour for comprehending Europe's evolving place in the global order. Through such an analysis, one can foster a more sophisticated understanding of the EU, challenging and enriching the discourse on its role in the international arena.

Did the European Union fail in Afghanistan?

With the EU being one of many actors engaged in Afghanistan, questions should arise as to whether EU external action failed and how we would understand this in a complex foreign policy environment. It is not sufficient to simply assert that the EU bears any responsibility, just as it is not sufficient to overlook EU actions. Notably, many EU officials themselves have conceded that their action failed. The most prominent of these was Josep Borrell Fontelles, High Representative of the European Union for Foreign Affairs and Security Policy, even if he was at a loss to explain how and why this was possible (Borrell 2021a, 2021b). Of course, alarm bells concerning EU failures had been ringing for years. Francesc Vendrell, the European Union Special Representative, was very vocal about the EU's systematic failures upon leaving office in 2008 (Vendrell 2008). Nevertheless, it is worth reflecting on what is meant by failure in this context. We could assess the EU's performance in terms of broad aspirations, for global peace, justice and the EU's adherence to universal human rights principles. Yet, the return of the Taliban reflects the grim reality that two decades of war in Afghanistan has not supported these higher goals. In 2021, the Taliban were emboldened by their swift return and the withdrawal of Western support. Perhaps a better benchmark for asserting that the EU failed in Afghanistan is the EU's own stated objectives. As EU institutions previously agreed, 'the overarching strategic goal of the EU's … role in Afghanistan should be the development of Afghanistan's institutions to provide the resilience needed to safeguard progress to date and provide a countrywide platform for a more effective and ultimately sustainable Afghan state' (Council 2014).

The resurgence of the Taliban not only underscores the fragility of the Afghan state but also highlights the unsustainability of progress made. When measured against the EU's defined objectives, EU engagement in Afghanistan must be perceived as unsuccessful. The return of the Taliban and the systematic collapse of the Afghan state demonstrates that 20 years of engagement in Afghanistan did not deliver favourable or desired outcomes to the EU or its Member States.[2] If we understand success and failure against the benchmark of stated EU goals and objectives, we can only conclude that Afghanistan was a failure.

Perhaps, we could consider the EU's failure in Afghanistan as trivial. It is entirely possible that the EU failed to meet its objectives, but that this was of little cost to the EU or Afghans themselves. Perhaps, what happens in Afghanistan could be considered of little importance to the EU and its

---

[2] For an excellent overview of defining success and failure in foreign policy see Baldwin (2000).

Member States? Perhaps, most Afghans will be better off under Taliban rule for the foreseeable future? This book argues strongly against this line of argument. The EU and its Member States are collectively the world's largest donors of international aid. They provide approximately EUR 50 billion per year to advance global development and overcome poverty. Moreover, the EU aims to increase its contribution and dedicate at least 0.7 per cent of its gross national income to development aid each year, to be split between development cooperation and humanitarian assistance (Hassan 2023). It is within this context that we should be acutely aware that as the EU financed its efforts in Afghanistan over two decades, Afghanistan became the largest recipient of EU aid in the world. Indeed, EU institutions increasingly held Afghanistan as a test case of EU integration and crisis management, coming to benchmark success in Afghanistan as an indicator of the EU's ability reach beyond its immediate neighbourhood. A failure of EU policy in Afghanistan is therefore not just significant in terms of the EU's credibility, but a crucial case study if we are to understand the implications of EU policy and its effectiveness. This case not only highlights the costly disconnect between the allocation of substantial resources and the realization of intended policy outcomes but also underscores the broader consequences of such disconnects on both the recipient nations and the EU's international standing. Failures in Afghanistan bring the EU's credibility as an international actor into question. Given the EU's commitment to promoting development, human rights and stability through its aid programmes, the failure in Afghanistan calls into question the mechanisms of accountability, strategy formulation and implementation within the EU's external action framework. This examination is pivotal for re-evaluating and enhancing the EU's approach to international aid, ensuring that future efforts are more aligned with achieving tangible improvements in the lives of those in recipient countries, while also safeguarding the EU's interests and global image.

Why does it matter that the European Union failed in Afghanistan?

Despite the EU's substantial investment in Afghanistan, sustained scrutiny of its performance and the EU–Afghanistan relationship remains sparse (Ferrié 2008; Theros 2010; Gross 2012; Burke 2014; Hassan 2020b, 2021, 2023). This analytical shortfall is stark given the scale of the EU's commitments, the breadth of specific EU interests in the region and Afghanistan's troubled political history. Beyond humanitarian concerns, the EU and its Member States have continued vested security interests in Afghanistan, ranging from regional stability to counterterrorism, weapons proliferation, drug trafficking, modern slavery, organized crime networks and irregular migration. Additionally, Afghanistan's rare earth metal deposits are increasingly significant for modern economies and the green transition. These are very practical policy relevant issues that self-evidently will remain of interest to the EU for the foreseeable future. How EU institutions and Member States seek to deal with these challenges in the future will matter to the people of Europe. Yet, just as these issues have policy relevance, they also have academic relevance and warrant further research and analysis, if we are to critically understand how the EU engages with the world and constructs its response to these issues. Just as policy issues have academic relevance; academic research has policy relevance.

In policy terms, unlike the US, which established the Office of the Special Inspector General for Afghanistan Reconstruction (SIGAR) to provide independent oversight, no comparable European body exists.[3] Moreover, despite calls for the equivalent of public enquires across Europe, as of 2024, these have not been undertaken. However, momentum is building. For the EU Parliament's Committee on Foreign Affairs, this author undertook the first lessons learned exercise evaluating EU policy over the last 20 years (Hassan 2023). In June 2023, the Foreign Affairs Committee of the Parliament of Finland released its lessons learned report undertaken by the Finnish Institute of Foreign Affairs (Mustasilta et al 2023). This is to be followed by a Dutch report undertaken by the Danish Institute for International Studies and further reports commissioned by the German Bundestag.[4] In the United Kingdom (UK), the Independent Commission for Aid Impact (ICAI) undertook a more bounded review of UK aid in Afghanistan, concluding that 'UK aid to Afghanistan lacked a credible and realistic approach to its central goal of building a viable Afghan state. While it provided valuable support to Afghan citizens, including women and girls, it failed to make substantial progress towards its strategic objectives' (ICAI 2022).

The ICAI report is part of a very fractured landscape of the UK attempting to learn lessons from Afghanistan. In contrast to the comprehensive, 12-volume Chilcot Inquiry on the Iraq War, this approach avoids a broader, in-depth examination of the failures underpinning UK

---

[3] There is minimal similarity between the oversight provided by SIGAR and for example the European Court of Auditors, which by 2024 had only produced three reports focused on the EU's relationship with Afghanistan: *Special Report No 07/2016: The European External Action Service's Management of its Buildings around the World*; *Special Report No 7/2015: The EU Police Mission in Afghanistan: Mixed Results*; and *Special Report No 3/2011: The Efficiency and Effectiveness of EU Contributions Channelled through United Nations Organisations in Conflict-affected Countries*.

[4] As part of the Global Affairs Canada's review, a literature review of Danish Evaluations was completed in 2019, for the purposes of helping to evaluate Canada's programming in Afghanistan (Klausen and Yurtaslan 2019).

policy in Afghanistan. This is despite the Afghanistan conflict being longer and substantially more deadly for UK forces.[5] Indeed, the UK's fractured approach comes with difficulties. For example, on 15 December 2022, the British Ministry of Defence announced a formal, independent inquiry established under the Inquiries Act 2005. This inquiry narrowly investigates claims of unlawful killings by British Special Forces between mid-2010 and mid-2013. In particular, the inquiry assesses claims that British soldiers summarily killed 80 Afghans. Yet, this has itself become marred in controversy. The inquiry and the UK's Afghan Relocation and Assistance Policy scheme have been tarnished by allegations that UK Special Forces blocked Afghan troops they had fought alongside from relocating to the UK, potentially preventing Afghan troops testifying to UK war crimes. This has left dozens of Afghan troops who served with British forces to be beaten, tortured or killed by the Taliban since their return in 2021 (BBC Panorama 2024). Hence, understanding what happened in Afghanistan and why is not a historical nor abstract exercise, but continues to be an issue of life and death.

It is because Afghanistan remains an issue of life and death for individuals and of significant importance to the future of Europe and its place in the world, however, that analysing what went wrong cannot be left exclusively to policy analysts and public enquiries. A lack of sustained academic analysis over the last 20 years has demonstrably narrowed the intellectual debate and pool of ideas needed by EU institutions to respond. With the return of the Taliban, EU institutions and Member States have been ill-equipped with academic expertise able to address the specific failures in Afghanistan and understand what went wrong and why. While policy-focused evaluations and lessons-learned reports offer crucial insights for foreign policy debates and recommendations, sustained academic research is essential for generating new knowledge and advancing our theoretical understanding.

It is worth reflecting here on why there is a considerable gap in the academic literature on the EU's involvement in Afghanistan, as this will ultimately help explain this book's focus on the longue durée and the need to adopt an interdisciplinary approach to explaining the EU's relationship with Afghanistan. Namely, there are two primary reasons why this academic field has been neglected. First, many working on the EU have necessarily been inward-looking, with European Studies largely analysing European societies' internal politics, history and economy. To the extent that European Studies scholars have been concerned with the 'outside', it has often been

---

[5]   UK formal involvement in the invasion of Iraq was from 2003 to 2009 resulting in the deaths of 179 British Servicemen and women. From 2001 to 2021 the war in Afghanistan resulted in the loss of 456 British Servicemen and women.

to reflect on how the outside perceives and constructs Europe itself. The same has been true of Afghanistan Studies, whereby area specialists have been concerned with internal political movements and the impact of great powers on Afghanistan. By necessity, Afghanistan scholars have been more outward-looking, but there has been remarkably little reflection on how the EU has engaged with the country. All this is to say that scholars researching Europe and Afghanistan have often worked in distinct silos of area studies. They have been guilty of their own provincialism (see Busse et al 2024). Furthermore, for the sake of clarity, there is no shortage of literature on the war in Afghanistan nor the US's involvement as the primary actor. There is also no shortage of excellent academic literature on peacebuilding, corruption or development policy in Afghanistan. The gap in the literature has been in connecting these issues specifically to the context of the EU's involvement. By necessity this involvement is more contextually specific and complex due to the tensions between transatlantic solidarity and European integration, the transitional and emergent nature of European external action, the limitation of European capabilities that do not match overwhelming expectations, and Europe's geographical proximity and shared history with Afghanistan. This book attempts to bridge this gap and add much-needed value to the literature by talking to these issues and the specific challenges faced by the EU in Afghanistan. By doing this, it hopes to provide new knowledge and theoretical understanding to explain why the EU failed in Afghanistan.

Second, as the editorial team of a highly ranked International Relations (IR) journal informed this author before the Taliban's return, work on the EU's relations with Afghanistan is "interesting" but "too parochial for academics and practitioners". This is unsurprising as academic research in the social science is often reactive, and issues garner more attention once crises emerge. However, it is also indicative of a long-documented phenomena, whereby high-quality research published in top IR journals often lacks policy relevance and is unable to bridge the chasm between theory and practice (Lepgold 1998; Baldwin 2000). It is also suggestive of what Desch (2019) termed the 'cult of the irrelevant' whereby scholars undertaking academically rigorous research relevant to policy have been disregarded because of fads and fashions stripping practical utility from academic work. Such attitudes have partially changed since the return of the Taliban. Still, they suggest the intellectual neglect and disinterest in the topic before the EU experienced the largest and most significant foreign and security failure in its history. This neglect is unfortunate given Afghanistan's substantial receipt of EU aid and the conflict witnessing 857 troop fatalities from EU Member States alone. It also neglects the importance of Afghanistan as a rich case study to explain how EU external action has evolved in the 21st century and how Afghanistan has again been impacted by Europe. Yet, it is precisely to starting a wider academic conversation about Afghanistan and its relationship with the EU that this book aims to begin.

How can we advance our understanding of why the European Union failed in Afghanistan?

Given the gap in the academic literature, the EU's relationship with Afghanistan has unquestionably been represented as a product of the 21st century. The EU's policy in Afghanistan is presented as if it was hastily derived following the 11 September 2001 terrorist attacks. Indeed, EU policy makers have themselves perpetuated this myth. In part, as later chapters will show, this is because after 11 September 2001, policy makers treated Afghanistan as a 'blank slate', and ignored lessons learned over the previous 60 years of collective European engagement. As a former EU diplomat informed this author, '[w]e didn't take into consideration we were not starting from a blank sheet … I was part of that … we thought that we could build from nothing' (Hassan 2023). Indeed, decontextualizing Afghanistan in this way proved to be *the* primary mistake in the EU's overall strategic approach. EU actors developed policy assuming that Afghanistan was a 'tabula rasa', and preconceived models of state-building and development could be applied without reference to Afghanistan's history, culture or political norms. It was taken for granted that through development a modern state structure would emerge. In effect EU actors and institutions stripped any sensitivity to the temporal and spatial dimensions of the Afghan state. This was an odd approach, for two reasons. First, it placed the EU at a disadvantage because EU institutions failed to draw on their own historical experience of engaging with Afghanistan, which included periods of civil war and the first period of Taliban rule in the 1990s. Second, and just as importantly, EU strategy was not designed to take into account the historical context and the realities in Afghanistan today. A policy that decontextualizes Afghanistan denies agency to the Afghans themselves, and their historical and political reality. Simply put, EU *conduct* failed to match the Afghan *context*.

To explain this phenomenon, it is worth briefly considering what can be termed *contextual consonance* and *contextual dissonance* in relation to foreign and security policy. This is because a central thesis of this book is that by acting towards Afghanistan as if it was a blank slate, EU external action was exposed to a high level of *contextual dissonance*. Accordingly, *contextual dissonance* occurs when foreign and security policy diverges from the dominant characteristics of the environment it is intended to operate within. As a result of this disharmony, policy implementation can experience a high level of social, political and economic friction; and fail to gain traction because of a mismatch between conduct and context. Notably, *contextual dissonance* can occur at the level of the international system through to local norms, as these contextualize the operationalization of policy. Conversely, *contextual consonance* in foreign and security policy occurs when conduct is aligned with the dominant characteristics of the environment it is operating in. As an objective, *contextual consonance* tries to align policy with the reality of local norms through to the structures of the international system.[6] It can be taken for granted that given the complexity of the international system, its subsystems and the complexity of interactions and dynamics, that no foreign and security policy will have perfect *contextual consonance*, and therefore we can consider this an ideal whereby both *contextual dissonance* and *contextual consonance* are a matter of degree. The implication of this for our analysis is that by necessity we must account for complexity, but also seek to abstract from it by looking at which phenomena are the most significant contributors to *contextual dissonance* and *contextual consonance* and why.

By introducing the concepts of *contextual dissonance* and *contextual consonance* into the analysis of foreign and security policy, this book aims to reconcile a practical issue of accounting for structure and agency. Introducing our two concepts, we can shift our focus of questions of ontology, and the ontological dualism that is suggested by the analytical separation of structure and agency. This can be done by focusing on *strategic actors* operating in a *strategically selective context* (see Hassan 2013). For those readers familiar with Bob Jessop's (2005) strategic-relational approach, and the concern of critical realists, these terms will be familiar. However, it is worth briefly unpacking the strategic-relational approach here as it helps explain the methodological choices that inform this book.

The *strategic-relational approach* provides a nuanced framework for analysing state power and policy in the context of changing social relations, strategic actions of diverse actors, and the structural constraints and opportunities these actors face (Jessop and Morgan 2022). It was originally conceived to provide a sophisticated tool for examining the complex interplay between the state, economy and society in a way that is sensitive to historical and geographical specificities (Hay 2002). At a methodological level, it can recognize the complexity of the structure and agency debate but talk to the real contexts of social and political interaction. As a result, some scholars have utilized this approach for the analysis of foreign policy (Hassan 2009,

---

6   For the sake of clarity here, by using the term 'reality', this author is advocating for a form of complex naturalism inspired by the arguments outlined in *The Reality of Social Construction* and *The Causal Power of Social Structures* (Elder-Vass 2010, 2012). This builds on my previous work inspired by *The Construction of Social Reality* (Searle 1996). Notably, I have maintained the strategic-relational approach of Bob Jessop as a heuristic way of utilizing debates around structure and agency. However, Elder-Vass has the advantage of accounting for emergence, which is a feature of my forthcoming work.

2013; Holland 2012; Bentley and Holland 2014).[7] Notably, this framework can blend seamlessly into the narrative provided in this book by focusing on the strategic content of action, and accepting the premise that,

> agents both internalise perceptions of their context and consciously orient themselves towards that context in choosing between potential courses of action. ... Yet for that action to have any chance of realising such intentions, it must be informed by a strategic assessment of the relevant context in which strategy occurs and upon which it subsequently impinges. (Hay 2002, 129)

Hence, *contextual dissonance* and *contextual consonance* can be understood as terms used to highlight the way in which actors' strategic assessments and conduct 'fit' to the relevant strategic context. They are an expression of 'strategic selectivity' and the way strategic objectives need to reflect the balance of social forces and power relations at any given moment.

Moving our analysis forward, there is a considerable disjuncture between, on the one hand, EU policy makers treating Afghanistan as if it was a 'blank slate', and on the other the *strategic-relational approach* demonstrating that all states need to be understood as social relations embedded in temporal and spatial dimensions (Jessop and Morgan 2022). The EU's decontextualization failed to recognize how the Afghan state has been shaped by different strategies of the Afghans themselves. EU institutions, therefore, failed to acknowledge that in their strategic actions, they needed to account for how Afghanistan's state strategies have been shaped over time and across different spatial scales, from the local to the global, and how these strategies, in turn, reshaped temporal and spatial relations. The EU failed to account for Afghans having agency and working as *strategic actors* operating in a *strategically selective context*.

Putting Afghanistan into European Union–Afghanistan relations

Known as the 'primacy effect', discovered by the Polish-American psychologist Solomon Eliot Asch in the 1940s, there is a propensity in human psychology to remember the first items in a list more than those in the middle or the end. As a result, the order in which things appear in a list matter and can often demonstrate an inclination to prioritize one element

---

[7]   The advantage of the approach is derived from its rejection of ontological individualism and pure ontological structuralism and can merge structure and agency at a methodological level.

over another. Using the term '*EU–Afghanistan*' relations means that there is not only a propensity to think of the EU and European Member States as the primary actors, but also as the dominant actors in the relationship. A logical consequence of this is that this book should start with the EU narrative and how collective European action in Afghanistan unfolded. We could perpetuate the inclination of making Afghanistan the secondary element of this narrative and cast Afghanistan in the background as the stage that we simply don't need to understand. Yet, when taken to its logical conclusion, this approach allows for the decontextualization of Afghanistan, which is precisely what this book sets out to avoid.

If we understand Afghanistan as a product of social relations embedded in temporal and spatial dimensions, as explained by the *strategic-relational approach*, then we should start by focusing on the development of the Afghan state; and not EU policy towards Afghanistan. Rather than assume Afghanistan is a 'blank slate', we need to prioritize our understanding of Afghanistan first, and not as an afterthought of EU policy or European history; we need to understand Afghanistan first as this informs our understanding of Afghanistan's relations with the world and the EU. The implications of this are that this book needs to start by focusing on Afghanistan and how it is situated in the international system and world history, before explaining how the EU attempted to engage with Afghanistan.

Unfortunately, the discipline of IR is poorly equipped to start our analysis of Afghanistan and how it is situated in world history and the international system. As Buzan and Little have illustrated at length, IR theories have overwhelmingly prioritized presentism, ahistoricism, Eurocentrism and state-centrism as the discipline has developed its conception of the international system (2000, 17–22). If we briefly unpack each in turn, we can strengthen the case for starting our analysis of Afghanistan and situating it within world history and the international system in the next chapter. Furthermore, these terms provide us with concepts in and through which we can explore the EU's approach to Afghanistan. As this book demonstrates, the EU's external action in Afghanistan embedded presentism, ahistoricism, Eurocentrism and state-centrism, and failed to question whether these created *contextual dissonance* and *contextual consonance*.

Presentism in IR is characterized by a preoccupation with contemporary events and policies, often at the expense of a deeper historical insight (Buzan and Little 2000, 18–19). This approach tends to emphasize similarities with modern European history, particularly periods of international anarchy like those of classical Greece and Renaissance Italy, thereby overlooking the broader and varied historical dynamics of the international system (Spoerhase 2008). This focus not only narrows the scope of analysis but also risks imposing contemporary norms and values on past events, perpetuating a form of ahistoricism (Cello 2018). As the narrative in this book develops throughout its chapters, we can see the ways in which presentism manifests itself in the EU's approach to Afghanistan. Yet what clearer indication of this approach could there be than the assertion that Afghanistan was to be seen as a 'blank slate' upon which a new modern state could be erected (see Hassan 2023).

By embedding presentism in its approach, the EU seamlessly espoused a form of ahistoricism. Observed in IR, *ahistoricism* signifies an attempt to identify universal, timeless principles governing international relations, much like the laws in natural sciences. This quest, predominantly pursued by positivist scholars and traditional approaches to IR, aims to abstract theories from historical context, assuming the unchanging nature of international politics (LaRoche and MacKay 2017). In accepting *ahistoricism*, the EU would deny the historicity of Afghanistan. This had a profound effect of the EU denying what Zarakol terms 'the presence of the past' and the importance of history in understanding, explaining or evaluating contemporary phenomena (Zarakol 2023, 291). By denying the historicity of Afghanistan, EU strategy failed to pay attention to how Afghanistan's past shapes its present. In turn, this reinforced a very Eurocentric approach that failed to recognize Afghanistan's distinctive strategically selective context.

This reinforces *Eurocentrism*, and the notion that the international system began in the 1500s with European colonization and European models of statehood and economy (Buzan and Little 2000, 20–1). This worldview simplifies and overlooks the contributions and interactions of non-European societies, thus distorting the understanding of the international system's origins (Duzgun 2022). It also, through its emphasis on universalism, seeks to promote the 'West' as the highest or ideal normative referent, not only at the exclusion of others, but through both imperialist and anti-imperialist conceptions of international theory (Hobson 2012). Embracing historicism is essential for overcoming Eurocentric biases and fostering a more nuanced comprehension of global historical dynamics. Historicism was not a position adopted by EU institutions. The failure to consider Afghanistan's position in world history, and how the Afghan state was formed, embedded both ahistoricism and Eurocentrism into the EU's strategic approach to Afghanistan. In turn, EU institutions developed strategies that failed to recognize the strategic selective context they were operating in, generating further *contextual dissonance* rather than *contextual consonance*.

In hand with *presentism*, *ahistoricism* and *Eurocentrism*, this book will also demonstrate that EU institutions adopted *state-centrism*, emphasising the state as the primary actor in international relations. This is consistent with traditional IR theories such as Liberalism and Realism (see Hobson 2000). Unlike the *strategic-relational approach's* emphasis on the state being a social construction built through social relations, *state-centrism* treats states as unopenable monolithic entities at the centre of world politics. This perspective, reinforced post-Second World War, has somewhat narrowed IR's analytical scope, sidelining the economic, social and environmental factors also at play. Indeed, IR has become anchored to state-centric frameworks that have limited the disciplines' ability to fully capture the complexities of global interactions in an era where non-state actors and transnational forces increasingly challenge the sovereignty and centrality of the state (Buzan and Little 2000, 21–2). EU institutions embedded *state-centrism* in their attempt to build a centralized Afghan state. This had a dramatic impact. As this book will show, *state-centrism* curbed the imagination of EU policy makers, who were unable to identify the need for pluralism, peacebuilding and tackling corruption, which would have challenged their state-building strategy. Moreover, unable to transcend this state-centric view, and without appreciating the strategic selectivity they were operating in, EU policy makers systematically failed to imagine that the Afghan state they were helping to build could fail.

While Buzan and Little (2000) have been able to identify the intrinsic problems with traditional IR theory, they did not stop at deconstructing the discipline. Rather, by engaging in explanatory critique, they provide a framework designed to challenge presentism, ahistoricism, Eurocentrism and state-centrism in IR. As a result, this framework is particularly well placed in allowing us to situate Afghanistan in world history and the development of the international system and reject the notion that Afghanistan should have been treated as a 'blank slate'. The value of Buzan and Little's contribution goes beyond what can be covered in this book and represents a forerunner to what is now referred to as 'global international relations' and efforts to widen international contributions to the field (Acharya and Buzan 2019).[8] For the purposes of this book, Buzan and Little offer three distinctive stages in which the systems in world history have developed. The three stages start with the origins of *pre-international systems*; the rise of *multiple international systems* in the ancient and classical world; and the evolution of the *global international system*. Mapping Afghanistan onto this three-stage framework is a novel element of this book. Yet its added value is in adding historicity to our narrative, and exposing exactly why the EU's approach ultimately failed in the latter chapters.

---

[8] Global International Relations (GIR) is a response to IR's narrow theories of global politics and the way in which 'they neglect the experiences and relationships in other parts of the world, or offer a poor fit for understanding and explaining them'. GIR attempts to widen IR to include 'ideas, approaches and experiences of both Western and non-Western societies'. The aim of GIR is to 'bring the Rest in' (Acharya 2017).

Theoretical overview

To redress the EU's oversight and demonstrate why treating Afghanistan as a blank slate is problematic, the first chapter of this volume places Afghanistan into Buzan and Little's (2000) *International Systems in World History* framework. This framework distinguishes between pre-international systems, the multiple international systems of the ancient and classical world, and the global international system we know today. In each of these periods, different 'units' came to define the systems they operated within. In pre-international systems, these units were hunter-gather tribes; in ancient and classical worlds units were constituted by city-states, nomadic tribes and their respective empires; and in the era of the global international system the dominant units are overwhelmingly modern states. Buzan and Little argue that:

> [I]f the units share a common identity (a religion or a language), or even just a common set of rules or norms (about how to determine relative status, and how to conduct diplomacy), then these intersubjective understandings not only condition their behaviour, but also define the boundaries of a social system. (Buzan and Little 2000, 104)

Indeed, within Buzan and Little's framework, norms play an important role in helping to define what constitutes a 'unit' and help establish the boundaries of a social system. To advance this point, and add a level of ontological clarity, this book centralizes the role of norms in the construction of social reality.[9]

For the sake of clarity, in general terms, 'norms' refers to 'social norms', which are a prescribed guide for conduct or action which is generally complied with in social groups (Ullmann-Margalit 1977, 12–13). However, critical realist research can add to the theoretical sophistication and the way norms are central to social reality. Thus, the aim of Chapter 2 is to contextualize Afghanistan and identify the social norms that have developed within each of the periods set out within Buzan and Little's periodization of world history. Those familiar with the history of Afghanistan or wanting an evaluation of EU policy may be enticed to skip this chapter. However, the chapter adds value to the current literature by tracing the development of 'meta-norms' through a diachronic analysis. Meta-norms are composed

---

[9] From this author's theoretical perspective, it is difficult to defend the assertion that a 'common identity' is distinct from a larger set of norms; such as religious norms or linguistic norms. As a result, this text has less of a focus on 'identity' than the operation of norms. For an important theoretical discussion on culture and national identity see Elder-Vass (2012, 163–82).

of other complexes of mutually referencing and mutually supporting norms advanced by people that make up 'norm circles' (Elder-Vass 2012, 166–7). For critical realists such as Elder-Vass, norms are ontologically significant, and are explained with considerable depth and rigour:

> Norms are expectations that people will and should conform with certain recognisable patterns of behaviour which we may call practices … there is a wide range of norms, some of which are rarely verbalised, while others may be quite formally documented. In many cultural contexts, for example, there is a norm that when a number of people are waiting for the same resource they should form a queue and follow certain related practices such as allowing the person at the front of the queue to access the resource first … for every norm there is a *norm circle*, a group of people who are committed to endorsing and enforcing that norm, for example by rewarding, praising, or otherwise honouring those who conform with the norm, and by criticising or punishing those who breach it. The effectiveness of norms depends on this groups backing. (Elder-Vass 2017a, 83–6; emphasis in original)

Notably, Elder-Vass' intervention is theoretically sophisticated, wide ranging in scope and set out in multiple volumes (Elder-Vass 2010, 2012, 2017b; Elder-Vass and Morgan 2022). There is little reason to rehearse the metatheoretical arguments for this critical realist position in full, except to explain the utility of understanding norms and their social role throughout this volume. We can see norms as ontologically grounded in social practices. Norms do not bubble from a swamp. Rather, they are the product of people's *collective intentions*. They are supported by groups of individuals, which Elder-Vass terms *norm circles*, that actively hold normative beliefs or a disposition endorsing certain practices.[10] From these social interactions and collective intentions, social institutions emerge that have more social power than the sum of the individuals (Elder-Vass 2010, 122–30).

The relevance of *meta-norms* to the analysis presented in this volume is that they allow us to address the emergent role of culture without essentializing that term. Rather, meta-norms allow us to see 'culture' as a political project, where social norms form the basis of collective intentions by particular norm

---

[10] For the sake of contextualizing the term *norm circles*, or normative circles in full, it is useful to understand how this term was derived. Originally, the term *normative communities* was used, but this was deemed to have many of the same problems as the term *society*. Working in the academic field of sociology, this carried disciplinary baggage. As such, Elder-Vass seized on Georg Simmel's use of the term circle and the way it was used to denote overlapping or cross-cutting social groups. Elder-Vass, however, applies the term to normativity, rather than identity (Elder-Vass 2010, 122).

circles. These norm circles are willing, through practices, to enforce, endorse and observe those norms in preference to others. As Elder-Vass outlines:

> Cultures ... are composed of articulated complexes of mutually referencing and mutually supporting norms and advanced by the corresponding norm circles. Practices, to put the point in another way, are not inherently tied to specific cultures; their attachment to a culture is itself a normative symbolic move. The definitions of cultural boundaries are themselves norms with norm circles enforcing them. (Elder-Vass 2012, 166)

In many respects, this book can be read without acknowledging this theoretical baggage. Yet, as the narrative in this book unfolds, having an appreciation of this theoretical position in advance will help the reader identify why certain analytical choices have been made and others have not. For example, given the ubiquity of social norms and practices, there must be a rationale for identifying meta-norms around political legitimacy rather than more distinct norms practised by local Afghan tribes. It is not that the latter is not interesting, or indeed, could have very important contextual relevance. However, it is the case that the former allow the questions driving the research in this book to be answered, whereas the latter do not.

Through articulating Buzan and Little's account of world history and the formation of the international system, with Elder-Vass' conception of meta-norms and norm circles, Chapter 2 provides an account of Afghanistan that is sensitive to normative change and geopolitics. This not only refutes the notion that Afghanistan could be treated as a blank slate, but it establishes the meta-norms that should have been taken into account in EU policy if the aim was to achieve contextual consonance in EU external action. As a result, Chapter 2 establishes a set of norms that needed to be considered but, as later chapters demonstrate, were not.

Chapter summary

Having established the theoretical framework for this book, each of the chapters that follows provides a theoretically driven but empirically rich account of Afghanistan and the EU's relationship with its people. It demonstrates that EU's engagement in Afghanistan ultimately faltered due to a multitude of strategic misalignments and oversight failures, exacerbated by a pervasive underestimation of Afghanistan's historical complexities and societal norms.

To demonstrate this, Chapter 2 unveils the EU's oversight of Afghanistan's intricate historical and normative landscape, emphasizing the disparity between European conceptual frameworks and Afghan realities. This chapter establishes the foundation by elucidating how the EU's ahistorical and Eurocentric stance, coupled with a commitment to normative power, failed to accommodate the diverse norms emerging from Afghanistan's historical interactions, both internally and with external powers. To establish this a thick contextualization of Afghanistan through three phases of world history is set out, and the development of complex norms is demonstrated. By revisiting and centralizing Afghanistan's rich historical narrative within the broader international system, the chapter advocates for a departure from Eurocentric policies towards a more inclusive understanding that acknowledges the complexities and resilience of Afghan society. Through a detailed examination of Afghanistan's place in world history – from its pre-international systems and formation of international systems to the modern global international system – the chapter underscores the importance of recognizing Afghanistan's active role and agency in shaping its destiny amidst the shifting dynamics of global power structures.

Progressing to Chapter 3, the focus shifts to Afghanistan's tumultuous transition from a decolonized entity to an independent state, embroiled in internal and external normative conflicts. This analysis spotlights the 1929 coup and the enduring battle between traditional Islamic norms and attempts to impose European modernity, underscoring the multifaceted nature of Afghanistan's 20th-century experience, far removed from linear narratives of development and modernization. The chapter intricately explores Afghanistan's interactions with the global international system, particularly with the European Union and its predecessors, tracing the evolution of relationships from trade and aid to a more complex engagement influenced by humanitarian concerns. This is contextualized within the broader narrative of Afghanistan's struggle with modernization, sovereignty and the impacts of Cold War dynamics, including the significant role of external powers in shaping its domestic and foreign policies.

Chapter 4 delves into the EU's strategic and operational missteps post-11 September 2001, detailing how initial solidarity with the US morphed into a scenario of marginalization and misaligned strategies, exacerbating the challenges in state-building and peace processes. This chapter critically evaluates the consequences of the EU's actions and inactions within the broader geopolitical dynamics and internal complexities of Afghanistan. The analysis delves into the ramifications of the Bonn Agreement and the international community's failure to establish a comprehensive peace process, which inadvertently empowered warlords and entrenched neopatrimonial norms. This misstep is framed as a critical oversight, which neglected the complex sociopolitical fabric of Afghanistan and exacerbated the challenges of state-building. The chapter also explores the impact of the Iraq War on the transatlantic relationship and the broader international strategy towards Afghanistan. The US's diversion of attention and resources to Iraq is critiqued for undermining the efforts in Afghanistan and contributing to the resurgence of the Taliban. The EU's inability to adapt its strategy in light of these developments is highlighted as a missed opportunity to assert a more autonomous and coherent approach.

In Chapter 5, the EU's state-building endeavours are outlined, demonstrating the contextual dissonance that emerged, as EU strategy demonstrated misalignments and oversight failures. The analysis demonstrates the adverse effects of attempting to transplant Western models onto Afghan soil, amidst a corruption eruption and the resultant deep-seated issues undermining international efforts and Afghan governance. The chapter underscores the necessity of a nuanced understanding of local contexts and historical dynamics in international state-building efforts, criticizing the oversimplified approaches that overlooked Afghanistan's deep-seated norms and the multifaceted nature of corruption. It serves as a reflective analysis on the EU's role in Afghanistan, offering vital lessons for future international engagements in complex, post-conflict state-building scenarios.

Transitioning to Chapter 6, the examination highlights the EU's limitations in contributing to security and peace in Afghanistan. Despite evolving engagements and responsibilities, European actions fell short, as detailed through the challenges faced by the European Union Police Mission (EUPOL) mission and the broader implications of deferred leadership and internal bureaucratic struggles on the peace process and the fight against the resurgence of the Taliban. The chapter critically assesses the EU's multifaceted role in Afghanistan, from its initial prioritization of transatlantic solidarity and partnership with the Government of Afghanistan to its eventual navigation of complex international relations, all while confronting internal challenges and external pressures.

Chapter 7 outlines the gradual resurgence of the Taliban, attributed to the Afghan government's legitimacy crisis, systemic corruption and inability to ensure security and political stability. The flawed 2019 presidential election, marked by historically low voter turnout, underscored the diminishing trust in the electoral process and governance structures. The subsequent US decision to withdraw troops, amidst an already tumultuous political landscape, exacerbated the situation, leading to a swift and largely unanticipated Taliban takeover. This has left dire consequences. The Taliban's return to power should lead to a period of introspection and evaluation of EU external actions. This chapter confronts the grim realities of human rights rollbacks, economic crises, and the broader geopolitical implications for EU policy making and strategic autonomy in the global international system.

In the endeavour to elucidate the reasons behind the EU's policy failures in Afghanistan, this research has ventured beyond conventional IR theories, challenging prevailing notions entrenched in presentism, ahistoricism, Eurocentrism and state-centrism. By embracing methodological pluralism and drawing on the theoretical frameworks of Buzan and Little, alongside the sociological insights of Elder-Vass, this study underscores the indispensability of historical context in understanding international relations. It hopes to illuminate the critical role of norm circles, norms and practices in shaping the sociopolitical landscape, thereby providing a nuanced understanding of the complex interplay between Afghanistan's rich historical tapestry and contemporary global politics. This approach not only offers a rigorous critique of the EU's external action but provides a comprehensive exploration of the complex relationship between Afghanistan and the EU.

More than a 'Blank Slate': Afghan Meta-norms in World History

'The Afghans do not have a history because anarchy has none.'
A French ethnologist in the late 19th century
(in Crews 2015, 3)

'We thought it was a tabula rasa, and we could implement our ready-made development solutions to build a modern state.'
Author's interview with senior EU official

Contemporary assertions that Afghanistan could be treated as a 'blank slate' uncomfortably echo 19th-century imperialist assertions that 'Afghans do not have a history'. These reverberations raise questions about historicity and the need for sociohistorical inquiry, but also whether Western attitudes and discourses towards Afghanistan have significantly changed across three centuries. Overt norms of European imperialism may have formally ended, but the idea that Afghanistan and its people can be stripped of their history has a long afterlife. It is within this context that European Union (EU) policy makers' assertions that they engaged with Afghanistan as if it were a 'blank slate' should not be seen as neutral, but rather as part of an attempt to diffuse EU norms.

Although EU policy makers have openly stated that they proceeded on the basis that Afghanistan is a 'blank slate', it is worth unpacking what is meant by this (Hassan 2023). At conceptual level, it has meant proceeding with EU external action on the basis that the tumultuous history that has shaped Afghanistan's present can be overlooked. At a practical level, it has meant prioritizing technical and managerial models embedded in EU external action, which are designed to create more efficient and stable sovereign states. These models exist primarily in the sphere of development and democracy assistance and are perceived as universally applicable even as they emphasize normative commitments to democracy, the rule of law and gender equality.

These models are often portrayed as scientific and ahistorical because they are elevated to the status of being 'universal' in appeal and application. Yet, multiple studies have outlined that the EU's 'one size fits all' approach, and the unreflexive way EU external action has sought to promote its own model, is based on Europe's historical experience and political practices (Bicchi 2006; Börzel et al 2008; Börzel 2022). Through the EU's developmental models, ahistoricism is intricately tied to conceptions of 'Normative Power Europe' and the way in which European norms are diffused into the international system (Manners 2002).

Understanding norms as collective expectations of behaviour that EU policy makers understand they should conform with, then the application of 'blank slate' ahistorical models can be better understood. Such models, contrary to being technical or managerially neutral, represent a form of normative practice in their own right. This practice is perpetuated by policy makers collectively operating as a norm circle. Internally, those who adopt and support these practices will be rewarded, and those that do not will be socially and professionally punished. The concept of Normative Power Europe can be comprehended as the outcome of the interplay between norms and the collective intentions of policy makers dedicated to advancing and disseminating these norms throughout the international system.

Understanding the EU's 'blank slate' approach as a norm of EU external action should raise concerns. Indeed, there is an inherent contradiction in this form of practice. On the one hand, the EU perpetuates its own norms through a 'one size fits all' model based on Europe's historical experience and political context. On the other hand, the EU's approach decontextualizes and denies the agency of others and overlooks the norms others have developed and maintained. The EU's normative position doesn't reflect upon the norms of others. Yet, if we understand norm circles as part of the emergent fabric of social institutions, then a failure to account for the norms of others in external action is extremely likely to result in a high level of contextual dissonance. This is because asserting that something is a 'blank slate' is tantamount to proclaiming that the EU's approach intentionally lacks contextual awareness. Not considering the norms of others is therefore likely to result in EU actors failing to identify the strategically selective context that norms and social institutions play in other contexts. Indeed, as scholars contributing at the intersection of security and development literatures have noted, this ahistorical approach lacks contextual understanding and is incapable of producing 'theoretically and historically informed strategies for the specific operational context' (Egnell and Haldén 2010).

To critique the EU's approach to Afghanistan, it is necessary to reject the ahistoricism at the centre of its Eurocentric 'blank slate' model and reintroduce sensitivity to the Afghan norms and historicity. This, it is argued, will provide a better understanding of why the EU failed in Afghanistan, and offer a way of achieving greater contextual consonance moving forward.[1] A central issue in this undertaking, however, is in determining when to start the analysis of Afghanistan to identify the development of pertinent norms and their formation. Buzan and Little's (2000) *International Systems in World History* provides a useful framework for this undertaking because of its ability to avoid presentism, ahistoricism, Eurocentrism and state-centrism. Indeed, this framework provides us with a periodization that recognizes as a starting point the temporal unity of past, present and future, rather than arbitrary assertions based on the European experience and the development of modern states.

The overarching periodization set out by Buzan and Little can be broken into three phases that situate the formation of the international system in world history. The aim of this chapter is to situate Afghanistan within these phases to identify the development of pertinent norms and add historicity, and, therefore, centralize and recontextualize Afghans and Afghanistan. The first of Buzan and Little's phases is defined by the existence of pre-international systems, where the dominant actors were mobile, egalitarian, hunter-gather bands. These hunter-gather bands interacted with other hunter-gather bands forming systems and connections through social institutions such as speech, marriage and gift giving. Within this period sedentary tribes and chiefdoms began to emerge as this era began to transition into the formation of multiple international systems across the globe. During this transitional phase, war and alliances became endemic processes, as competition and ethnic divisions began to emerge in sedentary units (Buzan and Little 2000, 111–33).

The second phase of this framework is marked by changes in the types of units across the globe, with the rise of city-states, nomadic tribes and their respective empires. Although elements of pre-international systems, such as hunter-gather bands, lasted into the 20th century, the formation of ancient and classical international systems across the globe emerged around 4000 BCE. As a result, the nature and capacity of interactions across the globe began to change, with the rise of new physical and social technologies. An

---

[1] Methodologically, this move has the added value of undertaking an empirical case study through the acts of retroduction and retrodiction. The aim of retroduction is to identify the interacting mechanisms and structures which generate a phenomenon (McAvoy and Butler 2017). In this case, particular sensitivity is being paid to norms and norm circles, among other physical, social and psychological phenomena. Retroduction therefore provides theoretical explanations which are empirically assessed. Related, but distinct, retrodiction looks back to identify powers interacting to cause specific events (McAvoy and Butler 2017). Elder-Vass brings the two terms together to complement one another whereby retroduction identifies the mechanisms and retrodiction analyses how the mechanisms interact in actual events (Elder-Vass 2007).

excellent illustration of this was the Silk Road that placed the Turko-Persian world in the centre of world history (Frankopan 2016). Along with changes in transportation and communication came the rise of universal religions, of which the spread of Islam is most pertinent to Afghanistan. Interaction capacity within ancient and classical international systems increased with the rise of diplomacy, money and bills of exchange, and trade diasporas. This made multiple international systems more regional in scale, which was reflected in the military-political institutions that emerged as empires expanded and contracted. Across the globe, nomads still sought to operate with autonomy, but empires began to change the nature of political autonomy. For some empires this meant the creation of suzerain powers, which were under imperial rule, but maintained elements of domestic control. For other empires, dominion systems were established, whereby the ruling empire extended its control into domestic governance (Buzan and Little 2000, 163–240).

The third phase of Buzan and Little's framework will be the most familiar to readers, as it involves the development of the global international system, which characterizes the current epoch. This phase is characterized by the rise of the modern state system as the dominant unit in global affairs starting from approximately 1500 CE, and certainly by 1648 CE with the Peace of Westphalia. As the European state system began to spill out of regional confinement the world order began to adapt and change. Indeed, technological advancement and utilizing new sea routes for voyages fundamentally altered the distribution of power within the world system. At first this allowed for greater economic interaction, and the formation of a global-scale economy underpinned by capitalism and industrialism. Yet, it also facilitated European colonialism and the rise of new European empires that stretched across the globe. As modern states began to exert pressure in the international system, this challenged old empires and the influence of nomadic systems. New international norms, rules and institutions were established, facilitated by revolutions at sea, land, air and communication. These have come to characterize the era of globalization and the global scale anarchic international system. Yet, multilateral institutions such as the EU have emerged within this international system, meshed by shared sovereignty and thick webs of common laws that govern trade and finance, human rights, environmental standards and increasingly military cooperation (Buzan and Little 2000, 241–345).

Setting out a framework to understand the international system in world history is a broad endeavour. However, the framework provides a larger historical context in which to situate the analysis of Afghanistan and the identification of pertinent meta-norms relevant today. Furthermore, in rejecting ahistoricism, this chapter goes beyond traditional International Relations (IR) theories and emergency epistemologies that have done little to help us understand Afghanistan (see Manchanda 2020). Buzan and Little provide a world-historical narrative that helps condense complex micro-histories and situate Afghanistan and its meta-norms within the macro-level international system(s) and broader global transformations.[2]

A benefit of situating Afghanistan within world history is that it provides a break from arbitrarily trying to fit it within artificially defined regions. As Crews explains, with Afghanistan not fitting neatly into the regions typically referred to as the 'Middle East' or 'South Asia', it has been treated as its own distinct world, unlike anywhere else and set apart from all other places (2015, 4). However, Afghans and the territory we now call Afghanistan have rarely been at the periphery of global history. Being marginal is not how Afghans have typically imagined themselves and recorded their own history. Crews' seminal volume, *Afghan Modern*, makes this point far better than this author would presume to:

> Afghans have rarely imagined themselves as peripheral to the rest of the world. One of the first histories of the Afghans placed them at the centre of a universal history. Composed in the seventeenth century, Nimatullah's *History of the Afghans* (Makhzan- i Afghānī) mapped their past onto a sacred landscape. It followed the contours of the geography of both the Bible and the Quran and portrayed Afghans in dynamic contact with these holy places. Their history began with Adam and Eve and their descendant, the Prophet Yaqub Israel. Their progeny included the original Israelites, and they ruled at Jerusalem, where one of them, Afghana, constructed the al-Aqsa Mosque. (Crews 2015, 11)

Indeed, Crews poses a broad challenge to current thinking about Afghanistan, asserting the need to understand what he terms 'Afghan globalism' (2015, 2). At its core, Afghan globalism illuminates the profound ties Afghans have fostered with international society, highlighting their physical, intellectual and rich cultural exchanges with the world over centuries. Expanding on this, it is clear that for thousands of years, Afghanistan has been a mosaic of diverse ethnicities, tribes and religious influences, each contributing to its intricate cultural fabric. Rather than simply proceeding on the basis that Afghanistan is a 'blank slate', it is imperative to recognize and appreciate this depth of history. Only by doing so can we begin to confront and dismantle

---

[2] For the best histories in this space, see Louis Dupree's (1980) *Afghanistan*; Ali Ahmad Jalali's (2021) *Afghanistan: A Military History from the Ancient Empires to the Great Game* and (2017) *A Military History of Afghanistan: From the Great Game to the Global War on Terror*; and Jonathan L. Lee's (2022) *Afghanistan: A History from 1260 to the Present*.

the Orientalist narratives that have historically clouded Western views of Afghanistan. It is to this that this chapter now turns, setting out Afghanistan's role from the pre-international systems period through the early formation of international systems and their linkages, its Islamization, and the arrival of the Mongol Empire.

Afghanistan in pre-international systems

The period before international systems arrived in world history is significant because we find the institutionalization of important structures and norms joining the peoples of the Eurasian continent. Notably, Buzan and Little date the start of this period 'back at least 40,000 years' to the 'fourth millennium BC[E]' (2000, 111). Over the past two decades, advanced scientific research has, however, shed more light on this timeframe, illuminating the central role of Africa in human evolution. Contemporary DNA analysis and skeletal evidence confirm that Homo sapiens emerged in Africa around 200,000 years ago.[3] A critical study shows the Makgadikgadi–Okavango palaeo-wetland in modern-day Botswana, Namibia and Zimbabwe as our probable origin point (Chan et al 2019). Prompted by environmental changes and evolutionary advancements in behaviour, these pioneers began their exodus from southern Africa about 60,000 years ago. Their migration routes onto other continents followed the Sinai or the Bab-el-Mandeb strait (Mellars 2006; Pagani et al 2015). Upon leaving Africa, they found crucial junctions in areas that now correspond to modern-day Iran and Iraq.[4] These junctures acted as dispersal epicentres. Moving at an estimated pace of less than half a kilometre a year, these groups branched out, gradually populating West Asia before diverging to other continents, including Europe, Central, East and South Asia, Australia, and the Americas. Whether parts of what is now called Afghanistan were a crossroads for populations migrating to Asia remains probable but a matter of speculation. The rugged terrains and variable climate patterns would have inevitably acted as a formidable barrier, potentially shaping the routes and adaptations of the early Homo sapiens migrating to the East. The region below the Hindu Kush could have been more aligned with South Asian populations, while its northern territory would likely have experienced Central Asian influences. However, as Davis demonstrates from archaeological records, '[t]here is no question that by

---

[3] I have abbreviated here from Homo sapiens sapiens, a subspecies of Homo sapiens. The necessity of designating a subspecies is contested, given that modern humans are the only living members of the genus Homo.

[4] Accordingly, today's global population has a common connection to a single group of Homo sapiens sapiens from 2,000 generations ago, as they crossed from Africa and through today's Middle East to settle the globe and replace other branches of early humans.

Middle Palaeolithic times [no later than 30000 years ago], Afghanistan was inhabited. During this period, there was an expansion of human populations into higher latitudes, and the movement into the continental interiors of Asia is well-documented' (2019, 97).

Besides highlighting the importance of topography and climate, this is important to our historical account as it dates the emergence of pre-international systems in the region we now call Afghanistan. Broadly, a defining feature of pre-international systems in world history is that they were dominated by 'mobile, egalitarian, hunter-gatherer bands' (Buzan and Little 2000, 112). To use Buzan and Little's terminology, mobile, egalitarian, hunter-gatherer bands were the basic *unit* to which people belonged; sharing norms that created the boundaries of a social system. These interdependent social formations were too small, mobile and insufficiently hierarchical to generate an 'inside' and an 'outside'; a feature that characterizes the present state system. Accordingly, hunter-gatherer bands stand apart from what IR theory has defined as an international system. Yet, the existence of hunter-gatherer bands and the way they operated challenges a fundamental Realist premise of IR theory. As Buzan and Little demonstrate, 'there has never been a pre-social Hobbesian world of human beings in which life was nasty, brutish and short. We know human beings have always lived in society because they evolved from primates, which are now all recognised to be innately social beings' (2000, 111).

Hunter-gatherer bands, which consisted of close-knit families, operated as norm circles and reinforced norms that underpinned social institutions such as speech, marriage and gift-giving. Again, to use Buzan and Little's terminology, these facilitated the *interaction capacity* of the period.[5] These norms and their emergent social institutions allowed hunter-gatherer bands to interact far beyond the boundary that circumscribed the members of their immediate band. Chains of social networks spread across continents because of these complex social institutions. Significantly, sociopolitical relations operated based on *authority* rather than military and economic power. This marks a distinct norm operating within pre-international systems. In the modern territories of Afghanistan, north of the Hindu Kush in the semi-arid steppe zone, there is evidence of hunter-gatherer bands operating, surviving off open steppe vegetation and hunting and operating in this way (Davis 2019). This time pre-dates the inside/outside dichotomy that structures the discipline of IR, along with the assumption of territorially fixed units (Buzan and Little 2000, 160–2).

---

[5]   Interaction capacity is defined as 'the level of transportation, communication and organisation capacity in the unit/system that determines what types and levels of interaction are possible' (Buzan and Little 2000, 441).

The pre-international period began to end once nomadic hunter-gatherers started to become settled agriculturalists. In northern Afghanistan, carbon dating evidence shows this starting to take place at approximately 8000 BCE, with the discovery of domesticated animals and agricultural tools (Dupree et al 1972). The Neolithic revolution would, however, take millennia to be fully institutionalized through its composite norms and technological innovations. The evidence base for the intervening years is sparse. However, through the Neolithic period, settlements were made, and early sedentary agriculturists in northern Afghanistan became linked to broad-scale interactive processes in neighbouring regions. Doubtless, however, was the fact that this was a period of *nucleation* as hunter-gatherer bands settled down into small villages, which became the dominant unit within pre-international systems as this period began to transition into a period of ancient and classical international systems (Buzan and Little 2000, 112). Within Buzan and Little's framework, hunter-gatherer bands settled in village communities, which they term '*tribes*'. This allowed more hierarchical domestic structures to emerge, with chiefs as new political actors. These *chiefdoms* were unstable units until the rise of city-states and the formation of the first international systems (Buzan and Little 2000, 134–5).

The importance of this period for the analysis presented in this chapter is that it is possible to discern that in the absence of anything resembling a concentrated urbanization or a state, norms of kinship and authority bound social units operating in both egalitarian and more hierarchical domestic structures. Residual traces of these norms continue today. Tribes continue to maintain high levels of autonomy inside Afghanistan. These groups continue to emphasize norms of kinship, egalitarianism and social solidarity, along with an emphasis on the norms of 'honour, respect, hospitality, and family solidarity' (Rasuly-Paleczek 2021). They are not ruled nor should they be defined by a Hobbesian 'state of nature'. They exist within social structures reinforced by norm circles and the practices they maintain. Notably, the social structures of groups inside Afghanistan differ, and anthropologists such as Noelle (1998) have provided more granular detail than what is required here. Nevertheless, anthropologists such as Barfield have utilized the broader typology set out by ibn Khaldun in his 14th-century sociological framework dividing *desert civilization* and *sedentary civilization*. Barfield demonstrates how tribal warriors inhibiting marginal zones inside Afghanistan continue to exhibit desert civilization characteristics through strong community solidarity (Barfield 2010, 77). This contrasts with sedentary civilization, which ibn Khaldun explained emphasized hierarchy, social classes and concentrations of wealth/residence-based identities. Sedentary civilization has little social solidarity but a strong economic interdependence. Barfield demonstrates that inside Afghanistan, people continue to ascribe to desert norms. As a result, he identifies that *desert civilization* and *sedentary civilization* have come to live as two worlds interacting but not integrating inside Afghanistan today (Barfield 2010, 10–11). The origins of this tension, which can be better understood as tensions between competing norm circles and practices rather than 'civilizations', began in the ancient and classical period when larger international systems emerged.

The formation of international systems: city-states, nomads and the norm of heterarchy

Pre-international systems began transforming into international systems in the fourth and third millennium BCE. This started as sedentary tribes and chiefdoms gave way to city-states, and the elements of international systems became nested into more expansive pre-international systems. The first of these were the Sumerian city-states of Akkad, Babylon, Girsu, Isin, Kish, Mari, Nippur, Sippar, Ur and Uruk in what is now southern Iraq. The expansion of these city-states was driven by new battles over fertile land and fresh water. With their expanding size and internal complexity, these city-states could generate something that would be recognized as a territorial 'inside/outside' distinction; along with this, came the introduction of wars and empires. Indeed, around 2340 BCE, Sargon, leader of the Akkadians, and his army overran the Sumerian city-states to unite Akkadian and Sumerian speakers under one rule. This would become the first empire in human history until its collapse around 2100 BCE (Duiker and Spielvogel 2002, 8). For Buzan and Little, the importance of this period, which ran from the Sumerian states through to the 16th century, is that it introduced city-states, sedentary empires, and nomadic tribes and empires as fundamental units of the world's international systems (Buzan and Little 2000b, 164–89). These would have a lasting impact on Afghanistan.

From around the third millennium BCE, Afghanistan was inhabited mainly by Iranic tribes. These were the descendants of the Indo-Aryan Iranian language groups that migrated south from Central Asia, only to displace the Dravidian people, who in turn moved south into the Indian subcontinent (Tanner 2009, 7). In this respect, what is now called Afghanistan fitted within Indo-Persia, which interconnected regions spanning Iran through to Bangladesh (Ludden 2021). This is an often-overlooked influence, because of a shift towards Turko-Persian dominance in Afghanistan from the 11th to 19th centuries. Significantly, when situated within Indo-Persia a *nucleation* process occurred.[6] South of the Hindu Kush, the 'Helmand civilization' maintained the largest prehistoric town of Mundigak, northwest of

---

[6] The oldest sedentary occupation recognized in northern Afghanistan dates to approximately 3500–2500 BCE (Francfort et al 2019).

Kandahar, which dates from approximately 4000 BCE. Over two millennia, Mundigak transformed from a small agricultural village to a major centre but was abandoned when Kandahar emerged as the major centre (Petrie and Shaffer 2019). The Helmand civilization had extensive links with the 'Indus civilization', belonging to the same 'interaction sphere' (Cortesi et al 2008; Jarrige et al 2011). In the north between 2250 and 1700 BCE, the Bactro-Margiana Cultural Complex (BMAC) or 'Oxus civilization' introduced two major innovations: an economy centred on domesticated plants and animals and the rise of stratified societies. Increased urbanization and interaction began a period of regionalization, where *desert norms* and newly emergent *sedentary norms* began to coexist. The material world played an important part in this process. That *nucleation* emerged along earthquake-prone tectonic fractures is not by chance. As the Indian plate crashed into the Eurasian plate, it formed the Himalayan mountain range, providing fertile agricultural sediment and water springs (Dartnell 2018, 25–8). Accordingly, the topography that provided the conditions for human settlement and allowed for food surpluses for trade and exchange divided the region along two sides of seismically active fault lines. It also shows how the region's topography had an early impact on shaping the social and political systems within the geographical space.[7]

Notably, the development of the Helmand civilization and Oxus civilization in the Indo-Persia region fits neatly into the world historical narrative set out by Buzan and Little. However, there is a need to add to this framework because of the Indus Valley civilization. This civilization spanned the region along the Indus River, from today's northeast Afghanistan into Pakistan and northwest India. The civilization developed in three distinct periods, starting with the Early Harappan Phase (3300 BCE to 2600 BCE), the Mature Harappan Phase (2600 BCE to 1900 BCE) and the Late Harappan Phase (1900 BCE to 1300 BCE). What makes the Indus Valley civilization distinct is that within its cities, there was a lack of religious architectural structures and political palaces, pointing to the lack of a clearly defined political hierarchy.

---

[7] As the reader will no doubt have discerned, this author has an ontological commitment to complex naturalism and a critical materialist position. This is in line with the origins of critical realism and scientific realism (Bhaskar 1975). As Elder-Vass explains: 'For critical realists … we are ourselves material beings who are not dualistically separate from the world "out there" but rather are part of the same material world of things and events of which we have empirical experience. We obtain (fallible) knowledge of these things and events through a material process of perception. This process is itself influenced – but not simply determined – by social interactions. But even those social interactions are material processes, and when, as often, they operate in discursive form, we can access the texts concerned only because they themselves are presented to us in material forms' (2012, 251).

Rather than cities in this region consolidating around political hierarchies, they were heterarchical with a distribution of authority (Ehrenreich et al 1995). This was a complex society living in complex city structures. Yet, archaeological research demonstrates that it was far more egalitarian than other early complex societies and assumptions around hierarchies of power and urbanization are problematic, with the Indus civilization revealing that a ruling class is not a prerequisite for social complexity (Green 2021). As Eltsov makes clear for the Indus Valley Harappans:

> There was no linear progression from the pre-Harappan to post-Harappan cultures. Nor is there a simple correlation between the sociopolitical organisation of Harappan culture and those of other cultures existing in the Eurasian world in the 3rd millennium BC. The notion of historical universality is equally unenlightening because the traits of Harappan archaeology demonstrate, if anything, the idiosyncrasy of Harappan society on the grand scale of historical process … attempts to deploy either the concept of the state or the concept of chiefdom in the analysis of the Harappan culture are doomed to fail unless one stretches their definitions to include any politically complex or socially differentiated system. (Eltsov 2013, 306–7)

As this suggests, the Indus civilization peoples organized and operated around fundamentally different norms to other units at the time (Possehl 1998; Eltsov 2013). As Possehl summarizes in rejecting the notion of historical universality, 'the reason for dissatisfaction … comes down to one point: there is an increasingly poor fit between the "facts" as we know them and traditional evolutionary constructs' (Possehl 1998, 279).

For the purposes of this book, the Indus civilization illustrates an early example of how a Eurocentric analysis and concepts do not neatly fit the historical trajectory and context of Indo-Persia. It also indicates that in this region more egalitarian norms operated for millennia within heterarchical–city formations; rather than anything resembling the more hierarchical city-states of Europe. As a result, it is possible to add a new type of unit to Buzan and Little's framework, which is more regionally specific. Namely, the heterarchical–city formations south of the Hindu Kush, where political and economic centralization were limited. Indeed, there is no evidence of government or military establishments, and religious practices were decentralized with no single religious authority. This is despite high-quality urban planning (Ramesh 2023).[8] With no

---

[8] Buzan and Little explicitly allowed for such adaptation, noting a high level of caution needed when applying their model across the world (2000, 160–2). As such, this adaptation should be seen as an enhancement to their model rather than a challenge.

kingship, the region operated under a system of governance norms that can be best described as arranged around heterarchical-cities and, therefore, a 'non-state' format. Power was not consolidated in a central authority's hands but distributed among various urban entities spanning multiple territories. This form of governance would have necessitated a fluid approach to political alliances, with groups forming cooperative bonds that were likely temporary and situational. The resolution of political matters would have been achieved via a network of local councils engaging in dialogue and negotiation, not by a centralized edict.

Despite these loosely territorialized 'city polities' existing within a heterarchical structure, they maintained complex social and economic structures. These societies demonstrated advanced engagement in crafts and commerce while lacking any entity with a monopoly on violence typically associated with sovereign archaic states (Possehl 1998, 287–9). Relatedly, sovereignty over territory was not expressed with the robustness of more centralized chiefdoms and city-states. Nevertheless, complexity emerged as a product of extended interactions, which produced the 'Middle Asian Interaction Sphere' (MAIS) around 2500–1900 BCE (Possehl 2002, 2007). Within the MAIS, intense interregional interaction crisscrossed the Iranian Plateau, going to the west through the Persian Gulf and Mesopotamia and to the east through Central Asia. Consequently, Amiet (1986) described this period as the *Age of Exchange* to characterize the importance of these interactions. In the waning years of the third and the onset of the second millennium BCE, a surge in connectivity across the Central Asian highlands began to bridge communities throughout Eurasia. This escalating engagement set the stage for what would, over millennia, evolve into the famed Silk Road (Spengler 2015).

Adding to Buzan and Little's framework is significant, as it enriches the historical context of today's Afghanistan. Although the region was characterized by its interaction capacity, the units undertaking this interaction operated with more egalitarian norms to the more hierarchical expectations of world history. The Indus Valley civilization was not constructed from the city-states, sedentary empires, and nomadic tribes and empires Buzan and Little describe. Yet, the nature of these heterarchical-city formations interaction within the MAIS situates them within the first international systems Buzan and Little describe. Heterarchical-city formations entrenched *heterarchy* as a sociopolitical norm for millennia, which was resistant to centralization and hierarchy. *Heterarchy* gave the Indus Valley civilization the benefit of being more egalitarian and less prone to war than other early complex societies (Kumar et al 2020; Green 2021). Indeed, in championing *heterarchy* as a norm the associated norm circles would have valorized the principles of shared power and collective responsibility. This is a different way of practising social relations compared to centralization and hierarchy, but allowed for the adaptation, resilience and survival skills needed within a difficult terrain. The reasons for the Indus Valley civilization's gradual decline and deurbanization remain contested but coincide with the climate changes of the late Holocene and subsequent changes in river courses (Lawler 2008; Dixit et al 2014; Kumar et al 2020). With heterarchy presenting itself as a dominant social and political norm for two millennia, it is evident that the Indo-Persian region developed in ways divergent to the European experience. Indeed, historical evidence has demonstrated that there were interlinkages between the Indus Valley civilization and the Oxus civilization, which included beliefs, political alliances and imitation/emulation (Mutin and Lamberg-Karlovsky 2021). Moreover, although norms must be inherited and learned anew, it is reasonable to see this norm of *heterarchy* as having a residual influence on the more remote parts of Afghanistan today, where group interests continue to trump individual interests.

The interlinkage of multiple international systems: meeting Europe

It was not until the rise of the Achaemenid Empire that Afghanistan and Europe would become entangled inside the same international system. As this Persian empire created a transcontinental imperium, lasting from 559 BCE to 331 BCE, it stretched from Europe in the west to India in the east. In the north, it extended from Afghanistan and Central Asia, reaching south to Egypt (Tavernier 2021, 39–40). This empire unified the Iranian plateau, linking Asia, the Mediterranean and southeast Europe. To use Buzan and Little's framework, through increased economic and political interaction the boundaries of a new 'inside' was constituted. Indeed, Persian power changed the course of history in Central Asia and Europe, as imperial power enveloped new territory and reconstituted the inside/outside (Young 1988).

For what is now Afghanistan this period added the complexities of transcontinental imperial rule. Although the modern myth is that Afghanistan is the 'graveyard of empires', this was not the case for most Afghanistan's experience of empire. Indeed, in the 6th century BCE, after founding the Achaemenid Empire, Cyrus the Great would gain authority over what is now Afghanistan. Originating from a semi-nomadic Pasargadae tribe, the Achaemenid Empire would abandon this heritage and establish settlements and major urban areas to facilitate the structured administration of the empire (Wiesehfer 2009). As a result, the first Persian empire fits neatly into Buzan and Little's framework of new units emerging in this period. Moreover, following a period of instability, power over Achaemenid territory was consolidated when Darius I seized the throne around 522 BCE. To expand imperial rule, the empire moved west into Europe, conquering Thrace and getting as far as crossing the Danube River before being forced to retreat. This was a prelude to the Greco-Persian wars between the Achaemenian Empire and the Greek city-states between 499 and 449 BCE (see Waters 2014, 73–91).

On the empire's eastern side, Darius I consolidated his rule by introducing *satrapies*. As with the rest of the Achaemenid Empire, Central Asia was subdivided into *dahyava* (countries), where largely pre-existing cultural units were reconfigured into satrapal administrative units (Tolman 1908, 5; Morris 2020). Derived from Old Persian, a 'satrapy' refers to a province led by a governor that answers directly to the monarch (Waters 2014, 101). This imperial encounter demarcated Aria, Bactria, Sattagydia, Arachosia and Drangiana as administrative units within the dominion of Achaemenid power (Ferrario 2022; Ali et al 2023; see also Maniscalco 2018).[9] This fits Watson's model of functional differentiation within empires, which underpins Buzan and Little's framework (Buzan and Little 2000, 179). Herein, the sway and control exerted by an empire over other entities diminishes with the growing distance from the central power. This framework differentiates among hegemony, characterized by de facto restrictions on external foreign policy caused by the influence of empire; suzerainty, wherein other units accept the empire's rightful authority over their foreign policy; and dominion, wherein the central power also dictates elements of the entities' internal governance (Watson 1992, 14–16). Being physically close to the imperial core, the Achaemenid Empire was able to exercise dominion over the early political and cultural landscape of what is now Afghanistan by imposing an imperial administration. In effect, bolstering the norms of ibn Khaldun's *sedentary civilization*, with a veneer of hierarchy and stratified administrative units over these territories.

For two centuries, the Achaemenid Empire faced diminutive challenges to its dominions. However, the empire would fall when confronted by the Macedonian king Alexander the Great's conquest. Between 330 BCE and 325 BCE, Alexander devoted much of his time to military campaigns in Afghanistan, Pakistan and India. The Macedonian Empire crossed what Buzan and Little term 'civilisational boundaries' as innovative military technology and organizational strategies accelerated forward advancement

---

[9]   Aria was located in modern-day Herat, the third largest city in present-day Afghanistan. Bactria, the most well-known satrap, was situated between the Hindu Kush mountains and the Amu Darya (Oxus) River in parts of what are now northern Afghanistan, Uzbekistan and Tajikistan. Sattagydia occupied the region around modern-day Ghazni, about 150km south of Kabul, Afghanistan's current capital. Arachosia was the southernmost satrap, located near present-day Kandahar, while Drangiana lay about 400km west of Kabul in today's Sistan region (Ali et al 2023).

and increased the interaction capacity between Europe and Asia (Buzan and Little 2000, 182; also see Worthington 2014).[10] In the wake of his conquests, he established Greek-style kingdoms and left a lasting imprint of Hellenistic culture in Afghanistan and the wider Indo-Persian region (Wallace 2016). Indeed, Alexander maintained the satrap system, even as this conquest marked a significant shift in the dynamics of power between Europe and Afghanistan (Holt 1988; Morris 2020). Yet, Alexander faced disorder from nomadic peoples when he attempted to circumscribe trade and close the borders of his empire in the east. Order was only restored when trade resumed and Alexander married Roxane, the daughter of the Oxyartes, a chief originating from a tribe near the Oxus River. As one historian noted, '[a]s much a bribe as a bride, Roxane brought the warring factions together' (Holt 2012, 57). While this maintained the norm of unity through marriage in the region, it was not a norm for Greeks and Macedonians that were alarmed by this practice. Over time, the first European attempt to transform Afghanistan collapsed. The reasons for this should be familiar to contemporary policy makers, as historians have long referenced strong resistance from the local population, the difficult terrain and climate, cultural and religious differences, and lack of effective governance and administration (Prevas 2004; Holt 2012; Wallace 2016). With the empire unable to exercise hegemony so far from the imperial core, the local population, practising the norms of heterarchy, resisted attempts to maintain systems of hierarchy in and through the satrap. Moreover, following Alexander's death, administrative control of the *satrapies* fell to the Seleucid Empire, founded by one of Alexander's generals. However, with growing pressures and the gradual erosion of its territories, the Greco-Bactrian Kingdom was declared independent around 250 BCE, becoming a major centre for trade and cultural exchange for three centuries on the Silk Road (Tarn 2010; Golden 2011, 25). Bactria stopped being an

---

[10] Thus far in this volume the term 'civilization' has been used uncritically, namely because it is used within the literatures being reviewed. However, there is some need for ontological clarity at this point because a tension could be perceived between the assertion of a critical realist framework emphasizing norm circles and the world historical narrative framework guiding the periodization of this chapter. Accordingly, it should be specified that this author adheres to 'civilization' only to the extent that it is shorthand for higher cultural norms and resultant practices. 'Culture', however, is being defined within the framework of norm circles wherein '[o]nly individuals have the power to hold beliefs; only groups have the power to designate those beliefs as elements of shared culture. Culture is not simply belief, but socially endorsed belief, and that social endorsement can only be brought about by a group – a norm circle' (Elder-Vass 2012, 44). Moreover, 'culture and structure are emergent from interactions between human individuals, through today's culture may be a product of such interactions of the past rather than in the immediate present. Culture, then, is ontologically distinct from human agency but (at least historically) dependent upon it' (Elder-Vass 2012, 41).

eastern imperial frontier and transformed into a new imperial territory in its own right (Morris 2020). What followed was a dynamic period of increased interaction within the region (see Kumar et al 2021). Cut off from Europe, art in Bactria reveals a confluence of Greek, Indian Buddhist and wider Eastern styles (Martinez-Sève 2014, 2015).

Islam and medieval Afghanistan: Islamization as discursive norm circles

Afghanistan remained central to world history and empire early in the first millennium. With the rise of the Kushan Empire, started by the nomadic Yuezhi tribe from the Central Asian steppe, Afghanistan fell under the rule of the new empire emanating from Bactria, and extending through the Indus Valley to the North Indian Plain. This introduced a more feudal structure with local rulers owing allegiance to the central authority but retaining a degree of independence. As Liu (2020) explains, the 'Kushan regime gave much autonomy to local institutions such as castes, guilds, and Buddhist monasteries and meanwhile won support from those local communities'. Indeed, although the Kushans were instrumental in spreading Buddhism, the empire was cosmopolitan in character and provided an economic bridge between the east and west. This was maintained by establishing new norms around diplomacy, which aided in the development of interaction capacity in the ancient and classical worlds more generally (Buzan and Little 2000, 209).[11] Nevertheless, over three centuries, the Kushan Empire fragmented, and by 300 CE, the Sasanian Empire seized Afghanistan, renewing Persian influence. The Sassanid had a significant impact on the cultural and socioeconomic development of the Afghan region, with Zoroastrianism becoming the dominant religion, even as Christians in Armenia and Transcaucasia survived persecution on the empire's border with Eastern Europe (Kerr and Wright 2015). However, it was the rise of Islam that would come to have the most profound normative transformation of the region from the mid-first millennium through to today.

As Buzan and Little outline, 'the rise of Islam, one of the world's greatest civilisations', was a product of nomadic tribes which played a unique role in the evolution of international systems (Buzan and Little 2000, 183). In Arabia, the Prophet Muhammad united the Bedonie in the 7th century CE, creating a state structure with a Bedonie identity and mission to spread

---

[11] Notably, as Buzan and Little set out, rudimentary forms of diplomacy were evident in pre-international systems. Drawing on Numelin's work, they demonstrate how many of the essential elements of modern diplomacy were exercised by hunter-gatherer bands (Buzan and Little 2000, 129–30).

Islam (Buzan and Little 2000, 186; Manz 2021). Facilitating this, nomads developed faster transportation systems by domesticating horses and camels, allowing greater mobility and the colonization of deserts and the steppe (Levine 1999). This expedited an increased interaction capacity, and Islam emerged as a significant global religion and cultural force.

Following the Prophet Muhammad's passing, successive *caliphs* assumed leadership over the Muslim populace (Donner 2000).[12] At its pinnacle, the caliphate stood as a geopolitical behemoth, overshadowing the territorial expanse and demographic makeup of the Roman Empire (Marsham 2021). Stretching from Spain to India, the caliphate represented the most dramatic expansion of faith and power since the rise of Christianity. It forged a geopolitical linkage between the Mediterranean and the Iranian Plateau through to Afghanistan.

The rise of the caliphate was facilitated by internal Arab dissent following the death of the Prophet Muhammad. Abu Bakr [al-Siddiq] took on the Prophet's former role as political leader and administrator of the Muslim community. This established the new office of the caliph. However, many Arab leaders renounced their allegiance to Islam and refused to pay *zakat*, the religious tax, to the central Islamic authority. This threatened the unity and authority of Islam and the nascent central authority based in Medina. The Ridda wars, or apostasy wars, were initiated to re-establish the caliph's central authority and unify Arabia (Qureshi 1981; Donner 1993; Gordon 2020). The significance of this is felt today, as waves of external conquests shaped the Eurasian and African continents.

Although a standing army was established for internal unification, it allowed the caliphate to project its power externally. The caliphate proceeded with simultaneous conflicts in Syria and Palestine while confronting the Sasanian Empire in today's southern Iraq. Sasanian defences were unsuccessful. Under the suzerain power of the *satrap* system, the Sasanian Empire maintained a relatively light footprint and its defences were unable to prevent invasion outside the capital (see Azad 2016). The pivotal battle in 637 CE at al-Qadisiyah led to a significant defeat for the Sasanians, allowing the occupation of what is now Iraq. By the mid-650s, the caliphate covered a vast region from Yemen to Armenia and Egypt to eastern Iran (Donner 2000, 12). As the caliphate and its associated international system grew, to the east lay Afghanistan and the fringes of Central Asia.

Incrementally, the caliphate began to encroach upon what is now Afghanistan, starting a process of 'Islamization'. That is to say, the spread of Islamic norms and associated practices by expanding the norm circles

---

[12] The term caliph is derived from the Arabic khalifa (خليفة), meaning 'successor' or 'representative'.

of people willing to enforce them. Nevertheless, as Green systematically outlines, 'there is no doubt that the initial coming of Islam to Afghanistan occurred through the conquests of Arab generals serving the Rashidun caliphs (r. 632–61) and the Umayyad dynasty (r. 661–750) based in Damascus' (2016, 3).

A landmark moment in this period was 652 CE, as the ancient city of Zarang (Zaranj in southwest Afghanistan on the border with Iran) surrendered, and Balkh, Badghis and the trade route city Herat were subdued (Bosworth 2007, 153; Azad 2016; Green 2016). By 709 CE, Balkh was placed under the direct rule of the caliphate and became an important centre for regional *Islamization*. Here Islam can be understood as a set of norms and normative institutions being enforced by a *discursive norm circles*. Discursive norm circles are 'specifically concerned with endorsing and enforcing discursive norms' such as 'norms about what sort of things may be said, must be said, and must not be said' (Elder-Vass 2012, 153).[13] As a result, we can understand Islamization as a process of recruiting people willing to enforce the discursive norms and support Islamic practices and institutions. The utility of this is that it helps account for why Islam took time to embed itself within the caliphate's dominions, and why in Afghanistan there was a 'repetitive pattern of submission, rebellion, and resistance' until 'eventually final submission' (Azad 2016, 47). Moreover, by seeing Islam being enforced by a *discursive norm circle*, it is possible to account for considerable variation of practices and their enforcement over time and space.

The caliphate was able to rule over the province of Khurasan, which spans what is now northeastern Iran, southern Turkmenistan and northern Afghanistan, by co-opting and eventually assimilating local power-holders into enforcing Islamic norms. Nevertheless, there were uprisings throughout Balkh, Herat and Sistan, mainly driven by new converts' resentment towards taxation by the central authority. By 749 CE, however, internal strife within the caliphate culminated in the Abbasid dynasty ousting the Umayyad dynasty, starting the third significant caliphate in Islamic history. In their quest for expansion and dominance, the Abbasid dynasty ventured eastwards, driven by the allure of acquiring access to new goods, wealth from trade, taxes, and enslaved people. The Abbasid dynasty's systematic and determined efforts bore fruit when they established control over Kabul by 870 CE. This marked a significant milestone in their eastward endeavours, allowing for the Islamization of the Kabul region in the 9th and 10th centuries (Bosworth 2007, 256–7). As Green's seminal volume demonstrates at length:

---

[13] Notably, this is considered to be a post-Foucauldian theory of discourse, even as Elder-Vass sets out this position in relation to Foucauldian principles. It is a realist theory of discourse (Elder-Vass 2012, 157).

It was not until almost 900 CE that Muslim political power was proclaimed over all the region's main cities. And it was not until some time afterwards that Islam reached the majority of the region's population. Remote mountain regions … remained beyond … reach … till the eleventh century, while so-called Kafiristan ('Land of the Infidels') held on to its indigenous religion till the conquests … in the late nineteenth century. … Some communities, including wealthy Jewish and Hindu merchant groups, avoided conversion entirely to survive into recent times … pre-Islamic cultural practices continued after nominal conversion … overall [our] understanding of the expansion and variety of Islam in the region remains … patchy. (Green 2016, 3–5)

Despite the intense scrutiny Afghanistan has received, our understanding of its religious lineage remains surprisingly superficial compared to our knowledge of Islamic history in the broader Middle East and South Asia. Nevertheless, it is worth illustrating that Islam took approximately two-and-a-half centuries to gain a firm foothold in Afghan urban centres and a staggering millennium to permeate Afghanistan's more secluded territories. This slow progression underscores the profound patience and time often required for *discursive norm circles* to entrench themselves and motivate widespread practices. Afghanistan stands out as particularly resistant because in other conquered lands of the caliphate the Islamization of the native inhabitants is largely considered 'extraordinarily rapid' (Finer 1999, 671). In and of itself, this points to an inability of centralized, hierarchical structures to impose norms on a terrain that favours heterarchy. This should have come as a cautionary tale for those seeking to diffuse Western norms inside Afghanistan in the 21st century, but such consideration was remarkably absent in light of casting Afghanistan as a 'blank slate'.

The impact Islamic norms have had on Afghanistan are abundant and have not escaped the pertinent issues of state centralization, political legitimacy and regional power. Here it is necessary to compress a fascinating period of history for the purposes of explaining these dynamics. The Tahirids in Khorasan, around 821 CE, were able to gain greater independence of the Abbasid caliphate.[14] This marked a period of decentralization in the caliphate where religious authority was no longer backed by direct imperial control, and suzerainty became normalized (El-Hibri 2021, 143). The Tahirids maintained a commitment to Sunni Islam but have a place in Islamic history

---

[14] Khorasan is an expansive region of the eastern Iranian plateau that encompassed today's northeastern Iran and the modern territories of Balkh and Herat through to the Oxus River.

for being the first provincial governors in the east to gain this suzerain status (Bosworth 1969). By 869 CE, regional power dynamics shifted with the ascension of the Saffarids, a dynasty indigenous to Sistan. The Saffarids supplanted the Tahirids and sought to establish a strong centralized system of governance, which would be the basis for the East Persian-Tajik identity to emerge (Negmatov 1998). The Abbasid caliphate recognized this transition, even though this brought an independent emirate to power that was a challenge to the authority of the Abbasid caliphate itself. Indeed, by 876 CE the Saffarids had advanced on Baghdad only to be defeated by the caliphate (Musa and Hamidi 2021). By 900 CE, the Saffarid dynasty crumbled and gave way to the Samanid dynasty. The Samanids consolidated their rule in Transoxania and extended their geopolitical influence to Khorasan and as far afield as Kandahar (Negmatov 1998).[15] Although the Samanids assembled a more centralized state, this began to collapse towards the end of the 10th century. As a result of these internal crises, and a growing reliance on Turkish slave troops, the Ghaznavid Empire was able to rise and reach its height between 998 and 1030 CE (Bosworth 1998).

The importance of the 9th and 10th centuries for the narrative of Afghanistan being presented in this chapter is three-fold. First, it was in this period that the region was becoming more autonomous within the Islamic international system. Second, that increasing attempts were made to build more centralized systems of governance to support this growing autonomy. Third, it set the stage for a shift in geopolitical alliance from Indo-Persia to Turko-Persia with the rise of the Ghaznavid Empire. As a result, the 10th to 11th centuries marked an important period of transitional consolidation, where these three norms gave rise to an emergent form of governance under the Ghaznavid Empire. To maintain more autonomous power and centralization, Bosworth demonstrates, 'the pattern of the despotic power-state introduced by the Ghaznavids became the norm for many of the subsequent pre-modern Islamic dynasties' (1998, 124). As Barfield illustrates, 'from the mid-tenth century to the mid-eighteenth century, every dynasty that ruled in the region was either of Turko-Mongolian origin or had a military that was dominated by Turko-Mongolian peoples' (2010, 66–7). Moreover, because the Ghaznavids had no indigenous legitimacy, they aligned their political goals with religious legitimacy and appealed to Islamic norms to legitimize their power. Indeed, the modern state of Pakistan stems from the Ghaznavid campaigns spreading Islamic norms across the Indus River (Tanner 2009, 77; Sanchooli and Hosseini 2021). Thus, even though the power of the Ghaznavids would fade, with the Seljuq Turks annexing

---

[15]   Transoxania approximately corresponds to present-day Uzbekistan and parts of Turkmenistan, Tajikistan and Kazakhstan.

most of the Ghaznavids' western territories, and eventually fragmentation of the empire into smaller successor states, their historical legacy is present today. Indeed, that legacy was felt even more keenly by the short-lived Ghurids and the Khwarazmian Empires rose to power until the 13th-century Mongol Conquest.

The Mongols and Afghanistan

Originating from the steppe of Central Asia, the Mongol Empire would span from the Pacific Ocean in the east to the Danube River in Ukraine. In the annals of world history, this is unique and allowed the Mongols to create vast networks across Eurasia while also refining and spreading imperial technologies that were later embraced by future regimes. Their uniqueness is further highlighted by their existence as a nomadic empire on a scale, unlike anything the world had ever seen. This empire relied on 'organised mobility' as its 'organised, mobile and self-sufficient armies' focused on invading the powers along the Silk Road (Burbank and Cooper 2010, 94–104). This meant going through Afghanistan en route to Europe.

By 1219 CE, the Mongols, under Chinggis Khan, had begun the invasion of the Khwarizm Empire, and by the 1220s CE reached Khurasan and Transoxania. This invasion was triggered by the failed diplomatic overtures to the Shah of Khwarezm in today's Iran and the execution of Chinggis' envoys and merchants (Burbank and Cooper 2010, 103). With no reverence for Islamic norms, the Mongols systematically slaughtered local populations to instil terror and prevent future insurrections. With the Mongols being a highly organized nomadic society, settled communities became targets for pillaging, but rather than assimilating these new urban populations into the Mongol Empire, entire populations were annihilated, leading to a period of depopulation and systematic destruction (Bira 1998). Yet, as Frankopan explains, '[a]lthough the Mongols seemed to be chaotic, bloodthirsty and unreliable, their rise was not the result of a lack of order but precisely the opposite: ruthless planning, streamlined organisation and a clear set of strategic objectives were the key to establishing the largest land empire in history' (2016, 128). Indeed, unlike the heterarchical norms that prevailed from the pre-international systems period, Chinggis Khan's empire spread hierarchical lineage norms to support centralized rule. This allowed bigger and more powerful empires to function. As Barfield explains:

> Turko-Mongolian tribal systems proved strong because their people, unlike the more egalitarian Bedouins and Pashtuns [in today's Afghanistan], accepted the legitimacy of hierarchical differences. Indeed, hierarchy was embedded into the very DNA of their social organization, with ranking distinctions between elder and younger

brothers, senior and junior generations, noble and common clans, and ultimately the ruling dynasty and everyone else. (Barfield 2010, 81)

In these circumstances political legitimacy was gained through conquest, which was then conferred via lines of succession. Norms of hierarchy began to dominate the empire being created and erode the norms of heterarchy that characterized pre-international systems. Thus, although Chinggis Khan died in 1226 CE, this did not stop the march of the Mongol Empire. Hulagu Khan, a grandson of Genghis Khan, was tasked with capturing Iran and defeating the Abbasid caliphate in Baghdad (Biran 2016). Herein, although the Abbasid caliphate was in decline long before the Mongols vanquished Baghdad in 1258 CE, the Mongols definitively ended the Islamic Golden Age (Biran 2016). Upon doing so, the Il-Khanid dynasty was established, and the Ilkhanate ruled what is now Iran and parts of Turkmenistan, Turkey, Iraq, Armenia, Afghanistan and Pakistan from approximately 1256 to 1335 CE. This situated the Ilkhanate next to the Mamluks based in Egypt and the Mongol 'Great State' of the Golden Horde that stretched from Eastern Europe to Siberia.

Over time, as Mongol leaders settled, 'they lost their tactical advantages over their rivals and motives for unity among themselves'. As a result, '[w]ar between the Mongol khanates became as promising as war at the edges of the nomadic empire' (Burbank and Cooper 2010, 112). In Buzan and Little's terms, the nature of the units changed when this happened, from nomadic empires to city-state systems of empire (Buzan and Little 2000, 167–89). This is borne out in the historical record, whereby the Ilkhanate leaders built and maintained several important cities, including Tabriz, Maragheh and Sultaniya, gradually transforming this nomadic Empire into city-states (Jackson 2017, 116–24). Transforming the nature of the unit had a significant impact on relations between the Mongols. In an attempt to generate a balance of power against the Golden Horde, the Ilkhanate sought closer cooperation with China, and there was also a willingness to seek cooperation with European powers such as England and Prince Edward's 1271 Crusade for the Holy Lands (Amitai 2007; Biran 2016). Indeed, even under the rule of Ghazan Khan, from 1295 to 1304 CE, who formally established Islam as the state religion of the Ilkhanate, diplomatic ties with China and Europe were maintained (Amitai-Preiss 1996; Biran 2015). However, as important as the Ilkhanate was in defining the region, it was short-lived. Following the death of Ghazan Khan in 1304, the Ilkhanate entered a period of instability marked by internal power struggles among his successors. This weakened the central authority and led to divisions within the empire, making it susceptible to external threats. Neighbouring powers like the Mamluks and the Timurids in Central Asia capitalized on this internal turmoil to assert their geopolitical interests and territorial expansion. The Ilkhanate's military efforts to counter these external challenges largely failed, exacerbating their weakened state. This combination of internal discord and external pressures created a cycle of decline for the Ilkhanate, undermining its ability to maintain control and defend its territories effectively (Morgan 2009). By 1335, however, Abu Sa'id's failure to leave a direct male heir led to the collapse of the Ilkhanate and its fragmentation. As a result, many settled Mongols merged into Turkic Muslim tribes across the fractured lands (Burbank and Cooper 2010, 112). In Afghanistan today, the Uzbeks, Turkmen and Hazaras all claim heritage from these settled Mongol tribes (Lee 2022, 16).

Although the Ilkhanate was relatively short, the importance of the Mongols cannot be underestimated. The Mongol Empire expedited Eurasian integration and ushered in the early modern era. As Biran argues, 'our globalised world can be viewed as a progeny of the Mongols' imperial enterprise' (2015, 555). Indeed, during the Middle Ages, Europe was a sideshow in global power struggles, but with greater economic openness and exchange, new opportunities for European traders and missionaries emerged. This interaction sparked a newfound European interest in Asia, elevating it from a peripheral concern to a central topic of discussion. This shift in focus had lasting effects on Europe, driving interest in trade, sea exploration and knowledge-sharing. In short, the era of the Mongol Empire was more than just a period of military conquest; it reshaped European thought and economic direction (Frankopan 2016). Indeed, when the Italian explorer Cristoforo Colombo led his Spanish explorations and the colonization of the Americas, he was in search of the land of the 'Great Khan' that he had read of in *The Travels of Marco Polo* (Biran 2015, 555).

It was not just a network of shared ideas and economies that the Mongol Empire facilitated. The pathways the Mongols carved in their quest for dominance became the conduits for something far beyond human control. The intricate network of trade and communication routes, once a testament to the Mongols' prowess, morphed into a dark harbinger of turmoil. The Black Death changed the course of global politics. The rise of the European international system would not just lead to the decline of Asian powers but start a process of globalization and the emergence of the global international system that has been central to the study of IR (Buzan and Little 2000, 241–346).

Transitioning to modernity and the global international system

Contemporary DNA research has placed the origins of the bubonic plague between 1338 and 1339 in what is now northern Kyrgyzstan (Spyrou et al 2022). Over its initial eight-year course, it claimed the lives of up to 60 per cent of the Western Eurasian population (Benedictow 2021). In

Europe, it killed millions and led to a period of depopulation. As Europe's population collapsed, wage labour rose along with challenges to the norms of the Church. As May (2013, 203) details, 'old beliefs and methods simply did not or could not function in post-plague Europe. In short, the plague, with its devastating death toll, fundamentally altered the European world'. Unfortunately, there are few primary or secondary sources dealing with the Black Death's impact on the fragmented territories of the Ilkhanate, leaving a considerable gap in our understanding of its impact. Nevertheless, it is widely accepted that it expediated the collapse of the Mongol Empire because, as Frankopan outlines, '[f]rom field to farm and city to village, the Black Death created hell on earth: putrid, rotting bodies, oozing with pus, set against a background of fear, anxiety and disbelief at the scale of suffering' (2016, 151). It is only through inference from contemporaneous Persian accounts, and those that followed in the Timurid era, that the Black Death's impact on Afghan territories can be discerned (see Fazlinejad and Ahmadi 2018).[16] Thus, not only would there have been a devastating depopulation effect in urban centres, but it is reasonable to suggest that this would have led to a period of counterurbanization as people escaped cities and returned to agrarian life. Moreover, unlike in Europe, there is evidence of an increase in religiosity which strengthened the relationship between rulers and the religious classes (Schamiloglu 2017, 337–8). As Zarakol notes of the early 15th century, 'in this period … we increasingly see a hybridisation between sacred and political orders and rulers'. This included Timur, who 'enjoyed a cult like following among a group of his soldiers who treated him as their spiritual guide' (Zarakol 2022, 100).

Timur is recognized as the final conqueror from Central Asia to accomplish significant military triumphs while commanding a coalition of nomadic warrior chieftains. Within Buzan and Little's framework, this is a testament to the diminishing nomadic empires drawing an end to the classical world of multiple interlinked international systems (Buzan and Little 2000, 241–76). Timur's governance extended across agrarian and nomadic populations on an imperial magnitude. Timur became the Emir of Transoxiana in 1370 CE, having conquered the territories of Iraq, Persia and Afghanistan, and starting the Timurid dynasty from 1370 to 1506 CE. With the empire's capital in Samarqand, in modern-day Uzbekistan, this vast territory was not controlled by city-states but by a centralized authority with Timur as the dominant ruler who never took up a permanent abode.

Timur's conquests caught the attention of Western European rulers, who viewed him as a potential ally against the Ottoman Turks, who were expanding their territory in Europe. Key figures, including the Byzantine

---

[16]   Such accounts include major breakouts of plague around 1426 CE in Herat.

emperor and French King Charles VI, sought Timur's support against the Turks, leading to diplomatic exchanges. King Henry III of Castile was particularly interested in Timur's empire, sending envoys to gather information and establishing brief contact. Though no formal relations were established, Timur wanted to build relations before he died in 1405, observing that 'peace is strengthened by trade'. Timur's death cut short the possibility of a strategic alliance with European powers, as the empire faced a struggle for succession (Ashrafyan 1998). Indeed, the empire faced extreme political fragmentation and decentralization following Timur's death, which characterized much of the 15th century (Subtelny 1988).

Within this period it is notable that the norms of royal succession were reinforced, and political competition occurred within the boundaries of this political elite. In essence, two sets of norms now operated, the political elite now garnered political legitimacy from conquest, lineage and adherence to Islam. Conversely, tribal norms of heterarchy were maintained favouring egalitarianism, and loyalties to tribe, kin and location. This set the stage for a professional political elite to be in contestation with what Barfield eloquently terms 'tribal republicanism' (Barfield 2010, 105). For example, although there was political contestation following Timur's death, it was Shah Rukh, the fourth son of Timur, who claimed Central Asia as his own. He declared himself the independent ruler of a large domain that included Khurasan and the Herat region. Indeed, Herat soon became the capital and rapidly evolved into a pivotal cultural and political hub (Ashrafyan 1998). During this period, Herat witnessed a transformation, emerging as a nexus of art, science and commerce that attracted scholars, artists and intellectuals from various parts of the world; a testament to the Turkic-Mongol dynasty becoming renowned for its revival of artistic and intellectual life (Dale 1998; Lee 2016; Allchin et al 2019). Indeed, Kabul, captured in 1398 CE, also undertook a revival. As Subtelny (2007) argues, 'the late Timurid period ... [had] sophisticated artistic and literary achievements that arguably make it the most outstanding period in the cultural history of the medieval eastern Islamic world'. Accordingly, the new political elite would focus on major urban areas and largely leave the 'tribal republics' to their own devices.

The demise of the Timurid dynasty was marked by fragmentation, instability and insecurity, culminating in its fall to Uzbek forces in Herat in 1507. Efforts to resurrect the dynasty were briefly undertaken with Kabul as the capital, but it was in India that the empire found its renaissance. In 1526, Zahir-ud-Din Muhammad Babur, a descendant of Timur, laid the foundation for the Mughal Empire following his triumph in Delhi. The Mughal ascendancy ushered in an era where they emerged as one of the three prominent Islamic 'Gunpowder Empires' of the 16th and 17th centuries, alongside the Safavids and Ottomans. These empires were distinguished not only by their extensive territories, affluence and formidable power but also by their innovative military tactics, notably using gunpowder weaponry like cannons and muskets. Afghanistan, positioned at the strategic nexus of Central Asia and India, became a coveted prize among these empires. The Mughals, Safavids and Uzbeks relentlessly competed for its dominion, resulting in an epoch marked by recurrent warfare and regional instability.

Pashtun resistance and national consciousness

Although the Mughal Empire's primary focus was the Indian subcontinent, it endeavoured to preserve its Central Asian ties through key Afghan cities, setting the stage for conflict with the Persian Safavids to the west and northwest. These tensions were further complicated by the Safavids' own challenges from the expanding Ottoman Empire and Tsarist Russia (Jalali 2021, 236–8). Further stirring the Central Asian geopolitical cauldron was the Uzbek khanate, situated to Afghanistan's north and northeast. The Uzbeks, too, were grappling with the growing threats posed by the Kazakh khanate and the ascendant Oirat Empire, with territories in northwest China and eastern Turkistan (Jalali 2021, 236–8). This intricate geopolitical tapestry in Central Asia during the 16th and 17th centuries set the stage for fervent imperial contention, with the Mughal Empire at the forefront. Its influence over Afghanistan was not merely a matter of prestige but a crucial component of its strategic calculus.

While these empires battled at their peripheries, Afghans were trapped fighting for survival across the fault lines of these empires. This produced an inherently unstable milieu. For example, at its height, direct Mughal influence extended to Afghanistan's central regions like Ghazni and Bamiyan. This influence was facilitated by the Mughal Empire deploying a combination of control of critical cities but often providing rural areas with financial appeasements. In a society where power and authority are distributed through heterarchical norms, such payments can buy allegiance from tribal and ethnic leaders instrumental in mediating disputes, providing social services and representing their communities. However, while such payments strengthened relationships between rural areas and the empire, this was temporary by its very nature. Accordingly, this did not stabilize Mughal rule in the long term, even though it was the most engaged empire within Afghan territory. Instead, revolts were constant, and after 1677, the Mughal influence was limited to cities and the main routes between them (Pillalamarri 2017). Wink's characterization of Afghans in the early 15th century continued to hold: 'In the Afghan homeland, statehood had been aborted by the parochial focus on tribal loyalty and blood feuds. Afghan chiefs were normally no more than first among equals, unwilling to submit to kings, and often too proud to tolerate any authority for long' (Wink 2003, 134).

Afghans refused to be subjugated by the Mughals, and in the late 16th century and throughout the 17th century, they engaged in an asymmetric war against the Mughal Empire (Jalali 2021, 260–2). This began to institutionalize norms of asymmetric warfare, which did not just include the practices of war itself, but the lionization of individuals engaged in practices of resistance. The Afghans used their knowledge of the terrain and guerrilla tactics against the Mughals. They often attacked Mughal caravans and outposts, then melted into the mountains. The Mughals were eventually forced to withdraw. The norm of heterogeneity proved a strategic advantage in fighting off attempts to centralize power, and the superior mobility of a nomadic tradition proved instrumental in repelling outside forces. This helped to further shape Afghan identity around modernized nomadic and heterarchical norms and fed into narratives that laid the foundation for eventual Afghan independence. Indeed, these narratives have remained even as Afghanistan has moved towards semi- and post-nomadic life, where people do not necessarily practice pastoral nomadism as their primary or secondary occupation.

While the Afghan-Mughal wars characterized the regional milieu, large global systemic forces were at play as a new global international system was established. Geopolitically, with the rise of European powers and the colonization of the Americas, the power of Central Asian empires began to decline. This shift in geopolitical power created a rise and fall dynamic within the more significant trends of world history and the emergence of the global international system. From the point of view of the emerging global international system, Afghanistan was becoming decentred. This was a result of the first revolution at sea, with the development of sailing ship technology, which made it possible to carry goods and soldiers around the planet and 'opened a 200-year period of transition from land- to ocean-centered international relations' (Buzan and Little 2000, 279–80). This geopolitical movement was reversing a trend that had begun around 2250 BCE and endured for over four millennia. As Jalali, who has undertaken the best work on how this impacted Afghanistan, explains:

> The period between the sixteenth and nineteenth centuries brought major changes to the political landscape of Central Asia. The region that fostered the emergence of several empires in the past gradually declined into one of history's backwaters [sic]. … The situation changed the historical trend in which Central Asia-based empires projected power to the south while expanding their rule to larger areas in the Middle East and India. (Jalali 2021, 234–5)

These large geopolitical movements had an emergent effect at the local level. Situated between multiple declining empires, Afghans were increasingly empowered locally in what Jalali terms 'village states' (Jalali and Grau 2001, xiii). Echoing Barfield's assertion of tribal republicanism, these village states existed in the *Yagistan* or 'rebel lands', which were 'ungoverned' territories (Barfield 2010, 69). Here, local agrarian, pastoral and more isolated populations would combat nomadic invasions and the rule of empires to maintain their local autonomy. Thus, a major global movement being driven by the formation of the global international system had the local effect of contributing to the awakening of Pashtun national consciousness in the 17th century (Misdaq 2008, 37–9).[17] At the local level, heterarchical 'village state' networks of Afghans began to emerge, supported by norm circles that refused to acquiesce to the norm that political legitimacy was derived through conquering their territory. Rather, they formed militias capable of undertaking asymmetric warfare in Afghanistan's difficult terrain. Misdaq goes so far as to compare these networks to the modern Taliban movement, which 'recruited from madrassas, seminary schools, and operate across the tribal and ethnic divide' (2008, 38). Once networked, groups of predominantly footmen were mobilized for war, even if they were difficult to keep together during times of peace (Jalali 2017, 57). These networks proved highly effective.

In the early 18th century, Afghan coalitions expelled foreign occupiers from their homeland and extended their military campaigns into the heart of these empires, compelling them to submit to Afghan authority. In 1709, Mir Wais Khan (or Amir Khan), leader of the Hotak of the Ghilzai Pashtuns in Kandahar, united a national Afghan army and established government institutions to rebel against the Safavid dynasty. Exploiting sectarian divisions between Sunni and Shia, Mir Wais was able to call a Loya Jirga (Grand Council) and manoeuvre an agreement with regional Pashtuns to remove the Persians (Misdaq 2008, 40). As a result, Kandahar was liberated from Safavid rule, and Mir Wais went about further uniting the Ghilizai Pashtuns. The Loya Jirga replicated the norms of the village Jirga convened to resolve local disputes at a national level. While based on a traditional model of norms designed to resolve local disputes, the Loya Jirga was a modern institution that reflected a new iteration of national consciousness and the spread of nationalist identities within the global international system (Smith 2019). The rise of Europe may have destabilized the empires of Central Asia, but it was creating nationalist ideologies that Afghans did not escape. Following Mir Wais' death, internal conflict threatened the Pashtuns' stability. Nevertheless,

---

[17] Around 300 CE, the term *Afghan* was first documented, which some have suggested meant 'noisy' or 'unruly' (Tanner 2009, 5). As evidenced in texts and inscriptions, the term originates from the region and refers to the Pashtun. Over time, this came to be adopted by other groups that had inhabited the land for centuries (Green 2008). Accordingly, there were Afghans for over a millennium before there was an Afghanistan. Indeed, there were Afghans before Islam was embraced within the region.

they rallied, toppling the Safavids and seizing Isfahan in 1722 and Tehran by 1725 (Misdaq 2008, 41). Their triumph soon waned under Persian counteroffensives. The Ghilizai Pashtuns were pushed back by the Persians through the 1730s, with Kandahar succumbing in 1738. This marked the end of decades of rule by a now-contracting Pashtun Empire as the Persian army moved forward, attacking the Mughal Empire in India. Afghans again found themselves ensnared in the vice of empires on the march.

The rise and fall of the Afghan empire

It was not until 1747 that an opportunity for Afghan rule would emerge again. Nader Shah, the leader of the Persian Afsharids who had beaten the Afghans back in the previous decade, was assassinated. This provided the political opportunity for a Loya Jirga, proposed by Afghans serving in the Persian army, to elect a leader to unify Afghans. After nine days of intense rivalry and discussion, Ahmad Khan was accepted as leader and coronated with the title Ahmad Shah Durrani. Over 26 years, Ahmad Shah Durrani would lead a holy war (jihad), engaging in imperial expansion to capture what he considered Afghan territory in India and Iran (Misdaq 2008, 42–7). This allowed the Durrani Empire to extract wealth from foreign invasion, buttressing the empire's economic power without extracting resources from the Pashtuns that were supplying political and military power. Yet, as Jalali explains, '[w]hat makes Ahmad Shah distinct from other local conquerors in the past was that he intended to conquer other lands to build his own state and not to follow the example of past Afghan rulers of India or the Hotaks, who chose to preside over empires in foreign lands' (2017, 68).

The aim was to establish borders and sovereignty over Afghan territory without overextending the military and undermining his power base. Building the infrastructure of the state was prioritized over foreign invasion. By 1772, the Durrani Empire extended from the north of modern Iran, Afghanistan, Pakistan and parts of northern India to Delhi. This domestic focus marked the start of the modern Afghan state. Afghans were not abandoning their 'village states', but increasingly, the pressures of the European model were starting to structure elite understandings of what was politically possible and desirable. Ideas of sovereignty and nationalism were beginning to add emergent pressures to restructure Afghanistan's political organization in a more European image (see Buzan and Little 2000, 330–4). This would exacerbate the tensions of centralized hierarchy in a world of emerging modern states and the localized heterarchy of 'village states'. The forces of the global international system were increasingly in tension with sociopolitical systems that had their lineage in pre-international systems. As Barfield argues:

It is true that by bringing the Durranis to power, Ahmad Shah is rightly seen as the founder of an independent Afghanistan that was no longer just a contested border region of Iran and India. But there remained a natural friction between the pretensions of the autocratic ruler who had founded an empire and a people whose politically egalitarian ethos rendered such claims of preeminence suspect. Ahmad smoothed over this problem by appointing a majlis (council) composed of Pashtun clan elders … the real conflict between royal pretensions and tribal republicanism, however, would not emerge until the reigns of Ahmad's successors, who never treated the tribes as partners. (Barfield 2010, 105)

The task of state-building continued after Ahmad Shah died in 1773. His heir, Timur Shah, further centralized the state by moving the capital from Kandahar to Kabul and increasingly included the employment of non-Pashtuns to make the state more autonomous. This required relying on the authority of Islamic norms to legitimate power (Rubin 1992, 46). Ultimately, however, this process of centralization was undermined by civil war and the rise of European colonialism in Asia.

Civil war, British colonialism and the Anglo-Afghan wars

The rise of the global international system devastated the development of Afghanistan as a state. On the one hand, the European model was exerting pressures within the international system for states to emerge, not only to enhance security against European empires but also by spreading European ideas and norms within its colonies (Buzan and Little 2000, 332). Indeed, up until the middle of the 20th century, the dominant unit in the global international system were empires with modern states at their core and layers of sovereignty afforded within the structures of empire (Buzan and Little 2000, 264). On the other hand, European powers were undermining indigenous efforts at state-building through colonization.[18] This was a particularly poor fit for Afghanistan, with its heterarchical norms, national consciousness and institutionalized norms of asymmetric warfare. With such norms, Afghans were not willingly going to acquiesce to European colonization. Herein lay a significant tension between the rise of the global international system and Afghan norms. Nevertheless, as Rubin outlines of

---

[18] As Buzan and Little illustrate, '[i]n 1500, Europeans controlled 7 per cent of the world's land area. By 1800, they controlled 35 per cent. By 1914, they had substantially empeopled three continents (North and South America and Australia) and controlled 84 per cent of the world's land' (Buzan and Little 2000, 257).

Afghan state-building efforts, 'decline was not due so much to the decay of tribal asabiyya [unity] as to a change in the international system. … By the end of the eighteenth century … the British were advancing towards northwest India from their base in Calcutta' (1992, 46).

With the rise of an all-water route to the East Indies in the 15th century, the Islamic barrier to European trade had been removed (see Buzan and Little 2000, 307). However, over the next two centuries, Asia would become instrumental in establishing and effectively operating new international trade networks. What is striking about the initial phase of the global international system being established is that the economic interaction between Europe and Asia was fundamentally symbiotic. Both regions were fully capable adhering to early capitalist norms and derive market-driven responses and logical decision-making processes (Prakash 1998). However, through the 1750s and 1760s, a new phase of European colonial expansion began to transform Europe–Asia relations. As the Mughal Empire started to disintegrate, European nations seized the opportunity to expand their political and economic spheres of influence. This transformed intra-European rivalry, particularly the Anglo-French rivalry, with European traders mobilizing naval and military resources and European powers militarizing their foreign engagements to exert power (Travers 2007a). The British East India Company increasingly emerged as the most powerful of the European traders, allowing it to evolve from a commercial entity into a governing body (P. Marshall 1998b). Under orientalist tropes of bringing 'civilization' and 'modernity', the East India Company, supported by the British state, began an enterprise of colonial state-building in India. This required building clients and removing local rulers that challenged British interests in India (see P.J. Marshall 1998a).

The importance of Britain expanding its sphere of influence cannot be overstated. Self-evidently, British colonialism impacted the future of India. However, it also led to meddling in Afghan affairs at the end of the 18th and the start of the 19th century. This meddling necessitated actively undermining indigenous attempts at state development to pursue British power in the global international system. Keen to counterbalance burgeoning French influence, Britain turned to Persia, forging an alliance designed as much to preoccupy the Afghans as to forestall any potential French overland incursions into India. However, this delicate balance of power was soon upended by Napoleon's successful courtship of Persia, which forced the British to make a defensive treaty with the Durrani monarch Shah Shuja in 1809 (Jalali 2017, 76–8). Less than a decade later, Afghanistan would be in civil war. Russian expansion became central to British concerns, setting the stage for Britain's colonial adventure in Afghanistan.

Timur Shah's death in 1793 opened the gateway for a power struggle for the Afghan throne, culminating in civil war and the fragmentation of the empire. One of Timur's sons, Shah Zaman, was named his successor, but this was disputed by his brother Shah Mahmud. Soon, rival factions emerged, with claims to the throne and declarations of independence from disloyal governors. Accordingly, as an Afghan civil war ensued, the kingdom was divided into semi-independent fiefdoms (Verma 1970; Nawid 1997). This instability increasingly drew the attention of Britain's East India Company, which had financial interests in northern India. Despite Afghan instability and succession dramas, Shah Zaman was able to launch campaigns in the Punjab and capture Lahore. Such action did little to alleviate fears that Afghans would form a coalition with France nor form an anti-British Muslim coalition of regional powers (Lee 2022, 159–61). Accordingly, by 1801, under the Anglo-Persian Treaty, British military aid was pledged in return for the Persians attacking the Afghan kingdom 'to ruin and humble the nation' (Lee 2022, 164).

Irrespective of British and Persian actions, it was also in 1801 that Shah Zaman lost the throne to Shah Mahmud. In turn, within an elite game of thrones, Shah Mahmud's reign was short-lived, ending in 1803. As the Persians sieged Herat and Shah Zaman's full brother, Shah Shuja' al-Mulk, marched on Kabul, the throne became unstable. Having imported the Turkish norm of royal succession, who ruled Afghanistan had become an issue of lineage among an elite (Barfield 2010, 11). So began a period of rivalry between Shah Shuja' al-Mulk and Shah Mahmud, who would rule the Afghan kingdom at various points throughout the early 19th century.[19] Indeed, the early 19th century was a complex historical period for Afghan rule, with the kingdom changing hands 12 times by 1840. Those competing for power, however, belonged to what Barfield terms 'professional rulers' who regarded themselves as 'elites who saw government as their business' (2010, 3).

Afghanistan's instability helped facilitated Britain's growing intervention. In 1809, British intervention in the Afghan kingdom occurred when Shah Shuja' al-Mulk allowed representatives from the East India Company to enter the royal court. This led to an agreement to provide military assistance and financial support to prevent French and Russian access to India. However, the East India Company's mission was to get an agreement and gather intelligence about the Afghans and potential invasion routes. The head of this mission, Mountstuart Elphinstone (1815), published *An Account of the Kingdom of Caubul* detailing portions of the intelligence gathered on the mission. For most of the 19th century, this remained the most influential

---

[19]   Shah Mahmud would add to his reign of 1801–3 with a second reign in 1809–18 and a third in 1818–26. Shuja' al-Mulk would reign from 1803 to 1809, again briefly in 1818, and from 1839 to 1842.

study on the Afghan kingdom and became the 'cornerstone of British colonial and Orientalist perceptions of Afghanistan and the Afghan tribes'. Indeed, in the British 'Elphinstone episteme', the term 'Afghanistan' was first used to describe the Durrani kingdom (Lee 2022, 171–2). This failed to capture the complexities of the kingdom, as 'Afghanistan' did not concur with European notions of sovereignty. Rather than having a single all-powerful sovereign, the kingdom maintained autonomous and independent local power structures in village states. These were more 'egalitarian and rejected the legitimacy of any outside authority', and of these, it was only the 'tribal warriors organised into segmentary descent groups who inhabited marginal zone' who could occasionally provide a challenge to Durrani power (Barfield 2010, 4). Without recognizing Afghanistan's underlying heterarchical norms, a century of British policy towards it was maintained without understanding the history and character of 'Afghanistan'. This was a recipe for failure, even though it would be replicated in the 20th and 21st centuries. Contextual dissonance between European policy and Afghan reality has not simply been a modern problem.

Afghanistan undertook a dynastic transition following fragmentation and a heightened phase of civil conflict from 1818 to 1826. With Dost Mohammad Khan taking the throne in Kabul in an 1826 palace coup, Afghanistan's dynastic rule shifted from the Durrani to the Barakzai. With both being Pashtun tribes, this maintained Pashtun power and the place of 'professional rulers' but changed the line of succession through to the 20th century. After this dynastic transition, Dost Mohammad Khan embarked on a rigorous campaign to stabilize the nation, asserting his authority in Kabul and decisively quelling familial opposition. Even so, his vision of a united Afghanistan soon encountered formidable obstacles, as British India would significantly thwart his unification efforts.

As the French Empire crumbled, the Congress of Vienna (1814–15) ushered in a new European political era, diminishing the French menace in British eyes. However, Britain's gaze quickly shifted to the burgeoning power of Russia, whose advances in Persia and Ottoman Turkey were perceived as ominous harbingers of future conflicts. Britain concluded that pre-emptive action was needed. This included an expansion of trade to promote 'civilisation … freedom, peace and good governance', but also the potential unilateral military occupation of critical cities across Afghan territory if necessary (Lee 2022, 191–2).[20] Ignoring local expertise and its

---

[20] This became known as the Ellenborough Doctrine after Lord Ellenborough set out to enact his vision in 1830 after being appointed President of the Board of Control of the East India Company. Thus, while the term 'Great Game' is attributed to Arthur Conolly, an intelligence officer in the East India Company, and the term was popularized by the British novelist Rudyard Kipling, it was Ellenborough who constructed the intellectual

own military and intelligence personnel with experience in India, London concluded that Russia posed a threat and could invade India through the Afghan city of Herat (Alder 1974a, 1974b; Lee 2022, 193–5). As a result, it was concluded that Britain should 'reunify' the territories of the Afghan Empire. For Britain, this would benefit its commercial interests. However, misunderstanding Afghan norms, British statesmen believed the Afghans would welcome this apparent benevolence. When this proved not to be the case, it 'baffled statesmen in London and Calcutta for a generation' (Alder 1974a, 186). This was an early harbinger of being involved in Afghanistan without understanding pertinent Afghan meta-norms, and was a notable demonstration of contextual dissonance from a European power. In and of itself this should have served as a warning nearly two centuries later.

After multiple missteps by Dost Mohammad Khan, the British launched the First Anglo-Afghan War in 1839, quickly taking southern Afghanistan. The emergent global international system, and the imperialism that underlined it, finally brought war between a European power and the Afghans; following a more than two-millennia hiatus from Alexander the Great's northern conquests (Holt 2012). After Kandahar, Ghazni and Kabul fell, the British assumed they were victorious. Afghanistan was understood to be pacified with the installation of Shah Shuja' al-Mulk once again to the throne, and because of this, British troops could quickly withdraw (Jalali 2017, 117). The British failed to recognize that they remained in a war zone and would soon face a regrouped opposition and resistance to the occupation. The sovereign may have been replaced, but the heterarchy of village states would adapt and resist. This ended in a humiliating loss for the British Empire, not seen since the end of the American Revolutionary War in 1783 (Dalrymple 2013).

Dost Mohammad Khan resumed the throne from 1842 until his death in 1863. Significantly, during his exile in India, Dost Mohammad Khan was exposed to the institutions of the modern state system advanced by the British Empire. Upon his return to the throne, this exposure galvanized his desire to modernize Afghanistan, if only to provide greater security (Rubin 1990). For Barfield, this was the moment that 'exclusive elite authority began to erode' as there was an 'increasing sway of Western colonial powers changing the political ecology of the region' (Barfield 2010, 5). Indeed, we can see this as an emergent effect of colonization and the rise of a global international system, which consisted of empires with modern states at their core. It was not the professional rulers that expelled the British, but the heterarchical warrior tribes organized into rural militias. The 'professional rulers' would encourage them to organize and expel the foreign invasion, but then refuse

---

architecture that would set the British–Afghan conflict in motion (National Archives 1840; Hansard 1843).

to share political power once victorious. This altered the norms of political legitimacy inside Afghanistan and began to alter the collective intentions of village states. Increasingly, because of mobilizing tribal republics, the norm circles accepting royal pretensions and dynastic privilege were eroding. Added to an ever-growing national consciousness, tribal republicanism had an increasing reluctance to acquiesce to the medieval norms of hierarchy and royal patronage.

Although expelled, the British Empire further undermined professional rule. Having consolidated British rule in India, the external source of revenue used to unite the Afghans was removed. Afghan rulers could no longer extract wealth from India and therefore could no longer consolidate their economic power without increasing feudal levies. They were also less capable of funding mercenary armies, which were a bulwark against popular support, and, therefore, the ruling elite needed to play groups against each other or receive aid from more powerful states if they were to survive. Importantly, as Rubin explains, '[t]he balance of power between state and tribes – in contemporary terms, the degree of autonomy of the state from social forces – repeatedly shifted, often because of changes in the relations between the state and the international system' (1992, 47).

Consequently, Afghanistan may have removed the British from their territory, but they now relied on military assistance from British India and Qajar Iran. The question for the British was exactly how should Afghanistan be dominated? Thus, while some historians have argued that 'under the second reign of Amir Dost Muhammad, Afghanistan became a stable political entity', this position suffers from myopia (Roy 2015, 87). From the systemic perspective of Afghanistan's position in the global international system, Afghanistan remained unstable in the postwar settlement of 1842. Indeed, some historians claiming Afghanistan was stable have themselves shown that there were power struggles fuelled by Persian influence throughout the 1850s (Roy 2015, 88). Moreover, upon Dost Mohammad Khan's death, the country fell back into civil war until Sher Ali Khan could reconsolidate some semblance of power in 1868.

Sher Ali Khan strived to establish Afghanistan as a neutral territory, serving as a buffer during the heightened strain between Russia and Britain. However, this strategy was unsuccessful. At the time, Britain wanted to maintain a 'Big Afghanistan' policy that maintained Afghanistan's territorial integrity. This was under the proviso that Afghanistan would be a lookout for Russian expansionism and act as a client state of the British Empire. This was an attempt to exercise hegemony over Afghanistan. The Big Afghanistan strategy collapsed when Sher Ali Khan denied unhindered access to British troops entering Afghan territory. In its place, Lord Lytton, the viceroy of India, became obsessed with a 'policy of disintegration' that would gradually weaken Afghanistan and split Herat from Kandahar and

Kabul (Duthie 1984).[21] Lord Lytton was planning to exacerbate ethnic and tribal tensions and undermine diplomatic efforts to avoid war so that Britain would partition Afghanistan. In 1878, with a lack of unity among Afghans, the Second Anglo-Afghan War was initiated when the British strategically invaded Afghanistan from three different directions (Klein 1974).

Following his father's death, Yakub Khan signed the *Treaty of Gandamak* in May 1879, marking a turning point in the war. This agreement recognized Yakub Khan as the emir but surrendered Afghanistan's sovereignty to Britain. Accordingly, Britain established permanent representation in Kabul and required that Yakub Khan cede control of Afghanistan's foreign relations to the British government. Afghanistan was to be a suzerain power of the British Empire. However, this semblance of peace was short-lived. A few months later, on 3 September 1879, Louis Cavagnari, the British resident in Kabul, was murdered in Kabul, prompting the dispatch of British forces (Palat 2005, 105). By the end of October, British troops had occupied Kabul and, facing overwhelming opposition, Yakub Khan abdicated (Fuoli 2018).

The power dynamics shifted again in 1880 when Amir Abdur Rahman Khan, a cousin of Sher Ali Khan, returned from exile in Central Asia. He proclaimed himself Emir of Kabul, ushering in a new era. The British finally withdrew from Kandahar in April 1881, marking the end of direct military conflict but the beginning of a new geopolitical landscape in the region (Ghose 1953). The effects of this conflict were devastating. As the viceroy of India summarized for the Secretary of State for India after the war in 1881, '[British military operations and occupation] have left the Civil government and the military resources of the Afghans in a state of dilapidation which will require a long time to repair' (in Ghani 1982). Indeed, in trying to repair Afghanistan from this devastation, Abdur Rahman would establish new norms of centralized violence that have left a lasting legacy from British imperialism in Afghanistan.

With British backing, Abdur Rahman was tasked with ending the civil war and building a centralized state within an increasingly defined territory that respected British interests in India (Barfield 2010, 146). This led to what Dupree (1980) termed 'internal imperialism', where a campaign of terror was unleashed as Abdur Rahman sought to build a centralized autocratic regime. Old state structures were dismantled in an expanding state-building exercise, drawing political power towards a centralized state and away from the more autonomous urban and regional power centres throughout the country (Ibrahimi 2019). Accordingly, by the turn of the 20th century, Afghanistan was an autocratic police state forged by the violence of British imperialism

---

[21] The policy of disintegration is attributed to Sir Henry Creswicke Rawlinson in his 1875 volume *England and Russia in the East* (in Duthie 1984).

and internal wars led by a violent autocrat. These were the agential drivers of modernization norms that began to reshape social institutions inside an emergent state. As the capital, Kabul, wrestled the rest of the country for political and economic power, the Afghan state was territorialized. Indeed, by 1893, British India determined that Afghanistan needed formal borders to demarcate their respective zones of influence. Sending the Indian Foreign Secretary, Sir Henry Mortimer Durand, the Durand Line was established (Omrani 2009). This border did not follow a natural path but was instead negotiated geostrategically. Consequently, as Dupree argued, the Durand Line was 'a classic example of an artificial political boundary cutting through a culture area' (1980, 425).

Afghanistan was increasingly becoming a modern state in the global international system. Ostensibly, territorial demarcations and the stronger veneer of a centralist state gave the appearance that Afghanistan was a pathway towards modernization. Village states remained, along with the heterarchical norms of semi-nomadic and post-nomadic life, but Afghanistan had also entered the modern state system.[22] To facilitate this, Abdur Rahman was willing to 'crush every autonomous group in Afghanistan one by one, aided by British subsidies that financed the creation of a powerful national army equipped with modern weapons that were purchased abroad or produced in his own factories [with imported machinery]' (Barfield 2010, 147). This is not the romantic image of Abdur Rahman that was portrayed before he died in 1901. As one biographer generalizes:

> I do not think it necessary to waste time in trying to prove that the Amir Abdur Rahman Khan is one of the greatest men now living. All the European Statesmen who have come in personal contact with him have formed this opinion, and his remarkable achievement in turning Afghanistan, which before his time was a mere barren piece of land full of barbarous tribes, into a consolidated Muslim Kingdom and centre of manufactures and modern inventions, speaks for itself, and shows his marvellous genius. (Khan 1900, vii)

---

[22] This dynamic is recognized by Buzan and Little, who argue, 'Because IR theory assumes that units are territorially fixed, that they are hierarchically structured (and functionally and structurally differentiated in their internal organisation), that they have robust and durable institutions, that they have an inside and an outside, and that they engage in sectorally differentiated activities such as diplomacy, war, and trade, it is unsurprising that IR has had such difficulty dealing with the many weak states that entered the international system with decolonisation. But for the fact that they are being held in place by strong patterns of international recognition and support, many of them (think of Afghanistan, Tadjikistan, Somalia, Liberia, Sierra Leone, Congo, and others) could almost be understood as chiefdoms' (2000, 161).

This image continued throughout the 20th century, with Abdur Rahman becoming known somewhat admirably as the 'Iron Amir', even by those detailing his systematic acts of violence (Edwards 1996). Having embedded norms of violence in the collective intentions of others, Barfield notes that '[t]he amazing thing is that to this day, governments in Kabul have emulated the Iron Amir despite the grief this has brought to the Afghan people' (2010, 163). As Lee explains, this is because 'one of the many legacies of [Abdur Rahman's] reign was the belief, espoused by both Afghans and Europeans, that the only way Afghanistan could be ruled was by an absolutist monarch backed by state terror' (2022, 421). Such sentiments fail to recognize that Abdur Rahman built a ruling Muhammadzai elite that would become the dominant ruling class in Afghanistan. It is important to note that the Muhammadzai elite, unlike tribal Pashtuns, periodically used the social institution of marriage outside of their lineage for social advancement and co-option. Although Pashtun, this was a new elite that grew economic power from state patronage and not feudal land ownership (Barfield 2010, 166–7). Nevertheless, Abdur Rahman would be the last Afghanistan head of state who was not violently killed or forced into exile, demonstrating that this is not a winning formula for modern governance.

Afghanistan's independence and the global international system

By the turn of the 20th century Afghanistan bore little difference from centuries earlier. Kabul had undergone a degree of modernization, evident in government-run factories, but there was little advancement elsewhere in the provinces or countryside. Even so, a radical political transformation had occurred, with Kabul becoming an unchallenged centre of political power. Abdur Rahman had centralized political power in ways that Afghans had never experienced before. However, such a high degree of political centralization would ultimately undermine the stability of later Afghan governments that have sought to mirror and maintain this centralized authority (Barfield 2010, 165–6).

Following Abdur Rahman's death, his eldest son, Habib Allah [Habibullah] Khan, was declared Emir in 1901 and reigned until his assassination in 1919. His transition to the throne was relatively peaceful because he entered a power-sharing agreement with his younger brother, Nasr Allah (Nasrullah) Khan. Nasr Allah would become the heir apparent, head of the Treasury, Revenue and Internal Affairs, minister of education, and army commander-in-chief (Lee 2022, 412–13). During his rule, Habib Allah declared an amnesty that allowed political exiles to return in an act of political reconciliation. He also sought to carry on his father's legacy of modernization, for example, by inaugurating Habibiyya College (Emadi 2010, 17–18). Modelled on

European schooling, the curriculum included 'basic science, mathematics, history and geography as well as Islamiyat' (Lee 2022, 419). This was seen as secularizing the curriculum, which was opposed by Nasr Allah, who was then allowed to fund madrassas with a traditional Islamic curriculum in key provincial centres. Indeed, a further compromise had to be reached, making admission into Habibiyya conditional on completing the primary and secondary stages of madrassa education. This exacerbated the differences between the elites in Kabul and those in the provinces and countryside. It also demonstrated that norms around education in Afghanistan remained highly contested because of the tensions between these other sets of norms. Indeed, this deeply politicized and highly contested nature of education has persisted into the 21st century (see Spink 2005).

During Habib Allah's rule, relations with Britain soured again. Russia was increasingly applying pressure on the northern border and bribing local governors. This soon erupted into the Herat frontier crisis in 1903, where Britain could not gain local cooperation in restoring boundary demarcations (Williams 1966, 361). Increasingly, Britain received a lack of cooperation from its client state. Habib Allah went so far as to suggest that previous treaties may not apply to Afghanistan, meaning that the Durand Line was now in contention and Afghanistan was an independent sovereign state. Accordingly, Britain wanted a new treaty, and in 1905, the Kabul Treaty was signed (Fahim 1988). This reconfirmed the Anglo-Afghan alliance in return for British subsidies and marked the first step in Afghanistan becoming independent. While Britain maintained control of Afghanistan's foreign affairs, the agreement was made with the 'State of Afghanistan' and its 'independent King' (Lee 2022, 425). Nevertheless, although this was the first time Afghanistan was officially conferred the position of a state, Britain did not behave as if this was the case when negotiating with Russia, much to the chagrin of Habib Allah and a rising tide of anti-British sentiment across Afghanistan. Gradually, this culminated in calls for a jihad against the British, discussions of invading India, and allowing British rifles to flow across the border (Fahim 1978).

As the First World War approached, Britain's unpopularity led to many Afghans calling for Habib Allah to join Germany and Turkey, and try to gain complete independence from Britain. However, Habib Allah positioned Afghanistan to be a neutral state, even though Germany and Turkey sent multiple missions to persuade him to join their efforts, along with interventions from Indian nationalists (Rasanayagam 2010, 17). This culminated in the German-Afghan treaty of 1916, even if it did not change the war's outcome. Soon, a more concerning issue for the British emerged with the October 1917 Bolshevik Revolution. This ended the threat of the Russian Empire invading India, but the British feared the spread of communism into Afghanistan through to India (see Druhe 1959).

Habib Allah's reign ended abruptly with assassination, ultimately bringing little substantive modernization. Major capital projects proved nearly impossible through a combination of incompetence, untrained oversight, spiralling costs and extensive corruption (Lee 2022, 449). Just the same, as Nasr Allah succeeded the throne in January 1919, and the Spanish Flu spread, killing thousands, a coup was being planned. After just one week, Nasr Allah was arrested, as his nephew Aman Allah (Amanullah) Khan seized power and prepared plans to invade India and liberate Afghanistan from British influence (Rasanayagam 2010, 17).

The start of the Third Anglo-Afghan War surprised the British, as Aman Allah would appeal to ethno-nationalist sentiment on both sides of the Durand Line and attempt to expel the British from the Punjab. Not long after, the British would deploy aerial warfare to gain a strategic advantage and force the emir to agree to a truce after just one month. Nevertheless, as a result of the war, the British were forced to recognize the independence of Afghanistan and relinquish control of its foreign affairs, signing the Rawalpindi Peace Agreement on 8 August 1919 (Rasanayagam 2010, 19). In return, Afghanistan accepted the demarcation of the Durand Line and official blame for the war. This significant blow for Afghanistan would have profound consequences into the 21st century. The more immediate problem for Afghanistan, however, was the breakup of the Ottoman Empire, which had been divided into Mandates by Britain, France and Imperial Russia. Generating concern in India, the Khilafat Movement emerged, and by the summer of 1920, tens of thousands migrated to Afghanistan in protest against the British government and trying to preserve the Ottoman caliphate (see Sultan-I-Rome 2004). Afghanistan was not equipped for the influx of migrants on this scale, many of whom perished, and Aman Allah's pan-Islamic credentials never recovered.

With Afghanistan being an independent state and fully recognized by the Anglo-Afghan Treaty of 1921, European powers were particularly interested in pursuing their interests through diplomatic relations and business. Italy signed its own treaty, but Germany and France also vied for a more formal stake. This benefited Aman Allah, who wanted to engage in a modernization process that transformed Afghanistan into a Europeanized state (Dupree 1980, 445–7). Physically, this manifested itself in the construction of Paghman, which features a mini-Arc de Triomphe and Opera House (see Crews 2015, 133–4). However, with no national infrastructure plan, European nations undertook various development projects with no coherent strategy. The French ran the postal service, secured a monopoly over archaeological exploration and established Afghanistan's first museum. German engineers constructed dams, irrigation systems, the Dar al-Aman Palace and railways. Little thought was being paid to the maintenance of these over the years, and ultimately, these projects crumbled in the following decades.

For all of Aman Allah's Europhile instincts, Turkey would provide the greatest inspiration for his attempted remodelling of Afghanistan in the interwar years. In attempting to draft Afghanistan's 1923 constitution, initial models drew upon Turkey's Tanzimat (Reorganization) period of the mid-19th century. Wherein, the Ottoman Empire attempted modernization reforms and the consolidation of its social and political foundations through the post-First World War secularization reforms of Mustafa Kemal Atatürk and the new Republic of Turkey (Ahmed 2013). *Atatürk's* secularization reforms, however, divided Afghan opinion and religious elites feared that Afghanistan would follow a similar path. This revealed a severe schism between elites in Kabul, pushing for modernization and secularization, and religious and tribal leaders throughout the country seeking to maintain traditional social and legal structures under Islamic law (Nawid 1999). Ultimately, the latter would win the constitutional struggle. After a period of revolt, Aman Allah agreed to embed Islamic norms into the constitution; once again reaffirming the relationship of Islamic norms and political legitimacy. Afghanistan was officially declared an Islamic state that included a codified role for the religious leaders to veto legislation that did not comply with Islamic law (Lee 2022, 478). The tensions between secularization and Islamization did not abate. Rather, tensions between different norm circles would come to characterize collective intentions and social institutions in Afghanistan, as issues over who had the political legitimacy to rule Afghanistan were tied to questions of how they ruled.

With the king's tour of Europe in 1927, he returned with the will to reinstate universal education and emancipatory women's rights. Meanwhile, Queen Soraya began challenging traditional assertions of the Islamic faith, arguing that Islam did not forbid women's education nor demand a full veil. Soon, such statements led to protests and revolt (Rasanayagam 2010, 21). Still, Aman Allah pushed for further reforms, allowing for primary education, compulsory co-education for all children, 'foreign run schools were to be opened in every province, and Afghan girls would be sent to study in Europe' (Lee 2022, 488). As tensions mounted, rebellions would soon spread throughout the country, culminating in the January 1929 coup and the rise of Habib Allah Kalakani (Habibullah). Seeking to regain the throne, Aman Allah sought help from British India, only to find Britain declaring its neutrality, and thus turned to the Soviet Union for support. Moscow agreed on a military and financial aid support package, yet Aman Allah, exiled in Italy, could not regain the throne (Hofmann 1979). Few of his reforms remained, demonstrating a strategic and political failure in imposing them quickly rather than seeking consensus and gradual introduction. The king, having spent more time trying to institutionalize European norms, had misread his own country and the contextual dissonance this created led to his downfall. Indeed, historians still debate the exact cause of Aman Allah's failures of modernization and their implications for Afghanistan today. However, Barfield concisely summarizes Aman Allah's reign, arguing that he had 'the dubious distinction of provoking a civil war against his own government by acting as if he were a foreign occupier himself' (2010, 191). Afghanistan may have entered the global international system. However, it was unwilling to reconcile to the trappings of hierarchy and modernization, setting the stage for a tumultuous century and new forms of international intervention.

3

Afghan Independence and European Union Humanitarianism in the Global International System

As Afghanistan gained its independence in the early 20th century it joined a growing number of decolonized states in the international system. Indeed, while it is commonplace to refer to modern states as the dominant unit of international relations, it is important to reflect that in 1914 there were only 44 states. Prior to the First World War colonies, dominions and protectorates characterized much of the global international system. By 1930 this had increased to 64 states, and as waves of formal independence took hold this grew to 107 in 1960, 148 in 1978, and over 190 by the turn of the new millennium (Buzan and Little 2000, 265). In this respect, Afghanistan gained the status of an independent state comparatively early in the global process of decolonization. Conversely, in the context of world history, Afghanistan's independence as a modern state is a novel phenomenon. Nevertheless, as Buzan and Little identify:

> Many of these [decolonized] states were not well made, and only a few of them were close to the leading edge in terms of shifting sovereignty from the rulers to the people. Some, most notably China, Indonesia, Pakistan, and Russia, had internal politics still reminiscent of empires even though formally constructed as modern states ... within the space of five centuries, ancient and classical empires, nomadic empires, city-states, and even the empires of early modern states had all disappeared, leaving a political landscape of unprecedented uniformity. (Buzan and Little 2000, 265–6)

The perception of outward uniformity has allowed traditional International Relations theory to attempt to 'close the historical box' on these decolonized states. However, in Afghanistan, gaining the formal status of a modern state did not suddenly eradicate the tensions between desert norms and sedentary norms that had developed over the previous millennia. Statehood, and the centralization of power that this implies, did not eradicate the heterarchical norms of tribal republics. On the contrary, in fighting for Afghan independence, many 'village states' began to question the imposition of power and hierarchy by the ruling elite that had come to rely on their mobilizations of resistance. The rise of Afghan national consciousness in the 17th century had fused with practices of resistance in the 18th and 19th centuries, and unsettled questions of political legitimacy.

The consequences of this were first demonstrated in the January 1929 coup, when Habib Allah Kalakani and his followers seized Kabul. From January to October 1929, Afghanistan was partially under Tajik rule, and the Pashtuns were effectively out of direct power for the first time since the mid-18th century.[1] Habib Allah Kalakani (Kalakan being the name of his village north of Kabul) and his followers began their period of rule in Kabul by terrorizing the population through sexual violence, theft and murder, dividing erstwhile Pashtun unity. Norms and norm circles lay at the centre of this political contestation. On the one hand, King Aman Allah and his associate norm circle of sedentary elites had been attempting to push for social reforms in the 1920s. These reforms attempted to introduce European social norms into Afghanistan and rebalance the role Afghanistan's traditional Islamic norms and practices played within the country. Central to this, but by no means exclusively, were norms around women rights and girls' education. On the other hand, Habib Allah Kalakani and his associate norm circle rejected European norms and practices in favour of a revolution and the instigation of renewed orthodox Islamic norms. These included the exclusion of the Shia population as unbelievers, the establishment of Sharia as the exclusive law in the nation, the direction of men to stop shaving and readopt the turban, and women to wear the hijab and not to exit their homes without a *mahram* (a male relative that a woman could not marry). These counter-reforms should be understood as the norm of resistance being fused with norms of conservative Islamic orthodoxy and instigated by one norm circle over another. Indeed, Roy argues, Habib Allah Kalakani was the 'candidate of a fundamentalist coalition' and the dominant historical narrative is thus problematic:

> For the majority of Afghan and Western historians … [this] affair represents a rather bizarre episode, an interruption in the course of

---

[1]   Official accounts of this interregnum portray these nine months as a purely Tajik rule, yet Lee convincingly contends that Tajik rule was backed directly and indirectly by Pashtun tribes (2022, 503).

traditional politics. But in fact, it should be interpreted as a visible manifestation of a deep structure: the fundamentalist network. Kabul does not fall, even in a period of anarchy, by mere chance. (Roy 1990, 66)

Moreover, Roy's work is particularly astute in tracing the origins of 'fundamentalist networks', or more precisely norm circles, back to the 16th century. Starting within the Mughal Empire, Sufi revivalist movements were a preamble to the rise of Islamist movements that would evolve throughout the 20th century as they came to terms with modernity and developed from a political critique of the fundamentalist movements that preceded them (Roy 1990, 68). Notably, the teachings of Shaikh Ahmad Sirhindi and his role in the Naqshbandī Sufi order are particularly important in this context, establishing norms of Islamic orthodoxy that challenged the religious tolerance of the Mughal Emperor Akbar and his calls for Sulh-i-Kull (universal peace) (Moin 2022; Ahmed 2023). While the Taliban are not direct intellectual decedents of this, norms of conservative Islamic orthodoxy have shaped the broader historical context within which groups such as the Taliban have emerged.

Once Pashtun elites had remobilized behind Nadir Khan, in October 1929 Habib Allah Kalakani's forces were crushed, and a dozen of his avid followers would find themselves shot and ceremonially hung. This marked a return of the Barakzai Muhammadzai dynasty and a more gradualist approach to social and political reform. As this chapter sets out, this began an important period of post-independence modernization and relative stability inside Afghanistan. However, emerging from the Second World War, Afghanistan was unable to escape the emergent forces of the global international system and the rise of superpowers competing in the Cold War. It was also unable to escape the emergence of new norms and the rise of *global international society*. It is because of this that, increasingly, as this chapter shows, Afghanistan and Europe began to interact more closely, and stages of European collective action began to take shape. As this chapter explains, it was in the 20th century that Europe developed a policy of trade and aid, followed by a more humanitarian approach. Indeed, while the EU did not exist at the start, by the end of the century it would find itself propagating norms in support of global international society and becoming the de facto coordinating body for humanitarian aid in Afghanistan.

The rise of Nadir Shah and the empowerment of Islamist norm circles

As the Pashtuns began to reunite, they backed Nadir Khan, who had returned from exile. As he recruited fighters, tribes in northern India proved pivotal in allowing the military balance to tip in his favour. A tribal *lashkar* (military unit) of 12,000 Wazir tribesmen from British India mobilized and took Kabul on 13 October (Barfield 2010, 195).[2] This would not be the last time that Pashtun border tribes would be called upon to secure Nadir Khan's reign, proving pivotal in the balance of Afghan politics over the next century.

Upon acceding to the throne, Nadir Shah represented a dynastic change, establishing the Musahiban dynasty that would rule until 1978. Indeed, Aman Allah tried to reassert his legitimacy for the throne, but by November 1929, the British recognized Nadir Shah and began providing financial and military aid to stabilize his government. To prevent rebellions from gaining momentum, Nadir Shah soon divided Afghanistan into a complex administration system. This took the form of seven major provinces, *wilayats*, created around major urban areas ruled by *walis* (governors). Minor provinces, *hukumat-i a'la*, were then established and subdivided into smaller administrative units. This allowed new provincial and military officials to be recruited and installed from the southern Pashtuns and locals to take lower civil service roles (Lee 2022, 510). What Nadir Shah effectively created was a gradual modernization programme that joined provinces with the central government, but this system also respected informal local institutions and actors while empowering the Pashtuns. A premium was placed on building a secure central government in Kabul while coexisting harmoniously with a relatively untouched periphery (Mukhopadhyay 2014). This was a conscious attempt to balance sedentary and desert norms by allowing conservative village states and their tribal republics to maintain a sense of sovereignty. As Saikal correctly notes, Nadir Shah adopted a 'concept of sober nationalism ... a gradual process of change and development, based on peaceful coexistence with conservative forces' (2004, 97). Afghanistan was to be united under broader Islamic norms while gradually attempting to become a progressive postcolonial state.

Veiled in the notion of balancing traditional norms and modernity, Nadir Shah engaged in a new Islamization project, culminating in the 1931 constitution.[3] This project introduced a raft of new measures, particularly around the justice system, giving more significant influence to Islamic law and sharia courts. As Gregorian notes, the 1931 constitution 'institutionalised the power of the religious establishment' (1969, 340). Moreover, as Tarzi illustrates, this was because Nadir Shah saw the kingdom's stability resting

---

[2] *Lashkars* are often composed of members of a particular tribe or ethnic group and are used for various purposes, including fighting against foreign forces, providing security in local areas, and enforcing local customs and laws.

[3] Officially titled: Osul-e asāsi-e dawlat-e ʿāliya-ye Afghānestān (Fundamental Laws of the Exalted Government of Afghanistan).

with primarily 'keeping the Pashtun tribal and religious leadership content' (2012, 215). This is because Nadir Shah ultimately drew legitimacy from the conservative religious scholars (*'ulama*) from eastern Afghanistan, who were mostly Pashtuns. In return, the king elevated the power of the *'ulama* and their tribes and furnished them with a level of political power they had not possessed since the 1890s under Amir Abdur Rahman Khan's centralization reforms (Tarzi 2012, 215). However, while doing this Nadir Shah abandoned his own appeals to pan-Islamism and began developing plans for the consolidation of a modern state. Counterintuitively, this strengthened the *'ulama*, by awarding conservative religious scholars a monopoly over endorsing and enforcing discursive pan-Islamic norms and appeals to the *umma* (Muslim community) (see Ahmed 1975; Roy 1990, 62). In terms of the dynamics of norm circles, the monarchy stopped endorsing and enforcing the boundaries of pan-Islamic norms and practice, which allowed the norm circle established by religious leaders to take ownership of defining and protecting these norms. This allowed pan-Islamic norms and practice to be far more conservative. Indeed, empowering the *'ulama* ushered in a new era of censorship and a retraction of women's rights by forcing women to wear the veil in public spaces and a loss of education outside of madrassas. As Lee correctly demonstrates, '[w]hat this meant in practice was the 1931 Constitution formalized an Islamization programme unprecedented in Afghanistan's history until the era of the Taliban' (2022, 512–15).

In return for Nadir Shah's Islamization programme, the norm of royal succession was codified in the constitution. Article Five 'recognised His Majesty as a fit and worthy King' and stipulated that 'the crown of Afghanistan will be transferred to the family of this King' (Nadir Shah 1931). This article would soon be enforced with the king's assassination in November 1933. Standing at the podium of a high school graduation, the king was shot by Abdul Khaliq who was apprehended and subsequently executed along with most of his relatives (Baker 1934; Castagne 1935). Acceding to the throne, Muhammad Zahir Shah, at only 19 years of age, would initially have power in name only, with Prime Minster Hashim Khan, the assassinated king's younger brother, wielding significant political power for the next two decades (Dupree 1980, 477–98).

The Second World War and Afghanistan in global international society

It was Hashim Khan who sought closer diplomatic relations with Nazi Germany in the run-up to the Second World War but who would ultimately be responsible for maintaining Afghanistan's declared neutrality upon the outbreak of war. Inexorably, just as this was a pivotal moment for the global international system, so too was it pivotal for the units that comprised it.

Afghanistan found itself engulfed in what began as a European crisis but enveloped Eurasia and the rest of the global international system. British influence in Afghanistan had certainly waned since recognizing Afghanistan's independence, and as a result the Soviet Union was attempting to build an Asiatic bloc in Turko-Persia. Soviet elites cast themselves as the protectors of 'the oppressed nations of the Orient' and attempted to build closer relations (Castagne 1935, 699). Notably, the United States (US) had recognized Afghanistan in 1921, but it was not until 1935 that diplomatic relations were established. Moreover, it was not until the US joined the Allies' efforts that the 1942 American Legation was established in Kabul (Office of the Historian 2023). Nevertheless, among the limited number of historians who have examined this period, Milan L. Hauner stands out for his argument that Germany had effectively established 'a subversive infrastructure of conquest' inside Afghanistan (1982, 483). This was particularly pronounced through commercial relations with Germany, which Hashim Khan believed could provoke an invasion from the Soviet Union and Britain. As a result, Afghanistan found itself in a delicate balancing act, playing 'the Switzerland of Asia', even as pro-German sentiment spread across the country (Dupree 1980, 482; also see Koplik 2015, 137–236).

Afghanistan's reliance on Germany was noticeable as economic development slowed abruptly once the war began. This would have profound implications for the country's integration into the global international system and its crisis-prone domestic economy. In 1938, Da Afghanistan Bank (State Bank of Afghanistan) was incorporated and began building branch links with European states and the US. However, by the end of the Second World War, Afghanistan was faced with economic disaster (Dupree 1980, 479). With the fall of Nazi Germany, one of Afghanistan's most important financial and military assistance providers abated. With exports collapsing, Afghanistan was forced to sell agricultural goods abroad, which created shortages at home and sparked a series of revolts. However, with the Afghan Army benefiting from technological advancements in warfare, state capabilities had an advantage, shifting the balance of power towards the centralized state and against domestic security challenges posed by the tribal republics. This imbalance was particularly pronounced in the 1945–7 rebellion of the Safi tribe in the eastern Kumar province but had been taking shape through the Katawaz rebellion in 1937–9, the Shinwari revolt of 1938 and the Alizai-Durrani unrest in 1939 (Jalali 2017, 336–7). Modern technology had shifted military capabilities enough to support the power of the ruling elite and quell rebellions from the tribal republics.

With added state resilience, Afghanistan took a further step towards integrating into the global international system by signing the Charter of the United Nations (UN) and becoming a member of the UN in November 1946 (United Nations 2016). This marked a significant milestone in Afghanistan joining what Buzan and Little term the 'global international society'. Notably, there is a need for some theoretical clarification on this point, as it is at the macro level that potential tensions between the historical framework set out by Buzan and Little could be perceived to be in tension with the use of norm circles as an explanatory mechanism of social reality. Thus, drawing on theoretical insights of the English School in International Relations, and the work of Hedley Bull, international society exists when states become conscious of certain common interests and values, and as a result, see themselves bound by a common set of rules and working within common institutions (Bull 1977, 13). For Buzan and Little, a *European international society* began to emerge with the rise of the Treaty of Westphalia in 1648. It was not until after the Second World War that a 'fully-fledge global international society' began to take shape, whereby 'its bottom line was the mutual recognition of its members as legal equals in the international community, with the exception of the "big 5" retaining a veto in the UN Security Council, and the recognised right to hold nuclear weapons under the NPT [Non-Proliferation Treaty]' (Buzan and Little 2000, 337).

Central to the notion of a global international society is that 'like units' of sovereign territorial states, irrespective of their wide ranging internal political differences, began to accept and act upon 'norms and rules' (Buzan and Little 2000, 337). At an initial threshold level this included adherence to non-proliferation norms and adherence to the norms of international trade. Indeed, economic interdependence and integration have been central to the emergence of the *global international system* and the *global international society* that accompanied it in the 20th century. While the use of the term *system* is complementary to the use of norm circles, the term *society* needs unpacking because of its ontological ambiguity (see Van Langenhove 2023).[4] As Elder-Vass explains at length:

> Society ... is an amorphous, poorly bounded and unclearly defined agglomeration that is more analogous to portfolio terms like nature or humanity than to any causally effective natural entity. The coherence of any bounded concept of society is extremely problematic. Those who use the concept often seem to assume that a society is coterminous with the territory controlled by a particular state. States themselves may well control territory with well-defined spatial boundaries, at least in some respects. But they do not map neatly onto societies; there are many potentially cross-cutting social systems that follow different boundaries, or none at all. ... One consequence of globalisation, for

---

[4] For the best work on the complementary nature of systems thinking and critical realism see John Mingers (2014).

example, is that fewer and fewer social entities are coterminous with states. But many – for example multinational corporations, religions and families – have never structured themselves on this basis. Given the lack of coherence of the concept of society, it is hard to see how such a poorly defined entity could have real causal powers. (Elder-Vass 2010, 82)

Given that Buzan and Little allow for considerable internal variability in states as 'units', a sensible reading of their work demonstrates that society, even at the global level, is not understood to be coterminous with state boundaries. Rather, a focus on norms provides common ground between the two theoretical frameworks guiding this book. As Elder-Vass continues:

Most of the powers that have usually been attributed to societies belong to somewhat smaller and more clearly definable social entities: structures at an intermediate level between individual and society that can have more specific effects. The neglect of these intermediate levels is a common problem in treatments of social structure … [as this] systematically ignores the complex hierarchy of actors that provides the bridge between individual role players on the micro-level, and systematic incompatibilities on the macro-level. (Elder-Vass 2010, 82)

Given the commitment to the role of norm circles as the mechanism of creating social institutions, it is necessary to unpack this further in relation to the global level. To do this, it is essential to add the concept of *intersectionality*. When a group intersects with one or more other groups, they possess the property of intersectionality. Applied to normative groups, intersectionality is a property that multiple norm circles (a norm-set circle) can have when the beliefs they endorse and enforce cut across one another. By virtue of this overlap, these intersectional norm circles are committed to the practice of a particular norm or a cluster of norms. As a result, 'to the extent that norm-set circles … are cross-cutting rather than congruent with each other, individuals become sites of normative intersectionality and *society* becomes a patchwork of overlapping and intersecting normative circles' (Elder-Vass 2010, 133; emphasis in original). Understood in this way, it is possible to be more precise over what is meant by *global international society* throughout this volume. Namely, *global international society* is a patchwork of overlapping and intersecting normative circles that consciously focus their collective intentions on operationalizing norms, through institutions, at the global level. This can include multilateral institutions such as the UN or the European Union (EU) but is not limited to the actions of states through such institutions. Indeed, as Buzan and Little identify, non-state units strongly contribute to *global international society*, which has been characterized by the development and contributions of international non-governmental organizations (INGOs) (2000, 272–4). Understood in this way, the selective and variable nature of how the norms of *global international society* are put into practice can be better explained. This may not be a concern for powerful states in the system, but it is for Afghanistan and other postcolonial polities. Indeed, it is through the development, and eventual thickening, of the norms of *global international society*, that Afghanistan would increasingly begin its interactions with the European Community and then the EU throughout the 20th century.

Daud's geopolitical manoeuvres and Pashtunistan

Following the end of the Second World War, Afghanistan's economic problems were not over, but the country was more internally stable, and Kabul had begun wrestling power back from the *'ulama* in a new round of centralization. This was accelerated with Shah Mahmud Khan acceding to the position of prime minister and regent. Shah Mahmud allowed modest attempts at democratization to move forward, with moderately free elections taking place (Suhrke 2007). This resulted in the 'Liberal Parliament' of 1949, which passed legislation allowing for the freedom of the press and allowed political associations that formed the basis of political parties and a student union (Dupree 1980, 494–8). Nevertheless, by 1953, Afghanistan's flirtations with more progressive and reformist norms faltered. By September of that year, King Zahir Shah allowed an internal palace coup and appointed Lieutenant General Muhammad Daud Khan, his brother-in-law and first cousin, as prime minister. Having returned from Stalin's funeral, Daud had been encouraged by the Soviet officials to depose Shah Mahmud (Lee 2022, 550–1).

Prime Minister Daud would initially attempt to alter Afghanistan's geopolitical orientation towards its local neighbourhood by promoting the creation of a separate independent state for the Pashtun spanning across the border region between Afghanistan and Pakistan (Bezhan 2014). As the British withdrew from India in 1947, it brought about an end to centuries of colonial rule. However, this also triggered India's partition and the creation of West Pakistan and East Pakistan (now Bangladesh), following demands for a separate homeland comprised of Muslim-majority provinces. The idea of creating a 'Pashtunistan' led to a clash of interests between Afghanistan and Pakistan over the status of the Pashtun territories. Britain's haste to exit left a power vacuum, ill-considered international borders and a legacy of bloodshed that continues to have profound consequences in the 21st century (see Meher 2012).

For Afghanistan, the British withdrawal from India and the decline of Pax Britannica was a surprise not considered even a decade earlier (Brown 1999).

Indeed, under 'Scheme Lancaster' from 1945 to 1947, Afghanistan received support from the British through arms, military equipment and training for Afghan forces to maintain a buffer for British India (see Government of Afghanistan 1948). Afghanistan was now in a position where it suddenly shared its longest border with a new neighbouring state. This generated considerable geopolitical tension and opened a debate about the Durand Line and historical sovereignty over the Pashtun tribes now inside Pakistan. In effect, the emergence of the global international system was straining fault lines between classical international systems and those imposed by empires as the global international system was forged.

The British dismissed Afghanistan's concerns, stating that Pakistan had legal authority over the former colonial territory. The British behaved as if they had the legitimacy to award sovereignty, and Afghanistan was challenging this postcolonial norm. Of course, the British obfuscated over the fact that even under the empire, British rule of these territories was tentative. Lord Birdwood (1953) summed up British policy rather concisely:

> For fifty years on the Indian Frontier, we were unable to decide whether to go forward to the Durand Line or come out of the country. A political officer would venture in and receive a bullet. A force would go in; a road would be made to maintain the force, and the force would then be kept there to protect the road. We became the servants rather than the masters of policy. (Birdwood 1953)

Rather than considering various options, the British ruled out an independent Pashtunistan and boundary adjustments to bring the tribes under Afghan sovereignty (see Bezhan 2014). Consequently, by the time Daud came to power, the future of Pashtunistan had become an emotive issue and persisted as a central point of international contention as Afghanistan began to connect with the norms of *global international society*. Under Daud, Afghanistan was challenging the territorial sovereignty of another postcolonial state. This put Afghanistan at odds with Pakistan, but also, within the Cold War context, the US, Britain, France and the multilateral security architecture established to prevent Soviet expansionism. Not endorsing Pakistan's agreed territorial sovereignty resulted in Afghanistan being ostracized from other international institutions. One of the reasons Afghanistan was not invited to join the Southeast Asia Treaty Organization (SEATO) or the Central Treaty Organization (CENTO) was because of Daud's persistent pursuit of Pashtunistan and conflict with Pakistan (Lee 2022, 553–4).[5] This was

---

[5]   The Baghdad Pact, established in 1955, was a defensive alliance initiated by Turkey, Iraq, Great Britain, Pakistan and Iran to advance mutual political, military, and economic

even though now declassified documents from the period show that under Foreign Minister Naim, some Afghan officials were attempting to work with the US and European powers on normalizing relations with Pakistan (US Department of State 1954). Failing to accept the norm of postcolonial sovereignty was punishable through the operating norm-circles of *global international society*.

Afghanistan's superpower relations

The geopolitical ascendance of the US, after the Second World War, led to significant adjustments within the global international system. The decline of Pax Britannica and the rise of US power was accompanied by greater engagement and the instigation of liberal norms into the global international system. As a result of this geopolitical ascendancy, US involvement in Eurasia increased (Hassan 2012, 2020a). In the mid-1950s this culminated in the US attempting to define what Secretary of State John Foster Dulles termed a 'Northern Tier' bordering the Soviet Union (Khalilzad 1979). While the US was reluctant to offer formal security assurances or assume the erstwhile imperial responsibilities of Britain in Afghanistan, it nevertheless stepped into a regional leadership position, acting as the primary mediator and overseer for geopolitical matters concerning Pakistan, Iran, Iraq and Turkey. This masked the US Department of State's assessment that Afghanistan was politically and economically fragile with limited defence capacities. In such circumstances, Afghanistan was not invited to join new security institutions. This allowed Afghanistan to present itself as geopolitically neutral in the early stages of the Cold War.

During the emerging Cold War, from the US perspective, Afghanistan was to be independent even if that meant it remained vulnerable to Soviet invasion. Britain had restrained Russian territorial ambitions for nearly two centuries, but this had led to the Anglo-Afghan wars. The US would not be drawn into the same pattern, and instead sought to contain Soviet ambitions through leadership over the 'Northern Tier'. However, from the Afghan perspective, this was a continuation of the 'Great Game', between 20th-century superpowers rather than 19th-century empires. Afghanistan was able to take advantage of the geopolitical tensions to find a new source of external rent, now the British Empire was in decline. As a result, the Soviet Union soon became Afghanistan's primary supporter in trade and aid. Afghanistan's professional ruling class had re-established an external

---

interests. Analogous to the North Atlantic Treaty Organization (NATO) and SEATO, its primary aim was to deter communist infiltration and promote stability within the Middle East region. Following Iraq's withdrawal in 1959, the alliance was rebranded as CENTO.

source of rent to support a system that had been reliant on external income since Dost Mohammad Khan's rule in the mid-19th century. As a result, norm circles in Afghanistan and the Soviet Union were soon aligning their normative positions in the global international system.

In 1955, Nikita Khrushchev, in his first foreign trip as leader of the Communist Party, visited Kabul and actively endorsed Afghan claims to Pashtunistan (Riedel 2014). Indeed, upon receiving loans, Daud quickly purchased Soviet arms and military equipment to counter Pakistan, which had been supported by the US as a buttress to Indian neutrality (see Dupree 1963). Afghanistan would also experience the largest boom in infrastructure investment in the 20th century, with civil engineering projects such as 'the construction of highways; the paving of Kabul's streets; hydroelectric plants; irrigation schemes; textile and cement factories; hospitals; post offices; soviet-style housing units for government officials, and the construction of Kabul's Polytechnic' (Lee 2022, 557). Daud was engaged in large-scale statism, underpinned by a Soviet-style five-year plan and funded by foreign aid and technical assistance (Emadi 2010, 59). As Saikal correctly assesses, 'Daud's skilful manipulation of the internal settings and the growing American-Soviet Cold War rivalry enabled him to put Afghanistan on an accelerated course of modernisation but at the cost of transforming the country into a "rentier state", with close ties with and ideological vulnerability to, the Soviet Union' (2004, 117). Far from being 'neutral', Daud was playing the 'Soviet card', and in return, the Soviets built political and military networks inside Afghanistan (Saikal 2004, 122). Indeed, by 1960, trade with the Soviet Union had accelerated, making it Afghanistan's largest trading partner. This was helping Afghanistan's adherence to the norms of *global international society*, even as Daud was sowing the seeds for decades of Soviet influence and, ultimately, the collapse of international societal norms with the Soviet invasion in December 1979 (Rubinstein 1980, 81).

This is not to say that Western nations were not present nor had influence. As the Cold War began, the US recognized the need to establish its hegemony and contain the Soviet Union. As such, under the Point Four Program, the US set out to aid capital investments and technical assistance in 'underdeveloped countries' (Truman 1949; Olden and Phillips 1952).[6] For Afghanistan, this included funding for an extensive hydroelectric and

---

6   The Point Four Program was named after the fourth point of President Harry S. Truman's 1949 inaugural address, committing the US to 'embark on a bold new program for making the benefits of our scientific advances and industrial progress available for the improvement and growth of underdeveloped areas … to help the free peoples of the world, through their own efforts, to produce more food, more clothing, more materials for housing, and more mechanical power to lighten their burdens' (Truman 1949).

irrigation project in the Helmand Valley.[7] US documentation declared that this was necessary to 'help in overcoming effects of ravages during the 12th and 14th centuries by Genghis Khan and Tamerlane' (in Rouland 2014, 54). Policy makers in this era were more acutely aware of historical legacies than their contemporaries. In addition, the US invested in Afghanistan's civil aviation and the expansion of Kandahar airport. Through the 1950s, and early 1960s, the US government invested heavily in Afghanistan trying to mitigate Soviet influence (Rouland 2014). Although, as a later USAID evaluation noted as a prescient but unlearned lesson:

> [W]hen a project becomes the donor's project and is no longer the host country's project, trouble will develop, so their common goals must be clearly defined, agreed upon, and planned on a long-term basis. ... There is no getting off cheap. Programs to make the desert bloom are enormous and expensive. If AID is involved in any way, its success is dependent on the success of the entire effort. (Clapp-Wincek 1983, viii)

Irrespective of US efforts, however, it was the Soviet Union that Afghanistan's sedentary professional elites were aligning to. This may have sat comfortably with the more secular elements in Afghanistan, but the intersectionality of these norm circles was unlikely to sit well with the Afghan desert norms, nor the subset of norms of conservative Islamic orthodoxy. Over the course of the next decades the tensions between these norms would build and finally erupt into a violent civil war.

The European consensus on trade and aid for Afghanistan

In the aftermath of the Second World War, European international society began to change dramatically, resulting in collective European action. As such, European norm circles became a fundamental part of bring the *global international society* into practice. Very quickly after the war, West Germany, France, Italy, the Netherlands, Belgium and Luxembourg adopted collective norms and postwar cooperation took hold. This led to the creation of the

---

[7]   Notably, this was inherited by the US government. In its first phase from 1946 to 1953, the Afghan government employed the US company Morrison-Knudsen Afghanistan and attempted to build a new system. This proved slow and problematic due to spiralling costs, budget cuts, hostility from Pakistan preventing equipment imports into Afghanistan, lack of local commitments and tensions with Iran. Nevertheless, the Arghandab and Kajaki Dams were completed, even as other work needed to be carried out (Dupree 1980, 482–5).

European Coal and Steel Community in 1951, the signing of the Treaties of Rome in 1957, and the birth of the European Parliament in 1958. Europe's growing normative cooperation had effects beyond the European international society and began contributing to the norms of global international society. Afghanistan was not immune from this. European nations had individually been engaging Afghanistan in technical assistance, with the French training lawyers and medical staff and Germans leading the Police Academy inside Afghanistan (Saikal 2004, 124). However, in the early 1950s, European-level engagement with Afghanistan was initiated by the European Community (EC) with small levels of trade (ECSC 1954; O. Hassan 2022). Like the US, this expanded in the 1960s. For Europe, however, this was due to the introduction of the Common Agricultural Policy (CAP) in 1962 and the rise of European food aid (ECSC 1962; Bergmann 1977). Unlike the US, the EC's relationship with Afghanistan was a by-product of the CAP and not one built around security concerns. The partnership offered a way to rectify imbalances in Member States' domestic agricultural sectors while reinforcing the EC's growing desire to play a more significant role in international affairs.

At the European level, a new consensus emerged around EC norms. A collective intention to engage in trade and aid was established to support Afghanistan in its modernization and development endeavours (Hassan 2020b). This consensus has been the foundational agreement that European norm circles have rallied around for decades. Europe's initial collective interaction with Afghanistan, through trade and aid, laid the blueprint for subsequent interactions through to the 21st century. Although the methods and intensity of European involvement have varied over time, this central norm has remained consistent since the 1960s (O. Hassan 2022). Indeed, from its inception this collective European practice was welcomed by Afghanistan. For Daud, this supported internal efforts to modernize Afghanistan and foster a developmental state (Suhrke 2007, 2, 7). Daud provided a drive to modernize and develop Afghanistan not seen since the aborted efforts of Aman Allah Khan in the 1920s (Dupree 1980, 485). Under Daud's influence Afghanistan began to reinstitutionalize more liberal norms in the form of women's rights and education, with women attending university and also enjoying rights that were on par with those in European countries. Furthermore, Kabul became the so-called 'Paris of Central Asia', with Afghanistan increasingly becoming a popular tourist destination (Bumiller 2009). However, unlike Aman Allah, it was not Daud's modernization agenda that brought his initial downfall but his policy on Pashtunistan.

As tensions with Pakistan increased, the issue of Pashtunistan led to border skirmishes in the early 1960s. This had a direct impact on Afghanistan's vulnerable and crisis-prone economy. As Pakistan sought to manage Afghanistan, it effectively created a blockade by cutting off trade, depriving Afghans of essential commodities and generating rampant inflation. Pakistan controlled most of Afghanistan's trade routes, and the blockade cut off the country's access to essential goods. As Afghanistan's economic crisis worsened, Afghanistan became more dependent on the Soviet Union for its survival, and the importance of the Soviet–Afghan relationship increased. Conversely, the Afghan–Soviet alignment constrained Afghanistan's relations with the US and European powers. For example, it made US aid programmes particularly difficult to deliver because the goods and materials needed were shipped through Pakistan. Finally, landlocked Afghanistan could ill afford the continued closure of its Frontier border with Pakistan, and ultimately, King Zahir Shah dismissed Daud in early 1963 (Haqqani 2005, 171–5). With Daud removed, the issue of Pashtunistan subsided. President John F. Kennedy and the Shah of Iran convinced Pakistan to reopen its border, resume the norms of international trade and allow for the resumption of US aid programmes (Riedel 2014, 14).

Afghanistan's constitutional period

Although Daud was no longer prime minister, he began rapidly preparing to seize power, planning a coup that would be a decade in the making. In the intervening years, however, King Zahir Shah became more active and was increasingly seeking to separate the royal family from the executive. As Dr Muhammad Yusuf took on the role of interim prime minister, there was agreement that there needed to be constitutional reform and a more representative system of government. Ultimately, this was not altruistic but derived from the emergent pressures of a growing modern state, which required greater professionalization within the state bureaucracy and the military and, therefore, higher education standards (Barfield 2010, 211). The 1931 constitution and its underlying norms of conservative Islamic orthodoxy were at odds with these emergent pressures. Once again, Afghanistan's desert norms and sedentary norms were in tension because of the desires for greater centralization and modernization. The emergent pressures of the global international system were exacerbating the tensions between these internal sets of norms.

Resolving these pressures culminated in adopting a new constitution in 1964, which built upon the liberalized constitutional drafts Daud had prepared before leaving office (Dupree 1980, 562–6). This was a significant moment in Afghan history. The new constitution was drafted with public involvement and approved in a relatively democratic process as Afghanistan ventured into limited representative democracy. Indeed, women regained the right to vote, initially gained in 1919 but repealed in 1929.[8] In addition,

---

[8] By comparison, women initially gained the right to vote in Afghanistan in 1919, one year after the United Kingdom (UK) and one year before White women in the US. This was lost in 1929 but regained in 1964 after adopting the new constitution.

Afghanistan was recognized as a constitutional monarchy, and sovereignty was placed in the hands of the Afghan people. This signalled a secular shift because although Article 2 confirmed Islam as Afghanistan's sacred religion and the new parliament was bound not to pass laws against Islam's basic principles, sharia had minimal emphasis within the new text. Thus, a pivotal shift from the 1931 constitution was the supremacy given to secular law over the sharia. Courts, under the new constitution, moved from being bound by the sharia to a secular legal framework, relegating religious law (Tarzi 2012, 219–22). These were transformative practices demonstrating a renewed attempt to give primacy to sedentary norms. They dissolved the codified Islamization project put in place by Nadir Shah and the 1931 constitution. The 1964 constitution sought to balance desert and sedentary norms, but ultimately embraced the latter in an effort to institutionalize social change and democratic reforms. The constitution was, for some, 'the finest in the Muslim world', standing out because it rejected the sovereignty of God over the state (Dupree 1980, 565).

Aligning with this new constitutional vision, 1965 was earmarked for elections. This necessitated a new delineation of provincial territories, giving birth to 29 *wilayats*, further subdivided into *wuluswalis* (districts). With elections looming, new political parties began to emerge in the shadows. Formally, these were not permitted. However, organizations such as the People's Democratic Party of Afghanistan (PDPA) began organizing for its Marxist-Leninist agenda. Islamist parties such as the Islamic Revolutionary Movement also began organizing, having long held the ambition of establishing a mass movement (Roy 1990, 70).[9] By the time parliament convened in early 1965, it would become a battleground for 'Leftists, Islamists, Pashtunists, Monarchists and representatives of ethnic and religious minorities' (Lee 2022, 566). The diverse range of norm circles this exposed in Afghanistan proved to be highly incongruent and resistant to intersectionality; Afghan society was divided. Fissures in this democratic experiment began to show in October of that year when members of the PDPA stormed the chamber and sparked protests in an attempt to get Prime Minister Yusuf and his cabinet to reveal their personal wealth. Prime Minister Yusuf would resign due to this episode, ending the reign of the first Afghan prime minister who was not part of the royal family.

Under the new prime minister, Muhammad Hashim Maiwandwal, Afghanistan began gravitating towards the US geopolitical orbit and attempted to make overtures towards adopting norms with a greater intersectionality

---

[9]   The Islamic Revolutionary Movement is particularly significant because it would facilitate the rise of Mullah Omar, who would establish the Taliban.

with the US. Maiwandwal was increasingly concerned with a growing communist movement and its influence among leftist students. Maiwandwal foresaw that Daud had opened the floodgates to Soviet aid and trade, which made inhibiting Soviet influence challenging. For their part, the Soviets began to view Maiwandwal as an American puppet, and rumours that he was a CIA agent were spread through the burgeoning Afghan press (Dupree 1980, 613–14; Emadi 2010, 76). This was not dispelled by Maiwandwal's meeting with President Johnson in the Oval Office. Maiwandwal declared:

> Although a considerable geographic distance separates our two countries, our common belief and devotion to liberty and respect for the inherent dignity of man has bridged this distance ... over the past 20 years, many Americans have been coming to Afghanistan to assist our country in its economic development ... Afghanistan is engaged in an all-out effort to develop its economy while at the same time modernising its political and social institutions. (Maiwandwal 1967)

Privately in the Cabinet Room of the White House, Maiwandwal was warning Johnson that as a result of Afghanistan having more 'democracy in the country', an 'explosive situation' was emerging that he 'feared might escalate into a bigger danger' (Spain 1967). Ultimately, the king refused to allow the formation of political parties, but this empowered communists and Islamists at the expense of moderate reformists (Bezhan 2013). The king's unpopularity was also becoming more entrenched as the veneer of democratic freedoms was not translating into effective political change. A deepening economic crisis exacerbated a political crisis as the system could not redress people's material needs. Afghanistan remained a repressive state, and the king was increasingly turning to well-established norms of authoritarianism.

By October 1967, Maiwandwal was forced to resign as he undertook cancer treatment. He would survive this health scare only to be tortured and beaten to death in prison under the suspicion of trying to counter the 1973 coup (CIA 1973). In the intervening years, King Zahir would make another misstep in appointing Nur Ahmad Etemadi as prime minister to replace Maiwandwal. Contemporaneously, historians such as Dupree disagreed with this assessment, arguing that the appointment and reappointment in 1969 demonstrated the king's 'political astuteness' (1980, 653). Nevertheless, it was clear that in seeking to quell urban protests, with West German–trained elite riot squads willing to unflinchingly beat protesters and bystanders alike, Etemadi's authoritarian leadership was exacerbating emergent militant norms. By way of background, Germany had provided police training advisors in the 1930s through to 1941 and West Germany from 1953 to 1979. While Afghanistan had sent some police to train in British India, this was abandoned after the British withdrawal. In 1957, the US signed an agreement allowing police officers to train abroad, which was quickly abandoned and fully returned to the Germans (Giustozzi and Isaqzadeh 2013, 22).

Environmental crisis and European food aid

By 1971, communists and Islamists openly battled in the streets of Kabul, generating domestic tensions in the most strategically significant city needed for the king to maintain power. This forced Etemadi's resignation as he faced a no-confidence vote in parliament. Prime Minister Abdul Zahir was appointed in June and inherited a mounting series of crises. On top of the growing political and economic crisis was an increasing environmental catastrophe. Afghanistan has been facing encroaching desertification for centuries, but since 1969, 'Afghanistan has experienced several extended droughts that have had severe consequences on the country's land and people' (Afghanistan National Environmental Protection Agency 2017). From the spring of 1969 to the autumn of 1972, the rain and snow seasons failed to fill Afghanistan's rivers. This compounded systemic environmental problems from overgrazing, poor soil maintenance, salination and deforestation (Shroder 2012). For the Afghan population, almost entirely reliant on domestic agriculture, this was devastating. By 1971, nearly a quarter of a million Afghans were on the edge of starvation, and Afghanistan was faced with a natural disaster (Lee 2022, 572).

With such devastating consequences awaiting, Abdul Zahir reached out for food aid and called on global powers to adhere to the norms of *global international society*. The US provided around 200,000 metric tons of wheat. In addition, the World Food Programme, Canada, China, Germany, Turkey, France and the EC contributed another 100,000 tons. This was a significant milestone in European-level engagement with Afghanistan, as it consolidated a new role for European-level action, whereby the norms of humanitarian aid began to embed themselves more deeply into bilateral cooperation. For example, in 1971, the EC declared through community action that it 'proposed to grant to the Kingdom of Afghanistan 10,000 metric tons of common wheat under its 1970/71 food aid programme'. This was followed in 1972 with agreed conditions on the supply of common wheat as food aid (OJ 1972, 8, 1973, 37–9). By 1975, EC food aid to Afghanistan was expanded from common wheat to include 300 metric tons of skimmed milk powder and 600 metric tons of butteroil (OJ 1975a, 33–7, 1975b, 26–30). Accordingly, the EC's relationship with Afghanistan in the mid-1970s was characterized by increasing engagement and cooperation, particularly in food aid, irrespective of Afghanistan's formal non-alignment in the Cold War and the the 1973 coup. A norm of humanitarian aid being apolitical began to articulate itself with expressions of *global international society*. Apolitical practices were not extended, however, to meeting Afghanistan's economic needs in light of the environmental crisis.

In the autumn of 1972, Abdul Zahir resigned after the US attempted to restructure its approach to foreign loans. Under the Nixon Doctrine, Afghanistan would need to apply for foreign loans from its rival Iran. This was a humiliation too far (Lee 2022, 575). The king appointed Muhammad Musa Shafiq as prime minister in December 1972. Facing a mounting foreign debt crisis, Shafiq quickly sought to restructure Afghanistan's debt payments. The Soviet Union agreed. However, short-sightedly, the US and European nations were less willing. Diplomatic relations were not helped by the discovery of heroin trafficking into the US and Europe by embassy staff and one of the king's closest advisors (Lee 2022, 576). Recognizing the structural problems Afghanistan faced, Shafiq also sought to deepen regional integration and reduce Soviet influence. This required a rapprochement with Iran and resolving territorial tensions and the distribution of the Helmand River's water. Tensions with Pakistan were also eased with President Bhutto's visits to Kabul (Saikal 2004, 170–2). Such efforts were in vain. After just seven months in office, Shafiq would be removed while the king was in Europe, and Daud would finally undertake his long-planned coup starting on 17 July 1973.

Daud's bloodless coup and the Saur Revolution

Daud declared himself president of a new Republic of Afghanistan in a *coup d'état*. Unlike previous coups that played out palace politics, Daud was brought to power by Soviet-trained military officers, some with links to the PDPA. This created an odd and ultimately unsustainable coalition of norm circles between monarchists and the Marxist-Leninist ideology of the PDPA. Internationally, such a coalition made Daud's claims of non-alignment unfeasible, with the US and European powers, at first, resisting recognition of the increasingly authoritarian regime. This was combined with a purge against liberals and Islamists alike. Many of the latter fled to Peshawar in Pakistan and began to regroup. Indeed, as Daud renewed calls for Pashtunistan, President Bhutto's government welcomed Islamists who opposed Daud's nationalist agenda (Lee 2022, 582). Pakistan began to fund these groups, providing training, financing and arms in their new safe haven.[10] Indeed, by 1975, Pakistan had covertly assisted an attempted Islamist

---

[10]   This included Gulbuddin Hekmatyar, who established a militia known as Hezb-e Islami, and another, Ahmad Shah Massoud. Both play a role in the EU's engagement with Afghanistan in the 21st century.

uprising, which forced Daud to temper his separatist position (Rubin 1992, 100). As Daud began to drop demands for Pashtunistan and build bridges with Western powers, along with Iran and Pakistan, he domestically began to reinforce the presence of monarchists over the PDPA members in his regime. In this respect, Pakistan's funding of Islamist groups was perceived to be in its national interest. It also placed the US and European powers on the same side as Islamist detractors of his regime. While aid continued to flow to Afghanistan as part of a 'business as usual' Cold War approach, there were already covert efforts to support a new regime. As Rubin demonstrates, links were being forged between 'American military and intelligence agencies … [and] Afghan insurgents through the ISI' (Rubin 1992, 101).

It was not just the US and Pakistan looking to remove Daud. Increasingly, Afghan–Soviet tensions began to rise as Moscow became particularly unhappy with the Afghan leadership. Between 1975 and 1977, the Soviets broadened their view of what was politically desirable and searched for alternatives to Daud. This led to the PDPA actively trying to destabilize Daud's regime. Nevertheless, Saikal demonstrates that, ultimately, 'Daud was a self-seeking, autocratic nationalist reformer, ultimately not prepared to share power with anyone' (2004, 176). Over time, tensions between Daud and the PDPA leadership became so strained that in April 1978, Daud ordered the arrest of the PDPA leadership. This attempted purge failed. In response, the PDPA initiated a coup. On 27 April 1978, Daud, his wives, children and aides were executed after the presidential palace was seized. Their bodies were unceremoniously dumped into a mass grave, not to be discovered until 2008 (Reuters 2008). The Saur [April] Revolution ended Afghanistan's centuries-long norm of dynastic rule.

Communist rule and the Soviet invasion

By dismantling the existing dynastic rule, the Saur Revolution unleashed a complex set of challenges around political legitimacy and governance. Ultimately the prevailing norm circle and its institutions of political power had been removed, and as a result a mechanism endowed with maintaining norms of political legitimacy removed. This ignited fundamental questions about who had the right to rule Afghanistan, and how they should do it. Initially, Nur Muhammad Taraki was president and prime minister of a new revolutionary government. However, extending political power beyond Kabul proved highly problematic. The PDPA lacked political legitimacy and a capable administration. As Taraki initiated land and social reforms, they were met with violent demonstrations and unrest, forcing the government to turn to the Soviet Union for assistance (Edwards 2002, 25–86). Not only were desert and sedentary norms in conflict, but more extreme subsets of norm circles were emerging. The political vacuum fuelled ideological extremism, particularly among Islamist groups. The PDPA were not just Marxist-Leninist, and therefore espousing an alien ideology birthed in Europe, but their atheism denied them political legitimacy beyond elites in Kabul. With the centralized state's political legitimacy removed, the country's heterarchical village states were empowered, and 'for the first time since the reign of Abdur Rahman Khan, violence emerged as the determining factor in state-society relations' (Saikal 2004, 187). Norms of resistance had been reawakened.

Despite the PDPA's lack of both political legitimacy and broad popular support, the Soviet Union remained committed to its survival, thereby exacerbating the crisis. By October 1978, people had started to rise against the new regime, and this soon spread across the country. However, Soviet assistance still began to make its way into the country, ultimately propping up an illegitimate regime. This included military aid, advisors and logistical support to plan and implement security operations, but also in the hope of building the state in a 'large-scale experiment of Sovietisation' (Zagorski 2007). This turned Afghanistan into a Cold War proxy battleground. This external backing further delegitimized the PDPA in the eyes of Afghans, who increasingly saw the government as a puppet regime. The Soviet Union's unwavering commitment to the PDPA, despite its glaring deficiencies in governance and public trust, only served to deepen the social and political fissures. By March 1979, the Herat Uprising had begun because of the 'government's affronts to Islam'. As testimonials recall:

> They changed the education. Suddenly, even the basic literacy curriculum was inundated with communist propaganda. ... They wanted our girls to be taught by men. We had no problem with girls being educated by female teachers, but male teachers was just too much at the time. ... These weren't just men, these were young men, not much older than many of their female students. ... [It] showed how little regard the communists had for Afghan customs. Religious leaders began to lash out against the policies in their sermons, eventually calling for a protest march to the provincial capital. ... The elders and religious scholars called for 'death or success'. There were no other options. (Latifi 2014)

It was also in March 1979 that Hafizullah Amin ascended from deputy prime minister to prime minister. Amin, a power-hungry autocrat, ruled through terror and, within months, undertook a coup to seize the presidency. After side-lining Taraki's loyalists, Taraki himself was placed under house arrest and was found murdered at his residence in October 1979. Amin's goal was 'to use the state apparatus to destroy all competition for social control in all sectors of Afghan society' (Rubin 1992, 115). Initially, the

Soviets sought to at least try and cultivate a relationship with Amin despite his brutal governance. However, witnessing the escalating unrest across Afghanistan, they concluded that the regime's collapse was imminent. In a decisive move in December 1979, the Soviet Union intervened militarily, aiming to supplant the regime and prevent it from falling into Islamist hands and falling out of the sphere of Soviet influence. On 27 December, Soviet forces attacked Kabul, killing Amin and members of his family, and installed Babrak Karmal as the new president. This move further alienated the Afghan populace and intensified resistance against the PDPA and foreign occupation.

The Soviet Union's decision to intervene in December 1979 marked a critical juncture for Afghanistan. The Soviets had planned the invasion on their experiences of Hungary in 1956 and Czechoslovakia in 1968 (Jalali and Grau 2001, xvii). However, repeating the mistakes of the British in the Anglo-Afghan War, they failed to account for the contextual norms of Afghanistan and develop a plan to subjugate the heterarchical village state and gain control beyond the cities. In failing to do this, the Soviet invasion demonstrated contextual dissonance, and a fundamental misunderstanding of Afghanistan. As Rubin's research has explained:

> In retrospect, as Russian and other former Soviet experts say today, they should have announced national reconciliation with the mujahidin on day one and used models compatible with Afghan society, but they knew nothing about that and were constrained by Soviet ideology. The Soviet leaders tried to do what they knew how to do: turn Afghanistan into a satellite state. (Rubin 2020, 55–6)

In attempting to impose Soviet norms without consideration for their contextual consonance, the Soviet's failed to account for the strategically selective context they were engaging in. Indeed, Zagorski's research on lessons learned from the Soviet experience in Afghanistan echoes this:

> The Soviet knowledge of Afghanistan was rather superficial and the reality on the ground could not be comprehended through a pre-set template. The readiness of the Afghan population to embrace social change was not to the extent that Soviet leaders had assumed. And the assumptions made about the ability to mobilise wider political support for social change in the country's Islamic society proved wrong as well. (Zagorski 2007, 21)

Inside Afghanistan, the Soviets found an uncoordinated resistance gaining momentum and embroiled themselves in a conflict that was militarily draining. The mujahidin (those who engage in jihad) consisted of several guerrilla groups from the countryside village states. They emerged in a similar pattern to centuries of protests in Afghanistan, namely with an action from the central government triggering a reaction from the religious leadership and local men, who would then seize local government institutions (Rubin 2020, 58–65). These local groups, however, needed support. Initially, this was supplied by Pakistan.

Following their successful covert action in 1975, Pakistan began a longer-term training programme for Islamist refugees and their leadership base in Peshawar. Under a doctrine of 'strategic depth', Pakistan aimed to promote a pan-Islamist agenda inside Afghanistan and transform its leadership, making it more favourable to Pakistan should a war with India break out. It was, therefore, seen as in Pakistan's regional interests to incubate norm circles of radical extremists opposed to Afghanistan's PDPA and its former royal dynasty. The Islamists would also help with Pakistan's own Islamization agenda, bolstering Pakistani President Muhammad Zia-ul-Haq's domestic interests. Accordingly, following the Saur Revolution, Islamists in Pakistan were prepared to aid local uprisings, and Pakistan had built roads to the Afghan border to help this happen. Over time, the US, China, Britain, France, Italy, Saudi Arabia, Egypt and the United Arab Emirates began providing military and humanitarian aid through Pakistan (Grau 2004). The EC, however, began to transform from a policy of trade and aid into an essential humanitarian actor in Afghanistan. Thus, while a common objective united the mujahidin in opposing the PDPA, the US and some EC Member States attempted to make Afghanistan ungovernable for the Soviets. The EC adopted a fundamentally different approach as it emerged as a significant international actor.

Transatlantic responses to the Soviet invasion

The Soviet invasion of Afghanistan in 1979 marked a watershed moment. The year started with the Shah of Iran being overthrown in an Islamic Revolution and Ayatollah Khomeini's fervently anti-Western regime upending the US approach to the Gulf region and Central Asia. Instability in the Gulf that same year would also see the rise of Saddam Hussein in Iraq through a Ba'ath party purge and Islamists seizing the Grand Mosque in Mecca. The sense of growing instability was furthered by the pro-US regime in Nicaragua being overthrown by the Sandinista rebels, bringing Soviet influence to Central America. This added to the blistering defeats and sense of decline faced by the Carter administration.

Before the Soviet invasion, in July 1979, the Carter administration had already agreed, in now declassified documents, to 'support insurgent propaganda and other psychological operations in Afghanistan; establish radio access to the Afghan population through third country facilities' and 'provide unilaterally or through third countries as appropriate support to Afghan insurgents, either in the form of cash or non-military supplies'. The objective was to 'expose the Democratic Republic of Afghanistan and its leadership as despotic and subservient to the Soviet Union' and 'publicise efforts by the Afghan insurgents to regain their country's sovereignty' (Office of the Historian 1979). This followed a souring of relations with Afghanistan after US Ambassador Adolph Dubs was taken hostage and subsequently killed. The US State Department concluded that at least three Soviet advisors were actively involved in arming the hostage takers and responded by cutting aid to Afghanistan. Indeed, by May 1979, the US concluded that while it was more likely that the Soviets would avoid direct involvement in Afghanistan's domestic turmoil, 'a 1968 Czechoslovakia-type situation' was becoming possible if domestic unrest threatened the 'Afghan Revolution' (DNSA 2015). Nevertheless, when the Soviets invaded, it was a watershed moment for the US and Europe.

In the US, President Carter proclaimed a Doctrine that conflated the crisis in Afghanistan with the implications of the revolution in Iran and the 1979 oil crisis. In his State of the Union Address on 23 January 1980, Carter unequivocally stated that any attempt to exert control over the Persian Gulf region would be treated as an attack on US vital interests and warrant US military intervention. This was in line with a long-term strategic framework to protect the flow of global oil production and transit routes (Yergin 1991; Hassan 2013). It thereby led to extensive US involvement in Afghanistan and Pakistan, culminating in the provision of military aid to Pakistan as a regional counterweight (Carter 1980). The Carter Doctrine set the stage for future US policy and military deployments, redefining America's relations with the Middle East and the geopolitics of the Cold War.

In Europe, leaders publicly supported the US and put out statements of solidarity. Indeed, practising the norm of solidarity is important for generating intersectionality between sets of norm circles in times of transatlantic crisis. For example, the British government, under Prime Minister Margaret Thatcher, adhered closely to American policy and was tacitly supported by the Dutch and the Belgians (Dale 1980). In direct conversations, Thatcher would agree with Carter that 'swift action was needed', and Britain went about severing high-level contacts with Soviet officials and endorsed trade sanctions, albeit without rigorous enforcement. The Soviet Union was to be punished for breaking the norm of sovereignty and failing to adhere to the norms of *global international society*. Furthermore, the British Foreign Secretary undertook diplomatic tours to drum up support, mirroring the US stance. However, in Brussels, British representation was concerned that the US was overstating the threat and disagreed that security capabilities should be diverted to a 'third theatre' of Cold War conflict at the expense of European security (Newell 1981; Dimitrakis 2012). Nevertheless, behind calls of solidarity, the Thatcher government was briefing that the European reaction was 'decidedly wet' and both the EC and the North Atlantic Treaty Organization (NATO) had failed to 'spawn one single specifically European act of reprisal against the Russians' (Wyles 1980a, 16).

In contrast, France and other European allies were more cautious, fearing that a strong response could damage détente and lead to a broader conflict with the Soviet Union. For example, the French position was wide-ranging, expressing solidarity with the US while demanding it adopt an independent policy. This was something of a dual approach, both aligning with and distinguishing itself from the US and Britain. While French policy called for an end to the Soviet occupation in joint statements with Western European allies, it also sought diplomatic nuances to navigate the crisis (Newell 1981). French President Giscard d'Estaing met with Soviet leader Leonid Brezhnev, advocating for an international conference to explore peaceful resolutions. The conclusion of the meeting in May 1980 was that the French and Soviet positions were 'far apart and remain[ed] far apart'; yet West Germany and Britain remained irked at only being informed of the meeting at the last minute (Koven 1980). Of course, the West German Chancellor, Helmut Schmidt, developed a novel line of expressing solidarity while simultaneously criticizing Carter's handling of the crisis. As Newell assessed, 'Schmidt was reportedly incensed by the inept coordination with European Governments and military posturing fuelled by American military pressures. He claimed to "stand solidly" with Washington but was compelled to find other means of developing his position' (1981, 179).

The Soviet invasion also presented a profound conundrum within the NATO alliance, precipitating a state of collective disarray. NATO members found themselves ensnared in a vexing paradox: their entrenched dependence on the Middle Eastern hydrocarbon endowments was at odds with their burgeoning ambitions to intensify commercial interactions with Eastern Europe. As such, the invasion presented a dilemma whereby the potential threat to oil supplies was vague and ill-defined, and NATO had no immediate answer to the problem being presented. Initially, members were divided between concerns that the US would drag them into an unnecessary war or, conversely, abandon European security altogether (Davy 1980, 14). It took months of political debate and assessment for NATO to finally coalesce around the idea that this was not Moscow's first move in attempting to cut off Middle Eastern oil but a response to events on the ground in Afghanistan (Dale 1980). Of course, these political dynamics also played out within the EC and shaped European-level action.

The European Community response and emergence of Civilian Power Europe

At the level of collective European action, the EC was initially incoherent and confused, as Member States' national interests surpassed any attempt to develop a coherent European approach (*Financial Times* 1980). The EC's initial response, representing the public positions of the Member States, was to note its 'solidarity' with the US. This was echoed in the European Parliament, which only months before held its first elections under direct universal suffrage, and new Members of the European Parliament (MEPs) passed a resolution condemning Soviet actions (European Commission 1980; European Parliament 1980; Jenkins 1980). However, over time, the Soviet invasion accelerated a significant shift in European-level norms. Through the lens of the Cold War, the collective European position began to shift away from its focus on trade and aid. The crisis had precipitated a reframing of the relationship, taking on more geopolitical and security concerns. The community swiftly responded within its jurisdiction by halting its food aid programme to Afghanistan, restricting agricultural exports to the Soviet Union in line with US policy, and allocating funds for Afghan refugees in Pakistan (Lakc 1980; Wyles 1980b; O. Hassan 2022). However, organizing collective European action beyond this proved problematic throughout the early 1980s.

By 1981, the European Council stressed the 'urgent need to bring about a solution which would enable Afghanistan to return to its traditional independent and non-aligned status free from external interference'. The proposal, made by the Council, was to lead an international conference in October or November of that year, consisting of two stages. First, to 'work out international arrangements designed to bring about the cessation of external intervention' and, second, to 'reach agreement on the implementation of the international arrangements … to assure Afghanistan's future as an independent and non-aligned state' (European Council 1981). Nevertheless, as the EC attempted to move forward, national governments refused to provide the EC with the authority or coherence for firm collective leadership. As Ham argues, '[n]either the EC nor the EPC [European Political Cooperation] were authorised more than in an informal way to deal with th[is] security issue' (Ham 2016, 115). This was a significant moment, exposing what has become a dominant strategic tension within the transatlantic relationship with Afghanistan (Robinson 1981). For the 'solidarity of the West' and a mixture of national interests, Member States forfeited the development of the EC's crisis management norms and instruments, and the EC was not endorsed by Member States to assert itself as a security actor in Afghanistan. Without the collective intentions of Member States facilitating a change in norms, the EC was unable to institutionalize security practices or to emerge as a security actor with traditional security instruments. This is because European integration was at odds with the norm of Member States maintaining sovereignty over security issues, and the norm of maintaining Atlantic solidarity.

That European integration and Atlantic solidarity are perceived as being in tension with one another reflects the structure of the global international system and the nature of state units. Buzan and Little's framework is instructive in illustrating this point. Self-evidently, the EC represents a new type of unit within a system dominated by states and is part of a wider 20th-century shift towards the norms of *global international society*. As Buzan and Little explain, the EC/EU is an example of a 'very fully developed international society, with many shared norms, rules, and institutions coordinating, constraining, and facilitating the relationships amongst its members' (2000, 122). Through a gradual integration process, the objective of collective European-level action was to foster norms of peace, unity and prosperity in Europe. As this was institutionalized, it became clear that states shared a range of common interests and common values, conceived themselves to be bound by a common set of rules, and began working within a common set of institutions. In this sense, the EC, conceptually and in practice, came to form a regional-level international society through the intersectionality of sets of norm circles. What is significant here, for both the EC and its relationship with Afghanistan, is that new norms of global international society were deemed necessary because of the inadequacies of the 'state-centric paradigm' and the diminishing role of using force in European relations.

In the 1970s and early 1980s, as intellectuals and policy makers grappled with what this meant for European-level external action, it translated into the notion of Civilian Power Europe (CPE) (Bull 1982; Whitman 1998; Orbie 2006). Drawing from Duchêne's concept of 'civilian power' (1972), European norms shifted the focus from power politics to global betterment and aiding impoverished nations. This, albeit vaguely, translated into the idea that Europe can exert its collective influence and achieve its goals through non-military means. To do this, European institutions needed to emphasize using civilian instruments and values to promote European interests globally. Within the global international system, this would allow Europe to practice a distinctive role, facilitating the collective needs of Member States without creating a European superpower but allowing Europe to act externally without being neutral (Orbie 2006).

The notion of CPE should not, however, be seen in a historical vacuum. Within the global international system, the ascendancy of the US was marginalizing European states' power and influence. After the Suez Crisis in 1956, it was abundantly clear that Pax Britannica had transformed into Pax Americana. As a result, the strategic direction of the global international system and the maintenance of international security were implicitly yielded to the US. The development of CPE can be seen as an emergent product of this structural transformation. Europe's external role in the world was to have a positive impact through its civilian capabilities and normative commitments. Europe remained a continent with considerable international power, even as the state-empire formation within the system transformed more coherently into a more extensive system of independent sovereign states. However, the US and Soviet Union had become the dominant international players within a world of bipolar superpowers. Without giving traditional instruments of power to the EC, the notion of CPE allowed a consensus to slowly emerge around normative power at the collective European level. Accordingly, an emphasis on the EC becoming a humanitarian actor emerged from within Member States (Hassan 2020b). This has become central to European norms and the emergence of European exceptionalism in European aid policies (Lorenzini 2019).

The European Community's Aid to Uprooted People programme

As much out of necessity as fitting with the zeitgeist, the EC moved towards being a humanitarian actor within Afghanistan in the mid-1980s. The EC adopted a humanitarian stance in its dealings with Afghanistan, developing an institutional norm of leaving conventional geopolitical matters to its Member States. In a state-centric world, transatlantic partnerships had marginalized collective European action but contributed to the emergence of a normative Europe devoid of traditional security mechanisms. Inside Afghanistan there was a growing urgency for EC to take up this role. While the brutality of Taraki and Amin's communist regime led to 400,000 individuals fleeing to neighbouring states, the Soviet invasion would cause an exponential increase. By the end of 1980, Pakistan alone hosted between three and four million Afghan refugees. Within the subsequent four years, this count escalated, exceeding five million across Pakistan and Iran (Schöch 2008; Amnesty International 2019).

Due to bureaucratic delays in the Pakistani government, the Office of the High Commissioner for Refugees (UNHCR) began contracting INGOs for projects in 1981, effectively making them implementing partners and, in some instances, allowing them to steer UNHCR programming (Baitenmann 1990, 67). By the end of 1985, Afghan refugees represented the largest displaced population in the world. Nevertheless, Sri Wijeratne, the UNHCR's Chief of Mission for Afghanistan in the 1990s, argued that:

> During the 1980s, the open-door policy of both Iran and Pakistan and their treatment of the refugees was exemplary. ... The example of Pakistan and Iran should be studied very carefully by many countries

who try to shut up shop when confronted with refugee caseloads a fraction of the size of the Afghans. … Both countries ended up with over three million Afghan refugees, and both countries responded with a generosity of spirit that has not been paralleled since. (Colville 1997)

It was within this context that the EC began institutionalizing a humanitarian approach towards Afghanistan and developing a role for civilian power. This took the shape of the Aid to Uprooted People (AUP) programme, funded under the DG-1 budget line, and the redelivery of aid to Afghanistan from a representative office in Peshawar, Pakistan (ICG 2005, 3). Through the AUP programme, humanitarian assistance attempted to meet the needs of refugees and prepare for their expected return to Afghanistan's eastern provinces (Sondorp 2004, 5). Instrumental to this was the influx of INGOs and the development of local non-governmental organizations (NGOs). This represented a thickening of the norms of *global international society*, as multilateral and non-state actors coalesced around humanitarian norms.

By way of background, European influence in developing INGO networks that operate in international emergencies has a historical precedence. In terms of the global international system, INGOs emerged from the civil societies of leading states. They thrived in the democratic, legal spaces that expanded internationally in the late 20th century. The roots of INGOs date back to 18th-century European and American societies, but 19th-century middle-class growth and advancements in international communication catalysed their formal emergence. Formal association between INGOs and international governmental organizations (IGOs) eventually grew internationally as INGO and IGO goals aligned. Thus, while there were only 176 INGOs in 1909, by 1994, these had increased to 4,928 (Buzan and Little 2000, 272). In this sense the emergence of these organizations 'thickened' the norms of *global international society* by adding to the interaction capacity within the global international system.

In Afghanistan, the Soviet invasion spurred a surge of IGO, INGO and local NGO activity, particularly in Peshawar, Pakistan, to assist Afghan refugees. This period saw the formation of new INGOs, significant financial support from private and governmental donors, and the unique emergence of local NGOs, some of which were backed by INGOs (Sondorp 2004, 5). A primary player in this was the EC (and later the EU), as Europe enhanced its normative agenda through civilian power and, therefore, sought to meet its primary humanitarian objective by funding INGOs and local NGOs as they gravitated towards Afghanistan. Accordingly, European NGOs came to dominate assistance programmes across the border of Afghanistan and Pakistan. Indeed, the US funded more European NGOs, as fewer US NGOs engaged in cross-border operations. Despite policy differences, many European NGOs accepted US funds, often channelled through the

International Rescue Committee, which had become the most extensive US-funded programme in Pakistan (Baitenmann 1990, 76). Rather than conflicting with the US, this reinforced the EC's humanitarian approach. As humanitarian norms became increasingly institutionalized, they laid the foundations for the EU to emerge as the most significant humanitarian coordinator in Afghanistan throughout the 1990s (O. Hassan 2022).

Soviet withdrawal and the Geneva Accords

During the early stages of the Soviet occupation, while the EC was developing its humanitarian approach, the US strategy was to fund the resistance and promote their cause. The aim was to make the occupation of Afghanistan so costly that the Soviets would not want to advance further. This fell short of trying to expel the Soviet troops and replace the communist government. It also meant that the US showed no strategic interest in preparing the groundwork for a future government, which would have required building Afghan unity. As Rubin argues:

> The common terms for this strategy were 'bleeding the Soviets' or 'fighting to the last Afghan'. Given this goal, it made sense to arm whatever Afghan group inflicted the maximum pain on the Soviets rather than to try to help the resistance transform itself into a coherent force, one that could present a political alternative to the Kabul regime and stabilise a future Afghanistan. (Rubin 2020, 72)

In terms of the US strategic approach, it is interesting to note that there was no regard for the contextual consonance of this strategy as it related to Afghans. The central focus was on developing a Soviet focused strategy within the Afghan context, with no regard for what followed. This was reflective of the US's normative myopia, whereby dominant policy-making circles practice short-term thinking and decision-making practices and neglect to consider the long-term consequences and broader impacts. By 1985, it had become abundantly clear that the US's strategic objectives were unattainable because Soviet dominance of the airspace acted as an effective counter to the rebellion. This strategic reality coalesced with a shift in the US administration's application of the Reagan Doctrine. Under President Reagan, Washington shifted from a containment strategy to overtly engaging in 'rolling back' Soviet power (Walcher 2015, 341). Having re-evaluated the strategically selective context, by September 1986, following Mohammad Najibullah's ascension as the PDPA's secretary-general, the CIA, Pakistan's Inter-Services Intelligence (ISI) and mujahidin successfully trialled shoulder-held Stinger anti-aircraft missiles. This led the US to expedite weapon deliveries, fostering a more direct relationship with the mujahidin and side-lining the ISI, which had been solely financing Islamist factions. This recalibrated the dynamics of regional alliances and changed the US's role in the conflict. By 1989, this strategic shift enabled the US to diverge from what it now regarded as 'extremist' entities (Rubin 2020, 73).[11]

The Soviets began withdrawing from Afghanistan in May 1988, following the signing of the Geneva Accords in April of that year. This had been planned since late 1986. Upon taking power in 1985, Mikhail Gorbachev changed Soviet policy to focus on modernizing the Soviet Union (Rubinstein 1988; Rubin 2020, 76). Indeed, this is one of the reasons Najibullah was brought to power. As the former head of KhAD (the State Information Service), the Soviets believed he was well-placed to strengthen Afghanistan's security forces and bring Afghans together through a national reconciliation process (Marshall 2007; Oliker 2011). Not only did this process fail, but the Geneva Accords failed to provide a structure for national reconciliation. There was no institutional structure developed to create intersectionality and help focus the collective intentions of divergent norm circles around normative commitments to peace. The Accords consisted of four key instruments:

1. A Bilateral Agreement between Afghanistan and Pakistan focused on principles of mutual relations, particularly non-interference and non-intervention.
2. A Declaration on International Guarantees signed by the Soviet Union and the United States, committing to respect the independence, sovereignty and territorial integrity of Afghanistan and Pakistan.
3. Another Bilateral Agreement between Afghanistan and Pakistan concerning the voluntary return of refugees facilitated by UNHCR.
4. An Agreement outlining the interrelationships between these instruments and providing a timeline for the phased withdrawal of foreign troops, to be completed within nine months starting from 15 May 1988.

While the Accords aimed to establish an inclusive Afghan government, they explicitly acknowledged that questions of governance were exclusively within Afghanistan's jurisdiction and to be decided by the Afghan people. However, Iran's Ministry of Foreign Affairs took exception to the Accords, declaring the agreement with Kabul as 'legally invalid' and criticizing the exclusion of the mujahidin. Overall, the Geneva Accords sought to achieve a political settlement in Afghanistan, discourage external interference and lay the groundwork for a government that would be representative of all segments of Afghan society (Shahi 2008).

---

[11] This included Gulbuddin Hekmatyar's Hizb-i Islami and Abd al-Rabb al-Rasul Sayyaf's Islamic Union, which were respectively funded by Pakistan and Saudi Arabia.

Nevertheless, as one lesson-learned exercise concluded, the Geneva Accords failed to include a mechanism to settle the internal conflict, global powers disengaged and 'Russia, Pakistan, Iran and ... Saudi Arabia supported their favoured Afghan groups in the civil war' (Suhrke et al 2002). Ultimately, the Accords' failure to include all factions in the talks and build mechanisms for peace led to their failure. Indeed, the Soviets continued to fund Najibullah's government, and the US continued to fund the mujahidin even as the Soviets withdrew. After the Soviet withdrawal, and with the Soviet Union facing collapse, the Najibullah government would fall, leaving Afghanistan in a state of further instability and civil war. Thus, as Barfield argues, 'the successful resistance strategy of making the country ungovernable for the Soviet occupiers also ended up making Afghanistan ungovernable for the Afghans themselves' (2010, 6). To be clear, this did not create an anarchic 'state of nature' whereby the history of Afghanistan was somehow eviscerated. Rather, it weakened the centralized state to such an extent that norms of political legitimacy were radically disturbed by disempowering previously dominant norm circles. This empowered village states tribal republicanism, which now had powerful international backers and external rents of their own. In short, the social and political fabric of Afghanistan had been deliberately destabilized to fight the Soviet Union, creating a legacy that endured into the 21st century.

The European Union's humanitarian leadership before the Taliban

Following the 1989 Soviet troop withdrawal, the EU's humanitarian role in Afghanistan evolved (Katzman 2005, 3). This reflected the political reality on the ground, and developed a contextual consonance with the needs of Afghans. The UN-brokered Geneva Accords left a weak communist government trying to face down mujahidin fighters that had benefited from a USD 3 billion influx of US weapons and assistance (Rashid 2000). The Najibullah government was increasingly under threat, and in March 1990, it survived a coup attempt inspired by the ISI. Nevertheless, it was not until the end of 1991, in the final throes of the Soviet Union itself, that the US and the Soviets withdrew aid to the mujahidin and the Najibullah government, respectively. As a result, Najibullah could no longer afford to pay the militias, which had devastating consequences. As Rubin outlines, '[o]nce Najibullah stopped paying them, these militias, led by Dostum, mutinied, allied with co-ethnics in both the army and the mujahidin, and seized control of the customs posts, from which they paid themselves' (Rubin 2020, 81). This created a similar situation in 1992 to that of the British in 1841, and without an external source of income, Najibullah was critically weakened. With his government destabilized, Najibullah was forced to resign under the terms of a UN peace plan. By April 1992, the government crumpled, setting the stage for a collapse of the centralized state and further civil war.

In the wake of a security vacuum left by the government's collapse, new strategic actors emerged and began exercising little restraint in committing widespread human rights violations and ignoring the rule of law. Often loosely referred to as *warlords*, these actors were increasingly powerful charismatic actors that rose to power locally by maintaining independent control over a military force. Buzan and Little are notably silent on warlords as actors in any stage of world history. They certainly date the emergence of 'warlords' as actors with the rise of tribes and nucleation of the pre-international systems period, but this is carried out almost by way of passing comment (Buzan and Little 2000, 147, 413). However, the term *warlord* in Afghanistan does not necessarily carry the same connotation as traditional tribal leadership, although some warlords may have also been tribal leaders. Indeed, because of the egalitarian nature of desert norms, the rise of warlords was particularly difficult in many local contexts of Afghanistan (see Giustozzi and Ullah 2006).[12] This confusion is symptomatic of a lack of analytical precision around the term. Giustozzi provides a particularly useful account of the debates around this term, demonstrating that while some have provided a historiography dating the rise of warlords as actors to ancient Rome, others have considered them a post-Cold War phenomena (Giustozzi 2005).

There is little room to evaluate this literature and set out points of stasis in the debate here, but it is possible to define some of the normative practices of such individuals to establish the boundaries of their respective norm circles. First and foremost, such individuals have a normative commitment to violence as a means of securing power. As a result, they will need to propagate norms associated with military functioning and hierarchy, including leadership and coordination norms. These norms are not pursued for a collective good of perceived higher entities, but rather for personal enrichment and the personalization of political power. It is possible to consider these to be part of larger neopatrimonialist norms. These include the blending of official and personal networks where resources are distributed as patronage, and the centralization of authority is placed within a single

---

[12] The best work on this has been carried out by Antonio Giustozzi and Noor Ullah (2006), who provide an overview of anthropological studies detailing the difference between the social organization of the Nang, whose norms correspond with the historically earlier egalitarian models, and practice the honour code of Pashtunwali. The Galang is a second type of normative social organization which is more hierarchical and where Pashtunwali plays a more modest role in patron–client relations. Indeed, Giustozzi and Ullah provide a significant overview of normative fragmentation between tribal units, which should be consulted by any reader wishing to garner more depth in this subject than could be afforded by this text.

leader who can operate beyond the formal legal frameworks of the primary unit (be that city-states, or centralized forms of empire and states). Herein, they operate within a strategically selective context that is more amenable to allow them to function. Often this is where central authority has been weakened or collapsed in a particular territory. To fill a political power vacuum, these individuals create a norm of personal loyalty and allegiance as the primary criteria for political and economic advancement, rather than merit or legal rationality. These norms manifest in practices such as clientelism, rent-seeking, and the extensive use of governance resources for personal or political gain, undermining formal institutions and contributing to governance challenges, including corruption and inefficiency. These were norms that, for example, epitomized the leadership of General Abdul Rashid Dostum in northern Afghanistan and the wider fragmentation of Afghanistan in the early 1990s. With strategic actors propagating these practices in Afghanistan, already serious humanitarian crises were exacerbated.

In a significant shift in the political landscape, a series of uprisings culminated in establishing a mujahidin regime in Kabul on 18 April 1992. This regime was predominantly composed of Tajik and Uzbek factions. This event marked a pivotal juncture where, for only the second time since the inception of the Afghan state in 1747, the Pashtuns were not at the helm of the capital. Although, this time, unlike the months of 1929, there was no tacit acceptance of Tajik rule. This challenge to Pashtun power and influence set the stage for a devastating civil conflict. Gulbuddin Hekmatyar, to reclaim Pashtun dominance, besieged Kabul. His tactics, characterized by indiscriminate violence, resulted in the deaths of thousands, leading to his infamous moniker, the 'Butcher of Kabul'. To exacerbate Afghanistan's growing crisis, drought and famine added to a growing level of human misery. Over five million Afghans lacked access to food and water, and less than 12 per cent of the population had access to sanitation. As a result of these combined factors, Afghanistan entered a renewed phase of humanitarian crises, and a refugee crisis followed, with increased movement inside Afghanistan and an increase in refugees fleeing to Pakistan and Iran (Rashid 2000, 21; Ruiz and Emery 2001).

EU humanitarian activity in Afghanistan was not insulated from the deteriorating insecurity inside the country. Afghanistan was an extremely complex environment in which to deliver aid. In response to the growing insecurity, the EU emerged as the most strategically situated actor prepared to undertake the role of humanitarian coordinator within the region, even as it emphasized normative commitments to multilateral crisis management (Agence Europe 1994). European institutions and the newly established European Community Humanitarian Office (ECHO) were instrumental in providing food, water, health care and shelter to the local population throughout the parts of Afghanistan they could reach (European Commission

2010). In 1993, ECHO commenced its operations in Afghanistan. Its projects were emblematic of core norms such as 'independence', 'neutrality' and 'relief', aligning with the established 'values and principles for the intervention of European humanitarian aid' (Hassan 2023). Conceptually, ECHO was envisioned as an entity with a robust operational capacity for direct interventions during humanitarian emergencies (Mowjee 1998). However, in practice, this operational capacity remained nascent. Instead of direct interventions, ECHO adopted a collaboration strategy, predominantly partnering with European NGOs. This approach sought to facilitate the efficient allocation of funds and underscore the importance of partnerships in humanitarian assistance.

Herein, the EU buttressed the UN, supporting UN-initiated activities and coordinating humanitarian assistance. However, although aligned with UN initiatives, the EU was willing to sidestep the UN when European NGOs directly sought EU funding (Donini 1996, 51; ICG 2005). This practice was not without its problems, as Strand identified, in some instances, 'NGOs shied[ed] away from being coordinated by the UN ... especially NGOs principally funded through ECHO, such as Médecins Sans Frontières' (Strand 2003, 111). The EU could circumvent the UN where it was deemed necessary because it emerged as the single largest humanitarian donor to Afghanistan, with over EUR 500 million in aid allocated throughout the 1990s (European Commission 2003). From its office in Peshawar, the EU began to take on a discreet role in 'coordinating the work of NGOs, particularly in the health sector, which was supported by UNICEF, WHO, and the governmental authorities', allowing the EU to become the 'de facto coordinating body' in a range of sectors, and particularly in the realm of humanitarian assistance (Burns 1995; Donini 1996, 38–51; Strand 2003, 96). This is significant because, as a lesson-learned study for the European Parliament would later conclude, 'There is a need for EU institutions to correct the narrative and assert the positive role Europe ... historically played in Afghanistan throughout the 1980s and 1990s' (Hassan 2023). The EU was a significant contributor to the norms of global international society, even if this role has not been largely recognized. Indeed, it was because the EU was in this role that tensions began to emerge between the EU and the Taliban in the mid-1990s.

European Union humanitarianism and engagement with the Taliban, 1996–2001

Following the Maastricht Treaty coming into force, the EU began to expand its global impact. In Asia, this was reflected in the release of the first regional strategic document, *Towards a New Asia Strategy*, in 1994. To have a regional impact, the Union wanted to assert itself and play a more significant role in 'the management of international affairs ... [and] a constructive and stabilising role in the world' through 'positive contribution to regional security dialogues' (Commission of the European Communities 1994). This buttressed the EU's vision of civilian power and its humanitarian efforts in Afghanistan. Institutions of the EU were increasingly articulating their humanitarian contribution to normative concerns and a more considerable contribution to international security and the stability of the global international system. Accordingly, in the latter half of the 1990s, EU institutions emerged as the predominant aid donor to Afghanistan, contributing 18 per cent of all official donor receipts, starkly contrasting to the US's 3 per cent. Within this timeframe, the EU's institutions were responsible for a remarkable 27 per cent of all humanitarian aid disbursements, juxtaposed with a mere 2 per cent from the US (Hassan 2023). This was a significant contribution that should not be understated, and independent assessments have lauded Europe's intervention in the region. A comprehensive evaluation of the AUP initiative underscored its profound impact on the uprooted populace and the host communities in Afghanistan. The initiative's adaptability was evident in its collaborations with diverse stakeholders, including the UNHCR, local governance structures, INGOs and Afghan NGOs. Furthermore, it operated across multiple sectors, such as health, agriculture, education and mine action, employing a range of mechanisms from direct delivery and capacity building to delegating responsibilities to local NGOs (COTA 2000, 17).

The EU's humanitarian engagement in Afghanistan during the 1990s was both significant and impactful, yielding tangible results on the ground. This demonstrated a degree of contextual consonance. The EU's humanitarian capacity, operating through NGO networks and formal assistance programmes, was instrumental in this success and created a normative consensus for Member States to unify around the EU's new capacities. Thus, unlike in the previous decade, where Member States were fragmented on collective European initiatives, the 1990s witnessed a unified European stance. However, this proactive role inadvertently positioned Europe in direct contention with the Taliban, especially as the latter ascended to power during the mid to late 1990s. Grasping the nuances of these tensions is pivotal for comprehending contemporary European interactions with the Taliban, as they reveal significant normative dissonance.

The 1990s were marred by the international community's failure to broker a peace settlement in Afghanistan. This shortcoming had dire ramifications for the Afghan populace. Despite sporadic multilateral efforts to alleviate the humanitarian crisis, the situation deteriorated, culminating in the world's most severe refugee crisis (Amnesty International 1995b,

1995a). Amidst the backdrop of pervasive human insecurity and rampant human rights violations, the Taliban, under the leadership of Mullah Omar, emerged in 1994. The Taliban began to contest the dominance of warlords, particularly in the Kandahar province. Capitalizing on the internal divisions among warlords and the disillusionment with the once-revered mujahidin leadership, the Taliban managed to carve a niche for themselves. Their ability to provide local security, anchored in their interpretation of sharia law and a punitive justice system, granted them a semblance of domestic legitimacy during the 1990s.

The Taliban's ascent to power in Afghanistan can be attributed to their ability to significantly reduce the rampant arbitrary violence that had become a hallmark of domestic life. Mullah Omar, through his confrontations with warlords and adept resolution of local disputes, began to be perceived by segments of the Afghan populace as a 'Robin Hood figure'. This image, juxtaposed with the prevailing instability of the civil war, positioned the Taliban as a potentially stabilizing political force (Bergen 2006). Their momentum was evident when, shortly after their emergence, they secured a substantial arms cache near Spin Baldak and subsequently captured Kandahar, Afghanistan's second-largest city. By early 1995, the Taliban, armed with repurposed Soviet weaponry, were advancing towards Kabul, eventually capturing the capital on 27 September 1996 (Katzman 2005). Their rapid rise can be attributed to various factors: combat skills acquired from mujahidin factions based in Pakistan; a potent blend of Pashtun nationalism; and appeals to Islamic tenets. This multifaceted approach enabled a set of norms that transcended tribal and ethnic affiliations. The Taliban projected themselves as a pan-Sunni religious movement, embracing all Afghan ethnicities yet strategically emphasizing their Pashtun identity when beneficial (Borthakur and Kotokey 2020).

The Taliban's capture of Kabul in the mid-1990s marked the beginning of a series of punitive and symbolic acts that would define their rule. Once Kabul had been seized, the Taliban's first act was to capture former President Najibullah from the UN diplomatic compound he had been residing in since 1992. Najibullah was transported to the presidential palace, castrated, dragged behind a jeep, shot dead and finally hung on a control post outside the palace (Rashid 2000; Katzman 2005). Punitive ceremonial displays of justice set the tone of the Taliban's practices inside Afghanistan. This was met with condemnation from the European Parliament, which expressed 'shock'. In addition, the Parliament expressed its concerns over the Taliban's 'absolute discriminatory regime against women', the committing of 'atrocities', an 'extreme interpretation of Sharia … implying inhumane forms of punishment', the attacking of 'humanitarian workers such as the Delegate of the International Red Cross Committee' and the burning of 'foreign films and books' (European

Parliament 1996). These became recurring themes discussed throughout EU institutions and the wider international community during the late 1990s (Hassan 2023).

Relations between the EU and the Taliban were, unsurprisingly, fraught. The EU, in line with most of the international community – with the notable exceptions of Saudi Arabia, the United Arab Emirates and Pakistan – did not recognize the Taliban as Afghanistan's legitimate government. This diplomatic stance culminated in a particularly tense incident on 29 September 1997. European Union Commissioner for Humanitarian Affairs, Emma Bonino, was threatened with a Kalashnikov rifle and arrested in Kabul. The Commissioner and her party had been touring a women's hospital when they were arrested, and some members were beaten for taking photos in violation of the Taliban's strict interpretation of Islamic norms (Shawcross 1997).

Following her release, Commissioner Bonino poignantly remarked on the pervasive 'random terror' that characterized daily life in Afghanistan. She further emphasized the need for Afghanistan to be prioritized on the international agenda, advocating for a political solution to the nation's challenges (Johnston 1997). While tensions with the Taliban intensified, the EU remained committed to its humanitarian mission in Afghanistan. Commission spokesman Klaus van der Pas underscored this commitment, asserting that EU aid was humanitarian, asserting that 'this money is given regardless of the government … it goes to the people, not the government' (Peters 1997). This stance highlighted the EU's dedication to alleviating the humanitarian crisis, even amidst escalating political tensions.

The Taliban's strict normative interpretation of Islamic law, particularly those concerning women and girls, often conflicted with the EU's humanitarian and development norms. Nevertheless, internal evaluations for the European Commission demonstrated that the EU could have a 'a tangible impact' supporting 'over 400 schools and over 200 basic health clinics, many offering services to women and girls' (European Commission 2003). This was possible because the EU was able to take advantage of the strategically selective context, and circumvent the Taliban. As a lessons-learned study conducted for the European Parliament would later note, this provides essential lessons for engaging with the Taliban, as humanitarian aid, with a political component, can be successful and have a tangible impact inside Afghanistan under Taliban rule (Hassan 2023). However, caution on development policy needs to be acknowledged. The European Commission's *2003–2006 Afghanistan Country Strategy Paper* outlined that during Taliban rule in the 1990s, 'the biggest impact has been more on reducing extremes of vulnerability rather than actual development, which has been largely impossible given the war and then Taliban policies, especially in relation to girls' education and women's mobility and employment' (European Commission 2003).

Significantly, this included a period where the Taliban actively undermined the EU strategy. In early 1998, the Taliban began imposing restrictions on NGOs, asking them to sign a Memorandum of Understanding and move their offices to Kabul's Polytechnic Centre if they wished to continue operating in Afghanistan (Strand 2003, 131). However, in the latter half of 1998, the Taliban directed all NGOs to vacate Kabul, posing a significant challenge to ECHO's activities. Removing NGOs damaged the primary mechanism through which the EU operationalized its humanitarian norms, as by 1998, all EU funds were distributed through NGOs, and the EU was forced to suspend aid provision (ICG 2005, 10). This situation was compounded by two major earthquakes and the Clinton administration's decision to launch cruise missiles at al Qaeda training camps in retaliation for the bombing of two American embassies in Africa. While ECHO recommenced its operations in Afghanistan by the close of 1998, its interventions were strategically focused on regions facing acute crises, such as Hazarajat, which was under a Taliban blockade (European Community Humanitarian Office 1998, 15).

Hence, throughout the 1990s, EU success was more than anecdotal. The EU moved away from a policy of trade and aid, cementing a policy of humanitarian assistance in the mid-1980s. Due to the EU's leading role, its humanitarian policy helped mitigate against the excesses of Afghanistan's unfolding crises. Moreover, through its relationships with INGOs and NGOs, the EU was remarkably well-informed about events in Afghanistan, even if it could not encourage development or generate meaningful structural change. For example, EU institutions were increasingly drawing links between instability in Afghanistan and the potential for international terrorism long before 11 September 2001 (Hassan 2010). Significantly, during the 1990s, the EU did have a positive impact through the realization of CPE, developing a positive impact in Afghanistan through its civilian capabilities and normative commitments. This was despite the EU needing more fungibility to utilize the capabilities of Member States (see Whitman 1998, 108). This is particularly important to acknowledge, given the return of the Taliban in 2021. Although the strategically selective context has changed, there are salient lessons that emerge from this period. What this period shows is that the EU can have an impact, even when the Taliban demonstrates a remarkable ability to resist political, social or economic pressures generated from within the global international system. Prior to the events of 11 September 2001, the EU had already established itself as a significant stakeholder with on-the-ground humanitarian capabilities, institutionalized through its IGO, INGO and NGO networks and formal aid programmes (Hassan 2020b, 2023). This was a human security role *par excellence* and harnessed Europe's normative commitment to civilian power. The problem was, in the aftermath of 11 September 2001, the EU was marginalized in the name of solidarity and its expertise was disregarded by the US and Member States in the name of counterterrorism and attempts at state-building.

Terrorism, Solidarity and European Marginalization

Throughout the second half of the 1990s, European Union (EU) institutions made declaratory statements linking ongoing violence in Afghanistan with regional instability, drug trafficking and international terrorism (Bulletin EU 1996). Under the EU's Common Foreign and Security Policy (CFSP) framework, these declarations mirrored the Union's escalating apprehension about Afghanistan's increasing instability and potential repercussions for the global international system (Hassan 2010). Notably, the EU's concerns contradicted many assertions that the importance of terrorism was waning. As Weinberg summarizes:

> By the mid-1990s, it appeared to some observers that terrorism was declining. The Cold War had ended. The Palestinians and Israelis had agreed to the Oslo Accords, calling for mutual recognition with outstanding differences to be resolved peacefully. The various Latin American urban guerrilla groups were on the wane as one country after another had restored their democracies as revolutionary terrorism had proved to be a dead end. As it turned out, however, peace was not at hand. (Weinberg 2018, 45–6)

In the United States (US), the Clinton administration sought to capitalize on the end of the Cold War 'peace dividend'. This entailed the US politically moving towards a more significant domestic focus, even after a bombing at the World Trade Center in February 1993. At the time, with over 1,000 injuries and six killed, this was the deadliest attack on American soil. Yet, the mastermind, Ramzi Yousef, was suspected of having ties to Iraq and not Afghanistan; there was no evidence of links between Yousef and the Iraqi regime (Mylroie 1995; Kean et al 2004). It was only later discovered that Yousef had received explosives training in Afghanistan in the early 1990s, which helped him make the truck bombs placed inside the World

Trade Center. Moreover, Yousef planned another series of attacks, including President Clinton's assassination in Manila, before being captured in Pakistan in 1995 (Kean et al 2004, 147–9).

Within the Clinton and subsequent Bush administration, significant concerns around terrorism and Afghanistan were only shared by narrow sections of their officials. This proved to be a catastrophic failure in intelligence for both administrations (Clarke 2004). What was initially perceived as a global terrorist 'network' subsequently came to be identified as 'al Qaeda'. This organization would be responsible for launching the deadliest terrorist attack in world history. Planned in Afghanistan, under the leadership of the Saudi national Osama bin Laden, 11 September 2001 directly claimed the lives of 2,977 individuals. Exposure at Ground Zero led to subsequent deaths of an additional estimated 5,000 survivors and emergency service personnel and a further 130,000 receiving ongoing care from the World Trade Center Health Program (Haelle 2021; WTCHP 2023). The beginning of the 21st century would be defined by the global response to these attacks, and place Afghanistan and the Taliban's relationship with al Qaeda in central focus. Indeed, the US response, and subsequent European support, would characterize the first two decades and create a shift in collective European action towards Afghanistan. What began as a relationship built on trade and aid in the 1950s, and subsequently evolved around normative commitments to humanitarianism in the 1970s and 1980s, would evolve again into attempts at state-building. Attempts that, from their inception, failed to evaluate the strategically selective context they were operating in, generating a considerable level of contextual dissonance between state-building policies and the realities on the ground.

Al Qaeda and Afghanistan

The link between al Qaeda and Afghanistan began with the Soviet invasion, but it is possible to draw a further connection to the development of the global international system. During the development of the global international system, it was commonplace until the latter half of the 20th century for states to colonize Muslim nations and dominate them within the structure of state–empire relations. Faced with imperialism and colonization, starting around the 1880s, Muslim reformers grappled with modernity, the implications of nationalism and how they could harmonize collective Islamic norms within the global international system. The answer to this, for many, was pan-Islamism. As Hafez explains, '[p]an-Islamism served as a defensive response to Western encroachment even as Islamic modernists sought to foster an indigenous modernisation that took its inspiration from Western scientific and material progress' (2023, 332).

The 19th century is important because Muslim communities around the globe tried to maintain the core or traditional elements of Islam while innovatively adjusting to new conditions and challenges presented by the connectivity of the global international system. At its heart was a struggle to maintain continuity in Islamic norms and practices, alongside the necessity for dynamism and change to remain relevant and functional. Indeed, the historian John Herbert Voll summarizes this perfectly with the notion that Islam was undergoing a period of 'creative preservation and active adaptation' and '[i]n some cases, the efforts were successful, and in others, there was failure. The most visible failure was the attempt to stop European military and economic expansion. By the end of the century, virtually all the Islamic world was under some form of European control' (Voll 1994, 149).

In this sense, the forging of the global international system gave rise to different forms of, and emphases on, pan-Islamism. On the *adaptationist side*, three types of pan-Islamist norm circles emerged. First, *Islamic modernism* placed Islamic norms at the centre while attempting to integrate Western norms into political, social and cultural life. This was an approach that emphasized the intersectionality of respective norm circles. In contrast, *Islamic secularism* accepted the division of mosque and state, prioritizing norms of individualism. A third saw the rise of *Islamic nationalism*, which prioritized nationalist norms of ethnicity and language rather than prioritizing religious identity. On the *preservation side*, pan-Islamism drew more heavily on 18th-century neo-Sufism and the idea that socio-moral reconstruction was the primary focus. *Islamic fundamentalism* draws upon this, legitimizing anti-modernist Islamic norms as a form of resistance to modernism and the structure of the global international system favouring Western power in the 19th and 20th centuries (Voll 1994, 2014). Whilst Afghanistan demonstrated a mixture of these forms of pan-Islamism throughout the 19th and 20th centuries, the Soviet invasion precipitated an influx of Islamic fundamentalists, precipitating a global jihadist movement that continued into the 21st century. Indeed, they added a considerable emphasis on violent norms, which supplemented the norms of conservative Islamic orthodoxy outlined in the previous chapter. Indeed, it was the presence of norm circles endorsing these later norms inside Afghanistan that made the strategically selective context amenable to Islamic fundamentalist norm circles.

For Osama bin Laden, the Soviet invasion was considered the most 'transformative event of his life' and allowed him to take up the 'full-time job helping the Afghan resistance' (Bergen 2006, 24). In 1980, bin Laden was drawn to the Afghan jihad against the Soviet Union and made his first trip to Pakistan. Inspired by his mentor, the Palestinian cleric Abdullah Azzam, they founded the 'Bureau of Services' in 1984, which placed Arab volunteers with relief organizations in Pakistan, arranged for Arab fighters to be placed with the mujahidin, and produced the monthly *Jihad* magazine that reported on events in Afghanistan (Bergen 2006, 24–33). Highlighting Arab contributions to fighting the Soviets, the magazine justified jihad towards the West based on references to European colonization as far back as the colonization of the Americas. To quote the magazine at length:

> Maybe Muslims forgot the wars that occurred in the last century between France, Britain, and other European countries. And maybe the Muslims forgot the hardships of two world wars, created by the West and lasting twenty-five years, which killed fifty million people, and left people injured, maimed, and wounded. … America is the New World leader, or better yet, a country that has built its empire on the backs of original inhabitants [the Native Americans] who they wiped out and who now number less than a million … jihad is a religious duty for the Umma, so as to free the people and give them Islamic justice and protection of the religion … we want to spread it over all four corners of the world … Jihad in God's will means killing the infidels in the name of God. (English translation in Bergen 2006, 35)

Published in February 1987, these remarks demonstrated the ambitions of a pan-Islamist global jihadi movement that had ambitions far beyond repelling the Soviets. Published and distributed globally, it encouraged travellers from all over the world to join its cause. As more Arab fighters travelled to Pakistan and Afghanistan, Osama bin Laden began to build his military force based in Jaji and engage in direct conflict with the Soviets. Accordingly, bin Laden was no longer simply acting as a donor and organizer. He was part of the mujahidin's efforts. By 1988 as the Soviets announced their intended withdrawal, the nucleus of al Qaeda formed at a meeting in Peshawar, Pakistan, rather than allowing the dissolution of the jihadi network (Hamid and Farrall 2015, 61).

Of course, bin Laden and the so-called 'Arab Afghans' contributions were primarily meaningless to the conflict and eventual withdrawal of the Soviet Union. They operated differently from the Afghan fighters, but this role did allow bin Laden to form a network of like-minded associates from around the globe. It also allowed bin Laden to build the 'Golden Chain' funding network to filter money into non-governmental organizations and supply arms to the mujahidin (Kean et al 2004; Hamid and Farrall 2015). By 1989, however, bin Laden moved back to Saudi Arabia and then to Sudan in 1991, from where he would build a global terrorist network and focus calls of war on the 'far enemy' of the US. It was in May 1996 that bin Laden would return to Afghanistan, where he was formally introduced to the Taliban leadership in Kandahar by Pakistani intelligence operatives. This did not cement the relationship, and bin Laden maintained contact with Gulbuddin Hekmatyar, who opposed the Taliban. It was only when the Taliban seized Kabul that al Qaeda would cement ties with them, and even then, this relationship was fraught. Through the Golden Chain funding network, however, bin Laden was able to support Mullah Omar's Taliban financially. Like the leaders of Afghanistan before him, Omar capitalized on the external financial support bin Laden and the Golden Chain provided. The Taliban provided sanctuary, and in return, al Qaeda provided funding, fighters, weapons and international networks to a regime with few international backers. Once again, the rulers of Afghanistan had addressed a structural problem and found external rents to support their regime. In return, US intelligence estimates believe that 10,000 to 20,000 of al Qaeda's fighters were trained in Afghanistan between 1996 and 2001 (Kean et al 2004).

By 1998, following the bombing of US embassies in Kenya and Tanzania, the US had concluded that the Taliban had 'not kept Afghanistan from being a platform for international terrorism', and 'Bin Laden and his network continue[d] to threaten US interests'. Significantly, these conclusions came with requests from both the US and Saudi Arabia for bin Laden to be extradited, but these were refused by the Taliban. The US State Department concluded that this was because of ties between Mullah Omar and bin Laden specifically, but that the Taliban was divided on the dangers of providing sanctuary. As such, the US informed the Taliban that 'we hold the Taliban and by implication its supporters responsible for bin Laden's activities while he is in Afghanistan' (Inderfurth 1998).

The US government in 1998 downplayed the connections between the Taliban and al Qaeda and believed that formally recognizing the Taliban could provide leverage to drive a wedge between them (Stenersen 2017, 76–85). Some academics have also sought to downplay the relationship between the Taliban and al Qaeda as a 'marriage of convenience' and stressed the importance of ideological differences (Pillar 2011). There certainly existed a difference of focus, with the Taliban concentrating internally within Afghanistan and al Qaeda having global jihadi ambitions. However, bin Laden had established himself as more than just a guest. Even after years of conflict and threats of further Western intervention, the relationship between al Qaeda and the Taliban has lasted into the 21st century (OFS 2020, 35). Accordingly, it is important to note that al Qaeda has pledged *bay'ah* (an allegiance grounded in sharia law) to the Taliban and, through the Haqqani network, has ties of family and marriage (Mir 2020; Hassan 2023). Accordingly, there are social institutions that bind this relationship, and therefore there are operable normative practices being endorsed and supported within the relationship. Some scholars have dismissed such issues, but these are critical institutional norms grounded in centuries of tradition that supplement various points of norm circle intersectionality between member of each group. This is far from deterministic. Although these social institutions are old, as our world history of Afghanistan has shown, the formation of collective intentions between al Qaeda and the Taliban are extremely new in terms of contemporary history and the emergence of the global international system. Indeed, there is no intrinsic nor long-term connection between Afghanistan and international terrorism demonstrable in the account of world history provided in Chapters 1 and 2.[1] As Pillar testified:

> The connection of this region with militant Islamist terrorism is rooted in the insurgency against the Soviets in Afghanistan in the 1980s. … Afghan nationals are conspicuously absent from the ranks of international terrorists. … In short, the link between this region and international terrorism is not based on inherent qualities of the region or of the conflicts that bedevil it. Instead, it is more of a historical accident related to an attempt by the Soviet Union to quell an insurgency in a bordering state. (Pillar 2011)

This analysis is significant, as it necessitates the disentanglement of Afghanistan's long-standing historical norms from the distinct challenges that have emerged in the post-1970s, particularly following the Soviet incursion. Such a dissection reveals a layered historical complexity, and even as Afghanistan will forever be associated with the 11 September 2001 terrorist attacks, its relationship with terrorism is not immutable.

The European Union and the transatlantic response to 11 September 2001

The G.W. Bush administration took two pivotal decisions that shaped the normative trajectory of US engagement in Afghanistan after the 11 September 2001 attacks. The first, encapsulated in *National Security Presidential Directive 9*, refused to differentiate between al Qaeda and the Taliban. Ostensibly, this ratified the warning the Taliban had received in 1998 about being held accountable for bin Laden's actions (Inderfurth 1998). Yet, this conflation precipitated further practices framed around a 'war on terror'. The US's engagement with Afghanistan proceeded based on military and security norms; sidelining legal and diplomatic norms. The ramifications of this were profound, establishing a path-dependency that directed the course of US foreign policy (Jackson 2005; Hassan 2013). Given the US's unparalleled status as the only superpower in the global

---

[1] Considering that al Qaeda was established in 1988 and launched attacks on the World Trade Center 13 years subsequently, it is pertinent to observe that the duration of the US military presence in Afghanistan, aimed at dismantling al Qaeda, exceeded the period for which the organization had existed prior to the attacks.

international system, this path-dependency significantly influenced EU Member States, EU institutions and other global alliance networks. Indeed, in trying to align collective intentions, respective norm circles would have to search for intersectionality with US military and security norms, while observing wider diplomatic practices.

The US concluded that it was at 'war' with international terrorism, and by 14 September 2001, had developed a White House paper titled *Game Plan for a Political-Military Strategy for Pakistan and Afghanistan*. This linked the war to Afghanistan and Pakistan, which amounted to recognition that the 'Pastunistan problem' had resurfaced from the very start of the conflict. The legacy of 19th-century British imperialism had resurfaced. The *Strategy for Pakistan and Afghanistan* detailed specific demands for the Taliban:

- Surrender bin Laden and his chief lieutenants, including Ayman al Zawahiri.
- Tell the US what the Taliban knew about al Qaeda and its operations.
- Close all terrorist camps.
- Free all imprisoned foreigners.
- Comply with all UN Security Council resolutions.

By 16 September, the US Departments of State and Defense had consulted the North Atlantic Treaty Organization (NATO), requested intelligence sharing, and designed a plan to approach allies based on their capabilities and resources. By 17 September, military objectives had been established, which included the use of ground troops (Kean et al 2004, 332–3). The US remained confident that the Taliban would not hand over bin Laden, just as they had not in the late 1990s. The Taliban sent mixed messages, demanding evidence that bin Laden was behind the terrorist attacks and making suggestions that bin Laden could be extradited for trial to a third country, even as Mullah Omar was saying there was no move to 'hand anyone over' (*The Guardian* 2001a). On 21 September, President G.W. Bush approved military plans with the operational name Enduring Freedom (OEF).

The choice made by the US to frame its response within the confines of conventional security norms and state-centric conflict resolution practices yielded far-reaching implications. Remarkably, this decision was reached within mere days and influenced policy trajectories spanning over two decades. It was not a well-considered strategy designed to succeed in a challenging, strategically selective context. As such, it was a crisis response and not a strategy designed to achieve contextual consonance. In retrospect, numerous George W. Bush administration members began to perceive this approach as excessively reductionist in its outlook. President Bush and Secretary of Defense Donald Rumsfeld would later concede, respectively:

We actually misnamed the war on terror. It ought to be the struggle against ideological extremists who do not believe in free societies who happen to use terror as a weapon to try to shake the conscience of the free world. (Bush 2004)

I don't think I would have called it the war on terror … I don't mean to be critical of those who have or did or … and certainly I've used the phrase frequently … it's not a war on terror. Terror is a weapon of choice for extremists who are trying to destabilise regimes and impose their … dark vision on all the people that they can control. So 'war on terror' has a problem for me. (Rumsfeld 2006)

As many active and retired US military leaders would argue, publicly and privately, the idea of a 'war on terror' was too simplistic in its prescriptions, and conveyed the impression that military power alone could address the threat. This echoed the initially private objections from EU officials and was a point of contention between the US and European institutions (Hassan 2023). There was normative dissonance created by two different normative approaches to dealing with terrorism.

During the Maastricht era, Europe predominantly embraced criminal justice practices in addressing terrorism. At the European level, the Trevi framework from the 1970s was incorporated into the Justice and Home Affairs (JHA) pillar of the EU (Monar 2008). Accordingly, by the time of the 2000 EU Convention on Mutual Assistance in Criminal Matters and the EU Mutual Legal Assistance Convention, terrorism was considered a criminal matter through which Member States would offer 'mutual assistance' (Wilkinson 2005). On issues of common security between 1975 and 2000, there was a greater level of European integration, which the 1997 Treaty of Amsterdam strengthened. The Treaty not only obligated Member States to establish a Union characterized by 'freedom, security, and justice' but also established the groundwork for the EU to embrace shared strategies and instruments. This, in turn, facilitated an expansion of the EU's external role in pursuing this overarching vision of security. As Sperling notes, '[w]hile the JHA has been the primary nexus of EU and Member State efforts, there has been a gradual elision of external and internal security policies, particularly the nascent linkage of Pillars III and II [Common Foreign and Security Policy] (CFSP) and [European Security and Defence Policy] (ESDP)' (2007, 122).

The difference between the US and EU norms towards terrorism was rooted in Europe's historical encounters that underscored the potential for the escalation of violence through the application of force. Consequently, the prevailing practices emphasized addressing the underlying catalysts of terrorism in conjunction with the engagement of law enforcement and judicial authorities (Hassan 2010; Baker-Beall 2017). This represented a significant alternative approach to the one pursued under the US-initiated 'war on terror'. Yet, a criminal approach was dismissed by the G.W. Bush administration at the time, even as calls domestically and internationally were voicing the need to reframe terrorism away from state-to-state conflict and towards criminal justice and international legal frameworks. Thus, in such a view, 'rather than fighting wars, the United States ... should adapt itself to living with vulnerability and to managing rather than solving the problem of terrorism, as Europe had long done' (Gordon and Shapiro 2004, 61).

Casting 11 September 2001 within the norms of criminal and judicial institutions provides a compelling alternative to the war on terror framework. Yet, US and EU officials, even after the return of the Taliban in 2021 and with the benefit of hindsight, contend that alternative strategies to the US war on terror were not 'possible' or 'imagined' at the time. As a study for the European Parliament laid out the view of a senior EU official:

> [I]t's not a secret that transatlantic solidarity played very strongly at the moment of engagement ... if we were requested to go to the moon, by the US, we would go to the moon ... if we were asked by the US to go to Madagascar, we will have been now discussing 20 years of EU involvement in Madagascar ... transatlantic unity and solidarity was much more important. And actually, it was the only reason why people [states] entered Afghanistan. It was not about democracy. It was not about state building. It was just to get rid of Osama bin Laden at that point ... initially, it was just EU member states, following the request of the US to get engaged. (Hassan 2023)

Indeed, Member States overwhelmingly prioritized the norm of solidarity, which, just as during the Cold War, was important for generating intersectionality between sets of norm circles in times of transatlantic crisis. The British prime minister, Tony Blair, declared that: 'This mass terrorism is the new evil in our world today. It is perpetrated by fanatics who are utterly indifferent to the sanctity of human life, and we, the democracies of this world, are going to have to come together and fight it together.' Similarly, the Spanish prime minister, Jose Maria Aznar, announced that 'We, who know well the insanity of terrorism, manifest our support and solidarity ... to all the citizens of the United States'. The German chancellor, Gerhard Schroeder, asserted that 'My government condemns these terrorist attacks to the utmost. I want to express ... my unqualified solidarity to you and the American people'. The Dutch prime minister, Wim Kok, confirmed that 'The bitter observation that this is apparently a terrorist attack obliges us to combat each form of terrorism both nationally and internationally with all force', and the Belgian prime minister, representing the EU presidency, proclaimed that, 'On behalf of the European Union, they condemn in the strongest possible terms this type of cowardly attack on innocent civilians' (*The Guardian* 2001b). These were strong expressions of solidarity, which, within less than 24 hours, were supported by NATO invoking Article 5, the collective defence clause of the Washington Treaty, for the first time in the organization's history (NATO 2009a).

Significantly, senior EU officials would later argue that transatlantic solidarity was deemed essential to European security itself, pronouncing that 'we wanted them [the US] to react as they are reacting now on the Eastern Flank of NATO [in Ukraine following the 2022 Russian invasion]. We wanted to be sure that the US will help us out whenever we have yet another problem with Russia' (Hassan 2023). This is testimony to the considerable power the US maintains through its alliance networks within the global international system. EU involvement in Afghanistan and the response to 11 September 2001 was premised on the norms of solidarity and reciprocity. This was a significant move for the EU and Member States, many of whom were conflicted about the appropriateness and feasibility of the US response yet would find themselves wedded for two decades to the conflict. Accordingly, EU norm circles operated two sets of norms that needed to reconcile. As a senior EU official detailed to this author, on the 'civilian side', the EU maintained 'a genuine EU commitment to values, but on the "security side", the EU deferred to the US and Member States' (interview with author). In the initial phases of the 'war on terror' in 2001, the EU began to shift its policy towards Afghanistan. It maintained an autonomous emphasis on humanitarian norms, which was carried through from its leadership in the 1990s. However, without security instruments of its own, the EU would be quickly marginalized. Echoing the early 1980s, the US and EU Member States would favour the norm of transatlantic solidarity over the progress of European integration.

The European Union's marginalization: relinquishing autonomy

Upon framing the war on terror within military norms and a state-centric approach to counterterrorism, the US regarded European-level assistance as undesirable. European powers were marginalized because the US saw them as needing more capabilities and having low expectations of what they could achieve. Consequently, the US decided that military operations in Afghanistan would not be executed within the broader NATO framework. This perspective was articulated by US Secretary of Defense Donald Rumsfeld, who emphasized that 'the mission needs to define the coalition, and we ought not to think that a coalition should define the mission' (Gordon and Shapiro 2004). The choice to proceed in an ad hoc manner epitomized the Bush administration's inclination to forge 'coalitions of the willing'. This strategic approach was emblematic of the administration's proclivity for unilateralism and was influenced by the experiences and lessons gleaned from engagements in Bosnia and Kosovo during the 1990s (Haass 1999; Perle 2003).

The significance of this decision extended to the EU. It entailed the rejection of NATO, the established institution for orchestrating European collaboration and coordination in defence, and posed a direct challenge to the European Security and Defence Policy (ESDP). The US's choice undermined the nascent Common Foreign and Security Policy (CFSP) and ESDP of the EU, as it encouraged EU Member States to align themselves with the US-led campaign against terrorism and OEF. In this context, Britain, France, and Germany sought to reaffirm the norm of solidarity with the US at the expense of EU integration and norms of European unity. Thus, as Eva Gross has noted about these Member States' decisions: 'This ... provoked resentment not only for compromising EU unity but also for engaging in what may be termed mini-lateralism: discussing contributions in closed meetings, often ahead of EU summits – thereby sidelining smaller EU member states, including Belgium, which held the EU presidency during the second half of 2001' (2009b: 39). The 'mini-lateral' approach undercut the EU's efforts to forge coherent autonomous security norms, as the alignment of key EU member states with the US initiative implicitly devalued the collective decision-making processes of the EU, intergovernmentalism and European integration. Transatlantic solidarity, in practice, had led to an undermining of collective European intentions and institutions.

Thus, although the EU appointed a European Union Special Representative (EUSR) in December 2001, this position was initially undermined. In what EU officials privately refer to as 'the wasted years', Member States acted independently of EU coordination, and there was little by way of tangible EU engagements. Thus, Germany resumed training the Afghan police force, the British took responsibility for counter-narcotics efforts, and the French established a constitutional committee. As Ambassador Klaiber, the first EUSR for Afghanistan, recalled, his efforts were hampered:

> Europe's culture is one of nation-states. I went back to Brussels after my third month in Afghanistan and told my Ministers that the CFSP will never succeed if the nation states' Foreign Ministers continue to discuss bilateral issues. Diplomacy must be pitched in multilateral terms if the EU's agenda is to be advanced. (Klaiber 2002)

Indeed, evident in Klaiber's role of having to lobby the Member States for more of an active European role, it was clear that the 'mini-lateral' approach had a profound marginalization effect on EU external policy. Mini-lateralism ultimately facilitated a geopolitical environment in which the EU's role in global security was diminished, and the EU became more dependent on US strategic preferences. As Shapiro (2021) correctly assessed, 'European contributions willingly, even eagerly, subordinated themselves to US strategy, regardless of whether it made sense'. This chimes with the findings of other studies that determined that the US was the 'major actor', but the EU,

> never tried strategic autonomy … it is not the EU's lack of capabilities that restrain[ed] it [the EU] from acting autonomously but political choices. In the case of Afghanistan, this was the political choice to follow US leadership for two decades … US military power underwrote the transatlantic campaign in Afghanistan because European powers lacked the political will to imagine an alternative to this scenario. (Hassan 2023)

Significantly, the relinquishing of autonomy was not because there was a lack of European alternatives at the start of transatlantic involvement in Afghanistan. UN Security Council Resolution (UNSCR) 1386 mandated a 5,000-strong International Security Assistance Force (ISAF) to be deployed in Kabul in December 2001. This deployment was a 'light footprint' mission comprising a 'coalition of the willing'. The low-level deployment was, however, 'quietly controversial'.

Before becoming the EUSR in June 2002, Francesc Vendrell was the UN Secretary General's envoy to Afghanistan. In his UN role, he managed to open dialogue between the Taliban and the warlords of the Northern Alliance, explaining that:

> [T]he Taliban were not particularly difficult people to meet … I wanted to hear the parties … I basically spoke to the Taliban, asked them questions, I talked to [Ahmed Shah] Massoud. And then I brought in the former King [Zahir Shah]. … Everybody was telling me that the King was still very respected in Afghanistan because, after all, he presided over the best period, particularly between 1946 and 1973. … Throughout 2001, I had been trying to encourage the Northern Alliance and the former King to get together. The King had legitimacy and quite a lot of popularity. (Loyn and Vendrell 2022, 640–50)

In contrast to his predecessor, Lakhdar Brahimi, who served as the representative for the UN Secretary-General between 1997 and 1999, Vendrell also opened dialogue on Afghanistan with European states. Brahimi operated under the 'six-plus-two' framework, which included Afghanistan's neighbours, China, Iran, Pakistan, Tajikistan, Turkmenistan and Uzbekistan, and the US and Russia (UN DGC 2001). Within the six-plus-two framework, participation from the United Kingdom (UK), France and Germany was actively rejected. However, Vendrell created a 'luncheon group' of seven ambassadors posted to Islamabad, which included the UK, France, Germany, Sweden, Norway and Japan. Sweden was unofficially intended to act as a representative for the EU, given its presidency in the first six months of 2001. These monthly dialogues in Islamabad were buttressed by information being derived from UN offices in Kabul, Kandahar, Jalalabad, Herat, Mazar-e-Sharif and Faizabad, which was under the Northern Alliance, as well as the ongoing six-plus-two framework (Loyn and Vendrell 2022).

Thus, while UN diplomacy was weakening through 2001 and collapsed after the 11 September attacks, Vendrell was remarkably well placed to understand the strategically selective context in Afghanistan and party to a considerably wide range of views from local, regional and global stakeholders. Significantly, Vendrell was able to testify to the marginalization of international institutions and European powers concerning the UNSCR 1386's mandated 'light footprint'. Vendrell (2008) outlined at length that:

> Some of us forcefully argued for a 'heavy footprint' on the model of Cambodia, East Timor, Bosnia, or Kosovo since we were convinced that its [Afghan] people were ready for some kind of international tutelage that would do away both with warlord and Taliban rule, reconstruct their country, and assist in building up the rule of law institutions. In the end, the day was won by those favouring a 'light footprint' and an 'Afghan-led' process – a politically correct slogan that, in practice, meant that the international community would be led not by genuine representatives of the Afghan people but a group of rapacious individuals. (Vendrell 2008)

The light footprint approach exemplified European marginalization; as Vendrell continued:

> The US deprived itself of a larger European contribution at a time when, with fresh memories of 9/11, many governments would have readily participated in ISAF. Two years later, when the US sought a larger involvement of its NATO partners, the momentum had slackened. In the meantime, Iraq had consumed the attention of both the United States and its allies. (Vendrell 2008)

The original tension between the US approach and the one outlined by Vendrell rests upon the US's original strategic objectives. With counterterrorism being the primary goal in Afghanistan early in the war, ISAF's light footprint was intended to facilitate this objective. This was seen as something other than a nation-building exercise. Indeed, President G.W.

Bush would recall in his autobiography that he agreed to the light footprint in line with the military advice he received, through fear of 'repeating the experience of the Soviets and the British, who ended up looking like occupiers'. However, Bush concedes that 'in retrospect, our rapid success with low troop levels created false comfort, and our desire to maintain a light footprint left us short of the resources we needed. It would take several years for these shortcomings to become clear' (Bush 2010, 207). The ramifications of the light footprint went beyond a lack of resources. The light footprint facilitated the failures in the Bonn Process, which many EU policy makers now call 'the original sin'.

The original sin and failures at Bonn

The initial military campaign in Afghanistan quickly removed the Taliban from power in November 2001. The Northern Alliance, with US support, was able to take the city of Mazar-e-Sharif by 9 November 2001 and then capture Kabul by 12 November 2001. They proved to be a significant fighting force, assisting US special forces with the targeted bombing of the Taliban. This set the stage for the Bonn Process, a UN-brokered conference in Germany in December 2001. Having been an active partner in track two diplomacy previously, Germany offered a neutral location for negotiations. On 22 December, an interim government was installed, headed by Hamid Karzai, a Popalzai Pashtun leader. However, the interim government came to be dominated by Tajiks from the Panjshir Valley (ICG 2003, 8). This was made possible because the Northern Alliance, backed by US military support, had taken over two-thirds of the country and could 'present participants in Bonn with a *fait accompli*'; to the victors belong the spoils. Accordingly, the Northern Alliance were able to take the 'lion's share of ministries in the Interim Administration', which,

> enabled the Northern Alliance's warlords and commanders to retain or be appointed to many provincial and district governorships and key positions in the Afghan National Army (ANA) and Afghan National Police (ANP). The return to power of persons widely despised and dreaded by most Afghans for the atrocities and sleaze that had characterised their rule during the mid-1990s ensured that bad governance and corruption became the norm from the very beginning. (Vendrell 2009)

From the perspective of norm circles, allowing Northern Alliance warlords to dominate the political process introduced a range of problematic norms into weak state institutions. These individuals had a demonstrable track record of neopatrimonialist norms and practices of violence to benefit their own personal gain. It soon became abundantly clear that the political rationale for the Bonn Process was negotiated to meet the US military objectives of eliminating the terrorist threat. The issue of creating a stable political entity in Afghanistan was secondary to this, and therefore concerns of contextual consonance were subjugated to the US normative myopia.

Accordingly, the Bonn Process was never intended to be an inclusive peace conference capable of establishing a peaceful settlement. This was evident in the exclusion of the Taliban, which removed the possibility of creating a broadly inclusive political framework. The Taliban's exclusion was a result of ongoing fighting, and the US conflation of the Taliban with al Qaeda. Perhaps there was space to disaggregate between various Taliban norm circles along various ethnic and tribal lines or political divisions along nationalist and fundamentalist lines, but this was an emergency process that was hastily put together. Myopic decisions were not accounting for the long-term consequences of military action, nor the strategically selective context in which continued military action was to take place. The Taliban were homogenized, and international negotiations proceeded erroneously on the assumption that the Taliban had been unequivocally defeated on the battlefield. In trying not to repeat the mistakes of the British and the Soviets, the US did in fact replicated the mistake of First Anglo-Afghan War and failed to recognize that they remained in a war zone. They would soon face a regrouped opposition and resistance to US occupation (see Chapter 1). The exclusion of the Taliban in its entirety undermined the potential for a comprehensive peace settlement and created a centralized power imbalance in the interim authority. As more than one EU representative interviewed for this research explained, international actors proceeded as if Afghanistan was a 'blank slate'. The Bonn Process is a product of an emergency epistemology hastily put together in a crisis, with little regard for the strategically selective context in which the Bonn Agreement was supposed to operate. From the very beginning there was little regard to the contextual consonance of the agreement, and as a result, 20 years would be spent trying to fix the subsequent contextual dissonance this created.

Not only was the Bonn Process empowering the neopatrimonialist norm circles, but it was doing so against the historical grain of Afghanistan's heterarchical village states and their tribal republic norms. A feature of modern states in the era of the global international system has been for norms of sovereignty to dictate that the rule of law applies uniformly inside its territorial borders. Afghanistan, throughout all Buzan and Little's stages of world history, has never functioned in this way. Over millennia, as outlined in Chapter 1, Afghanistan's rules have had to balance the tensions between desert and sedentary norms. The working assumptions of the Bonn Process failed to account for this, operating under the assumption that building a strong central government was not only achievable but necessary. A failure to account for Afghan norms created significant contextual dissonance, and there was little by way of a plan to move the strategic dial and achieve greater contextual consonance. Moreover, just as the Soviet invasion made the mistake of drawing historical analogies with the experiences in Hungry and Czechoslovakia prior to the invasion in 1979, Western powers were making mistaken historical analogies with their own experiences in Yugoslavia in 1992. An operating assumption was that a centralized state was needed to prevent the fragmentation of Afghanistan and creation of ethnically divided regional states (Barfield 2010, 8). Yet, with norms of heterarchy being so prevalent throughout all stage of Afghanistan's development in world history, there is no evidence base to suggest this would be the case; on the contrary, there is very strong historical evidence that unity and stability would require local practice and solutions being needed to provide political legitimacy. Afghan history should have provided a warning about creating a centralized power imbalance that would perpetuate a cycle of factional dominance and marginalization of other groups, including the Pashtuns. Afghanistan's diversity and heterarchy were not accounted for, nor were the Pashtun perceptions of marginalization and declining power. Rather, Bonn institutionalized a highly centralized Kabul-centric government that empowered the warlords to embed neopatrimonialist norms at the cost of stability. The post-2001 system empowered the very individuals that the Afghan people rejected in the 1990s by allowing the Taliban to come to power. Twenty years later, Afghanistan would repeat this, having endured further occupation and neopatrimonialist practices from within.

Moreover, it is important to note that the US approach was not part of its 'Freedom Agenda', aiming to spread democracy around the Middle East (Hassan 2013). Support for democratic elections in Afghanistan was not a foregone conclusion of the Bonn Process. Ambassador James F. Dobbins, the inaugural US Special Envoy to Afghanistan, was clear in his memoir that neither the US nor European nations proposed the concept of democratic elections during the initial drafting phase of the agreement. Ambassador Dobbins was tasked primarily with facilitating the formation of a broad-based government. Instead, it was Iranian representative Javad Zarif who raised the democratic deficit in the Bonn Agreement, leading to a refocusing on elections and democratic processes being integrated into the Bonn Agreement (Dobbins 2008, 83).

In contrast to demands for democracy, European powers and some Washington, DC policy makers wanted to see King Zahir Shah's return as a unity figure. Indeed, when meeting US representatives in Rome, the frail 87-year-old expressed a desire to facilitate the formation of a representative broad-based government. However, from the US perspective, this was seen as potentially undermining the Northern Alliance, who were being granted impunity for their activities in the 1990s because of the sacrifices they had made in opposing the Taliban (Dobbins 2008, 4, 53). From the UN perspective, having appointed Lakhdar Brahimi to lead its reconstruction efforts in Afghanistan, the king was effectively blocked in favour of gerrymandering support for Hamid Karzai in an 'Afghan-led and Afghan-owned' process (Loyn and Vendrell 2022, 654).

The objectives of the Bonn Agreement were primarily focused on the swift establishment of a political settlement to forge a legitimate state authority, thereby facilitating international collaboration in the war on terror. This process aimed to ensure a lasting political transition rather than laying the groundwork for a comprehensive peace settlement. In choosing to prioritize the creation of a political ally over a holistic peace agreement, the process inadvertently rendered Afghanistan excessively dependent on international backing, both politically and financially. This is unsurprising, as Afghanistan has needed an external source of rent to remain stable since the end of the 18th century. The British had fulfilled this role in the 19th century, followed briefly by Nazi Germany, then the Soviet Union in the 20th century. In the 21st century, the US, Europe and wider members of global international society would come to fulfil this function.

The dependencies Bonn created significantly compromised the sovereignty and self-reliance of the interim Afghan government and subsequent governments. In the long term, such reliance proved counterproductive, undermining the stability and functionality of the government and its institutions. This outcome highlights a critical oversight in the Bonn Process, where the immediate goal of establishing a political framework overshadowed the need for a sustainable peace strategy. In doing this, it laid the conditions for persistent insecurity and violence in Afghanistan once the Taliban were able to reorganize and adapt. Because of the path-dependency the Bonn Process set in motion, EU policy makers have come to regard it as the primary contributor to undermining the EU's bilateral efforts at state-building after 2001 (Hassan 2023).

The significance of the Bonn Agreement in undermining state-building efforts should not be understated. Creating a political settlement and a pathway for governance hindered and obscured the need for a peaceful settlement. By doing so, Bonn ignored the lessons of other international experiences and the need for peacebuilding and national reconciliation (Maass 2006). It allowed for historical impunity of human rights violations and created a missed opportunity to build trust with the Afghan people. Indeed, as a study for the European Parliament concluded, 'even if international prosecution of the warlords such as Hekmatyar and Dostum was improbable, it is feasible that justice could have been obtained through domestic institutions in the longer term' (Hassan 2023). Unfortunately, neither the US nor the EU prioritized a genuine peace settlement, believing that facilitating elections instigated by the Bonn Agreement would be sufficient. Peace was seen as a by-product of political legitimacy generated through electoral norms and processes. Peace was not in and of itself seen as something that required a specific normative commitment and associated practices. As an EU election observation mission would later declare of the 2004 Parliamentary and Provincial Council Elections, these were considered 'an important step in a transition process designed to put in place a representative government and thereby help bring peace to Afghanistan after a quarter-century of conflict' (EUEOM 2005b). Accordingly, there was a persistent failure of international peacebuilding efforts over decades, accompanied by a strikingly apparent inability to recognize, much less address, the deeply entrenched sources of internal conflict. This oversight points to a fundamental deficiency in the US and EU peacebuilding strategies, which have tended to overlook the complex, underlying factors that fuelled and sustained internal conflicts in Afghanistan. The emphasis was on immediate, superficial solutions rather than a comprehensive understanding and resolution of the root causes, leading to recurring patterns of unrest and instability. Contextual dissonance reigned supreme. As the US Special Inspector General for Afghanistan Reconstruction (SIGAR) concluded in 2021:

> US government decisions in Afghanistan helped ensure there would be no peace to keep in the first place. For perspective, Bosnia benefitted from a proper peace settlement in 1995 that has prevented mass violence ever since. In contrast, in Afghanistan, the US government refused opportunities to reconcile with the defeated Taliban and declined to implement an inclusive, post-conflict peace process, so the Taliban soon rebuilt itself as a powerful insurgency. ... As a result, simply maintaining security levels—a goal that did not seem ambitious early in the war—proved very ambitious and poorly aligned with the ways and means the US government planned to use. (SIGAR 2021, 16)

From the EU perspective, as one senior EU diplomat told this author, it 'wasn't ready for peace. Nobody was ready for peace. Nobody wanted to upset the Americans' (interview with author). Accordingly, EU marginalization and the abandonment of any semblance of European autonomy came at the expense of international peace.

The Iraq War and calculated neglect

In addition to the problems instigated at Bonn, the EU and its Member States faced further problems in maintaining transatlantic solidarity. The rapid collapse of the Taliban regime was taken as vindication for Defense Secretary Donald Rumsfeld and US Central Command leader Army Gen. Tommy Franks' military strategy, which combined US air power and Special

Forces with the Northern Alliance (Call 2007, 25–41). This created a sense of renewal for US military power. Candidate G.W. Bush, in the 2000 US presidential election, had deemed the US to be in decline, overstretched and unable to project power worldwide. Afghanistan transformed this perception of decline into hubris (Hassan 2013). As President Bush argued:

> These past two months have shown that an innovative doctrine and high-tech weaponry can shape then dominate an unconventional conflict … our military are rewriting the rules of war … real-time intelligence, local allied forces, special forces, and precision air power. … The conflict in Afghanistan has taught us more about the future of our military than a decade of blue-ribbon panels and think-tank symposiums. (Bush 2001)

In the wake of what was perceived as a rapid military triumph in Afghanistan, in November 2001, and less than two weeks after the fall of Kabul, President George W. Bush directed Secretary of Defense Donald Rumsfeld to shift his focus to Iraq for an evaluation of potential military strategies. In now declassified documents, next to the bullet point 'regime change' is the handwritten question 'What do forces do coming out of Afghanistan?' followed by the bullet point 'Unlike Afghanistan, important to have ideas in advance about who would rule afterwards' (Rumsfeld 2001). Accordingly, Afghanistan played a pivotal role in contextualizing the Iraq War, as the swift success of military operations presented a cost-effective model for regime change, setting a precedent for future military interventions. The George W. Bush administration now believed that America could fight two wars simultaneously: a low-level conflict in Afghanistan and a larger war in Iraq.

With planning for the Iraq War being conducted in silos of the US Department of Defense and the Central Intelligence Agency, European powers were unaware of the build-up to a new war. Solidarity with the US shifted dramatically once the US publicly moved its focus from Afghanistan to Iraq. The normative dissonance created between transatlantic norm circles was significant. For the US, this was the start of an 'intentional' period of 'calculated neglect', which the US's own assessments confirmed allowed the Taliban to resurge (SIGAR 2021). For Europe, just one year after invoking the norms of solidarity in the invasion of Afghanistan, the Iraq conflict engendered the most substantial rift in transatlantic relations since the Second World War. As a result of European failures to endorse the war, breaking the norm of solidarity, the US openly sought to castigate European powers. The US increasingly sought to divide EU Member States, publicly rebuking Germany and France as 'Old Europe' and comparing Germany to Libya and Cuba. In response, France threatened to block 'New' Central European states' accession to the EU (Gordon 2003).

With transatlantic tensions running high, the US increasingly challenged the EU and its Member States' commitment to Afghanistan. Within NATO, for example, Europe's contribution was seen as lacking, and as Burke outlines, '[i]f the war [in Afghanistan] was going badly, it was because Europe was not paying enough attention. … The perception in Washington was that this was the war Europe was supposed to manage, while the USA focused on Iraq' (2014, 4–5). This US perspective was, however, disingenuous. The Bush administration forced the US into a situation where it had to choose between substantially resourcing Iraq or Afghanistan. US policy makers chose Iraq, as the situation there deteriorated quickly. This decision resulted in several years of calculated and intentional neglect in Afghanistan, whereby the US struggled with resource allocation. This was another example of the US normative myopia, and the impact was devastating. As SIGAR concluded:

> Simply maintaining security levels [in Afghanistan]—a goal that did not seem ambitious early in the war—proved very ambitious and poorly aligned with the ways and means the US government planned to use … this kind of misalignment represents 'the most common cause for failure of nation building efforts'. … This gap became particularly acute starting in 2003 when the USA diverted troops and reconstruction funds to the invasion and reconstruction of Iraq. (SIGAR 2021)

The ramifications of the Iraq war extended beyond the US, profoundly impacting other nations, including the UK. This was exemplified in a 2009 evaluation report by the UK's Department for International Development, which underscored the diversion and depletion of resources initially allocated for Afghanistan (Bennett et al 2009). By forcing the UK to reallocate resources and shift attention to Iraq, the UK's capacity and commitment to Afghanistan were undermined. The US created broader and demonstrably unintended consequences by shifting focus to Iraq. Indeed, UK evaluations demonstrate that:

> [The] US-led intervention in Iraq provided the Taliban with a political foundation on which to draw both resources and recruits from the wider Islamic world on the grounds that Afghanistan was subjugated by a 'US-led invasion'. … Afghanistan thus became a cause célèbre within the global Islamic community, alongside Iraq, Palestine, Lebanon and Chechnya. (Bennett et al 2009, 9)

The US had not only misjudged the impact the Iraq War would have on its capacities but also those of its allies. Moreover, in the context of the global international system, the US also misjudged the interconnected nature of global conflicts and their ability to influence each other, particularly in terms of narrative and perception. The intervention in Iraq inadvertently bolstered the Taliban's position in Afghanistan by providing them with a potent narrative to attract support. However, what is particularly curious about this episode is that 'there is no evidence of the EU recognising or adapting its approach to Afghanistan in light of the growing risk the US strategy was accumulating due to the war in Iraq' (Hassan 2023). Not only were EU institutions not adapting to the strategically selective context in Afghanistan, but there was no attempt being made to adapt to changing normative practices of the US. As involvement in Afghanistan moved forward, there was not only contextual dissonance of EU strategy in Afghanistan but growing contextual dissonance between EU and US strategy.

5

European Union State-building Efforts and the Corruption Eruption

To understand the European Union (EU)'s path to being involved in Afghanistan's development, it is essential to contextualize its growing role in Afghanistan. Conterminous with EU marginalization, Ambassador Dr Klaus-Peter Klaiber was appointed European Union Special Representative (EUSR) in December 2001. Under a political mandate, Klaiber sought to support the new interim government, ensure the rights of women and minorities were upheld, fight the trafficking and production of drugs and 'convince Afghanistan's neighbours that their interference in this process was unwelcome' (Klaiber 2002). Under an economic mandate, the EUSR's role was to represent European-level interests and reassure Afghanistan that European cooperation would be sustained over the long term. Following an international conference in Tokyo, the EU pledged USD 1 billion in humanitarian aid over the next five years, making it the largest donor at the conference and continuing its humanitarian role from the 1980s and 1990s (Klaiber 2002).

With the EUSR based in Kabul, Klaiber would often need to explain the EU's role and the nature of its action, which was often misunderstood. Before the Bonn Agreement was enacted, the EUSR attempted to persuade the interim Afghan Authority that various political measures should be adopted. Ambassador Klaiber detailed that early on, the most important of these was 'impressing the importance of a Human Rights Commission, a political assembly, a judicial commission to consider the new constitution and a new legal system' (Klaiber 2002). Klaiber was able to lobby EU Member States for a more active political role rather than simply making financial contributions (Gross 2009a, 2009b). Yet, with Germany taking responsibility for training the Afghan police force, British counter-narcotics efforts, and French leadership establishing a constitutional committee, this was unheeded. In addition, the EUSR was to act as a voice for Afghanistan in Europe and ensure that Afghanistan did not slip down the political agenda of Member States. The EUSR's ability to speak with 'one voice' was especially helpful in furthering international coordination efforts and European integration, both of which were needed given that the EU was a marginalized international actor in a crowded and complex environment dominated by the United States (US). By the time Klaiber left the role of EUSR in June 2002, the EU predominantly remained a humanitarian actor with limited influence.

As the US strategy towards Afghanistan began to change, so did the role the EU could play. By April 2002, President G.W. Bush expanded US plans for Afghanistan. Increasingly, this reflected what was becoming known as the Freedom Agenda. This drew on the idea that democratization would deliver international peace and secure American hegemony, whether imposed from above or developed from below (Hassan and Hammond 2011; Hassan 2013). Accordingly, Bush acknowledged the complexities and challenges associated with military engagement in Afghanistan and outlined his expectations for a resurgence of militant activities with the onset of spring 2003. This was an explicit acceptance that the original counterterrorism strategy was failing. Recognizing the contextual dissonance resulting from the strategy, the president's norm circle articulated normative values and commitments to define a more contextually consonant strategy. For Bush, the reason Afghanistan was facing a resurgence of violence was because the Afghan people were disempowered. As a result, empowering all of Afghanistan through democracy and a centralized state would empower Afghans and provide a route to achieving peace. In turn, this entailed the US adopt a normative commitment to the functioning of electoral democracy for the establishment of a stable centralized government, the development of a national army, and the creation of an inclusive education system for both boys and girls. These components were presented as integral to fostering lasting peace and setting the US on a track of promoting state-building, democracy and development. Indeed, President Bush went so far as to suggest that the US was establishing a Marshall Plan for Afghanistan, recommending that military victory needed to be followed by a 'moral victory' and long-term commitment to Afghanistan, promising that '[w]e will stay until the mission is done' (Bush 2002).

Remarkably absent from the Freedom Agenda, as it came to be applied to Afghanistan in 2003, was that it demonstrated a fundamental disregard for Afghan norms and an active disregard for the history of Afghanistan. For example, there was no awareness of the norms surrounding state centralization, nor recognition that strong central governments have either accommodated desert norms or been removed from power relatively quickly. As shown in Chapter 1, the early onset of norms around centralization was conditioned by the formation of heterarchical–city formations as far back as the Indus civilization. Questions of how modern state norms of centralization would have contextual consonance with norms of *heterarchy* were not asked. Indeed, because of a lack of awareness of norms, such questions were not even imagined and the possibility that modern state norms were not universally accepted was never considered. Of course, arrays of norms are adaptive, but given that Afghanistan has maintained a history of resisting the formation of a centralized state, alternative models to state centralization should have been considered. In practice, after Bonn, Afghanistan continued to operate with more of an informal federalism that represented the norms of heterarchy and allowed village state tribal republic norms to continue to function (Murtazashvili 2016).

Nor was there any demonstrable awareness of Afghan norms around education. For example, in many respects, issues around the education of girls were conflated with Taliban rule. There were no broader considerations of the strategically selective context. Had the Taliban's position on education been seen as relying on norm circles endorsing wider practices of conservative Islamic orthodoxy, then more historical context could have been afforded. Such consideration would have demonstrated that girls' education was a source of tension between modernist secularization norms and norms of conservative Islamic orthodoxy. This was evident throughout the 20th century. Indeed, this tension unfolded between Habib Allah and Nasr Allah, and subsequently Nadir Shah's Islamization project and the ratification of the 1931 Constitution, and again in the 1979 Herat Uprising (see Chapters 1 and 2). Rapid modernization of education for girls may have suited elites in Kabul and Western capitals, but it alienated important norm circles in the provinces and countryside. There was a greater need to take a gradualist systemic approach that dealt with this as an evolving normative issue and local and regional power sharing; and not a universalist principle imposed uniformly from outside without existent norm circles willing to adopt such practices over the long term. Within the EU, some policy makers expressed concerns with a universalist approach to girls' education, arguing, for example:

> I'm not very impressed by what happened. I have to say that … the basic reality was people are not evil … they want good outcomes; they want the best for Afghan girls … but strategic reality doesn't exist in those discussions … we had, even after all those years, Afghanistan was still the next worst place to be a woman. (Interview with author)

This proved to be an unpopular position within EU norm circles. Some policy makers informed this author that they were unable to express this view in public and private meetings over two decades and had to 'make sure nobody suspected' that they privately deviated from EU norm circles.

Indeed, others argued that an inflexible commitment to women and girls' education inhibited their ability to start a comprehensive peace process with the Taliban because compromises on issues such as girls' education would have had to be made. As one senior EU diplomat outlined,

> If we want[ed] peace, we were going to have to pay a price. You don't get what you want. It hurts it. It's painful. You have to talk to people who don't like ... having the Taliban come in [to a peace process] ... we would have had to make compromises. (Interview with author)

However, it was the Bush administration's insistence that the US would stay the course and make sure that these state-building efforts were done that was particularly disingenuous. To US allies, this suggested that the norm of transatlantic solidarity had committed them to a long-term, open-ended mission in Afghanistan. Unclear to these allies was that the US believed it had won the war after just six months and was planning to withdraw troops from Afghanistan by 2004. This was US hubris and normative myopia *par excellence*. Islamic norms had taken over 250 years to gain a foothold in cities and a millennium to spread throughout Afghanistan. The Barakzai Muhammadzai lineage had attempted to instil the norms of a modern state for over 150 years. The US, however, was working on the absurd assumption that it would install democratic norms and build a peaceful and secure Afghan state in just three years. As the US Ambassador to Afghanistan, Robert Finn, recalls in a lessons-learned interview with the Office of the Special Inspector General for Afghanistan Reconstruction (SIGAR): 'We can't think beyond the next election. When we went into Afghanistan everybody was talking about a year or two, and I said to them we would be lucky if we were out of here in twenty years' (Finn 2015).[1]

Nevertheless, as Bush declared under the banner of 'MISSION ACCOMPLISHED' – 'In the battle of Afghanistan, we destroyed the Taliban', and the US moved to 'stability operations' as it focused on Iraq (Bush 2003). What was initially a limited counterterrorism operation had expanded to a state-building exercise, even though it received less attention from the US administration. This reflected the expectation that there would only be a brief overlap between the wars in Afghanistan and Iraq. However, whereas the US was initially reluctant to pay for reconstruction, it would spend USD 145 billion over 20 years to rebuild Afghanistan, including its security forces, civilian government institutions, economy and civil society.

---

[1] After a three-year legal battle, *The Washington Post* won the release of more than 2,000 pages of 'Lessons Learned' interviews conducted by SIGAR. These comments were never intended to be made available beyond SIGAR.

In addition to this, the Department of Defense spent USD 837 billion on warfighting activities during this period. The human cost of this endeavour was also significant, with 2,443 American troops and 1,144 Allied troops killed and 20,666 US troops injured. The toll on Afghan forces and civilians was even higher, with at least 66,000 Afghan troops killed and more than 48,000 Afghan civilians killed, alongside at least 75,000 injuries from 2001 to 2021. The numbers provided for Afghan casualties are likely underestimations (SIGAR 2021).

International Security Assistance Force

In the first years of the campaign, between 2002 and 2003, EU officials largely agreed that successfully engaging in state-building was feasible. This reflected an initial hiatus in intense levels of combat across the country. Indeed, US officials separately agreed with this assessment, arguing that 'in 2002 to 2003, there weren't very many security problems. We could have been everywhere' (Finn 2015). However, the initial focus on counterterrorism undermined the possibility of capitalizing on this operating space. Indeed, attempting to engage in counterterrorism through military norms was counterproductive to normative commitments to state-building. This became evident with the establishment of the International Security Assistance Force (ISAF), which was established following the Bonn Conference to help the Afghan Transitional Authority provide governance. Provided a United Nations (UN) mandate, ISAF was only designed to maintain security around Kabul, effectively protecting the new Afghan authorities and UN personnel (NATO 2022a). Counterterrorism objectives led the US to conclude that it had more autonomy if ISAF's mandate was limited to Kabul and ISAF command was assumed by nations on a rotational basis. In effect, the US wanted strategic and operational autonomy and the impunity it affords.

It was not until 11 August 2003 that the North Atlantic Treaty Organization (NATO) took the lead on ISAF, thereby ending six-monthly national rotations, and not until October 2003 was ISAF's mandate expanded to cover the whole of Afghanistan. Before this, Coalition Humanitarian Liaison Cells (CHLCs) and US Army Civil Affairs Teams–Afghanistan (CAT-As) supported humanitarian assistance, relief and reconstruction efforts throughout Afghanistan. CHLCs typically comprised military personnel liaising with various civilian humanitarian agencies, non-governmental organizations and International organisations (IOs). However, the absence of an integrated interagency political-military plan in Afghanistan led to confusion in roles and missions, with a lack of coordinated strategy among agencies and military units resulting in unclear objectives and responsibilities. There was significant uncertainty over the nature of US military humanitarian assistance, with the ambiguity between a 'wholesale' approach of limited logistics support outside Afghanistan and a 'retail' approach involving direct provision within the country. This uncertainty hindered the determination of military involvement in humanitarian efforts, affecting the coordination and effectiveness of aid delivery (Oliker et al 2004).

The United States Agency for International Development (USAID) and US Central Command developed Joint Regional Teams plans following this initial strategy. The Afghan Transitional Authority and interim president Hamid Karzai supported these. As a result, in January 2003, a new structure termed Provincial Reconstruction Teams (PRTs) were established. PRTs combined military and intelligence personnel with civilian reconstruction specialists, bringing expertise in diplomacy and economic development together with representatives of the Afghan Ministry of Interior. The deployment of PRTs grew to 25 units, which were attached to military engagements and spread throughout Afghanistan. For those PRTs operating under the US-led coalition for Operation Enduring Freedom, the United Kingdom (UK) was the only European Member State to make a significant contribution. PRTs led by NATO, under the control of ISAF, had greater European involvement, with Germany, Italy, the Netherlands and the UK taking responsibility for operations. The experiences and effectiveness of PRTs varied considerably depending on the security context and the operational mission, often deployed to insecure environments where few development or humanitarian operations were underway.

International Security Assistance Force expansion

Gradually, NATO's mission expanded to take over command of the PRTs. In December 2003, authorization was granted for NATO to expand north. This expansion involved taking over the command of the PRT in Kunduz, which Germany previously led. Six months after this, on 28 June 2004, at the NATO Summit held in Istanbul, leaders of the Alliance declared intentions to set up an additional four PRTs in the northern region of Afghanistan. These were to be in Mazar-e Sharif, Meymaneh, Feyzabad and Baghlan. Completed on 1 October 2004, this signified the fulfilment of ISAF's first phase of expansion, where French and German forces were predominant. Agreed in 2005, second stage expansions to the west began in May 2006, when ISAF command expanded to include two additional PRTs in Herat and Farah provinces. In this area, Italian and Spanish forces formed the core of NATO forces. The north and west remained relatively stable. The third phase of NATO expansion was to the south, bringing NATO forces into Taliban-dominated areas. This phase was implemented on 31 July 2006, following multiple delays caused by insurgent violence and attempts to obtain further troop commitments from allied nations. On 5 October 2006, Stage Four commenced, which included the US transferring around 12,000 troops to ISAF under US General Stanley McChrystal's command. This stage expanded ISAF's mandate to encompass all of Afghanistan (Morelli and Belkin 2009, 9–10; NATO 2022b).

Early expectations within NATO were that stages three and four would be consistent with the previous stages. However, increasingly under attack, allies demanded more robust capability, necessitating a strategic shift in the mission's focus. Not only were allies facing confrontation with the Taliban, rooted in southern Kandahar province but around Helmand, there was a prevalence of poppy cultivation, which posed a problem for British forces. In Uruzgan, dominated by Dutch troops, further complexities presented themselves. The Taliban were able to generate considerable instability. However, the Dutch were reluctant to work alongside the US because of the Abu Ghraib prison scandal and the US treatment of prisoners at Guantanamo Bay (Morelli and Belkin 2009). Moreover, echoing the Italians, the Dutch view favoured an emphasis on reconstruction over combat operations. In the opinions of one EU official interviewed for this research, this emphasis was why Dutch forces often came under attack and suffered casualties – where the Taliban would use completed development projects to advance their fighting capabilities.

By the end of 2006, as ISAF's role expanded across Afghanistan, it became apparent to the allies that the mission demanded a more robust combat capability than initially anticipated, necessitating a strategic shift in its focus. This was not forthcoming. Indeed, in December 2006, British Defence Secretary Desmond Browne sent a letter to Rumsfeld arguing that a strategy needed to be implemented. Rumsfeld deferred to incoming Secretary of Defense Robert Gates. However, as Gates later recalled privately, he had three priorities: 'Iraq, Iraq and Iraq'. As then Commander of ISAF forces, General Dan Kelly McNeill, would declare, '[i]n 2007, there was no NATO campaign plan, a lot of verbiage and talk, but no plan ... the instructions were kill terrorists and build the [Afghan Army]. Also, don't fracture the Alliance, and that was it' (Whitlock 2021, 108–9).

Afghanistan was not only secondary to Iraq, but transatlantic policy in Afghanistan was adrift. This was reflected in NATO's lessons learned process that diplomatically warned against the problems of mission expansion:

[T]he wider ambition of building a stable Afghanistan, while not without important gains, proved extremely challenging. When planning and conducting future operations, Allies should continuously assess strategic interests, remain acutely aware of the dangers of mission expansion, and seek to avoid taking on commitments that go well beyond assigned tasks. (NATO 2001)

With EU Member States in NATO deferring to the US, this profoundly impacted the EU's bilateral engagement in Afghanistan during this period. Not least, because with a growing insurgency from the Taliban, the EU would miscalculate its policy development to support US and NATO efforts at state-building.

The European Union's long-term state-building strategy

As European involvement in Afghanistan grew, and the US shifted focus to Iraq, differing perceptions between the US and EU regarding the timeline for state-building in Afghanistan became increasingly evident. EU institutions perceived Afghanistan as a commitment for the long haul. This involved a normative commitment to maintaining a steady flow of development cooperation and humanitarian aid. This was a shift in EU policy from the trade and aid of the 1950s to 1970s and commitment to humanitarian norms of the 1980s and 1990s. Civilian Power Europe, meeting the norm of transatlantic solidarity, was to direct its energies towards state-building. US and EU norm circles aligned, and the intersectionality resulted in practices that would attempt to transform Afghanistan into a functioning democratic state. This intersectionality was reinforced by European norms already committed to advancing development worldwide, and a commitment to the norms of global international society. Indeed, the EU remains the world's largest international aid donor, providing approximately EUR 50 billion per year. The EU aims to increase its contribution further, dedicating at least 0.7 per cent of its gross national income to development aid each year (European Commission 2023).

Split between the more immediate needs of humanitarian assistance and the longer-term demands of development cooperation, the EU aims to maintain long-term horizons that build sustainable economic growth and eliminate poverty. This is a crucial distinction. Humanitarian aid, such as that provided in the 1980s and 1990s, is designed for rapid deployment in more immediate crises, addressing the basic needs of civilians in conflicts or natural disasters. Humanitarian aid is never channelled through government or armed groups and is allocated to humanitarian partners. In contrast, development cooperation is often given directly to governments, wherein EU institutions cooperate on priorities and monitor its expenditure in collaboration with those governments. It is within this context that Afghanistan became the world's largest recipient of EU aid.

Between 1980 and 2001, Afghanistan received around EUR 1.6 billion in Official Development Aid (ODA) and Other Official Flows (OOF). However, in the subsequent period from 2002 to 2020, there was a substantial increase, with Afghanistan receiving approximately EUR 65 billion (see Figure 5.1).

Figure 5.1: Official Development Aid and Other Official Flows to Afghanistan

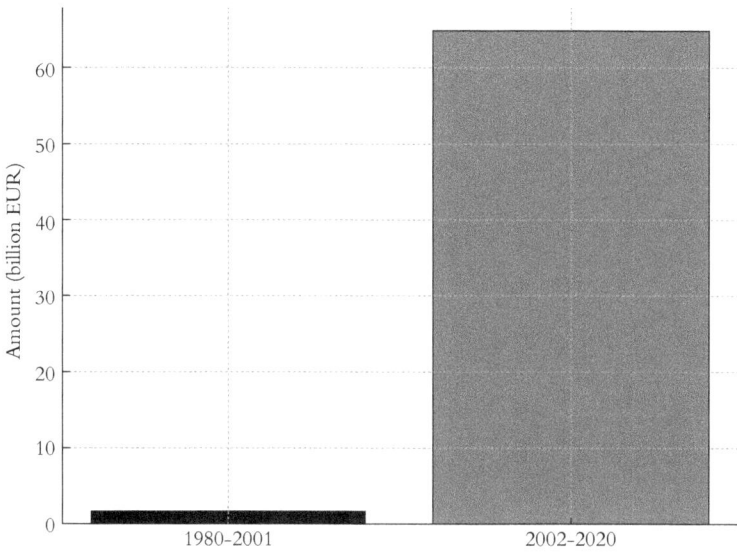

Source: Data adapted from OECD, https://stats.oecd.org/OECDStat_Metadata/ShowMetad
ata.ashx?Dataset=REF_TOTALRECPTS&ShowOnWeb=true&Lang=en

Around EUR 6 billion in ODA and official bilateral transactions came from European institutions. Additionally, within the same period, Afghanistan received EUR 20 billion bilaterally from EU member states, with the most significant contributors being Germany (EUR 6.6 billion), the UK (EUR 5.9 billion), Sweden (EUR 1.7 billion), the Netherlands (EUR 1.6 billion) and Denmark (EUR 1.1 billion). This sum of EUR 26 billion from the EU and its Member States is juxtaposed against the EUR 32 billion provided by the US in ODA and OOF (see Figure 5.2).

Hence, from 2002 to 2020, the EU and its Member States accounted for approximately 40 per cent of all ODA and OOF to Afghanistan, compared to 49 per cent from the US (see Figure 5.3). These figures do not include an additional EUR 1.2 billion in aid for 2021–5 pledged by the EU at the Afghanistan Conference in Geneva in 2020. This aid was intended to complete the support of Afghanistan's 'Transformational Decade' between 2015 and 2024.

Given that Afghanistan became the world's largest recipient of EU aid, it is extraordinary that the strategic risk posed by the US operating on short-term horizons was never considered in relation to the EU's long-term development objectives (Hassan 2023). Having observed the norm of solidarity, the EU nested its strategy towards Afghanistan inside that of the US. As a result the EU would also come to rely on increasingly centralized

Figure 5.2: Contributions of Official Development Aid by EU institutions, Member States and the US from 2002 to 2020

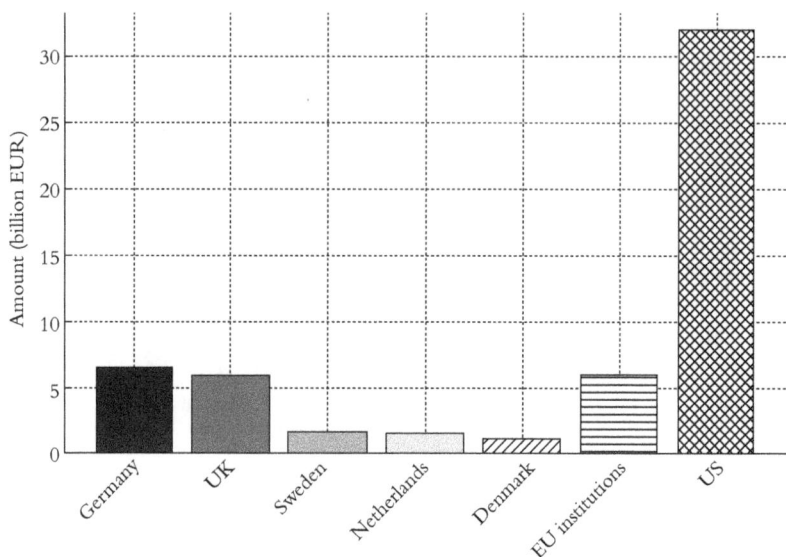

Source: Data adapted from OECD, https://stats.oecd.org/OECDStat_Metadata/ShowMetad ata.ashx?Dataset=REF_TOTALRECPTS&ShowOnWeb=true&Lang=en

Afghan government institutions populated by strategic actors dedicated to neopatrimonialist norms. As the EU developed the most extensive, and expensive, development portfolio it has ever undertaken there was considerable contextual dissonance between what it was trying to achieve and the strategically selective context on the ground. This problem was exacerbated by the US, in addition to ODA, using short-term military deployments to carry out development projects in a sporadic 'feast and famine' manner.

European Union and United States coordination and divergent timelines

The manner in which US and EU policy makers overlooked divergent timelines for their engagement in Afghanistan was highly problematic. In an attempt to maintain the norm of solidarity, neither partner challenged the working assumptions of the other. Thus, while the US was working within the time horizon of months and years, the EU operated within a timeframe of decades. The latter certainly maintained greater contextual consonance with the development needs of Afghanistan. However, with the US being the primary strategic actor and EU strategy being nested inside US strategy,

Figure 5.3: Total contributions of Official Development Aid by the EU including Member States and the US from 2002 to 2020

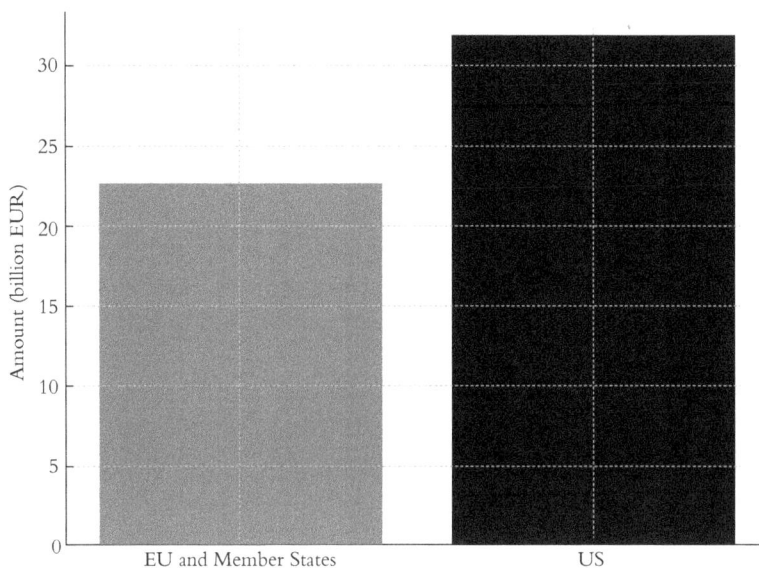

Source: Data adapted from OECD, https://stats.oecd.org/OECDStat_Metadata/ShowMetad ata.ashx?Dataset=REF_TOTALRECPTS&ShowOnWeb=true&Lang=en

EU institutions had misread the strategically selective context they were operating within. The US operated with a 'perpetual sense of imminent departure', which 'reduced the ability of US officials to plan for the long term', while EU development thinking was geared towards a long-term commitment. Thus, interviews with EU officials consistently highlight a strong partnership with the US, marked by continuous collaboration and significant strategic alignment. As elucidated by a senior EU diplomat:

> [W]e aligned everything we were doing. So, we aligned what we were doing on the security side with what we were doing on the development side, what we were doing on the [hand gesture and so forth] and what we would do regionally. So, everything started working in the same direction. (Hassan 2023)

The perceived extent of alignment between the EU and the US was so significant that EU policy makers have suggested that there needed to be greater unity or coordination within EU institutions and between Member States to assert a more independent stance and challenge the US approach. Such comments are exemplified by the EU's post-2021 debates around strategic autonomy and adopting a Strategic Compass (EEAS 2022).

What is distinct about this situation is that the US view of the EU and Member States' contributions differ wildly. US officials often regarded European contributions as largely extraneous. As one US official outlined, 'it just became easier to go it alone ... from the US perspective, Europe didn't matter as much. It's just the hard, painful truth' (Hassan 2023). Indeed, criticism of Member States contributed to this view. Germany, for example, garnered an abysmal reputation. Not only were German troops not permitted to join combat operations and patrol at night from the relative haven of northern Afghanistan, but troops gained a reputation for being drunkards because of excessive beer consumption. Moreover, their early efforts at training the Afghan National Police were regarded as woeful in terms of funding, staffing, speed and overall quality of officers coming through the programme (Whitlock 2021, 65, 106). Germany may have had vast experience training Afghan security services throughout the 20th century, but this had little bearing on successful training in the 21st century.

Paradoxically, EU officials, from the Delegation to those in the Commission and later the European External Action Service (EEAS), believed they had been coordinating and strategically aligning with the US. They failed to account for the significant problems with US policy making that undermined the coordination of these efforts. As one US official highlighted, pointing to US lessons learned reports in Afghanistan, US strategy was a moving target:

> The conceptual requirement of developing an effective strategy is a bar even lower than coordination. We couldn't even hit the basics of understanding how to build a long-term strategy. And by long term, even five years ... identifying the way forward, the kinds of programmes that would be necessary, the theories of change, all of that, we couldn't even do that. And so, coordinating ... seems like a much higher bar than what we were able to hit ... it's, in some ways, much worse than you think. That is really the source of this problem, we couldn't even conceptually understand what would be required of an effective strategy. And, so, we never even got to the point of asking, 'Well, who do we need to build this strategy with?'. (Hassan 2023)

This was echoed by British Lt. Gen. David Richards, who, upon taking charge of NATO forces, recalled that 'there was no coherent long-term strategy ... instead, we got a lot of tactics' (Richards 2017). A lack of a military strategy filtered through into the US overall development practices, which was being run conterminously.

To briefly summarize, US lessons learned reports have consistently shown that the US struggled with development because of failures in strategy, timelines, sustainability, personnel, context, monitoring and evaluation. Strategically, there was no coherent strategy that would enable a division of responsibilities among agencies that aligned with their strengths and weaknesses. Regarding timelines, the US repeatedly underestimated the time needed for reconstruction, creating unrealistic timelines and expectations prioritizing rapid spending. These efforts were often unsustainable. US-built institutions and infrastructure projects intended as foundations for long-term development often went unused or fell into disrepair due to a lack of long-term planning. Specific examples of unsustainable projects include a USD 36 million command and control facility at Camp Leatherneck that the Marines did not want, a USD 34 million soybean processing facility that was unused, and a USD 3 million poultry feed mill that closed after one day. A USD 2.89 million C-130 hangar on Bagram Airfield was also unused. There were also considerable personnel issues within the civilian and military sides of US development. Personnel were unqualified or poorly trained, and those who were qualified were difficult to retain. The US government's lack of understanding of the Afghan context led to a failure to tailor efforts effectively. This included imposing Western models onto Afghan institutions, mismanagement of security force training, and misunderstanding local cultural dynamics. Finally, US government agencies rarely conducted sufficient monitoring and evaluation to understand the impact of their efforts, leading to situations where projects were considered successful based on completion rather than actual impact (SIGAR 2021).

The problems identified by US lessons learned reports are salient to the EU. Not only was EU policy nested within and operating alongside US strategy, but Afghanistan was not a closed system. US practices had an impact on the success and failure of EU practices in Afghanistan. Recognizing this, the EU sought to coordinate with the US. However, this proved impossible and was frustrated by incompatible timelines for development. Problematically, for the EU, the risk of diverging timelines was not identified nor assessed from 2001 through to 2021. As one US official explained, the 'US was the 800-pound gorilla in the room'; it was able to 'bulldoze' its counterparts, and that is why there was 'this divergence in what we [USA and Europe] were trying to accomplish' (Hassan 2023).

European Union and Government of Afghanistan cooperation on development aid

The EU's growing role in Afghanistan began to take shape under a new EUSR. Having left his role at the UN, Francesc Vendrell became the second EUSR to serve in Afghanistan. Serving from July 2002 to August 2008, Vendrell was the longest-serving EUSR in Afghanistan and presided over a period of increasing involvement for the EU. In 2003, the Country Strategy Paper for Afghanistan was released, followed by the 2005 EU Joint

Declaration. In May 2007, the European Council established a Common Security and Defence Policy mission in Afghanistan (EUPOL). Within this timeframe, the EU delegation garnered a reputation for having genuine expertise and extensive knowledge of Afghanistan. This is unsurprising, given Vendrell's previous role and the expertise he brought to the office of the EUSR. As Edward Burke (2014) noted about the EU: 'From that time, one diplomat reflected, "It is hard to quantify political skill or knowledge. It doesn't fit into an Excel chart or PowerPoint very well. But it is indispensable … And we had all the advantages".'

Vendrell proved particularly adept at the 'ever-expanding' EUSR role and pushing for greater cooperation with Afghanistan at the EU level. This role grew because the political environment in Afghanistan itself was changing, and the EUSR role was forced to adapt. Some have portrayed this adaptation as a weakness, but navigating a complex and evolving strategically selective context requires adaptation if contextual dissonance is to be reduced. The institutionalization of the EUSR role was suited to these needs, even if some confusion resulted from an ill-defined set of structures (ICG 2005).

In 2004, under the terms of the Bonn Agreement, Afghanistan elected its first president. With 55.4 per cent of the vote, Hamid Karzai won an election that was marred by the threat of violence and resurgence by the Taliban. On this occasion, the EU did not send an Election Observation Mission (EOM) because of the security situation; it sent a more compact Democracy and Election Support Mission. Nevertheless, as Hedi Annabi, Assistant Secretary-General for Peacekeeping Operations, told the UN Security Council: 'Taking place against the backdrop of extremist threats, difficult terrain and sometimes adverse weather conditions, Afghanistan's first-ever presidential election … while not perfect, had placed under the best auspices the Afghans' journey towards a vigorous democracy' (UNSC 2004). Similarly, Afghanistan returned to elections in 2005, holding parliamentary and provincial council elections, leading to the inauguration of the National Assembly in December. Emma Bonino, who headed the EU EOM at the time, concluded that this was:

> [A]n essential step in a transition process designed to put in place a representative government and thereby help bring peace to Afghanistan after a quarter-century of conflict. The elections were held in extremely difficult conditions and to a timetable that was very tight. … Overall, given their complexity and the operational challenges, the elections are an accomplishment, although there were notable shortcomings which will need to be addressed in the future. (EUEOM 2005a)

It is widely considered that Vendrell's extensive experience provided the EU with a credible and competent voice as these important political milestones were achieved. This allowed the EUSR role to grow in influence and, with it, the EU's credibility inside Afghanistan. This was evident when Vendrell gained access to the elite Policy Action Group chaired by President Karzai, consisting of officials from the Afghan government and various international bodies (Quigley 2007). Contemporary evaluations of the EU's efforts suggested that:

> Many believe the EU gets a place at the table in Afghanistan because of his [Vendrell's] personal standing rather than his EU title. He has far more Afghanistan-specific experience than most member state representatives in Kabul, his multilingual staff is well versed in the region, and the political reporting of his office is widely seen as the best – and most realistic – available. (ICG 2005)

The election of the Afghan National Assembly marked the completion of the Bonn Process, and with this, the EU endeavoured to strengthen its relationship with the Afghan government. On 16 November 2005, the Council of the European Union took the significant step of signing the EU–Afghanistan Joint Declaration (Council, 2005a).

The Joint Declaration outlined a loose framework for a new post-Bonn partnership with Afghanistan, committing to democratic reforms, economic growth, fighting corruption and ending drug trafficking. This sought to establish norms of partnership with the Government of Afghanistan (GOA). The EU reaffirmed its support in these endeavours and encouraged international cooperation. This reiterated much of what was envisioned in the Afghan Constitution of 2004 but committed EU institutions to a leading role. Ostensibly, this was an attempt to decentre Member States that had marginalized European-level policy since 2001 but whose citizens were becoming increasingly fatigued by the war. Accordingly, the Joint Declaration highlighted the progress made since the Bonn Agreement. It stated the role of EU institutions and Member States in Afghanistan's reconstruction, presenting a more integrated and unified picture of European involvement. Indeed, between 2002 and 2006, the EU and Member States had already contributed around EUR 3.1 billion in aid, which would proliferate over the next decade.

The Joint Declaration also set out normative commitments, including political and economic governance reforms, security and justice sector reform, counter-narcotics efforts, and development objectives aligned with the Millennium Development Goals. The agreement also emphasized the importance of human rights, civil society development, and the return and integration of Afghan refugees. The document concluded with commitments to education and cultural dialogue, formalizing regular political dialogue through annual ministerial-level meetings, solidifying the EU's and Afghanistan's dedication to mutual goals, and continuing cooperation (Council 2005a).

For the most part, this is a standard document that is thin on detail. However, the Joint Declaration was significant, as it was the foundational document between the EU and the GOA. It marked a new moment in EU–Afghanistan bilateral relations at the end of 2005. Moreover, as the US paid greater attention to Iraq and NATO expanded the ISAF mission, the EU was afforded a more significant role in Afghanistan. As a signal of less US interest in the war and growing fatigue from Member States, the EU was no longer as marginalized as it was in 2001. This certainly provided a political opening for greater autonomy in the civilian space, which Member States increasingly afforded. The EU cooperated more on development and state-building, with the objective of underpinning Afghanistan's security, stability, freedom, prosperity and democratic governance (Council 2005a).

The intent to build on this development relationship is evident in the Joint Declaration itself. The headings are approximately derived from the Afghanistan National Development Strategy (ANDS), which originated from the Afghan Development Forum. These provided the contextual background for developmental cooperation, with the ANDS establishing three National Development Headings:

1. security
2. governance, rule of law and human rights
3. economic and social development.

The ANDS also identified five 'crosscutting themes', namely:

1. gender equity
2. counter–narcotics strategy
3. regional cooperation
4. anti-corruption
5. environment.

Regarding the GOA's role, the ANDS process was initiated in 2004, beginning with consultations involving Afghan policy makers. Following this, an ANDS Working Group was constituted, which conducted informal consultations with a significant number of community representatives. This group engaged with '400 Community Development Council (CDC) leaders', who collectively represented the interests of over 10,000 villages across Afghanistan (ANDS 2005). During the development of the ANDS, the GOA facilitated consultations with international stakeholders, including donor countries, and received written inputs from civil society on various drafts. Despite this international engagement, the GOA was keen to assert the indigenous and Afghan-owned nature of the ANDS, underscoring that it was tailored to reflect the specific development needs of Afghanistan as a whole (Hassan 2023).

By 2003, there was a noticeable shift in the international community's approach, moving away from the donor-centric meetings and initiatives that characterized the period of 2001–2. The GOA began to assume 'full leadership' in reconstruction efforts and aid coordination. This shift was evident even though entities like the World Bank advocated for more funding channelled through government budgetary mechanisms, aligning with national priorities. Concurrently, there was a significant focus on 'capacity building by doing' and altering mindsets concerning the National Development Budget, reflecting the Afghan government's more active and direct involvement in managing and directing the development process (World Bank 2003).

Over time, the GOA advanced its developmental agenda by introducing three additional strategic documents: the 2008–2013 Afghanistan National Development Strategy; the 2017–2021 Afghanistan National Peace and Development Framework; and the subsequent 2021–2025 iteration of the same framework. These documents expanded the initial 2005 ANDS, delineating specific timelines and objectives for the country's development trajectory. Paramount among these objectives was a vision set for Afghanistan by the year 2020, outlining key milestones and targets for the nation's progress:

- A stable Islamic constitutional democracy at peace with itself and its neighbours, standing with full dignity in the international family.
- A tolerant, united, pluralistic nation that honours its Islamic heritage and deep-seated aspirations toward participation, justice and equal rights for all.
- A society of hope and prosperity based on a strong, private sector-led market economy, social equity and environmental sustainability (ANDS 2008).

On the face of it, this was an ambitious agenda contingent upon the GOA's ability to enhance a broad spectrum of national capabilities; including improvement of the security landscape, the facilitation of reconciliation processes, and the advancement of justice systems. The implementation of this agenda was structured into two critical phases: a transition period spanning from 2012 to 2014, followed by a transformative decade from 2015 to 2024.

During the transition period, the focus was on establishing a robust framework for transferring responsibilities from international forces to Afghan authorities, ensuring a seamless progression towards self-reliance in security matters. Concurrently, efforts in political and socioeconomic spheres aimed to lay the groundwork for the subsequent transformative decade.

The transformation decade was supposed to be a phase of sustained development, where the foundational efforts of the transition period were expected to yield tangible progress. This decade was supposed to be pivotal for consolidating state institutions, economic growth and fostering a resilient civil society, ultimately leading to a self-sufficient and prosperous Afghanistan. This long-term vision underscored the depth of commitment from both the GOA and the EU, highlighting their joint aspiration for a stable and thriving Afghanistan.

In broad terms, approximately 50 per cent of EU development cooperation was dedicated to governance and security under the categories of policing and rule of law, along with democratization and accountability. A further 20 per cent was dedicated to agriculture and rural development, and a further 20 per cent to health and social protection. In precise terms, funding was disbursed within 161 sectors, the five most extensive of which were 'public sector policy and administrative management' (+/-10 per cent), 'material relief assistance and services' (+/-9 per cent), 'civilian peacebuilding, conflict prevention and resolution' (+/-6 per cent), 'security system management and reform' (+/-6 per cent) and 'legal and judicial development' (+/-6 per cent) (see Figure 5.4). Combined, these five disbursement categories covered over one-third of all EU aid.

From the European Commission's perspective, the 2005 EU–Afghanistan Joint Declaration established a framework to cooperate with the GOA and realize the ambitions set out in the ANDS. This allowed the Commission to emphasize that development was under 'Afghan ownership' and the GOA provided 'leadership' in 'promoting economic and social development, including the development of poverty reduction strategies and in state-building'. Despite acknowledging the essential role of the GOA in making substantial progress in these areas, the EU's reliance on the Afghan government for implementing progressive reforms was markedly evident. The success and failure of these projects were tied to the GOA's competence and endurance, with development initiatives, therefore, coming from the centre rather than, for the most part, being derived beyond major urban centres. If the GOA was successful, development cooperation would have established a symbiotic relationship where both partners benefit from a close association. Theoretically, Afghanistan would have been transformed into a more secure, prosperous and democratic state, and Europe would have benefited from a more stable region. However, this was different from the outcome in practice. With development assistance struggling to reach widespread areas of Afghanistan, power over development norms became centralized within the GOA. This provided significant difficulties for EU development aid, which was channelled not only through the national

Figure 5.4: EU and Member State distribution of disbursements across various sectors

Distribution of disbursements by sector (with <2% as 'other')

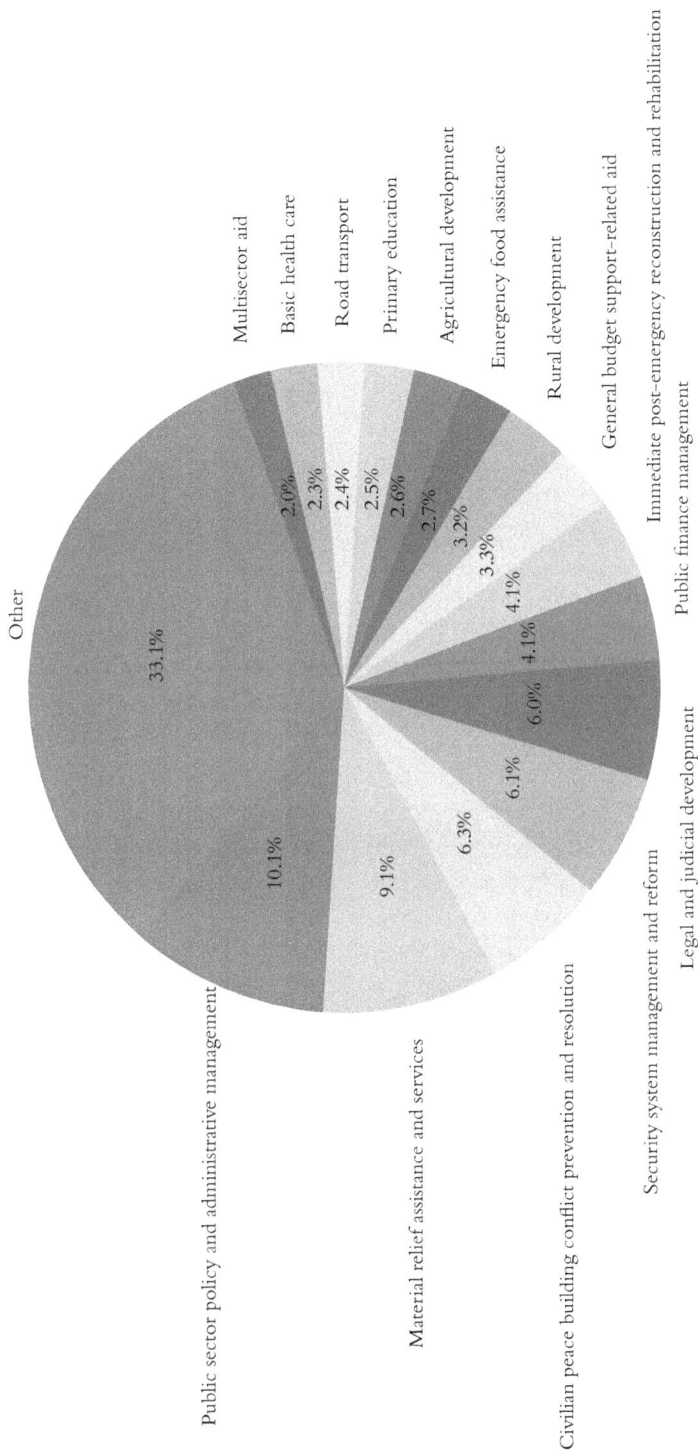

Other

Multisector aid

Basic health care

Road transport

Primary education

Agricultural development

Emergency food assistance

Rural development

General budget support-related aid

Immediate post-emergency reconstruction and rehabilitation

Public finance management

Legal and judicial development

Security system management and reform

Civilian peace building conflict prevention and resolution

Material relief assistance and services

Public sector policy and administrative management

33.1%

10.1%

9.1%

6.3%

6.1%

6.0%

4.1%

4.1%

3.3%

3.2%

2.7%

2.6%

2.5%

2.4%

2.3%

2.0%

Source: EU Aid Explorer (nd)

143

programmes of the Afghan government but also through the multi-donor trust funds that contribute to the government's central budget.

European Union contributions to multi-donor trust funds

The intensification of cooperation between the European Commission and multilateral organizations, as part of the former's commitment to better aid coordination, is evidenced by the substantial increase in the amount of EU aid channelled through the World Bank and UN organizations. As part of this effort, there was a notable shift in the European Commission's approach to aid distribution and its reliance on international organizations for implementation. This shift represented a complementary system to the EU's bilateral efforts, setting out multilateral frameworks to maximize the efficiency of EU development aid. It also represents an innovation in development that is part of the thickening institutional arrangements of global international society in the 21st century.

The EU's substantial role in international reconstruction funding for Afghanistan, particularly through the Afghanistan Reconstruction Trust Fund and the Law-and-Order Trust Fund for Afghanistan (LOTFA), underscores the strategic importance and financial weight the EU placed on multilateral aid mechanisms in conflict-affected regions. By 2020, the EU's position as the fourth highest contributor to these funds, following the US, UK and Japan, reflected its commitment to stabilizing and rebuilding Afghanistan through these multilateral channels and the EU's broader foreign policy objectives of promoting stability, peace and development through collective international efforts (Hassan 2020b). Indeed, the EU and Member States contributed 40 per cent of Afghanistan Reconstruction Trust Fund funds and 32 per cent of LOTFA funds, which was higher in both cases than the US contribution to these multilateral efforts (see Figure 5.5).

Within these multi-donor trust funds, the EU embraced the norm of 'Country Ownership', but multilateral organizations would administer funds and facilitate host government cooperation. The Afghanistan Reconstruction Trust Fund administration was undertaken by the World Bank, and LOTFA by the UN Development Programme (UNDP). However, the European Court of Auditors highlighted severe problems with the efficiency and effectiveness of these multilateral funds. Indeed, the EU was experiencing similar issues to those of the US, and the Auditors' report was damning. The Court identified information gaps and project design weaknesses, demonstrating that reports to the Commission were typically delayed, needed more detail and focused more on activities than results. Also prevalent were project

Figure 5.5: US and combined EU Member States' cumulative contributions to the Afghanistan Reconstruction Trust Fund and the Law-and-Order Trust Fund for Afghanistan

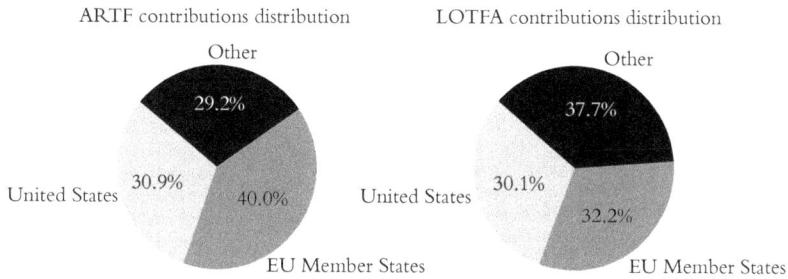

Source: Derived from Hassan (2020b)

design flaws, which adversely impacted their implementation and evaluation. There were also efficiency concerns, illustrating that the Commission's focus on efficiency was insufficient. The cost assessments conducted were limited and not systematically documented. Almost half of the sampled projects showed shortcomings in this area, with incomplete information available for several projects. There was also a failure to undertake risk management in Afghanistan, compounded by conflict conditions restricting the evaluation of the project's effectiveness, efficiency and sustainability. Correctly, the audit highlighted that taking this considerable risk was a political choice. This was particularly concerning, given deficiencies in the budget details within contribution agreements. Notably, during a project's duration, the Commission's attention was primarily on cost eligibility over efficiency, missing systematic documentation and thorough assessment. More widely, the audit found instances where implementing partners, typically other UN organizations, incurred indirect costs surpassing the permitted 7 per cent of direct costs and significant problems with inefficiencies in cost management (Court 2011).

Compounding these problems were numerous projects with prolonged implementation periods, requiring increased project time and costs, which depleted funds for essential activities, thus affecting effectiveness and efficiency. Moreover, just as the US discovered, the sustainability of project results was a key concern and the likelihood of projects lasting beyond their funding was limited. This was due to project outcomes not being sufficiently integrated with the local beneficiaries' needs and capacities, undermining stakeholders' desire to continue seeking the project's benefit. There was also poor consideration of the availability of further funding beyond the initial funding periods, a lack of necessary expertise, and a failure to consider the stability and receptiveness of the political environment and how this would greatly influence the sustainability of project results (Court 2011). Yet, one of the significant absences in the audit was any focus on corruption. For example, the audit identified that LOTFA was at risk of being unsustainable, noting: 'The main objective of the Law and Order Trust Fund is to pay salaries of police officers in Afghanistan. Due to the limited financial capacity of Afghanistan the fund will, in the medium to longer term, remain dependent on further donor funding to continue its activities' (Court 2011).

Yet, just a few years after the audit, it was discovered that LOTFA could not account for USD 200 million in deductions (Guilbert 2014). With LOTFA being the UNDP's largest and most complex project and dealing with very high levels of donor financing, the UNDP sought to expand and strengthen its oversight of funds. This, combined with LOTFA's strategy, aimed to improve Afghan National Police's (ANP) accountability and oversight, fund the shift from counterinsurgency to community policing and integrate women into the police force (Paldi 2015). These initiatives were seen as vital for Afghanistan's stability and socioeconomic development, but LOTFA's oversight proved insufficient around payroll management issues. This damaged the reputation of the multilateral fund, even though this deficiency was a symptom of a much broader corruption issue. Indeed, with international actors asleep at the wheel, there was a failure to account for the 'corruption eruption' that was fuelling a growing insurgency and undermining international efforts for security and development.

The corruption eruption and aid absorption capacity

Addressing corruption was raised in the EU-Afghanistan Joint Declaration. In forming this 'new partnership', the EU outlined its support for shared priorities and stated that EU institutions would 'continue to help Afghanistan build strong and accountable institutions at national and provincial level free from corruption' to promote the rule of law and democratic oversight (Council 2005a). This is related to the EU institution's focus on state-building and addressing political corruption. However, within the Joint Declaration, the GOA was conferred responsibility for accelerating progress towards sustainable state finances, fighting corruption and ending the trafficking of drugs (Council 2005a). Indeed, by the end of 2005, it was widely recognized that systemic levels of corruption were inhibiting Afghanistan's development.

Strikingly, the Afghan Interim Authority and, subsequently, the GOA overcame the stigma of talking about corruption as early as 2002. Initiated by then Chairman of the Interim Authority, Hamid Karzai, high-level discussions revolved around the need to take a hard stance on tackling all forms of corruption:

Coming back to corruption, I remarked to Secretary Powell that we will be going towards an Afghanistan where the people will have the choice to choose their own government. People will be empowered, will be free there, absolutely. But one area where we'll be extremely tough and rather oppressive will be against corruption ... We will be very very very rough there. There is no way that we can allow that. No way because we know if we allow that, the country will not do well. (Karzai 2002)

Statements about adopting a hard-line approach towards corruption were welcomed by the US and the wider international donor community, as, ostensibly, Afghanistan looked like it was putting structures in place to tackle corruption at multiple levels. Internationally, Afghanistan ratified the United Nations Convention against Corruption in 2004, which is the only legally binding universal anti-corruption instrument set in the framework of international law, and covers the areas of 'preventive measures, criminalisation and law enforcement, international cooperation, asset recovery, and technical assistance and information exchange' (UNODC 2004). This was to be strengthened with the promulgation of specific legislation in 2004 and the establishment of the General Independent Administration for Anti-Corruption in the same year. The legislation was specifically intended to tackle bribery, administrative corruption and money laundering (AsianLII 2004).[2] Thus, an institutional and legislative approach to tackling corruption was put in place.

What is notable, however, is that whereas EU institutions failed to characterize corruption and its causes, the GOA was able to present corruption as part of a historical legacy. Thus, the 2005 ANDS placed the origins of corruption in Afghanistan within the communist period; as opposed to the introduction of neopatrimonialist norms introduced through the Bonn Process. Corruption was presented as a hangover from the economic collapse of the communist era. The narrative provided by the GOA detailed the communist expansion of state control in the economy and the replacement of skilled elites with technocrats trained in Soviet ideology. Following the Soviet withdrawal, it was argued that successive governments failed to generate domestic financial resources due to a lack of capacity and legitimacy. This resulted in the printing of large amounts of currency, causing hyperinflation. Hyperinflation severely devalued government salaries,

---

[2] These included the Law on the Campaign Against Bribery and Administrative Corruption – Official Gazette No. 838, published 2004/10/11 (1383/07/20 AP), and the Law on the Campaign Against Money Laundering and Its Proceeds – Official Gazette No. 840, published 2004/10/31 (1383/08/10 AP).

undermining the living standards of public servants, including teachers, police and the judiciary. Consequently, their commitment and performance declined, and corruption spread due to the politicized and factionalized administration. It was argued that public servants, earning less than USD 20 per month, stayed in their jobs but often resorted to corruption, trading, remittances or additional jobs to supplement their income. This scenario further weakened the economy and good governance (ANDS 2005, 33–4).

Attributing corruption to the communist period had the value of absolving those in power and the Bonn Process of responsibility for corruption. Indeed, within the parameters of the ANDS historical schema, the GOA sought to demonstrate how it would tackle corruption in multiple areas, including state capacity for revenue collection, addressing the informal economy, increasing police wages, professionalized civil service, and addressing centralized regulatory frameworks. Similarly, the GOA recognized corruption as the third most constraining factor for private sector growth, below the reliability of electricity supplies and access to land. Corruption was seen as substantially more debilitating than even security issues. Indeed, citing a World Bank Investment Climate Survey, the ANDS reiterated that:

> 58% of firms cited corruption as a major or severe problem, especially threatening to foreign investors or returning Afghans. Firms, on average, pay 8% of sales as bribes, and this is more than four times the average reported in Pakistan and other countries. … Clearly, minimising the costs of doing business is vital to competitiveness, growth, market expansion and greater employment and prosperity. The current approximately 18% combined 'security and bribery transaction' costs that Afghan companies incur over other private sector operators in the region impedes the emergence of a strong export-oriented formal economy. (ANDS 2005, 62)

Thus, with the ANDS referring to 'corruption' no fewer than 133 times in 260 pages, the crosscutting issue was not seen as peripheral to Afghanistan's overall development strategy. Moreover, by early 2006, following a large international conference in London, the Afghanistan Compact was issued, articulating the international community's commitment towards Afghanistan, alongside Afghanistan's dedication to state-building and reform, for the forthcoming five-year period. Again, corruption was addressed with Afghanistan and the 'international community' committing to 'combat corruption and ensure public transparency and accountability' (Afghanistan Compact 2006).

Rubin's (2006) account of the Afghanistan Compact is instructive, demonstrating that the US, UK and other donors vehemently opposed language that would hold attendees directly responsible for the Compact's implementation. This is notable because the Compact set out benchmarks and because the European Commission and the EU were listed separately as participating organizations, along with 18 participating Member States and two Accession States.[3] This was over a third of all participants. Yet, while the GOA was to be held directly accountable for shortcomings in meeting those benchmarks, the vaguely defined 'international community' could not. In practice, this empowered the GOA to set the scope and agenda for dealing with corruption, even when large parts of the GOA were under suspicion and implicated in corrupt practices. Ultimately, as a legacy of the Bonn Process neopatrimonialist norms had become part of the institutional fabric of the centralized state, but members of the 'international community', including the EU and Member States, actively worked to absolve themselves of this responsibility. Indeed, by 2007, as the Taliban resurgence was growing, there were increasing concerns that corruption in Afghanistan was growing and embedding itself into regular day-to-day practices. Thus, while corruption to varying extents is present in every state, the grand corruption of senior officials was being matched by smaller-scale petty corruption at a systemic level (UNODC 2007).

Grand corruption specifically refers to abusing high-level power, which advantages a select few while detrimentally impacting the majority. This can involve large-scale exchanges of resources, access to economic rents, or other advantages by high-level officials, privileged firms and their networks. Grand corruption is characterized by significant monetary value and often involves senior officials receiving kickbacks in exchange for directing lucrative government contracts to favoured companies. It can also include manipulating policies, institutions and procedures, allowing high-level officials to benefit at the expense of the public good. This form of corruption includes 'political corruption', which profoundly impacts governance and the rule of law.

In contrast, petty corruption is regarded as the routine misuse of power by public officials during their dealings with everyday citizens, typically occurring when these individuals seek access to fundamental necessities or services at locations such as hospitals, educational institutions, law enforcement offices and various other public agencies (SIGAR 2016). Significantly, by 2007, international organizations began to outline a radically different understanding of corruption and its causes. Whereas the GOA

---

[3] Austria, Belgium, Bulgaria (joined the EU on 1 January 2007 but was in the process of accession in 2006), Czech Republic, Denmark, Finland, France, Germany, Greece, Hungary, Italy, Lithuania, Luxembourg, Netherlands, Poland, Portugal, Romania (similar to Bulgaria, joined on 1 January 2007 but was in the accession process in 2006), Spain, Sweden, United Kingdom.

laid the blame on Afghanistan's communist past and the Taliban, multilateral organizations began highlighting that:

> Available data on perceptions and anecdotal evidence indicate that corruption is seen to be very widespread and most likely increasing in recent years (from the apparently relatively low base under the Taliban regime pre-2001, reflecting, among other factors, more limited opportunities for corruption at that time due to small resource flows and the de-facto quasi-legal status of the opium economy). (UNODC 2007, 7)

The perception that corruption in Afghanistan was worsening bore out in annual indexing by Transparency International, which consistently ranked Afghanistan as one of the ten most corrupt countries in the world. Indeed, although Afghanistan was outside the top 40 in 2005, between 2008 and 2015, it was ranked in the world's top five most corrupt countries (Transparency International 2022).[4]

To explain this phenomenon, it is essential to briefly recall Afghanistan's history of state development from previous chapters. Afghanistan's modern corruption problem rests on an interplay of a strategically selective context produced by an intersection of historical events. With Afghanistan maintaining a heterarchical power structure outside of Kabul, local power structures continued to exist even as post-Bonn centralization attempted to engage in state-building. The 19th- and 20th-century attempts at centralization by Abdul Rahman Khan, Amanullah, Zahir Shah and Daud could not give the state enough reach to challenge village states. This created the co-existence of a centralized hierarchy and a distributed heterarchy of power, which have never been reconciled. Within circles of elites, practices of nepotism, patronage and clientelism were social norms that empowered and reinforced royal privilege and dynastic rule. In the communist period, and especially following the Soviet invasion, the state's legitimacy was questioned, and the civil war represented a legitimation crisis. The Najibullah regime could never overcome this crisis, and removing Soviet clientelism and rents eroded the state further. The Taliban were never able to overcome this state legitimation crisis, even as they installed theocratic norms in the 1990s. Without legitimate state institutions, the public domain was readily exploited for personnel

---

[4] Data for overall international ranking by Transparency International: 2005 117/159; 2007 172/180; 2008 176/180; 2009 179/180; 2010 176/178; 2011 180/183; 2012 174/176; 2013 175/177; 2014 172/175; 2015 166/168; 2016 169/176; 2017 177/180; 2018 172/180; 2019 173/180; 2020 165/180; 2021 174/180; 2022 150/180.

and group benefits. Individuals and groups pursued their own political power and financial interests within weak state institutions while seeking to marginalize others.

The historical context of Afghanistan's state development should have been a critical consideration in designing Afghanistan's development programmes and the reliance on centralized state institutions for the design and distribution of aid frameworks. It was not. Instead, as set out in Chapter 1, Afghanistan was treated as a 'tabula rasa'. Interviews with multiple senior officials at the EEAS and other EU institutions repeated this point. As a former EU ambassador to Pakistan argued: 'We didn't take into consideration we were not starting from a blank sheet … I was part of that … we thought that we could build from nothing' (Hassan 2023, 4). Similarly, another EU official explained: 'We thought it is a tabula rasa, and we [could] implement our ready-made development solutions to build a modern state' (Hassan 2023, 35). The importance of this is that because Afghanistan was treated as a blank slate, questions surrounding sources of corruption and the suitability of development strategies were not factored into the EU's development strategy and overall programme designs for Afghanistan. This contextual dissonance had a direct impact on levels of corruption in Afghanistan. As an EU ambassador informed this author, one of the biggest mistakes made in Afghanistan was that the international community 'incentivised corruption, spending more than [Afghanistan's] GDP', which led to 'elite capture of aid' and a failure for aid to reach beyond major urban centres. This was supported by the testimony of another EU official who pointed to a problem with aid absorption and fuelling corruption:

> It wasn't a question of lack of money … there was an absorption problem since day one. Afghanistan was washed with money from all donors, not only EU donors, and this money hasn't been spent wisely because there were too many donors with too much cash and [and] no structures to implement that assistance. It's catered to the ever-present corruption culture in Afghanistan. So, money that was supposed to install modern institutions modelled on the Western idea of independent civil service, free of corruption, actually, were used, not with our consent, but it's just that this is what happens … [we made the] problem even bigger … money was stolen … we knew that the government will not be able to deliver …we just wanted to spend the money … we're not that happy with the outcome that we bought with European taxpayers' money … we contributed to this culture of clientelism and corruption by not addressing it properly. Not reacting when we would see that it is happening on our account, or on the account of another donor. (Hassan 2023, 35)

Discernibly, the problem of aid absorption was not immediately recognized throughout the first decade of involvement in Afghanistan. As one scholar argued in the leading journal *International Affairs*, 'by March 2003 Afghanistan had received the lowest per capita aid for post-conflict reconstruction, and a large share of that aid has been emergency assistance ... there is a serious risk that in 2006, with no further additional allocations, funding for Afghanistan will dry up' (Woods 2005, 395). Similarly, Rupp argued that 'considering Afghanistan's staggering needs, the expenditure by the US government of $1.4 billion during this crucial period [2001–2005] seems limited' (2006, 290). Such statements do not sit well with EU policy makers' assertions that there was a detrimentally high level of funds allocated to Afghanistan. However, they help elucidate the initial academic and donor debates surrounding Afghanistan's needs and capabilities in the early 2000s. While some argued that large injections of aid funding were needed to generate momentum for development and, therefore, that there was insufficient aid allocation, others were concerned that the Afghan government would not have the capacity to manage large sums of money nor be able to implement programmes (see Marsden 2003). While the former won the initial argument, it became increasingly clear over the next decade that this approach was causing serious problems.

As Suhrke noted of the US mission in Afghanistan, in the aptly titled *When More is Less*, over the initial stages of the intervention, '[b]ureaucratic momentum, organizational interests, aid lobbies and a cascading of objectives further deepened the commitment, making it progressively harder to turn around and change course' (2011, 5). In many respects, what this describes is a global international society that has developed norms prioritizing self-sustaining volumes of aid over contextual consonance.

There were growing concerns that an unprecedentedly large quantity of international assistance was flowing into Afghanistan, accompanied by pressure to spend it quickly (UNODC 2007, 7). Thus, while the UK was a strong initial advocate for Afghanistan to receive large injections of aid by 2009, the UK's Department for International Development recognized that Afghanistan had a 'low absorptive capacity' and was only spending 23 per cent of what it had been granted for the development budget, of which 'for every $100 spent only $20 actually reaches Afghan recipients' (Bennett et al 2009). Despite these findings, the UK's House of Commons International Development Committee would note three years later that:

> [T]he Afghan Government has a limited absorptive capacity. The Afghan Government is currently able to spend only an estimated 18 to 20% of the aid allocated to it by the US Government ... where aid had gone through the Afghan Government, it was not sufficiently reaching the provinces ... which meant that funds coming through

the line ministries were directed on ill-informed priorities or to corrupt individual and institutions. (International Development Committee 2012)

Again, in evaluations for the period 2014 to 2020, Global Affairs Canada's International Assistance Evaluation Division would conclude:

[T]here was a pressure to spend, and it was too much and too fast in the context of Afghanistan … it was sometimes difficult to find good initiatives in Afghanistan to disburse the amount of money available. Many other donors also perceived their development assistance spending in Afghanistan as ambitious and exceeding the absorption capacity of Afghan institutions. (Global Affairs Canada 2020)

Concerns around Afghanistan's aid absorption capacity were not limited to US allies. As early as 2011, USAID estimated that approximately 30 per cent of its contracted project costs were lost to corruption, and the Congressional Research Service demonstrated that corrupt officials and criminal syndicates were misappropriating significant amounts of aid funds directed to Afghanistan. These funds were then transferred outside of Afghanistan and into bank accounts in Dubai and other foreign locations (Schwartz 2011). Indeed, SIGAR concluded as early as 2014 that '[i]n Afghanistan, absorptive capacity [was] reached in the first year of operations' and going above absorption capacity 'led to the corruption eruption' (SIGAR 2014). SIGAR's conclusions noted that massive amounts of military and aid spending overwhelmed the Afghan government's ability to absorb it, along with the Afghan economy, and a point of saturation was exceeded. Beyond this point, extra inputs were often diverted elsewhere, frequently leading to illicit capital flight. In addition, high levels of aid lacked adequate oversight, as the levels of aid grew far beyond what 'US agencies themselves could effectively absorb, disperse, and oversee' (SIGAR 2021). Although there is discussion regarding the theoretical limit at which the threshold for aid absorption is reached, estimated to be between 15 and 45 per cent of gross domestic product, from 2004 to 2013, US allocations for Afghanistan's reconstruction consistently surpassed this upper limit. In 2006 and 2010, the funds appropriated by the US exceeded 100 per cent of Afghanistan's gross domestic product (SIGAR 2021).

Concerns that the aid level was detrimental to Afghanistan's reconstruction were not limited to governments and international organizations. Within the academic and think tank literature, there were growing levels of concern around the detrimental effects of aid to Afghanistan and, in particular, the way aid was fuelling patronage and corruption because of a reliance on warlords (Goodhand 2002; Marquette 2011; Peceny and Bosin 2011;

Zürcher 2012; Suhrke 2013). For example, a report released by the Danish Institute for International Studies highlighted that 'the US's initial support of warlords, reliance on logistics contracting, and the deluge of military and aid spending ... overwhelmed the absorptive capacity of the Government of the Islamic Republic of Afghanistan [and] created an environment that fostered corruption and impeded later [counter- and anti-corruption] efforts' (Andersen 2016).

Significantly, even after it was publicly recognized that US reliance on local military commanders and local drug networks was proving detrimental and undermining the government of Afghanistan, the US continued instigating this policy as part of the routine practice of the war on terror. The Central Intelligence Agency continued to pay warlords, governors, parliamentarians and religious leaders to purchase loyalty and information, and the US military continued to pay local actors in an attempt to purchase stability (Whitlock 2019). The influx of funds through the military empowered militias and strongmen beyond Kabul. The US was, therefore, as reliant on the hierarchical system in Kabul for state-building as it was on the heterarchical system outside of major urban centres for security. This was an explicit contradiction held together by American military power and rents and would ultimately collapse in 2021. The dynamics of this contradiction were exemplified in the US House of Representatives Subcommittee on National Security and Foreign Affairs report entitled *Warlord, Inc.* The report estimated that by 2010, US military funding alone had 'injected a good portion of a $2.16 billion contract's resources into a corruptive environment' just in Host Nation Trucking contracts (Tierney 2010). In doing so, the US established a parallel economy and financial system lacking the rigorous oversight typical of conventional development institutions. This parallel structure remained unaddressed by the US military, partly due to 'a perpetual sense of imminent departure'.

Notably, EU institutions were aware of this situation but failed to act upon it and adjust their policy accordingly. As one senior EU official described:

> Now I worked with the Americans on this, so you know, it's not like I didn't talk to our American friends about it. The vast amount of money is coming from the US. Now, who in the US is using the vast amount of development mode? The US military ... their generals, colonels and lieutenants, were given very big bags of money, and on the rotation scheme, they had six months to spend all the money. And they did. ... You have four and a half million dollars in your pocket, and you want to spend it in six months – that created corruption because that money was spent very, very poorly. It fuelled corruption to an extreme point; to an unthinkable extent. Basically, these were

unguided money missiles raining down over Afghanistan left, right and centre. (Hassan 2023, 37)

In the case of military spending dedicated towards development objectives, it was not audited, and there was poor oversight. On the contrary, volumes of expenditure were equated with success. As one EU official explained:

If we look at the traditional development agencies – Danish DANIDA, GTZ, and even USAID, this was better controlled, and they understood they had to look after that money. But we're talking about 10%, or whatever 15% of the total sum; it was nothing. It was all the other money that the military was spending there; that was just crazy money. Millions to spend in six months. Development projects in six months? It's completely insane. I mean, anybody who knows about development knows that it's completely insane. (Hassan 2023, 38)

Significantly, the US's militarized development practices impacted the EU's civilian approach to development. There was no aid coordination at this level, and for the US, lines were blurred between military and development objectives. This generated corruption, empowered warlords, developed an alternative economy and undermined the GOA. But providing alternative rents that 'dwarfed' EU development contributions reduced the EU's overall leverage and, indeed, that of the wider global international society. Moreover, a diachronic timeline constructed by SIGAR is instructive. Between 2001 and 2005, the US established this harmful spending pattern. However, between 2006 and 2008, spending was 'ramped up', and from 2009 to 2011 in an 18-month surge, Afghanistan was 'flooded with cash'. It was not until 2012 through 2014 that these efforts revealed themselves to be problematic, and from 2015 to 2020 the US came to terms with reducing troops, assistance and overall influence in Afghanistan (SIGAR 2021). As one State Department official disclosed, up until 2015, '[m]oney … poured in – [the US was] so desperate to have the alcoholics to the table, we kept pouring drinks not knowing/considering we were killing them' (*Washington Post* 2015). In the name of transatlantic solidarity, EU institutions and Member States similarly looked the other way. Political decisions were made to ignore European taxpayers' money being stolen, misused and helping to fuel an insurgency.

By 2018, General Nicholson, Commander of US Forces–Afghanistan, explained that the US believed the Taliban had 'evolved into a criminal or narco-insurgency'. This was affirmed by the Council of the European Union's (2021) *Afghanistan: Counter-Terrorism Action Plan*, which raised concerns about the Taliban's relationship with narcotics, criminality and terrorism. Yet, what is striking about this is that upon leaving office in 2008, EUSR Vendrell made this exact charge. In his candid and profoundly critical assessment of EU policy, he argued that the 'EU is rather pitiful' and that 'we [the EU] look pretty pathetic at times' because the US 'ignored' EU concerns and left EU officials 'frustrated'. He continued that the EU only in 'small ways had some impact' and despite the considerable levels of aid being contributed to Afghanistan, 'we [the EU and the international community] have all failed', allowing Afghanistan to turn into a 'criminal narco-state'. In framing his argument about Western strategy more widely, he argued that:

> I don't leave with a sense of failure … but I do leave with a sense of regret that we made so many mistakes. I don't believe the situation will lead to failure, but we have got to do a hell of a lot to get things right. … In 2002, we were being welcomed almost as liberators by the Afghans. Now, we are being seen as a necessary evil, perhaps something that they need to put up with because our departure would probably mean a civil war. (Vendrell 2008)

Unfortunately, Vendrell was proven wrong, and the return of the Taliban in 2021 demonstrated the most significant failure of EU external action to date. Indeed, while there was some progress in EU policy over the intervening years, and the Lisbon Treaty added to EU competencies, EU institutions needed to do more to prevent the return of the Taliban.

European Union Diplomacy, Democracy and Security Assistance

When challenged with widespread corruption, European Union (EU) institutions prioritized the norm of solidarity with the United States (US) and a norm of partnership with the Government of Afghanistan (GOA). This was not without consequence for other aspects of EU engagement. With absorption capacity greatly exceeded, and corruption fuelling an insurgency, insecurity throughout Afghanistan grew. This had a counterintuitive effect on EU-level relations with Afghanistan. As corruption and insecurity took hold, EU Member States would start to pass on more responsibilities to EU institutions, to counter growing fatigue with the ongoing conflict. As a result, having marginalized norms of EU integration at the start of the conflict, EU institutions would be drawn further into a relationship with Afghanistan and take on new responsibilities. Importantly, the EU increasingly had to operate in a strategically selective context, whereby it not only had to navigate Afghanistan, but demands and previous responsibilities of Member States, along with the larger transatlantic relationship with the US and the North Atlantic Treaty Organization (NATO). All while remaining a secondary partner in all these relations. The complexity of being in this position is reflective of how norms and the interaction capacity of global international society have evolved in the early 21st century.

The complexity of having to negotiate the norms of global international society was compounded by the problems accumulated from previous contextual dissonance. As a marginalized partner in the ongoing conflict, EU institutions were sceptical about casting counterterrorism operations within military norms. EU actors had also been sceptical about empowering the Northern Alliance and embedding neopatrimonialist norms within the institutions of state and the decision to invade Iraq. Yet, the EU was being asked to do more and work around the accumulation of problems that had been generated throughout the conflict. This required going beyond the blank slate development policies as EU institutions became more active in Afghanistan in the second decade of the conflict. This started with a contribution to Afghan security and the establishment of the European Union Police Mission in Afghanistan (EUPOL) in 2007. Indeed, the EU became more engaged in offering bilateral assistance, political dialogue and peacebuilding efforts from 2007 to 2017. This chapter details those efforts, starting with the EUPOL mission and how EU external action adapted to transatlantic demands for greater European involvement. Even as Member States demonstrated fatigue with the war, and pushed for the start of the Kabul Process, the EU remained committed and helped keep Afghanistan on the international agenda. However, by 2017, this began to fall apart as the Trump administration broke with the norms of transatlantic solidarity, and internal bureaucratic battles within the EU began to mount. As a result, EU policy makers were not well prepared for the re-emergence of the Taliban and the collapse of the GOA.

The European Union Police Mission in Afghanistan: too little, too late

Although Germany was tasked with police reform in 2002 and then supported by the US, it was widely acknowledged that there were no significant improvements in the quality of policing and insecurity in the country continued to grow (Murray 2007). Although Germany was eager to assert solidarity with the US in the early stages of the war, there was a reluctance to politically invest in an increasingly unpopular conflict among the German public (Eckhard 2016). Thus, between 2002 and 2007, Germany provided the German Police Project Office with approximately EUR 12 million annually for police-building in Afghanistan (EU Committee 2011). By early 2006, police reform was so neglected that the training pillar of its funding was switched to gender support as a 'pragmatic move to attract donor money known to be available for gender projects' (Murray 2007). This switch also reflected significant tension within security sector reform and the Afghanistan National Police (ANP). Namely, should the ANP reflect the more immediate military security needs to fight a growing insurgency or the need for a civilian police force able to compel everyday compliance with the law? In both cases, there was a need for greater gender representation within the ANP, but having a civilian force necessitated greater gender equality and a focus on human rights to act effectively as a civilian force within local populations (Ansorg and Haastrup 2018).

This provided the context upon which EUPOL was established by the Council of the European Union in 2007. Although the mission was framed in reference to EU-level commitments as signatories to the 2005 Joint Declaration and the 2006 Afghanistan Compact, there was more to the

EU's growing involvement.[1] As the German-led mission faltered, an EU-level police mission became increasingly appealing. Thus, EUPOL grew from the German mission's failures and the decision to pass responsibility to the EU (Hassan 2020b). Indeed, when interviewing EU policy makers for this research, there was a recurring theme of Member States passing responsibilities to the EU when they ran into difficulties and continued involvement became domestically unpopular. As one EU diplomat critiqued, the EU was useful for Member States wanting to 'get rid of difficulties' as it was 'easier to pass them over' (Hassan 2023). As such, when EUPOL was initiated in 2007, it was not just a result of the deteriorating security situation but also because the elevation of EU-level action was politically expedient in Berlin and other major European capitals. Six years after the start of US-led action and declarations of transatlantic solidarity, European integration was on the agenda for Member States' missions in Afghanistan. This was reflected in EUPOL's objectives:

> EUPOL AFGHANISTAN shall significantly contribute to the establishment under Afghan ownership of sustainable and effective civilian policing arrangements, which will ensure appropriate interaction with the wider criminal justice system in keeping with the policy advice and institution-building work of the Community, Member States and other international actors. Further, the Mission will support the reform process towards a trusted and efficient police service that works in accordance with international standards, within the framework of the rule of law, and respects human rights. (Council 2007a)

Overall authority for EUPOL rested with the High Representative for Foreign Affairs and Security Policy. The Political and Security Committee provided strategic direction and political control, and the Civilian Planning and Conduct Capability Brussels oversaw the operational level (Gross 2010, 230).[2] Initially granted three years to operate, EUPOL would carry out 'monitoring, mentoring, advising and training' under the day-to-day management and operational control of Head of Mission Brigadier General Friedrich Eichele (Council 2007a). However, after three months, the German Brigadier General quit because of an apparent turf war with other

---

[1]   See Council Joint Action 2007/369/CFSP of 30 May 2007, on the establishment of the European Union Police Mission in Afghanistan (EUPOL AFGHANISTAN).

[2]   From 1999 to 2009, the Office of the High Representative for Foreign Affairs and Security Policy was held by Javier Solana, followed by Catherine Ashton from 2009 to 2014, and Federica Mogherini from 2014 to 2019. EUPOL was overseen by all three, running from 2007 to 2016.

officials at the EU delegation in Kabul and an inability to secure basics such as computers, cars and furniture (Dempsey 2008). He was replaced by German Brigadier General Jürgen Scholz, who had led EU police missions in Macedonia and had experience training police in Africa and former Soviet states. Eleven months later, in October 2008, Scholz was replaced by Police Commissioner Kai Vittrup of Denmark.

EUPOL's senior leadership changing so frequently proved to be profoundly problematic and hindered coordination efforts with the European Union Special Representative (EUSR) for the first two years of its operation. In terms of norms, a frequent changing of norm circles naturally inhibited intersectionality and undermined the collective intentions of the institution. Nevertheless, EUPOL improved its efforts to develop a collaborative strategy aligned with the Afghanistan Compact and the Afghanistan National Development Strategy (ANDS). This was an attempt to help foster connections between the police force and the broader issues around the rule of law (Council 2007a). By 2009, EUPOL had established six strategic priorities:

1. Develop police command, control and communications for the Ministry of Interior and the Afghan National Police.
2. Develop intelligence-led policing.
3. Build the capabilities of the Criminal Investigations Department.
4. Develop anti-corruption capacities.
5. Improve cooperation and coordination between the police and the judiciary, with a particular emphasis on prosecutors.
6. Mainstream gender issues and human rights within the Ministry of Interior and the ANP (EU Committee 2011).

However, despite having its mandate extended, the mission was vexed from the start, leading one United Kingdom (UK) House of Lords Select Committee to conclude that: '[T]he mission was too late, too slow to get off the ground once the decision was made, and too small to achieve its aim; or perhaps, worst, too small to receive respect from other actors. ... Despite achieving local successes, overall, there is a strong risk of failure' (EU Committee 2011). While much of this conclusion proved to be accurate, it was not the case that EUPOL received little respect. Under more stable leadership, the Head of Mission could better coordinate with the EUSR following the implementation of the Lisbon Treaty in December 2009. This benefited Brigadier General Jukka Savolainen of Finland, who took over as Head of EUPOL Afghanistan in July 2010, and Police Commissioner Karl Åke Roghe of Sweden, who became Head of EUPOL Afghanistan in August 2012. Indeed, at its height in 2012, EUPOL had 350 staff members. This fell short of its 400 staff target, primarily due to Member States' hesitance in assigning personnel. Still, EUPOL officers were collectively known to 'punch above their weight in terms of influence' at, for example, the International Police Coordination Board of Afghanistan (SIGAR 2022a). EUPOL did not face a lack of respect, but rather, it was undermined by norms and perceptions. This was exposed by the European Court of Auditors, who identified that EUPOL was seen internally as a 'European effort' lacking an overarching European approach. There was a low level of intersectionality between norm circles, and therefore no set of European level collective intentions emerged within the institution. Externally, international members refused to buy into the EUPOL mission because it was seen as an attempt by EU institutions to take the lead in police development (European Court of Auditors 2015).

The accusation that EUPOL was too small and too late was a legitimate concern that came to fruition. In terms of being too small, a brief comparison between EUPOL Afghanistan with the EU mission in Kosovo is fruitful. EUPOL was the EU's second most expensive civilian mission, surpassed only by the European Union Rule of Law Mission in Kosovo (EULEX Kosovo). However, the EULEX mission started in 2008 and grew to 2,170 staff in 2012, more than six times the EUPOL staffing in the same year (European Court of Auditors 2012, 52). Geographically, Afghanistan is 60 times larger, with a population more than 20 times the size of Kosovo's. With this as a comparator, it should have been evident that EUPOL was too small to succeed and would be unable to act meaningfully within such a large-scale strategically selective context. This demonstrated a lack of European-level strategy and ambition for Afghanistan's future security.

Now, declassified reviews of EUPOL demonstrate considerable concern, by 2012, around the safety of EUPOL personnel in what was deemed to be a 'highly volatile and unstable security environment' (Council of the European Union 2016a). As one EU diplomat noted, EUPOL was primarily seen as a failure, and given its limited size and budget, it ultimately had little impact (Hassan 2023). EUPOL's mission was fine-tuned in 2014 under a revised Operation Plan, which reflected the end of Operation Enduring Freedom and the start of the Resolute Support Mission (RSM). EUPOL's mission was circumscribed to three primary areas:

1. institutional reform of the Ministry of Interior;
2. the professionalization of the ANP;
3. developing justice–police linkages.

Yet, there was an inescapable sense of retrenchment despite EU declarations of a continued commitment. In January 2015, Counsellor Pia Stjernvall was appointed the Head of Mission, having served as the deputy to this position from June 2014. The government of Finland eagerly pointed out that 'Stjernvall is the only woman to head an EU civilian crisis management mission', yet with no military or policing background, there was an impression that this was now a custodial role as EUPOL approached liquidation (Ministry of Foreign Affairs 2015). Throughout 2015, nearly all EUPOL field offices had been closed, staff had suffered fatalities from terrorist attacks and widespread activities were being ceased (Ashton 2014; Harooni and Johnson 2015). EUPOL maintained its annual budget, but its mandate was deemed to have reached its conclusion, and the EUPOL mission ended on 31 December 2016 (Council of the European Union 2016b). Unable to achieve contextual consonance and institutionalize a European set of norms, EUPOL had failed in its efforts to help build effective civilian policing.

Responding to insecurity: Af-Pak, the surge plan and the EU–Afghanistan Action Plan

The design of EUPOL did not allow contextual consonance to be achieved, because it failed to acknowledge the reality of growing insecurity on the ground. EUPOL was run parallel to a growing level of insecurity and an adapting strategically selective context. Starting its mission in 2007, EUPOL failed to acknowledge that the low-level resistance in 2002 had grown into a full-blown insurgency by 2006. Although conceived as a vital function of peacekeeping in the United Nations (UN) Brahimi Report in 2000, and driven in Afghanistan by the demands of Member States such as Germany, it is difficult to see how civilian policing norms would function as intended in an active war zone (Brahimi 2000; Shilston 2012). Indeed, as Jones demonstrated:

> During this period [2002–6], the number of insurgent-initiated attacks rose by 400 per cent, and the number of deaths from these attacks by more than 800 per cent. The increase in violence was particularly acute between 2005 and 2006 when the number of suicide attacks quintupled from 27 to 139; remotely detonated bombings more than doubled from 783 to 1,677; and armed attacks nearly tripled from 1,558 to 4,542. Insurgent-initiated attacks rose another 27 percent between 2006 and 2007. The result was a lack of security for Afghans and foreigners. (Jones 2008, 7–8)

By mid-2006, Afghanistan witnessed a marked deterioration in its security landscape, characterized by escalating terrorism, violence and a burgeoning Taliban-led insurgency. Just as local knowledge had allowed institutionalized norms of asymmetric warfare to be used against the Mughal Empire in the late 17th century, and the British in the 19th, these were now being used against the US and its NATO allies. The norm of heterogeneity once again proved a strategic advantage in fighting centralized powers, and the superior mobility of a semi-nomadic tradition proved instrumental in limiting the International Security Assistance Force (ISAF)'s regional control. This forced a gradual erosion of mobility, and just as Mughal control became limited to critical cities, this was increasingly the case of the US counterterrorism operations and ISAF (see Chapter 1). Although the modern warfare technology is vastly different in the 21st century to the 17th, technology used to uphold norms of resistance had also adapted. Tactics employed by the Afghan insurgency increasingly mirrored those seen in Iraq, particularly the growing use of improvised explosive devices (IEDs) and suicide bombings. Thus, while suicide bombings were rare until 2005, increasingly young men were drawn from madrassas across the border in Pakistan (UNAMA 2007). By 2008, a year after the establishment of EUPOL, 85 per cent of the weekly reports from the Afghan police documented attacks involving suicide bombers or IEDs. This escalation in violence was evident in the rising fatality rates affecting various groups, including US military personnel, coalition forces, contractors, members of the Afghan National Army and ANP, humanitarian workers and Afghan civilians (Gollob and O'Hanlon 2020). For Member States contributing to the ISAF, the growing insecurity was evident in a sudden rise in troop casualties. Whereas from late 2001 to 2006, all Member State fatalities totalled 44, in the following two years alone, fatalities more than doubled to 93. These were overwhelmingly British forces, who would go on to see more fatalities in Afghanistan than all other Member States combined (see Table 6.1).

With the worsening security conditions in Afghanistan, there was an increasing demand for more robust European intervention. In a notable instance during October 2009, EUSR Sequi, in his initial discussion with the European Parliament's Committee on Foreign Affairs, emphasized the necessity to reinforce EUPOL, which was already showing signs of strain. He underscored the importance of transitioning the security forces to Afghan control as a critical step towards improving the security situation on the ground. Sequi highlighted to the European Parliament that since 2007, the areas under threat had expanded, with insurgents gaining ground in regions previously deemed secure. He attributed this to the lack of an 'institutional dimension of security' and pointed out that the state's failure to provide local services enabled the Taliban's growth and influence (European Parliament 2009). Sequi correctly linked the insurgency to the preponderance of weak governance. In Afghanistan, the government's failure to deliver fundamental services, coupled with corruption, impunity and a lack of security forces capable of enforcing law and order, created an environment that the insurgency was able to exploit (Jones 2008). Poor governance was

Table 6.1: EU Member State coalition troop fatalities by country

EU Member State	2001	2002	2003	2004	2005	2006	2007	2008	2009	2010	2011	2012	2013	2014	2015	2016	2017	2018	2019	2020	2021	Total fatalities
Belgium	–	–	–	–	–	–	–	–	1	–	–	–	–	–	–	–	–	–	–	–	–	1
Croatia	–	–	–	–	–	–	–	–	–	–	–	–	–	–	–	–	–	1	–	–	–	1
Czech Republic	–	–	–	–	–	–	1	2	–	–	2	–	–	5	–	–	–	4	–	–	–	14
Denmark	–	3	–	1	–	–	6	13	7	9	3	–	1	–	–	–	–	–	–	–	–	43
Estonia	–	–	–	–	–	–	2	1	4	1	1	–	–	–	–	–	–	–	–	–	–	9
Finland	–	–	–	–	–	–	1	–	–	1	–	–	–	–	–	–	–	–	–	–	–	2
France	–	–	–	3	2	6	3	11	10	16	26	8	–	–	–	–	–	–	–	–	–	85
Germany	–	10	6	–	4	–	7	3	7	8	7	–	1	–	–	–	–	–	–	–	–	53
Hungary	–	–	–	–	–	–	–	2	–	2	3	–	–	–	–	–	–	–	–	–	–	7
Italy	–	–	–	1	2	6	2	2	9	12	8	5	1	–	–	–	–	–	–	–	–	48
Latvia	–	–	–	–	–	–	–	1	2	–	–	–	–	–	–	–	–	–	–	–	–	3
Lithuania	–	–	–	–	–	–	–	1	–	–	–	–	–	–	–	–	–	–	–	–	–	1
Netherlands	–	–	–	–	–	4	8	6	3	4	–	–	–	–	–	–	–	–	–	–	–	25
Poland	–	–	–	–	–	–	1	7	8	6	13	–	4	1	–	–	–	–	–	–	–	40
Portugal	–	–	–	–	1	–	1	–	–	–	–	–	–	–	–	–	–	–	–	–	–	2
Romania	–	–	2	–	1	1	1	3	3	6	2	–	2	–	–	2	1	1	–	–	–	25
Slovakia	–	–	–	–	–	–	–	–	–	–	–	3	3	–	–	–	–	–	–	–	–	3
Spain	–	–	–	–	18	1	4	2	1	4	4	–	–	–	–	–	–	–	–	–	–	34
Sweden	–	–	–	–	2	–	–	–	–	3	–	–	–	–	–	–	–	–	–	–	–	5

Table 6.1: EU Member State coalition troop fatalities by country (continued)

EU Member State	2001	2002	2003	2004	2005	2006	2007	2008	2009	2010	2011	2012	2013	2014	2015	2016	2017	2018	2019	2020	2021	Total fatalities
United Kingdom	–	3	–	1	1	39	42	51	108	103	46	44	9	6	3	–	–	–	–	–	–	456
Annual combined total of EU Member State fatalities	**0**	**16**	**8**	**6**	**31**	**57**	**79**	**105**	**163**	**174**	**116**	**57**	**21**	**12**	**3**	**2**	**1**	**4**	**2**	**0**	**0**	**857**

Notes: Data was derived from http://icasualties.org and cross-referenced with official national figures and newspaper reports where possible. Figures vary slightly based on the methodology of recording fatalities and the cause of death. Britain left the EU on 31 January 2020. The Member States of Austria, Bulgaria, Greece, Ireland, Luxembourg and Slovenia are excluded from the table because they suffered zero troop fatalities.

fuelling insecurity, and insurgent groups could exploit this, which fuelled further insecurity and conflict and generated a downward cycle of violence and instability.

With growing violence, newly elected President Obama, and his norm circle, sought to adapt US strategy to the changing context. This was derived in two stages that impacted the EU and its Member States. The first was announcing a new Af-Pak strategy, and the second was the announcement of a surge in US combat troops at the end of 2009. Notably, while President Obama had long opposed the war in Iraq as a 'dumb war' that sought to 'shove … [an] ideological agenda down our throats', this was not the case with Afghanistan (Obama 2002). Obama had argued on the campaign trail that while Iraq was a 'war of choice', more focus should be placed on Afghanistan as a 'war of necessity'. Obama explained:

> Our troops and our NATO allies are performing heroically in Afghanistan, but I have argued for years that we lack the resources to finish the job because of our commitment to Iraq. That's what the Chairman of the Joint Chiefs of Staff said earlier this month. And that's why, as President, I will make the fight against al Qaeda and the Taliban the top priority that it should be. This is a war that we have to win. I will send at least two additional combat brigades to Afghanistan and use this commitment to seek greater contributions – with fewer restrictions – from NATO allies. (Obama 2008)

Entering the White House, Obama quickly realized that the previous administration had not conducted an interagency assessment of Afghanistan nor considered a wider regional strategy. There had simply been no due diligence in developing a strategy that outlined the strategically selective context in an attempt to achieve greater contextual consonance. In less than a month, Bruce Riedel was appointed to assemble a team, review US policy towards Afghanistan and Pakistan, and produce a strategic review before the April 2009 NATO Summit in Strasbourg and Kehl (Fair 2010).

On 27 March 2009, Obama announced a 'comprehensive new strategy for Afghanistan and Pakistan', emphasizing the interconnectedness of the situation in both countries with global security. He acknowledged the perilous situation, with the Taliban's influence in parts of Afghanistan and Pakistan and the presence of al Qaeda. The strategy focused on disrupting, dismantling and defeating al Qaeda in both countries. It called for a stronger, smarter and comprehensive strategy, including military support, enhanced governance and economic development, focusing on training Afghan security forces. The plan also emphasized the importance of international support and partnerships and the need for responsible, accountable use of resources to support these efforts (Obama 2009b). What the 'comprehensive new strategy' did not do was evaluate the basic assumptions of international involvement in Afghanistan and question the ahistorical assumption of US policy. It was a myopic attempt to achieve contextual consonance that was ultimately flawed because it doubled down on the norms embedded in the Bonn Agreement.

Responsible for this new Af-Pak strategy, senior diplomat Richard Holbrooke was appointed the head of the Special Representative for Afghanistan and Pakistan office within the US Department of State. Soon after, the UK, France, Germany, Sweden and Denmark appointed their own Af-Pak representatives (Dirkx 2017). Indeed, NATO also stressed this more regional approach, declaring its four guiding principles of 'long-term commitment; Afghan leadership; a fully comprehensive and a regional approach' (NATO 2009b). The EU soon followed suit by altering EUSR Sequi's mandate. It was long the case that the EUSR's role was to 'encourage positive contributions from regional actors in Afghanistan and from neighbouring countries to the peace process in Afghanistan and thereby contribute to the consolidation of the Afghan State' (Council 2008). Council Joint Action enhanced this on 15 June 2009:

[T]he mandate of the European Union Special Representative for Afghanistan should be expanded to include Pakistan. … The mandate of the EUSR shall be based on the policy objectives of the European Union (EU) in Afghanistan and Pakistan, taking into account the comprehensive approach of the EU towards cross-border and wider regional cooperation. … More specifically, the EUSR shall … contribute to the implementation of the EU–Pakistan Joint Declaration, as well as the relevant UN Security Council Resolutions (UNSCRs) and other relevant UN Resolutions. (Council 2009a)

Of course, what this mandate obscured was that EU institutions had no comprehensive regional strategy and very little concrete cooperation with Pakistan. Indeed, the 2007 EU-Pakistan Joint Declaration consisted of five paragraphs interrupted by four bullet points and referred back to the 2004 Cooperation Agreement between the European Community and the Islamic Republic of Pakistan. The cooperation agreement was primarily concerned with norms around trade and commercial cooperation, development cooperation and economic cooperation (Council 2004, 2007b). Nevertheless, the EU Council explained the rationale behind the expanded role and the international debate at the time:

The conflict in Afghanistan cannot be solved without addressing the complex situation in Pakistan. The Government of Pakistan has an important role to play as a neighbour and friend of Afghanistan. Regional integration and economic cooperation must be developed while borders must be better managed and the cross-border flow of insurgents, drugs, weapons and illegal goods stopped. The situation in Afghanistan and Pakistan has a direct impact on Europe. Many of the most serious global threats facing us today are present in the region. (Council 2009b)

Strikingly, this statement did not reflect upon the EU's history of superficial engagement with Asia, a product of focusing on internal integration and European interests in their immediate neighbourhood. Notably absent from the EU's relationship with Asia was anything by way of substantive security cooperation on the issues now deemed to directly impact Europe. In its 1994 publication, *Towards a New Asia Strategy*, the European Commission highlighted the need for the EU to elevate its prioritization of Asia, emphasizing the need to bolster its regional economic footprint. This strategy underscored the importance of dialogues on arms control, non-proliferation, human rights and drug issues, particularly with India and China. Afghanistan was not a focal point of any regional strategy, even though the EU was showing humanitarian leadership at the time (European Commission 1994). In 2001, the European Commission's *Europe and Asia: A Strategic Framework for Enhanced Partnerships* acknowledged the need for further efforts, citing only modest advancements in EU–Asia relations during the 1990s (European Commission 2001). After the 11 September 2001 attacks, just days after the new strategy being released, there was no regional shift in EU-level policy. The EU's approach towards Asia remained primarily driven by trade and aid objectives, lacking in strategic bilateral and regional depth. Indeed, an independent evaluation of the EU's regional cooperation with Asia released in 2014 concluded that despite the relevance of individual programmes and projects to Asian partners, the overall strategy failed to craft a cohesive regional approach (European Commission 2014).

By late October 2009, the EU Action Plan for Afghanistan and Pakistan was approved by EU foreign ministers at the External Relations Council Meeting. The Action Plan was designed to revitalize a dedication from the EU and enhance EU-level coordination and assistance. It was intended to harmonize Member States' national-level initiatives at the civilian level with programmes in Afghanistan and Pakistan. However, the EU's more regional approach was short-lived.

With the appointment of Vygaudas Ušackas as EUSR in April 2010, the EUSR position jettisoned the oversight of Pakistan, with the position's mandate stating that the role would 'contribute to the implementation of the EU-Afghanistan Joint Declaration and lead the implementation of the EU Action Plan on Afghanistan and Pakistan, *in so far as it concerns*

Afghanistan' (Council 2010; emphasis added). This contraction of the EUSR's role, made just ten months after its inclusion, marked the cessation of the EUSR's oversight of Pakistan. This move represented a departure from the momentarily more regional Af-Pak strategy and diverged from the US strategy, which continued to uphold the Special Representative for Af-Pak. Indeed, Obama's Af-Pak strategy was supposed to compel allies, EU institutions included, into placing Afghanistan and Pakistan into a 'regional strategy'. Therefore, the EU downgrading of the Af-Pak strategy led by the EUSR in Kabul could be seen as an attempt to assert a more autonomous and independent European strategy. However, it reflected the complexities involved in integrating a broader range of voices into the policy-making process. Ušackas' mandate was to ensure the implementation of the Action Plan, harmonizing EU assistance efforts. Ultimately, the European Commission focused on enhancing the coordination of EU efforts rather than expanding to a broader regional approach. Thus, if at the end of 2006, the EU was no longer marginalized by the US and Member States, it was by the end of 2009 that there were consolidated attempts to unify an EU position (Dirkx 2017; Hassan 2023).

This attempt at creating an integrated European approach to Afghanistan was perhaps too little, too late. However, moving towards integration was necessary in advance of the Treaty of Lisbon and its associated norms coming into effect on 1 December 2009. The collective intentions of the Treaty set in motion a new institutionalization process that culminated in the establishment of the European External Action Service (EEAS) on 1 January 2011.[3] This was highly significant. Although the EUSR mandate no longer included Pakistan, the role was expanded when it merged the office of the EUSR and the Commission's Head of Delegation into a single role. This created a 'double-hatted' EUSR/Head of Delegation position. The objective was to facilitate:

A more active role of the EU in the policy dialogue with the Government of Afghanistan, matched by improved cooperation amongst the EU MS and increased capacity of the EU Missions to effectively deliver assistance. ... For the first time, the EU is combining its substantial development assistance with its growing political weight in the country. (Council 2010)

---

[3] A Council decision established the organization and functioning of the EEAS. The Council acted on a proposal from the High Representative after consulting the European Parliament and obtaining the Commission's consent. https://www.eeas.europa.eu/eeas/creation-european-external-action-service_en#8621

Accordingly, the Action Plan was a significant milestone in the EU's policy formation and recognized that efforts to resolve the conflict in Afghanistan also needed to address the complex issues faced in Pakistan, while engaging regional stakeholders in 'India, China, Russia, Iran, Turkey, Central Asian nations, Saudi Arabia and other Gulf countries, including the SCO [Shanghai Cooperation Organisation]' (Council 2009b). This may have added more complexity, but the double-hatted EUSR role demonstrated the EU's growing efforts to establish coordination, bilateral assistance and political dialogue norms.

Little more than a month after the Action Plan was announced, the Obama administration announced the second part of his plan for Afghanistan and requested contributions to his planned surge in troops. This came after a campaign by the White House, through 2009, that added significant pressure on European Member States to do more in Afghanistan. For example, with transatlantic solidarity waning, the Obama administration used the EU–US Summit in Prague and the NATO summit to make the case that instability in Afghanistan was a threat to European security (Dawar 2009; Obama 2009a). Accordingly, the objective of the troop surge, announced on 1 December 2009, was to reverse the Taliban's momentum and stabilize the country but also to share the burden with NATO allies. Thus, US troop numbers grew from approximately 30,000 in 2008 to a peak of nearly 100,000 in 2011 (Thomas et al 2021). This was accompanied by a shift from counterterrorism to a more comprehensive counterinsurgency approach. Indeed, in early 2009, ISAF was comprised of 71,000 military personnel drawn from a coalition of 42 nations. This included significant troop contributions from EU Member States, including the UK, Germany, Italy, France, the Netherlands, Poland and Spain.

As a result of the surge, Member States would contribute, albeit very unevenly, a 12 per cent increase in troop numbers to ISAF over the next two years. Indeed, Bulgaria, the Czech Republic, France, Germany, Italy, Poland, Romania, Spain and the UK primarily contributed to the European Member States' surge in troops (see Table 6.2). As a result, 2009 through 2011 would be the most dangerous years for European Member States contributing to the coalition. This overwhelmingly impacted UK troops, totalling over 56 per cent of Member State fatalities in the three bloodiest of years. Thus, despite all the momentum built up throughout 2009, as these fatalities took their toll, considerable fatigue with the war took its toll in European capitals.

Member State fatigue and the Kabul Process

Soon after Obama's surge had been announced and European powers had confirmed their commitments, it became widely acknowledged that Europe

Table 6.2: Troops committed to NATO's International Security Assistance Forces by EU Member States

EU Member State	Oct 2007	Oct 2008	Oct 2009	Nov 2010	Oct 2011	Oct 2012	Oct 2013	Nov 2014
Austria	3	1	4	3	3	3	3	1
Belgium	368	420	530	491	520	283	193	33
Bulgaria	401	460	460	516	597	572	416	319
Croatia	199	280	290	299	317	260	187	79
Czech Republic	233	415	480	468	623	422	213	228
Denmark	454	750	690	750	750	613	249	128
Estonia	128	120	150	140	159	155	160	2
Finland	85	80	165	150	156	136	100	91
France	1,073	2,730	3,095	3,850	3,932	2,418	235	89
Germany	3,155	3,310	4,365	4,341	5,000	4,737	4,400	1,318
Greece	146	130	145	80	153	12	8	8
Hungary	225	240	360	502	415	555	151	79
Ireland	7	7	7	4	7	6	7	7
Italy	2,395	2,350	2,795	3,688	3,952	4,000	2,826	1,371
Latvia	97	70	175	189	174	40	141	18
Lithuania	195	200	250	219	236	221	96	47
Luxembourg	9	9	8	9	11	10	10	0
Netherlands	1,516	1,770	2,160	242	183	500	400	30
Poland	937	1,130	1,910	2,519	2,580	1,800	1,553	310
Portugal	162	70	145	95	140	141	154	32
Romania	536	725	990	1,648	1,873	1,762	1,022	273
Slovakia	70	70	245	250	309	343	199	32
Slovenia	42	70	130	78	77	77	35	2
Spain	715	780	1,000	1,576	1,526	1,450	414	273
Sweden	340	280	430	500	500	506	259	12
United Kingdom	7,740	8,330	9,000	9,500	9,500	9,500	7,900	2,837
Total EU Member State contributions to ISAF	**21,231**	**24,797**	**29,979**	**32,107**	**33,693**	**30,522**	**21,331**	**7,619**

Notes: Data compiled from NATO Afghanistan ISAF Placemats Archive: https://www.nato.int/cps/en/natolive/107995.htm. The Member States of the Republic of Cyprus and Malta contribute zero troops in each year and have not been included in the table.

was experiencing war fatigue. By the end of 2008, the US had already suffered 630 fatalities, compared to 302 of the Member States combined (see Table 6.3). Nor was it because 2009 would become the most deadly year to date, witnessing a further 480 casualties. Rather, weakened by the 2008 global financial crisis, European powers created economic stimulus packages that grew their fiscal deficits. These deficits contributed to the 2009 Eurozone debt crisis, exposing debt and trade deficits, which threatened to collapse the single currency and, some feared, the EU itself (Tooze 2018, 93–119). The so-called PIIGS (Portugal, Italy, Ireland, Greece and Spain) were particularly affected, but there was fear of economic contagion across the Eurozone. In response to the crisis, the imposition of deep-cutting austerity measures transformed an economic crisis into a political crisis, with reduced public spending, rising unemployment and economic recessions leading to political protests. Indeed, the Greek government collapsed in the autumn of 2009, and a new Panhellenic Socialist Movement (PASOK) government was formed (Verney 2014). This was the first, but certainly not the last, European government to fall because of the crisis, but there was a 'de-Europeanisation' of Greek foreign policy (Raimundo et al 2021). Herein, Obama's request for additional commitments in Afghanistan was poorly timed. The prevailing mood in Europe was retrenchment and not increased commitments abroad.

With the Eurozone crisis colouring the European milieu, along with mounting casualties, European governments were under considerable pressure from their citizens and parliaments to bring military involvement in Afghanistan to an end. This was unquestionably evident with the collapse of the Dutch coalition government in February 2010, after the two largest parties failed to agree on withdrawing Dutch troops from the Task Force Uruzgan mission in southern Afghanistan (Dimitriu and de Graaf 2010; Dombey et al 2010). The Dutch were not alone in no longer wishing to place their troops in harm's way. Britain, France and Germany put pressure on the UN to organize an international conference in January 2010. Held in London, the conference was publicized as an international attempt to renew commitments towards Afghanistan's security, prosperity and democracy. A plan for the 'Afghanization' of the conflict emerged by transitioning security from NATO to the Afghan leadership over the next five years (Borger 2010). Henceforth, there was the gestating plan allowing European troops to withdraw. This was coupled with the GOA's commitment to construct a peace plan. As President Karzai declared, the GOA was to '[o]ffer an honourable place in society to those willing to renounce violence, participate in the free and open society and respect the principles that are enshrined in the Afghan constitution, cut ties with al-Qaeda and other terrorist groups, and pursue their political goals peacefully' (Foreign and Commonwealth Office 2010).

The London Conference was, therefore, a crucial moment in shaping the norms within the two-tiered framework of the 'Kabul Process'. The process began with the Afghan Government's Consultative Peace Jirga (CPJ) on 2–4 June 2010. Brought together under the banner of 'Those who love peace will support the peace jirga', representatives from across Afghanistan were drawn from multiple stakeholders in government and civil society (Clark 2010a, 2010b). The Jirga was intended to provide a platform for Afghan citizens to express their opinions on integration and reconciliation. As a result, participants formulated a declaration appealing for insurgents to cease hostilities and initiate negotiation processes. It also provided the GOA with the mandate to pursue peace and reconciliation and establish a High Peace Council (HPC) to facilitate the implementation of these initiatives. The HPC was created in September 2010 with 70 members, predominantly consisting of former jihadi commanders, Provincial Peace Committees and a Joint Secretariat, and chaired by former president and Jamiat leader Burhanuddin Rabbani (Clark 2018).

In addition to the CPJ, the Afghan Peace and Reintegration Programme (APRP) was announced at the Kabul Conference held on 20 July 2010. The HPC would be a key element of the APRP throughout its intended three phases. First, *Social Outreach, Confidence-Building, and Negotiation* involving community engagement and grievance resolution. Second, *Demobilization*, entailing assessment, vetting, weapon management and potential humanitarian aid. Third, the *Consolidation of Peace*, focusing on community-specific recovery options, varying in access and needs. These were to be focused on provinces such as Helmand, Kandahar, Nangarhar, Khost, Baghlan, Badghis, Kunduz and Herat in the first instance (Foreign and Commonwealth Office 2010). Ultimately, however, as Quie's (2013) research illustrated, the multifaceted nature of the insurgency, coupled with communication deficiencies within and among international and local stakeholders, significantly impeded the APRP initiative. What became abundantly apparent as the APRP moved forward, was that there was a tension between pursuing the APRP and promoting democracy, demonstrating the widely detailed tensions between peacebuilding and democracy assistance (see Call and Cook 2003). Indeed, explorations of amnesties and power-sharing were met with the Taliban renewing its campaign against the government and the assassination of Burhanuddin Rabbani on 20 September 2011.

The second tier of the Kabul Process, announced at the Kabul Conference, was a military transition, whereby the GOA would take responsibility for security development and reconstruction. Accordingly, at the NATO Summit in Lisbon in November 2010, a consensus with the Afghan government was reached on the transfer of complete security responsibility in Afghanistan from ISAF to Afghan forces by the end of 2014. This was to be a gradual transition launched in 2011, allowing for surge troops to be withdrawn by 2012 as Afghan security forces filled the vacuum. Indeed, by early 2012, the GOA and the US signed the Strategic Partnership Agreement laying out the bilateral relationship between the two states. At the May NATO summit in Chicago, an agreement was reached for the future funding for Afghanistan's security, a plan for troop withdrawal and the longer-term presence of NATO to assist in Afghanistan's transformational decade (Obama 2012). This was followed up in July at the Tokyo conference, which brought international actors together to agree on the levels of development support needed through 2017 (Ministry of Foreign Affairs of Japan 2012).

Accordingly, in late 2012, France withdrew combat troops, ending its battlefield role, and throughout the drawdown phase in 2013, Belgium, the Czech Republic, Hungary, Lithuania and Slovenia halved their troop commitments (see Table 6.2). This followed the *Inteqal*, the Dari and Pashtu word for transition, a process comprising five stages of Afghan provinces and districts being handed over to Afghan forces, coordinated by the Joint Afghan-NATO Inteqal Board. The fifth and final transition occurred on 18 June 2013, whereby NATO handed over the security responsibilities of a final tranche of 11 provinces to Afghan forces (NATO 2022b). This paved the way for the start of RSM on 1 January 2015, which aimed to continue training, advising and assisting the Afghan security forces and institutions. Indeed, over the next seven years, Member States would contribute approximately 30 per cent of all RSM committed troops until 2020, and peak at 42 per cent of RSM committed troops in 2021. This was a combined annual average of 4,500 troops to RSM (see Table 6.4).

The impact of the Lisbon Treaty and the elements for a European Union strategy in Afghanistan

The Lisbon Treaty significantly enhanced the EU's approach to Afghanistan, setting in motion a more successful phase in EU engagement and political dialogue. The institutionalization of the EEAS was a key development, which, combined with the double-hatted EUSR position and the 2009 Action Plan, acted as a force multiplier for EU coordination and action. As one EEAS officer interviewed for this research explained: "With the Lisbon Treaty, we became a standalone diplomatic actor ... it's something EU officials value more than the outside world." Indeed, another went further to explain that:

'In the middle of this effort to bring stability, democracy and peace and prosperity to Afghanistan, the EAS added an additional player, able to coordinate the EU Member States presence on the ground. Now EU member states and institutions, implementing ideas put forward politically by Member States, were able to play a bigger role.'

Table 6.3: US, UK and EU Member State coalition troop fatalities by year

	2001	2002	2003	2004	2005	2006	2007	2008	2009	2010	2011	2012	2013	2014	2015	2016	2017	2018	2019	2020	2021	Total fatalities
US	12	49	48	52	99	98	117	155	317	498	415	310	128	55	22	13	15	14	24	11	13	2,465
UK	–	3	–	1	1	39	42	51	108	103	46	44	9	6	3	–	–	–	–	–	–	456
Other EU Member State	–	13	8	5	30	18	37p	54	55	71	70	13	12	6	–	2	1	4	2	–	–	401
Total EU Member State fatalities	–	16	8	6	31	57	79	105	163	174	116	57	21	12	3	2	1	4	2	–	–	857
Total fatalities by year	12	65	56	58	130	155	196	260	480	672	531	367	149	67	25	15	16	18	26	11	13	3,322

Source: Data from Table 6.1, with additional US information from http://icasualties.org

Table 6.4: Troops committed to NATO's Resolute Support Mission, EU Member States, US and other contributing nations

	2015	2016	2017	2018	2019	2020	2021
EU Member States	4,021	3,883	4,165	4,775	5,962	4,980	4,029
US	6,827	6,954	6,941	8,475	8,475	8,000	2,500
Other contributing nations	2,351	1,976	2,226	2,373	2,597	3,571	3,063
Total	**13,199**	**12,813**	**13,332**	**15,623**	**17,034**	**16,551**	**9,592**

Source: https://www.nato.int/cps/en/natolive/107995.htm

At the global international society level, the Lisbon Treaty provided the EU with full legal personality, allowing the EU to become more of a strategic actor in external action. The EU could now sign international treaties in areas of its attributed powers and join international organizations. The Treaty removed the intergovernmental structure of the three pillars, while compelling Member States to limit signing international agreements to only those compatible with EU law (Blockmans and Wessel 2009; Ziller 2019). This had a gradual impact on the EU's collective action in Afghanistan, as elucidated by an EEAS officer:

> [Initially] the EU presence on the ground was always spread out across different boroughs. For a long time, we had a police mission. We had an EU delegation that was responsible for economic assistance. And then we had an EU Special Representative since 2002, that was helping with political reporting and unifying member states. This was the case for a long time. Three different operations, three separate offices within Kabul; one office having the money, the other having the policeman, and another having the political influence. So, the idea was always to consolidate these different roles. And once the Lisbon Treaty was ratified, you know, the delegations also became functional embassies. Legally, that meant that the head of delegation had ambassador-like functions. (Hassan 2023, 46)

After a decade of attempting state-building in Afghanistan, the EU now possessed new institutional capacities. This institutional change was significant because the High Representative for Foreign Affairs and Security Policy, combined with a European diplomatic service, laid out new norms for greater European integration, more effective coordination, and, between 2015 and 2017, more effective EU leadership in Afghanistan. Furthermore, combining the Office of the EUSR and the Commission delegation also allowed for more effective EU representation in Afghanistan, for example, preventing confusion over two EU officials participating in Afghanistan's

Joint Coordination and Monitoring Board (Dirkx 2017). As new norms embedded themselves within institutional changes, and the ISAF mission came to a close, the EU was able to develop the most concise articulation of EU strategy throughout the 20 years of engagement.

To better coordinate EU institutions and Member States' civilian engagements, the new *Elements for an EU Strategy in Afghanistan 2014–16*, communicated in April 2014, provided the clearest, boldest and most succinct articulation of EU strategy to date. Repeated and underlined within the document, the EU Council confirmed that 'the overarching strategic goal of the EU's future role in Afghanistan should be the development of Afghanistan's institutions to provide the resilience needed to safeguard progress to date and provide a countrywide platform for a more effective and ultimately sustainable Afghan state' (Council 2014). Underpinning the EU strategy were international frameworks, particularly the Tokyo Mutual Accountability Framework (TMAF), which provided the wider international community and GOA with a donor agreement for the transformational decade 2014–2024. Herein lay an important crystallization within EU strategy: a new emphasis on 'systemic reform' to enable 'progress in Afghanistan'.

To achieve systemic reform the EU appealed to four sets of norms to focus its collective intentions. First, 'promoting peace, stability and security in the region'; second, reinforcing democracy; third, encouraging economic and human development; and finally, 'fostering the rule of law and respect for human rights, in particular the rights of women and children' (Council 2014). These were certainly not a new set of normative commitments. For the EU institutions they were to provide greater directional clarity and allow the EU to 'focus its efforts in areas in which it adds most value' and allow it to 'take into account the regional dimension and maintain the flexibility to respond appropriately to potential changes in Afghanistan' (Council 2014).

With a critical lens, it is apparent that this simply did not provide a systemic evaluation of the issues Afghanistan faced. It was a reiteration of what the EU and other global international society actors had been trying to accomplish over the previous decade. Norms of global international society had been reiterated as if they were going to gain more traction in the second decade of the conflict than they did the first. Yet, it is difficult to provide a rationale for why greater contextual consonance would result from doing the same practices again and expecting different results. The asserted norms lacked any contextual adjustments that would reconcile normative tensions within Afghanistan. Nevertheless, the EU would briefly have a more successful period. Indeed, following the *Elements for an EU Strategy*, the EU would have the most successful and high-profile period of engagement with Afghanistan since the 1990s. However, this was not because of the *Elements for an EU Strategy*, but a result of the US beginning to disengage from Afghanistan and undermining EU integration. As the norm of transatlantic solidarity began to dissipate, the EU was able to become a more significant and strategic actor.

EU efforts to promote peace and stability

The *Elements for an EU Strategy in Afghanistan 2014–16* aimed to promote peace, stability and security in the region. As such, the EU was externally projecting a commitment to embracing a role in peacebuilding. This was necessary because, as a workshop for the European Parliament's Committee on Foreign Affairs noted in early 2014:

> ISAF had been involved in increasingly more intensive combat operations in southern and eastern Afghanistan. Despite these efforts, the Taliban, al-Qaeda and factional warlords have effectively carved out mini-caliphates for themselves beyond the control of the central government and outside the reach of international troops and donor organisations. Anno 2013 Afghanistan is a fragmented country. (Blockmans et al 2014, 11)

With the APRP still operating along a two-tier reintegration and reconciliation pillar, the GOA operated an Afghan-led peacebuilding process. Indeed, EU Member States Denmark, Germany, Italy, Spain and the Netherlands were key donors, with funds handled by the GOA. Overall, the scheme successfully reintegrated 11,074 insurgents and their commanders and mobilized nationwide debate about peace through coordination, engagement and outreach in communities. From 1 August 2010 to 31 March 2016, APRP received a total of USD 140 million in donor contributions (UNDP 2017). There were core problems with APRP, not least in APRP funds themselves, which helped to fuel corruption further. The absence of a comprehensive peace agreement significantly undermined reintegration programmes, especially those targeting Taliban fighters, and illustrated the problems of reintegrating ex-combatants during active insurgency. None of the reintegration programmes significantly weakened the Taliban insurgency or contributed meaningfully to reconciliation efforts (SIGAR 2019). More widely, there were serious issues with insufficient security for those reintegrated and APRP staff and members. This was exacerbated by increases in insurgency activities and attacks, and further complicated with the emergence of the Islamic State of Iraq and Syria (ISIS) inside Afghanistan. Herein, there were concerns throughout its operation that Afghanistan's political leadership was neither committed to nor invested in APRP, which undermined the programme (UNDP 2017).

There were similar concerns about the GOA's indifference to the reconciliation pillar, whereby at the national level, talks with the Taliban were always kept open but unable to turn into meaningful action. That talks remained open was unsurprising. The heterarchical norms of Afghanistan's sociopolitical landscape is characterized by fluid, often ambiguous fault lines, where adversaries frequently maintain multifaceted connections through tribal, historical or personal ties (see Bijlert 2010). These complex relationships enabled a unique dynamic of negotiation and influence, transcending conventional opposition, but were never able to create a tipping point towards successful Afghan-led peace. This was despite several trust-building mechanisms, including key measures such as releasing Taliban prisoners, removing UN sanctions and blacklists against former members, and creating a political platform for their participation in mainstream politics. Additionally, the strategy included allowing Taliban representatives to engage in track two diplomacy and offering them non-elected roles within the state's power structure. These steps aimed to transition the Taliban from armed opposition to political stakeholders, which was integral to achieving peace and stability in Afghanistan, but ultimately failed to produce a comprehensive peace agreement (Safi 2014).

In this context, the EU's involvement in peacebuilding efforts stands out. In September 2016, the GOA and Hezb-e Islami Gulbuddin (HIG) finalized a landmark peace agreement. This process, initiated in 2008, was lauded as 'historic' by the US government upon its conclusion. The GOA viewed this agreement as a potential template for future negotiations with the Taliban. Initially, the US was reticent to talk with HIG and its leader, Gulbuddin Hekmatyar, 'the Butcher of Kabul', and thus played a limited role in the negotiations. During the Soviet–Afghan War, HIG emerged as one of the most prominent resistance factions against the Soviet occupation. However, following the Soviet withdrawal and the subsequent Afghan civil wars, HIG became embroiled in factional fighting and gained a reputation for human rights abuses. By 2010, HIG emerged as the second-largest group of insurgents (Osman 2013). However, the breakthrough came when HIG consented to disarm, disband and sever ties with terrorist and illegal armed groups, leading to Hekmatyar's removal from the UN sanctions list and his return to Kabul in May 2017. Significantly, EUSR Mellbin played a crucial role in this process, acting on behalf of the EU and intervening at critical junctures to prevent the collapse of the peace deal (Hassan 2023). Indeed, his role included providing 'constructive input on wording of several articles of the final agreement', helping maintain dialogue and bringing 'the deal over the finish line' (Johnson 2018). At one point in the negotiations, there was discussion of having the EU monitor the agreement's implementation, which helped push the parties towards an agreement, even though this was not adopted. Negotiators for HIG and the GOA didn't want the outward acknowledgement of the international community's involvement to detract from the deal being sold to Afghans more widely. If this was to be a larger model to encourage the Taliban, international involvement would undermine this; the Taliban had long rejected the international support of a 'puppet regime' and used this as a reason not to fully engage with a peace process.

The EU's involvement in the peace deal between the GOA and HIG is significant. EUSR Mellbin was able to demonstrate an astute understanding of the strategically selective context and formulate a strategy with considerable contextual consonance. For the EU, it demonstrated an ability to engage in a significant peacebuilding exercise and the importance of having a double-hatted EUSR capable of operating reactively inside Afghanistan while coordinating European-level efforts. This was operationally significant for the EU. However, a US lessons learned process identified the US government's non-opposition to the peace process with HIG as a key factor in the successful conclusion of the agreement (SIGAR 2019). The systemic importance of this in the global international system is worth noting. The absence of US marginalization facilitated EU external action; European success was achieved when the absence of American hegemony facilitated EU autonomy. Within the EU, what is notable about this episode was that it was controversial with some policy makers inside the EEAS. The episode demonstrated the tension between norms of peacemaking and a normative commitment to human rights. One senior EU diplomat argued that it was this tension that led to there being little acknowledgement of this achievement within EU institutions itself. Norm circles committed to universal human rights and retributive justice were in tension with the more pragmatic norm circles committed to peacemaking and dialogue. Although these are not necessarily in tension, there was little intersectionality between these two norm circles within the EU.[4]

The Brussels Conference in October 2016 marked a significant continuation of the EU's peace-making efforts in Afghanistan. Under the theme of 'prosperity and peace', representatives from over a hundred states and international bodies attended to reaffirm their sustained commitment to Afghanistan. For the EU, this was needed to confirm its long-term commitment in a period of declining global focus on the country. Indeed, the focus of global international society on Afghanistan had begun to wane, and this was the EU's attempt to reignite collective intentions. The Brussels Conference successfully secured renewed commitments and attention towards Afghanistan. The international community pledged to uphold EUR 13.6 billion in development aid, with the EU and its Member States contributing nearly EUR 5 billion, accounting for almost 40 per cent of

---

[4] Conducting interviews with EU policy makers, this author's overwhelming impression was that this tension still exists, and there continues to be antagonism over this issue within the EU.

this total. Moreover, building on prior mutual accountability frameworks, first introduced in 2012 with the TMAF and the 2015 Self-Reliance through Mutual Accountability Framework, the Brussels Conference identified 24 'SMART' objectives for 2017 and 2018.[5] This framework established a robust foundation for Afghanistan's self-reliance, incorporating a comprehensive approach to governance, economic stability, gender equality and institutional reforms (Brussels Conference 2016). Ultimately, it was acknowledged that Afghanistan's developmental progress hinged on continued international support, and donors committed to supporting Afghanistan's national budget through 2020. This involved pledges to cover about 69 per cent of the country's USD 6.5 billion fiscal budget for the year through grants (SIGAR 2017). Additionally, the conference featured high-level discussions on women's empowerment and regional cooperation, including a keynote speech by First Lady Rula Ghani at the 'Empowered Women, Prosperous Afghanistan' event. The GOA agreed to greater reporting of these issues through National Action Plan reports (Hassan 2023).

With regard to peacebuilding, the Afghanistan National Peace and Development Framework (ANPDF) was introduced, replacing the ANDS that expired in 2013. The document overwhelmingly prioritized the need to accelerate and consolidate development initiatives. Yet, the ANPDF made clear that much of its economic and development was contingent on 'the prospects for achieving peace and reconciliation … [because] until Afghanistan has peace, large scale new private investment is unlikely … [and] the prospects for peace are the spectres that shadow all development' (Islamic Republic of Afghanistan 2016). For the EU, co-hosting the Brussels Conference, the declared expectations were that the narrative would change from 'winning the war to winning the peace' as 'regional actors take more responsibility for Afghanistan's peace and stability' (Mellbin 2016). Indeed, while the focus was on development, it was confirmed that 'Brussels will help align our [EU] collective political, security, economic, development and regional efforts towards building the conditions for a lasting peace in Afghanistan' (Mellbin 2016).

At first glance, the HIG peace agreement and the Brussels Conference seemed remarkably successful compared to the EU's previous efforts. These events represented significant EU milestones in pursuing peace and stability, showcasing a commitment to diplomatic solutions and international cooperation. However, a senior EU diplomat's insight suggests a more nuanced reality. While ceremonially lauded, the Brussels Conference was marred by an increasing lack of international engagement after the event, indicating a gap between its perceived success and the underlying interest of

---

5 SMART stands for Specific, Measurable, Achievable, Realistic and Time-bound.

global international society. In 2017, there was a notable shift in the approach of both the US and the EU regarding their stated objective of securing an Afghan-led negotiated peace settlement. A senior EU diplomat provided further clarification on this shift in approach, offering insights that shed light on the underlying reasons and implications of this strategic reorientation after the Brussels Conference:

> We also had this extraordinary first regional meeting. All the key stakeholders in the neighbourhood on Afghan peace. There was a peace which is about the Afghans agreeing. And then there's the peace with the externals. Especially Pakistan and Iran. Of course, but also China [and] India. The USA and EU hosted. You have the north-south dichotomy between China and India to a certain extent. Russia played a role but it was more marginal. I mean, there were all kinds of intersections. We got people together at a very high level. And so, there was on that level also a foundation to go for peace. The Americans said they were not ready to sit down at the conference and open the door for peace talks. On the final day, John Kerry said the USA was willing to discuss peace talks with the Taliban. It was a breakthrough – there was optimism. But the reality afterwards was it fell apart quickly from there. Clearly, the political will for peace did not exist. (Hassan 2023, 51)

Pushed on the EU's role, it was reported that the 'the [Commission and the] EEAS wasn't ready for peace. Nobody was ready for peace. Nobody wanted to upset the Americans'. This was highly problematic, as it revealed an abandonment of EU autonomy even when it was clearly in the EU's and Member States' stated interests to pursue peace in Afghanistan. Nevertheless, the US effectively standing in the way of a comprehensive peace was reinforced in US lessons learned exercises carried out by the Office of the Special Inspector General for Afghanistan Reconstruction: 'US government decisions in Afghanistan helped ensure there would be no peace ... refus[ing] opportunities to reconcile with the defeated Taliban. It declined to implement an inclusive, post-conflict peace process, so the Taliban soon rebuilt itself as a powerful insurgency' (SIGAR 2021).

As accounted in a study for the EU Parliament, in early 2017, the EU faced internal deliberations over the strategic course of its policy in Afghanistan. A pronounced division arose among the EUSR office, the EEAS and the Member States. The central disagreement revolved around a strategic choice: whether to focus on a peacebuilding strategy to address the growing insurgency or to continue with a state-building approach, supporting established partners while avoiding further upheaval. The strategic choice being presented was whether to prioritize peacebuilding or development in the sequencing of EU policy. The latter was chosen because the EU 'bureaucracy had its own track', and the Commission's aid strategy was a 'big ship' which was unable to 'adapt'. Indeed, the Commission was negotiating what became the 2017 EU-Afghanistan Cooperation Agreement on Partnership and Development and was unwilling to explore a peace agreement that diminished cooperation with the GOA (Hassan 2023). As the former EU ambassador to Pakistan asserted, 'EU colleagues were not listening and not reading the reports about the deterioration'; therefore, development was prioritized over security. As another EU official confirmed, the Commission failed to recognize 'realistic strategic options'; 'the EU wasted several years, and then the Americans started the peace process' (Hassan 2023, 52). Thus, 2017 presented an opportunity for the EU to reassess its strategy and try to align it with the strategically selective context. It proved unable to undertake this task, and as a result a policy that was demonstrating considerable contextual dissonance was maintained. The failure to adapt to a complex environment ultimately proved fatal and resulted in EU policy failing in Afghanistan.

In large part, much of the doubt EU officials expressed when interviewed for this research related not only to the prioritization of development over security but also to the prioritization of the GOA as a legitimate international partner. Most notably, there was a sharp divide within and between EU institutions regarding the importance of democratic elections. Ultimately, national elections were a product of the Bonn Process and were intended to confer legitimacy to a new Afghan government. Yet, this was never the case, and national elections proved insufficient to provide the government with legitimacy (Lierl 2021). Indeed, the Commission had been assisting with the development of governance, the rule of law and elections, from 2002, and Afghanistan had become a beneficiary of the European Instrument for Democracy and Human Rights.[6] In addition, the Commission provided funds for the UN's electoral support and Election Observation Missions (EOM). For example, while an EOM was not sent to the first presidential election in 2004, which Hamid Karzai won with 55.4 per cent of the vote, the EU did dispatch an EOM in the 2005 parliamentary and provincial council elections. In 2009, another EOM was dispatched as Afghanistan conducted its presidential election, with the primary contenders being incumbent President Karzai and his main challenger, Abdullah Abdullah. However, this election was widely seen as flawed, with widespread reports of irregularities. Indeed, the EOM report was acutely critical of the election,

---

[6] This was the successor to the European Initiative for Democracy and Human Rights, which ran from 2000 to 2006 and was started in 1994 by the European Parliament.

having calculated that 1.6 million votes were 'suspect or fraudulent, the vast majority of which were for Mr Karzai' (EUEOM 2009). Indeed, with the announcement of a runoff election, Dr Abdullah declared his withdrawal, citing a lack of transparency and independent checks and balances to allow an election to be held. This significantly undermined the legitimacy of the Karzai government (Dorronsoro 2009).

The 2014 presidential election fared much better. The Taliban were increasing the ferociousness of their attacks to delegitimize the government and strategically position themselves for potential peace talks with the GOA in Qatar. Similarly, the elections were marred by widespread corruption and inconclusive results, necessitating a second round between Abdullah Abdullah and Ashraf Ghani. The results remained unresolved in the subsequent voting phase, prompting electoral authorities to initiate a recount followed by an audit. This culminated in a deadlock. The impasse was eventually resolved on 21 September 2014, with the two contenders reaching a consensus to establish a National Unity Government (Jalali 2015). Ashraf Ghani would become president and Abdullah Abdullah the chief executive officer, marking the first peaceful transfer of power in Afghanistan's modern history. For some within the EU, and despite the collapse of the GOA in 2021, the 2014 presidential election remains an important milestone. As one senior EU diplomat stressed at length:

Democracy gained a lot during the time that we were there. We had an amazing situation. There is absolutely no doubt that Afghans turned out in very large numbers to elect the government that became the coalition government between President Ghani and Doctor Abdullah. Yes, it wasn't a great government, and the elections were flawed. But the elections were very, very interesting from a democratic point of view. They created a new political reality in Afghanistan. And that's what democracy does; it changes where the power is. So, if you look before the elections, as much as they were chaotic, neither has a strong indigenous power base. Then you have elections happening ... the vote gave them legitimacy to become the rulers of the country. And that is democratic success. ... I hear a lot of people discounting this. ... I think it's a very dangerous thing to say, you know, democracy didn't play a role or was discounted in Afghanistan, or the Afghans didn't care. This is simply untrue. And we know it's untrue because we saw it happen ... [it was a] democratic triumph. ... Mr Ghani and Doctor Abdullah were the two people the Afghan people voted for. This is completely uncontested. So, the two people that the Afghans wanted to lead the country came into power. Got legitimacy, got political power through the vote. (Hassan 2023, 41)

Significantly, the tensions over how strongly the GOA should be supported were symptomatic of the growing conflict within EU institutions. As the practices between state-building, development and peacebuilding began to create tensions, the intersectionality between norm circles within EU institutions began to fracture. This was acutely the case between the Office of the EUSR and the EEAS, which was carried over to tensions with EU member states. In early 2017, the conflict between norm circles resulted in a downgrading of EU policy in Afghanistan.

The European Union downgrading the European Union Special Representative to Special Envoy

With 2016 being the highwater mark of EU engagement in Afghanistan, 2017 brought with it a striking difference; and highlighted the inherent dilemma of prioritizing development over peace. This was made evident in two contrasting events: the signing of the EU-Afghanistan Cooperation Agreement on Partnership and Development, symbolizing a commitment to development and collaboration, and, in stark contrast, a major explosion in Kabul, targeting the German Embassy. As one of the deadliest since 2001, this attack on a Member State killed 90 people and wounded 461 others. These incidents underscored the complex and often conflicting nature of pursuing development goals in the context of ongoing violence and instability. For some EU policy makers, the German Embassy bombing was a significant turning point for EU policy. It was explained that:

> [A]s a result of this attack, most diplomatic missions were significantly downgraded. At the time we [the EU] were trying to establish a different sort of diplomatic presence … our presence in Afghanistan was significantly reduced because of the security [situation] … five or six people in the delegation was not enough to do proper reporting or be engaged with the government on the reform agenda. (Hassan 2023, 52)

Thus, growing insecurity, disengagement from peacebuilding and a failure to tackle corruption ultimately caught up with EU policy and prevented effective development cooperation and diplomacy.

It was not, however, just events inside Afghanistan that were causing a downgrading and disengagement in Afghanistan. Internally, a growing inertia and policy battle was being played between the Office of the EUSR and Delegation in Kabul and the Commission in Brussels. The first signs of this internal conflict appeared with the Foreign Affairs Council's request to update the 2014–2016 EU Strategy for Afghanistan. Through a Joint Communication document, it was made clear that the 2014–2016 EU

Strategy would not have an impact assessment carried out, and a new strategy would 'mostly update and enhance the existing EU strategy'. There was no appetite for a full evaluation to be carried out, which was a missed opportunity. As the UK's European Scrutiny Committee responded: 'While many of its objectives may be straightforward, their means of delivery are not. Given the deteriorating security and economic situation in the country, the priorities set by the Commission and the EEAS seem highly ambitious' (FCO 2017).

Moreover, the Joint Communication stated that its main source of information would be through the missions, delegation reports and implementation reports. Yet, serious tensions were demonstrated between the Office of the EUSR and the EEAS. A senior EU diplomat recalled, 'I remember that paper, I was quite disgusted when I got a draft', and although written feedback was provided, it was subsequently edited out, whereby staff on the ground in Kabul later concluded that 'I'm not going to touch it' (interview with author). Indeed, an anecdote about the tensions was given to this author to provide insight into the relationship:

> I'll give you an anecdote which I think is very telling about, you know, [about] what happened ... because it was a shocking experience to me. We're sitting at a meeting and there's some very high-end people involved and we're talking about Afghanistan. ... We start talking about where a lot of the Member States are and where they want to go. And then somebody says 'who gives a f★★k what the Member States want'. This was the exact language 'who gives a f★★k what the Member States want'. (Hassan 2023, 47)

Similar reports were provided over EUSR engagement on issues of corruption, where the EEAS were at odds with confronting the GOA, which was in tension with EU delegations in the region and the Member States, highlighting the connections between the insurgency, corruption, drug production and the wider illicit economy.

As a result of tensions between norm circles, there was a downgrading of the EU's policy towards Afghanistan. This manifested itself in the EUSR 'double-hatted' position being abandoned. Indeed, norm circles do not just endorse and enforce, they also punish. There was animosity between the Asia Directorate and the final EUSR for Afghanistan Ambassador Mellbin, who had been very effective in steering EU policy in 2015–16. However, it was felt that because the EUSR could circumvent the system and go 'directly' to HR/VP Mogherini, the position needed to be downgraded to the level of EU Special Envoy. Having demonstrated the ability to achieve greater contextual consonance and calibrate EU policy to the strategically selective context, the EUSR role was to be abandoned because of the tensions this caused.

The EU Special Envoy role is embedded within the EEAS, reporting directly to the directorate. As a senior EU diplomat explained, this was an 'internal trick'. It was counterintuitive given the EU's policy momentum established through 2016, whereby EUSR Mellbin steered the EU through its most successful period. This was not just an inconsequential bureaucratic reshuffle. The downgraded Special Envoy position deprived the Member States of a 'privileged channel' at the Political and Security Committee and fragmented a coherent line of intelligence reporting (Hassan 2023). As one senior EU diplomat recalled:

> [I]t was a big advantage to have the EUSR mandate, but it frustrated the EEAS a lot. And that's also why they killed it … they [took] the EUSR position back and [got] a bureaucrat to do that work. Then what happens when you split it? The EU becomes nobody. It happened immediately… they should have kept the structure. (Hassan 2023, 48)

EUSR Mellbin was replaced in August 2017. In his place, Roland Kobia was appointed as a new Special Envoy and would work with the nominated Head of the European Union Delegation in Afghanistan, Mr Pierre Mayaudon (EEAS 2017).

Abandoning the norm of transatlantic solidarity

The weakening of the EU's role in Afghanistan was compounded by the Trump administration's August 2017 announcement of a 'new Afghan strategy'. This added pressure on Pakistan to enhance its counterterrorism measures while increasing pressure on the Taliban to enter comprehensive peace negotiations with the GOA. The US was removing any preconditions for peace talks between the Taliban and the GOA, with Secretary of State Rex Tillerson arguing that 'the Government of Afghanistan and the Taliban representatives need to sit down and sort this out. It's not for the U.S. to tell them it must be this particular model; it must be under these conditions'. The Trump administration was keen to get a 'political settlement' to the conflict and withdraw its commitment to Afghanistan. Simultaneously, the US began to consider proposals to broaden RSM and deploy additional ground forces because it became clear that the Taliban were advancing. The GOA's geographical areas of control were diminishing in what General John Nicholson, Commander of U.S. Forces–Afghanistan, was openly declaring as a 'stalemate'. Indeed, echoing EUSR Vendrell ten years earlier, General Nicholson had determined that 'We believe that the Taliban, in some ways, have evolved into a criminal or narco-insurgency'. Over time, international unity was weakened, exacerbated by growing transatlantic tensions between the Trump administration and European capitals. By July 2018, the Trump administration had entered into direct negotiations with the Taliban without consultation or representation from the GOA. This action not only reversed the long-held international position that all peace should be 'Afghan-owned and Afghan-led' but also abandoned a cornerstone of the US-initiated war on terror.

National Security Presidential Directives (NSPD-9) set out that there was to be no distinction between terrorists and those that harboured them, a proposition that helped justify the war in Afghanistan in 2001. The Trump administration made exactly that distinction, ending a central principle of US policy that had been in place for 17 years. In September 2018, Ambassador Zalmay Khalilzad was appointed as Special Representative for Afghanistan Reconciliation and, by January 2019, declared that 'The Taliban have committed, to our satisfaction, to do what is necessary that would prevent Afghanistan from ever becoming a platform for international terrorist groups or individuals'. With this confirmation, it became clear that the US was preparing for a full withdrawal. Special Envoy Kobia subsequently stated that 'we need to be ready. ... This diplomatic and political activity has created totally new dimensions you never know – it could take long, or it can go fast' (Mashal and Nordland 2019). This was a tacit admission that the EU was not being updated or consulted about events in Doha. As one EU official set out:

> I haven't seen European Union institutions being consulted by the Americans or the Taliban on what to do in Doha. I haven't seen any document or analysis of the additional annexes of the Doha agreement. So, in that respect, my answer is the European Union when we look at the EU situations was not consulted, whether one or two other member states were consulted about the process, you have to go to Member States. (Interview with author)

Another EU official confirmed this situation:

> [O]n the peace process, and on talking with the Taliban, I think the US always kept a close hold on that. There wasn't much sharing or consultation on that particular issue area. There were a few countries that were more in the know than others, like Germany or Norway, for example, the UK with extensive contacts, but the EU was never really part of the club. (Interview with author)

While conducted discreetly in 2019, Special Envoy Kobia has confirmed that there were separate talks with the Taliban and the EU (Kobia 2022). The Taliban spokesperson confirmed one such meeting in May 2019. This places the overall timeframe of EU engagement with the Taliban after Khalilzad's

12 March 2019, announcement that an agreement 'in the draft' had been made but considerably before the September 2019 presidential election and the 29 February 2020 signing of the Doha Agreement.

Special Envoy Kobia described talking to the Taliban as a very difficult lesson for the EU to learn but stated that a wider lesson needs to be taken away from this process: 'As somebody who's been involved in peace processes and peace talks for over 20 years, if I have learnt one thing, it is that you need to talk to everyone. … I think at a certain time you need a change of paradigm' (Kobia 2022). Indeed, it is now with regret that several EU officials interviewed for a parliamentary study confirm that a mistake was made in not engaging the Taliban earlier. As one official argued, 'the issue of corruption could have been taken into consideration more … also the perception of corruption' and 'have a more inclusive government from the start … meaning dealing with the Taliban from the beginning' (Hassan 2023). Of course, there were those within the EU that had long called for such action. For example, the EU's second most senior official in Kabul, Michael Semple, was expelled from Afghanistan for communicating with the Taliban in December 2007 (Boone 2007). In 2013, even as the GOA was suggesting that they would engage in peace talks with the Taliban in Qatar, President Karzai halted security talks with the US because they had announced possible peace talks with the Taliban. However, there was a missed opportunity for the EU to engage the Taliban between 2015 and 2017 when the Office of the EUSR 'begged' for greater engagement and conference invitations, which senior officials declined at the EEAS in Brussels. The option of EU peace talks with the Taliban was particularly pronounced after the peace agreement with HIG and Gulbuddin Hekmatyar. The EU and its member states did not want to provide perceptions of legitimacy to the Taliban and favoured unity in the international approach. International unity would itself break down shortly after this window, and the norm of solidarity was eroded by the Trump administration.

Special Envoy Kobia identified the way international unity broke down as the tipping point that allowed the Taliban to gain power in 2021 (Kobia 2022). Similarly, in NATO's lessons learned report, a key finding was that 'Allies would have benefitted from more meaningful discussions on the negotiations of the US–Taliban agreement'. Throughout 2019, a 'waiting game' emerged. In August, President Trump expressed his desire to get out of Afghanistan 'as quickly as we can'. In February 2020, the US and the Taliban signed a formal agreement and a timetable for withdrawal was announced. The US would draw down its forces by mid-July 2020 and complete the withdrawal by April 2021 (Thomas 2021). For some within EU institutions, it was hoped that President Biden's election would change the strategic calculus. As one EU official detailed, there was genuine concern that the country would collapse once 'President Biden confirmed the withdrawal of US troops when he was elected ... that was the moment we started knowing, the entire international community knew that, it was going to be the end'. Indeed, the extent of EU failure was exacerbated by its conflict analysis exercises between October 2020 and February 2021. Many inside the process did not believe the US would genuinely leave Afghanistan; 'they were bluffing'. For many involved in that analysis, Afghanistan was considered 'too big to fail', and scenarios whereby the Taliban retook the country were 'refused' and not considered in full. This was as much a failure of imagination as it was 'blindness ... denial ... and an unwillingness to listen to bad news' (Hassan 2023, 53–54). As the strategically selective context began to change, EU institutions once again demonstrated an inability to adapt, exacerbating the contextual dissonance of EU policy. Far from the EU's stated aim of creating resilience and safeguarding the progress of the Afghan state, the Taliban returned to power in August 2021. After a 20-year hiatus, the return of the Taliban marked the largest failure of EU external action to date.

The Fall of Kabul and New Challenges for the European Union

The return of the Taliban in August 2021, while abrupt, was not an unforeseen phenomenon. Although European Union (EU) policy makers refused to accept the scenario in advance, the Taliban's return was the culmination of a protracted process marked by the gradual expansion of their influence and control over territories in Afghanistan. The withdrawal of United States (US) troops was merely a tipping point. Still, the Taliban's progression was observed and documented over several years, indicating a complex interplay of regional, political and military dynamics. It was also the result of the failures of the Government of Afghanistan (GOA), which lacked legitimacy and fundamentally was unable to tackle corruption, improve security and provide political stability within the country. The 2019 presidential election exemplified this. Unfolding amid a challenging backdrop and delays, voting commenced on 28 September 2019. The election was marked by the lowest voter turnout in modern Afghan history, highlighting the profound impact of electoral insecurity on political participation. This low turnout was a clear indicator of the challenges and apprehensions faced by the Afghan populace, reflecting concerns over safety and the credibility of the electoral process (SIGAR 2021). With President Ghani's constitutional tenure expiring four months prior and the US already engaged in negotiations with the Taliban in Doha, there were suggestions of postponing the elections and establishing an interim government until the peace talks concluded. Despite these circumstances, President Ghani proceeded with the elections, a move widely seen as an effort to bolster his international legitimacy rather than in the best interest of the Afghan state (Cookman 2020). Following prolonged disputes and delays, the election results were finally announced in February 2020. President Ghani was re-elected with 50.64 per cent of the vote compared to Abdullah Abdullah's second place, 39.52 per cent of the vote (BBC News 2020).

February 2020 was the same month President Trump announced the unilateral decision to withdraw US troops following the conclusion of the Doha Agreement. Rather than Afghanistan being prepared for this announcement, the election result threw Afghanistan into political turmoil. The election further undermined the legitimacy of Afghan political institutions. Abdullah rejected the outcome and sought to establish a parallel government. This political standoff led to both Ghani and Abdullah holding separate inauguration ceremonies, further deepening the political divide in Afghanistan. Rather than bolstering Ghani's international reputation, the election deprived the global community of a legitimate partner. The situation demonstrated that despite two decades of international involvement and substantial aid in Afghanistan, persistent security issues significantly undermined democratic processes. The perception that democratic elections could effectively influence governance was eroded due to growing insecurity nationwide. This insecurity and a faltering constitutional system contributed to the weakening of democratic norms within the country. The EU's prioritization of state-building and development norms over peace and security was once again shown to lack contextual consonance.

In reaction to the political impasse and the establishment of rival governments, the US responded by announcing a significant reduction in aid. This reduction amounted to USD 1 billion, with an additional warning that further cuts could be implemented if necessary (Cookman 2020). This move was indicative of the US's stance on the political situation and its implications for continued support to Afghanistan. By May 2020, amidst the challenges posed by the COVID-19 pandemic, President Ghani agreed to appoint Abdullah as the head of a newly formed High Council for National Reconciliation (HCNR). This appointment was a crucial step towards political unity and was particularly significant as it granted Abdullah the authority to lead future peace negotiations with the Taliban. Indeed, the European External Action Service and the EU Delegation were eager to push for the swift establishment of the HCNR, noting the increasing level of violence targeted at civilians and the need for a comprehensive ceasefire (EEAS 2020).

This was followed by a concerted effort by Member States, choreographed by the EU, to apply pressure on the formation of the HCNR (Adili and Sorush 2020). Having initiated meetings with the Taliban over 2019, EU policy makers were coming to the realization that more needed to be done to secure a lasting peace process. This was, however, far too little, far too late.

The HCNR was intended to have the final say on the GOA signing a peace deal with the Taliban after what was expected to be a series of negotiations. Inter-Afghan talks were the expected pathway to peace, even as consistent delays proved to be a problem (Faiez 2020). Under further international pressure, the HCNR was finally inaugurated on 5 December 2020. This was a critical loss of time, given that talks with the Taliban had started two months earlier without an authoritative body to guide them (Adili and Sorush 2020). As Ghani dithered, the Taliban advanced. Indeed, the Taliban were taking advantage of the hesitancy of the GOA, but also the considerable international confusion about the timetable for US troop withdrawal. Various contradictory communications were made within the Trump administration, which had more to do with the US presidential election timetable than the strategically selective context in Afghanistan or, indeed, the US military's capacity to withdraw in an orderly fashion. This situation was little better under the newly elected Biden administration. In March 2021, Biden remarked that he couldn't 'picture' US troops in Afghanistan in 2022, but there was no solid timeline. In April, it was declared that the 'final withdrawal' would begin on 1 May 2021 and be completed by 11 September 2021. By July 2021, most North Atlantic Treaty Organization (NATO) allies and US partners had withdrawn, and hence, it was concluded that the military mission would end on 31 August 2021 (Thomas 2021; Thomas et al 2021).

Ahead of schedule, as US troops withdrew, the Taliban seized power. Their war of attrition had been won, and having delegitimized the GOA and strengthened their legitimacy in Afghanistan's rural areas, they were able to seize power on 15 August 2001 (Sakhi 2022). From the EU's perspective, one official explained, 'It was a shock; it wasn't part of our imagination or what we believe to be possible' (Hassan, 2023, 55). This is because, while EU officials believed the Taliban would become part of the strategic equation and potentially come to power, the speed at which this occurred was not predicted. As one EU official outlined, 'there were no analyses showing that the moment the West switches off the light, the next day, you will have a completely new regime. If we were sure of that happening, we would have reacted differently' (Hassan, 2023, 55). As another EU official was eager to illustrate, '[t]he EU has no intelligence of its own. I just want to make a very strong point that the EU has no intelligence agency. … We always rely on EU member states and allied countries' intelligence being shared with us' (Hassan 2023). Indeed, with Tomas Niklasson becoming the EU Special Envoy to Afghanistan in June 2021, two months before the Taliban's return, there was no suggestion that the departure of US troops would precipitate the return of the Taliban. Nevertheless, he was faced with a worsening humanitarian situation, economic crisis and worsening human rights violations, while acknowledging on behalf of the EU that 'Afghans have accepted that the Taliban are here as part of the Afghan reality, and they are seeking solutions and ways through their daily life' (Niklasson 2022). Accordingly, the EU had a new bilateral phase in its relationship with Afghanistan thrust upon it. With the sudden collapse of the GOA, a hastily established strategy emerged trying to institute new norms of engagement and focus the collective intentions of EU institutions and Member States. What emerged were the *five benchmarks for engagement* coupled with what the EU institutions termed 'Basic Needs'. Yet, remarkably absent from this was reflection of what had gone wrong and why. As Josep Borrell Fontelles, the High Representative for Foreign Affairs and Security Policy, asserted:

> We're facing a new and painful reality on the ground in Afghanistan. … This is a catastrophe, a catastrophe for the people, for Western values and credibility, and for international relations. … We have been doing a lot in order to build the state in Afghanistan … today twenty years on, we can say that we … failed. We have to ask ourselves some difficult questions to understand why this was possible. And why what has happened has happened. (Borrell 2021a)

Perhaps what was more extraordinary was not the collapse of the GOA and the return of the Taliban, but that the EU had failed to see this approaching and could not explain why it had happened. This was a remarkable admission. EU institutions had failed to understand the strategically selective context in which they were operating. Just as it points to a fundamental lack of understanding about Afghanistan, it also points to what some in the EU have suggested is a failure of imagination.

Sudden collapse and a challenge of imagination

The Taliban's return was influenced by a combination of factors, which have been reflected in the broader academic and policy debates on this issue. There is a consensus that the precipitating event sparking the collapse of the GOA was the withdrawal of US and allied troops, which created a vacuum allowing the Taliban to seize power. However, there is more significant disagreement over the underlying causes precipitating the Taliban's return and the swift collapse of the GOA. No school of thought is monocausal, as scholars and policy makers widely acknowledge that multiple failings contributed to this multicausal event. As such, the issue is one of emphasis rather than identifying an isolated cause. As a result, it is helpful to see the arguments relating to different levels of analysis, starting with the global international system and geopolitical considerations, followed by the state-level weaknesses of the GOA and the strengths of the Taliban at the local level.

International system level arguments have primarily revolved around the geopolitics of the primary international actors engaging with Afghanistan. The US, and as this book has shown, the EU and Pakistan are often highlighted because of the way they provided rentier functions for the GOA and Taliban, respectively. With Pakistan, it is repeatedly stressed that Pakistani actors have played a covert role supporting the Taliban and al Qaeda. Sakhi (2022) demonstrates that the Taliban's resilience and influence in Afghanistan can be attributed to several key factors, but receiving continuous weaponry and strategic guidance from sponsoring countries was crucial. This external backing significantly bolstered the Taliban's operational capabilities. Indeed, it is keenly illustrated by this school of thought that Osama bin Laden was found in Abbottabad, Pakistan when the 'manhunt' ended with his death in 2011 (Lahoud 2022; Ruback and Carlson 2022). Similarly, Ullah has deployed a particularly interesting 'security-cum-rentier state framework to explain Pakistan's double game', demonstrating that Pakistan's reliance on friendly relations with the Taliban results from Pakistan's security needs (Ullah 2022). This position is in concurrence with one senior EU diplomat who argued that:

> The withdrawal changed the balance of power, with the GOA, the US and allies on one side and the Taliban and Pakistan on the other. The GOA was entirely reliant on Western intervention, and so, with the withdrawal, you changed that balance of power. Pakistan's involvement with the Taliban helps explain the quick collapse. (Hassan 2023, 55)

Counterintuitively, relations between the Taliban and Pakistan soured shortly after their return to power. Yet, as some scholars have shown, and as we saw in previous chapters, the Taliban's support base is in Pakistan's Federally Administered Tribal Areas (FATA), which has long been seen to provide 'strategic depth' against India (Abbas 2014). As Jan (2022) illustrates, this in itself has meant the return of the Taliban has encouraged militant groups and terrorist organizations inside Pakistan, marking a striking level of 'blowback', as Tehreek-e-Taliban Pakistan, Islamic State of Khurasan (IS-K) and the Baloch Liberation Army pose a security threat to Pakistan.

It is possible to concur with these assertions through both a historical lens and an understanding of norm circles. Having maintained a long history of tribal independence the FATA consists of heterarchical village states. These were originally introduced to Islamic norms when the Ghaznavid Empire interacted with them at the end of the 10th century. Variations of these norms were carried through the Ilkhanate in the 13th and 14th centuries. Permeating village states, these norms were articulated with norms of resistance in the era of the global international system. This was particularly pronounced in relation to resisting the British empire in the 19th century, and again in a fight against the Soviet Union in the 20th century. It is within that context that norm circles have emerged, and bonded due to the intersectionality of tribal republican norms. However, there is also a subset of norm circles within this area, that have combined norms of conservative Islamic orthodoxy and norms violence, which have culminated in practices of modern terrorism, and the intersectional formation of militant groups and terrorist organizations. This thick contextualization demonstrates that Pakistan is an important part of the strategically selective context that needs to be considered in attempts at achieving contextual consonance. This was acknowledged by the EU in 2009 but largely jettisoned in 2010.

Nevertheless, while Pakistani relations with the Taliban are undoubtedly significant in the continuation of the Taliban's campaign, they are but one element of the complex imbrication of norm circles and their practices that resulted in failures in Afghanistan. It is important to understand that Pakistan's relations with the Taliban intersected with other factors within the global international system. It is important to note that this is an open system where different factors interact, and not a closed system where interactions can be limited and controlled (see Bhaskar 1975). For example, it was clear that there was a structural overdependence on the US for military power, economic support and political stability. The EU had nested its strategy within that overdependent dynamic, but so too had other strategic actors supporting the norms of global international society. Yet, in nesting their approach to Afghanistan inside US strategy, they exposed themselves to a reliance on US norm circles and norms. A norm of solidarity failed to account for the US normative myopia and hubris. The US, and as a result, the EU, having relinquished its autonomy, developed the intention of transforming Afghanistan but withdrew when it became a liability at home and fatigue set in. This was interspersed with what Stewart (2021) defined as a fluctuating pattern of 'ruinous overinvestment and complete neglect'. Thus, it was not simply the case that the Taliban was able to outlast the US with Pakistani support. Rather, there were failures inherent in the venture from the beginning. Herein, the return of the Taliban represents a failure of liberal peacebuilding, which Dodge (2021) concludes was fundamentally flawed from the outset, primarily due to its disregard for the nuances of Afghan history and culture and an underestimation of the limitations faced by the US and its allies.

However, as tempting as it may be for the EU and Member States to exclusively blame Pakistan or the US for the Taliban's return, this would be a mistake. Over two decades Member States allowed their positions, and that of EU institutions, to be aligned with a myopic strategy. When European norms and commitments to long-term practices diverged, the EU had the opportunity to re-evaluate their strategy but failed to act. Contextual dissonance was, in this sense, not just an outcome of poor policy decisions, but a political choice. The decision not to adapt and formulate an independent strategy highlights a fundamental limitation in the EU's approach to Afghanistan, and international conflicts and interventions more broadly. As Youngs' (2021) analysis illustrates, the EU's restraint in acting autonomously is often not due to a lack of capabilities. Instead, it is primarily driven by political choices. In Afghanistan, this manifested as the EU's decision to align with and follow the leadership of the United States for two decades. This strategic choice to support US policies and initiatives, rather than pursuing a more independent or distinct approach, reflects the political dynamics and considerations within the EU regarding its role in global affairs. Kaldor (2021) reinforces this point, arguing that a European force could have remained in Afghanistan to bolster the Afghan National Security Forces (ANSF) in 2021, and Member States could have facilitated European autonomy in Afghanistan. However, there was a lack of political will. Indeed, there were more European Member State troops on the ground contributing to the Resolute Support Mission in 2021 than there were US troops (see Table 6.4). Nevertheless, a disagreement between France and Germany about European involvement led to a decision not to become embroiled in further conflict once Kabul fell. This was a damning indictment of the EU's attempts to instil norms of 'EU Strategic Autonomy' (EU-SA) in response to 'a hostile geopolitical environment, marked by Brexit, the Trump Presidency and China's growing assertiveness' (Damen 2022, 1).

Remarkably, both the US and EU failed to learn lessons from their previous engagements with Afghanistan and understand historical patterns. This was not a mistake on the part of the EU; it was a deliberate policy to treat Afghanistan as a 'blank slate'. As a result, there was a failure to recognize the need for Afghanistan to be reintegrated into the regional economy because of its loss of position in the global international system. Without a domestic revenue source and reintegration into the global international system, Afghanistan was structurally vulnerable because of its dependency on foreign aid as a form of rentierism. One EU official highlighted the lack of self-sufficiency as central to the speed of the GOA's collapse. Thus:

> The direct reason was the withdrawal of US troops, followed by the withdrawal of NATO. The problem was, the government was never completely, independently, self-subsistent. It was never able to fulfil basic duties without borrowing subsistence in terms of money, technical support, and security. That is why the collapse happened quickly. (Hassan, 2023, 56)

There was also a failure, as the early victors in the conflict, to reconcile with regional actors and geopolitical rivals such as China. The EU actively sought to prevent regional powers playing a role early in the conflict (Klaiber 2002). This practice later reversed, but the damage had been done. Indeed, once the GOA collapsed, China seized the opportunity to expand its influence into Afghanistan specifically and Central Asia more broadly (Murtazashvili 2022; Wieringen and Claustre 2023). Indeed, in early 2024, Chinese President Xi Jinping became the first head of state to official recognize the Taliban government (Dawi 2024). European inaction and lack of global leadership norms, despite assertions of EU-SA, has allowed China to realize its more assertive norms in Afghanistan.

It was not just the importance of regional players that the EU underestimated. The political decision not to pursue a comprehensive peace and reconciliation process led to the US and EU underestimating the insurgency's resilience. It demonstrated a failure to recognize the heterarchical nature of the strategically selective context. Abandoning the GOA in August 2021 failed to recognize this reality, and as a result, a lack of international unity and commitment led to the return of the Taliban. As one EU official argued:

> This was not a monocausal event; it was years in the making. Several factors were in play. Firstly, an overdependence on the US. For international presence and support for ANSF. The US withdrawal took away capacities and capabilities. Secondly, the Taliban negotiations broke the trust and confidence of the Afghan military and the political class. It undermined the position of the Afghan government and the security forces. The broader legitimacy of the Afghan government in the eyes of the people was also damaged. Thirdly, in August 2021, you had a government that was abandoned by the international community. So initially, the US, but then NATO's withdrawal. Fourthly, the Taliban advance shifted the military balance on whether to support the government. Fifthly, there was an intelligence failure. This was something that we underestimated across the board over the years: the strength of the Taliban. Not just militarily but also the support they were able to gain from non-government-controlled areas. Sixth, a lack of imagination, we didn't want to allow for this to be a possibility. (Hassan 2023, 56)

This assessment is insightful and reconciles with the Special Inspector General for Afghanistan Reconstruction (SIGAR)'s review of *Why the Afghan Government Collapsed*. A confluence of pivotal factors shaped the evolving situation in the lead-up to the US withdrawal. First, there was a widespread misjudgement by the GOA regarding the likelihood of a US withdrawal. This resulted in a lack of preparedness by the Afghan government. Like the EU, members of the GOA simply did not believe that the US would withdraw. This was compounded by the second problem, in that the US–Taliban negotiations significantly undermined the Afghan government's authority, simultaneously encouraging the Taliban to pursue a military victory. Third, intra-Afghan negotiations were impeded by the weakened government's insistence on integrating the Taliban into the existing republic, a demand that proved to be a significant obstacle. Fourth, the Taliban's reluctance to engage in meaningful compromise hindered the prospects of a negotiated political settlement. Fifth, the internal dynamics within the GOA contributed to its instability, particularly at the critical junctures in 2021, as President Ghani's reliance on a narrow circle of loyalists limited the government's political inclusivity and effectiveness. Lastly, long-term factors include the 'Afghan government's high level of centralisation, struggle to attain legitimacy, and endemic corruption' (SIGAR 2022b). These factors collectively underscored the complexities and challenges that defined this period in Afghanistan's political history.

Significantly, SIGAR's assessment also reconciles with the academic literature that highlights the weaknesses of the GOA as the primary source of collapse. Plagued by corruption, incompetence and a lack of legitimacy, the GOA was unable to provide basic services to the Afghan people, and it was deeply unpopular among many Afghans. This made it difficult for the government to mobilize support to resist the Taliban. For Williams (2022), this was symptomatic of a failure of governance, whereby Bonn created a centralized government that was markedly efficient in resource extraction but notably deficient in providing services. Previous chapters concur with Williams' assessment that this imbalance was further exacerbated by the dynamics of development aid and the burgeoning opium economy, which, combined with a lack of political accountability, gave rise to new and particularly harmful forms of corruption. As a former EU ambassador to Pakistan argued:

> Twenty years of mistakes by the international community and the Afghans themselves were made. Firstly, corruption was incentivised, leading to elite capture of aid. Second, impunity. NATO, for the first year ten years, never dealt with 'collateral damage' and compensated families. Then the same was done by Afghan security forces, that were corrupt. This benefited the Taliban. Thirdly, the peace dividend was never shared. Wealth and aid never trickled down outside of the cities. (Hassan 2023, 55)

With an ineffectual centralized government, wealth failed to trickle down to the village states, and Afghans outside the cities were never adequately represented. The needs of remote provinces were never met. Centralization contributed to a growing disconnect and mistrust between the government and the populace, creating a vacuum that the Taliban were able to fill (Sakhi 2022). To once again draw on Ibn Khaldun, the imposed model of centralization failed to create a sustainable bridge between desert and sedentary norm circles. This is not just a damning indictment of the GOA, but also of the current iteration of norms constituting global international society. There was not a lack of aid to Afghanistan; on the contrary there was too much for a centralized state model to absorb.

A multicausal explanation of how the Taliban were able to return so quickly after NATO's withdrawal, resonates with the heterarchical understanding of Afghanistan set out in previous chapters. It helps to explain the swiftness at which the Taliban were able to make rapid advances throughout the country's rural areas from May 2021. This included some northern regions that were able to resist the Taliban in the 1990s but succumbed to Taliban control in 2021 (Thomas 2021). The Taliban adeptly exploited the Afghan government's shortcomings in providing security and addressing public grievances. With the GOA and international partners unable to create norms around who had the legitimate right to rule, the Taliban worked to erode the government's authority and delegitimize state institutions. Aligning themselves with local leaders in remote areas, they could leverage relationships and utilize religious institutions as platforms to disseminate anti-foreigner sentiments, resonating with segments of the population and norms of Afghan identity. These elements enabled the Taliban to maintain and expand their influence. Thus, the withdrawal of US and allied troops precipitated the fall of the GOA. However, it is also important to recognize that responsibility lies with the international community, of which the EU is but one actor, in addition to the weaknesses of the Afghan government, the strengths of the Taliban and their ability to act within the strategically selective context. Recognizing international shortfalls and the Taliban's strengths is important, as this is part of the new context shaping EU involvement as EU institutions couple the five benchmarks for engagement with meeting 'Basic Needs'.

Five benchmarks and a challenge of engagement

At an informal meeting in Slovenia on 3 September 2021, the EU ministers of foreign affairs agreed to the five benchmarks of engagement. Along with agreeing to maintain a minimal presence on the ground in Kabul, it was decided that there would be a continuation of humanitarian aid and monitoring the humanitarian situation so that the EU could play a significant role in Afghanistan's future. This has included assisting with coordinating and supporting the safe, secure and orderly departure of all foreign nationals and Afghans who wish to leave the country (Council 2021a). Such efforts demonstrate that the EU has undoubtedly not abandoned Afghanistan, as it continued close collaboration between various international entities, non-governmental organizations (NGOs) and local Afghan institutions to effectively address the complex challenges brought about by the return of the Taliban.

The introduction of the five benchmarks of engagement sought to ensure that the Taliban live up to international obligations and the criteria set out in the Doha Agreement. Once sufficient progress on the benchmarks is met, EU and Member States are committed to engaging with the Taliban beyond basic operational necessities. As a result, the new stage of EU external action in Afghanistan is on hiatus in terms of bilateral engagement with the Taliban. To qualify for engagement, the Taliban is required, per UN Security Council Resolutions, to facilitate the orderly departure of foreign nationals and Afghans. Simultaneously, the Taliban is required to ensure the protection and respect of all human rights, particularly those of women, girls, children and minorities, and uphold fundamental principles such as the rule of law and freedom of speech and media. The EU requires the Taliban to enable unhindered humanitarian operations strictly adhering to humanitarian principles and International Humanitarian Law, ensuring the safety and access of humanitarian staff and aid recipients. In terms of security, the five benchmarks require concentrated efforts to prevent Afghanistan from becoming a haven for terrorism, which includes severing all ties between the Taliban and international terrorist groups. Finally, the establishment of an inclusive and representative Afghan government, inclusive of all minorities and with significant participation of women, is essential for ensuring lasting peace and regional stability (Council 2021c).

While diplomatic engagement with the Taliban requires that the five benchmarks be met, operational engagement with the Taliban has taken place. Operational engagement with the Taliban has been assisted by the EU abandoning nearly two decades of not talking to the Taliban. Since the Taliban's takeover in August 2021, the EU's dialogue with them has continued, albeit the nature of these talks has evolved to reflect the changed political landscape. Additionally, there are ongoing, albeit limited, technical discussions with the National Resistance Force (NRF). These discussions are crucial in determining the extent to which the EU can continue to provide humanitarian assistance in Afghanistan under the new regime. This engagement indicates a pragmatic approach by the EU, adapting to the new realities on the ground while attempting to maintain humanitarian norms.

EU policy has become reminiscent of the EU's humanitarian approach in the 1980s and 1990s.[1] A policy that was initially referred to as 'Humanitarian aid +', was hastily constructed to deal with the new reality inside Afghanistan. Upon consultation with stakeholders, the policy was later termed *Basic Needs*, as the former name implied a level of political impartiality that did not accurately reflect the nature of the approach. The term development

---

[1] Interestingly, when interviewing EU policy makers, they demonstrated a remarkable lack of awareness of what the EU had undertaken in the 1990s. A lack of historical awareness characterized the interviews, even around issues of former EU policy. In many respects this demonstrates a reliance on core norms of the EU in the 1990s and in the 2020s.

was not considered, as the EU no longer engaged with the governing powers. This is instructive because it demonstrates a return to the EU, combining humanitarian norms with more political funding where necessary. Simultaneously, the EU not only aligned their policy objectives with those of UN organizations, but members of the Commission were highly active in putting together a new aid architecture and initiating an Afghanistan Coordination Group. Once again, as the US turned its attention away, the EU demonstrated a higher degree of leadership and autonomy, building on the norms of global international society. This demonstrates a remarkably consistent pattern that has emerged throughout the late 20th and early 21st centuries. In discussions with policy makers, it was substantiated that the EU Delegation, the sole Western entity with a physical presence in Kabul, has regained its status as the most well-informed body. Consequently, Member States and allies in the post-2021 context now rely on the Delegation to obtain clear insights into local conditions inside Afghanistan, albeit with the Delegation's visibility being limited outside of Kabul.

By the end of 2023, the EU renewed its commitment to Afghanistan with a EUR 142.8 million package to 'focus on health, nutrition, education, clean water and sanitation, in particular for women, girls, displaced populations and those affected by displacement' (International Partnerships 2023). This financial commitment follows an August 2021 pledge, culminating in mobilizing a significant aid package totalling EUR 1.2 billion. This package includes EUR 676 million in newly adopted aid, supplementing an existing EUR 554 million dedicated to humanitarian assistance (International Partnerships 2023). This considerable allocation of funds demonstrates the EU's ongoing commitment to assisting the Afghan population in the face of persistent challenges. Contrary to fears of EU disengagement, this financial support offers insight into the EU's medium-term policy trajectory in Afghanistan, indicating a continued focus on providing aid and support in the region. Indeed, when interviewing NGOs and local organizations, it was apparent that organizations feared global abandonment, especially as attention turned to the war in Ukraine. However, as an EU official confirmed:

> Yes, lots of fear that due to the war in Ukraine, money would be diverted to Ukraine and not to Afghanistan. This is not at all the case. Not one cent has been diverted, even to Central Asia. This is really the money that was allocated for Afghanistan at the beginning of the Multiannual Financial Framework, and it is still there ... we still think that the money is needed, and we keep it. This is thanks to the rigidity of the Multiannual Financial Framework, when allocations are fixed, they are there. (Hassan 2023, 62)

Nevertheless, humanitarian conditions in Afghanistan have deteriorated under the Taliban. For women and girls in particular, the UN's Special Rapporteurs and Independent Experts concluded that within two years, the Taliban had eradicated all progress made since 2002. Girls have been barred from secondary education, and women from tertiary institutions. Restrictions extend to public spaces, with women and girls prohibited from amusement parks, public baths, gyms, and sports clubs and from working in NGO offices. The exclusion of women from public office and the judiciary is complete, and women are subject to stringent dress codes and travel restrictions, requiring a male guardian for journeys over 75km and compelling them to stay at home. Across Afghanistan, women report feelings of invisibility, isolation and suffocation, likening their conditions to imprisonment. The lack of employment opportunities and access to aid severely hampers their ability to meet basic needs, including medical and psychological support, especially for victims of violence, including sexual violence (OHCHR 2023).

The deterioration of humanitarian conditions inside Afghanistan has been accompanied by economic isolation, with up to 97 per cent of Afghans living in poverty. A retaliatory focus has accompanied this on extrajudicial executions of former government officials, members of armed groups such as the NRF, IS-K and those allegedly not following the Taliban's rules (Amnesty International 2023). This has been complemented by enforced disappearances, torture, the targeting of minorities and the eradication of freedom of speech (T. Hassan 2022).

By the end of 2023, seeking to leverage international recognition for adherence to the five benchmarks was failing. Moreover, just as in the 1990s, the EU's humanitarian approach was only able to mitigate the worst of the humanitarian disaster; two years of Basic Needs appeared to have the same effect. As one EU official stressed:

> I think just like for the 20 years before, it's an illusion to think that the EU itself can have any leverage or influence [on the Taliban]. It's more the international community as a whole if we remain united … it's only by being united that we can have some influence. This is why the EU has had influence, by really putting lots of pressure on the UN system to organise itself. Officially, I mean, it's clearly [showing as] the UN in the data, [but] it's only by being united that we can have some influence. (Hassan 2023, 59)

Accepting limited influence with the Taliban has not, however, stopped the EU from developing broader policies to deal with the issues of terrorism, narcotics and irregular migration.

The challenge of counterterrorism and narcotics

The return of the Taliban has heightened the EU's concerns about international terrorism. As a result, on 29 September 2021, the Council of the EU announced the *Afghanistan: Counter-Terrorism Action Plan*. The plan details four key areas of action: security checks to prevent terrorist infiltration into the EU; strategic intelligence and foresight to prevent Afghanistan from becoming a haven for terrorist groups; monitoring and countering propaganda and mobilization; and tackling organized crime as a source of terrorist financing. The plan includes specific recommendations for action in each area and emphasizes the importance of international cooperation, information sharing, and strategic coordination among EU member states and global partners (Council 2021b). The plan's implementation and effectiveness are subject to regular review and adjustments based on evolving circumstances and threats.

The overarching characteristic of the plan is on internal protection rather than external action, as the focus pertains to actions and measures within the EU. The *Counter-Terrorism Action Plan* does not explicitly detail actions to be taken inside Afghanistan. Instead, it concentrates on preventing the spread of terrorism from Afghanistan to the EU, enhancing security measures within the EU, and addressing the broader implications of the Taliban takeover for EU security. This is unsurprising given the EU institution's absent focus on counterterrorism in Afghanistan over the previous two decades (Hassan 2010; Hassan and Hammond 2011). Throughout that time, with the EU abandoning its autonomy, counterterrorism was deferred to the US and NATO. To the extent that the EU was engaged in counterterrorism inside Afghanistan, this was primarily seen as the result of state building and development; the EU was, to quote Keohane (2008), 'The Absent Friend'.

Internally, the EU talks of taking 'a whole-of-society approach' to prevention, which relies on the role of civil society and other non-governmental actors (EEAS 2023). This began with the 2005 EU Counter-Terrorism Strategy, which focuses on the pillars of Prevent, Protect, Pursue and Respond (Council 2005b). However, externally, action has been limited because EU capabilities have been left wanting, and the EU's emphasis has been on trying to undermine terrorism by promoting peace and security. This was the primary focus of the European Agenda on Security and the EU's 2016 Global Strategy. Moreover, there has been some movement on increasing the EU's capabilities with adopting the Strategic Compass for Security and Defence, particularly with a boost in EU intelligence analysis capabilities. However, EU counterterrorism depends on Member States' contributions through the COTER Working Party on Terrorism (International Aspects). The working party conducts threat analyses regarding non-EU countries, and therefore Afghanistan, seeking to enhance EU cooperation with these countries in combating international terrorism (EEAS 2023). Without a political partner in Afghanistan, the EU's approach to counterterrorism is limited, even if counterterrorism dialogue with Pakistan is viable and ongoing.

Notably, the 2021 *Afghanistan: Counter-Terrorism Action Plan* identifies narcotics as one of the Taliban's primary sources of income, encompassing opium production, poppy cultivation, and the production and trafficking of synthetic drugs. Narcotics, notably opium, often travel through the Balkans, and there is a noted correlation between increased opium production in Afghanistan and the availability of heroin in EU markets. As such, the Council of the European Union recognizes a significant connection between Afghan narcotics, the Taliban, and the threat of terrorism in Europe. This was elaborated upon in the Commission's EU Agenda and Action Plan on Drugs 2021–2025, underscoring the linkages between organized crime within the EU and the global and regional nature of drug markets. It highlighted the need for a comprehensive understanding of these markets and their implications for security and public health within the EU (Commission 2020). This approach reflects a broader recognition of the complex interplay between narcotics trafficking, terrorism and organized crime. Necessarily, tackling these issues requires coordinated international practices and the development of effective norms. However, on 25 June 2023, Haibatullah Akhundzada, the Taliban supreme leader, announced the eradication of poppy cultivation. As a result, the production of opium has dropped to levels not seen since a Taliban ban on production in 2000–2001. In Helmand, known for its extensive poppy cultivation, there was a dramatic decrease of almost 99 per cent from April 2022 to April 2023. Similarly, Nangarhar, another major poppy-producing province, experienced an 84 per cent reduction in cultivation over the same period (SIGAR 2023).

Post-2021 counterterrorism cooperation in Afghanistan should acknowledge the limited capabilities and possibilities of engagement with the Taliban. Despite these constraints, it remains crucial to critically examine the current state of the terrorist threat in Afghanistan. Although countering terrorism was the primary objective of Western intervention and a pillar of the EU's justification for state-building, this objective was not achieved. The ongoing character of terrorist capabilities remains unclear. In April 2022, the US Department of State acknowledged progress in the Taliban's adherence to counterterrorism commitments outlined in the Doha Accords. However, reconciling this assessment with the emergence of al Qaeda leader al-Zawahiri in Kabul in August 2022 presents a significant challenge. One of the most wanted terrorists in the world felt confident enough to appear at an open window in the centre of Kabul before a US drone missile strike killed him (Thomas 2022). This discrepancy raises questions about the effectiveness of the Taliban's counterterrorism measures and the extent of their commitment to the Doha Agreement.

Notably, after the US withdrawal from Afghanistan, it has maintained an 'over the horizon' approach to monitoring how the terrorist threat in Afghanistan evolves. In addition, the US shares counterterrorism intelligence with the Taliban, especially details concerning IS-K activities (SIGAR 2023). Assessments after August 2021 have shown that al Qaeda was regrouping and could build a capability to launch foreign attacks in one to two years, absent of any sustained pressure. However, other groups, including the Haqqani Network, Tehrik-e-Taliban Pakistan, Islamic Movement of Uzbekistan and Eastern Turkistan Islamic Movement have all been highlighted as operating within or having strong ties to Afghanistan. A leaked Central Intelligence Agency report in 2023 confirmed that the worst fears of early assessments had come to fruition, with Islamic State of Iraq and Syria (ISIS) leaders in Afghanistan coordinating plans for attacks across Europe and Asia while plotting targets in the US. Specific efforts included targeting embassies, churches, business centres and the FIFA World Cup held in Qatar (Lamothe and Warrick 2023). In early 2024, two Afghan nationals were arrested in Germany on suspicion of belonging to ISIS and plotting attacks on the Swedish Parliament (Leven 2024). Moreover, strategic assessments have demonstrated that al Qaeda and the Taliban have maintained close ties, even while observing a 'strategic silence' that allows the al Qaeda members to remain in Afghanistan so long as they do not attack the US or its allies. Thus, the Taliban and al Qaeda are distinct, but they are linked through 'intermarriage and other personal bonds between members ... official assessments concur that [al-Qaeda] AQ-Taliban ties remain close' (Thomas 2022). From this perspective, the counterterrorism objective in Afghanistan was unsuccessful, and those espousing norms of violence, pan-Islamism and conservative Islamic orthodoxy remain a threat to Europe.

The issue of counterterrorism in Afghanistan has been further complicated by the fact that coalition partners left behind substantial stockpiles of weapons during their withdrawal. These stockpiles included a range of armaments such as 'AK-47s, medium-range rocket launchers, M-14s and M-16s', as well as advanced equipment like 'night-vision gear, thermal imagers, and steel-penetrating bullets' (UNSC 2022). The presence of these weapons has sparked serious concerns. The potential acquisition of such weaponry by terrorist groups could significantly enhance their offensive capabilities, posing a heightened security risk both within Afghanistan and potentially beyond its borders. These weapons have already been used in Kashmir, including M4s, M16s and US-made arms and ammunitions (Kathju 2023). Similarly, in Pakistan's Khyber Pakhtunkhwa province, militants have directly targeted the police force using US weaponry. In one such incident, six police officers were killed (Economic Times 2022). The spread of small arms has not been limited to Afghanistan's neighbours. In June 2023, concerns were raised that small arms had been transported to Ḥarakat al-Muqāwamah al-ʾIslāmiyyah (Hamas) in Gaza and as far afield as the US-Mexican border in the hands of Mexican cartels (House Committee on Oversight and Accountability 2023; Virgin 2023). The movement of small arms from Afghanistan to foreign terrorist groups and crime organizations, as confirmed by the UNSC (2022), represents a clear and immediate threat to the EU. This situation poses a significant challenge, particularly given the EU's lack of a dedicated intelligence agency. The task of locating, monitoring, tracking and ultimately neutralizing this technology as it moves among malign actors across the Eurasian continent is daunting.

The challenge of irregular migration

The challenges of countering narcotics, terrorism and small arms are not the only immediate challenges to Europe. As the EU has sought to come to terms with the humanitarian crisis inside Afghanistan, it has also had to come to terms with the implications this has had on irregular migration from Afghanistan. This is perhaps the largest challenge to the EU's norms and conception of itself as a civilian power dedicated to the norms of global international society. This is not a new challenge, but the impact this issue has had on new European practices is profound.

In the early 2000s, the EU focused on strengthening border controls and harmonizing asylum procedures, dealing with irregular migration through the emerging Common European Asylum System. The overall focus was on managing migration flows while protecting those in need. Over time, this developed into more structured asylum and immigration policies through 2015, when increased migration led the EU to seek further cooperation with the GOA (Dimitriadi 2018). Increasingly defined as a 'migrant crisis', the EU opted for an approach that emphasized 'migration management' in attempts to address the 'root causes' of irregular migration. The EU's approach aimed to mitigate underlying issues, reducing the impetus for individuals to migrate irregularly. In Afghanistan this led to the The Joint Way Forward, signed by the EU and the GOA in 2016. This was one of the first migration partnership agreements instigated by the EU and tried to implement measures to deter migrants from entering Europe through unofficial channels. In addition, the agreement tied the continuance of development assistance to the return of Afghans who have been refused protection or settlement in the EU (Quie and Hakimi 2020). Indeed, in 2016, the Commission pressured Afghanistan on this issue. As Ekil Hakimi, Afghanistan's finance minister, told the Afghan parliament: 'If Afghanistan does not cooperate with EU countries on the refugee crisis, this will negatively impact the amount of aid allocated to Afghanistan' (Amnesty International 2019).

A significant driver of the EU's policy in 2015 was a surge in immigration from predominantly Muslim countries, which was changing the political landscape by allowing right-wing populists to gain traction. Mudde (2016) outlines a particularly pertinent instance, when Hungarian Prime Minister Viktor Orban was able to undermine German Chancellor Angela Merkel's advocacy for a *Willkommenskultur*, or 'culture of welcoming', and instead prioritized national security and stringent immigration controls. Evidently, this was a tension between norm circles, and a battle between norms relating to immigration. This conflict over norms highlighted the widespread European debate regarding approaches to immigration and refugee integration.

Since 2016, the European Commission has acknowledged the necessity of collaborating with countries of origin and transit to tackle the underlying causes of irregular migration and to ensure the repatriation of irregular migrants. This 'regional cooperation' strategy has been at the centre of the Commission's approach to managing irregular migration. In 2017, notable strides were made in executing this regional cooperation strategy, establishing readmission agreements with three partner nations: Afghanistan, Pakistan and Bangladesh. These agreements marked a crucial step in the Commission's efforts to build norms and practices around irregular migration in collaboration with these countries. In addition, the EU has sought to outsource and push back irregular migration to Turkey through a refugee facility, which the Commission termed 'one of the swiftest and most effective EU support mechanisms' (Commission 2018). Turkey has played a vital role with Syrian refugees, but it is also the most prevalent route for Afghans into the EU flowing through Iran into Turkey using the 'Urmia to Van' and 'Maku to Degubeyazit' routes (Mohammadi et al 2001).

The resurgence of Taliban control in Afghanistan is projected to significantly impact the EU and its Member States, escalating irregular migration and an increase in asylum applications. The convergence of a worsening human rights environment and economic instability in Afghanistan is poised to drive many Afghans to undertake hazardous journeys in search of refuge. Although the majority of Afghan refugees initially seek asylum in adjacent countries, data from Frontex indicates that Afghan nationals rank among the top three nationalities involved in unauthorized border crossings into the EU (Frontex 2022). This trend highlights the broader implications of Afghanistan's political upheaval on European migration dynamics and poses a complex challenge to the EU's migration and asylum policies. Moreover, the number of first-time asylum applications from Afghanistan has started to grow, although it has remained considerably below the peak of 2015 (Eurostat 2024).

These trends underscore the broader impact of the situation in Afghanistan on European migration patterns. The EU faces the dual challenge to its normative character, responding to the humanitarian needs of Afghan refugees while also managing and securing its borders. This situation necessitates a multifaceted response that balances humanitarian norms inherent in the obligations of global international society, and the practicalities of irregular migration management in an EU that is increasingly uncertain about developing traditional security norms in the 21st century. Germany, France, Austria and Sweden emerged as principal hosts for a substantial proportion of Afghan refugees. However, in 2021, many Afghans who secured legal status in the EU were primarily received by Germany, Greece, France and Italy (Mentzelopoulou 2021). How to balance the norms of global international society against a resurgence of far-right and populist movements wishing to challenge those norms has not proved easy (see Bennhold and Erlanger 2021). The situation in Afghanistan, therefore, not only poses a humanitarian challenge but also has significant implications for the EU's migration policy, border management, social integration frameworks, and the political composition of the EU itself. As a result, a cost of failing in Afghanistan is being exacted, within the EU and its Member States, and the norms of global international society.

The challenge of heritage and division

Although this volume began by outlining the EU's ahistoricism and 'blank slate' approach, it is worth noting that Afghanistan's ancient and classical history poses a new challenge for the EU. The return of the Taliban has helped further new normative concerns around Afghanistan's archaeological heritage, and the way it can be used to exacerbate conflict and crisis. In 2021, the European Council concluded that protecting cultural heritage can help promote 'peace, democracy, and sustainable development'. As a result, the EU's new strategic approach to cultural heritage in conflicts and crises was established. The rationale for this was that promoting tolerance and mutual understanding is crucial for harmonious coexistence within diverse societies. Reconciliation and intercultural dialogues serve as proactive measures to alleviate social tensions and prevent violent conflict. Under this new approach, initiatives around protecting cultural heritage are seen as essential for stabilizing and enriching pluralistic communities. This is recognition that cultural heritage can be weaponized and exploited to fuel conflict (European Council 2021).

For the EU, focusing on cultural heritage is now seen as an addition to its foreign policy toolbox and a 'symbolic front' to its external action (EEAS 2021). Although the EU had for two decades operated a 'blank slate' approach in Afghanistan, its new 'symbolic front' was in part inspired by the Taliban's treatment of the Buddhas of Bamiyan prior to US military action. During the 4th and 5th centuries CE the colossal Buddha statues – measuring 53 and approximately 40 metres in height – were hewn into the cliffside of the Bamiyan Valley in central Afghanistan. These awe-inspiring sculptures fell victim to the Taliban's attempts at pre-Islamic cultural erasure in 2001 (Lee

2006; Ball 2008). As Mir Ghulam Navi, a curator at the National Museum of Afghanistan, described in March 2001, '[t]hey [the Taliban] came with ten men with hammers and began smashing the sculptures of human forms. We couldn't stop them—they said they would kill us if we tried' (Shorthose 2003, 9). Contrary to the Taliban's claims that this was undertaken because of religious necessity, the most sustained analysis has demonstrated that the Taliban's attacks were a '*modern phenomenon* performed under the name of Islamic Iconoclasm' (Reza 'Husseini' 2012; emphasis added). Indeed, comparative studies have shown that there is no single normative 'Islamic' approach to the cultural heritage of pre-Islamic civilizations (Michael Feener 2017). The treatment of these religious artefacts was a product of Taliban norm circles and practices, motivated by a political desire to attack world heritage in the name of Islam.

One of the primary motivations for the destruction of the statues was the Taliban's frustration with the UN for imposing sanctions against them and recognizing the Rabbani government-in-exile as the legitimate Afghan authority. In addition, the Taliban were also encouraged by al Qaeda and Pakistani fundamentalists looking to expand norms of conservative Islamic orthodoxy and pan-Islamism. The Taliban's rejection of historical pluralism and trans-culturalism served political purposes: as revenge for their failure to gain UN recognition and as a way to portray themselves as staunch defenders of Islam to extremist factions (Shorthose 2003; Reza 'Husseini' 2012; Hussain 2015). Such acts were more than a demonstration of the Taliban's puritanical Islamic revivalism, even as they inspired similar acts by the Pakistani Taliban, such as damaging the rock-cut Buddhas at Jahanabad in the Swat Valley of Pakistan in 2007 (Wijesuriya and Lee 2013).

While efforts to restore the Buddhas at Jahanabad have been successful, international efforts continued at the Bamiyan Valley, where teams sifted through 400 tons of rubble in an attempt to conserve the remains of the Buddha statues and protect the Bamiyan Valley World Heritage property (Gruen et al 2003; Kakissis 2011; Khaliq 2016; Nagaoka 2020). The return of the Taliban in 2021 has complicated these efforts, for example, with the Taliban allowing coal mining on the site and gunmen using the remnants of the Buddhas for target practice (Radio Free Europe 2023). Accordingly, Afghanistan's pre-Islamic history remains a point of tension between the Taliban and international institutions of world heritage, such as the United Nations Educational, Scientific and Cultural Organization (see Azoulay 2021).[2] Today, Afghans are still trying to come to terms with the legacy

---

[2] Since 2003, there have been growing efforts towards criminalizing the intentional destruction of cultural heritage. For example, in 2016, the International Criminal Court convicted Ahmad Al Faqi Al Mahdi for intentionally directing attacks against religious and historic buildings in Mali, the first such ruling by the court (ICC 2021).

of historical divisions and as a result its pre-Islamic history has become politicized; this is a central sight of contemporary struggles with the Taliban. Yet, this also serves as an important reminder that history still matters in Afghanistan, no matter how much Western powers choose to ignore it. Afghanistan has entered the global international system, but that does not mean that it has forgotten or erased the historical lineage it has had into the ancient and classical world. Had Western powers been more appreciative of this point, perhaps the Taliban would not have been able to once again challenge the norms of global international society.

8

Conclusion

In addressing why European Union (EU) policy in Afghanistan failed, this research has aimed to shed new light on the EU's external action. To do this, it has not used a traditional International Relations theory, but sought to challenge many of the working assumptions of approaches that prioritize presentism, ahistoricism, Eurocentrism and state-centrism. This has required a commitment to methodological pluralism. Guiding this research has been a sense that three key theoretical commitments not only matter, but that they can help explain the social world and in doing so identify why EU policy failed. The first, using Buzan and Little's framework, is that in trying to understand international relations, world history matters and can provide an important lens for looking at world politics today. Rather than accepting contemporary logics and structures, it is important to put them within a larger historical context and see how they developed in different place and at different times. This certainly had the benefit of allowing the chapters of this book to recontextualize Afghanistan and reject notions that it is in any way a 'blank slate'. Notions that anywhere can be considered a *tabula rasa* do not just resonate with neocolonial ways of looking at the world, but as this book has shown, they have enormous potential to damage and endanger the world around us. The Taliban may well physically want to eradicate Afghanistan's pre-Islamic history, but Western powers should not commit the same mistake by eradicating history from their psychological consciousness. It is in this context that Chapter 1 necessarily challenged the profound misperception of Afghanistan as a 'blank slate', a perspective that disregards the rich tapestry of Afghan history and norms shaped over millennia. This fallacy has perpetuated a misunderstanding and underestimation of Afghanistan's complex sociopolitical fabric and its people's agency.

The second key theoretical commitment has been in explaining how norm circles, norms and practices help us explain the social world. This has not only been applied to Afghanistan, but as the narrative unfolded, as a point of entry for explaining EU, United States (US) and other actors' actions at multiple levels of analysis. This author willingly accepts that utilizing norm circles, norms and practices to explain complex sociopolitical fabrics and social institutions has required some intellectual heavy lifting. As the chapters developed, it has been necessary to lean on Elder-Vass' sociological research and critical realist framework, to define culture and society in a way that was compatible with Buzan and Little's framework, but that maintained an ontological commitment to complex naturalism. Yet, it is in maintaining this ontological commitment that the third theoretical commitment in this text has maintained theoretical consistency. Assertions that the strategic relational approach can help capture the complex dynamics of the structure and agency debate, require that a 'real world' exists and contextually textures human agency. It is this that allows the concepts of contextual consonance and contextual dissonance to have meaning, and any theoretical utility. As these three elements have combined, they have helped weave a theoretically driven but empirically rich account of Afghanistan, the EU and the nature of transatlantic relations together. They have also allowed a thick contextualization of world history and contemporary relationships to draw out the emergence of norms and practices in a rigorous diachronic explanation. This has revealed that EU policy failed in Afghanistan because the gap between what it was trying to do, and the reality it was operating within were so dissonant that the chance of success was derisory.

In the first chapter it was shown that the EU's ahistoricism, Eurocentrism and commitment to normative power failed to recognize the myriad of norms that have shaped, and been shaped by, Afghanistan's history, its interactions with external powers, and its own internal dynamics. These norms span across all three historical periods set out by Buzan and Little, reflecting the complex interplay between local traditions, external influences and the evolving landscape of global politics. By casting aside the history of Afghanistan, the tensions between centralization and local autonomy were cast aside. So too were norms of tribal egalitarianism, heterarchy, social cohesion, kinship, resistance through asymmetric warfare, colonial resistance and a multifaceted relationship with Islamic norms. These norms have meant that the way Afghanistan has dealt with questions of sovereignty, nationalism and imperial legacies simply do not fit into European understandings of these terms derived from the European experience.

The dissonance with the European experience was made evident in Chapter 2, as the complex transition of Afghanistan from a decolonized state into an independent entity within the global international system demonstrated. Afghanistan faced inherent issues in state formation and sovereignty transfer, that it never resolved. Central to this narrative is the analysis of Afghanistan's internal contestations between desert and sedentary norms, particularly in light of the 1929 coup. This event underscored the deep-rooted normative battles within Afghanistan, highlighting the tension between efforts to introduce European modernity and the resistance rooted in traditionally orthodox Islamic norm circles. Thus, Afghanistan's experience of the 20th century was not a liner transition to industrialization, modernization and development. On the contrary, as the chapter showed, it was characterized by normative conflicts coupled with internal violence, as external influences prepared to shape Afghanistan's political landscape to their will. In this respect, there is very little 'post' nor 'state' in the notion that Afghanistan was a postcolonial state in the 20th century. Yet, as the interaction capacity of the global international system increased, Afghanistan found its 'inside' norms increasingly encountering the 'outside' norms of international actors and global international society. Herein, internally sedentary and desert norms were in conflict, raising a plethora of issues about how to deal with questions of political legitimacy, resistance to modernity, the role of Islamic orthodoxy and national consciousness. Externally, having to deal with the Soviet Union added to this already complex situation. First as the Soviets provided an external source of revenue, but then as two dissonant sets of norms vied for power as the Cold War turned hotter and sparked a civil war. Afghanistan is still trying to recover from this historical legacy, even as external actors such as the EU have sought to mobilize the norms of global international society. To this extent, the EU has a proud record of humanitarianism in Afghanistan throughout the 1990s; its ahistoricism has meant that the EU has not drawn on those lessons of that period. Yet, in moving from an initial European Community relationship built on trade and aid, to a championing humanitarian norms, it was the EU that became the de facto coordinator in Afghanistan and helped multiple uprooted people and refugees.

With EU institutions hosting significant strategic actors in Afghanistan, their marginalization after 11 September 2001 was problematic. Indeed, in many respects, EU policy towards Afghanistan never recovered from this original marginalization in the name of transatlantic solidarity. Chapter 3 stressed this point, even as it became clear that the EU was willing to support the US and get involved in state-building efforts. What emerged was a considerable contextual dissonance between the EU's intentions and the complex dynamics within Afghanistan. In responding to the 11 September 2001 terrorist attacks, the US entered Afghanistan without a long-term plan and a myopic commitment to leave as soon as 2004. A consequence of this was the Bonn Agreement and the failure to establish a comprehensive peace process, which inadvertently empowered warlords and entrenched neopatrimonial norm circles into state institutions. Rather than helping achieve transatlantic goals, this exacerbated the challenges of state-building. Moreover, the US's diversion of attention and resources to Iraq undermined efforts in Afghanistan and contributed to the resurgence of the Taliban. Only this time, the insurgency had become the *cause célèbre* of pan-Islamist groups who had the benefit of learning lessons in Iraq and developed more deadly capabilities in their resistance efforts. The failure to comprehensively address the root causes of instability and terrorism, coupled with strategic misalignments and the impact of external factors like the Iraq War, significantly hampered the effectiveness of the international community's engagement in Afghanistan. For the EU, failing to recognize the calculated neglect and misjudging US levels of commitment predestined their efforts to failure. Indeed, lessons from the EU's experience in Afghanistan should not only concern the need for greater EU strategic autonomy, but the recognition that US short-term operational horizons and myopic outlook raise questions about US global leadership in the 21st century.

Nevertheless, as Chapter 4 illustrated, even as a secondary actor in Afghanistan the EU has its own burden of responsibility to bear. The EU's state-building efforts ultimately faltered due to a multitude of strategic misalignments and oversight failures, exacerbated by a pervasive underestimation of Afghanistan's historical complexities and societal norms. Having deliberately and consciously nested EU policy inside US leadership, EU institutions failed to critically assess the feasibility of transplanting Western democratic and state-building models onto Afghan soil, which significantly diverged from local practices and expectations. The complications of this only deepened when the corruption of neopatrimonial networks began to spread into the wider economy and the so-called 'corruption eruption' took hold. Fuelled by the influx of international aid far exceeding Afghanistan's absorptive capacity, the EU chose not to challenge neopatrimonialist norms, even when it involved the theft of EU aid. Failing to challenge the pervasive influence of corruption has become a policy that many EU policy makers regret; especially as it came at the expense of pursuing peace. Nevertheless, the result was a deeply entrenched corruption that undermined the legitimacy and effectiveness of both the Afghan government and international efforts.

With corruption helping to fuel insecurity in Afghanistan, Chapter 5 detailed how the EU was unable to meaningfully address the growing insecurity. As EU engagement evolved from a marginal role to taking on increased responsibilities, it was clear that European actions were too little too late. The European Union Police Mission in Afghanistan (EUPOL Afghanistan) mission aimed at police reform, but it faced numerous challenges from being an insufficient size and lacking coordination. Indeed, it did little to move the needle towards significantly improve policing and security in Afghanistan. In such circumstances, the EU should have paid greater attention to peacebuilding, but instead it deferred to US leadership and the Government of Afghanistan (GOA), as it grappled with its own internal bureaucratic battles, the re-emergence of the Taliban, and the eventual collapse of the GOA. In this context, 2016 was certainly a positive moment, with the European Union Special Representative (EUSR) Mellbin helping to push forward the peace deal between the GOA and Hezb-e Islami Gulbuddin. The Brussels Conference was also valuable in initially refocusing the attention of global international society. Yet, just as the EU had the opportunity to lead in Afghanistan, and re-evaluate its strategy, EU actors in Brussels chose not to. Worse still, the EUSR position that had proved successful under both Vendrell and Mellbin was downgraded to a Special Envoy position. This was neither shrewd nor expedient in helping the EU resolve mounting issues inside Afghanistan. Indeed, the EU became so irrelevant over time, that the norm of solidarity was broken, and the Trump administration moved forward with plans to remove US troops. That the EU was not consulted, nor aware that this was a genuine option, speaks directly to the state of the transatlantic relationship. This is not a trivial point. Over the two decades 857 troops from EU Member States were fatally wounded to uphold transatlantic solidarity and help build an Afghan state.

It is not just the loss of human life on all sides that makes this episode in Afghanistan so tragic. As Chapter 6 demonstrated, there are onward consequences for Afghanistan and the EU as they move forward through the 21st century. In Afghanistan, the return of the Taliban has not silenced questions about who has the right to rule. The Taliban have been able to pause that question, but they have certainly not resolved it. As a result, Afghans now face human rights and gender inequality in a drastic roll-back in human rights, especially for women and girls; including access to education, employment and participation in the public sphere. Compounding this problem, Afghanistan faces an exacerbated humanitarian crisis, with up to 97 per cent of the population living in poverty. Rather than tackling these problems the Taliban has become preoccupied with vengeance and enforcing norms of conservative Islamic orthodoxy. All the while engaging in education and cultural erasure. In return, Afghanistan has faced international isolation and economic crisis. This is an abysmal record for 20 years of action, and should raise serious questions over how accountable practices around EU aid are given that Afghanistan has been its largest recipient. Nevertheless, the Taliban's return should mean that the EU will be forced to evaluate its practices pertaining to EU external action. Already challenges around terrorism, narcotics, small arms and irregular migration have been elevated as the EU comes to terms with this new strategic reality. Although the war in Ukraine has quickly drawn attention away from what happened in Afghanistan, EU policy makers should engage in a period of evaluation and introspection, as a reassessment of what has gone wrong and why takes place. It is only by doing this that the EU and its calls for strategic autonomy will be better able to navigate the strategically selective context of the global international system with any contextual consonance.

Theoretical and practical implications

With this research being theoretically driven but empirically rich, it is worth reflecting on the implications for future research. Combining the three key theoretical commitments presented in this research will inevitably take more time and experimentation to add sophistication and depth. Indeed, there has been much of what both Buzan and Little, Elder-Vass and Jessop have refined left out from this already complex examination. However, moving forward it is hoped that in fusing these literatures in and through thick contextualizations of case studies a critical realist approach will emerge that can speak to a wide range of issues in world politics. Indeed, it is hoped that by looking outside of the Western context, a critical realist theory of decolonization will emerge. Nevertheless, as an initial start to this project, the case study in this book has already opened a range of theoretical questions that a future research agenda needs to address. It has done so by challenging the prevailing Eurocentric and ahistoric approaches within International Relations and advocating for a more nuanced understanding of non-Western contexts and historical dynamics. This has important implications for conceptualizing international policy making and engagement and urges scholars and practitioners to adopt a more historically informed and context-sensitive approach to identifying the important role norms play in maintaining and perpetuating social reality. Indeed, where this research falls short is in explicitly identify the causal mechanisms of how norms perpetuate and impact the world over long periods of time. However, this should not detract from the challenge this theoretical framework has tried to pose in trying to move beyond disciplinary boundaries and a traditional Western-centric focus, to opening up new avenues for research that are more inclusive of diverse histories and sociopolitical realities.

Key to opening new avenues, in this research agenda, is the reasonable assumption that while people share a common origin in Africa around 200,000 years ago, people do not maintain widespread intersectionality of norms. Given this, the dynamic interplay between norm circles and practices needs to be taken into account and be grounded in historical contexts. For example, the myth of a 'state of nature' is one that permeates IR literature. That there has never been a state of nature is surely an important fact of reality but tends to be treated as incidental. The theoretical implication of the framework presented here is that International Relations theory is better served trying to contribute to an understanding of how norms shape international relations, and in doing so provide empirical evidence of norm contestation, adoption and transformation. Understanding the complexity of normative landscapes, and their impact, can enrich our theories of the world with detailed case studies. Indeed, using this lens on Afghanistan, it was possible to explore the contestation as Afghanistan attempted to transition from a tribal society to a sovereign state. This certainly challenges theories of state formation and sovereignty, and for example, the role Indus Valley civilization norms play in this is certainly worth further exploration. Afghanistan does not fit the traditional Westphalian model of statehood. However, rather than asserting this is the case, the theoretical framework presented in this volume helps to explain why this might be the case with reference to complex norms operating in internal dynamics and external interventions. It is this that may allow it to contribute more definitively to postcolonial and decolonial theories moving forward, in addition to debates about Global International Relations.

The ambition of this volume was not, however, to produce an exclusively theoretical text and contribute to exclusively theoretical debates. One of the main appeals of critical realism and the complex naturalism it ascribes to, is that it helps speak to empirical content and bridge the analytical distinction between social and material worlds. As such, it is important to draw out and highlight the practical implications from this case study as they relate to the EU. While the reader may have already drawn these lessons out, it is useful to recap them explicitly here as concisely as possible. To this extent it is worth considering five clusters of practical implications.

Strategic foresight and intelligence

The Afghanistan experience underscores the need for the EU to prioritize long-term analysis, enhance intelligence gathering and restructure information-sharing mechanisms. A 'blank slate approach' has not served the EU well. Indeed, rather than waiting for crisis to emerge, the EU should try to proactively capture the knowledge within its networks of delegations and non-governmental organization networks. In 2002, the EU had enormous information advantages that it could have drawn upon in Afghanistan. Making sure that these are linked to deeper understanding of geopolitical contexts and trends will better serve the EU and the people its institutions are engaging with.

Peacebuilding and local empowerment

Decades of experience in Afghanistan demonstrate the futility of top-down state-building and ignoring community-level conflicts. The EU must shift its focus, prioritizing grassroots peacebuilding, indigenous pluralism and strengthening local mediation capacities. This may require new instruments to be part of the array of the EU's commitment to strategic autonomy, and work with the EU in its commitments to global international society. Indeed, the EU should learn the lesson that peace is not an afterthought of development, but a necessary condition of development success.

European Union autonomy, diplomacy and partnerships

Navigating volatile regions demands strategic autonomy for the EU, with clear external action goals independent of immediate US influence. This entails enhanced security capabilities, greater resolve and a focus on building strategic depth in regions like Central Asia. Simultaneously, the EU must nurture transatlantic solidarity where interests align and actively reinforce diplomatic ties with regional powers like India and Pakistan. More probingly, the EU needs to reflect on its global role and the leadership it can offer through its normative commitments.

Rethinking aid distribution and conflict sensitivity

Afghanistan showcases how poorly monitored aid fuels corruption and undermines development goals. The EU needs stricter conflict sensitivity in its aid distribution, focusing on impact, resilience and accountability. This means establishing parallel support structures, prioritizing systemic reform early on, and potentially using aid conditionality linked to anti-corruption and peacebuilding efforts.

Counter-narcotics and counterterrorism

The Taliban's return highlights ongoing regional threats of terrorism, the illicit drug trade and links to organized crime in Europe. The EU must proactively explore regional counter-narcotics cooperation and discreet, limited cooperation with the Taliban where necessary. This includes addressing the trafficking of small arms and potentially expanding the EU's regional training programmes. Existing EU intelligence capabilities should be scrutinized and adapted to effectively counter these threats.

The Afghan experience offers the EU a stark but invaluable opportunity to recalibrate its approach to future conflicts and crises. These lessons demand a fundamental shift in norms across EU institutions – moving from reactive to anticipatory, from externally driven to strategically autonomous, and from Eurocentric values-driven engagement to contextually sensitive engagement. Intelligence reform, localized peacebuilding, conflict-sensitive aid and the development of nuanced regional diplomacy are not mere options, but prerequisites for the EU to effectively navigate the complex landscape of future global challenges. Europe has a critical role to play in championing global change, but it needs to ensure that policy decisions are driven by hard-earned knowledge, strategic foresight and a commitment to building genuine resilience in the world's most vulnerable regions. Contextual consonance should not just be a vague ambition, but a central goal in setting collective intentions.

Reflections beyond Afghanistan

Moving beyond Afghanistan, the EU has an unprecedented opportunity to reimagine its role on the global stage. The failure in Afghanistan serves as painful but instructive ground upon which a more historically informed, norm-sensitive and strategically nuanced EU approach can flourish. The principles outlined here, though born of difficult lessons, point to a future where the EU acts as an indispensable force for positive change in the world's toughest corners.

This transformation must extend beyond crisis zones to shape the EU's overall approach to global affairs. Applying the principles of thick contextualization should enhance intelligence, localize peacebuilding, delineate the direction of strategic autonomy, and reimagine how aid across diverse contexts could have far-reaching implications. Similarly, the EU's commitment to democracy, human rights and sustainability should be grounded in a deep understanding of local contexts and a willingness to adapt strategies for greater contextual consonance among diverse stakeholders. Utilizing partnerships and normative diplomacy as levers of influence requires sensitivity to historical legacies, regional power dynamics and the differing priorities of partners.

Ultimately, the EU's transformative potential rests on its ability to embrace complexity and nuance as cornerstones of its engagement, both in immediate crises and broader long-term global trends. This means investing in the internal capacity to understand diverse histories, cultures and worldviews. It also demands a willingness to challenge established assumptions within EU institutions and foster a culture of constant learning and adaptation. The result won't simply be a more effective EU, but one that acts as a beacon of hope, demonstrating that positive global change is possible even in the face of immense challenges.

References

Abbas, Hassan. 2014. *The Taliban Revival: Violence and Extremism on the Pakistan-Afghanistan Frontier*. New Haven: Yale University Press.

Abbas, Hassan. 2023. *The Return of the Taliban: Afghanistan After the Americans Left*. New Haven: Yale University Press.

Acharya, Amitav. 2017. 'Towards a Global International Relations?'. *E-International Relations*. https://www.e-ir.info/2017/12/10/towards-a-global-international-relations/.

Acharya, Amitav and Barry Buzan. 2019. *The Making of Global International Relations: Origins and Evolution of IR at its Centenary*. Cambridge: Cambridge University Press.

Adili, Ali Yawar and Rohullah Sorush. 2020. 'Afghanistan's New – But Still Incomplete Cabinet: No End Yet to Acting Ministers'. *Afghanistan Analyst Network*. https://www.afghanistan-analysts.org/en/reports/politi cal-landscape/afghanistans-new-but-still-incomplete-cabinet-no-end-yet-to-acting-ministers/.

Afghanistan Compact. 2006. *The Afghanistan Compact*. London. https://www.europarl.europa.eu/meetdocs/2004_2009/documents/dv/afghan istancompactfin/afghanistancompactfinal.pdf.

Afghanistan National Environmental Protection Agency. 2017. *Second National Communication under the United Nations Framework Convention on Climate Change (UNFCCC)*. Kabul.

Agence Europe. 1994. 'Communique by Council Presidency on the Situation in Afghanistan'. *Agence Europe*.

Ahmed, Faiz 2013. 'Rule of Law Experts in Afghanistan: A Socio-Legal History of the First Afghan Constitution and the Indo-Ottoman Nexus in Kabul, 1860–1923'. UC Berkeley.

Ahmed, Manzooruddin. 1975. 'Umma: The Idea of a Universal Community'. *Islamic Studies* 14(1): 27–54.

Ahmed, Zahid. 2023. 'Sufi Revivalism in South Asia: A Study of the Role of Pir Syed Jamaat Ali Shah'. *QJSS* 4(4): 225–31.

Alder, George J. 1974a. 'The Key to India? Britain and the Herat Problem 1830–1863: Part 1'. *Middle Eastern Studies* 10(2): 186–209. doi:10.1080/00263207408700270.

Alder, George J. 1974b. 'The Key to India? Britain and the Herat Problem, 1830–1863: Part II'. *Middle Eastern Studies* 10(3): 287–311. doi:10.1080/00263207408700277.

Ali, Mohammad, Louis Dupree, Marvin G. Weinbaum, Nancy Hatch Dupree, Victor P. Petrov and Frank Raymond Allchin. 2023. 'Afghanistan'. *Britannica*. https://www.britannica.com/place/Afghanistan.

Allchin, Raymond, Warwick Ball and Norman Hammond. 2019. *The Archaeology of Afghanistan: From Earliest Times to the Timurid Period: New Edition*. Edinburgh: Edinburgh University Press. doi:10.1515/9781474450478.

Amiet, Pierre. 1986. *L'âge Des Échanges Inter-Iraniens: 3500–1700 Avant J-C*. Paris: Éditions de la Réunion des Musées Nationaux.

Amitai, Reuven. 2007. *The Mongols in the Islamic Lands Studies in the History of the Ilkhanate*. Oxon: Routledge.

Amitai-Preiss, Reuven. 1996. 'Ghazan, Islam and Mongol Tradition: A View from the Mamlūk Sultanate'. *Bulletin of the School of Oriental and African Studies* 59(1): 1–10. doi: 10.1017/S0041977X00028524.

Amnesty International. 1995a. 'Afghanistan: International Responsibility for Human Rights Disaster'. *ASA 11/09/95*. https://www.refworld.org/reference/countryrep/amnesty/1995/en/57236

Amnesty International. 1995b. 'Afghanistan: The Human Rights Crisis and the Refugees'. *ASA 11/002/1995*. https://www.refworld.org/docid/3ae6a9a613.html.

Amnesty International. 2019. *Afghanistan Refugee: Forty Years of Dispossession*. London. https://www.amnesty.org/en/latest/news/2019/06/afghanistan-refugees-forty-years/.

Amnesty International. 2023. *Amnesty International Report 2022/23: The State of the World's Human Rights*. www.amnesty.org.

Andersen, Louise Riis. 2016. *International Lessons from Integrated Approaches in Afghanistan, Part I*. https://papers.ssrn.com/sol3/papers.cfm?abstract_id=3387396.

ANDS. 2005. *Afghanistan National Development Strategy: An Interim Strategy for Security, Governance, Economic Growth & Poverty Reduction*. Kabul. https://mof.gov.af/sites/default/files/2021-05/ANDS.pdf.

ANDS. 2008. *Afghanistan National Development Strategy 2008–2013: A Strategy for Security, Governance, Economic Growth & Poverty Reduction*. Kabul. https://www.imf.org/external/pubs/ft/scr/2008/cr08153.pdf.

Ansorg, Nadine and Toni Haastrup. 2018. 'Gender and the EU's Support for Security Sector Reform in Fragile Contexts'. *JCMS: Journal of Common Market Studies* 56(5): 1127–43. doi:https://doi.org/10.1111/jcms.12716.

Ashrafyan, Klara Zarmairovna. 1998. 'Central Asia under Timur from 1370 to the Early Fifteenth Century'. In *History of Civilizations of Central Asia, v. 4: The Age of Achievement, A.D. 750 to the End of the Fifteenth Century*, edited by Muhammad Seyfeydinovich Asimov and Clifford Edmund Bosworth. Paris: United Nations Educational, Scientific and Cultural Organization, pp 323–49.

Ashton, Catherine. 2014. 'Statement by EU High Representative Catherine Ashton on Fatalities in EUPOL Afghanistan Following Yesterday's Attack in Kabul – News – EULEX – European Union Rule of Law Mission in Kosovo'. *EULEX*. https://www.eulex-kosovo.eu/?page=2,11,2062.

AsianLII. 2004. '2004 Afghan Laws Legislation'. *AsianLII*. http://www.asianlii.org/af/legis/laws/toc-2004.html.

Azad, Arezou. 2016. 'The Beginnings of Islam in Afghanistan: Conquest, Acculturation, and Islamization'. In *Afghanistan's Islam: From Conversion to the Taliban*, edited by Nile Green. Berkeley: University of California Press, pp 41–55. doi:10.1515/9780520967373-006.

Azoulay, Audrey. 2021. 'Afghanistan: UNESCO Calls for the Protection of Cultural Heritage in Its Diversity'. *UNESCO*. https://www.unesco.org/en/articles/afghanistan-unesco-calls-protection-cultural-heritage-its-diversity.

Baitenmann, Helga. 1990. 'NGOs and the Afghan War: The Politicisation of Humanitarian Aid'. *Third World Quarterly* 12(1): 62–85. http://www.jstor.org/stable/3992448.

Baker, Robert L. 1934. 'The Passing of an Afghan King'. *Current History (1916–1940)* 39(4): 505–8. http://www.jstor.org/stable/45334549.

Baker-Beall, Christopher. 2017. 'Introduction: The Language of the European Union's "Fight against Terrorism"'. In *The European Union's Fight against Terrorism*, Manchester: Manchester University Press, pp 1–27. https://doi.org/10.7228/manchester/9780719091063.003.0001.

Baldwin, David A. 2000. 'Success and Failure in Foreign Policy'. *Annual Review of Political Science* 3(1): 167–82. doi:10.1146/annurev.polisci.3.1.167.

Ball, Warwick. 2008. *The Monuments of Afghanistan: History, Archaeology and Architecture*. London: I.B. Tauris.

Barfield, Thomas. 2010. *Afghanistan: A Cultural and Political History*. Princeton: Princeton University Press.

BBC News. 2020. 'Afghanistan Presidential Election: Ashraf Ghani Re-Elected'. *BBC News*. https://www.bbc.co.uk/news/world-asia-51547726.

BBC Panorama. 2024. 'Special Forces Blocked UK Resettlement Applications from Elite Afghan Troops'. *BBC News*. https://www.bbc.co.uk/news/uk-68332923.

Benedictow, Ole J. 2021. *The Complete History of the Black Death*. Woodbridge: Boydell & Brewer. doi: 10.1017/9781787449312.

Bennett, Jon, Jane Alexander, Douglas Saltmarshe, Rachel Phillipson and Peter Marsden. 2009. 'Evaluation Report EV696 Country Programme Evaluation Afghanistan'. Department for International Development https://assets.publishing.service.gov.uk/media/5a7485e9e5274a7f9c586 aa4/afghan_eval.pdf

Bennhold, Katrin and Steven Erlanger. 2021. 'Why Europe's Leaders Say They Won't Welcome More Afghan Refugees'. *The New York Times.* https://www.nytimes.com/2021/08/18/world/europe/afghanistan-refug ees-europe-migration-asylum.html?action=click&module=RelatedLi nks&pgtype=Article.

Bentley, Michelle and Jack Holland. 2014. *Obama's Foreign Policy.* London: Routledge.

Bergen, Peter. 2006. *The Osama Bin Laden I Know: An Oral History of al-Qaeda's Leader.* New York: Free Press.

Bergmann, Denis. 1977. 'Agricultural Policies in the EEC and Their External Implications'. *World Development* 5(5): 407–15.

Bezhan, Faridullah. 2013. 'The Emergence of Political Parties and Political Dynamics in Afghanistan, 1964–73'. *Iranian Studies* 46(6): 921–41. doi:10.1080/00210862.2013.810074.

Bezhan, Faridullah. 2014. 'The Pashtunistan Issue and Politics in Afghanistan, 1947–1952'. *The Middle East Journal* 68(2): 197–209. doi: https://doi.org/10.3751/68.2.11.

Bhaskar, Roy. 1975. *A Realist Theory of Science.* London: Verso.

Bicchi, Federica. 2006. '"Our Size Fits All": Normative Power Europe and the Mediterranean'. *Journal of European Public Policy* 13(2): 286–303. doi:10.1080/13501760500451733.

Bijlert, Martine van. 2010. 'Are Talks with the Taliban Snow-Balling?' *Afghanistan Analyst Network.* https://www.afghanistan-analysts.org/en/repo rts/war-and-peace/are-talks-with-the-taleban-snow-balling/.

Bira, Shagdaryn. 1998. 'The Mongols and Their State in the Twelfth to the Thirteenth Century'. In *History of Civilizations of Central Asia*, edited by Muhammad Seyfeydinovich Asimove and Clifford Edmund Bosworth. Paris: Multiple History Series UNESCO Publishing.

Biran, Michal. 2015. 'The Mongol Empire and Inter-Civilizational Exchange'. In *The Cambridge World History: Volume 5: Expanding Webs of Exchange and Conflict, 500CE–1500CE*, edited by Benjamin Z. Kedar and Merry E. Wiesner-Hanks. Cambridge: Cambridge University Press, pp 534–58. doi:10.1017/CBO9780511667480.021.

Biran, Michal. 2016. 'Il-Khanate Empire'. In *The Encyclopedia of Empire*, edited by John M. MacKenzie. Chichester: John Wiley & Sons, Ltd. doi:10.1002/9781118455074.wbeoe362.

Birdwood, Christopher. 1953. 'The International Situation'. *Hansard* 183. https://hansard.parliament.uk/Lords/1953-10-21/debates/6b22ebf3-5890-4677-b8bd-65951fd16584/TheInternationalSituation

Blockmans, Steve and Ramses A. Wessel. 2009. 'The European Union and Crisis Management: Will the Lisbon Treaty Make the EU More Effective?' *Journal of Conflict and Security Law* 14(2): 265–308.

Blockmans, Steven, Rebecca Davis, Seed Parto, Rachel Reid and Hekmat Khalil Karzai. 2014. *Afghanistan and Central Asia: Prospects and Challenges after Withdrawal of NATO/ISAF Forces*. Brussels. https://www.europarl.europa.eu/RegData/etudes/STUD/2015/457127/EXPO_STU(2015)457127_EN.pdf.

Boone, Jon. 2007. 'Envoys Expelled for "Talks with Taliban"'. *The Financial Times*. https://www.ft.com/content/a311138c-b3b0-11dc-a6df-0000779fd2ac

Borger, Julian. 2010. 'Afghanistan Conference Sets out Plan for Two-Tier Peace Process'. *The Guardian*. https://www.theguardian.com/world/2010/jan/28/afghanistan-london-conference-analysis.

Borrell, Josep. 2021a. 'Afghanistan: Speech by the High Representative/Vice-President Josep Borrell at the EP Debate'. *European Union External Action*. https://www.eeas.europa.eu/eeas/afghanistan-speech-high-representativevice-president-josep-borrell-ep-debate_en.

Borrell, Josep. 2021b. 'European Parliament Joint AFET: DEVE Committee Meeting with the Delegation for Relations with Afghanistan'. https://multimedia.europarl.europa.eu/en/webstreaming/joint-afet-deve-committee-meeting_20210819-0900-COMMITTEE-AFET-DEVE.

Borthakur, Anchita and Angana Kotokey. 2020. 'Ethnicity or Religion? The Genesis of the Taliban Movement in Afghanistan'. *Asian Affairs* 51(4): 817–37. doi:10.1080/03068374.2020.1832772.

Börzel, Tanja A. 2022. 'EU Democracy Projection: Does the EU Practice What It Preaches?' *Mediterranean Politics* 27(4): 553–62. doi:10.1080/13629395.2021.1915738.

Börzel, Tanja A., Yasemin Pamuk and Andreas Stahn. 2008. 'The European Union and the Promotion of Good Governance in Its Near Abroad. One Size Fits All?' *SFB-Governance Working Paper Series* 18. http://edoc.vifapol.de/opus/volltexte/2009/1976/.

Bosworth, Clifford Edmund. 1969. 'The Tahirids and Arabic Culture'. *Journal of Semitic Studies* 14(1): 45–79. doi:10.1093/jss/14.1.45.

Bosworth, C. Edmund. 1998. 'The Ghaznavids'. In *History of Civilizations of Central Asia*, edited by Muhammad Seyfeydinovich Asimov and Clifford Edmund Bosworth. Paris: Multiple History Series UNESCO Publishing, pp 102–24.

Bosworth, C. Edmund. 2007. *Historic Cities of the Islamic World*. Leiden: Brill. doi:https://doi.org/10.1163/ej.9789004153882.i-616.

Brahimi, Lakhdar. 2000. 'A/55/305–S/2000/809 General Assembly Security Council General Assembly Comprehensive Review of the Whole Question of Peacekeeping Operations in All Their Aspects'. UN General Assembly Security Council. https://peacekeeping.un.org/sites/default/files/a_55_305_e_brahimi_report.pdf.

Brivati, Brian. 2022. *Losing Afghanistan: The Fall of Kabul and the End of Western Intervention*. London: Biteback Publishing.

Brown, Judith M. 1999. 'India'. In *The Oxford History of the British Empire: The Twentieth Century*, edited by Judith M. Brown and W.M. Roger Louis. Oxford: Oxford University Press, pp 421–46.

Brussels Conference. 2016. 'Self-Reliance Through Mutual Accountability Framework'. https://www.consilium.europa.eu/media/23645/agreed-smaf-smart-deliverables-final.pdf.

Bull, Hedley. 1977. *The Anarchical Society*. London: Macmillan Press. doi:10.1007/978-1-349-24028-9.

Bull, Hedley. 1982. 'Civilian Power Europe: A Contradiction in Terms?' *JCMS: Journal of Common Market Studies* 21(2): 149–70. doi:10.1111/j.1468-5965.1982.tb00866.x.

Bulletin EU. 1996. *European Union Statements and Presidency Statements on Behalf of the European Union, Bulletin EU 10–1996; Common Foreign and Security Policy (7/16)*. http://europa.eu/archives/bulletin/en/9610/p104007.htm.

Bumiller, Elisabeth. 2009. 'Remembering Afghanistan's Golden Age'. *The New York Times*. https://www.nytimes.com/2009/10/18/weekinreview/18bumiller.html

Burbank, Jane and Frederick Cooper. 2010. *Empires in World History: Power and the Politics of Difference*. Princeton: Princeton University Press.

Burke, Edward. 2014. 'Game Over? The EU's Legacy in Afghanistan' (February). https://www.nytimes.com/1995/02/22/world/as-us-aid-ends-need-of-afghan-war-victims-persists.html

Burns, John F. 1995. 'As U.S. Aid Ends, Need of Afghan War Victims Persists'. *The New York Times*.

Bush, George W. 2001. 'President Speaks on War Effort to Citadel Cadets'. *The White House*. https://georgewbush-whitehouse.archives.gov/news/releases/2001/12/20011211-6.html.

Bush, George W. 2002. 'President Outlines War Effort'. *The White House*. https://georgewbush-whitehouse.archives.gov/news/releases/2002/04/20020417-1.html.

Bush, George W. 2003. 'President Bush Announces Major Combat Operations in Iraq Have Ended'. *The White House*. https://georgewbush-whitehouse.archives.gov/news/releases/2003/05/20030501-15.html.

Bush, George W. (2004) 'President's Remarks to the Unity Journalists of Color Convention'. Washington Convention Center, August 6. https:// georgewbush-whitehouse.archives.gov/news/releases/2004/08/20040 806-1.html

Bush, George W. 2010. *Decision Points*. London: Virgin. https://go.exlib ris.link/8X7WNb1X.

Busse, Jan, Morten Valbjørn, Asel Doolotkeldieva, Stefanie Ortmann, Karen Smith, Seteney Shami, et al. 2024. 'Contextualizing the Contextualizers: How the Area Studies Controversy Is Different in Different Places'. *International Studies Review* 26(1): viad056. doi:10.1093/ isr/viad056.

Buzan, Barry and Richard Little. 2000. *International Systems in World History; Remaking the Study of International Relations*. Oxford: Oxford University Press.

Call, Charles T. and Susan E. Cook. 2003. 'On Democratisation and Peacebuilding'. *Global Governance* 9(2): 233–46.

Call, Steve. 2007. *Danger Close: Tactical Air Controllers in Afghanistan and Iraq*. Texas: Texas A&M University Press.

Carter, Jimmy. 1980. 'Jimmy Carter State of the Union Address 1980'. *Jimmy Carter Presidential Library and Museum*.

Castagne, Joseph. 1935. 'Soviet Imperialism in Afghanistan'. *Foreign Affairs* 13(4): 698–703. https://heinonline.org/HOL/P?h=hein.journals/for a13&i=719.

Cello, Lorenzo. 2018. 'Taking History Seriously in IR: Towards a Historicist Approach'. *Review of International Studies* 44(2): 236–51. doi:10.1017/ S0260210517000432.

Chan, Eva K.F., Axel Timmermann, Benedetta F. Baldi, Andy E. Moore, Ruth J. Lyons, Sun-Seon Lee, et al. 2019. 'Human Origins in a Southern African Palaeo-Wetland and First Migrations'. *Nature* 575(7781): 185–9. doi:10.1038/s41586-019-1714-1.

CIA. 1973. 'Afghanistan: Death of Former Prime Minister Mohammad Hashim Maiwandwal'. *Intelligence Information Cable NSC/S*. https://www. cia.gov/readingroom/docs/DOC_0000200633.pdf.

Clapp-Wincek, Cynthia. 1983. *The Helmand Valley Project in Afghanistan*. USAID: Washington, DC. https://pdf.usaid.gov/pdf_docs/Pnaal028.pdf

Clark, Kate. 2010a. 'PEACE JIRGA BLOG 2: Peace Jirga Goes to Washington: Whose Opinions Count on Reconciling Taliban?'. *Afghanistan Analysts Network*. https://www.afghanistan-analysts.org/en/reports/war- and-peace/peace-jirga-blog-2-peace-jirga-goes-to-washington-whose- opinions-count-on-reconciling-taliban/.

Clark, Kate. 2010b. 'PEACE JIRGA BLOG 8: The Afghan Jungle's Big Beasts and "Lively Debate"'. *Afghanistan Analysts Network*. https://www.afghanistan-analysts.org/en/reports/war-and-peace/peace-jirga-blog-8-the-afghan-jungles-big-beasts-and-lively-debate/.

Clark, Kate. 2018. 'Graft and Remilitarisation: A Look Back at Efforts to Disarm, Demobilise, Reconcile and Reintegrate'. *Afghanistan Analysts Network*. https://www.afghanistan-analysts.org/en/reports/war-and-peace/graft-and-remilitarisation-a-look-back-at-efforts-to-disarm-demobilise-reconcile-and-reintegrate/.

Clarke, Richard A. 2004. *Against All Enemies: Inside America's War on Terror*. New York: Free Press.

Colville, Rupert. 1997. 'Afghanistan: The Unending Crisis – The Biggest Caseload in the World'. *Refugees Magazine*. https://www.unhcr.org/uk/publications/refugees-magazine-issue-108-afghanistan-unending-crisis-biggest-caseload-world.

Commission. 2018. *Progress Report on the Implementation of the European Agenda on Migration*. Brussels.

Commission. 2020. *Communication from the Commission to the European Parliament, the Council, the European Economic and Social Committee, and the Committee of the Regions. EU Agenda and Action Plan on Drugs 2021– 2025*. Brussels.

Commission of the European Communities. 1994. *Towards a New Asia Strategy*. Communication from the Commission to the Council. COM (94) 314 final, 13 July 1994. http://aei.pitt.edu/2949/

Cookman, Colin. 2020. *Assessing Afghanistan's 2019 Presidential Election*. Washington DC. https://www.usip.org/sites/default/files/2020-08/pw_166-assessing_afghanistans_2019_presidential_election-pw.pdf.

Cortesi, Elisa, Maurizio Tosi, Alessandra Lazzari and Massimo Vidale. 2008. 'Cultural Relationships beyond the Iranian Plateau: The Helmand Civilization, Baluchistan and the Indus Valley in the 3rd Millennium BCE'. *Paléorient* 34(2): 5–35.

COTA. 2000. *Evaluation of the European Commission Aid in the Fields of Social and Rural Development: Evaluation of Budget Line 'Aid for Uprooted People in ALA Countries 1997–1999 (Council Regulation 443/97)*. Bruxelles.

Council. 2004. 'Council Decision of 29 April 2004 Concerning the Conclusion of the Cooperation Agreement between the European Community and the Islamic Republic of Pakistan (2004/870/EC)'. *Official Journal of the European Union* 378(22).

Council. 2005a. *EU-Afghanistan Joint Declaration Committing to a New EU-Afghan Partnership*. Strasbourg. https://data.consilium.europa.eu/doc/document/ST-14519-2005-INIT/en/pdf.

Council. 2005b. 'European Union Counter-Terrorism Strategy'. *Council of the European Union*.

Council. 2007a. 'Council Joint Action 2007/369/CFSP of 30 May 2007 on Establishment of the European Union Police Mission in Afghanistan (EUPOL AFGANISTAN)'. *Official Journal of the European Union.* https://eur-lex.europa.eu/legal-content/EN/TXT/HTML/?uri=CELEX:32007E0369.

Council. 2007b. 'EU-Pakistan Joint Declaration Berlin, 08 February 2007'. *Consilium.europa.eu Newroom.* https://www.consilium.europa.eu/uedocs/cms_data/docs/pressdata/en/er/92681.pdf.

Council. 2008. 'Council Joint Action 2008/612/CFSP of 24 July 2008 Concerning the Appointment of the European Union Special Representative for Afghanistan'. *Official Journal of the European Union L 197/60 – EUR-Lex – 32008E0612 – EN – EUR-Lex.* https://eur-lex.europa.eu/legal-content/EN/TXT/?uri=CELEX%3A32008E0612&qid=1701256033831.

Council. 2009a. 'Council Joint Action 2009/467/CFSP of 15 June 2009 Appointing the European Union Special Representative for Afghanistan and Pakistan and Repealing Joint Action 2009/135/CFSP'. *Official Journal of the European Union EUR-Lex – 32009E0467 – EN – EUR-Lex.* https://eur-lex.europa.eu/legal-content/EN/TXT/?uri=CELEX%3A32009E0467&qid=1701258042045

Council. 2009b. 'Strengthening EU Action in Afghanistan and Pakistan'. *Consilium.Europa/Newsroom.* https://reliefweb.int/report/afghanistan/strengthening-eu-action-afghanistan-and-pakistan-2971st-external-relations.

Council. 2010. 'Council Decision 2010/168/CFSP of 22 March 2010 Appointing the European Union Special Representative in Afghanistan'. *Official Journal of the European Union.* https://www.europarl.europa.eu/meetdocs/2009_2014/documents/sede/dv/sede030510cdeusrafghanistan_/sede030510cdeusrafghanistan_en.pdf.

Council. 2014. 'Joint Communication to the European Parliament and the Council: Elements for an EU Strategy in Afghanistan 2014–16'. https://data.consilium.europa.eu/doc/document/ST-9467-2014-INIT/en/pdf.

Council. 2021a. 'Afghanistan: Council Conclusions Set out the EU's Position and Next Steps'. https://www.consilium.europa.eu/en/press/press-releases/2021/09/21/afghanistan-council-conclusions-set-out-the-eu-s-position-and-next-steps/pdf.

Council. 2021b. *Afghanistan: Counter-Terrorism Action Plan.* Brussels. https://data.consilium.europa.eu/doc/document/ST-12315-2021-INIT/en/pdf.

Council. 2021c. 'Council Conclusions on Afghanistan'. *General Secretariat of the Council to Delegations.* https://data.consilium.europa.eu/doc/document/ST-11713-2021-REV-2/en/pdf.

Council of the European Union. 2016a. *15379/12 Restreint UE/EU Restricted – CIVCOM Advice on the Strategic Review of EUPOL Afghanistan.* Brussels. https://data.consilium.europa.eu/doc/document/ST-15379-2012-DCL-1/en/.pdf.

Council of the European Union. 2016b. *Council Decision Amending Decision 2010/279/CFSP on the European Union Police Mission in Afghanistan (EUPOL Afghanistan), Providing for Its Liquidation.* Brussels. https://data.consilium.europa.eu/doc/document/ST-12412-2016-INIT/en/pdf.

Council of the European Union. 2021. 'Afghanistan: Counter-Terrorism Action Plan'. *Europa.* https://www.consilium.europa.eu/media/52758/st_12315_2021_init_en.pdf.

Court. 2011. *The Efficiency and Effectiveness of EU Contributions Channelled Through United Nations Organisations in Conflict-Affected Countries European Court of Auditors.* Luxembourg. doi:10.2865/41651.

Crews, Robert D. 2015. *Afghan Modern: The History of a Global Nation.* Cambridge, MA: Harvard University Press. doi:10.4159/9780674495746.

Dale, Reginald. 1980. 'NATO Strategy after the Invasion of Afghanistan'. *The Financial Times.* 18 April.

Dale, Stephen Frederic. 1998. 'The Legacy of the Timurids'. *Journal of the Royal Asiatic Society* 8(1): 43–58.

Dalrymple, William. 2013. *Return of a King: The Battle for Afghanistan.* London: Bloomsbury.

Damen, Mario. 2022. *EU Strategic Autonomy 2013–2023: From Concept to Capacity.* Brussels.

Dartnell, Lewis. 2018. *Origins: How the Earth Made Us.* London: The Bodley Head.

Davis, Richard S. 2019. 'The Palaeolithic'. In *The Archaeology of Afghanistan From Earliest Times to the Timurid Period: New Edition,* edited by Raymond Allchin, Warwick Ball and Norman Hammond. Edinburgh: Edinburgh University Press, pp 61–98.

Davy, Richard. 1980. 'Has Nato Now Stopped Arguing over Afghanistan?'. *The Times Newspaper.* https://0-go-gale-com.pugwash.lib.warwick.ac.uk/ps/retrieve.do?tabID=Newspapers&resultListType=RESULT_LIST&searchResultsType=SingleTab&retrievalId=b99d800f-0520-4d97-a89b-3531d9df8ea8&hitCount=2&searchType=BasicSearchForm&currentPosition=2&docId=GALE%7CCS235112190&docType=Article&sort=Relevance&contentSegment=ZTMA-MOD1&prodId=GDCS&pageNum=1&contentSet=GALE%7CCS235112190&searchId=R2&userGroupName=warwick&inPS=true.

Dawar, Anil. 2009. 'Barack Obama Warns Europe Faces Greater Threat from Al-Qaida'. *The Guardian.* https://www.theguardian.com/world/2009/apr/03/obama-russia-nato-al-qaida.

Dawi, Akmal. 2024. 'China's President Accepts Credentials From Afghan Representative'. *Voice of America*. https://www.voanews.com/a/china-s-president-receives-afghan-ambassador-taliban-seek-recognition-from-russia-iran-/7463837.html

Dempsey, Judy. 2008. 'Europe Lagging in Effort to Train Afghan Police'. *The New York Times*. https://www.nytimes.com/2008/05/28/world/asia/28iht-letter.1.13274908.html.

Desch, Michael C. 2019. *Cult of the Irrelevant: The Waning Influence of Social Science on National Security*. Oxford: Princeton University Press.

Dimitrakis, Panagiotis. 2012. 'The Soviet Invasion of Afghanistan: International Reactions, Military Intelligence and British Diplomacy'. *Middle Eastern Studies* 48(4): 511–36. doi:10.1080/00263206.2012.682304.

Dimitriadi, Angeliki. 2018. *Irregular Afghan Migration to Europe: At the Margins, Looking In*. Cham: Palgrave Macmillan.

Dimitriu, George and Beatrice de Graaf. 2010. 'The Dutch COIN Approach: Three Years in Uruzgan, 2006–2009'. *Small Wars & Insurgencies* 21(3): 429–58. doi:10.1080/09592318.2010.505471.

Dirkx, Toon. 2017. *State-Building in the Shadow of War: EU Capabilities in the Fields of Conflict Prevention and Peacebuilding in Afghanistan*. Utrecht: Centre for Conflict Studies, Utrecht University.

Dixit, Yama, David A. Hodell and Cameron A. Petrie. 2014. 'Abrupt Weakening of the Summer Monsoon in Northwest India 4100 Yr Ago'. *Geology* 42(4): 339–42. doi:10.1130/g35236.1.

DNSA. 2015. *Afghanistan: The Making of U.S. Policy, 1973–1990*. Washington, DC: Digital National Security Archive (DNSA).

Dobbins, James F. 2008. *After the Taliban: Nation-Building in Afghanistan*. Virginia: Potomac Books.

Dodge, Toby. 2021. 'Afghanistan and the Failure of Liberal Peacebuilding'. *Survival* 63(5): 47–58. doi:10.1080/00396338.2021.1982197.

Dombey, Daniel, James Blitz and Michael Steen. 2010. 'Crisis Highlights War Fatigue in Europe'. *The Financial Times*. https://www.ft.com/content/61bf12be-1f22-11df-9584-00144feab49a.

Donini, Antonio. 1996. *The Policies of Mercy: UN Coordination in Afghanistan, Mozambique and Rwanda*. Providence: The Thomas J. Watson Jr. Institute for International Studies, Brown University.

Donner, Fred M. 1993. 'The Growth of Military Institutions in the Early Caliphate and Their Relations to Civilian Authority'. *Al-Qantara (Madrid)* 14: 311–26.

Donner, Fred M. 2000. 'Muhammad and the Caliphate: Political History of the Islamic Empire up to the Mongol Conquest'. In *The Oxford History of Islam*, edited by John L. Esposito. Oxford: Oxford University Press. https://www.oxfordreference.com/display/10.1093/acref/9780195107999.001.0001/acref-9780195107999-chapter-1

Dorronsoro, Gilles. 2009. 'Already Illegitimate'. *Carnegie Endowment for International Peace*. https://carnegieendowment.org/2009/10/21/already-illegitimate-pub-24026.

Druhe, David. 1959. *Soviet Russia and Indian Communism, 1917–1947*. New York: Bookman Associates.

Duchêne, François. 1972. 'Europe's Role in World Peace'. In *Europe Tomorrow: Sixteen Europeans Look Ahead*, edited by Richard Mayne. Fontana/Collins, pp 32–47. https://www.scirp.org/(S(lz5mqp453edsnp55rrgjct55.))/reference/referencespapers.aspx?referenceid=3515872.

Duiker, William J. and Jackson J. Spielvogel. 2002. *The Essential World History: Comprehensive Volume*. London: Wadsworth.

Dupree, Louis. 1963. 'A Suggested Pakistan-Afghanistan-Iran Federation'. *Middle East Journal* 17(4): 383–99.

Dupree, Louis. 1980. *Afghanistan*. Princeton: Princeton University Press.

Dupree, Louis, J. Lawrence Angel, Robert H. Brill, Earle R. Caley, Richard S. Davis, Charles C. Kolb, Alexander Marshack, Dexter Perkins and Alan Solem. 1972. 'Prehistoric Research in Afghanistan (1959–1966)'. *Transactions of the American Philosophical Society* 62(4): 1–84. doi:10.2307/1005969.

Duthie, John Lowe. 1984. 'Lord Lytton and the Second Afghan War: A Psychohistorical Study'. *Victorian Studies* 27(4): 461–75.

Duzgun, Eren. 2022. 'Radicalising Global IR: Modernity, Capitalism, and the Question of Eurocentrism'. *The Chinese Journal of International Politics* 15(3): 313–33. doi:10.1093/cjip/poac012.

Eckhard, Steffen. 2016. 'The German Contribution to Police Reform in Afghanistan'. In *International Assistance to Police Reform: Managing Peacebuilding*, edited by Steffen Eckhard. London: Palgrave Macmillan, pp 123–57. doi:10.1057/978-1-137-59512-6_5.

Economic Times. 2022. 'US Weapons Left in Afghanistan Being Used by Militants in Pakistan, Say Local Police'. *The Economic Times*. https://economictimes.indiatimes.com/news/defence/us-weapons-left-in-afghanistan-being-used-by-militants-in-pakistan-say-local-police/articleshow/95586264.cms.

ECSC. 1954. *Informations Statistiques (CECA) = Statistical Information (ECSC)*. No. 6, April–May 1954. http://aei.pitt.edu/43909/

ECSC. (Foreign Trade of the Community) 1962. *Commerce Exterieur de La Communaute (CECA). Resultats Annuels 1961*. Annual results for 1961 http://aei.pitt.edu/44106/

Edwards, David B. 1996. *Heroes of the Age: Moral Fault Lines on the Afghan Frontier*. Berkeley: University of California Press.

Edwards, David B. 2002. *Before Taliban: Genealogies of the Afghan Jihad*. London: University of California Press.

EEAS. 2017. 'European Union Strengthens Engagement with Afghanistan through the Appointment of a Special Envoy'. *European Union External Action*. https://www.eeas.europa.eu/node/28512_en.

EEAS. 2020. 'Statement on the Establishment of the High Council of National Reconciliation'. *European External Action Service*. https://www.eeas.europa.eu/delegations/afghanistan/statement-establishment-high-council-national-reconciliation_en.

EEAS. 2021. 'Building Peace by Cultural Heritage: A New EU Approach in Conflicts and Crises'. *Europa*. https://www.eeas.europa.eu/eeas/building-peace-cultural-heritage-–-new-eu-approach-conflicts-and-crises_und_fr#:~:text=On%20June%2021%2C%20the%20Foreign,on%20cultural%20heritage%20for%20peace

EEAS. 2022. 'A Strategic Compass for Security and Defence'. *Europa*. https://www.eeas.europa.eu/eeas/strategic-compass-security-and-defence-1_en.

EEAS. 2023. 'Counter-Terrorism: What We Do Policies and Actions'. https://www.eeas.europa.eu/eeas/counter-terrorism_en.

Egnell, Robert and Peter Haldén. 2010. 'Contextualising International State-Building'. *Conflict, Security & Development* 10(4): 431–41. doi:10.1080/14678802.2010.500505.

Ehrenreich, Robert M., Carole L. Crumley and Janet E. Levy. 1995. *Heterarchy and the Analysis of Complex Societies*. Arlington: American Anthropological Association.

Elder-Vass, Dave. 2007. 'Social Structure and Social Relations'. *Journal for the Theory of Social Behaviour* 37(4): 463–77. doi:https://doi.org/10.1111/j.1468-5914.2007.00346.x.

Elder-Vass, Dave. 2010. *The Causal Power of Social Structures: Emergence, Structure and Agency*. Cambridge: Cambridge University Press.

Elder-Vass, Dave. 2012. *The Reality of Social Construction*. Cambridge: Cambridge University Press.

Elder-Vass, Dave. 2017a. 'How Do Norms Work? Critical Realism and the Causal Power of Social Structures'. In *Critical Realism Meets Kritische Sozialtheorie: Ontologie, Erklärung Und Kritik in Den Sozialwissenschaften*, edited by Urs Linder and Dimitri Mader. Bielefeld: Verlag, pp 77–94.

Elder-Vass, Dave. 2017b. 'Material Parts in Social Structures'. *Journal of Social Ontology* 3(1): 89–105. doi:10.1515/jso-2015-0058.

Elder-Vass, Dave and Jamie Morgan. 2022. '"Materially Social" Critical Realism: An Interview with Dave Elder-Vass'. *Journal of Critical Realism* 21(2): 211–46. doi:10.1080/14767430.2022.2028233.

El-Hibri, Tayeb. 2021. *The Abbasid Caliphate: A History*. Cambridge: Cambridge University Press. doi:10.1017/9781316869567.

Elphinstone, Mountstuart. 1815. *An Account of the Kingdom of Caubul*. London: Longman, Hurst, Rees, Orme and Brown et.

Eltsov, Piotr A. 2013. 'The Ghost of the State in Deep Antiquity'. In *Connections and Complexity: New Approaches to the Archaeology of South Asia*, edited by Shinu Anna Abraham, Praveena Gullapalli, Teresa P. Raczek and Uzma Z. Rizvi. Walnut Creek: Taylor & Francis, pp 299–314.

Emadi, Hafizullah. 2010. *Reform and Rebellion in Post-Independence – Dynamics of Political Development in Afghanistan: The British, Russian, and American Invasions*. New York: Palgrave Macmillan. doi:10.1057/9780230112001_2.

EU Aid Explorer. nd. 'Recipients'. https://euaidexplorer.ec.europa.eu/explore/recipients_en

EU Committee. 2011. *European Union Committee: Eighth Report the EU's Afghan Police Mission*. London. https://publications.parliament.uk/pa/ld201 011/ldselect/ldeucom/87/8702.htm.

EUEOM. 2005. *Final Report on the Parliamentary and Provincial Council Elections*. https://eeas.europa.eu/archives/eueom/pdf/missions/final_rep ort._10-12-2005.pdf.

EUEOM. 2005. *Afghanistan Parliamentary and Provincial Council Elections: Final Report*. Kabul. https://eeas.europa.eu/archives/eueom/pdf/missions/final _report._10-12-2005.pdf.

EUEOM. 2009. *Islamic Republic of Afghanistan Final Report: Presidential and Provincial Council Elections 20 August 2009*. https://eeas.europa.eu/archi ves/eueom/pdf/missions/2010_election_observation_afghanistan_final_ report_0809_en.pdf.

European Commission. 1980. 'SEC(80)333 – Resolution of the European Parliament of 15 February 1980 on Community Measures Following the Soviet Invasion of Afghanistan Response by the European Commission (ENG)'. https://eur-lex.europa.eu/legal-content/EN/TXT/PDF/?uri= URISERV:1980_0016_SEC_1980_0333_package

European Commission. 1994. *Towards a New Asia Strategy*. https://eur-lex.europa.eu/legal-content/EN/TXT/PDF/?uri=CELEX:51994DC0 314&from=en.

European Commission. 2001. *Europe and Asia: A Strategic Framework for Enhanced Partnerships*. https://eur-lex.europa.eu/legal-content/EN/TXT/ PDF/?uri=CELEX:52001DC0469&from=en.

European Commission. 2003. 'Country Strategy Paper (CSP) Afghanistan 2003–2006, Including National Indicative Programme 2003–2004'. *Directorate-General for External Relations*. http://www.eeas.europa.eu/afgh anistan/csp/03_06_en.pdf.

European Commission. 2010. *Afghanistan State of Play January 2010*. : http:// ec.europa.eu/europeaid/where/asia/documents/state_of_play_afg_2010-jan.pdf (Accessed 13 March 2013).

European Commission. 2014. *Evaluation of the European Union's Regional Cooperation with Asia, Final Report. Volume 1.* https://www.oecd.org/derec/ec/Evaluation_of_the_European_Union_regional_co-operation_with_Asia_Vol1.pdf.

European Commission. 2023. 'International Development Aid'. *Europa.* https://economy-finance.ec.europa.eu/international-economic-relations/international-development-aid_en.

European Community Humanitarian Office. 1998. *Caught in the Eye of the Storm: ECHO Annual Review.* http://aei-dev.library.pitt.edu/38571/

European Council. 1981. *The Luxembourg European Council Publishes an Official Statement on the Political and Military Situation in Afghanistan.* Luxembourg. https://ec.europa.eu/dorie/fileDownload.do?docId=202275&cardId=202275.

European Council. 2021. *Council Conclusions on EU Approach to Cultural Heritage in Conflicts and Crises.* Brussels.

European Court of Auditors. 2012. *European Union Assistance to Kosovo Related to the Rule of Law: Special Report No 18.* Luxembourg. doi:10.2865/31965.

European Court of Auditors. 2015. *The EU Police Mission in Afghanistan: Mixed Results.* Luxembourg. doi:10.2865/699786.

European Parliament. 1980. 'Parlement Europpen, Documents de Seance 1979–1980'. *Communautes Europeennes.* https://ep-archives-archibot.s3.eu-central-1.amazonaws.com/root/vol1/686/N20170118214644382-628E6E22307F4.pdf.

European Parliament. 1996. '51996IP1106: Resolution on Afghanistan'. *Official Journal of the European Union* C347 ((18/11/1996):0156).

European Parliament. 2009. 'Afghanistan: "EU police force must be beefed up", says Ettore Sequi', Press Release No 20091005IPR61856. https://www.europarl.europa.eu/RegData/presse/pr_info/2009/EN/03A-DV-PRESSE_IPR(2009)10-05(61856)_EN.pdf

Eurostat. 2024. 'Asylum Applications: Monthly Statistics'. https://ec.europa.eu/eurostat/statistics-explained/index.php?title=Asylum_applications_-_monthly_statistics.

Fahim, Mohammad. 1978. 'Afghanistan and World War – 1'. *Journal of the Pakistan Historical Society* 26(2): 107–115.

Fahim, Mohammad. 1988. 'Anglo-Afghan Relations (1880–1919)'. *Journal of the Pakistan Historical Society* 36(4): 337–342.

Faiez, Rahim. 2020. 'Afghan President Names Council for Peace Deal with Taliban'. *The Diplomat.* https://thediplomat.com/2020/08/afghan-president-names-council-for-peace-deal-with-taliban/.

Fair, C. Christine. 2010. *Obama's New 'Af-Pak' Strategy: Can 'Clear, Hold, Build, Transfer' Work?* Washington, DC. www.cigionline.

Farhadi, Adib and Anthony Masya. 2023. *The Great Power Competition Volume 4 Learned in Afghanistan: America's Longest War*. Cham: Springer International Publishing. doi:10.1007/978-3-031-22934-3_1.

Fazlinejad, Ahmad and Farajollah Ahmadi. 2018. 'The Black Death in Iran, According to Iranian Historical Accounts from the Fourteenth through Fifteenth Centuries'. *Journal of Persianate Studies* 11(1): 56–71. doi:https://doi.org/10.1163/18747167-12341321.

FCO. 2017. *Joint Communication: Elements for an EU Strategy on Afghanistan*. London. https://publications.parliament.uk/pa/cm201719/cmselect/cmeuleg/301-iii/30133.htm.

Ferrario, Marco. 2022. 'Far Away from Pārsa: Empire, Borders, and Ideology in Achaemenid Bactria'. *Iran and the Caucasus* 26(1): 1–16. doi:https://doi.org/10.1163/1573384X-20220101.

Ferrié, Jean-Noël. 2008. 'The Uncertainties of Democratic Promotion in Afghanistan'. In *EU Foreign Policy in a Globalized World: Normative Power and Social Preferences*, edited by Zaki Laïdi. Oxon: Routledge, pp 134–42.

Financial Times. 1980. 'Weak Voice of Europe'. *The Financial Times*, 21 February, p 24.

Finer, Samuel E. 1999. *The History of Government from the Earliest Times: Volume II: The Intermediate Ages*. doi:10.1093/acprof:oso/9780198207900.003.0003.

Finn, Robert. 2015. 'Robert Finn, Lessons Learned Interview'. *The Washington Post*, 22 October.

Foreign and Commonwealth Office. 2010. *The UK's Foreign Policy towards Afghanistan and Pakistan: Written Evidence from the Foreign and Commonwealth Office*. London. https://publications.parliament.uk/pa/cm201011/cmselect/cmfaff/writev/afpak/afpak01.htm.

Francfort, Henri-Paul, Bertille Lyonnet, Cameron A. Petrie and Jim G. Shaffer. 2019. 'The Development of the Oxus Civilisation North of the Hindu Kush'. In *The Archaeology of Afghanistan: From Earliest Times to the Timurid Period: New Edition*, Edinburgh: Edinburgh University Press, pp 99–160.

Frankopan, Peter. 2016. *The Silk Roads: A New History of the World*. London: Bloomsbury.

Frontex. 2022. *Risk Analysis for 2022/23*. Warsaw. https://www.frontex.europa.eu/assets/Publications/Risk_Analysis/Risk_Analysis/ARA_2022_Public_Web.pdf.

Fuoli, Francesca. 2018. 'Incorporating North-Western Afghanistan into the British Empire: Experiments in Indirect Rule through the Making of an Imperial Frontier, 1884–87'. *Afghanistan* 1(1): 4–25. doi:10.3366/afg.2018.0004.

Ghani, Ashraf. 1982. 'Afghanistan Administration'. *Encyclopaedia Iranica*, 558–64. http://www.iranicaonline.org/articles/afghanistan-xi-admin.

Ghose, Dilip Kumar. 1953. 'The "Liberal Policy in Afghanistan" during 1880–84'. *Proceedings of the Indian History Congress* 16: 333–41.

Giustozzi, Antonio. 2005. *The Debate on Warlordism: The Importance of Military Legitimacy*. London: LSE Crisis State Research Centre.

Giustozzi, Antonio and Noor Ullah. 2006. *'Tribes' and Warlords in Southern Afghanistan, 1980–2005*. London: LSE Crisis State Research Centre.

Giustozzi, Antonio and Mohammad Isaqzadeh. 2013. *Policing Afghanistan: The Politics of the Lame Leviathan*. Oxford: Oxford University Press. doi:10.1093/acprof:oso/9780199327942.003.0002.

Global Affairs Canada. 2020. *Evaluation of International Assistance Programming in Afghanistan 2014/15 to 2019/20*. Final Report, International Assistance Evaluation Division. https://www.oecd.org/derec/canada/afghanistan-evaluation-report.pdf.

Golden, Peter B. 2011. *Central Asia in World History*. Oxford: Oxford University Press.

Gollob, Sam and Michael E. O'Hanlon. 2020. *Afghanistan Index: Tracking Variables of Reconstruction and Security in Post-9/11 Afghanistan*. Washington, DC: Brookings. https://www.brookings.edu/wp-content/uploads/2020/08/FP_20200825_afganistan_index.pdf.

Goodhand, Jonathan. 2002. 'Aiding Violence or Building Peace? The Role of International Aid in Afghanistan'. *Third World Quarterly* 23(5): 837–59. doi:10.1080/0143659022000028620.

Gordon, Matthew S. 2020. 'The Early Islamic Empire and the Introduction of Military Slavery'. In *The Cambridge History of War: Volume 2: War and the Medieval World*, edited by Anne Curry and David A. Graff. Cambridge: Cambridge University Press, pp 17–49. doi:10.1017/9781139025492.002.

Gordon, Philip H. 2003. 'The Crisis in the Alliance'. *Brookings*. https://www.brookings.edu/articles/the-crisis-in-the-alliance/.

Gordon, Philip H. and Jeremy Shapiro. 2004. *Allies at War: America, Europe and the Crisis over Iraq*. London: McGraw-Hill.

Government of Afghanistan. 1948. 'Coll 7/48 "Afghanistan: Col. Lancaster's Suggestion Re Military Equipment and Training for Afghan Army; Supply of Military Equipment"'. British Library: India Office Records and Private Papers IOR/L/PS/12/2218. https://www.qdl.qa/archive/81055/vdc_100000000555.0x0002f4.

Grau, Lester W. 2004. 'The Soviet-Afghan War: A Superpower Mired in the Mountains'. *Journal of Slavic Military Studies* 17(1): 129–51.

Green, Adam S. 2021. 'Killing the Priest-King: Addressing Egalitarianism in the Indus Civilization'. *Journal of Archaeological Research* 29(2): 153–202. doi:10.1007/s10814-020-09147-9.

Green, Nile. 2008. 'Tribe, Diaspora, and Sainthood in Afghan History'. *Journal of Asian Studies* 67(1): 171–211. doi:10.1017/S0021911808000065.

Green, Nile. 2016. 'Afghanistan's Islam: A History and Its Scholarship'. In *Afghanistan's Islam: From Conversion to the Taliban*, Berkeley: University of California Press, pp 1–37.

Gregorian, Vartan. 1969. *The Emergence of Modern Afghanistan*. Stanford: Stanford University Press.

Gromes, Thorsten. 2023. 'Zum Scheitern Des Internationalen Einsatzes in Afghanistan'. *Politische Vierteljahresschrift*. doi:10.1007/s11615-023-00508-9.

Gross, Eva. 2009a. *Security Sector Reform in Afghanistan: The EU's Contribution*. Occasional Paper. European Union Institute for Security Studies Occasional Paper 78, http://publications.europa.eu/resource/cellar/97278876-629d-41ac-a889-c0f33382fe7f.0001.03/DOC_1#:~:text=The%20EU%20enga ges%20in%20aspects,reform%20in%20the%20coun%2D%20try

Gross, Eva. 2009b. *The Europeanization of National Foreign Policy: Continuity and Change in European Crisis Management*. Hampshire: Palgrave Macmillan.

Gross, Eva. 2010. 'Towards a Comprehensive Approach? The EU's Contribution to Security Sector Reform (SSR) in Afghanistan'. *Sicherheit und Frieden (S+F) / Security and Peace* 28(4): 227–32. http://www.jstor. org/stable/24232769.

Gross, Eva. 2012. 'The EU in Afghanistan'. In *The European Union as a Global Conflict Manager*, edited by Richard G. Whitman and Stefan Wolff. London: Routledge, pp 107–19.

Gruen, Armin, Fabio Remondino and Li Zhang. 2003. 'Image-Based Reconstruction of the Great Buddha of Bamiyan, Afghanistan'. *Proc. SPIE* 5013: 129–36. doi:10.1117/12.473091.

The Guardian. 2001a. 'Bush Rejects Taliban Offer to Hand Bin Laden Over'. *The Guardian*. https://www.theguardian.com/world/2001/oct/14/afgh anistan.terrorism5.

The Guardian. 2001b. 'World Leaders Express Outrage'. *The Guardian*. http:// www.guardian.co.uk/world/2001/sep/11/september11.usa10.

Guilbert, Kieran. 2014. 'UN Agency Lax over Afghan Police Fund Misspent Millions: Watchdog'. *Reuters*. https://www.reuters.com/article/foundat ion-afghanistan-corruption-un-idINKCN0HY1WV20141009.

Haass, Richard. 1999. *Transatlantic Tensions: The United States, Europe, and Problem Countries*. Washington, DC: Brookings Institution Press.

Haelle, Tara. 2021. 'Health Effects of 9/11 Still Plague Responders and Survivors'. *Scientific American*. https://www.scientificamerican.com/arti cle/health-effects-of-9-11-still-plague-responders-and-survivors/.

Hafez, Mohammed M. 2023. 'The Elusive Dream of Pan-Islamism'. In *The Cambridge Companion to Religion and War*, edited by Margo Kitts. Cambridge: Cambridge University Press, pp 332–48. doi:10.1017/ 9781108884075.021.

Ham, Peter van. 2016. *The EC, Eastern Europe and European Unity: Discord, Collaboration and Integration Since 1947*. London: Bloomsbury.

Hamid, Mustafa and Leah Farrall. 2015. *The Arabs at War in Afghanistan*. London: Hurst & Company.

Hansard. 1843. 'Lord Ellenborough's Proclamation – Somnauth. House Of Commons'. *Hansard* 67: 581–702.

Haqqani, Husain. 2005. *Pakistan: Between Mosque and Military*. Washington, DC: Carnegie Endowment for International Peace.

Harooni, Marwais and Kay Johnson. 2015. 'Car Bomb on EU Vehicle Kills at Least Three in Afghan Capital'. *Reuters*. https://www.reuters.com/article/uk-afghanistan-blast-idAFKBN0O203H20150517/.

Hassan, Oz. 2009. 'George W. Bush, September 11th and the Rise of the Freedom Agenda in US-Middle East Relations: A Constructivist Institutionalist Approach'. PhD thesis, University of Birmingham. https://etheses.bham.ac.uk/id/eprint/399/.

Hassan, Oz. 2010. 'Constructing Crises, (In)Securitising Terror: The Punctuated Evolution of EU Counter-Terror Strategy'. *European Security* 19(3): 445–66. doi:10.1080/09662839.2010.526935.

Hassan, Oz. 2012. Constructing America's Freedom Agenda for the Middle East: Democracy and Domination *Constructing America's Freedom Agenda for the Middle East: Democracy and Domination*. doi:10.4324/9780203102541.

Hassan, Oz. 2013. *Constructing America's Freedom Agenda for the Middle East: Democracy and Domination*. New York: Routledge.

Hassan, Oz. 2020a. 'Crisis, Narratives, and the Construction of US-Middle East Relations: Continuity and Change in World History and Trump's America First'. *Global Affairs* 6(1): 121–41. doi:10.1080/23340460.2020.1745084.

Hassan, Oz. 2020b. 'The Evolution of the European Union's Failed Approach to Afghanistan'. *European Security* 29(1): 74–95. doi:10.1080/09662839.2019.1679773.

Hassan, Oz. 2021. 'Reassessing the European Strategy in Afghanistan'. *Carnegie Europe and European Democracy Hub*.

Hassan, Oz. 2022. 'EU-Afghanistan Relations'. In *Routledge Handbook of EU-Middle East Relations*, edited by Dimitris Bouris, Daniela Huber and Michelle Pace. Oxon: Routledge, pp 344–55.

Hassan, Oz. 2023. 'Afghanistan: Lessons Learnt from 20 Years of Supporting Democracy, Development and Security'. *European Parliament Study Requested by the AFET Committee*. https://www.europarl.europa.eu/thinktank/en/document/EXPO_STU(2023)702579.

Hassan, Oz and Andrew Hammond. 2011. 'The Rise and Fall of American's Freedom Agenda in Afghanistan: Counter-Terrorism, Nation-Building and Democracy'. *The International Journal of Human Rights* 15(4): 532–51. doi:10.1080/13642987.2011.561986.

Hassan, Tirana. 2022. 'Afghanistan: Events of 2022'. *Human Rights Watch*. https://www.hrw.org/world-report/2023/country-chapters/afghanistan.

Hauner, Milan L. 1982. 'Afghanistan between the Great Powers, 1938–1945'. *International Journal of Middle East Studies* 14(4): 481–99.

Hay, Colin. 2002. *Political Analysis*. Basingstoke: Palgrave.

Hobson, John M. 2000. *The State and International Relations*. Cambridge: Cambridge University Press. doi:10.1017/CBO9780511612442.

Hobson, John M. 2012. *The Eurocentric Conception of World Politics: Western International Theory, 1760–2010*. Cambridge: Cambridge University Press. doi:10.1017/CBO9781139096829.

Hofmann, Paul. 1979. 'Afghan King, in Rome Exile, Tightens Belt'. *The New York Times*. https://www.nytimes.com/1979/04/29/archives/afg han-king-in-rome-exile-tightens-belt-daud-sent-money-to-family.html

Holland, Jack. 2012. *Selling the War on Terror: Foreign Policy Discourses after 9/11*. London: Routledge.

Holt, Frank L. 1988. *Alexander the Great and Bactria: The Formation of a Greek Frontier in Central Asia*. Leiden: Brill.

Holt, Frank L. 2012. 'Into the Land of Bones: Alexander the Great in Afghanistan'. University of California Press, Oakland. doi:10.1525/j.ctt1png5d.

House Committee on Oversight and Accountability. 2023. *Comer & Greene Press DOD on U.S. Military Aid and Weapons Falling into Terrorist Hands*. Washington, DC.

Hussain, Zahid. 2015. 'Destruction of the Past'. *Dawn*. https://www.dawn.com/news/1168714

Ibrahimi, S. Yaqub. 2019. 'Afghanistan's Political Development Dilemma: The Centralist State Versus a Centrifugal Society'. *Journal of South Asian Development* 14(1): 40–61. doi:10.1177/0973174119839843.

ICAI. 2022. *UK Aid to Afghanistan*. London.

ICC. 2021. *Policy on Cultural Heritage*. International Criminal Court, Office of the Prosecutor. https://www.icc-cpi.int/sites/default/files/itemsDo cuments/20210614-otp-policy-cultural-heritage-eng.pdf

ICG. 2003. *Afghanistan: The Bonn Process: Afghanistan and the Problem of Pashtun Alienation*. International Crisis Group. http://www.jstor.org/sta ble/resrep45990.6.

ICG. 2005. *Rebuilding the Afghan State: The European Union's Role*. http://www.operationspaix.net/DATA/DOCUMENT/6257~v~Rebuilding_ the_Afghan_State__The_European_Unions_Role.pdf.

Inderfurth, Karl F. 1998. 'Your Meeting on Usama Bin Laden – Unclassified: Briefing Memorandum'. https://nsarchive2.gwu.edu/NSA EBB/NSAEBB253/19981124a.pdf.

International Development Committee. 2012. *Afghanistan: Development Progress and Prospects after 2014, Sixth Report of Session 2012–13*. London. https://publications.parliament.uk/pa/cm201213/cmselect/cmintdev/403/403.pdf.

International Partnerships. 2023. 'Afghanistan: EU Reinforces Basic Needs Support to the Afghan People with a New €142.8 Million Package'. *The European Commission Directorate-General for International Partnerships.*

Islamic Republic of Afghanistan. 2016. *Afghanistan National Peace and Development Framework (Anpdf) 2017 to 2021.* https://www.refworld.org/pdfid/5b28f4294.pdf.

Jackson, Peter. 2017. *The Mongols and the Islamic World: From Conquest to Conversion.* Cumberland: Yale University Press.

Jackson, Richard. 2005. *Writing the War on Terrorism: Language, Politics, and Counter-Terrorism.* Manchester: Manchester University Press.

Jalali, Ali. 2015. *Forging Afghanistan's National Unity Government.* US Institute of Peace. http://www.jstor.org/stable/resrep20198.

Jalali, Ali Ahmad. 2017. *A Military History of Afghanistan: From the Great Game to the Global War on Terror.* Kansas: University Press of Kansas.

Jalali, Ali Ahmad. 2021. *Afghanistan: A Military History from the Ancient Empires to the Great Game.* Kansas: University Press of Kansas.

Jalali, Ali Ahmad and Lester W. Grau. 2001. *Afghan Guerrilla Warfare: In the Words of the Mujahideen Fighter.* Minneapolis: Zenith Press.

Jan, Attaullah and Fakhr-ul-Islam. 2022. 'The Rise of the Taliban in Afghanistan in 2021 and Its Security Implications for Pakistan'. *Pakistan Journal of Social Science* 4(4): 1059–67.

Jarrige, Jean-François, Aurore Didier and Gonzague Quivron. 2011. 'Shahr-i Sokhta and the Chronology of the Indo-Iranian Regions'. *Paléorient* 37(2): 7–34.

Jenkins, Roy. 1980. 'Statement on Afghanistan by E.C. Commission President Roy Jenkins'. *European Community News* 7. http://aei-dev.library.pitt.edu/59642/

Jessop, Bob. 2005. 'Critical Realism and the Strategic-Relational Approach'. *New Formations* 56: 40–53.

Jessop, Bob and Jamie Morgan. 2022. 'The Strategic-Relational Approach, Realism and the State: From Regulation Theory to Neoliberalism via Marx and Poulantzas, an Interview with Bob Jessop'. *Journal of Critical Realism* 21(1): 83–118. doi:10.1080/14767430.2021.1995685.

Johnson, Casey Garret. 2018. *The Political Deal with Hezb-E Islami: What It Means for Talks with the Taliban and Peace in Afghanistan.* Washington, DC. https://www.usip.org/sites/default/files/2018-07/pw_139_the_political_deal_with_hezb_e_islami.pdf.

Johnston, T. 1997. 'Taleban Arrest, Then Release EC Commissioner'. *Reuters News.* 29 September.

Jones, Seth G. 2008. 'The Rise of Afghanistan's Insurgency: State Failure and Jihad'. *International Security* 32(4): 7–40. http://www.jstor.org/stable/30129790.

Kakissis, Joanna. 2011. 'Bit By Bit, Afghanistan Rebuilds Buddhist Statues'. *NPR*.

Kaldor, Mary. 2021. 'Autonomous in Afghanistan: How the Europeans Could Have Stayed after US Withdrawal'. https://ecfr.eu/article/autonom ous-in-afghanistan-how-the-europeans-could-have-stayed-after-us-wit hdrawal/.

Karzai, Hamid. 2002. 'Remarks with AIA Chairman Hamid Karzai'. *US Department of State Archive*. https://2001-2009.state.gov/secretary/former/ powell/remarks/2002/7334.htm.

Kathju, Junaid. 2023. 'U.S. Arms Left in Afghanistan Are Turning up in a Different Conflict'. *NBC News*. https://www.nbcnews.com/news/world/ us-weapons-afghanistan-taliban-kashmir-rcna67134.

Katzman, Kenneth. 2005. *Afghanistan: Post-War Governance, Security and U.S. Policy*. Washington, DC: Congressional Research Service.

Kean, Thomas H., Lee H. Hamilton, Richard Ben-Veniste, Bob Kerrey, Fred F. Fielding, John F. Lehman, et al. 2004. *The 9/11 Commission Report*. http://www.9-11commission.gov/report/911Report.pdf.

Keohane, Daniel. 2008. 'The Absent Friend: EU Foreign Policy and Counter-Terrorism'. *JCMS: Journal of Common Market Studies* 46(1): 125– 46. doi:https://doi.org/10.1111/j.1468-5965.2007.00770.x.

Kerr, Anne and Edmund Wright. 2015. 'Sassanian Empire'. *A Dictionary of World History*, Oxford: Oxford University Press. https://www.oxfordre ference.com/view/10.1093/acref/9780199685691.001.0001/acref-978019 9685691-e-3246. doi:10.1093/acref/9780199685691.013.3246.

Khalilzad, Zalmay. 1979. 'The Superpowers and the Northern Tier'. *International Security* 4(3): 6–30. doi:10.2307/2626692.

Khaliq, Fazai. 2016. 'Iconic Buddha in Swat Valley Restored after Nine Years When Taliban Defaced It'. *Dawn*. https://www.dawn.com/news/ 1294246#:~:text=3%2DD%20technology.-,Italian%20experts%20co nducted%20the%20conservation%20and%20restoration%20process%20us ing%203,process%20conducted%20by%20Italian%20archaeologists.

Khan, Sultan Mahomed. 1900. 'Preface'. In *The Life of Abdur Rahman, Amir of Afghanistan*. London: J. Murray, pp vii–xi. https://www.loc.gov/resou rce/gdclccn.01027174v1/?st=gallery

Khosravi, Ali Reza and Ali Naghi Fayaz. 2023. 'Afghanistan's Iinternal Developments and the Change in the US Foreign Policy Strategy [تالوحت خاد‌ىل افغانستان و رد‌بهار درسايت خراجى آمريکا]'. *Central Eurasia Studies* 16(1): 99–123.

Klaiber, Klaus-Peter. 2002. 'The European Union in Afghanistan: Impressions of My Term as Special Representative'. *National Europe Centre Paper No. 44*. https://openresearch-repository.anu.edu.au/bitstream/1885/41711/ 4/klaiber.pdf.

Klausen, Anne-Lise and Ayla-Kristina Olesen Yurtaslan. 2019. *Review of Danish Evaluation Findings and Lessons Learned in Afghanistan*. Copenhagen.

Klein, Ira. 1974. 'Who Made the Second Afghan War?'. *Journal of Asian History* 8(2): 97–121.

Kobia, Roland. 2022. 'EU Ambassador Roland Kobia: Taliban Negotiations'. *Room for Discussion SEFA*. https://www.youtube.com/watch?v=0s1m bAn2F2s

Koplik, Sara. 2015. *A Political and Economic History of the Jews of Afghanistan*. Leiden: Brill. doi:10.1163/9789004292383.

Koven, Ronald. 1980. 'Giscard Comes Under Fire for Holding Talks With Brezhnev'. *The Washington Post*. https://www.washingtonpost.com/arch ive/politics/1980/05/20/giscard-comes-under-fire-for-holding-talks-with-brezhnev/2f4b7b40-f648-4e06-a701-b69912630175/#

Kumar, Suneel, Muhammad Ali and Pasand Ali Khoso. 2020. 'Emergence and Decline of the Indus Valley Civilization in Pakistan'. *Global Sociological Review* 5(2): 9–22.

Kumar, Vikas, E. Andrew Bennett, Dongyue Zhao, Yun Liang, Yunpeng Tang, Meng Ren, et al. 2021. 'Genetic Continuity of Bronze Age Ancestry with Increased Steppe-Related Ancestry in Late Iron Age Uzbekistan'. *Molecular Biology and Evolution* 38(11): 4908–17. doi:10.1093/molbev/ msab216.

Lahoud, Nelly. 2022. *The Bin Laden Papers: How the Abbottabad Raid Revealed the Truth about al-Qaeda, Its Leader and His Family*. New Haven: Yale University Press.

Lake, Michael. 1980. 'Delegation of the Commission of the European Communities to the United Nations'. *ECN*. European Communities Newsletter http://aei.pitt.edu/60270/

Lamothe, Dan and Joby Warrick. 2023. 'Afghanistan Has Become a Terrorism Staging Ground Again, Leak Reveals'. *The Washington Post*. https://www.washingtonpost.com/national-security/2023/04/22/afgh anistan-terrorism-leaked-documents/.

LaRoche, Christopher David and Joseph MacKay. 2017. 'The Conduct of History in International Relations: Rethinking Philosophy of History in IR Theory'. *International Theory* 9(2): 203–36. doi:10.1017/ S175297191700001X.

Latifi, Ali M. 2014. 'Remembering Afghanistan's Herat Uprising: Twenty-Five Years after the Soviet Withdrawal, Those Who Took Part in the Herat Uprising Look Back'. *Aljazeera*. https://www.aljazeera.com/features/2014/ 2/13/remembering-afghanistans-herat-uprising.

Lawler, Andrew. 2008. 'Indus Collapse: The End or the Beginning of an Asian Culture?' *Science* 320(5881): 1281–3. doi:10.1126/science.320.5881.1281.

Lee, Jonathan. 2006. 'Monuments of Bamiyan Province, Afghanistan'. *Iran* 44: 229–52.

Lee, Jonathan L. 2022. *Afghanistan: A History from 1260 to the Present*. London: Reaktion Books.

Lee, Joo-Yup. 2016. 'The Historical Meaning of the Term "Turk" and the Nature of the Turkic Identity of the Chinggisid and Timurid Elites in Post-Mongol Central Asia'. *Central Asiatic Journal* 59(1–2): 101–32. doi:10.13173/centasiaj.59.1-2.0101.

Lepgold, Joseph. 1998. 'Is Anyone Listening? International Relations Theory and the Problem of Policy Relevance'. *Political Science Quarterly* 113(1): 43–62. doi:10.2307/2657650.

Leven, Denis. 2024. 'Germany Arrests 2 Afghans over Swedish Parliament Attack Plot'. *Politico*. https://www.politico.eu/article/germany-arrests-two-afghan-people-allegedly-planning-attack-sweden-parliament/

Levine, Marsha A. 1999. 'Botai and the Origins of Horse Domestication'. *Journal of Anthropological Archaeology* 18(1): 29–78. doi: https://doi.org/10.1006/jaar.1998.0332.

Lierl, Malte. 2021. 'Elections and Government Legitimacy in Fragile States'. *German Institute for Global and Area Studies* 7. https://www.giga-hamburg.de/en/publications/giga-focus/elections-and-government-legitimacy-in-fragile-states

Liu, Xinru. 2020. 'The Kushan Empire'. *Oxford Research Encyclopedia of Asian History*. Retrieved 9 May 2024, https://oxfordre.com/asianhistory/view/10.1093/acrefore/9780190277727.001.0001/acrefore-9780190277727-e-227. doi:10.1093/acrefore/9780190277727.013.227.

Lorenzini, S. 2019. 'At the Origins of European Foreign Policy: European Exceptionalism and the Case of Development Aid'. In: Antoniolli, L., Bonatti, L., Ruzza, C. (eds) *Highs and Lows of European Integration*. Springer, Cham. https://doi.org/10.1007/978-3-319-93626-0_2

Loyn, David and Francesc Vendrell. 2022. 'Francesc Vendrell in Conversation: Mediation in Afghanistan 2000–2008'. *Asian Affairs* 53(3): 639–70. doi:10.1080/03068374.2022.2081429.

Ludden, David. 2021. 'The Centrality of Indo-Persia in Global Asia and Historical Formation of Afghanistan'. *Afghanistan* 4(1): 57–9. doi:10.3366/afg.2021.0065.

Maass, Citha D. 2006. 'National Reconciliation in Afghanistan: Conflict History and the Search for an Afghan Approach'. *Internationales Asienforum* 37(2): 5–35.

Maiwandwal, Muhammad Hashim. 1967. 'Remarks of Welcome at the White House to Prime Minister Maiwandwal of Afghanistan'. *The American Presidency Project*. https://www.presidency.ucsb.edu/documents/remarks-welcome-the-white-house-prime-minister-maiwandwal-afghanistan

Maley, William. 2023. 'Ukraine, Afghanistan and the Failure of Deterrence'. *Australian Journal of International Affairs* 77(4): 407–14. doi:10.1080/10357718.2023.2219628.

Maley, William and Ahmad Shuja Jamal. 2022. 'Diplomacy of Disaster: The Afghanistan "Peace Process" and the Taliban Occupation of Kabul'. *The Hague Journal of Diplomacy* 17(1): 32–63. doi:https://doi.org/10.1163/1871191X-bja10089.

Manchanda, Nivi. 2020. *Imagining Afghanistan: The History and Politics of Imperial Knowledge*. Cambridge: Cambridge University Press. doi:10.1017/9781108867986.

Maniscalco, Francesco. 2018. 'A New Interpretation of the Edicts of Asoka from Kandahar'. *Annali di Ca Foscari Serie Orientale* 54: 239–63. doi:10.30687/AnnOr/2385-3042/2018/01/011.

Manners, Ian. 2002. 'Normative Power Europe: A Contradiction in Terms?' *JCMS: Journal of Common Market Studies* 40(2): 235–58. doi:https://doi.org/10.1111/1468-5965.00353.

Manz, Beatrice Forbes, ed. 2021. 'Nomads in the Establishment of the Caliphate'. In *Nomads in the Middle East*. Cambridge: Cambridge University Press, pp 28–54. doi:10.1017/9781139028813.004.

Marquette, Heather. 2011. 'Donors, State Building and Corruption: Lessons from Afghanistan and the Implications for Aid Policy'. *Third World Quarterly* 32(10): 1871–90. doi:10.1080/01436597.2011.610587.

Marsden, Peter. 2003. 'Afghanistan: The Reconstruction Process'. *International Affairs* 79(1): 91–105. doi:10.1111/1468-2346.00297.

Marshall, Alex. 2007. 'Managing Withdrawal: Afghanistan as the Forgotten Example in Attempting Conflict Resolution and State Reconstruction'. *Small Wars & Insurgencies* 18(1): 68–89. doi:10.1080/09592310601173238.

Marshall, P.J. 1998a. 'The British in Asia: Trade to Dominion, 1700–1765'. In *The Oxford History of the British Empire: Volume II: The Eighteenth Century*, edited by P.J. Marshall, Alaine Low and Wm. Roger Louis. doi:10.1093/acprof:oso/9780198205630.003.0022.

Marshall, Peter. 1998b. 'The English in Asia to 1700'. In *The Oxford History of the British Empire: The Origins of Empire*, edited by Nicolas Canny, Wm Roger Louis and Alaine Low. Oxford: Oxford University Press, pp 264–285.

Marsham, Andrew. 2021. 'The Caliphate'. In *The Oxford World History of Empire: Volume Two: The History of Empires*, edited by Peter Fibiger Bang, C.A. Bayly and Walter Scheidel, Oxford: Oxford University Press, pp 355–79. doi:10.1093/oso/9780197532768.003.0012.

Martinez-Sève, Laurianne. 2014. 'The Spatial Organization of Ai Khanoum, a Greek City in Afghanistan'. *American Journal of Archaeology* 118(2): 267–83. doi:10.3764/aja.118.2.0267.

Martinez-Sève, Laurianne. 2015. 'Ai Khanoum and Greek Domination in Central Asia'. In *Central Asia and Iran: Greeks, Parthians, Kushans and Sasanians*, edited by Edward Dąbrowa. Krakow: Jagiellonian University Press, pp 17–46.

Mashal, Mujib. and Rod Nordland. 2019. 'U.S. and Taliban Make Headway in Talks for Withdrawal from Afghanistan'. *The New York Times*. https://www.nytimes.com/2019/01/24/world/asia/usa-taliban-afghanistan-deal.html

May, Timothy 2013. *The Mongol Conquests in World History*. Reaktion Books, London.

McAvoy, John. and Tom Butler. 2017. 'Causal Framework through Retroduction and Retrodiction'. In *Proceedings of the 25th European Conference on Information Systems*. Guimarães, Portugal, June 5–10, pp 1314–26. https:// aisel.aisnet.org/ecis2017_rp/85/.

Meher, Jagmohan. 2012. 'Pakistan's Strategic Obsession and the Road to Catastrophe: Is There a Way Out?' *India Quarterly* 68(4): 345–62. doi:10.1177/0974928412467248.

Mellars, Paul. 2006. 'Why Did Modern Human Populations Disperse from Africa ca. 60,000 Years Ago? A New Model'. *Proceedings of the National Academy of Sciences* 103(25): 9381–6. doi:10.1073/pnas.0510792103.

Mellbin, Franz-Michael Skjold. 2016. 'The Brussels Conference on Afghanistan: Between Aid and Migration – Afghanistan Analysts Network – English'. https://www.afghanistan-analysts.org/en/reports/international-engagement/the-brussels-conference-on-afghanistan-between-aid-and-migration/.

Mentzelopoulou, Maria-Margarita. 2021. *Evacuation of Afghan Nationals to EU Member States*. Brussels: European Parliamentary Research Service. https://www.europarl.europa.eu/RegData/etudes/BRIE/2021/698776/EPRS_BRI(2021)698776_EN.pdf]

Michael Feener, R. 2017. 'Muslim Cultures and Pre-Islamic Pasts: Changing Perceptions of "Heritage"'. In *The Making of Islamic Heritage: Muslim Pasts and Heritage Presents*, edited by Trinidad Rico. New Jersey: Palgrave Macmillan.

Mingers, John. 2014. *Systems Thinking, Critical Realism and Philosophy: A Confluence of Ideas*. London: Routledge.

Ministry of Foreign Affairs. 2015. 'Pia Stjernvall Appointed Head of Mission of the EU Civilian Crisis Management Mission in Afghanistan'. https://valtioneuvosto.fi/en/-/pia-stjernvall-eu-n-siviilikriisinhallintaoperaation-paallikoksi-afganistaniin.

Ministry of Foreign Affairs of Japan. 2012. 'Tokyo Conference on Afghanistan. The Tokyo Declaration Partnership for Self-Reliance in Afghanistan from Transition to Transformation'. https://www.mofa.go.jp/region/middle_e/afghanistan/tokyo_conference_2012/tokyo_declaration_en1.html.

Mir, Asfandyar. 2020. *Afghanistan's Terrorism Challenge The Ties That Bind*. Middle East Institute. Washington, DC. http://www.jstor.org/stable/resrep28475.7.

Misdaq, Nabi. 2008. *Afghanistan: Political Frailty and External Interference*. London: Routledge.

Mohammadi, Abdullah, Hanh Nguyen and Jennifer Vallentine. 2001. *The Impact of the Afghanistan Crisis on Migration: Increasingly Securitized Borders Will Only Make Migration Riskier and More Dangerous*. Mixed Migration Centre, 18 October. https://mixedmigration.org/the-impact-of-the-afghanistan-crisis-on-migration/

Moin, A. Azfar. 2022. 'Sulh-i Kull as an Oath of Peace: Mughal Political Theology in History, Theory, and Comparison'. *Modern Asian Studies* 56(3): 721–48. doi:10.1017/S0026749X2100041X.

Monar, Jörg. 2008. 'The European Union as a Collective Actor in the Fight against Post-9/11 Terrorism: Progress and Problems of a Primarily Cooperative Approach'. In *Fresh Perspectives on the War on Terror*, edited by Miriam Gani and Penelope Mathew. Canberra: ANU E Press, pp 209–234. https://www.jstor.org/stable/j.ctt24hf7j.18

Morelli, Vincent and Paul Belkin. 2009. 'CRS Report for Congress'. www.crs.gov.

Morgan, David. 2009. 'The Decline and Fall of the Mongol Empire'. *Journal of the Royal Asiatic Society* 19(4): 427–37. doi:10.1017/S1356186309990046.

Morris, Lauren. 2020. 'Central Asian Empires'. In *Handbook of Ancient Afro-Eurasian Economies*, edited by Sitta Reden. Berlin: De Gruyter Oldenbourg, pp 53–94. doi:10.1515/9783110607741-004.

Mowjee, Tasneem. 1998. 'The European Community Humanitarian Office (ECHO): 1992–1999 and Beyond'. *Disasters* 22(3): 250–67. doi:https://doi.org/10.1111/1467-7717.00090.

Mudde, Cas. 2016. 'Europe's Populist Surge: A Long Time in the Making'. *Foreign Affairs* 95(6): 25–30. http://www.jstor.org/stable/43948378.

Mukhopadhyay, Dipali. 2014. *Warlords, Strongman Governors, and the State in Afghanistan*. Cambridge: Cambridge University Press. doi:10.1017/CBO9781139161817.001.

Murid Partaw, Ahmad. 2023. 'The Failure of Democracy in Afghanistan'. *British Journal of Middle Eastern Studies*: 1–20. doi:10.1080/13530194.2022.2164480.

Murray, Tonita. 2007. 'Police-Building in Afghanistan: A Case Study of Civil Security Reform'. *International Peacekeeping* 14(1): 108–26. doi:10.1080/13533310601114327.

Murtazashvili, Jennifer Brick, ed. 2016. 'Federalism, Afghan Style'. In *Informal Order and the State in Afghanistan*, Cambridge: Cambridge University Press, pp 213–45. doi:DOI: 10.1017/CBO9781316286890.010.

Murtazashvili, Jennifer. 2022. 'China's Activities and Influence in South and Central Asia'. *Carnegie Endowment for International Peace*. https://carnegieendowment.org/2022/05/17/china-s-activities-and-influence-in-south-and-central-asia-pub-87146.

Musa, Mashreq Dhiaa and Hussein Karim Hamidi. 2021. 'Political Relations Between the Abbasid Caliphate and Transoxiana During the Rule of Saffarid Emirate (259-296 Ah/873-908 Ad)'. *Palarch's Journal of Archaeology of Egypt/Egyptology* 18(8): 4557–73.

Mustasilta, Katariina, Tyyne Karjalainen, Timo R. Stewart and Mathilda Salo. 2023. *Finland in Afghanistan 2001–2021: From Stabilization to Advancing Foreign and Security Policy Relations*. Helsinki: Finnish Institute of International Affairs. https://www.fiia.fi/wp-content/uploads/2022/12/report72_finland-in-afghanistan-2001-2021.pdf.

Mutin, Banjamin and Clifford Charles Lamberg-Karlovsky. 2021. 'The Relationship between the Oxus Civilisation and the Indo-Iranian Borderlands'. In *The World of the Oxus Civilisation*, edited by Bertille Lyonnet and Nadezhda A. Dubova. London: Routledge, pp 551–89.

Mylroie, Laurie. 1995. 'The World Trade Center Bomb: Who is Ramzi Yousef? And Why It Matters'. *The National Interest*, winter. https://irp.fas.org/world/iraq/956-tni.htm.

Nadir Shah. 1931. 'Fundamental Principles of the Government of Afghanistan'. http://www.dircost.unito.it/cs/docs/Afghanistan 1931W.htm.

Nagaoka, Masanori. 2020. *The Future of the Bamiyan Buddha Statues: Heritage Reconstruction in Theory and Practice*, edited by UNESCO. Kabul/Cham: UNESCO Publishing, Springer.

National Archives. 1840. 'Papers and Correspondence Relating to the Indian Army and the Afghan Campaign'. PRO 30/12/32/2.

NATO. 2001. 'Afghanistan Lessons Learned'. *Factsheet*. https://www.nato.int/nato_static_fl2014/assets/pdf/2021/12/pdf/2112-factsheet-afgh-lessons-en.pdf.

NATO. 2009a. 'NATO and the Fight Against Terrorism'. http://www.nato.int/cps/en/natolive/topics_48801.htm.

NATO. 2009b. 'NATO Expands Its Role in Afghanistan'. *Newsroom*. https://www.nato.int/cps/en/natolive/news_52799.htm.

NATO. 2022a. 'NATO: ISAF's Mission in Afghanistan (2001–2014)'. https://www.nato.int/cps/en/natohq/topics_69366.htm.

NATO. 2022b. 'NATO: Topic: Inteqal: Transition to Afghan Lead (2011–2014)'. https://www.nato.int/cps/en/natohq/topics_87183.htm.

Nawid, Senzil. 1997. 'The State, the Clergy, and British Imperial Policy in Afghanistan during the 19th and Early 20th Centuries'. *International Journal of Middle East Studies* 29(4): 581–605. doi:10.1017/S0020743800065211.

Nawid, Senzil K. 1999. *Religious Response to Social Change in Afghanistan, 1919–29: King Aman-Allah and the Afghan Ulama*. Costa Meza, CA: Mazda Publishers.

Negmatov, Numna Negmatovish. 1998. 'The Samanid State'. In *History of Civilizations of Central Asia*, edited by Muhammad Seyfeydinovich Asimov and Clifford Edmund Bosworth. Paris: UNESCO Publishing, pp 83–102.

Newell, Richard S. 1981. 'International Responses to the Afghanistan Crisis'. *The World Today* 37(5): 172–81. http://www.jstor.org/stable/40395288.

Niklasson, Tomas. 2022. 'Interview with EU Special Envoy Tomas Niklasson'. *TOLOnews*. https://www.youtube.com/watch?v=4Rho ZL1o0mY.

Noelle, Christine. 1998. *State and Tribe in Nineteenth-Century Afghanistan: The Reign of Amir Dost Muhammad Khan (1826–1863).* London: Routledge.

Obama, Barack. 2002. 'Transcript: Obama's Speech Against the Iraq War'. *NPR.* https://www.npr.org/templates/story/story.php?storyId=99591469.

Obama, Barack. 2008. 'Obama's Remarks on Iraq and Afghanistan'. *The New York Times.* https://www.nytimes.com/2008/07/15/us/politics/15t ext-obama.html.

Obama, Barack. 2009a. 'Remarks by President Barack Obama in Prague as Delivered'. *The White House.* https://obamawhitehouse.archives.gov/ the-press-office/remarks-president-barack-obama-prague-delivered.

Obama, Barack. 2009b. 'Remarks by the President on a New Strategy for Afghanistan and Pakistan'. *The White House.* https://obamawhitehouse. archives.gov/the-press-office/remarks-president-a-new-strategy-afghanis tan-and-pakistan.

Obama, Barack. 2012. 'Remarks by President Obama and President Karzai of Afghanistan After Bilateral Meeting'. *The White House.* https://obam awhitehouse.archives.gov/the-press-office/2012/05/20/remarks-presid ent-obama-and-president-karzai-afghanistan-after-bilateral.OECD.Stat. 2023. 'Total receipts by country and region (ODA+OOF+private)'. https://stats.oecd.org/OECDStat_Metadata/ShowMetadata.ashx?Data set=REF_TOTALRECPTS&ShowOnWeb=true&Lang=en

Office of the Historian. 1979. 'Summary of Conclusions of a Special Coordination Committee Meeting'. *Foreign Relations of the United States, 1977–1980, Volume XIII, Afghanistan.* https://history.state.gov/historic aldocuments/frus1977-80v13

Office of the Historian. 2023. 'A Guide to the United States' History of Recognition, Diplomatic, and Consular Relations, by Country, since 1776: Afghanistan'. *The State Department.* https://history.state.gov/countr ies/afghanistan.

OFS. 2020. *Operation Freedom's Sentinel: Lead Inspector General Report to the United States Congress.* Washington, DC. https://media.defense.gov/ 2020/May/19/2002302407/-1/-1/1/LEAD%20INSPECTOR%20 GENERAL%20FOR%20OPERATION%20FREEDOM'S%20SENTI NEL.PDF.

OHCHR. 2023. *Afghanistan: UN Experts Say 20 Years of Progress for Women and Girls' Rights Erased since Taliban Takeover.* https://www.ohchr.org/en/ press-releases/2023/03/afghanistan-un-experts-say-20-years-progress- women-and-girls-rights-erased.

OJ. 1972. *Agreement between the European Economic Community and the Kingdom of Afghanistan on the Supply of Common Wheat as Food Aid*. Journal officiel des Communautés européennes.

OJ. 1973. *The Issue of a New Invitation to Tender for the Mobilization of Common Wheat as Food Aid for the Kingdom of Afghanistan*. Official Journal of the European Communities.

OJ. 1975a. *Agreement between the European Economic Community and the Republic of Afghanistan on the Supply of Butteroil as Food Aid*. Official Journal of the European Communities.

OJ. 1975b. *The Conclusion of the Agreement between the European Economic Community and the Republic of Afghanistan on the Supply of Skimmed-Milk Powder as Food Aid*. Official Journal of the European Communities.

Olden, Herman and Paul Phillips. 1952. 'The Point Four Program: Promise or Menace?' *Science & Society* 16(3): 222–46.

Oliker, Olga. 2011. 'Mol and KhAD Security Forces During the 1980s'. In *Building Afghanistan's Security Forces in Wartime: The Soviet Experience*. Arlington: RAND Corporation, pp 25–36. http://www.jstor.org/stable/10.7249/mg1078a.12.

Oliker, Olga, Richard Kauzlarich, James Dobbins, Kurt W. Basseuner, Donald L. Sampler, John G. McGinn, et al. 2004. *Aid During Conflict: Interaction Between Military and Civilian Assistance Providers in Afghanistan, September 2001–June 2002*. Santa Monica, CA: RAND Corporation. https://www.rand.org/pubs/monographs/MG212.html. Also available in print form.

Omrani, Bijan. 2009. 'The Durand Line: History and Problems of the Afghan-Pakistan Border'. *Asian Affairs* 40(2): 177–95. doi:10.1080/03068370902871508.

Orbie, Jan. 2006. 'Civilian Power Europe: Review of the Original and Current Debates'. *Cooperation and Conflict* 41(1): 123–8. doi:10.1177/0010836706063503.

Osman, Borhan. 2013. *Adding the Ballot to the Bullet? Hezb-e Islami in Transition*. http://www.afghanistan-analysts.org/wp-content/uploads/wp-post-to-pdf-cache/1/adding-the-ballot-to-the-bullet-hezb-e-islami-in-transition.pdf.

Pagani, Luca, Stephan Schiffels, Deepti Gurdasani, Petr Danecek, Aylwyn Scally, Yuan Chen, et al. 2015. 'Tracing the Route of Modern Humans out of Africa by Using 225 Human Genome Sequences from Ethiopians and Egyptians'. *The American Journal of Human Genetics* 96(6): 986–91. doi:10.1016/j.ajhg.2015.04.019.

Palat, Madhavan K. 2005. 'The British in Central Asia'. In *History of Civilizations of Central Asia, v. VI: Towards the Contemporary Period: From the Min-Ninenteenth to the End of the Twentieth Century*, edited by Madhavan K. Palat and Anara Tabyshalieva. Paris: UNESCO, pp 99–120.

Paldi, Boaz. 2015. 'UNDP Responds to LOFTA Criticisms'. *Foreign Policy*. https://foreignpolicy.com/2015/02/04/undp-responds-to-lofta-criticisms/.

Peceny, Mark and Yury Bosin. 2011. 'Winning with Warlords in Afghanistan'. *Small Wars & Insurgencies* 22(4): 603–18. doi:10.1080/09592318.2011.599166.

Perle, Richard. 2003. 'United They Fall'. *The Spectator*. http://www.aei.org/article/16730.

Peters, Gretchen. 1997. 'Taliban Briefly Detain EU Commissioner, Journalists'. *Associated Press Newswires*, 29 September

Petrie, Cameron A. and Jim G. Shaffer. 2019. 'The Development of a "Helmand Civilisation" South of the Hindu Kush'. In *The Archaeology of Afghanistan: From Earliest Times to the Timurid Period*, edited by R. Allchin, W. Ball, and N. Hammond. Edinburgh: Edinburgh University Press, pp 161–259.

Pillalamarri, Akhilesh. 2017. 'Why is Afghanistan the "Graveyard of Empires"? A Brief History of the Empires That Were Broken in the Hindu Kush'. *The Diplomat*. 30 June. https://thediplomat.com/2017/06/why-is-afghanistan-the-graveyard-of-empires/

Pillar, Paul R. 2011. 'Al Qaeda, the Taliban, and Other Extremist Groups in Afghanistan and Pakistan'. *Hearing Before the Committee on Foreign Relations, United States Senate, One Hundred Twelfth Congress, First Session - S. Hrg. 112–70.* https://www.govinfo.gov/content/pkg/CHRG-112shrg67892/html/CHRG-112shrg67892.htm

Possehl, Gregory L. 1998. 'Sociocultural Complexity without the State: The Indus Civilization'. In *Archaic States*, edited by Gary M. Feinman and Joyce Marcus. Santa Fe: School of American Research, pp 261–91.

Possehl, Gregory L. 2002. *The Indus Civilization: A Contemporary Perspective*. Walnut Creek: AltaMira Press.

Possehl, G.L. 2007. 'The Middle Asian Interaction Sphere. Trade and Contact in the 3rd Millennium BC'. *Expedition* 49(1): 40–2.

Prakash, Om. 1998. *The New Cambridge History of India: European Commercial Enterprise in Pre-Colonial India*. Cambridge: Cambridge University Press. doi:10.1017/CHOL9780521257589.

Prevas, John. 2004. *Envy of the Gods: Alexander the Great's Ill-Fated Journey Across Asia*. Cambridge, MA: Da Capo Press.

Quie, Marissa. 2013. 'Peace-Building and Democracy Promotion in Afghanistan: The Afghanistan Peace and Reintegration Programme and Reconciliation with the Taliban'. In *Conflicting Objectives in Democracy Promotion: Do All Good Things Go Together?*, edited by Julia Leininger, Sonja Grimm and Tina Freyburg. London: Routledge, pp 165–86.

Quie, Marissa. and Hameed Hakimi. 2020. *The EU and the Politics of Migration Management in Afghanistan*. London: Chatham House. https://www.chathamhouse.org/2020/11/eu-and-politics-migration-management-afghanistan

Quigley, John. 2007. 'EU-Asia Relations and the Role of the European CFSP Special Representatives'. In *The European Union and Asia: Reflections and Re-Orientations*, edited by P. Anderson and G. Weissala. Amsterdam: European Studies, pp 193–214.

Qureshi, Saleem. 1981. 'Military in the Polity of Islam: Religion as a Basis for Civil-Military Interaction'. *International Political Science Review / Revue internationale de science politique* 2(3): 271–82.

Radio Free Europe. 2023. 'Fears Mount Over the Future of Afghanistan's Historic Bamiyan Valley'. *Radio Free Europe*. https://www.rferl.org/a/afghanistan-bamiyan-fears-collapse-buddha-statues/32297553.html.

Raimundo, António, Stelios Stavridis and Charalambos Tsardanidis. 2021. 'The Eurozone Crisis' Impact: A De-Europeanization of Greek and Portuguese Foreign Policies?'. *Journal of European Integration* 43(5): 535–50. doi:10.1080/07036337.2021.1927014.

Ramesh, Sangaralingam. 2023. 'The Indus Valley Civilisation: 3000 BC to 1600 BC'. In *The Political Economy of India's Economic Development: 5000BC to 2022AD, Volume I: Before the Indus Civilisation to Alexander the Great*, edited by Sangaralingam Ramesh. Cham: Springer International Publishing, pp 37–75. doi:10.1007/978-3-031-42072-6_2.

Rasanayagam, Angelo. 2010. *Afghanistan: A Modern History*. London: I.B. Tauris.

Rashid, Ahmed. 2000. *Taliban*. London: I.B. Tauris.

Rasuly-Paleczek, Gabriele. 2021. 'What is Afghan Culture? Some Reflections on a Contested Notion'. In *Temporary and Child Marriages in Iran and Afghanistan*, edited by Seyedeh Behnaz Hosseini. Singapore: Springer, pp 87–107.

Reuters. 2008. 'Afghans Find Body of Ex-President Slain Decades Ago'. *Reuters*. 4 December.

Reza 'Husseini', Said. 2012. 'Destruction of Bamiyan Buddhas Taliban Iconoclasm and Hazara Response'. *Himalayan and Central Asian Studies* 16(2): 15–50

Richards, David. 2017. 'David Richards, Lessons Learned Interview'. *Washington Post*. https://www.washingtonpost.com/graphics/2019/investigations/afghanistan-papers/documents-database/share/pdf.html?document=richards_david_ll_07_67_09262017.

Riedel, Bruce. 2014. *What We Won: America's Secret War in Afghanistan, 1979–89*. Washington, DC: Brookings Institution Press.

Robinson, Anthony. 1981. 'Solidarity: A Test for the West'. *The Financial Times*, 29 December, p 12.

Rouland, Michael R. 2014. *Great Game to 9/11: A Concise History of Afghanistan's International Relations.* Washington, DC: Air Force History and Museums Program.

Roy, Kaushik. 2015. *War and Society in Afghanistan: From the Mughals to the Americans, 1500–2013.* Oxford: Oxford University Press. doi:10.1093/acprof:oso/9780198099109.003.0002.

Roy, Olivier. 1990. *Islam and Resistance in Afghanistan*, 2nd edn. Cambridge: Cambridge University Press. doi:10.1017/CBO9780511563553.

Ruback, Timothy and Jon Carlson. 2022. 'Militarized Interstate Manhunts, "Absent/Presence" and the Spectral Logic of the U.S. War on Terror: The Ballad of Pancho and Bin Laden'. *Journal of International Political Theory* 19(1): 21–48. doi:10.1177/17550882221090993.

Rubin, Barnett R. 1990. 'Afghanistan: Political Exiles in Search of a State'. *Journal of Political Science* 18(1): 63–93.

Rubin, Barnett R. 1992. *The Fragmentation of Afghanistan.* New Haven: Yale University Press.

Rubin, Barnett R. 2006. 'Introduction: The Afghanistan Compact'. Afghanistan's Uncertain Transition from Turmoil to Normalcy'. *Council on Foreign Relations* pp 1–4. JSTOR, http://www.jstor.org/stable/resrep05 730.7 (Accessed 8 May 2024).

Rubin, Barnett R. 2020. *Afghanistan: What Everyone Needs to Know.* Oxford: Oxford University Press.

Rubinstein, Alvin Z. 1980. 'Soviet Imperialism in Afghanistan'. *Current History* 79(459): 80–104.

Rubinstein, Alvin Z. 1988. 'The Soviet Withdrawal from Afghanistan'. *Current History* 87(531): 333–40. http://www.jstor.org/stable/45316120.

Ruiz, Hiram and Margaret Emery. 2001. *Afghanistan's Refugee Crisis.* http://www.merip.org/mero/mero092401.html.

Rumsfeld, Donald. 2001. *Unclassified: November 27, 2001.* https://nsarchive2.gwu.edu/NSAEBB/NSAEBB326/doc08.pdf.

Rumsfeld, Donald. 2006. '*Interview with Secretary Donald Rumsfeld and Cal Thomas of Fox News Watch*'. 7th December, Location Undisclosed. https://www.twincities.com/2006/12/14/defense-secretary-talks-about-the-war-in-iraq-and-the-long-fight-to-come/

Rupp, Richard. 2006. 'High Hopes and Limited Prospects: Washington's Security and Nation-Building Aims in Afghanistan'. *Cambridge Review of International Affairs* 19(2): 285–98. doi:10.1080/09557570600724587.

Safi, Mariam. 2014. *Afghanistan, US and the Peace Process: A Deal with the Taliban in 2014?* Kabul: Afghan Institute of Strategic Studies.

Saikal, Amin. 2004. *Modern Afghanistan: A History of Struggle and Survival.* London: I.B. Tauris.

Sakhi, Nilofar. 2022. 'The Taliban Takeover in Afghanistan and Security Paradox'. *Journal of Asian Security and International Affairs* 9(3): 383–401. doi:10.1177/23477970221130882.

Sanchooli, Doostali and Seyyed Baqer Hosseini. 2021. 'The Political-Religious Role of Abu Bakr Hasiri Sistani Faqih Shafei in the Court of Ghaznavid Based on Two Literary and Historical Sources'. *International Journal of Multicultural and Multireligious Understanding* 8(3): 415–24. doi:http://dx.doi.org/10.18415/ijmmu.v8i3.2436.

Schamiloglu, Uli. 2017. 'The Impact of the Black Death on the Golden Horde: Politics, Economy, Society, Civilization'. *DOAJ* 5(2): 325–43.

Schöch, Rüdiger. 2008. *Afghan Refugees in Pakistan during the 1980s: Cold War Politics and Registration Practice*. UNHCR. https://www.unhcr.org/media/afghan-refugees-pakistan-during-1980s-cold-war-politics-and-regis tration-practice-ruediger.

Schwartz, Moshe. 2011. *Wartime Contracting in Afghanistan: Analysis and Issues for Congress*. Washington, DC. https://crsreports.congress.gov/prod uct/pdf/R/R42084.

Searle, John R. 1996. *The Construction of Social Reality*. St Ives: Penguin.

Shahi, Agha. 2008. 'The Geneva Accords'. *Pakistan Horizon* 61(1/2): 143–64. http://www.jstor.org/stable/23726021.

Shapiro, Jeremy. 2021. *The Fall of the Afghan Government and What It Means for Europe: Security and Defence*. https://ecfr.eu/publication/the-fall-of-the-afghan-government-and-what-it-means-for-europe/.

Shawcross, W. 1997. 'Welcome to New-Style Afghanistan and Don't Come Back'. *International Herald Tribune*. https://www.nytimes.com/1997/10/07/opinion/IHT-welcome-to-newstyle-afghanistan-and-dont-come-back.html

Shilston, Timothy. 2012. 'Police Development in a War Zone: Lessons from Afghanistan'. In *Policing Global Movement*, edited by Caroline S. Taylor, Daniel J. Torpy, and Dilip K. Das. New York: Routledge, pp 91–103.

Shorthose, Jim. 2003. 'Unlawful Instruments and Goods: Afghanistan, Culture and the Taliban'. *Capital & Class* 27(1): 9–16. doi:10.1177/030981680307900102.

Shroder, John F. 2012. 'Afghanistan: Rich Resource Base and Existing Environmental Despoliation'. *Environmental Earth Sciences* 67(7): 1971–86. doi:10.1007/s12665-012-1638-7.

SIGAR. 2014. *Quarterly Report to the United States Congress*. Virginia. https://www.sigar.mil/pdf/quarterlyreports/2014-04-30qr.pdf.

SIGAR. 2016. *SIGAR 16-58-LL Corruption in Conflict: Lessons from the U.S. Experience in Afghanistan*. Virginia. www.sigar.mil/investigations/hotline/report-fraud.aspx.

SIGAR. 2017. *Special Inspector General for Afghanistan Reconstruction Quarterly Report to the United States Congress*. Virginia. https://www.sigar.mil/pdf/quarterlyreports/2017-01-30qr.pdf.

SIGAR. 2019. *SIGAR 19-58-LL Reintegration of Ex-Combatants: Lessons from the U.S. Experience in Afghanistan*. Virginia. https://www.sigar.mil/pdf/lessonslearned/SIGAR-19-58-LL.pdf.

SIGAR. 2021. *What We Need to Learn: Lessons From Twenty Years of Afghanistan Reconstruction*. Virginia. https://www.sigar.mil/pdf/lessonslearned/SIGAR-21-46-LL.pdf.

SIGAR. 2022a. *Police in Conflict: Lessons from the U.S. Experience*. Virginia. https://www.sigar.mil/pdf/lessonslearned/SIGAR-22-23-LL.pdf.

SIGAR. 2022b. *SIGAR 23–05-IP Why the Afghan Government Collapsed*. Virginia. https://www.sigar.mil/pdf/evaluations/SIGAR-23-05-IP.pdf

SIGAR. 2023. *Recent Developments Report*. Virginia. https://www.sigar.mil/pdf/quarterlyreports/2023-07-30qr.pdf

Smith, Scott S. 2019. *Loya Jirgas and Political Crisis Management in Afghanistan*. Washington, DC: US Institute of Peace.

Sondorp, Egbert. 2004. *Service Delivery in Difficult Environments: Case Study 1: Afghanistan*. London: Department for International Development Report on Service Delivery in Difficult Environments, undertaken by the DFID Health Systems Resource Centre.

Spain, James W. 1967. '539 Memorandum of Conversation: The President's Conversation with Afghan Prime Minister Maiwandwal'. *Foreign Relations of the United States, 1964–1968, Volume XXV, South Asia*. https://history.state.gov/historicaldocuments/frus1964-68v25/d539.

Spengler, Robert N. 2015. 'Agriculture in the Central Asian Bronze Age'. *Journal of World Prehistory* 28(3): 215–53. doi:10.1007/s10963-015-9087-3.

Sperling, James. 2007. 'Policies of Protection: Meeting the Challenge of Internal Security'. In *EU Security Governance*, edited by Emil. Kirchner and James Sperling. Manchester: Manchester University Press, pp 120–84.

Spink, Jeaniene. 2005. 'Education and Politics in Afghanistan: The Importance of an Education System in Peacebuilding and Reconstruction'. *Journal of Peace Education* 2(2): 195–207. doi:10.1080/17400200500185794.

Spoerhase, Carlos. 2008. 'Presentism and Precursorship in Intellectual History'. *Culture, Theory and Critique* 49(1): 49–72. doi:10.1080/14735780802024257.

Spyrou, Maria A., Lyazzat Musralina, Guido A. Gnecchi Ruscone, Arthur Kocher, Pier-Giorgio Borbone, Valeri I. Khartanovich, et al. 2022. 'The Source of the Black Death in Fourteenth-Century Central Eurasia'. *Nature* 606(7915): 718–24. doi:10.1038/s41586-022-04800-3.

Stenersen, Anne. 2017. 'The Troublesome Guest'. In *Al-Qaida in Afghanistan*. Cambridge: Cambridge University Press, pp 69–95. doi:10.1017/9781139871501.006.

Stewart, Rory. 2021. 'The Last Days of Intervention: Afghanistan and the Delusions of Maximalism'. *Foreign Affairs*: 60–73.

Strand, Arne. 2003. 'Who's Helping Who? NGO Coordination of Humanitarian Assistance'. The University of York. https://open.cmi.no/cmi-xmlui/bitstream/handle/11250/2474522/Who%27s%20helping%20Who%3FNGO%20Coordination%20of%20Humanitarian%20Assistance.%20With%20Special%20Reference%20to%20Afghanistan%20%281985%20-2001%29?sequence=1&isAllowed=y.

Subtelny, Maria Eva. 1988. 'Socioeconomic Bases of Cultural Patronage under the Later Timurids'. *International Journal of Middle East Studies* 20(4): 479–505.

Subtelny, Maria. 2007. *Timurids in Transition: Turko-Persian Politics and Acculturation in Medieval Iran*. Leiden: Brill.

Suhrke, Astri. 2007. *The Democratisation of a Dependent State: The Case of Afghanistan*. Madrid: Chr. Michelsen Institute (CMI Working Paper WP 2007: 10).

Suhrke, Astri. 2011. *When More Is Less: The International Project in Afghanistan*. London: Hurst & Company.

Suhrke, Astri. 2013. 'Statebuilding in Afghanistan: A Contradictory Engagement'. *Central Asian Survey* 32(3): 271–86. doi:10.1080/02634937.2013.834715.

Suhrke, Astri, Kristian Berg Harpviken, Are Knudsen, Arve Ofstad and Arne Strand. 2002. 'Peacebuilding: Lessons for Afghanistan This Series Can Be Ordered from: Indexing Terms Peacebuilding Rehabilitation Aid Afghanistan'. *Chr. Michelsen Institute Development Studies and Human Rights*. https://www.cmi.no/publications/file/831-peacebuilding-lessons-for-afghanistan.pdf.

Sultan-I-Rome. 2004. 'The Role of the North-West Frontier Province in the Khilafat and Hijrat Movements'. *Islamic Studies* 43(1): 51–78.

Tanner, Stephen. 2009. *Afghanistan*. Philadelphia: Da Capo Press.

Tarn, William Woodthorpe. W.W. 2010. 'The Greeks in Bactria and India'. Cambridge: Cambridge University Press. doi:10.1017/cbo9780511707353.

Tarzi, Amin. 2012. 'Islam and Constitutionalism in Afghanistan'. *Journal of Persianate Studies* 5(2): 205–43. doi:https://doi.org/10.1163/18747167-12341244.

Tavernier, Jan. 2021. 'Peoples and Languages'. In *A Companion to the Achaemenid Persian Empire*, edited by Bruno Jacobs and Robert Rollinger. Wiley Blackwell: Oxford, pp 39–52. doi:https://doi.org/10.1002/9781119071860.ch3.

Theros, Marika. 2010. 'A Human Security Strategy for Afghanistan: What Role for the EU?' In *The European Union and Human Security*, edited by Mary Martin and Mary Kaldor. London: Routledge, pp 145–58.

Theros, Marika. 2023. 'Knowledge, Power and the Failure of US Peacemaking in Afghanistan 2018–21'. *International Affairs* 99(3): 1231–52. doi:10.1093/ia/iiad092.

Thomas, Clayton. 2021. *U.S. Military Withdrawal and Taliban Takeover in Afghanistan: Frequently Asked Questions*. Washington DC: Congressional Research Service. https://crsreports.congress.gov.

Thomas, Clayton. 2022. *Terrorist Groups in Afghanistan*. Washington DC: Congressional Research Service.

Thomas, Clayton, Cory R. Gill, Tyler F. Hacker, Kathleen J. McInnis and Heidi M. Peters. 2021. *U.S. Military Drawdown in Afghanistan: Frequently Asked Questions R46670*. Washington, DC: Congressional Research Service. https://crsreports.congress.gov.

Tierney, John F. 2010. *Warlord, Inc. Extortion and Corruption Along the Supply Chain in Afghanistan*. https://www.cbsnews.com/htdocs/pdf/HNT_Report.pdf.

Tolman, Herebert Cushing. 1908. *Ancient Persian Lexicon and Texts*. Nashville: Vanderbilt University.

Tooze, Adam. 2018. *Crashed: How a Decade of Financial Crises Changed the World*. London: Penguin Random House.

Transparency International. 2022. 'Corruption Perceptions Index'. https://www.transparency.org/en/cpi/2022.

Travers, Robert. 2007. *Ideology and Empire in Eighteenth-Century India: The British in Bengal*. Cambridge: Cambridge University Press. doi:DOI: 10.1017/CBO9780511497438.

Truman, Harry S. 1949. 'Inaugural Address'. *The National Archives*. https://www.trumanlibrary.gov/library/public-papers/19/inaugural-address#.

Ullah, Zahid. 2022. 'Contextualising the Taliban Redux (2021): Is the Taliban Takeover of Afghanistan a Pyrrhic Victory for Pakistan?' *Small Wars & Insurgencies* 33(7): 1177–1202. doi:10.1080/09592318.2022.2118417.

Ullmann-Margalit, Edna. 1977. *The Emergence of Norms*. Oxford: Oxford University Press.

UNAMA. 2007. *Suicide Attacks in Afghanistan (2001–2007)*. Kabul. https://www.securitycouncilreport.org/atf/cf/%7B65BFCF9B-6D27-4E9C-8CD3-CF6E4FF96FF9%7D/Afgh%202007SuicideAttacks.pdf.

UN DGC. 2001. 'Afghanistan: "Six Plus Two" Group Urges Warring Sides to Pursue Dialogue – Afghanistan'. *News and Press Release*. https://reliefweb.int/report/afghanistan/afghanistan-six-plus-two-group-urges-warring-sides-pursue-dialogue.

UNDP. 2017. *Afghanistan Peace and Reintegration Programme (UNDP Support): Project Completion Report*. https://www.undp.org/sites/g/files/zskgke326/files/migration/af/APRP-finalreport.pdf.

United Nations. 2016. '70th Anniversary of Afghanistan's Membership in United Nations'. *UN Missions*. https://unama.unmissions.org/70th-anni versary-afghanistan's-membership-united-nations.

UNODC. 2004. *United Nations Convention Against Corruption*. New York. https://www.unodc.org/documents/treaties/UNCAC/Publications/Con vention/08-50026_E.pdf.

UNODC. 2007. *Fighting Corruption in Afghanistan a Roadmap for Strategy and Action: Draft for Discussion by Staff at Asian Development Bank, UK Department for International Development, United Nations Development Programme, United Nations Office on Drugs and Crime, and The World Bank*. https://www.unodc. org/pdf/afg/anti_corruption_roadmap.pdf.

UNSC. 2004. *Afghanistan's First Presidential Election Not Perfect, But Sets Stage For Journey Towards Vigorous Democracy, Security Council Told*. https://press. un.org/en/2004/sc8216.doc.htm.

UNSC. 2022. *Letter Dated 11 July 2022 from the Chair of the Security Council Committee Pursuant to Resolutions 1267 (1999), 1989 (2011) and 2253 (2015) Concerning Islamic State in Iraq and the Levant (Da'esh), Al-Qaida and Associated Individuals, Groups, Undertakings and Entities Addressed to the President of the Security Council*. https://www.securitycouncilreport.org/atf/cf/%7B65BFC F9B-6D27-4E9C-8CD3-CF6E4FF96FF9%7D/S%202022%20547.pdf.

US Department of State. 1954. 'The Chargé in Afghanistan (Little) to the Department of State'. *789.00/7–1054: Telegram*. https://history.state.gov/ historicaldocuments/frus1952-54v11p2/d856.

Van Langenhove, Luk. 2023. 'The Idea of Society: The Spoken World Theory and the Ontological Conceptualization of Society'. *Front Sociol* 8(1241355).

Vendrell, Francesc. 2008. 'BBC HARDtalk, Interviewed by Stephen Sackur'. http://news.bbc.co.uk/1/hi/programmes/hardtalk/7606022.stm.

Vendrell, Francesc. 2009. 'What Went Wrong After Bonn'. *Middle East Institute*. https://www.mei.edu/publications/what-went-wrong-after-bonn.

Verma, Birendra. 1970. 'Indian Solicitations for Afghan Military Intervention, 1793–1800'. *Proceedings of the Indian History Congress* 32: 38–43.

Verney, Susannah. 2014. '"Broken and Can't Be Fixed": The Impact of the Economic Crisis on the Greek Party System'. *The International Spectator* 49(1): 18–35. doi:10.1080/03932729.2014.877222.

Virgin, Yami. 2023. 'U.S. Bombs Left in Afghanistan Are Ending up in the Hands of Mexican Cartels'. *Fox San Antonio*. https://foxsanantonio.com/ news/yami-investigates/us-bombs-left-in-afghanistan-are-ending-up-in-the-wrong-hands-retired-hsi-agent-warns-explosives-maximum-dam age-special-inspector-united-states-mexico-cartels.

Voll, John Obert. 1994. *Islam: Continuity and Change in the Modern World*, 2nd edn. Colorado: Syracuse University Press.

Voll, John Obert. 2014. 'The Middle East in World History'. In *The Oxford Handbook of World History*. Oxford: Oxford University Press, pp 437–54.

Walcher, Dustin. 2015. 'The Reagan Doctrine'. In *A Companion to Ronald Reagan*, pp 339–58. Oxford: Wiley Blackwell. doi:https://doi.org/10.1002/9781118607770.ch19.

Wallace, Shane. 2016. 'Greek Culture in Afghanistan and India: Old Evidence and New Discoveries'. *Greece and Rome* 63(2): 205–26. doi:10.1017/S0017383516000073.

Washington Post. 2015. 'State Department Official, Lessons Learned Interview'. *The Washington Post*. https://www.washingtonpost.com/graphics/2019/investigations/afghanistan-papers/documents-database/?document=background_ll_03_dc_06172015.

Waters, Matt. 2014. *Ancient Persia: A Concise History of the Achaemenid Empire, 550–330 BCE*. Cambridge: Cambridge University Press. doi:10.1017/CBO9780511841880.

Watson, Adam. 1992. *The Evolution of International Society*. London: Routledge.

Weinberg, Leonard. 2018. 'A History of Terrorism'. In *Routledge Handbook of Terrorism and Counterterrorism*, edited by Andrew Silke. Boca Raton: Routledge, pp 34–56. doi:10.4324/9781315744636.

Whitlock, Craig. 2019. 'U.S. Tolerated Corruption in Afghanistan, Officials Admit in Confidential Documents'. *The Washington Post*. https://www.washingtonpost.com/graphics/2019/investigations/afghanistan-papers/afghanistan-war-corruption-government/.

Whitlock, Craig. 2021. *The Afghanistan Papers: A Secret History of the War*. London: Simon & Schuster.

Whitman, Richard G. 1998. *From Civilian Power to Superpower? The International Identity of the European Union*. Hampshire: Macmillan.

Wieringen, Kjeld Van and Julie Claustre. 2023. 'Future of Sino-Afghan Relations on EU Interests and Strategic Autonomy'. *European Parliamentary Research Service*. https://www.europarl.europa.eu/RegData/etudes/BRIE/2023/747434/EPRS_BRI(2023)747434_EN.pdf.

Wiesehfer, Josef. 2009. 'The Achaemenid Empire'. In *The Dynamics of Ancient Empires: State Power from Assyria to Byzantium*, edited by Ian Morris and Walter Scheidel. Oxford: Oxford University Press, pp 66–98.

Wijesuriya, Gamini and Sujeong Lee. 2013. *Asian Buddhist Heritage: Conserving the Sacred*. Seoul: ICCROM-CHA International Forum on Conservation.

Wilkinson, P. 2005. *International Terrorism: The Changing Threat and the EU's Response*. Paris: Chaillot Papers.

Williams, Beryl J. 1966. 'VI. The Strategic Background to the Anglo-Russian Entente of August 1907'. *The Historical Journal* 9(3): 360–73. doi:10.1017/S0018246X00026698.

Williams, Phil. 2022. 'US Intervention in Afghanistan and the Failure of Governance'. *Small Wars & Insurgencies* 33(7): 1130–51. doi:10.1080/09592318.2022.2120299.

Wink, André. 2003. *Al-Hind, Volume 3 Indo-Islamic Society, 14th-15th Centuries*. Boston: BRILL.

Woods, Ngaire. 2005. 'The Shifting Politics of Foreign Aid'. *International Affairs (Royal Institute of International Affairs 1944–)* 81(2): 393–409. http://www.jstor.org/stable/3568895.

World Bank. 2003. 'Afghanistan Development Forum March 13–14'. *World Bank Statement*. https://web.worldbank.org/archive/website00811/WEB/PDF/ADF.PDF.

Worthington, Ian. 2014. *By the Spear: Philip II, Alexander the Great, and the Rise and Fall of the Macedonian Empire*. New York: Oxford University Press. https://warwick.summon.serialssolutions.com/2.0.0/link/0/eLvHCXMwfV3BSgMxEB1qexEvVitWreTkrUvIZpvsSVpxKcVLVdBbyW4mR5FVKfv3nWyypQh6DIFAhszMm5m8GYBUJHz6yyaUubROoEJnLEFaS6AD0ZC2yExwV3mucvEyWz3rp3e97kHRUWPaimH8pph0tnJfS92aehu_WiaBBnBvA7IlGEyRwxHFYpy0dTCfv60XB6kXzy7VocFOTvhAKxl78XRr3nJ4aj_N_MDdFKcwQM9BGEIPP85gFFp5NOyO-T6xpp3F25zDyaJhBN_Y1ye91hGw4vH1YTmN521iXmZTpqkiNEB45gL6FOvjJTCNHJUoMfd81JmzxmmTcZKZUKXMqmoM4z-Pufpn7xqOydPLkDu4gf53_YOT_RVvo4R26g94bQ.

WTCHP. 2023. 'Program Statistics: World Trade Center Health Program'. https://www.cdc.gov/wtc/ataglance.html#enrollmentWTC.

Wyles, John. 1980a. 'A Wet Response from Europe'. *The Financial Times*, 31 January, p 16.

Wyles, John. 1980b. 'EEC Still Considering Anti-Soviet Measures'. *The Financial Times*, 1 February, p 4.

Yergin, Daniel. 1991. *The Prize: The Epic Quest for Oil, Money, and Power*. New York: Simon & Schuster.

Young, T. Cuyler, Jr. 1988. 'The Early History of the Medes and the Persians and the Achaemenid Empire to the Death of Cambyses'. In *The Cambridge Ancient History: Volume 4: Persia, Greece and the Western Mediterranean, c.525 to 479 BC*, edited by D.M. Lewis, John Boardman, M. Ostwald and N.G.L. Hammond. Cambridge: Cambridge University Press, pp 1–52. DOI:10.1017/CHOL9780521228046.002.

Youngs, Richard. 2021. *The EU's Strategic Autonomy Trap*. Brussels: Carnegie Europe.

Zagorski, Andrei. 2007. 'Lessons from Soviet Experience of Socialist Modernisation in Afghanistan (1978–89)'. In *Readings in European Security*, edited by Michael Emerson. Brussels: Centre for European Policy Studies, International Institute for Security Studies & Geneva Centre for the Democratic Control of Armed Forces, pp 211–24.

Zarakol, Ayşe. 2022. *Before the West: The Rise and Fall of Eastern World Orders*. Cambridge: Cambridge University Press. doi:10.1017/9781108975377.

Zarakol, Ayşe. 2023. 'Can Historicism Win over IR?' In *The Historicity of International Politics Imperialism and the Presence of the Past*, edited by Klaus Schlichte and Stephan Stetter. Cambridge: Cambridge University Press, pp 291–302.

Ziller, Jacques. 2019. *The Lisbon Treaty: Oxford Research Encyclopedia of Politics*. Oxford: Oxford University Press. doi:10.1093/acrefore/9780190228637.013.1066.

Zürcher, Christoph. 2012. 'Conflict, State Fragility and Aid Effectiveness: Insights from Afghanistan'. *Conflict, Security & Development* 12(5): 461–80. doi:10.1080/14678802.2012.744180.

Index

Praise for *The Wives of Halcyon*

'Eirinie Lapidaki's storytelling prowess shines through this masterfully crafted narrative about strength, solidarity and faith. It's in the quiet whispers of strength that we find our loudest roars, reminding us of our shared human resilience.'

RUBY SLOANE, @xrubyreadsx

'An enthralling tale of female strength, vulnerability, and solidarity in a dangerous and unpredictable universe. The author has created such beautifully complex and flawed characters. It's definitely one of the best books I've read this year.'

MATINA TZOUMERKA, @breathing_pages

'A uniquely compelling and profound book with real and raw characters, I felt totally transported into the setting and emotionally absorbed by the story. It is an insightful tale of female fortitude in the face of manipulation and coercion.'

POPPY SMITH, @poppysreads

'An extraordinary debut novel... This is an astute and gripping tale of coercive control, about power and about misplaced trust. The isolated Scottish setting adds such depth to the narrative and the bonds of motherhood are beautifully portrayed. A novel that raises questions about power that can be gained by one man's charisma and words. Female characters who are precisely drawn, exposing their flaws and vulnerability, but most especially, their strength.'

ANNE CATER, Random Things Through My Letterbox

'A fascinating story.'

ILONA BANNISTER, author of *When I Ran Away*

'A brilliant and completely addictive read.'
Ruth Hogan, author of *The Keeper of Lost Things*

'An astonishing and extraordinary debut.'
Charlie Carroll, author of *The Lip*

'What a gripping journey this was! Hats off to Eirnie for this fabulous book. A stunningly written, powerful tale of power and control, and what happens when people lose themselves in the face of coercion.'
Jessica Ryn, author of *The Extraordinary Hope of Dawn Brightside*

'*The Wives of Halcyon* is a worthy addition to the 'cult' novel genre – a gripping page-turner which celebrates the strength and resilience of women, in even the most desperate of circumstances.'
Carole Hailey, author of *The Silence Project*

'I loved this fierce and perceptive book. It questions female solidarity, faith and redemption and answers with skill, wit and not a little provocation. Clever and satisfying!'
Janet Ellis, author of *The Butcher's Hook*

The Wives
of Halcyon

Eirinie Lapidaki

Legend Press Ltd, 51 Gower Street, London, WC1E 6HJ
info@legendtimesgroup.co.uk | www.legendpress.co.uk

Print ISBN 9781915643193
Ebook ISBN 9781915643209
Set in Times.
Cover design by Rose Cooper | www.rosecooper.com

Born in the north-east of England, Eirinie Lapidaki studied English Literature at St Andrews and completed her MLitt at Newcastle University.

She began writing her debut novel, *The Wives of Halcyon*, while working as a bookseller at Waterstones, and early chapters won a Northern Writers Award from New Writing North. Eirinie is currently working on her next novel, about the wellness industry and its impact on women's bodies, inspired by her battle with the chronic condition adenomyosis.

She lives in Gateshead with her husband, her daughter and her dog.

Follow Eirinie on Instagram
@eirinie.writes

For my Nell

Elijah

(m) Aoife   (m) Ruth   (m) Deborah

Constance	Eli	Jonah
Faith	Abraham	Noah
Halcyon	Leah	Susannah
Humility	Moses	
	Abigail	

Can man make for himself gods? Such are not gods!

Jeremiah 16:20

Prologue

Revelation

Halcyon is gone now. The farmhouse where three of my children were born has been demolished; cold stones once covered in flaking whitewash turned to rubble, floorboards taken up, grey roof slates reclaimed. And our meagre belongings – worn-out boots, mugs and plates, bed linens – taken away to some evidence room. They could still be there, those relics of our old way of life, gathering dust. Most likely they have been thrown out, to lie in a skip or a landfill site awaiting the End of Days. The barns and outbuildings have also been dismantled, taken for scrap, the poured concrete floors where worshipful knees once knelt jackhammered into oblivion so no trace is left behind. Caravans towed. Charred remnants of the fire vanished, like we were never there at all.

Halcyon was erased to deter the gawkers, the obsessives, the surviving believers. But the one-track road from Abercraig is still there, narrowing as it winds away from the village towards the old settlement. You could follow it still, admiring the undulating hills broken through with patches of heather and harsh grey rock, stopping to photograph the snow-capped mountains which rise in the distance. Two streams break the road, narrow and pretty and cold. They are two distributaries from the larger stream which formed one of the borders of our land, so although you can't stand in the same river twice you could get out of your car and walk the length of either of them and know that you were close to the spot where we lived. The surviving livestock were sold, so you won't see any of the sheep which once grazed the hardy grasses, but maybe you will spot a stag or an eagle in the distance. If you decide to drive on and take your chances on the road, which is paved with small stones that dislodge and catch in the wheels of your car, you will end up driving through the spot where our gate was and into the old heart of Halcyon. If you are very prepared, really invested in your trip, you might have a copy of those grainy aerial shots which got published during the trial. There are no landmarks any more, but you could pace it out roughly – this is the farmhouse where the wives lived, this is where their church was, here's where all of the children slept. Such people do exist, I've learned. People who will take that road and record themselves tramping over the land, looking for ghosts or souvenirs. Telling a story which isn't theirs to tell.

I tell my story as infrequently as I can. I'm still ashamed by the part I played in it all, embarrassed by my stupidity, frightened by how far astray I was led. I have spent enough time in therapy to see myself as a survivor, and enough time in the tangled web of my mind to see myself as a perpetrator. When I've spoken to other people about it, people who weren't there, it's obvious that they see me as a fool. They nod sympathetically and say all the right things, but behind their careful words and kind eyes I can sense the question they most want to ask – how did you not see it coming? They are desperate to know how so many people could walk headlong into such an obvious disaster waiting to happen. To follow a man with such unquestioning obedience, oblivious to the writing which must surely have been on the wall from the beginning, like the signs in *The Wizard of Oz*: *I'd turn back now if I were you.*

Most people, the ones who have spoken to me and the ones who have spoken about me, come to the conclusion that we were all brainwashed. He had brainwashed us. A pied piper, marching us away from our homes and jobs and along the craggy road to Halcyon. Personally, I don't hold with the brainwashing idea, but I do like to think about the word. Brainwashed. If I didn't know what it meant, if I'd just heard it for the first time with no context, I would think it sounded like a good thing. I imagine a brain, as grimy as a city dweller's lung, being submerged in a glittering Highland spring. The fresh water runs over the brain, washing away the dirt, smoothing it like a stone until it emerges unburdened, unworried and clean.

Part One

Chapter One

Aoife

Mostly, I forgot about the life I had lived before we moved to Halcyon, in the same way that you forget what winter feels like on a balmy summer day. It wasn't so much that I couldn't remember the world outside our compound, or the things I had done there; I just had no reason to. Occasionally, a memory would pop up in my mind – the sound of my boots against the paving slabs as I walked to work; the particular smell of chip fat and coffee and smoke which clung to my hair and clothes after a shift. Collapsing onto the sofa at the end of the day, too tired to do anything except turn on the TV and lie there, half watching, half dozing, until it was time for bed. What struck me when those memories surfaced was just how small my life had been, how empty, how *boring*. Halcyon had given me a purpose. It had made my life fuller. It had made it interesting.

For as long as I had known Elijah, he had dreamed of building a community, somewhere far away from the evils of the modern world, where like-minded people could live and work and worship together in peace. Halcyon was the realisation of his vision, but it was our shared achievement – our baby. He was the ideas man, but the details, the logistics, were all me. It was his job to say something like 'we need to be fully off grid, I want us running on wind power', and it was my job to make it work. And I did. Every time.

Our hard work had paid off, and we were thriving. Our farmhouse, squat and sturdy, was the centre of Halcyon, and at the centre of the farmhouse was the temple.

I was the last one to arrive at temple that morning, and when

I opened the door everyone was already seated for prayer. The temple was a small room, with damp emanating from the dark stone walls. Elijah wanted the space to be sacrosanct, free from any markers of the twenty-first century, so unlike the other rooms in our farmhouse, this one had not been wired with electricity. The only source of light came from a small window above his pulpit, the Scottish morning sun travelling weakly through it down into the space, illuminating the motes of dust which floated and eddied in its path. Elijah's pulpit faced the room's entrance, but he acted as though he hadn't noticed me and continued to stare up to the heavens, his arms remaining outstretched as the door creaked closed behind me.

I took my place next to Ruth, at the end of the row, and settled onto my knees. Even then, over ten years after our first meeting, I could not get my fill of Elijah. He was older of course, but still the same striking figure he had always been. When we'd first met, I had been taken by his shock of black hair, his broad, strong shoulders, his calm, assured stance. This was a man, I had thought, built to bear the weight of God's instructions. From my kneeling position he looked more imposing than he did in the old days, readier to face his challenges. He was the only man I could imagine who could wear ancient jeans and an argyle jumper and still look as though he had stepped straight out of the Old Testament.

'Lord!' he began, his voice reverberating against the unadorned walls, 'We thank you for granting us another day in our Heaven on Earth, and pray that we might do you service today. We thank you for granting us your bounty here at Halcyon, and for protecting us from the sins of the world outside its safe walls.'

Elijah expressed the same sentiments every morning at temple, and then again later on at church, and at evening worship. It was our mantra, our Lord's Prayer. We responded:

'Thanks be to God and our Holy Prophet.'

Other than the opening prayer, things were very different at temple to how they were at church and evening worship. At temple, it was just the four of us, the innermost family: Elijah at the helm, then me, then Ruth, then Deborah. We were his disciples, and because of our privileged position within Heaven on Earth his decisions and his prophecies were shared with us first. At the start, these prophecies had filled me with joy, but

God's latest revelations had been more difficult for me to accept, and slowly there had been less dialogue. I prayed a great deal.

'Some troubling news.'

I looked up in alarm, and for the briefest moment my eyes met Ruth's. Elijah continued, his low voice rumbling.

'The Devil has brought doubt and fear into the minds of our sinful neighbours. Since our mission reached out to Abercraig several weeks ago, our success there has raised concerns with some of the villagers. I have prayed, and decided to stop all of our local missionary work. God has told me not to waste any more time on these sinners; they have lost their chance at salvation. We need to remain vigilant, as some threats have been made to our property. Let me know the instant you see anything or *anyone* amiss.' He paused and gave us a knowing smile which did not quite reach his eyes.

Elijah bowed his head to indicate the start of silent prayer. I looked down at my knees. At almost ten miles away, the people of Abercraig were our closest neighbours, and we had had run-ins with them before. When we first bought the farm there were some rumours spread which caused a bit of a stir, but Elijah went over and charmed the village council and everything was sorted. If it came to it, I was sure he would go out and speak to them again.

Out of the corner of my eye I could see Deborah, her hands clasped virtuously in her lap, as unfazed by the revelation as she had been by Elijah's bombshell the previous week. Ruth was now breathing steadily, apparently focused on her prayers, but I had seen her flash of concern. The three of us were still, glassy pools of water, the gentle ripples left by the glance Ruth and I had shared had already faded into our depths. Deborah remained as shallow and unmoved as a puddle. I closed my eyes and prayed that the villagers would leave us alone, and not get anyone else involved. I also prayed about his bombshell, and wondered if Ruth was praying for the same thing.

Once temple was over and Elijah had gone, Ruth and Deborah and I rose to leave. Deborah clutched her swelling stomach with one hand and supported herself against the wall with the other. Although she was only around five or six months along, she already seemed fit to burst and the buttons of her dress strained against the force of her belly. Whenever I picture Deborah, she is always pregnant, like the Virgin in a nativity scene, only I'm sure Christ's mother was never so smug. She even looked like the Virgin, or at least the Virgin as she had appeared in every nativity play I'd seen – long fair hair, wide-eyed, angelic. Although her pointy little nose reminded me of a pig's snout.

'How are you feeling, Deborah?' asked Ruth, extending a hand to pull her upright. 'How's your back?'

'Much better thanks,' she said, 'the willow was a massive help. Like really, really helpful. I slept better last night than I've slept in a long time.'

Once upon a time, when pregnancy was something that happened to me, Ruth had offered me willow and pressed my stomach to feel the position of the baby. She had been a midwife before she'd married Elijah. All of the babies born in Halcyon were delivered by her steady hands and had their first cries lulled by her low, lilting voice.

It had been my idea to bring Ruth into our family. Elijah and I were four years, two children, and one church deep into our relationship. Faith, our youngest, was almost two years old and there was no sign of a little sibling making their way to join her. Elijah was stuck in a spiritual cul-de-sac; unsure of the direction we needed to take the church, and concerned that God's reluctance to bless us with another child was an indication of some misstep he had made or a sign he had unintentionally ignored. Grey clouds had gathered above our once happy little unit, and every day I would wake with a knot in my stomach, terrified of the impending flood. At home in the flat, we barely spoke. We went on as normal in the church, but even there the undercurrent of love which I had relied on seemed to be fading and I was becoming a colleague, not a wife. I had reached breaking point, but the failure of my marriage was not an option. It was Helen, the wife of John, Elijah's right-hand man, who had pointed me in the direction which had saved us. I had been unsure of Helen at first; John had developed something of a reputation in the café where I had worked, and surely any woman who would marry a man like him must be a little off-kilter herself? But she was kind and wise, and by that point, my closest friend.

'I know this might sound obvious, sweetheart,' she had said as we worked alone in the church hall kitchen, preparing snacks for the playgroup children, 'but have you turned to your Bible?

God wants you to be happy in your marriage. I know he'll point you to your answer if you look.'

So I looked. And I found. Elijah had started preaching more and more about the old patriarchs, and their many children from many wives, but even he seemed surprised when I broached the subject with him over dinner when Constance and Faith were in bed. Surprised, but intrigued. Surprised, but happy. Surprised, but satisfied. We spoke about the potential for jealousy, and although it was something I prepared for, I never felt it. Or at least, not at first; watching Ruth then, though, with her tender hand on Deborah, I couldn't help but feel a little pang of envy. I missed our gentle, easy camaraderie. I missed being the one that people cared about the most.

We walked out of the temple and into the kitchen together, removing our headscarves as we went. I knew I should go to the office for an hour before church and run through the finances, but instead I sat down and let out my relief with a slow exhale. The log book could wait a moment.

'Oh Aoife,' Deborah said as she sat next to me, 'that's exactly how I feel. Still, are you looking forward to the Feast of the Prophet tomorrow?'

I closed my eyes. Deborah would be the wrong person to talk to about my worries, with her exhausting optimism and holier-than-thou attitude. She had been a member of the church since she was a teenager, her and her mother, before the mother had died of liver failure or some such thing. At twenty-six she was almost ten years my junior, but she seemed far younger. So much of the work had already been done by the time Deborah was able to understand the church, and even more had been done before she joined our family. The foundations of Halcyon had been laid, and she seemed to think that meant there was no longer any urgency in our mission. She seemed to forget, as she mixed her home-made soaps and oversaw the children's lessons and crafts, that we were living in the End of Days.

Before she could speak again, I raised myself up out of the sagging folds of the sofa and walked out of the room without turning to say goodbye. Sequestered in the dim hallway, I allowed myself a moment of quiet contemplation before beginning my working day. The devil, after all, makes work for idle thumbs. My own thumbs had been far from idle for many years, and in the early days of our community I had spent my days side by side with the rest of them, renovating the crumbling barns, fixing up rusty caravans, and building our kennels and coops.

More recently, I had kept myself occupied with less strenuous, but equally vital, matters in the farmhouse office. The office sat at the back of the house, and if there had been a window it would have overlooked the deep, velveteen mountains and dancing streams which guarded our horizon. But there was no window; the sash had been rotted through so thoroughly when we moved in that we'd had to take it out and board up the gap with a sheet of ply. Instead, the whitewashed stone walls were adorned with glossy prints depicting Bible scenes. There were twelve, one for each month of the year. This was because each image had been carefully cut out of an old calendar and pasted up with water and flour. The picture of Christ in His manger, surrounded by the Virgin Mary – this one dark-haired – Saint Joseph, and an array of livestock, was my favourite. I liked the awed way that Joseph looked at Mary. In the bottom-right corner, cursive print read: 'December'. They were my only decorations.

In the place of ornaments and knick-knacks, there were stacks of heavy ledgers in which I kept track of our finances, noting every expenditure, every donation, every tithe from the early days of Heaven on Earth up to the present. Before we moved north, when I had use of a computer, I could manage all of my week's work on a Thursday afternoon and be finished in time for evening service. Of course, we were a smaller group then, and our members lived in their own homes and held down jobs with regular incomes coming into our account. Even so, the past few months had been harder work than they should have been. The little rows of numbers which once came together so easily had become reluctant to add up, and I spent many fruitless hours staring at the page, willing myself to spot the simple mistake which, when remedied, would solve all of my problems.

Chapter Two

Ruth

Stepping out of the farmhouse and into the yard was a religious experience. The cobbled stones under my feet had been there for over one hundred years, but the craggy green mountains which surrounded our settlement had been there even longer, since God Himself shaped them for us with His loving hands. They were darker in places now, rust red, burgundy, plum, where the patches of fern and heather grew, reminding us all of the turn in the year; an endless cycle of death and resurrection which played out around us in technicolour glory. I loved to look at those mountains in the mornings, especially in Fall, when the mist still lingered around their ragged peaks – God's curling, frosted breath. Occasionally, I would spy a stag a little way in the distance, and we would watch each other with interest until one of us moved away. Almost as magnificent to my eyes were the barns and outbuildings we had breathed life into when we'd arrived five years ago; the church, the schoolhouse and the community barn stood around the yard like three stone hives. They were not as beautiful as the land they were built on, not by a long way, but they were a reminder of our own little miracle of Creation.

Pulling the hem of my skirt out of my boots, I walked away from the centre of the settlement to the barn where I spent most of my days. In theory, I was the colony's resident medic, but we were mainly a healthy group. Aside from attending to the odd birth or injury, I found myself spending most of my time turning my nurses' training to our livestock. I grew up surrounded by farms, and although I couldn't get away fast enough at the time,

I'd begun to take great pleasure in dealing with the animals once we'd moved to Halcyon.

There was something serene about the huge beasts which walked slowly and gracefully towards me each morning; sometimes I even allowed myself to fuss them, running my hand over the pelt of one of our cows before settling down with my stool and bucket, or brushing out the donkey's coarse grey fur. Of course, the animals weren't there to be fussed. I did not name the chickens before we slaughtered them, just like I didn't name the cows or sheep. 'Adam already named the animals on the sixth day,' Elijah reminded us when we first moved to the farm, 'you do not need to name them again.' He was looking at the children when he said that. City-stifled, until that moment they had only seen animals in picture books, and they had barely been able to contain their excitement.

I milked the cows first thing, losing myself in the gentle and familiar rhythm of their breathing, the steady movement of my hands. It was a good time to pray, sitting there on my low wooden stool, listening to the spurts of milk hit the metal bucket by my feet. Once my work there was done and the milk had been poured into our little silo, I took the three halters from their hooks on the wall and one by one attached them to the cows' heads. They were padded, but still heavy and old-fashioned, and I worried that they must be uncomfortable. I wanted to talk to the cows as I fastened the buckles, to apologise for the inconvenience, to reassure them that we were headed right out to pasture, but I didn't. 'You can be so sentimental, Ruth.' I could hear Elijah's voice in my head as I knotted their lead lines. 'Everyone says so. No wonder Aoife doesn't take you seriously.' He said it so often that I could imagine the exact tone of his voice – gently reproachful. I would always nod. 'I'll work on that.' And then I tried my best, but whatever I did I could never manage to be as efficient as Aoife.

The three lead lines gathered into my right hand, I pulled open the gate which kept the cows in their pen and walked them out of the barn. I took another breath of the cold morning air and set off up the gentle slope to their pasture. I had made this journey so many times that my boots had begun to wear away a little trail in the hill's mossy earth, revealing patches of the stone beneath, and I could walk it without thinking even once about where to put my feet. The cows followed behind, their own hooves sure against the uneven ground. Once we reached the top of the hill, I lingered for a while before unfastening the cows. All of Halcyon lay before me like a picture postcard; our stone buildings and shiny white caravans, and then further out the fields where we grew our crops. Already people were hard at work – I could see them going about their business, hear as they sang hymns and chatted as they checked the hives and reinforced the bunker.

I was watching the cows drink from the stream when I was startled by a series of loud bangs and yells coming from down the other side of the hill, which made me drop the lead lines to the ground. It was only when the sound continued, this time louder and more intense, that I realised what was happening. Behind me, a little way down the slope, was an old coal bunker that the children had dragged out there to use for their games. It had become a kind of training ground for Halcyon's younger inhabitants to prepare for the End. The possibility of seeing my children was too much to resist, so selfishly I gathered the cows' lines and picked my way down to the source of the noise.

As I'd expected, the miniature bunker was surrounded by a group of children. A quick scan of their faces told me that none of my biological kids were amongst them, but I could see Constance and Faith – Aoife's oldest girls – and a cluster of others. I tried not to let myself be disappointed, but the feeling sat in my stomach like a stone. They were hitting the sides of the box with long pieces of firewood, making the corrugated steel thunder and shake. Constance was taking running leaps to kick at it with her boots. Some of the smaller children were smacking it with the palms of their hands and screeching through the cracks in the metal. I hugged myself against the chill as I continued towards them.

Ryan, the oldest in their crowd, was the first one to see me. He handed a small silver stopwatch to another boy, Ollie, and bounded over to where I was standing.

'Sorry, Sister Ruth,' he panted, 'I hope we didn't give you a fright. We were just practicing.'

I smiled. I remembered Ryan from when I had joined the church, and whenever I looked at him I could still see the chubby four-year-old he'd been then – all big eyes and dark curls. His voice broke a little when he spoke, and I wanted to reach out and ruffle his hair.

'No need to apologise, honey, I was just coming down to see

how you all were doing. Whose turn is it now?' I asked, pointing to the coal bunker which the other children were still battering.

'Oh, it's Humility, Sister.'

Humility, another of Aoife's; her youngest. Halcyon, her third daughter who was the same age as my Abraham, was nowhere to be seen.

'And? How's she doing in there?'

Ryan turned to Ollie, who was still clutching the stopwatch in his bony white hands.

'How's Humility getting on, Ollie?' he called.

Ollie glanced down at the watch, and then back up at me and Ryan. I had to strain to hear him over the ruckus as he spoke.

'She's only been in a couple of minutes,' he said, 'but she's already crying.'

Ryan shook his head. 'Females.'

The way he said it made him sound like Elijah, and I shivered. The game was something that had made me uncomfortable when it had been first introduced, but it was the invention of one of the more senior church members – not Elijah himself, but John, his assistant – and there wasn't much I could do. I'd been convinced, eventually, that it was good for them to practice for the End. That it would make the real thing less scary for them.

A second later, the lid of the coal bunker creaked open and Humility emerged, wet and dirty, her small face red and blotchy and streaked with tears. She struggled to climb out, her feet catching at the bottom of her dress, which reached down to the tops of her boots. My instinct was to comfort her, but I managed to fight it. Word would certainly get back to Elijah if I did. The children stopped their attack on the little tin hut, but as she rejoined their group they started up with a chorus of boos and jeers. Somebody threw a small stone, which bounced off her shoulder and made her cry even harder, and I watched with a lump in my throat as she gulped and wiped the tears from her eyes.

'Honestly, Humility, that was pathetic,' said Constance, rolling her eyes, 'you're four now. You're getting too big to be acting like such a baby. What are you going to do when the End comes? God isn't going to stop sending his wrath down to Earth because you're *crying*. Isn't that right, Ryan?'

She turned to where Ryan and I were standing and gave us both a smile.

'Yeah,' said Ryan, 'the hordes of sinners won't just turn away if they hear a cry-baby. It'll probably make them even more angry.'

Humility sniffed again and rubbed her shoulder. 'Will not.'

'It will, too,' said Constance. 'Anyway, it's my turn next. I'll show you how to be brave.'

With that, she closed herself into the coal bunker and the banging started again. Ryan handed Humility a stick of her own, which she took with a gleeful smile, tears forgotten. Content that all was well, I took my cue to leave.

'You all watch out with those sticks now,' I said as I waved, 'I don't want to have to give anyone here any stitches.'

The threat of stitches sent a thrilled shriek through the little gathering, and I could still hear them long after I started my descent down the other side of the hill. Even though my own children hadn't been there, it had been good to see the rest of them up close and at play. Adults made me nervous, unsure of myself – how to act, what to say – but babies and kids were different. They were easier to understand, more like animals in that sense, and I could always find my voice around them.

The children had been my first responsibility. With God's guidance, I had brought the smaller ones into the world, frightened only by the secrecy which shrouded the whole practice within Heaven on Earth. In the hospital, or even in my routine home births, a doctor was never far away. One could be called in to assist if something were to go wrong. Even before we came to Halcyon, when I delivered the Heaven on Earth babies who were born in the city, I did not have that luxury.

Midwifery was never my calling, but I was desperate to leave home and my father was a pastor, so he had firm views as to what was appropriate for a young woman to do with her time. My godmother, who lived in London, suggested I come stay with her and study midwifery. This was deemed a suitable career for me, better even than just plain old nursing because I would not have to deal with any men 'up close', as my father would say. It was either that or stay in the Midwest, plus I liked babies, so I got my visa and I went. I visited home just once after that, for Christmas during my second year of training. My godmother made me stay in London for my first Christmas; she was anxious that I would be overcome with homesickness and never come back. When

I finally returned to the States, I watched my father preach his Christmas sermon, and ate the food my mother cooked alongside my grandparents and my siblings and counted the days until I could be back in London, where interesting things happened to interesting people.

Back home, my mother braided my hair into cornrows in silence while we listened to the radio or watched some soap opera on TV, but in London I went to a real hairdresser who created intricate coiled designs against my scalp with her long, manicured fingers. She would gossip to me about the other customers and about her life, complaining about her boyfriend and her boyfriend's mother, who liked to interfere with her business and tell her how to raise her kids and what she should wear. Michelle, my hair lady, and the other girls at the hospital opened up a whole new world to me. I liked to listen to their stories about wild nights out, although when they invited me along I turned them down. It was one thing to hear about their adventures, and something very different to participate in them myself. I loved those girls when we worked side by side, but the thought of them after work, when their uniforms were swapped for high-heeled shoes and short leather skirts, frightened me. Their lives out of the hospital seemed messy and exhausting. The only other black trainee midwives both went to extra efforts to include me, but after a while their invitations dried up before stopping altogether, leaving me equal parts lonely and relieved. It wasn't too long before I started going back to church, where people were always on their best behaviour and I knew exactly what to expect from them.

Chapter Three

Aoife

As I sat in the front row of our church at Halcyon, I resisted the urge to turn my head and watch the other congregants as they made their way in to worship. When I first joined Heaven on Earth, church services had taken place in the living room of Elijah's first-floor flat, which stood unexceptionally within a terrace of identical Victorian homes in the leafy outskirts of the city. There were only around fifteen of us at that time, including myself, but even so there was hardly enough room for us all. Elijah would stand and preach in the bay window, so that the comings and goings of students and harried families which played out on the street below formed a background to his sermons. Despite its inhospitable size, the flat had been furnished for this very purpose, and chairs and sofas of all descriptions had been laid out in the approximation of pews in an ordinary church, with a small aisle down the centre leading to Elijah's window pulpit. A collection of mugs, just as cosily mismatched as the living room furniture, were laid out in the kitchen along with bags of herbal tea for after. Our refreshments were often supplemented with the home baking of various congregants, namely Helen, Lois, and Pauline, all of whom came with us to Halcyon. The effect of the homely setting and informal furnishings, combined with the provision of food and drink, was that I felt instantly welcome when I first joined the church. Before I'd found them, I had been homesick and desperately lonely. After, they became a second family, and then, my only family.

Helen took me under her wing from the first, and every service in the flat was subsequently spent by her side. In the weeks between my engagement and my wedding, I'd stayed with Helen and John at their house in the suburbs, and on my wedding day it was Helen who'd helped me to get ready. I even wore her wedding dress; a high-necked, long-sleeved gown, white of course – Elijah had absolved me of my one prior fumble with a boy from back home – in which I felt as beautiful and as grown up as I ever had. The ceremony took place in Elijah's flat. There was no paperwork, no documents to suggest that our union was sanctioned in the eyes of the law. It was witnessed, Elijah said, by God, not man, because the purpose of our marriage was to honour God, not man. It sounds like a cliche, but our wedding was truly the happiest day of my life. Standing there in the bay window of our church, surrounded by friends and pledging myself to a good and Godly man, all felt right with the world. I had been so happy that I hadn't even minded that John was the one officiating.

Many things had changed since the days of cramped church services in our living room; our congregation had grown, our family had grown, we had moved from the flat to the hall and then north from the city, and settled in the Highlands, where life was harsh and beautiful and closer to God. Our new church was a barn, larger and grander, certainly, although some things remained the same. The haphazard collections of furniture. The devotion of the people.

Deborah's long blonde plait swished from side to side as she turned her head towards one person and then another, and I did my best not to roll my eyes. She was just striking up a conversation with Helen, who sat behind her, when Elijah entered and a hush descended. My seat at the very front of the room meant that I could see his face clearly. The two wrinkles which had recently appeared on his broad forehead were deepened with concern, and his hands were balled into tight, tense fists. He barely relaxed for the opening prayer, which reverberated against the empty walls: 'God! We thank you for granting us another day in our Heaven on Earth, and pray that we might do you service today. We thank you for granting us your bounty here at Halcyon, and for protecting us from the sins of the world outside its safe walls.'

'Thanks be to God and our Holy Prophet.' The voices of our congregation rose together in response. Almost one hundred joined together as one.

Elijah began.

'We say this prayer every day. We know its words as well as we know ourselves. God gifted this prayer to us so that we could praise Him and thank Him. I thought to myself today that our prayer is like a diamond. Precious, valuable, and multi-faceted. Just like different colours and aspects of a diamond reveal themselves as the light moves, so it is with our prayer. It is a great sign of God's wisdom that the words which He revealed to me have many meanings, meanings which reveal themselves to us as our situations change, as we move through different seasons of our life's journey. He has recently drawn my focus to the final line of our beautiful prayer. The line with which we thank Him for protecting us from the sins of the world which lie outside Halcyon's safe walls.

'You are all aware of our recent outreach mission to Abercraig. Last night, this mission ended. Brother John had been in the village to collect two Godly young people who had wished to join our community here and in the next life. Unfortunately, the parents of these young people intercepted this mission, and we were forced to leave them behind. Brother John was waiting at the bottom of the driveway in the car, ready to bring these new recruits to Halcyon, when he was viciously attacked. Threats of violence were made to his person, our vehicle, and the community as a whole. We are taking this very seriously. I ask that you keep these two young people in your prayers, but also that you pray for the safety of our community. The threats made against us betray a gross ignorance about Heaven on Earth and our mission here at Halcyon, and I fear that we have not felt the last of their anger. I have prayed for guidance, and God showed me the answer in our own prayer. We will no longer be reaching out to Abercraig and the surrounding areas on missions, and I ask you all to be vigilant of outsiders or anything out of the ordinary. Remember, it's your sacred duty as citizens of this holy land to report anything, anything at all, that goes against our way of life.'

I knew that there was a man from Abercraig within the congregation, Aaron, who had joined us a year or so before. He had been saved during a mission trip there, and his own parents had also been angry about his decision to join us in Halcyon. He was one of the few colonists who had not come up with us from the city. He was a pleasant man, young and Godly and hardworking, and I hoped that Elijah would reach out to him and make sure he understood he was one of us, not an outsider, and still a welcome and loved member of our community. I was considering that this could be a pastoral duty which might feasibly fall to me, when Elijah took a breath and continued his sermon.

'Let this also be a lesson to us all,' he said, his eyes meeting mine for the briefest moment, 'of the dangers of the so-called *traditional* family. Parental bonds should never be stronger than the bonds between us and our Father God. These cruel parents may have denied their children the opportunity for eternal salvation, and for what reason? Because they value their earthly love over His heavenly love. They were frightened that their children loved God more than they loved them!'

Before, Elijah's delivery had been deliberate and sombre, but this new direction had filled his words with the passion and vigour which had first inspired me all those years ago. He had always had strong feelings about so-called 'nuclear families', and they were a subject which never failed to inspire him to righteous anger. Couples in Halcyon were married, but lived apart from one another in gender-segregated caravans, coming together only for pre-approved 'private' visits when Elijah decided that the schoolhouse was looking empty. I secretly wondered if his control over this most intimate aspect of his congregants' lives stemmed from his desire to have the most children of them all. Between us three wives, he'd fathered twelve children – my four, Ruth's five, and the three which Deborah had given him, not including the baby currently floating in her obnoxiously young and healthy womb. Unlike the others, our children knew who their father was – he was our Prophet after all, and what would be the point of so many heirs otherwise? But even for my oldest girls, the concept of 'mother' must have become a lost word in a dead language – as it had for me.

'How selfish can a person be,' he continued, 'that they value their meagre earthly happiness over the eternal happiness of others? Are they animals, that they don't understand anything other than what they see in front of them? Satan lives in these people and their shallow understanding of love. If they were not so very dangerous to us, we could almost pity them. Sadly, they are determined to push their warped beliefs onto us. They think *we* are the dangerous ones!'

A less dangerous group of people you could never hope to meet. We were a collective of all ages, all races, all backgrounds, all of us united by our faith in our Prophet and in God, and of course by our steadfast belief in the Halcyon project. We were parents, some of us grandparents. Of the eighty members of the community, almost thirty were children and babies. I wondered what the villagers thought we could possibly do to cause anyone any harm.

Once the sermon had finished, I shifted and stretched my neck as subtly as I could, all while trying to avoid John's gaze. John was the administrator, the lackey, the man on the ground, and he was stepping up to the rostrum to give the day's orders.

'Thank you, Elijah, for another powerful sermon,' he said, running a hand through his greying blond hair. 'I wanted to follow up on the point Elijah made there about reporting anything you see which goes against our way of life here – I hope you all remember that Elijah doesn't just mean any strangers you might spot around the compound. It's your duty to come to me if you see one of your fellow Brothers or Sisters in Christ straying from our path, if you hear someone say something which goes against our teachings. Let me know. We're in the final days here, people, and we can't be running the risk of inviting Satan into Halcyon when we're all so close to salvation.'

I felt a twinge of annoyance. He was right, of course, but the delight he seemed to take in rooting out sin was unbecoming. Many an evening we had been sitting in the farmhouse eating dinner when John had scuttled in, desperate to divulge to Elijah – and Elijah alone – the most recent infraction which he had uncovered. We wives would be forced to stand in the hallway, our dinners congealing on our plates, for the duration of the interruption which *just couldn't wait*.

Reading from a sheet of handmade paper – yet another ill-fated experiment of Deborah's, the clumpy fruits of which we were compelled to use up – he called out names and tasks. Mark and Niall to repair the roof of caravan M-3. Lisa, Annie, and Lois to the greenhouses and beehives. Alfie to lead the same group of men as yesterday to reinforce the roof of the bunker. And so on, everyone listening keenly for their name, careful not to drift off and miss their assignment. It was a crisp autumn day, cold but not freezing, clear and bright. Ideal weather for much of the outdoor work on the schedule, and people were keen to get outside and make the best of it. Two children whose faces I could not quite make out held the great barn doors wide open, and I turned to watch the exodus.

Elijah, too, stood by the exit, but instead of blessing the congregation as they left, he was focused on one person alone. They were shorter than Elijah, and although my position at the far end of the room obscured my view, I could guess who had captured his attention so entirely. We exited row by row, and following this convention I would be the last to leave. Elijah knew this too, and while it was possible that he was too engrossed in his conversation to pay attention to the other people passing him by, I knew him well enough to realise that this was a calculated move, and he would dismiss his mystery companion before Ruth, Deborah or I could get to the front of the church. With the entire congregation facing the other way, and Ruth and Deborah engrossed in their own private, whispered conversation, I took my chance and leaned out into the aisle, craning my neck to see around the bobbing heads of the people filing out ahead of me. A gap emerged for long enough for me to spy the person who was so captivating to my husband.

After we moved to Halcyon, I found myself predicting worst-case scenarios. Poor crop yields. Trouble with electricity. Arrest. I took a perverse pleasure in it, because if the worst were to happen, at least I would have the small satisfaction of having been right. I had guessed by the intent look on Elijah's face, the particular angle at which he tilted his head, a gesture visible even from across the barn, that he had been speaking to Jemima. Somehow my usual self-satisfaction at a correct guess was not enough to soften the blow of what I saw before me. It was as though the room went out of focus, like a scene in a film where a woman looks across a crowded bar and sees the love of her life, one clear figure in the centre. Except there were two figures, one tall, handsome man and one small, bird-like girl tucking her hair behind her ears in the absent way that teenagers have, and hanging on to every word the man was pouring into her head. She looked down shyly and laughed at something he had said, and he leaned even closer to her. My face already felt flushed, but when he reached out and touched her arm, it burned. I had had my suspicions before, but now I was certain. When Elijah had dropped his bombshell, when he had told us about God's desire for him to take another wife, he didn't tell us exactly who he had in mind. But I knew. It didn't take a genius to work it out. The only single women in Halcyon were either older – not Elijah's style – or they were teenagers. And there was only one of those who would fit the bill: petite, quiet Jemima.

The row of women ahead of me began to file out, and I turned to see if Ruth or Deborah had noticed that I had moved. Ruth was still turned towards Deborah – she hadn't even realised that it was almost time for us to leave – but Deborah was staring straight over her shoulder and directly at me. Her expression remained blank, but she maintained eye contact for just long enough that I knew she understood what I had been looking at. It was too late to deny it. All I could hope was that she wouldn't speak to Elijah about it. I returned her cold stare, hoping that my countenance was just as inscrutable as her own; perhaps I could convince her that she had been wrong, and that I had nothing to hide. In earlier days, I might have even taken the time to change the story completely, and have her feel as though she was the one who ought to feel guilty for staring at *me*. But I had grown too tired to play such games, as satisfying as they had been, and in all honesty I had also grown a little too worried that I would no longer come out on top.

Instead of challenging Deborah, I allowed myself to lead our row down the aisle and towards the door, my posture straight, my eyes looking fixedly ahead. I noted that I had been correct about Elijah; by the time I reached him, he had dismissed Jemima and had turned his attention fully onto John. As I drew closer to him, I prepared my face with a smile, waiting for him to wish me a blessed day, but he was too distracted to notice me and I passed by without acknowledgement. I turned my face away before anyone noticed that I had been ignored. Outside, I spotted Jemima standing by the schoolhouse. She was taking a headcount, watching carefully as each child returned indoors for their morning lessons. Occasionally, one would stop to talk or hug her, and she would lean in and smile. I spotted Humility, wrapped up in a trailing scarf and a little red hat that I'd not seen before, holding hands with a slightly older girl. When she reached Jemima, my youngest daughter let go of her friend's hand and flung her arms around Jemima's skinny legs.

Chapter Four

Ruth

We were all stifling yawns as we shuffled, one after the other, into the church barn after a long day of work. My eyes were bleary and stinging from tiredness, but I was glad to be there. My own, lonely bed promised nothing but hours of exhausted wakefulness. Elijah told me he had mentioned my insomnia to Deborah and Aoife, who had both agreed I couldn't sleep because I wasn't doing enough work during the day, and I agreed with them. My dread of the nights made evening worship even more appealing – there was plenty of opportunity to tire myself so much that by the time my head hit my pillow, I wouldn't be able to do anything *but* sleep. In theory, anyway. In practice, it never worked, no matter how much energy I put into worship. Still, just like Deborah likes to say: God loves a trier.

The chairs had been set out ready for the night in two concentric circles. I took my place next to Aoife and Deborah on the women's side of the inner circle, and waited for Elijah to arrive. All of the adults were there, shifting to get comfortable on their seats and talking quietly, when he made his entrance. John followed in after him, and the chatter subsided as Elijah took his place in the centre. He was the only one of us who didn't look tired; instead, he was almost vibrating with energy. I could sense it coming off him as he looked around the room, doing that thing he had always done where he seemed to meet everyone's eye at once, making sure that everyone felt included. I felt a giddy thrill as he looked my way. The room felt smaller with him in it, more compact. When he started to speak, his voice echoed.

'Before we start our worship tonight,' he said, pacing the

centre of the circle of chairs like a lion in a cage, 'we have some business to attend to.'

The congregation sat up a little straighter, and I felt Aoife turn to look at me. I wondered what she thought I had done.

'The world is full of sinners. We know that. The Bible tells us that.' He patted the heavy black book in his hand. 'But the reason that we, the Church of Heaven on Earth, came to Halcyon was so we could *escape* the sins of the world.'

I nodded, and a few people around me made some sounds of agreement.

'So I am sure you can all begin to imagine how very,' he paused, '*disappointed* I was to find that one of our number here, one of *you*, has brought sin into this most holy place.'

Again, he cast his eyes around the circles of chairs. This time they were searching, and when they lingered on me my stomach turned over. Had I committed a sin without realising? Had someone seen me talking to the children that morning, and told John that I'd been looking for my own kids? If that was true, there would be nothing I could even say to defend myself, because they would be right. I knew deep down that I had no reason to worry – even if someone had held me accountable to John, wives' sins never got aired out at evening worship. We'd be punished, sure, but in private. We were always careful to keep our dirty laundry safely inside the farmhouse. And yet my stomach still turned somersaults as the congregation squirmed and Elijah continued to pace. Last week, one of the women had been accused of stealing bread. Shanti. She and her husband had joined Heaven on Earth a year or so before we left for Halcyon, and her family had been angry about it. She was quiet and smiled a lot; I had always liked her. Elijah had drawn her into the centre of the circle to make her confession, and she had spent each mealtime since then with her hands tied behind her back.

'We know that the End times are coming, and they're coming quickly. Next year, next week, tomorrow – we can't be sure when, which means we can't afford for one of our number to tempt Satan into Halcyon. We need to be pure, and cleansed of sin, so that when God brings his wrath down on the world, we can be assured that *we* will be safe. When someone here sins, they threaten to bring the righteous vengeance of God down on *all of us*.'

His voice rose as he spoke those last three words, and I jumped a little in my seat. The words were still reverberating around the barn when he continued on.

'And so,' he said, 'this sinner amongst us must atone, before they seal our fate with their actions. Do you agree?'

The cheer started in the men's half of the room, and spread outwards until everyone was clapping and stamping. Some of the men whistled, but of course none of us women did.

'Good!' roared Elijah, picking up his pace around the circle. 'Now, whoever in this room has sinned, I need you to stand up and confess so we can absolve you!'

Across the room where the men were sitting, there was a murmur. Elijah changed the direction of his pacing, and strolled over to the source of the disruption.

'Stand up and speak up, please.'

I chewed my bottom lip.

It was Colin who stood up and walked into the centre, the men parting away from him like he was a leper. Colin was about ten years my senior, just over forty or so, and looked so much like my father that the first time I'd met him I'd been lost for words. He even wore the same type of glasses, the old-fashioned kind with those thick tortoiseshell rims, although Colin's were wrapped with Scotch tape around the sides where they'd broken while he'd been working on the bunker a few months ago. He'd been an optician, I remembered, when we'd still lived in town. He'd given us all free eye tests before we left for Halcyon, after his store had closed for the day.

'Brother Colin,' said Elijah, 'please can you speak out and tell the congregation what sin it is you have committed?'

Colin cleared his throat.

'I am sorry, Elijah. During our most recent visit together two nights ago, I expressed to my wife Lois that I missed being able to see our children whenever I liked. I said I wished that we could live together with them, like we'd done before we came here.'

Elijah gave a big, exaggerated nod. 'And how, Brother Colin, did you describe our arrangement of children living in the schoolhouse?'

Colin shuffled and looked down at his feet. He was a little taller even than Elijah was, but he looked so much smaller.

'I said it was ridiculous, Elijah. I'm sorry.'

The room was filled with the sound of fifty adults drawing a sharp, shocked breath all at once.

'You have four children, Colin, isn't that right?' Elijah gave no time for Colin to answer, but continued, pacing around him. 'And by all accounts, they're very good, Godly children. They do as they're told, they say their prayers, they work hard. Do you love your children, Colin?'

This time he did pause, and Colin nodded.

'Of course you do,' said Elijah. 'We are almost all of us parents here. We all love our children. We love every child of Halcyon, just as we all love one another. So, why, I wonder, Colin, do you want your children to burn in hell?'

Colin spoke, though his head was bent so low that it was impossible to hear him. I felt my muscles tense. Elijah bent so he was looking right up into Colin's downturned face.

'Say again, Colin? Do you want your children to burn in hell? To spend eternity in torment, away from God and the rest of the church?'

'No, Elijah.'

'Then why do you want them to love you more than they love God?'

I could hardly watch what was happening, but I couldn't bring myself to look away. Deep down in the very pit of my stomach, I knew that Colin's sin was not so far from my own, and my cheeks grew hot with shame as Elijah went on. I had never been dumb enough to say it out loud, to broadcast my sin like Colin had, but the deep, empty longing for my babies hollowed me out every night as I lay alone in my bed. On either side of me, Aoife and Deborah sat still. I could hear their easy, regular breaths. Their consciences must have been clear.

Elijah turned to the congregation as Colin stood, motionless, waiting to see what would happen. When Elijah pointed at Lois, I saw Colin wince. 'Lois,' he said, 'can you stand up for a moment, please?'

Behind me, Lois's chair scraped the floor as she stood. Everyone turned to look at her, but I kept my eyes on Colin. Beads of sweat were beginning to form on his temples.

'Sinners,' said Elijah, 'never just endanger themselves. Sin drags down everyone it touches. That's what makes it so dangerous.'

Around me, everyone nodded. I nodded too.

'When you exposed your wife to your sin, you put her in danger. Fortunately, Lois did the right thing, but women are more susceptible to sin than men, and we could easily be telling a different story tonight if your wife had less fortitude. I think it's important that you remember that.'

I could feel Lois shifting on her feet. She knew what was coming – we all did.

'Lois, in order for your husband to learn his lesson, he needs to see you punished. Please can you take your coat off and stand outside?'

Colin's shoulders sagged as he watched his wife pick her way through the circle of chairs to reach the door.

'Because of you, Lois will stay outside for the rest of worship. And for the next three days,' he held up three fingers to Colin, and then to the rest of us, 'I want none of you to speak to Lois. You may not look at her. You may not acknowledge that she exists. Colin needs to learn that his actions have consequences for others.'

Even though I knew Elijah was right, and it was important for Colin to learn his lesson, I still struggled to shake my guilt. Elijah once pretended that I didn't exist for a whole week, a punishment that still made me feel sick when I thought about it.

Later that night, just as I was beginning to spiral further away from any possibility of sleep, I was disturbed by a loud bang, followed by the sound of footsteps in the hallway outside. For one shameful moment, I let myself hope that Elijah had felt my sadness and was coming to check on me. I promised myself that if it was him, I would come right out and tell him about my sin and take whatever consequences came after. I pulled back my quilt and slid my feet into the thick pair of knitted socks which I used as slippers. I sent up a prayer – *please let it be him.* And then another, more cowardly part of my heart sent up another – *please don't let it be him.*

We all kept wind-up torches in our rooms in case of emergencies, and I fumbled under the bed for mine, knocking over an empty and rarely used chamber pot in the process. Conscious of the creaking floorboards beneath me, I picked my way across the room and opened the door onto the landing. There was no Elijah. Instead, I looked down to see the sharp little face of Russell the ratter blinking in the torchlight. Dazzled by the sudden light, it took the dog a moment to realise that the door was open, but once her eyes adjusted, she scampered straight past my legs. A couple of weeks before during a routine check-up, I had discovered Russell was carrying a litter, and by this time she was as round as a ball; so round, in fact, that I couldn't believe my eyes when she took a running leap and jumped straight onto my bed.

Elijah had very strong feelings about the difference between animals and humans; even Russell's name had been something of a compromise. Our two sheepdogs were both nameless, but she spent so much of her time with us, keeping our buildings and stores free from vermin, that we couldn't just keep calling her 'the dog'. At first, Elijah had been reluctant to name her, quoting the same Genesis passage which he had used with the children about the farm animals, but eventually he had relented just enough to name her Russell. He reasoned that by naming her after her breed, we weren't over-humanising her. She was allowed into the farmhouse only as a working dog. No petting her, no loving on her, no feeding her. There was no point in anyone making a rule about letting her on the furniture – we would have been no more likely to let Russell sit on the couch than to invite one of the sheep to stand on the kitchen table. But there she was, illuminated by the pale stream of torchlight, curling up on the pillow where my head had been resting just moments ago as though she had done it a thousand times before.

I closed the bedroom door and padded over to the bed. Russell raised her head slightly in acknowledgement before settling again as I slipped between the sheets and lay my head down on the pillow next to her. She smelled of fresh air and straw. I knew all of the animals in Halcyon: all of their individual quirks, what they liked to eat, which ones were jumpy, and which were calm. They were my daily companions as I went about my business on the farm, but I realised that I had never once reached out and touched that dog just for the sheer joy of it. Although the room was cold, I brought my hand out from beneath the quilt and placed it on her rough little back. She stretched a little and readjusted herself so that she was as close to me as possible. That night, with Russell's cold, wet nose against my ear, I slept better than I had in years.

Chapter Five

Aoife

After almost six years at Halcyon, the night-time routine was something the four of us had reduced to a fine art. Once evening worship was over, we would take it in turns to use the outhouse; Elijah first, followed by me, then Ruth, and finally Deborah. Returning to the house, we would make our individual cups of heather tea and take them to our rooms, where a filled basin lay in wait for washing faces and brushing teeth. It was rare to bump into another wife tramping along the garden path to the toilet, but I always made sure to time it so I would pass Elijah as he made his way back to the house. Sometimes he would brush his hand against mine, and I would relish the thrill of his touch on my skin. It was a stolen moment, and our carefully honed schedule meant that these fleeting extra-curricular meetings could only be afforded to me. On the nights Elijah and I shared, I would usually return to my bedroom to find him waiting for me on the bed, half-dressed and deeply engrossed in his Bible. I loved how easily and quickly he could focus his mind – he would have been alone in the room for no more than ten minutes, and already be oblivious to anything other than the words on the page in front of him. Eventually, he would look up at me and smile, as though my presence was the most delightful and unexpected surprise. *It's you*, his eyes would seem to say, *of all the people in Halcyon, how wonderful that it's you*. He'd always been very good at that. Then the Bible would be closed and laid to one side and one rough hand would move to unbuckle his heavy leather belt, his eyes staying on me, moving up and down my body.

That said, no such thing had happened now for three months.

I would open my bedroom door and he would barely glance up from his Bible. I would undress, slowly, my body aching in need of him, willing him to put the holy text to one side, to reach for me – even just to look at me. But when he finally laid his Bible down, it was just to turn off the light. Our last ten nights together had ended in quiet, heavy darkness, my hand desperate to reach out across the no man's land between us. *Still,* I thought, pulling on my boots – *there's always tonight.*

The anticipation was already building as I opened the door onto the crisp autumn night. I was almost certain that he hadn't returned to the house yet, as he'd still been speaking with John in church when I left, so the question was less *if* we would cross paths, but *when.* Feeling for the washing line we used to guide ourselves through the darkness, I made my way carefully along the cobbled path. As I walked, I listened, hoping to hear something that would indicate his approach; instead, all I could hear was the crunch of gravel beneath my feet, the shallow rhythm of my breath, and the familiar sounds of the farm settling itself down for the night. I had been so certain that I would meet Elijah along the path that I was surprised when my feet made the final step off the gravel and onto the hard slab of stone paving that indicated I was nearing the outhouse door. I knocked. Silence. I knocked again, pausing just a second before trying the handle – I did not want to stand there for too long, knowing that Ruth would not be far behind me.

It was quiet in the outhouse. The little stone room was empty of life, except for one large black spider clinging to the whitewashed wall like a full stop. I hoisted my skirt and pulled down my knickers. The sound of urine drumming against sawdust broke the silence of the night. There was a basket of newspaper next to the toilet, cut into neat little squares. I was never sure how old the newspapers were – the odd words which caught my eye could have been from any time – and I never had any interest in reading them. I didn't even know exactly where they came from, other than the obvious fact that they must have been imported into Halcyon from the outside world. With Elijah's recent decision to cease all missions to the neighbouring villages, I wondered where we would get our toilet paper from now on. Once I was finished, I took a handful of clean sawdust from the bucket and sprinkled it into the bowl, erasing the evidence of my visit.

My return journey to the farmhouse was much faster, the guiding line barely skimming my hand as I headed towards the gentle glow of the porch light. It was my night, so even if there was to be no sex, no intimacy of any kind, at least I didn't have to lie there, sleepless and angry, picturing him with Deborah. And still, some hope lingered until I arrived back in my room to find the bed empty, Elijah entirely absent. Somewhere along the garden path, my eagerness to see him had mingled with frustration. He had disregarded our nightly routine, a routine which was almost as sacred to me as the Halcyon earth beneath us. An image flashed before my eyes of a scene from earlier in the day – Elijah and Jemima standing together by the church door, looking intently at one another. I took off my clothes hurriedly and clumsily, tossing my skirt and blouse and jumper onto the floor by my side of the bed, trying not to wonder where he was. Standing naked in the middle of the rug, the rest of my many garments in a pile at my feet, my resentment grew further. I took such pleasure in undressing in front of him. We had no mirrors in Halcyon. Instead, I saw my reflection through his reaction to my body. His eyes were my mirror. If he wasn't there to see me, then where was I? I pulled on my nightgown, a flannel creation which was ugly but warm, and reluctantly got into bed alone. Despite our attempts to conserve electricity as much as possible, I left the lightbulb blinking dully above me, reluctant to fall asleep and miss his arrival.

It wasn't just the nights; we had been spending our days apart more than we ever used to. In the time before Halcyon, we shared a cluttered office space in the corner of our living room. We organised our soup kitchen there, our free community nursery, bingo for the old folk and Christmas collections for the food bank. It was there that we'd laid plans to rent out the old community centre to house our growing congregation, and there where we'd stayed up late into the night discussing the prospect of inviting Ruth into our inner circle of two. After that, Halcyon became the next project to consume our waking hours. Now, I saw him for worship, surrounded by other people, and at our silent mealtimes. One night in every three was all we had to be together, and now he'd thrown that away too. Maybe he'd decided to stay another night with Deborah instead.

I woke to the sound of my bedroom door bursting open. I

jumped, and it took a moment for my heart to slow down enough to realise where I was and what was happening. When I came to my senses, I saw him there in the doorway, a reverse silhouette against the darkness of the hallway behind him. It was truly night-time now, and the rest of Halcyon must have been fast asleep in their beds. His hair was wild and unbrushed, sticking up in the way it always did after he had run his hands through it, and he now wore an old nightshirt over his jeans, his heavy workman's boots caked in flaking mud. With one hand he held the heavy wooden door open, and in the other he clutched his heavy old Bible – dog-eared and bursting with fluorescent sticky notes and sheets of paper turned black and blue with his heavy hand writing. His eyes were dark and unfocused.

'What's the matter?' I asked, sitting up in bed.

Bleary-eyed as I was, I could tell from the flare of his nostrils and the narrowing of his eyes that I'd said the wrong thing. With a slam of the door he entered the room proper, and I flinched automatically at the sound. He turned off the light with the smack of his fist and we were plunged into darkness. I heard my own voice, a scolding stage whisper:

'What are you doing?' I hissed. 'You'll wake the whole house!'

I felt myself flush – I hadn't meant to speak, and I saw my words flutter in the space between us like a great red rag. Until then, there had still been a chance that the night could be salvaged, the anger channelled to lust, but of course I'd ruined it. *Silly bitch,* came the voice in my head, *silly nagging bitch. You just had to open your mouth.* He was silent, and for a moment I believed he had snapped out of the rage which had overtaken him. Instead, it morphed into a different mood, a mood which had once been rare, but which was now becoming increasingly more common. He went from explosive anger, the reverberations of which still buzzed in the air, to an electric form of fear which I was frightened to touch. He clambered onto the bed, still in his boots, like a terrified child. I no longer wanted to be close to him. Instinctively, I retreated as far as I could into my pillows.

'I'm the last thing this house has to worry about,' he whispered, his voice low and conspiratorial. 'This house is in about as much danger as it's possible to be in, but not from me. This whole *place*,' he gestured wildly around himself, 'is hanging by a fucking *thread* and I'm the only one who's trying to do something about it.'

My heart dipped in my chest, and visions of the End flashed through my mind. We knew it would be coming soon, some awful event which would force us down into the bunker to await The Rapture. What did he know? He was close enough to me now that I could see the whites of his eyes in the darkness, and feel his hot, heavy breath on my face. The sound of his teeth grinding anxiously gave me goosebumps, but as scared as I was there was an excitement there too. A little thrill of pleasure that he was talking to me again, trusting me, just like the old days. I tried not to let it carry through into my voice:

'What's going on?'

He grabbed me by the shoulders.

'What's going on, Aoife, is that the parents of those two brats from the village told John they were going to call the police. The government have had it in for me from the very start. They know who I am, and they know I'm here. They hate what I'm doing here. You know that; they'll take any sniff of a scandal and come bursting through the gates and take me away. This is my Gethsemane, Aoife.'

'Okay,' I said, almost disappointed. 'Well, you know, even if that's true about the parents of those kids from Abercraig calling the police, what can they do? This is our property. We're living peacefully on land that we own. They don't know what we're doing here, and they've no grounds to take you away or harm you, or any of us.'

The silence that followed was a heavy one, and I could almost hear Elijah's mind trying to reconcile my words with his paranoid fantasy. I knew that what I was saying was less than true – the police might not have any idea what was happening in Halcyon, but as Godly as our lives were, we were going against the law of the land. Ruth, Deborah and I shared a husband. With every unregistered child here, we had broken the law. And only God knew the whole raft of other minor infractions: taxes unpaid, the uninsured jeep. I prayed that he didn't think of those things, that what I had said would at least pull him out of the state he was in. Eventually, he spoke.

'They don't care about whether or not I've actually done anything wrong. What had Christ done wrong? They had to stop him because he was preaching the truth, and there's nothing they feared more. If everyone was like us, they would have no power. And it's the same people. They're terrified of me.'

'What?' I said, struggling to follow his jumbled line of argument, 'Who are the same people? The same as what?'

'The same people who killed Christ, you stupid woman. You don't understand anything important. The Order, they're in charge of everything and they'll kill me just like they killed him. They can't have another Prophet on their hands. If you don't understand that, I don't even know what you're doing here.'

His words were hard now, and venomous. I would have preferred a shout, a smack, to the seething disdain I heard when he spoke in that moment. Even the unfamiliar fear which had been there before would have been better. I took a sharp breath in, as though I'd been punched in the gut. In the darkness I watched his mouth, which had been contorted in rage and fear, twist into a cruel smile.

'Are you going to cry?' he asked, fake sympathy dripping from his lips. 'Go on then, cry. I don't know what you think you have to cry about.'

Elijah had been right. I had been about to cry. I couldn't remember the last time I had cried. I blinked the prickling tears back and swallowed the lump in my throat. *Pull it together, Aoife.* I focused back on my husband. His energy was shifting between terror and rage, as if he couldn't decide whether he wanted a fight or an embrace. I chose for him, reaching out and taking him in my arms. I expected him to resist at first, but instead he yielded immediately, and we lay down together, holding on to each other as if for dear life. I was still just about awake when his breathing began to slow, but not by much, and I'm not sure who fell asleep first.

Chapter Six

Ruth

When I came into the kitchen that morning the porridge was already beginning to congeal in its pot on the range stove, and the fire which warmed it was dwindling. I was downstairs later than usual; my deep, heavy sleep had carried me past the dawn, and I had slumbered through the cockerel's crow and the morning activities of the rest of the house. Elijah, Aoife and Deborah's bowls had already been washed and were drying on a threadbare tea towel by the sink. It would have been a quick meal, with everyone rushing to get their daily chores done before the Feast of the Prophet, but the thought of them all sitting together without me for any length of time made tears prick in the corners of my eyes.

I poked at the dying flames, hoping that I could revive them for long enough to warm my breakfast. The more I prodded, the more ash appeared and the fire started to smother itself, so I spooned out what was left in the pot into my bowl and sat down at the table. Our meals were now usually silent affairs, although we rarely took them alone. We tended to sit at the big kitchen table, one of us on each side, chewing in silence. The sound of knives and forks scraping plates was our only soundtrack. Dinner times in particular reminded me eerily of childhood meals at my grandparents' house. My grandfather was a disciplinarian, even more than my father was. There was no talking at dinner. My siblings and I would sit in silent terror, trying to remember all of the rules: elbows off the table, no yawning, no wriggling, never put your cutlery back on the table once you'd picked it up. Most importantly of all, and this was also a major rule for mealtimes in Halcyon, finish every scrap on your plate. Food production was too difficult, produce too scarce, to leave anything but the barest bone behind.

Once, early enough into one of my pregnancies that I didn't even know I was pregnant yet, I had been so sick that I had barely been able to eat a bite of food. We were having mashed potatoes, I can remember clearly, with boiled carrots and offal. The potatoes had been too thick, the carrots slimy and sweet and cold, the offal spongy and strong. My stomach had turned. Elijah and Aoife and Deborah were slowly clearing their plates while mine remained almost untouched. All eyes were on me and I forced myself to take one more mouthful of everything. I had barely swallowed when my mouth began to fill with saliva and I was hit with a wave of nausea so overpowering that I couldn't do anything to stop myself vomiting. Deborah gasped, and Aoife's eyes widened in shock or perhaps embarrassment. Elijah barely looked up from his meal. Weak as a kitten, I had cleaned up my mess as my sister wives looked on in stunned silence. Once I had finished, I took myself off to bed, thinking of nothing but my sudden overwhelming need to lie down and close my eyes against the whole day. I was woken several hours later by Elijah coming into my room; I remember being surprised to see him, because it wasn't our night together. He passed me my dressing gown and took me by the hand. Together we walked down the stairs and around to the back of the house where our compost bin sat waiting, barely visible in the twilight. He opened the lid and lying on top of a slurry of eggshells and bones and garden waste was my dinner. Even before Elijah took the knife and fork out of his pocket, I knew what he wanted me to do. He must have stood there for over an hour watching me eat. The sky darkened around us, and as it grew colder, he took off his own jacket and placed it gently over my shoulders. Once I had finished every last morsel, he walked me back into the house and tucked me gently into my bed. 'You're forgiven,' he had said. 'I love you.'

The memory was almost enough to put me off my breakfast, but I shut down the part of my mind that cared and ate the porridge as quickly and unthinkingly as possible. All I wanted at that moment was to get out of that cold, empty kitchen. It was time to be a good, productive member of the community.

There was no church or temple that morning, because of the

Feast, and everyone was working through their chores as quickly as they could. When I finished up with the animals, I came right back to the house to take my bath and get ready. One of the older children had already been in and filled up our tin tub with water boiled on the stove, and the kitchen door was closed. We usually just washed ourselves in basins, so the tub was a rare treat. I stood in the hallway clutching my towel and bar of soap, listening to the sounds of water as Aoife took her turn. Eventually, the door creaked open and Aoife peeked her head out of the crack. Her black hair was dripping wet, and she was wearing an old bathrobe which I recognised right away as Elijah's.

'I hope you weren't waiting there for too long, Ruth,' she said, pulling the robe tighter around her neck, 'it's all yours now. I'm heading back into my room to get ready. Just give a wee knock when you're done so I know when I'm all right to come out.'

She swung the door fully open and turned to walk back to her bedroom, which led off of the kitchen. Her feet left damp prints on the stone floor, and I tried not to look at her. It felt too intimate, seeing her bare legs sticking out from under the thick navy fabric. I waited until I could hear her opening her wardrobe before I undressed and lowered myself into the water. It was already cooling down, so I took a deep breath in before lying back fully until I was totally submerged. We had to be completely clean for the Feast. It was our biggest celebration, Easter and Christmas paling in comparison. October twenty-fifth: Elijah's birthday. He would be forty years old, not that we ever mentioned his age. I re-emerged from the water, rubbed the sliver of homemade soap across my body, moving as quickly as possible before the water had a chance to get any colder. I could hear Deborah shuffling around outside the door, waiting for her turn.

Dried and dressed, I pushed open the door to the community barn. The noise was nearly overwhelming after the quiet of our kitchen: people talking, dragging benches across the concrete floor, setting out platters of food. Four rectangular tables, each long enough to seat around twenty, had been laid with knives and forks. Each place setting was identical, and the wooden benches were bare, except for at the spaces where the inner circle would be sitting – Elijah, John, Aoife, Deborah, and I all got to sit on cushions.

Along one wall, women were busy arranging food on trestle tables ready to serve to the queue of diners. I could smell the savoury scent of chicken stew, the rich yeasty bread, steaming buttery vegetables, some kind of steaming dessert with preserved fruit. This was a special occasion. Soon, hungry colonists would be lining up, and an equal portion of everything would be set on their plates.

Helen banged the dinner gong and the few people who hadn't already been inside came chattering through the doors. Lois walked in alone and deflated, and sat at the edge of a bench as far away from Colin as she could get. Alfie and Adam, who were at the same end of the table, carried on their conversation as though she wasn't there at all. Other than the cushioned bench, there was no seating plan, although there was an unspoken rule that parents did not sit by their biological children. My five trooped in quietly with the others from the schoolhouse. Eli and Abraham had been born in the city, but the youngest were all Halcyon born. Moses, who was almost three, had one of his sweet hands clasped in Deborah's. I was stung by a pang of jealousy, which made me feel ashamed. Still, I desperately wanted to be the one to take his little hand in my own, to feel the grip of his small fingers. Constance, Aoife's eldest, was carrying Abigail. *My* Abigail. She was sucking on the end of one of Constance's long brown braids, and her own curly hair had been pulled away from her face into a topknot. I felt my eyes become hot with tears, and I blinked them away before anyone could notice.

'Busy morning, Ruth?' asked Aoife. Her hair was still damp from her bath, and she hardly looked at me when she spoke.

I wanted to tell her that I'd milked the cows, taken them to pasture, fed the chickens. Assure her that I was no sloth. But there was still a lump in my throat and the words got stuck behind it, so I just smiled again and nodded, hoping she wouldn't ask me anything else. By that time, Deborah was heaving her legs over the bench to sit down at her place across from us. She had barely got herself settled when the doors swung open again to reveal Elijah and John. The room rose to its feet.

Chapter Seven

Aoife

Despite everything which had happened the night before, my heart soared at the sight of Elijah. He had been gone by the time I'd woken up that morning, and I had worried that he would still be as distressed as he was when I last saw him. The Feast of the Prophet was too big an occasion in our church. It could not be spoiled.

I was pleased that my fears had been unfounded. I could tell as soon as he smiled his wide smile at the cheering congregation that everything would be all right, that he was back to his normal self. It was the fear of the End, I reassured myself; it was getting to him. He had such a burden to bear, and all things considered, he bore it beautifully. I had known him for years, and in that time those heavy moods had come and gone – it had always been me who had been able to save him from them. I watched with pride as he stopped and shook hands with various people on the way to his seat, the room ringing out with applause. I was clapping too, my palms buzzing. With all his stops, it took him a while to reach his spot to my left. I turned and looked up at him, still clapping, as he surveyed his kingdom. The whole barn was turned in our direction, and I smiled too, not just at Elijah but at the knowledge that as they looked at him they were also seeing me by his side. Seated at his right hand, just where I belonged.

Elijah liked it when we wives looked at him a certain way, eyes wide, interested, smiling. He said it showed respect. Recently, I'd had to make a concerted effort to get the look just right – the combination of our vanished sex life and the possibility of a new wife had made it difficult – but in that moment, it came as naturally as breathing. Jemima, I was aware, was standing at the far table by the door, surrounded by a gaggle of other children, out of sight, his sight, and I hoped, out of his mind. *I* had almost forgotten about her as I gazed up at his grinning face. Even his eyes were smiling, those beautiful delicate creases betraying true joy. He had the most wonderful eyes; brown and gleaming and wise, under thick brows and long lashes. His lashes, longer even than my own, were almost feminine. They didn't make him girlish, though – nothing could do that – just even more striking than he already was. His skin still carried a light tan, even though we were reaching the end of October, from all the time he spent outdoors. Mentally, I traced every line, every mark, every freckle. Just two more nights and he'd be mine again. And we'd be back to normal.

He raised his arms. The applause stopped, and the congregation sat down.

'My wonderful, loyal friends,' his voice boomed and bounced off the corrugated walls, 'we are here today to celebrate the Feast of the Prophet. I know for certain that this will be our final feast in this life – the End will be upon us soon, and by next October we will be feasting with our Lord in Heaven!'

The room burst out into applause once again, and some of the men stamped their feet and whooped. I had to resist the unladylike urge to whoop myself.

'Look at this bounty we have before us, friends, and look at what we've built here! They said it couldn't be done. They said we were fools when we made this journey, that we'd be back before the end of our first winter. Well, they were wrong!' With the word 'wrong', he leaned down and banged his fist on the table with such force that the crockery jumped into the air. 'We showed them! We showed them just what can be done when you have an Almighty God on your side!'

His eyes were wide with passion, and little beads of sweat had broken out on his forehead.

'Now,' he went on, 'I know we can all smell the delicious food which our women have so lovingly prepared for this Feast, and I'm sure we're excited to tuck in. But before we queue to be served, I would like us to offer up a prayer through song. God, we thank you for granting us another day in our Heaven on Earth, and pray that we might do you service today. We thank you for granting us your bounty here at Halcyon, and for protecting us from the sins of the world outside its safe walls.'

'Thanks be to God and our Holy Prophet.'

'Psalm twenty-three,' he said, and began to sing.

I had always associated that particular Psalm with funerals, *though I walk through the valley of the shadow of death, I will fear no evil*, but I sang along with the rest of the congregation, enjoying the sound of our voices all joined together.

When we finished, Elijah called for everyone to take their place in the queue for our meal. None of us in the inner circle had to queue, of course – this was the Feast of the Prophet and we were the wives of the Prophet. Annie took our plates for us and filled them, giving Elijah a little more than everyone else. The food was just a slightly better version of what we usually ate in the farmhouse, better probably just because Deborah had had nothing to do with the preparation of it, but I had a feeling it was significantly more than the general population of Halcyon was used to getting. As it was a special occasion, talking was very much allowed, but everyone was too distracted by the food on their plates so the main sound in the room was the scraping of cutlery against enamel.

I barely tasted my meal, so focused was I on my proximity to Elijah. I could feel the warmth coming off his body, our sides almost touching on the bench. I moved my foot so it rested against his. When he didn't react, I allowed myself to move my leg too, so it pressed into his own. That was when he turned to look at me. He gave a small smile, and gestured for me to lean in so he could whisper something in my ear. The feeling of his breath on my skin sent waves of heat through my body, and I had to inhale deeply through my nose to calm down.

'Aoife,' his lips were almost brushing my ears, 'I need you to do something for me.'

I nodded. I would have done anything.

'Go and fetch Jemima.'

My ears were ringing, suddenly, with the sound of my own blood, and I worried I might faint with the toxic combination of rage and grief which had engulfed me as soon as those three syllables came out of his mouth. Je-mi-ma. That was how he had said it, as though he was savouring the taste of her name on his tongue.

I rose, moving slowly to avoid tripping over my skirt or the bench. I was vaguely aware of Ruth and Deborah watching me go, but my full concentration was on staying upright, putting one foot in front of the other, and not screaming. Jemima was helping one of the smaller children cut up their food when I reached her. I couldn't bring myself to touch her bony little shoulder, so instead I coughed. She looked up, wide-eyed and frightened. *Good*, I thought, *you should be frightened, you little harlot.*

'Follow me,' I said, making my voice as terse and sharp as I could.

I didn't even wait for her to disentangle herself from the bench before I strode back towards Elijah. I liked the thought of her scampering along behind me, struggling to catch up.

Elijah barely looked at me when I got back. His eyes were focussed on her. When I went to retake my seat by his side, he shook his head.

'Let Mim sit there. You can go around the other side, next to Deborah.'

And then he was gone. Leaning in towards her, that whorish girl, that nasty child, whispering. What was he saying? And why was he calling her Mim? For the duration of our marriage he had never called me anything but my full Christian name. My stomach twisted into a knot of rage as I sat down next to Deborah, my buttocks feeling the hard wood of the bench for the first time.

I forced myself to take another deep breath. I wanted to be like a swan, serene and calm, no hint of the crazed paddling feet beneath the surface. Serene and calm and – but weren't swans vicious? I turned to Deborah, who was mopping up the last of her stew with a piece of bread. I waited until she was just about to pop it in her pretty pink mouth before I spoke.

'Well, you've certainly polished that off, haven't you, Deborah?' I heard my own voice, hard and cool, amid the low chatter and scraping of plates. My accent, usually subdued after years of living away from County Kildare, always pitched up when I was angry, and I could hear it rising then. Elijah and Jemima did not look up from their whispered discussion.

The bread was already in Deborah's mouth by that point, and I watched as she froze, holding it there.

'Although you know that eating for two is a myth, don't you?' I said. 'No need to turn into a greedy guts just because you're expecting.'

I let out a venomous laugh. Deborah's watery grey eyes had widened, but she didn't say anything. I leaned in and spoke in a stage whisper:

'If I were you, I'd watch your figure a bit more. You'll not be the youngest model for much longer, and when all you have to offer is your looks ... No offence meant of course, *Sister*.' I spat the word. 'Of course, I'm just looking out for you. But when all you have is a pretty face and a young body, it's awfully easy to be forgotten about when a prettier face and a younger body comes on the scene.'

I looked meaningfully over at Jemima. Elijah had his arm around her shoulders. The sight made me do a double-take, but no one else seemed to think anything of it; Ruth was staring at her plate, and John appeared to have vanished. I turned back to Deborah, watching her eyes for tears. *Come on you little cow, cry.*

I was just about to open my mouth again when Elijah stood and the room fell into silence.

'I hope we have all enjoyed our delicious meal?' He paused, allowing the congregation to answer him.

'Yes!'

'Good!' he said, 'I'm glad. I said before we ate that this will be our last Feast of the Prophet here on Earth, so I think we ought to make it a special one. Do you agree?'

'Yes!'

The answer was loud enough that I didn't have to respond myself. Instead, I opened and shut my mouth in time with everyone else, my silence lost in their voices.

'Excellent! I have a surprise for you all, one which I think you'll enjoy.' He smirked and I prayed that the surprise had nothing to do with Jemima, who was looking up at him wide-eyed, interested, smiling. 'But first, I think this is a good opportunity to share some testimony.'

Elijah pointed at one person after another, and they rose and spoke. I had heard everyone's stories so many times that they all blurred into one.

'I met Elijah just after I had got a new job, I was stressed, everything I did was about money. He showed me that there was more to life.'

'Thank you, Elijah. You brought God into my world just when I needed Him the most.'

'I was thinking about ending my life when Elijah invited me to a service in the community centre back in town.'

'I'd never felt so much love in a room before.'

'Elijah saved my mother's life. He turned her away from sin and he reunited us, and I'll always be so grateful.'

That was Deborah; Elijah loved getting her to trot out her sad little story on occasions like this. He stood and watched, beaming as the compliments rained down on him. When Deborah had finished speaking, he didn't point at anyone else. Instead, he spoke up again himself.

'Thank you to everyone who shared,' he said. 'I think it's so important to speak our testimonies. They remind us of the importance of faith, of placing our trust in God. Even when we ourselves can't see how something might end, we have to remember that God knows. That *I* know. And that we won't let you come to harm. With that in mind, I would like to share with you my surprise.'

Please don't let it be about Jemima, please don't let it be about Jemima, please, please.

'While we've been testifying, Brother John has been laying out glasses of water by your plates. I have noticed that some of you have taken sips already – don't worry if that's the case, but if you haven't, I would appreciate if you could wait until I've finished speaking before you do.'

John appeared at my left, a greasy waiter, and set a glass for me and a glass for Deborah down on the table.

'This isn't just ordinary water – well, most glasses glasses are full of ordinary water. But five,' he held up a hand, fingers splayed, 'contain something else too. You won't be able to taste or smell the difference, but after a few moments you'll notice… something. The glasses have been given out at random, although I've told John not to give any of the *special* glasses to the children. To make it fair, I've also asked John to make sure that one of the special glasses be served to one of the inner circle.' He gestured to Ruth, Deborah and me. 'I don't want to be accused of playing favourites.'

The room watched in silence. I couldn't believe what I was hearing. 'Special' glasses? What on Earth could be in them? I wracked my brains – LSD? Cyanide? Surely not. He had never spoken to me about anything like this. But then, he had not spoken to me properly for so long. My mind flashed back to the previous night. He had been out of his mind then. If he had been speaking with John just before…

'The End is coming so soon, friends. We need to be ready. I need to know that everyone in this room has faith, and so, when I give the command, I want you to pick up your glasses and drink. Show me your faith! Show everyone in this room that you deserve your place amongst us in these very final days!'

He raised his own glass to his lips, and drank. My heart was hammering so hard in my chest that I worried for a moment that I might have some kind of attack. Everyone around me was lifting their glasses and drinking. Next to me, Deborah had already downed her drink and was sitting serenely, hands patiently folded in her lap. With both hands I picked up my own glass. Elijah looked down at me, his brow raised expectantly, one hand clutching his empty glass, the other resting heavily on Jemima's shoulder.

I brought my glass to my lips and swallowed the cool, flavourless liquid. I held his gaze as behind me the coughing and spluttering began.

Chapter Eight

Ruth

Back in 2008, after I qualified as a midwife, I decided to move out of my godmother's place in London and try out somewhere new. I applied for about ten positions in hospitals and birthing centres around the country, but none in London; an omission that I didn't share with my godmother. I had been living with her for the whole duration of my studies, and was starting to get worn out. My father's rules had been too rigid, but Therese, my godmother, had no rules at all – a choice she worked hard to keep from my parents. Back home, I could leave the house for church and pre-approved church-related activities, school, and to help my mom run errands. I had to keep my hair just so, my nails filed way down, and the room I shared with my sister immaculate. Trying to please him had been difficult and exhausting, but it was possible. Therese wanted me to 'live my life' and 'have fun' and 'stop being so uptight', and pleasing her was difficult and exhausting in a whole different way. After four years of being dragged out to bars and parties where I was simultaneously the youngest and most boring person, having my orange juice and coffee spiked with liquor, and being set up on dates with men who painted murals, I had had enough. Moving to Newcastle was my chance to start again; I was twenty-two years old, and ready to begin life on my own terms.

It was my roommate Chrissy, another nurse, who told me about the Church of Heaven on Earth.

'You'd like them, I think. They seem like your kind of people.'

'My kind of people?' I wrinkled my nose, unsure what she was trying to say.

'Oh, you know I didn't mean…' Chrissy blushed. 'I just meant, they seem nice. Like, they do nice things. Lois from work, her and her husband go there. They run a free creche and do a soup kitchen, and I think some other stuff too? I'm like, not religious or anything, but they definitely seem like the kind of church I would join if I was, you know, going to join a church.'

I had been in the city for three weeks by then, and had tried three different churches, none of which had seemed right. On my fourth Sunday in Newcastle I took the bus from my apartment to the hall where Heaven on Earth held their services, and knew straight away that Chrissy had been right. These were my kind of people. First off, they welcomed me with open arms. Lois, one of the receptionists from work, recognised me right away and called me to sit with her and her husband and their little boy. Everyone there seemed so incredibly *nice*. Elijah was a draw, too. I liked the way he talked about faith, and what it meant to live like a Christian in the modern world. When the service was over, he filled my mug with tea from the urn and asked me about myself. When I talked, he seemed interested. He said he hoped he would see me again soon.

Eleven years later, I pulled myself out of bed, a dull throbbing pain pulsing behind my eyes. Elijah had not come to bed, and I'd been relieved. He'd scared me with his stunt with the water, in a way he hadn't ever scared me before.

He had waited until everyone had taken a drink before clapping his hands together. He kept them clasped as the room looked back up at him, waiting to be told what five of them had just drunk.

'I am so proud of you all,' he said, his knuckles turning white, 'so, so proud. You've shown your faith today, shown me that you all deserve to be here with us at the End. I'm pleased to say you have all passed the test.'

He smiled.

'Each and every one of your glasses contained nothing more than God's own Highland water.'

I hadn't realised that I had been holding my breath until I felt the air rush back into my lungs. Just water. Nothing more. Elijah would never harm us. Those terrifying coughs from the congregation, the urge I'd had to clutch at my throat, had been from fear, not poison.

On the other side of Elijah, John let out a loud and hearty laugh, as if Elijah had just pulled the funniest prank he'd ever seen. At first the sound echoed emptily around the room, until Elijah laughed too – then everyone joined in. Even little Jemima, next to me, put her hand to her mouth and giggled. My own laugh came out sounding like a rough honk, not a laugh at all really, just the strangled sound of relief. The only person who was silent was Aoife. She'd had her gaze fixed on Elijah since he had issued his instruction, and now she was staring up at him with thunder in her eyes. Had she been in on it, I wondered? Had Deborah? Was that why they had both finished their glasses so eagerly? My own glass was still almost full; I had barely swallowed any of it.

I took the opportunity while everyone was laughing to drink the rest, so if anyone checked afterward they would think I'd been just as obedient as my sister wives. The laughter went on for what felt like forever. Every time it slowed, someone would laugh louder and everybody would start up again. It was contagious, and by the end I let myself get swept up too, just glad that it was over, that no one had been hurt, that Elijah hadn't really wanted to harm us. Relieved too, I guess, that we had all done as we were told. I didn't like to think what punishment Elijah would have brought down on anyone who had stood up and refused.

The Feast went on for hours after that. We sang more hymns, Elijah preached, and when the autumn sun went down the women lifted the lid off the cabbage soup and brought out another platter of bread and we ate some more. By the time we were dismissed, everyone seemed to have forgotten about the test, as if it didn't bear thinking about. People laughed and talked all the way back to their caravans, their voices fading into the night as we wives walked back to the farmhouse in silence. I waited and waited for Elijah that night, keeping my door shut to Russell even though I could hear her padding around on the landing, running through what I would say to him when he arrived. Thinking about what he might say to me. Would he even want to talk? Would he just want to make love and then fall asleep, as he usually did? The cool grey light of dawn was coming through my window by the time I realised he wasn't coming.

The following morning, after work, I decided to visit the schoolhouse. It had been a long time since I had been inside. Like all of the farm buildings in Halcyon, the schoolhouse had been renovated lovingly but inexpertly by the many hands of our church. We had an architect and two engineers in our midst, but they had been too busy working on the bunker to spare much time for anything else. Inside, tarpaulin had been strung up to separate the sleeping quarters from the school. These hanging tarps had been used as canvases by Deborah, who at Elijah's request had spent painstaking days writing a selection of 'child-focussed' Bible verses on them in huge black letters. I always forgot just how imposing the great banners were, and how stern they made God's loving words.

FROM THE LIPS OF CHILDREN YOU, <u>LORD</u>, HAVE CALLED FORTH YOUR PRAISE.

LIKE ARROWS IN THE HANDS OF A WARRIOR ARE CHILDREN.

FOLLY IS BOUND UP IN THE HEART OF A CHILD, BUT THE ROD OF DISCIPLINE WILL DRIVE IT FAR AWAY.

LET THE LITTLE CHILDREN COME TO ME FOR THE KINGDOM OF GOD BELONGS TO SUCH AS THESE.

Even the last verse, which had been my favourite ever since I was a little girl, sounded harsh thanks to the heavy black text in which it was written. Elijah was proud of the banners, but although Deborah pretended to be pleased with how they had come out, I could tell she felt that they did not look exactly how she had intended. I wondered what the children made of them, or if they noticed them at all.

The porch opened up into the classroom side of the building, where rows of children sat cross-legged on the floor listening intently to Jemima, who at barely sixteen was one of the barn's older residents. Jemima. She had been there yesterday, had taken Aoife's seat at Elijah's side. I'd tried not to look as she'd leaned into Elijah, whose strong, familiar arm had encircled her shoulders. I did my best not to think about it as I watched her from across the room; she was demonstrating something, but I was too far away to see what. I was amazed by the children's undivided attention, especially as Helen and Danielle were busy laying out lunch on a trestle table nearby. Annie, who was tending to a little cluster of gurgling toddlers in another corner, looked up as I closed the door behind me and gave me a quizzical stare. Abigail was sitting on her lap, playing with the buttons on her cardigan. With a tentative wave in Annie's direction I ducked through an opening in the tarp into the dormitory, trying not to think about Abigail or Jemima or the Feast.

If it had been a long time since I had been in the school, I doubted if I had ever been into the children's sleeping quarters even once. The first thing that struck me was the smell, which transported me back into the changing rooms in my high school gym in Illinois. The second thing that stood out was the order in which the space was kept. Bunk beds and cots were lined up as neatly as soldiers, and bins of folded clothes labelled by contents did not look as though they had been rifled through by twenty-five children a few hours ago. Unable to resist, I came to the first bed and inspected the sheets – although the linens and blankets were mismatched, the little bed was made up as neatly as could be. I was so impressed by the hospital-like precision, which surely couldn't have been achieved by a child, that I didn't even notice Deborah until she spoke. She was sitting on the floor.

'Hey, Ruth! Is everything okay?' Her stage whisper, presumably to stop her voice carrying through the tarpaulin divider, sounded cheerful enough, but she looked concerned. It was only then that I realised she must have thought I was there for a particular reason, and I wished I'd never come at all. What if she thought I wanted to talk about the Feast of the Prophet? What if she brought it up herself?

'Oh,' I said, 'yeah of course, everything's fine.'

She looked at me expectantly until I spoke again.

'I got done a little earlier than usual this morning so I thought I would take a walk. Can I help with anything?'

Deborah gestured to the little piles of folded clothes around her with a gentle smile.

'You've timed that pretty well, Ruth. These have come back from being washed but I've just this minute finished folding them.'

'Oh, I'm sorry,' I said.

Deborah let out a sweet peal of laughter which echoed around the room, then put her hand to her mouth in mock embarrassment.

'Don't be daft! You're too sweet, Ruth, but you know I'm just teasing. Although…' she paused for a second, 'there is actually something I could use your help with.'

'Sure, anything!' I said quickly, stepping towards her.

'You can help me get up.' She reached up her arms to me like an overgrown toddler, and I heaved her onto her feet. Once upright, Deborah shook her head, 'I'm getting too pregnant for this.'

I wouldn't have dared agree with her out loud, but she was looking particularly large and I was keeping a close eye on her during her check-ups, doing my best to figure out if she was having twins again. I thought it was a miracle that she had managed to get down on the floor in the first place. Instead, I smiled and said, 'Well, looks like I came along at just the right time after all.'

My usefulness apparently exhausted, I was just about to make my excuses to leave when a burst of chatter from the classroom signalled the end of lessons and the beginning of lunch.

'That sounds like my cue to head next door,' said Deborah, 'I like to lead their mealtime prayers when I can.'

But instead of making a move in the direction of the schoolroom, she stayed where she was.

'Why don't you join me? It'll only take five minutes, and then we can head back to the farmhouse together for a bite to eat?'

Before I could answer, Jemima peeked her head through a gap in the tarp. She must have been completely engrossed in her lesson when I'd come in earlier, because she looked surprised to see me.

'Oh, err, hi,' she said, blushing slightly, 'am I all right to, I mean, please may I come in?'

Deborah nodded and beckoned her forward with a smile. 'You're very welcome to join us, Mim, but we were just about to head through ourselves.'

It took me a second to figure out that Mim must have been short for Jemima, and I wondered if any of my children had been granted schoolhouse nicknames of which I was unaware.

'I didn't know you were here, Sister Ruth. I'm sorry. I didn't mean to interrupt.'

She could barely look me in the eye, and I realised with wonder that she was waiting for me to grant her some kind of pardon. I supposed it made sense – in the hierarchy of Halcyon I was, somehow, the most senior person in the room.

'That's quite all right,' I said. I was so unused to any show of power that I had to borrow my words from Aoife, and they tasted foreign in my mouth.

Jemima – Mim – looked relieved, although she still kept her

gaze low. She had grown up in the church and I had seen her most days since she was five years old, but I suppose I hadn't really studied her for a long time. Even yesterday, when she had taken Aoife's place next to me, I had done my best not to look at her at all. Up close, I was surprised by how pretty she was, even with the peppering of acne across her chin.

'What can we do for you, Mim?' asked Deborah.

Was I imagining it, or did her pleasantness, usually so natural, seem slightly forced? Maybe she was just anxious to go say grace with the children, and was a little resentful of the hold-up. Nothing to do with Elijah's announcement last week, or Mim's seat on his right the day before. No. Nothing like that.

'I just wanted to catch you before you went for lunch,' said Mim, managing to lift her head high enough to look at Deborah while she spoke. 'I wanted to say thank you for letting me run the scripture lesson today. It was fun.'

'You're very welcome, sweetheart,' said Deborah, softening slightly, 'I'm sure you did a lovely job.'

Mim smiled, relieved.

'Off you go then, get yourself some soup before there's none left. I'm coming through just now to say a prayer with you all.'

With a nod at Deborah and a strange little half curtsy to me, Mim scurried back through to the classroom. We watched her go in silence.

'Sweet kid,' I said.

Deborah raised an eyebrow. 'She certainly is.'

Chapter Nine

Aoife

Schoolgirl stuff. That's what it was. Stupid, silly, petty schoolgirl stuff that should have been as far beneath me as it was possible for anything to be. But it still bothered me. The three of them standing there, chatting, pally as anything. I had been looking for Ruth, and when I was told that she'd last been seen going into the schoolhouse I had thought there must be some mistake. Only, there she was. And not just her, but Deborah too, and worst of all there *she* was. The girl. Jemima. Or what was it that he was calling her now, some sickly-sweet diminutive? Jem? Mim? Mim. When he said that at the breakfast table that morning I had almost choked on my porridge. It had been just the two of us there, and I had taken the opportunity to bring her up in conversation – conversation being allowed on occasion at breakfast, although never at dinner.

'Your idea with the water glasses at the Feast of the Prophet yesterday was really inspired, my love,' I said, choosing my words carefully. 'What a clever way to make sure everyone is faithful and ready for the End.' No hint of criticism. No shouting. Not a whisper of my real feelings about the whole thing, which were … what exactly?

He let out a pleased grunt of recognition.

'It was nice of you to let Jemima sit up with you, too. Did she have anything interesting to say?'

Elijah looked up and I thought I was in for it, but instead he tilted his head. 'Jemima? Oh, you mean Mim.'

Her name was like a spell – as soon as it escaped his lips he was transformed into a teenager with a crush. He flashed me a smile.

'Oh,' he said, 'Mim was just fine.'

I could have spat.

Seeing them all together had just been salt in the wound. Only the Lord himself knew what they were saying about me, huddled in their little coven. Deborah, especially, was very free with Elijah, telling him just what she thought of me at every opportunity she got – it made sense that she would be doing the same with Ruth and Jemima, trying to turn them against me. At least Elijah was honest, careful to relay her spiteful words with compassion and love. I could rely on him for that. For all his faults, at least he cared enough to tell me the truth. *Maybe they weren't talking about you at all*, came the voice in my head, venomous and wise, *maybe they were talking about his trick with the water. Maybe they were all in on it, and that's why they polished off their glasses so loyally. He probably ran it by them all first.*

I walked out again quickly, before any of them could spot me and accuse me of spying on them. To my shame, I felt tears prickling in my eyes and heat rising to my face. How could I let two women and a teenage girl make me feel this way? *Pathetic*, piped up the voice in my head, *you're absolutely pathetic, Aoife.* The voice was right. Why did I care if they hated me? Why should I mind if Deborah thought I was bossy and stuck-up and past my best? Who cared if Elijah had shared his plans with them and not me? It had felt like two against one for a while, so why was it important that I would soon have three sister wives against me?

Before I could come up with a concrete plan of what to do next, I found that I had passed out of the centre of Halcyon and was walking towards the perimeter fence. Instead of turning back, I decided to keep on walking, hoping that it would clear my head. I took a breath, inhaling the fresh Highland air. I tramped on by the caravans, which were mainly empty at that time of day, and the hives and the greenhouses, my eyes fixed purposefully ahead. I had learned a long time ago that a little confidence can take a person a long way – if I'd been shuffling, looking shifty or wary or lost, someone would have come up to me and asked where I was going, or they would have gone to tell Elijah or John that I was wandering. If I looked like I knew what I was doing, I could do anything that I wanted.

Without my noticing, Halcyon had burst into an autumnal flame. It happened every year – I would pay no attention at all to the land around me until it was almost too late to appreciate the changing colours. The deergrass and heather were a blazing russet red, and I let myself admire them as I picked my way towards the perimeter, carefully avoiding the stones and hard tufts of spiked grass which stuck out at random intervals. It wouldn't be long until winter came, and the golds and oranges and reds were replaced with dead browns and greys, covered with snow and treacherous with ice. I had wandered so far that the only sign that I was still in Halcyon at all was the chain-link fence (to keep the livestock *in* and the nosey neighbours *out*), and the wooden watchtower which stood, quaint and empty, waiting patiently for the End of Days. The sheep grazed, placid and uninterested in anything but the mossy grass at their feet, occasionally meandering over to one of Halcyon's winding streams for a drink. An eagle swooped high overhead in the wide grey Highland sky, circling gracefully through the air. I looked out ahead to see how far I was from the edge of our land, and that was when I noticed the car. It was a big four-by-four, fancier than ours, the sort that belonged to wealthy landowners and gentleman farmers across the British Isles. I was surprised that I hadn't noticed it before, even though it was parked at quite a distance from the perimeter and obscured slightly by a mound in the earth. Without thinking, I picked up my pace and strode towards it. I don't know what I expected to do when I reached the edge of Halcyon – dig out under the fence to investigate? Fortunately, the decision was made for me; as I continued my approach in the direction of the vehicle its door swung open and a figure leapt out. I stopped. This was the first person from outside of Heaven on Earth that I had encountered in a long time. Perhaps they sensed my unease from afar, because they bounded towards me with an exaggerated show of friendliness. It was a man, I realised, not quite as tall as Elijah but still broad and imposing in his own way. He gave a long, languid wave.

'Hullo!' he called.

I responded with a tentative wave and continued on my path towards him. We both reached the edge of the perimeter fence at the same moment and I was able to study him properly. My initial assumption that this person was some kind of wealthy landowner was reinforced when I saw him up close. He wore a waxed jacket, unbuttoned enough to reveal a woollen jumper and a red and white checked shirt underneath, and he had the floppy, public-schoolboy haircut and lazy grin of someone who lived a carefree and privileged life. I thought he might have been out on a fishing trip, but I couldn't see a rod anywhere on his person, and he wasn't wearing the sort of waders you'd need for the river which bordered us. Maybe he had left them in the car.

'Who are you?' I asked, surprised at the breathiness of my voice. 'What are you doing here?'

He let out a hearty laugh and shook his head.

'Malcolm,' he said, 'pleased to meet you.'

His voice was rich and warm, like a smoky Scotch whisky.

'Pleased to meet you,' I echoed.

'I would shake your hand, but...' he gestured to the fence between us.

'Oh, that's okay.' I looked down, embarrassed by my embarrassment, and noticed his wellington boots, expensive-looking and squeaky clean, through the gaps in the fence. I wondered what he was noticing about me.

I scolded myself internally. I had complained earlier about the rest of them acting like a bunch of schoolgirls, and there I was, unable to look a man in the eye. *Pathetic. Pull yourself together.*

'What did you say you were doing here, Malcolm?' I tried to convey breeziness and assertiveness all at once in my tone, but breezy was something I rarely tried to be, and I worried that the effect made me sound more demanding than I would have liked.

He laughed again, and I couldn't help but feel pleased. He lifted both hands up in a jovial surrender. 'You got me there. I didn't. I've recently inherited the land around here. Not your land, of course, but the rest of it.'

We looked at one another in silence for a short moment before he spoke again.

'I've heard a bit about the man who owns *your* land,' he nodded at the expanse of Halcyon behind me, 'and I thought he might be interested in some kind of offer.'

'I'm not so sure about that. I know him fairly well and I don't think he'd be interested in selling or buying. We've got just about the right amount of land for us. And you wouldn't want this land anyway, when the weather is bad the river floods and half of the pasture is under water.'

I could see him thinking, trying to figure me out. I'm ashamed to say that I enjoyed it.

'Do you think I might be able to chat with him anyway? I always thought that you should get to know your neighbours.'

I shook my head and turned to leave. 'He's not much of a people person, I'm afraid.'

'Wait!' he called.

I turned back around.

'I'm so sorry,' he said, 'that wasn't very neighbourly of me.'

'It was not.' Although I tried to sound hurt, I was secretly almost giddy with pleasure. I wasn't used to receiving apologies.

'I do think it's good to know your neighbours though, and if…'

'Elijah.'

'Elijah. If Elijah isn't much of a people person, then maybe I could get to know you? That way if I need to borrow a cupful of sugar or a bag of flour one day, I know who to go to.'

I smiled.

'That certainly sounds sensible to me,' I said. 'I shall keep an eye out for you coming along with your mug of tea.'

A dimple appeared in the left corner of his mouth when he grinned.

'Perhaps it would be a good start if you told me your name?'

'Aoife,' I said.

'Nice to meet you, Aoife.' He lifted his right arm as if he were about to shake my hand, and awkwardly stuck his forefinger through a hole in the chain link. He looked at me expectantly, and with a sheepish giggle I placed my own finger next to his. We linked them together and shook as best we could, separated as we were by the great metal fence. Other than my husband, he was the first man to touch me in almost twelve years.

I stayed out a little longer than I had planned to, and returned to the farmhouse with a sick, guilty knot in my stomach. I counted the things which I had done wrong. Number one, I had wandered off in the middle of a working day. Number two, I had stood and talked to a man, unchaperoned. Number three, that man was not a member of Heaven on Earth. Number four, I had let that man touch me, albeit with an entirely innocent part of his anatomy on an entirely innocent part of my anatomy. And worst of all, number five, I had enjoyed myself in his company. Not only was that sluttish and immodest, but with the End looming it was a potentially dangerous waste of time. The End. Somehow, speaking to someone new had made the End seem less – final.

Less urgent. Less *real*. Which was ridiculous. What had I been living in preparation for these past twelve years if that was the case? I shook my head, trying to dislodge the thoughts before I opened the front door.

When I walked into the kitchen where Deborah was preparing our evening meal, I expected her to notice some kind of difference in me, as though my transgressions would be branded onto my forehead. I had braced myself for an interrogation – *where have you been? With who? Why?* – and was relieved and disappointed in equal measure when she barely looked up from her chopping board.

'Hi, Aoife,' she said, returning almost instantly to her work, 'you all right?'

I made a small noise in response, although what it was supposed to mean I couldn't say, and busied myself by setting out four lots of cutlery. It was typical of her to be so oblivious. She was too simple to even still be annoyed with me about the way I'd spoken to her at the Feast. If she had talked to me that way, I certainly would not be looking at her now. Outside, I could hear the rest of the colony chatting as they traipsed to the community barn for their tea, tired but happy after a day of hard work. We were soon joined by Ruth, who filled a jug with water before taking her place at the table. Every sound was amplified by our silence as we waited for Elijah to arrive, each of us sitting patiently in our designated spot. Occasionally, Deborah rose to check the food, which smelled like it might be beginning to burn.

'Well, Deborah,' I said, leaning back in my chair to look at her as she stood by the stove, 'that certainly smells interesting. You really do just follow your own rules with cooking, don't you?'

I watched, stomach fluttering, as her shoulders froze. When she didn't say anything, I decided to keep going.

'I'd say it was admirable, if we weren't the ones who had to eat it every single day.'

Deborah's hand clenched around her wooden spoon as I let out a high-pitched laugh.

'You know, I remember reading something in a newspaper years ago about how burned food can give you cancer. Let's hope for our sakes that the corrupt media didn't get something right for once!'

I looked over at Ruth, but she didn't meet my eyes. My words kept ringing in my ears, and I had just opened my mouth to speak again when Deborah interrupted me.

'Wow, thanks, Aoife. I really value your opinion. Maybe, if you're so keen for a change from my cooking, you could give it a try once in a while. I'm sure Ruth and I would enjoy whatever five-star cuisine you'd manage to rustle up with our daily rations.'

'Well, I hardly think there's any need for that attitude, *Deborah.*' I stood up. 'I do plenty of work, not that you'd notice, actually keeping Halcyon running. It's not easy, you know, managing the accounts for a place like this.'

'Oh, I'm sure you're right,' she said, the corner of her mouth twitching, 'but we can't all be as clever as you. Saying that, I'm pretty certain you didn't bother yourself with cooking or housework before we came here, either. Didn't you just get Ruth to do it all for you?'

Before I could think of a retort, Ruth spoke up.

'Not that I minded a bit, Aoife. I was happy to do it.'

I forced a smile, trying not to wonder what else they said about me behind my back.

'That's nice of you to say,' said Deborah to Ruth, 'but you know, I wonder sometimes how happy Elijah could have been. Poor man, only the Lord knows how he coped before you and I came along.'

It wasn't like her to talk back, and my hand rose, reflexively, to slap her. It would have been worth whatever punishment Elijah dished out, and it would have been a big one I was certain, given Deborah's condition. The only thing that stopped me was the sound of the front door opening, followed by Elijah's familiar footsteps in the hallway. When he appeared in the doorway, he seemed surprised to see us there, waiting for him.

'Elijah!' Deborah chirped, turning to him with a smile as she took her seat. 'You must be famished. Why don't you sit down?'

He shook his head gruffly, as though he couldn't believe how stupid she was. As much as I was pleased to see it, his manner with her took me by surprise – he'd never acted so brusquely with Deborah before.

'I'm not staying,' he said.

'Oh?' I could hear a strain in Deborah's voice as she tried to remain cheerful. She was usually so effortless.

'I have to go and pray. About adding Mim to our family. I need to speak with God and I can't hear Him over your infernal *chat.*'

They were staring at each other so intently that I began to feel as though I was intruding on a private conversation.

'Do you know when we can expect you back?' she asked.

Once again, he fixed her with a look of pure distaste.

'No.'

The tension in the kitchen crackled, as though we were all waiting for lightning to strike.

'Oh, okay,' said Deborah, 'that's fine, but if you could just give a sort of rough ide—'

Elijah was not a violent man in the traditional sense. He dished out his punishments cold, when the heat of the moment had died away and you thought your indiscretion might have been quietly forgiven or forgotten. He had never smacked me in a temper, never bruised my face or blacked my eye. Which is why, I think, we were all so shocked when he interrupted Deborah's prattling request by picking up a heavy stoneware dinner plate from the kitchen worktop and throwing it so it soared inches above her head, before smashing against the kitchen wall. If she hadn't ducked, it would certainly have grazed the top of her scalp. Had he meant for it to get so close to her? Surely he hadn't intended to actually hit her? The electricity had gone from the air, and the three of us sat in stunned silence. Elijah was panting a little, and he hadn't taken his eyes off Deborah, who was white as a sheet and gripping the edge of the table with what I could only assume was fear.

'I will come back,' he said, 'when I decide that I want to come back. I am not beholden to you. Don't ever tell me what to do again.'

He spoke deliberately, almost calmly, waiting for Deborah to nod in agreement before leaving the kitchen. He closed the front door gently, but the sound of the latch clicking into place echoed down the corridor and made me wince. Nobody said a word as Deborah mechanically began to plate up our dinners, and we sat and ate in silence. One by one we finished our charred food, ignoring the ceramic shrapnel which had been scattered across every surface.

Part Two

Chapter Ten

Deborah

I wanted to kill him. I imagined how it would feel to leap onto his back as he left the room – in my fantasy I was nimble and not almost six months pregnant – and tear his hair so his head snapped backwards. I could almost feel the soft flesh of his throat giving way under my nails, the warm spurt of blood. He would be too shocked to do anything but fall to the floor, clutching at his neck, writhing under my weight as I straddled him and pummelled his face with my balled-up fists until he lay still and lifeless on the kitchen floor. 'How dare you do this to me?!' I would scream, raising my voice louder than I'd dared to for years, as Aoife and Ruth looked on.

At the very least, I should have left when he did. Packed a bag, picked up Jonah and Noah and Susannah, and followed him straight out of the open gate, into the Highland night. What would they have done? What *could* they have done? Nothing. But it was like something turned off in my brain when it happened, and I couldn't do anything at all any more. How dare he, after everything? Especially after his disgusting stunt at the Feast of the Prophet – that evil bullshit with the drinks, making my babies watch on, thinking that people around them were going to die. I'd almost killed myself trying to be normal and pleasant after that, and for what? For years I had played along, keeping everything in, and when it finally clicked that I was playing a losing game and the time came to let it all out, I realised that I couldn't. It's like when people say to kids, 'stop pulling faces or the wind will change, and you'll be stuck like that'. I'd played the cowed wife for so long that the wind had changed without me even noticing, and I was suddenly unable to be anything else.

That was the danger of my survival technique. The chameleon, quick-change, be-who-they-want-you-to-be personality which I had had down from the day I realised, as a child, that not everyone's life looked like mine. That to stay safe, wherever I was put, I needed to mask up and play whatever part was needed. It had kept me going through the early years with my mother and a childhood in care, but then in Heaven on Earth it had got a bit stuck. There was no need to change it up, because everyone needed the same from me, so I just kept the 'Prophet's Wife' mask on all the time. It had actually started to get comfortable, and when I needed to take it off, I couldn't, because there wasn't really a normal Deborah face underneath any more.

The next few days passed in a hazy dream, which was almost lucky really, because it meant I couldn't beat myself up too much about what had happened, or what hadn't happened. My mam used to say I was a 'nervous sleeper', because any kind of emotional surplus always exhausted me, and that was how I passed the days after Elijah left. Sleeping on my feet, walking around Halcyon like a pregnant zombie. I hadn't even realised that I'd been doing it until I returned to my body one morning, all of a sudden. I was midway through scrubbing the kitchen floor, and I woke up so abruptly that I actually felt a bit frightened. I had no way of telling exactly how long it had been since Elijah had left, how many days and nights I'd managed to pass without being present in my body or my mind. I had a sense it had been a few – two, three, four? Time passed differently in Halcyon, anyway.

Crouched there on the floor I stared at my hands. The cold water had turned them as red as the kitchen tiles and they seemed to belong to someone much older. I was clutching a rag, and my knuckles looked chapped and sore. After not feeling anything for however long I had been out, all of my emotions flooded back at once with an intensity that I hadn't felt since I was a teenager. Since moving to Halcyon, I had been a lot of things: frightened, miserable, desperate, lonely. And I was still all of those things, but I was something else as well, something that I hadn't been for such a long time that I almost didn't recognise the feeling as it simmered and bubbled inside me – I was angry.

With great care, I manoeuvred myself up off the floor; my legs had gone numb, and I had to regain my balance by gripping the countertop. The windowpane was beaded with condensation and outside the morning sky was just beginning to lighten, a peaceful blanket of mist still hanging in the air. The rest of Halcyon would be waking up very soon, but for now the colony was still asleep. Suddenly, I couldn't bear to stand there in the stillness any longer. Abandoning my sodden rag in the sink, I crept out of the silent farmhouse and across the garden path towards the outhouse. It was the only place in all of Halcyon that I could be certain of some privacy. Within its whitewashed stone walls, I wasn't Deborah the Third Wife; I wasn't a wife at all. I could almost begin to imagine that I was somewhere else altogether. I sat on the cold floor with my back against the wooden door, oblivious to the spelks of wood which pierced through the loose knit of my cardigan. The outhouse was the place that I came to cling on to myself, although I would have to start trying harder. If the scene in the kitchen the other night had proved anything, it was that I was no better than the rest of them. Ruth was once brave enough to emigrate halfway across the world, and now look at her; it was as though she'd been lobotomised. Even Aoife. When I first joined Heaven on Earth, she had terrified me. She had reminded me of a pagan queen, or an ancient warrior saint, black hair streaming down her back and blue eyes like something from a fairy tale. I had thought Halcyon would have been the making of her – really it should have been, she wasn't made for domesticated city life. When we first moved here, she had come into her own, some dormant pioneer blood bubbling to the surface. The graft of building a settlement from almost nothing had made her even more beautiful and terrible than she had been before, but once it was done, once we fell back into a routine, it was like she withered before my eyes. Seeing Aoife disappear into herself like that was the real worry, the real shock. If it could happen to her, how could I be surprised that it was happening to me? I could furiously read as many squares of recycled newspaper as I liked and sing as many pop songs under my breath as I could possibly rescue from the fog of my lost teenage years, and it wouldn't be enough.

My anger rose again, and I was relieved. With anger, I thought, would come the will to do something, *anything*, that would improve my situation. I needed it, and to keep it up I would have to force the flames to burn bright and hard enough to swallow me up, so I could burst up from the ashes like a whole new woman, like a – I wracked my brains for the word for the magical fiery bird I'd seen on TV as a kid. But it had vanished, along with a million other little bits of pre-Halcyon knowledge. *Never mind.* I shook the disappointment out of my head and I slid the bolt back to open the door. If I wanted to fan the flames of my rage I knew exactly where I would have to go.

I managed to make it to the schoolhouse without seeing another soul, although I could hear Aoife and Ruth moving around in their bedrooms when I returned to the house to change into some clean clothes. Everyone else must have still been in their caravans because of the cold. I wondered if the kids would even be up yet – I was rarely over there at this time of day – and if they weren't, what I would do. The door to the barn opened with a creak. Inside, the weak morning light was beginning to come through the high windows, making the children look sickly and pale. They were lined up for their morning exercises, led by Mim and under the watchful eye of Helen, who was leaning against the wall with her arms crossed tightly around her chest. I spotted Jonah and Noah straight away; they were two of the smallest ones there, their dark shaggy heads bouncing up and down as they star jumped in time with the others. As soon as I saw them my heart swelled, and I remembered why I had gone along with the whole thing in the first place. I'd had to convince Elijah that I was the most loyal, the most trustworthy, or he would never have let me spend so much time in the schoolhouse. Except for Helen, all of the other women in Halycon had to take turns working their shifts there to avoid spending too much time around their own children, just in case. Aoife and Ruth were lucky to see their kids from across the room at church, but I got to see mine every day. Even if it did piss me off that they looked so much like their father. Even if they knew they were his, but didn't really, fully know that they were mine. When I found out that I was pregnant with Susannah, I hoped that she would inherit something of mine – blonde hair, grey eyes, the shape of my mouth, anything at all – but when she was born, she came out with the same shock of brown hair as the other two. And now, at a year and a half, it was obvious that she was the spit of him.

I was so distracted watching them that I didn't notice that Helen had moved from her spot until she put her hand on my arm.

'Deborah? What are you doing here? You're awfully early!'

'Oh,' I said, 'I had an early start today. Sorry to disturb you. I hope you don't mind?'

Helen stifled a yawn. 'Not at all. Elijah usually pops in around this time to check on the children, see how they're getting on. You know?'

I did not know.

'They love it,' she said, gesturing at the kids, 'especially Jonah and Noah. And Susannah too, actually. The way she clings on to him when he picks her up, we always have such a job tearing her away.'

My fists clenched. I thought back to all the mornings that I had turned up at the schoolhouse to find little Susannah tearful and distressed, only for her to twist herself out of my arms. As betrayed as I was, I felt vindicated by the rare acknowledgement that I would be more interested to hear about Jonah and Noah and Susannah than any of the other children. That they belonged to me. Oblivious, Helen carried on.

'The boys have been asking when he'll be calling in to see them since they woke up this morning. He hasn't been for a few days and they really miss him.' She stopped herself and gave my arm a gentle squeeze. For a second, I hoped she would say that they'd miss me too if ever I wasn't there, but why would they? 'Of course, they're too small to understand that he has more important things to be worried about at the moment. He's in my prayers, Deborah. You are too.'

Helen's revelation about Elijah's morning visits had left me reeling, so it took me a second to realise that she had finished speaking and was waiting for a response from me.

'Thanks, Helen.'

'Are you going to stay for breakfast?'

'No. I don't think so. I need to sort a few things out back at the house, but I'll be back before too long.'

The kids had stopped their star jumps and were jogging on the spot when I turned to go, still in their military straight lines. I tried as hard as I could not to look at the boys again before I left. For the first time in my life, I didn't want to see them. When I got outside, I put my hand on my stomach. I felt my anger growing. Something had to be done.

Chapter Eleven

Aoife

Things seemed strangely light after Elijah left, but as the days went on his reason for leaving started to weigh heavily on us all, and the scene in the kitchen kept playing over in my head when I least expected it. I barely saw Ruth, who spent every daylight hour with the animals, and for the first time ever, Deborah looked downright miserable. I kept seeing her wandering around Halcyon like a lost puppy, her face drawn, eyes completely blank. Elijah and I had had our disagreements before, particularly in recent years, but as far as I knew he and Deborah had never had so much as a cross word for as long as they had known each other. I almost felt sorry for her.

Almost, but not quite, because I had more pressing things on my mind than the state of Deborah and Elijah's relationship. Or maybe I should say that the cracks appearing in their foundations had inspired me to up my game slightly, and to use the time Elijah was away wisely enough so that when he returned, he would be reminded of my – for want of a better phrase – overall superiority to Deborah. I couldn't stand for any more surprises, and so I needed to work my way back into the little circle of trust which had closed me out without my noticing.

I began to spend most of my waking hours cloistered in my office at the back of the farmhouse, wrapped in a quilt to keep away the encroaching October chill, surrounded by all of our ledgers from the past twelve years. I stared at the neat lines of numbers, written by me, until they were all I could see even when my eyes were closed. I knew I must be missing something somewhere. When we had moved from Newcastle to Halcyon, I had transcribed all of our records from the old computer onto paper. Could I have made a mistake? I combed through every line, trying to see if I had written something glaringly incorrect, but there was nothing. I counted the money in the petty cash safe so many times that my hands became grubby, even though I knew too much was missing to be found there. Far too much, in fact. We seemed to be down almost one hundred thousand pounds, somehow. A figure which seemed to grow each time I recalculated it, as though week by week our savings were just leaking out of some invisible hole. Elijah had been away for four days, and I had nothing to show for my efforts at all. The missing money was nowhere to be found. On my excursions from the farmhouse I could hardly look anyone in the eye. I thought of everything these people had done for us, donating their wages, selling their furniture, their cars, their homes, all so we could build Halcyon from practically nothing. They had given so generously and trusted us so deeply, and I had repaid them by losing their hard-earned money. When I had spoken with Elijah about it in the past, he had simply shrugged. 'There's more to life than money,' he had said. But I knew him well enough to notice the darkening of his brow. He was, deep down, concerned.

When the office walls seemed to be closing in, and the air became too stuffy for me to concentrate any more, I would take walks. The best route, the one where I was less likely to be disturbed by other church members, was the one I had taken previously around the perimeter fence. I would be lying if I tried to claim that the hope of meeting Malcolm again hadn't crossed my mind as I set out one early afternoon following a lonely lunch at my desk, but it wasn't as though I was heading out with the single aim of crossing his path. Plus, it seemed absurd to think that he would be there a second time, especially when he hadn't appeared the day before or the day before that. He was a busy man, I reasoned, as I trudged beneath the big white sky. It must take a lot of work to manage such a huge amount of land.

The blazing beauty of autumn which I had only just been admiring was already fading to ash. It was practically November now, winter-time drawing in like a familiar beast to wipe away the colour from our small world. Soon the sun, already setting earlier and earlier each night, would barely show its weak pale face, and the colony would settle into a sad hibernation until the gold and purple and green of spring arrived in April. It would soon be too cold to justify a walk around the perimeter, and I would be stuck in the farmhouse.

I had just about talked myself out of the idea of ever bumping into Malcolm again when his car slowly rolled into view from behind the hillock where it had been parked last time. I wondered how long he'd been waiting there, and if he had come out just to talk to me. We both reached the fence at the same moment, and I did nothing to hide the smile which twitched at my lips.

'Well hello, Aoife,' he said, still zipping up his coat, 'fancy seeing you here.'

'I was just out for a stroll, you know. This is my route.'

'Oh?'

'Yes,' I said, 'I've been stuck in my office all morning and thought I might go mad if I didn't get out to stretch my legs.'

I looked right at him as I spoke this time, searching his face. He had very fine laughter lines around his eyes, and they creased when he smiled – the only thing about him that reminded me of Elijah.

'Well, I'm certainly glad to see you. I actually came out this afternoon with the express hope of bumping into you again.'

Then it was my turn to say, 'Oh.'

'I enjoyed our chat the other day. This part of the world is beautiful, but it can get rather lonely. And you're an interesting person to speak to.'

'Well, I'd hardly say interesting. We don't do much of anything here that would be interesting to the rest of the world.'

I could tell, from the way he spoke, that he was trying to flatter me; I had lived thirty years outside of Halcyon after all. Still, just because I knew what he was doing didn't mean that I couldn't enjoy it. So what if he was still only interested in our land? I twisted a loose strand of hair around my finger and tucked it behind my ear.

'You say that, but we've been talking here for hardly a minute and I'm already intrigued as to what you've been doing in an office all morning. I didn't realise you sold produce from here.'

'No, we don't, everything we grow or make stays here in Hal— on the farm. But I run the accounts for our church.'

'Really?' he said, 'and is it interesting work? I can't say I envy you, accounts are my worst nightmare.'

I let out a little laugh. 'Mine too. I'd always thought of myself as pretty good at numbers and things, I did half of a degree in business studies once upon a time, but I just can't seem to get the numbers to add up at the minute. It's as though the money has just... sorry, I'm being boring. Not even *I* like talking about the accounts, and they're my job.'

I realised, of course, that he might actually be very interested in our accounts. I didn't think it could do too much harm for him to get the hint of an idea that we were struggling to balance the books, if he was interested in buying the land. If he thought there might be a chance we'd sell, and that I was the woman holding the purse strings, he might keep stopping by.

'Not boring at all,' he scratched the back of his neck with his gloved hand, 'but I wonder how a woman like yourself, with no less than half of a business degree, found herself doing accounts for a church in the back end of nowhere?'

'Well, now that really is a boring story.'

I had only ever told Elijah about my half-degree. It was the biggest shame of my life that I'd given it up. Homesickness for Grainne and my mother had sent me into despair, and I had fallen so far behind on my work that I had failed every end-of-year exam. The thought of retaking had made me feel sick, and so I quit. The irony was that I was too embarrassed to tell my family what I'd done – they had been so proud of me for going – that I didn't ever go back home. I wrote letters talking about lectures I never attended and classmates I barely remembered, and sent through the dates and times of exams which I saw posted on the campus notice board. I kept meaning to tell them, promising myself that I would, but it felt easier not to. My mother, who came very late to parenthood and was well on in years, suffered from poor health and couldn't travel, and Grainne couldn't leave her, so they never visited. I think Grainne might have guessed, but she never said anything, and my mother died thinking that her younger daughter was going to be a graduate. I promised myself, after that, that I would never give up on anything else – a dramatic, teenage promise, but one I kept.

He laughed. 'I don't believe you for one minute, you know. But even if it is. Indulge me.'

'Oh, well, all right then,' I said, trying to make my voice nonchalant, 'I dropped out of university after my first year. It wasn't really for me, but I couldn't just go back home, so I hung on in Newcastle where I'd been studying and I was working as a waitress—'

'In a cocktail bar? Sorry, that was awful.'

'Oh, no, nothing like that. It was a horrible little café that was open all hours of the day and night, so we got all of the drunks and junkies. And that was where I met Elijah.'

'Your husband?'

I nodded, pleased that we had skipped forward to a subject I knew I could speak on without shame. Elijah. I'd never given up on *him*.

'And was he a drunk or a junkie?'

I blushed. 'Oh certainly not,' I said, 'he was ministering to them. He'd come in and buy them a meal and sit and talk with them. I would stand there behind our horrible Formica counter and just listen to him talk, it was incredible. Eventually, he started to talk to me too, and I remember being absolutely beside myself. The other girls who worked there were so jealous, they all had a thing for him. Back then, he was so, well, he was so good. Just in every way. He took me on a date once, when we were first courting, and he bought a *Big Issue* from every seller we passed on the way from my flat to the restaurant. He cared about people. He made me feel like I was a better person just for being around him. Have you ever met anyone like that?'

'I'm not sure,' he said, when he eventually spoke.

'You would know if you had,' I said. 'Back then it would just glow off him, the good. I felt, and you might think this is silly, but I felt like I was spending time with Christ himself. He just drew people, he always knew what to say or do or ask to make someone comfortable. I've never met anyone else quite like it.'

When I stopped talking, Malcolm's face was still and serious. I had said too much, scared him off. But I couldn't help myself. It was nice to remind myself of how Elijah had been in the old days, when the weight of the world wasn't laying quite so heavily on his shoulders. When he shared his plans with me.

'And now?' he asked.

'What do you mean?'

'Twice there you said "back then". I just wondered, and you can tell me to shove off if this is too personal, what's changed?'

'Well, we don't have any homeless people in Halcyon.'

The word 'Halcyon' tasted different on my tongue when speaking it to a stranger – something I had never done before, and I must have sounded stern because Malcolm took a step backwards and shook his head. The sky overhead was turning from white to grey, and it began to drizzle.

'Sorry, Aoife, that was so rude of me. It's really none of my business. Let's talk about something else.'

And so we did. He asked me whereabouts in Ireland I was from, and told me he'd been born in Edinburgh but that his family had owned land in the Highlands for centuries. We talked for so long that by the time I was turning to leave, we were both flushed with cold and beaded with rain.

'Maybe I'll see you again soon?'

'Maybe,' I said, 'I hope so. I walk this way most days, after lunch.'

'That's good to know.' He smiled again, and I watched for the creases by his eyes. 'Oh, and Aoife? About your accounts. I'm no expert, but I find with things like that, the worst thing you can do is keep going over the same things again and again. It might help for you to try something different.'

'Thanks,' I nodded, 'I'll give that a go.'

And so, on the evening which marked four full days since Elijah had stormed out, I decided to change my approach. My fears about some possible mistake I'd made in the transcription of our accounts had kept me up the night before, and an afternoon of fruitless number crunching had left me feeling restless and fed up. I was just about to call it a day when I remembered the trouble Elijah had had in selling the old computer before we'd left the city. And I couldn't remember us leaving it in the flat with the desk and the other bits and pieces we were unable to sell or move. Which made me think that possibly, for some reason known only to him and God, Elijah had decided to bring it up to Halcyon after all. And *if* he had brought it with us, there was only one place it could possibly be – his office. As I returned all of the ledgers to their shelf, I weighed up my options. I had never been in there before, and there was an unspoken rule which put the space out of bounds for everyone but him. The possibilities turned over in my mind. On the off chance that the computer was in Elijah's office, and that he hadn't wiped the floppy disk which held our accounts, and that I was able to find where the missing money had gone, would he be pleased enough with me that he would neglect to ask how I'd found it? And if I got to his office and the computer wasn't there, he would never have to know that I had been in at all.

The more I thought about it, the happier I was with my idea. I would have to time it properly though. Ruth and Deborah didn't know that the money was missing in the first place, and even if they did, I couldn't trust them not to tell Elijah. Deborah especially would not be above using such an indiscretion to win favour with him – she was on shaky ground herself, after all. I would have to get through the evening like normal, and then find a way into the office once they were in bed.

After the lamplight of my own little office, it took my eyes a moment to adjust to the brightness of the kitchen, where a single electric bulb hung, naked, over the table. Ruth was washing her hands in the sink using a clump of Deborah's hand-made soap, while Deborah stood in front of the oven. Even with her back to me I could tell that she had cheered up slightly since the last time I had seen her; her hair was freshly plaited, and she stood a little taller than she had before.

'Hi, Aoife.' She turned her head and gave me a smile. 'You're just in time. I was just getting ready to plate up.'

Since Elijah had left, Deborah's communication had been monosyllabic at best, so I was almost surprised to hear her speaking normally again. In the interest of appearing normal myself, I forced a response.

'Lovely,' I said, wrinkling my nose while her back was turned, 'what are we having?'

I had used my lightest tone, but Deborah and Ruth exchanged a brief glance before Ruth spoke up.

'Deborah has made a barley and vegetable stew. And we have some boiled eggs, and some fresh bread.'

I rummaged through the cutlery drawer for knives and forks,

trying not to grimace. For as long as I lived, I would never ever get used to Deborah's cooking: rubbery meat; vegetables boiled until they were grey; dense, stodgy loaves. For someone so desperate to play the dream wife, she put on a poor show in the kitchen. I kept my mouth closed, though, this time around.

Ruth and I took our places at the table, and Deborah laid our plates out before us, setting mine down with a little more force than she did Ruth's. I pushed the stew around with my fork, trying to identify any of the ingredients which had gone into it.

'Thank you, Deborah, this looks delicious. Shall we say a word of thanks?'

Deborah blinked.

'Yes, let's,' said Ruth. 'Deborah, would you like to lead us?'

I gripped my knife and fork so hard that my nails dug into my palms. Deborah tossed her plait over her shoulder and gave a benevolent smile.

'For what we are about to receive, may the Lord make us truly thankful.'

'Thanks be to God and our Holy Prophet.'

As we spoke those final words together, I couldn't help but look over at the empty chair where Elijah usually sat. Where, I wondered, was our Holy Prophet now? And most importantly, what was *he* praying about?

Despite it being almost inedible, I managed to finish my meal without retching. Even without Elijah there I couldn't bear to leave a morsel on my plate; we had all learned our lesson about that the hard way. Ruth began to clear the dishes, and Deborah put the kettle on the stove to boil. Outside, I could hear John leading the rest of Halcyon in evening worship, the voices of the congregation carrying across the darkness from the warmth and light of the church. The three of us listened in silence. We should have been there ourselves, really, spending time amongst the congregation instead of sitting in the kitchen. But there we were, sipping our mugs of heather tea, not saying a word. All I had to do was wait for them both to go to bed.

Deborah was the first to break the spell when she rose from the table to fetch the sewing box.

'Does anyone have anything they need mended?' she asked.

'I do,' said Ruth, 'but I won't bother you with it. I can do my own.'

Before Deborah could say anything more, Ruth had already disappeared upstairs. She returned moments later with an armful of clothes piled so high that it almost obscured her face.

'Crikey, Ruth, you'll be on forever getting through that lot!' Deborah's eyes widened.

'I don't mind,' Ruth replied, 'I'm not tired.'

'Well, my stuff can wait. I'll help you,' said Deborah. For once I was glad of her.

'Yes,' I agreed, 'I'll help too, or you'll be mending until two in the morning.' I had no intention of waiting up that long.

Deborah and I reached into Ruth's pile of mending, ignoring her half-hearted protest. There was no clock in the kitchen, or anywhere else in Halcyon, but we must have been there for hours before we had finally worked through the lot, because it was pitch black outside and my eyes were stinging. When I stood up, my exhausted reflection stared back at me through the window. I was relieved when Ruth finally yawned and excused herself to go to bed. Deborah, though, remained seated.

'You look exhausted,' I said, 'why don't you get yourself off to bed too?'

She shrugged, but didn't move. 'I think I'm okay here for a bit. You go, though.'

I drummed my fingernails on the kitchen counter. The noise they made was the only sound in the room.

'It can't be good for the baby for you to be up this late. Go to bed.'

Deborah stared over at me, and for a moment I worried she might say no. Instead, she pushed back her chair and rose, unsteadily, to her feet. The woman really did look wrecked. She turned and left the room without saying a word.

'Goodnight,' I said, but she was already gone.

From down the hallway, I heard her bedroom door close with a bang.

Alone at last, I decided to retire to my own room for long enough to give the others a chance to fall asleep properly. The last thing I wanted was for one of them to hear me clattering about and come to investigate. My bedroom was dark and cold, and my heavy duvet looked too cosy to resist. I slipped off my shoes and slid under the covers, just to keep warm while I was waiting. Time passed, although I couldn't guess how much, and by some miracle I managed to keep myself awake. Even so, it was so difficult to leave the warmth of the bed behind that I was tempted to abandon my mission for another time. Only the threat of Elijah's impending return, which could come at any moment, gave me the motivation to leave my cocoon.

I closed the door behind me as quietly as I could. My room led straight into the deserted kitchen and I followed my instincts through the blackness towards the hall. Elijah's office was upstairs, which meant that not only did I risk waking Deborah, whose bedroom was directly next to the staircase, but also Ruth, who slept just off the landing. My stockinged feet made no noise on the hardwood floor, but I knew that the creak of a single board could give me up. Being caught in the kitchen was one thing, but it wouldn't be so easy to explain being upstairs in the middle of the night.

The farmhouse felt different in the dark. Unfamiliar and eerie. For some reason, the darkness made me feel more exposed than the light – like anyone could be watching me as I tiptoed like a child towards the one room I had never visited.

When we were young, Grainne and I had a book of fairy tales, and we would sit in her bed and read them together. She did voices better than anyone I'd ever met. We joked that she could have been on the stage. The book we shared was full of what Grainne called 'proper' stories.

'None of that Walt Disney rubbish,' she would laugh as we poured over gruesome illustrations of bleeding feet and crow-faced witches.

She liked the gory parts best. The scary parts. She could build the tension to the point that I would be clinging to her arm, white-knuckled, my knees pulled to my chest. Her favourite story, and the one she read most impressively, was 'Bluebeard'. As I walked towards Elijah's office, I could almost hear Grainne's childish voice, filled with the tantalising combination of fear and barely disguised glee, narrating my every step. It wasn't until I reached the door that I remembered the key. In the story, of course, Bluebeard gives his young wife a bundle of keys, the smallest of which opens the door to his secret room. Elijah, when he left, had given me no such gift. I had no key. I had no idea of where to find the key, and for all I knew he'd taken it with him. After all that. If I wasn't being so careful to keep quiet, I would have screamed. I reached out a hand to give the handle a dejected, frustrated rattle, but instead of stopping with the lock, my hand continued moving downward, taking the handle with it. Noiselessly, the door swung open.

I held my breath and stepped inside, half expecting to brush up against the hanging bodies of Bluebeard's murdered wives. What I did not expect to see was Deborah, her startled face illuminated by the blue-tinged light emanating from an unfamiliar computer.

Chapter Twelve

Ruth

I made my bed in the dark, tucking the loose sheets under the mattress as neatly and quietly as I could. It would have been faster to leave it, but I was feeling guilty enough and didn't want to add leaving an unmade bed to the ever-growing fog of shame which hung heavily in my head. I looked out of the window to where Mim was waiting, the white of her nightgown reflecting the moonlight like a ghost. I grabbed an extra sweater from my wardrobe for her and headed down the stairs and out the door.

'Hey,' I whispered, 'are you ready?'

'Yeah,' she said, 'all the towels and blankets and stuff are in the barn where the cows are. I wasn't sure where to leave them.'

The cattle barn was probably not the most suitable place; it was too open and exposed though the day.

'That's okay. We can find somewhere quieter together. I don't want to disturb the cows.'

Even with the moonlight it was difficult to make her out properly, but I thought I could see her nod. We walked side by side, as close as we could be without touching, along the worn dirt path between the farmhouse and the barn. It was a quiet night, and with every step something seemed to crunch underfoot. Even our breathing, shallow and nervous, seemed deafeningly loud to my sound-starved ears. It wasn't until that moment, surrounded by darkness halfway between the house and the barn, that I realised what a dumb thing it was that we were doing. Not even just dumb. It was a sin. I thought about how poor Aoife and Deborah had ended up helping with my big pile of mending, the pile I had brought down to give me an excuse to stay up until I could be sure they had gone to bed, and felt like the most awful person in the world. And if that wasn't bad enough, I would have to keep this secret from them, and from Elijah, for goodness knows how long. It wasn't even as though we'd had the good sense to make a proper plan. If I was the type of woman to curse, I would have cursed then. As it was, I gritted my teeth and kept on, slowly, carefully, towards the barn.

The whole mess had started when Elijah left. I had slept badly that night, tossing and turning so much that when I woke my sheets were tangled around me and my hair was damp with sweat. I had been raised in the firm belief that everything would look better in the morning, but when the three of us gathered around the kitchen table for breakfast without him, everything just seemed much worse. At the time we should have been filing down the hall for temple, Aoife and Deborah took off for work as though they didn't even notice there was a huge chunk missing from our morning. I sat in the empty temple room alone and closed my eyes, pretending that we were all there together in silent prayer. Even though I left the farmhouse at the same time I always did, and sat in my usual seat for church, the whole day was off. John delivered the sermon, but I found it hard to concentrate on what he was saying. I spent the service picking at a hangnail on my thumb and casting occasional glances at Deborah. Her hair looked as though it hadn't been brushed, and she had heavy purple bags under her eyes. She was looking up at John, fixing him with a dull, unblinking stare.

Once everyone was dismissed, I headed straight to the cattle barn. The scent, thick and sweet, calmed me from the very second that I stepped inside, and I took my time greeting each cow, patting their soft brown necks and looking into their big wise eyes. We kept three cows, big, beautiful Jerseys, but only two of them were giving milk at the moment. The oldest, who I took the most time with, had stopped producing several months ago and would most likely be slaughtered by Christmas, and when the next lot of calves were born we would not sell them all, like we usually did, but keep one to replace her. The methodical process of milking soothed me further, and by the time I was done I had almost convinced myself that Elijah would be back before the day was out if only I could follow our normal routine and keep on as though nothing was the matter. I reminded myself that Elijah often left Halcyon alone to do missionary work, although then he always said when he would be back. And he never stormed out.

Even though the milking was finished, I was still perched on my wooden stool with my head pressed against the cow's warm stomach when Mim arrived. She announced her entrance with a gentle knock on the lintel of the barn door, and I jumped to my feet, startling the cow in the process. Mim flushed and looked away. It took me a second to realise that she was not going to speak first.

'Can I help you?' My words sounded blunt, but I was too flustered to try and soften them with any sort of follow-up.

'Helen sent me over. We've run out of milk in the schoolhouse. It got spilled. And now there's none, and we were wanting to get prepared for lunch.' She looked down at her feet as she spoke, and her voice was so soft that I had to strain to hear her.

I looked at my pail, which was still full of milk.

'You can take this,' I said, 'will it be enough?'

Mim leaned forward from her place in the doorway, but her feet remained stuck to the floor. Really, I should have taken the bucket to her so she could examine it properly – I could see that she was nervous – but I always took personal offence when people were frightened of the cows and I wanted to show her that there was nothing to be scared of. I beckoned her in with my free hand, and reluctantly she came forward, keeping as far away from the animals as she could. Eventually, she was close enough to peer into the bucket.

'I think so,' she said.

Her eyes darted nervously from cow to cow, and they looked back curiously. I'd never had very much to do with cattle at all until we came to Halcyon, other than seeing them from a distance or maybe on TV. Their gentleness had surprised me. I had thought that they would be dopey, bovine being an insult as far as I was concerned, but it hardly took me any time at all to figure out that they had their own little quirks, and that they were friendly and sweet. Eventually, I came to see them as big, gentle dogs.

'They like you,' I said.

Mim looked unconvinced and wrinkled her freckled nose.

'Look,' I put the heavy milk pail down on the ground and stepped closer to the oldest cow, who was tethered to her post, 'look how interested they are in you.'

They were lined up together, blinking gently at us with

their thick lashes. Mim didn't respond but she did inch towards them, gingerly.

'I always think they look like genteel old British ladies,' I said, looking at the cows instead of Mim, 'as though they should be wearing flowery straw hats.'

By her silence, I could tell that she remained unconvinced. I turned to look at her, and she made a polite face.

'I guess I must have got the idea from a movie or something.'

Once I said it, I realised that Mim would never have seen a movie, and that her frame of reference for them would have come from one of Elijah's sermons. Fortunately, the comment seemed to go right over her head.

'Do they bite?'

'No,' I said, 'no, they're very sweet natured.'

She reached out a tentative hand and laid it on the neck of the youngest cow, the one I had delivered myself.

'It's quite pretty,' she said. 'Are they boys or girls?'

At first, I thought she might have been trying to make a joke, but when I looked at her face I could tell that she was completely serious.

'They're all girls,' I said, 'that's how we get the milk from them.'

She gave a serious nod. 'They look like girls.'

I wasn't sure what else to say, and really I just wanted her to leave so I could get them out to pasture. I was trying to come up with a tactful way to end the conversation when we were interrupted by the clacking of Russell's little feet on the concrete floor. She was a common fixture in the barn because it was her job to keep the rats away from the feed and I was used to her being there, but her arrival startled Mim, who pulled her hand away from the cow with a jerk. I had no idea how someone who lived on a farm could be so jumpy around animals.

'It's just Russell,' I said, bending down to nearer the dog's level. She waddled towards me.

'Russell?' Mim's voice betrayed her surprise. 'It has a *name*?'

My stomach turned over. Russell's name was not general knowledge in Halcyon. I fought the temptation to babble. *Play it cool*, I thought, *what would Aoife do?*

'Yeah,' I said, 'she does.'

That seemed to be enough for Mim, who had now turned her attention fully from the cows to the dog.

'Is there something wrong with her?'

It was a fair question. She was pacing up and down the barn, looking for a place to settle, and letting out a small, low whine. Even when I patted my thigh to call her over, she kept her distance, turning in circles as if she was about to lie down, and then picking herself up again and moving to a different spot. She was a pitiful sight.

'She's carrying a litter,' I explained, 'she might be getting ready to start whelping soon.'

'Whelping?'

'Having her pups,' I said.

'Oh!' Mim suddenly looked properly interested for the first time. 'Can I help?'

'Well, she's not having them right this moment,' I paused and took a closer look at Russell, who had finally curled up on a pile of hay, 'or I don't think she is.'

We were both kneeling down to get a better look at the dog when there came another knock on the wall of the barn. I turned to see Helen standing in the doorway. Mim turned too. As soon as she saw who it was, she shot to her feet.

'Mim! You're still here!' Helen's voice startled Russell, who raised her little head in weary surprise.

Mim stood there, silently staring at her feet.

'I'm sorry, Helen,' the sound of my own voice took me by surprise, 'this is my fault.'

'Oh no, Ruth, please don't apologise. I just wanted to make sure that Jemima wasn't bothering you. Jemima... do you think you might have taken up enough of Sister Ruth's time this morning?'

After that, things went back to normal very quickly. Mim collected the pail and followed Helen back to the schoolhouse. I finished my brief examination of Russell, and when I was satisfied that her pups weren't going to arrive any time in the next couple of hours, I got back to my work. I didn't even think about Mim again until the next morning, when she followed me to the barn after church. Before I could even ask her what she was doing there, she burst out:

'I just wanted to check on the dog.'

'Does Helen know you're here?'

Mim shook her head so vehemently that the two plaits which hung down by her ears lifted into the air.

'Look,' I said, 'I don't want to get you in any trouble.' I also didn't want to get *myself* into any trouble, but I thought it might be best not to say that part out loud.

'You won't, I promise.'

Famous last words. By this time, Russell had taken herself off into a quiet corner of the barn, and after some close inspection I predicted that she would be ready to have her litter later that day.

'Can you come and get me when she does?' Mim asked.

She didn't look at me when she spoke, but this time she wasn't staring at her feet; instead, she was looking right into Russell's face, their noses almost touching. For someone who had jumped at the sight of the dog the day before, she certainly had warmed to her.

'Dogs usually don't have their pups during the day,' I said, 'a bit like ladies. They tend to come along in the middle of the night.'

She looked up at me, crestfallen.

'Well, honey, I won't be here either. She'll just have them on her own.'

Mim's mouth fell open. 'On her own?' There was more emotion in her voice than I had ever heard there before.

'Honey, she's a dog. It's not like a human giving birth. Dogs are made to do this sort of thing without any help.'

I couldn't help it; my mind turned to Aoife ten years before, sitting in the living room of her and Elijah's flat, squatting with her back to the wall as I counted her contractions. It was wintertime, and Elijah had just returned from church. I could feel the cold radiating from him, smell the sharp freshness of outside which clung to his coat.

'How is everything progressing?' he asked, glancing at his labouring wife.

It touched me to see his vulnerability. He usually wore his confidence like a second skin.

'Perfectly,' I said. 'Textbook.'

Aoife looked up at us with a weary smile, 'What can I say? I know what I'm doing.' She closed her eyes for a moment, and I noted the time on my pad. 'So does Ruth.'

'How many babies have you delivered, Sister Ruth?' Elijah asked, 'I'm sure I've asked you this before.'

I could see his confidence was returning, and he looked me straight in the eyes as he spoke. This was a habit of his which I was still getting used to, and it sent a rush of hot blood to my cheeks. I lowered my gaze.

'Oh,' I said, busying myself with the contents of my medical bag, 'too many to count! Plenty.'

'More than one, then?' he smiled.

I nodded.

'Well, Aoife, she trumps you, so make sure you pay attention,' he said. 'I just called back to check in on you both, I have to run back to the church. Before I go, Sister Ruth, can I speak to you for a second?'

Aoife rolled her eyes and smiled at me as I followed Elijah into the corridor. I enjoyed being called Sister Ruth, not in the medical sense, but in the religious sense. I liked the idea that in God's eyes, the church of Heaven on Earth was one big family.

Once we were alone, his jovial attitude disappeared. The mood in the living room had been one of eager anticipation and nervous excitement, but out in the dim light of the hallway things felt more serious. Suddenly, I was very conscious that I had only officially completed my midwifery training the year before, and that this was my first delivery outside of the hospital. He ran a hand through his dark hair and shook his head gently. I allowed myself to make eye contact with him.

'I can't tell you how much I appreciate this, Ruth, your presence here is a real blessing. And I know that Aoife appreciates it too, despite her bravado.'

I felt my cheeks grow hot and my breath come out short. I think I must have been a little in love with him, even then.

'We have every faith in you, and your confidence is very reassuring.' He paused. 'However, I realise you're still new to our church and our life, so I feel I need to be very clear about what we need from you.'

'Sure,' I said. 'I mean, of course.'

'You know our beliefs. We follow God, and we turn away from what is not Godly. There are many things in this world that go against our teachings, including those in charge.'

I nodded, unsure where this impromptu sermon was leading.

'And you know that nobody outside of the church knows that Aoife is pregnant. No midwives, no doctors, not a soul. That can't change, Ruth, no matter what happens here tonight. I need this baby to live free, free from government tracking and Western medicine and the whole nightmare – I need to do that for him, I need to give him that gift. So hospital is not an option.'

He looked at me searchingly, waiting for me to say that I understood, holding my gaze.

'I understand.'

Elijah smiled and left. When I opened the door to the living room of their small flat, I saw Aoife, my patient, pacing in front of the window. Imposed against the darkness of the night outside, she looked even whiter than normal. Her fine black hair was plastered to her forehead with sweat. Her eyes were the very lightest blue I'd ever seen. I was only twenty-two at the time, so she couldn't have been much more than twenty-four or twenty-five, but she was my hero and I wanted to be just like her: Godly and beautiful.

When I entered the room, she looked straight across at me.

'Did he tell you about the hospital?' she asked.

'Yeah.'

I was still overwhelmed, both by my responsibility and how close I was to Aoife. This was the longest time we had ever spent together. I tried not to let it show in my voice.

'Who needs hospitals? We have everything we need right here.'

She smiled. 'That's what I like to hear. Oh, and Ruth?' but before she could speak, Aoife was interrupted by a contraction. My training eclipsed my nerves, and I imagined that I was in an ordinary delivery room, with trained professionals with years and years of experience waiting just outside the door.

Once the surge of pain was over and she had regained the ability to speak, she picked up from where she had been forced to leave off.

'Ruth, I want to apologise about before, if you thought I was being proud. I certainly didn't mean to suggest that I was as experienced as you. I only meant... Well, I only said it, because last time it was just me by myself, and I managed all right. Not that I'm not grateful for you being here, Ruth, you're a blessing...'

Back in the barn, Mim spoke again.

'But she's so little!' There was no petulance in her voice, no hint of a whine, which I appreciated.

I looked down at Russell. She really did look very small, lying there in her nest of hay.

'Okay,' I sighed, 'if she starts through the day I'll come and fetch you.'

'And if it happens at night?'

I deliberated for a second, but only a second. 'And if she's not started by the time I'm finishing up for the day, we can come check on her in the night.'

Mim let out a squeal of delight, and then immediately covered her mouth with her hand. Her reaction took me by surprise. I guess I thought it was a bit childish, although I really shouldn't have been shocked at that. She *was* a child. Gleefully, she planted a kiss on Russell's head and made her exit. For the rest of the day I kept a close eye on the dog. She paced and whined, but when I examined her I saw nothing that indicated the imminent arrival of her litter.

That was how I ended up walking in silence with Mim by my side, too frightened to even turn on my torch while we were still outside, towards the barn in the middle of the night. By the time we arrived, Russell was lying flat on her side, four tiny wriggling pups suckling at her teats in the torchlight.

'We missed it!' Mim's disappointed whisper filled the barn.

I was too busy kneeling at Russell's side to respond, trying to feel her stomach as gently as I could to make sure she was all done. 'What a clever girl you are,' I whispered. She turned her tired eyes up to meet mine. I wished all the labours I was responsible for went this smoothly.

I could feel Mim close behind me, her breathing loud by my ear.

'What do we do now?'

I gritted my teeth. Mim, who had once been so quiet, so reluctant to talk, to make a pest of herself, was suddenly hanging on to me like a little lost puppy. The irony was not lost on me, but I wanted to stand up and shake her off. Instead, I took a deep breath.

'Now we need to take her out for some air, so she can... potty. And then we need to move them all somewhere a bit out of the way, so they can rest up.'

'Oh, they're so *sweet*! I wonder if Elijah would maybe let us give them names too, like Russell?'

She clearly hadn't listened to a word I had said, but that wasn't what made me stand up so suddenly. At the mention of Elijah's name, it was as though an icy finger had touched my spine and turned my entire body cold. Even Elijah's absence could not make me forget a very frustrating and very relevant conversation we had had when I'd first discovered that Russell was carrying a litter. He had been adamant, then, that we did not have reason to keep an entire litter of pups, nor did we have the resources to feed them. He said we could keep just one. All of this had been before his decision to cut us off from the outside world, so I had assumed we would sell the puppies to someone in Abercraig when the time came. Now, though, I had no idea what he would want to do with them. I looked at Mim, who was carefully scooping water from the cows' trough into her small pale hand and carrying it across to Russell, who lapped at it gratefully. *Shit*, I thought, *shit shit shit.*

Chapter Thirteen

Deborah

It wasn't as though I hadn't thought of going into Elijah's office before. I don't know of anyone who could live in a house with a locked door and not wonder what was behind it, but for a long time I was the sort of person who could resist a lot for the sake of a simple life. I would walk past that locked door every time I went to clean upstairs, never going in, because the only way I could imagine life in Halcyon being much worse was if I actively went against Elijah's wishes.

Still, even though Elijah was a clever man, at times scarily quick and intelligent, when it came to hiding places he was almost disappointingly unimaginative. I found the ring which held the spare office key while clearing out his underwear drawer, tucked inside a balled-up pair of woollen socks in a chest of drawers on the upstairs landing, outside Ruth's bedroom and just along from his office. That was just a few months after we'd settled in Halcyon. It took me all of two seconds' thought to figure out what the key was for, but I dutifully returned it to its hiding spot. I can see now how idiotic I was being, but things were very different in those days. I was newly married, and even if I didn't necessarily *love* Elijah, I certainly cared enough to respect his privacy. My mother had been completely devoted to him, and I was still looking at him through her eyes. It was for the sake of her memory that I decided to believe that he had nothing to hide, because for her, he could do no wrong.

When I was seventeen years old, my mother took ill in our flat. We had only just moved in, and she had been tired and sick since the landlord – one of the men from the church – handed over her keys.

'Bloody typical,' she had said from the bathroom floor as I unpacked our things. Heaven on Earth had done a big donation drive for us, and I was suddenly in possession of more stuff than I ever had owned in my life before.

'Are you okay in there? You're missing out on all the fun.'

I entered the bathroom, a reinforced shopping bag of towels and loo rolls and toiletries in hand, just in time to see her empty her guts into the avocado toilet bowl.

Three days later, when Elijah called round to put up some shelves, she was lying in bed. I'd never really spoken to Elijah outside of church before. He was in his thirties and strict, and he scared me a little bit, with his heavy dark eyebrows and stern, unsmiling eyes. Still, I was glad to see him.

'I think there's something really wrong with her,' I said. We were standing outside her bedroom door, so I kept my voice low. 'She's been sick so much even her skin looks weird. She's hardly eaten anything since we moved.' Elijah left his toolbox on the floor and knocked gently.

'Cheryl? It's me. Deborah says you're under the weather. May I come in?'

There was a little murmur from inside the room, and I pushed the door open.

My mother had always been a skinny woman, but three days of illness had turned her into a skeleton. Her skin, usually pale, had taken on a yellowish tinge. She hadn't seemed so bad until Elijah had got there – it was only now that I saw her through his eyes that I realised what a state she was in. Sensing his shock, I felt like a kid again, standing next to a social worker and noticing, suddenly, just how bad things were.

Elijah took my arm and guided me gently back into the hall.

'Has your landline been installed yet?'

I nodded.

'Good,' he said, 'because I think you need to phone an ambulance.'

I had sat through enough church services to know that Elijah did not trust hospitals. For him to say we needed an ambulance, meant this must be serious.

Elijah sat by my side at the hospital that day as the doctors ran tests on my mother. When a nurse or doctor questioned if we both needed to be there, he shut them down straight away.

'This girl is a child,' he said, 'she can't be expected to do this on her own.'

The day ran on, and every so often when it seemed like it might be about time to eat, Elijah would excuse himself and return with food – sandwiches, crisps, scalding cups of soup from vending machines.

'Look at all this shit,' he said, pointing at the list of ingredients on the back of the sandwich box, 'no wonder everyone in this place is ill.'

By the time the evening staff came on shift, we had started to talk. He asked me about what it was like living with my mother again after so long, and I actually answered him. At first, I did it because it felt like I owed him something for being so good to us, but then the words kept on coming and soon I had told him everything – what it had been like growing up with her, then being moved around, never feeling quite at home anywhere. He nodded and listened. By the time I had finished my throat was hoarse from talking and exhaustion.

'Why don't you try and get some sleep? I'll wake you if there's any news.'

I shut my eyes against the harsh fluorescent hospital light and leaned my head back against the wall. When I woke up a few hours later, it was resting on his shoulder.

There was nothing the doctors could do about her kidneys, but Elijah had done something irreversible for her soul that night and she saw him as more of a saviour than ever before. His most loyal disciple, she would say over and over: 'This is what a really good man looks like, Debbie. I can't believe it took me forty years to meet one.' She'd say it after services, when he dropped her to the hospital for dialysis, whilst watching him play with his kids in the park next to the church hall. Her final words to me had been about him. How she was sorry she wouldn't get to be at our wedding, and how happy she had been to see us engaged. 'I know he'll keep you safe, pet.'

Now, when things got worse in Halcyon, I would return to the key. I would hold it in my hands, the cold metal acting as a reminder that if things got bad, like *really* bad, I would be able to use it. There were days when I was tempted, once or twice I even got as far as slipping the key into the lock, but I never turned it, never touched the door handle. Things were bad, but never really bad. Never as bad as they'd been before, not even as bad as the stuff I'd grown up watching on telly. Yeah, everything I did was an act, but I was safe in Halcyon. My kids might have been living in a different building and might not understand I was their mam, but I got to see them every day. And maybe some days Elijah scared me, but he never smacked me about or screamed at me. If I went in, I'd have to admit that things had got bad enough that I was ready to go against him, to step away from Halcyon and Heaven on Earth and everything I had there. Which was everything I had at all.

As soon as I left the schoolhouse, I felt the pull of the spare key calling me. All I could think of was putting one foot in front of the other on the hard, frosty earth, and making my way to its hiding place. Halcyon was waking up around me, but I was too focussed on my goal to stop and talk to the people leaving their caravans. I didn't even bother to look in on the kitchen to check if Aoife and Ruth were there before heading up the stairs. If I had ever wavered at the thought of entering the office in past, that fear was gone. Once my mind was made up, my only worry was whether or not Elijah would have thought to take the key with him, wherever he had gone. The original was worn on a loop on his belt, along with the keys to all of Halcyon's other locks, and if his departure had been as unplanned as it had seemed, he surely wouldn't have thought to take the spare one with him. I held my breath as I pulled open the drawer, but at first glance things seemed hopeful – the neatly folded rows of underwear and balled up socks looked undisturbed from the last time I had tidied them, which made me think that Elijah hadn't had a rifle through before leaving. The socks I was looking for were always kept in the same place, pushed up against the far right corner. I didn't even need to look; my hand knew exactly what to feel for. I would be able to recognise the exact shape, the particular bristle of the fibres, if I was blindfolded. And there they were, exactly where I had left them, an innocent looking woolly bundle containing, quite literally, the key to everything.

I moved as if I was in a dream, slowly and purposefully unrolling the socks and slipping the key out and into my hand. I was at the office door, key poised by the lock, when the front door banged open. *That's him,* I thought, *he's back.* My heart hammered so fiercely that it ached, and I worried that I would have a heart attack and collapse on the spot. The protective aura of my pregnancy would not be enough to save me from Elijah's wrath if he found me there. The rules had been changed, after all, the second he had lobbed a plate at my head. The key was back in its rightful place before I knew where I was, panic making the time skip.

'Elijah?' I called down the stairs, clinging on to the banister to stop myself falling, 'Elijah, is that you?'

Did my voice give me away? Would he know as soon as he heard it that I'd been up to no good? I listened out for his response, planning my excuses for being upstairs, rehearsing what I'd say when I saw him.

'No,' came the reply, 'sorry Deborah, honey, it's just me.'

Ruth. Not Elijah. Just Ruth. Just lovely Ruth. I felt the hard floor under me as I sat down heavily on the top step, one hand still clinging to the banister, the other gripping my head.

I don't know what I hoped to find inside the locked office, the inner sanctum, the Holy of Holies. Throughout the day my brain swam with possibilities – piles of Bibles, stacks of girlie mags, files of boring legal documents – but I didn't really care. I wasn't going in there to find anything specific; all I wanted and needed was one less secret in my life. The chance to take away a little bit of Elijah's power, to put my disobedient thoughts into action, so that I didn't lose myself completely. The thought of it thrilled me so much that I spent the whole day on a knife-edge, my brain too jittery to settle on a single thought or task. Every time someone turned to look at something behind me, I thought Elijah must be standing there. After he delivered the church service, John told us that he had an announcement, and when it didn't relate to Elijah at all, just the new bunking arrangements for the caravans, I let out an actual sigh of relief. When Aoife came in late for tea, I worried that she was caught up in talking to him, that they would stroll in together, hand in hand. I became so convinced that Elijah would be coming back that evening that I even prepared enough food for four. Through the scraping of plates and the chewing of food, I listened out for the noise of the gate opening or the car pulling in. By the time we finished eating I couldn't sit still any more. I lifted the kettle onto the hob, boiling water for cups of heather tea that nobody had asked for, worried that the whistling of the steam would cover up any sounds that might warn me of his return.

After hours and hours and the latest night the three of us had had in a long time, Aoife pushed her pile of mending to the side and told me to go to bed, almost like she knew what I was going to do and wanted to stop me. I could have stood my ground and told her no, but I didn't want to raise suspicion. If I started talking back, she would notice and remember, and she would suspect something was going on. Also, I'm not ashamed to say that a big part of me was properly frightened of Aoife. As she towered over me, arms folded, eyes bloodshot with exhaustion, I did not fancy my chances. And so I took myself into my bedroom and changed into my nightdress, not even daring to make my usual journey to the outhouse and using my chamber pot instead. I stopped short of actually getting into bed, though. Instead, I waited until I was sure that everyone was safely turned in for the night, and made my way carefully upstairs.

I gripped the banister tightly, waiting until both feet were firmly planted on the bare wood before taking another step, counting my way up. My biggest risk at this point, other than Elijah suddenly coming home and deciding to go straight upstairs or to my bedroom, was Ruth. Of the three of us she was the only one who slept up there, and I knew that she was a light sleeper. She could step out at any time and she'd find me where I had no right to be. As risks went, this one didn't worry me too much. Although the chances of Ruth finding me were fairly high, she was the sort of person who only cared to see the good in others. I imagined that if she saw me looming over Elijah's sleeping body, brandishing a butcher's knife, she would wait patiently for me to explain myself and then nod and leave me to it. She and Aoife were also barely speaking, which made it unlikely that she would grass me up the next day. There *was* the chance that concern for my wellbeing would lead her to tell Elijah, if he ever came back, but I would cross that bridge if I came to it.

I stopped outside Ruth's door, my ears straining to hear anything other than the sound of my heart slamming into my chest at double time. When I was as satisfied as I could be that she was sleeping I allowed myself to slide the drawer open, lifting it up from its mount to avoid the sound of wood sliding against wood. I kept the key inside the sock until I reached the office door, frightened that my shaking hand would drop it and wake Ruth. The keyring held one key and a flimsy plastic crucifix charm. The darkness and my shaking hand made me miss the keyhole so many times that by the time I finally felt the key slot in I could feel tears of frustration and relief stinging my eyes. The heavy metallic click of the turning lock echoed in the hallway and I froze, ready for Ruth's door to creak open. For a second, the absolute madness of the situation hit me. I didn't let myself get caught up in that madness for too long, though – it was a thread I didn't want to pull, and anyway, I had other things to worry about.

Opening the door was an anti-climax because the room was almost as dark as the hallway had been; the milky half-light cast by the full moon was barely bright enough to penetrate the glass in the window, let alone illuminate anything of interest inside. I closed the door gently behind me and leaned against the sturdy wood while my eyes adjusted. Before too long, some familiar shapes began to emerge from the gloom. A filing cabinet. A chair. A desk. Something else, resting on the desk, a frame? A box? I took a step closer, careful not to lift my feet too far from the ground in case I tripped. It wasn't until I was right on top of it that I could see what it was, and I had to reach out and touch it to be sure. It seemed to be a computer, but nothing like any computer I had seen in real life before. It was slim, and there was no big boxy hard drive. I felt its edges. It didn't even seem to have a mouse attached. It was only then that I realised it wasn't a proper computer, of the sort we had had in the labs when I was at school, but a portable laptop with its lid open. Taking the greatest care not to scrape the legs against the floor, I pulled out the chair and sat down. I felt the baby turning somersaults in my belly. Computers were not my area of expertise, fancy new computers in the dark even less so. Hell, it had been about ten years since I had sat at a desk. I ran my hand lightly across its surface, searching for something that felt like an 'on' button. It must have been much more sensitive than any machine I had used at school, because I barely grazed a little indentation at the top of the keyboard when the whole thing sprang to life. All at once the room was bathed in electric light from the screen, and a tinny tune burst from some concealed speaker. My heart leapt into my throat and stayed there long after the sound had stopped. A blue screen told me that it was 00:17. I couldn't even think when I had last known what the exact time was. It felt strange to remember that we shared a world with people who might need to know that it was precisely seventeen minutes past midnight, and that once upon a time, when I had lived in a world of buses and metro trains and appointments instead of chickens and babies and prayers, I had been that kind of person myself.

The keyboard glowed invitingly, but the lack of a mouse had thrown me and I wasn't sure how I was supposed to actually get the thing to work. I was still deciding what to do next when the door creaked open.

Chapter Fourteen

Aoife

I couldn't even begin to guess how long we stayed there in silence, blinking at each other in the near darkness. It was as though what was happening was too strange, too unlikely, for either of us to comprehend it, and so we had to wait for our brains to catch up. When the silence was finally broken, it was because we both spoke at once.

'This is ridiculous. I'm turning on the light.'

'You were supposed to be in bed.'

Even though I knew she couldn't see me, I shook my head and pressed my hand to my temple. I didn't know what to say, so I felt along the wall for a switch, certain that Elijah had thought to have the room wired with electric lights. The darkness heightened my senses, and the cold of the stone travelled from my fingertips and into my core. I was glad the light was still off, so Deborah couldn't see me shiver. My hand found the switch-box, unmistakably smooth and hard and plastic, jutting out of the wall. I knew that as soon as I flicked the switch, the situation would go from an absurd dream, from which I could wake at any time, to something very real. It was as though I was about to skim a pebble into a still and quiet lake, without any way of knowing how far the ripples in the water would spread, or what the pebble might hit on its way down.

'I thought you said you were going to switch the light on.' She was whispering, but I could hear something in her voice that I had never noticed there before. Fear, maybe? Or defiance.

Before she could say anything more, I turned on the light. The switch turned out to be attached to a single bulb which hung bare and dim in the centre of the room, directly above Elijah's desk. And above Deborah, who was perched as daintily as a pregnant woman could perch on the edge of a high-backed leather chair. Her mouth hung open as if she had been about to say something more before deciding against it. She had changed clothes since I'd seen her last, into a long flannel nightgown much like my own, and her hair was loose, its blonde waves crimped into the shape of the plaits she had been wearing all day. I had waited years to see what was in that room, but all I could see was her.

'I can't believe it.'

'Look, Aoife, I'm really sorry...' her voice cracked as she spoke, and she shook her head as though she was in disagreement with the whole situation.

'Shut up,' I snapped. 'Just shut up.'

I knew I had spoken too loudly, but as soon as Deborah widened her eyes and drew her finger to her lips to shush me, a vicious heat rose inside me. I could feel it colouring my cheeks, which prickled like flames. I stepped towards her and slammed my hands onto the desk. She winced.

'How *dare* you? How *dare* you tell me to lower my voice? How dare you tell me what to do *at all*?!' Despite my protest and my rage, I was careful to keep my voice to a whisper. Even so, I must have frightened Deborah, because she curled into herself, drawing her hands around her swollen stomach on instinct. That made me even angrier, and I leaned in further, until I was as close to her as I could get without climbing onto the desk. 'What are you flinching for? You think I'm going to hit you? I'm not going to hit you! Sit up properly and get a grip on yourself!' Tears were starting to burn the back of my eyes, and I banged the desk again. My palms stung.

The sound of my hand hitting the wood must have stirred something in Deborah, because she rose up out of the chair and looked me straight in the eye as she spoke.

'You must be kidding?' she asked, 'Why wouldn't I think that? Bashing around, shouting on. You're definitely bloody acting like someone who wants to hit me.'

'Really?' I said, 'Well, I'm not going to. So, stop acting like a baby, and start explaining yourself.'

I tried to prepare myself for what she was about to say, but I couldn't imagine what Elijah had been thinking when he decided to let her in there instead of me. What little plan could they have been brewing together?

'Please don't tell Elijah.'

I had not prepared myself for that. I stared at her, silently, waiting for her to go on. It didn't take long, and when she started speaking, it was as though she might never stop.

'I found the spare key in the drawer. I found it ages ago. I'm sorry. I just wanted to see what was inside, and it had to be tonight, because I don't know when he'll be home, and I just couldn't go any longer not knowing. And I don't know what's going to happen when he gets back. I'm so sorry, Aoife, I don't know what else to say, I'm so sorry.'

Finally, she fell silent. It was like she had just run out of words. She looked stunned, as if she couldn't quite believe what she had said. I couldn't believe it either.

'He doesn't know you're here?' I asked, hardly daring to hope that I had understood her correctly.

'No,' she said. 'Please don't tell him.'

My face must have given something away, or maybe she just put two and two together based on the surprise in my voice, but it looked like the reality of the situation had begun to dawn on her too.

'He doesn't know you're here either, does he?' she asked.

I shook my head. There was no point in lying. I could tell that, like me, she was trying to think of what this meant for the both of us. I was still toying with the possibility that she was hiding the truth from me when she let out a peal of hysterical laughter.

Then it was my turn to put my finger to my lips. She had looked ashen before, but all of a sudden there was colour in her face. She sat back down in the chair with a heavy *thump* and leaned back so she was looking at the ceiling. I stared in disbelief as her entire body shook with the effort of keeping the laughter in.

I hardly knew what to say. This frenzied, trembling woman in the chair in front of me was not the Deborah I knew. Where was her infuriating calmness? Her serene piety? I put my hands to my hips and tried to keep some authority in my voice.

'I don't know what you think is so funny! You look like you're having a fit!'

She heaved herself forwards, gripping on to the arms of the chair, until she was sitting upright. With a trembling hand, she wiped tears of mirth from her eyes.

'Oh, drop it, Aoife!' She had stopped laughing, but it was as though the laughter had left a trace of itself behind and it lingered in her voice. She went on, 'You can drop the act now. We're both just as bad as each other. You don't have a leg to stand on any more with that attitude.'

She was right, really. We were both sneaking around our house in the middle of the night, going behind our husband's back. Still, I wasn't ready to give up all of my authority. We were there in that room together, yes, but one of us had to be in charge, and by God and His Holy Prophet, that person was going to be me.

I cast my eyes around the room, looking for some inspiration. It was small and dark, even with the glow of the electric blub and the computer screen, and had the dank, cloying smell of damp. The walls had obviously been plastered once, but this had flaked and crumbled to reveal great patches of dark stone. On the wall behind the desk there was a large map of what appeared to be Halcyon, and the other two walls were lined with homemade shelves – the sort you put together when you're a skint student and all you have are a few planks of wood and some bricks. The shelves themselves were bursting with books, their spines turned inwards. Ordinarily, the books would have been my first port of call, but there was something else that drew my attention even more, and that I was desperate to explore. Something that made up for the ordinariness of Elijah's cell. His laptop.

'What have you found so far?' I asked, gesturing towards it.

Deborah shook her head. 'Nothing. Nothing yet. I don't even know how to use it.'

I could feel the smugness in my smile.

'Let me try.'

I made my way around the desk to where Deborah was sitting, and together we looked at the blue screen, on which the time had just changed to 00:30. She turned to look at me expectantly.

'It doesn't have a mouse,' she said. 'And the screen looked different before.'

I leaned forward and touched the tracker pad with a tentative finger. It had been such a long time since I had touched something like that, not since I'd left university fourteen years before, and it felt cool and artificial against my skin. The screen with the clock disappeared and was replaced by a cluttered desktop. Deborah looked impressed, and I tried my best to conceal my pride.

'Easy,' I said, 'look, look at all this stuff.'

'What is it all?' Deborah asked, squinting at the screen.

'Let's find out.' I clicked on a document called 'Timeline FINAL' and held my breath.

A little grey box popped up on the screen.

'Please insert removable drive D,' Deborah sounded the words slowly and deliberately.

'Thanks, Deborah, I can read,' I snapped.

This was not supposed to happen. He was not supposed to have a load of secret files stored on a secret laptop in a locked room. We were supposed to be a team. I was meant to be his *wife*. Halcyon had been *our* dream, *our* project. And now, clearly, it was just his. And where did that leave me? I no longer cared about the missing money, no longer wanted to win back his trust. It was too late. The realisation didn't enrage me the way I thought it might. Instead, it hollowed me out and brought a sinking emptiness which made my chest ache.

Deborah raised her eyebrows, but all she said was, 'What's "removable drive D"?'

I didn't answer. Instead, I tried another file. 'Strategy_optA'. What the hell was that supposed to be?

'It's just saying the same thing again,' said Deborah, pointing at the box which had popped up again on the screen, 'that removable drive D thing. What's that? Do we have one of those?'

I tried another, and another. I tried every file which I could see on the desktop, and for each one, the same message appeared.

'It must be the floppy disk,' I said, weakly, feeling around the sides of the machine for a slot, 'or a CD-ROM. Or something.' But I couldn't feel anything the right size or shape.

'Well,' said Deborah, 'should we have a look in the drawers?'

Elijah's desk had three deep drawers, all of which were locked. Deborah pulled and rattled each one hopelessly and then swore under her breath.

The desk was a cheap, lightweight one, and if we had really wanted to, we could have broken the lock with a few sharp blows, but then there would be no hiding what we had done.

'What do we do now?' she asked.

But I was one step ahead of her. I clicked the familiar blue 'e', the only other button I recognised, and said a silent prayer. If I couldn't read any of his files, the least I could do was try to get on the internet, maybe take a look at his search history. I knew it was a long shot, and to be perfectly honest I had no idea how I thought it was going to work. There was no wire attached to the laptop, and I couldn't see a router box anywhere. If I really thought about it, I would have realised that we had never had anyone come to install any such thing, but I was determined and practically giddy at the prospect of connecting with the outside world. The time might have passed for me to please Elijah, but now I was even more determined to drag him down.

A blank webpage appeared. I had expected it, but that didn't stop the disappointment winding me like a blow to the chest. I was just about ready to close the machine and take a look around the rest of the room when Deborah raised her finger to the screen again, this time pointing at a little icon in the bottom right corner.

'What's that?' she asked. 'That one there, that looks like a signal with a cross through? Is that something?'

I clicked on it.

'Look,' said Deborah, leaning close to read what was on the screen, 'it's got an internet thing, a connection or whatever! That bit that says, "portable Wi-Fi network". Click on it!'

'No,' I said, 'that's just what the laptop has connected to before. See, when I press it, it says it can't connect. "Portable Wi-Fi network not present".'

I could see from Deborah's face that she was puzzling something out.

'That can't be right though, can it?'

'Of course I'm right. What do you mean?' I said.

'No, I don't mean you. I just mean, if it's saying this laptop has been connected to Wi-Fi, that can't be right, can it? I've only just thought. Because we're not allowed to use Wi-Fi.'

Deborah was right. We weren't allowed to use Wi-Fi. Even when we lived in the city, Elijah had been adamant that it was dangerous, that it allowed the government to see everything you were doing, that it gave off radioscopic waves which messed with your mind and gave you tumours and miscarriages. I remembered one sermon in particular, which Elijah delivered after one of the congregants bought a mobile phone. *The rays from things like this,* he had said, holding the phone between his finger and thumb as though it was a dirty nappy, *are the government's most effective method of population control.* Deborah had only just joined us when that happened. It might have even been her phone for all I could remember. Either way, the perils of wireless internet and the mind-bending carcinogenic rays emitted by mobile phones were common subjects in Elijah's preaching.

'Why would he use something that he thinks is so dangerous?'

I shrugged. There were so many possible answers. Maybe he sat there in a tinfoil hat. Maybe he didn't care. Maybe he had changed his mind about the whole thing. Maybe it was simply one rule for him, and one rule for us. Once I would have puzzled it over, desperate to find a possible scenario that painted Elijah in the best light, determined to understand his thinking, but that time had certainly passed. He was no longer a man I could recognise. I closed the laptop's lid and took myself across the room to the thin window. If it had been daytime, I would have been able to see almost all of Halcyon's populated zone from there, but it was night and the moon was obscured by a cloud, so as it was, all I could see were the faint outlines of caravans and outbuildings. Behind me I could hear Deborah rising from her seat, the floorboards creaking gently as she walked over to study something else in the room. I knew that I should be doing the same – taking the opportunity to explore Elijah's secret space – but I no longer wanted to. I suppose I was worried about what else I might find, but I was also suddenly very tired, and the bright digital glare of the laptop screen had incited a throbbing pain behind my left eye. So instead of looking around the room with Deborah, I stayed at the window, gazing out over the sleeping colony below.

'Huh,' I heard her say quietly, 'hey, Aoife, did you know that Elijah still has his passport? It's in his old name, even.'

It must have been the movement that caught my eye. It was only slight, but in the stillness of the night any motion was hard to ignore. At first, I thought it must have been a trick of the darkness, or a side-effect of my headache, but a sliver of moon had found its way out from behind a cloud and I was suddenly certain.

'Turn off the light.' I moved away from the glass as quickly as I could.

'What?' said Deborah. She was busy flipping through the passport.

'Turn off the light! I think there's someone outside!'

Her face grew ashen, and she lumbered across the room to the light switch.

Neither of us spoke again until we were in the kitchen. I sat at the table, resting my head in my hands as Deborah made us cups of tea in the flickering candlelight. I was amazed at how swiftly she had locked the door behind us, how efficiently she had returned the key to its hiding place, how silently she had come down the stairs. I had lit the candle for us, reluctant to risk turning on another electric light in the middle of the night. The sound of boiling water did something to soothe my jangling nerves, and by the time I was holding the mug in my hands, inhaling the rising steam as the warmth seeped into my bones, I felt almost normal. Whatever normal was, then.

'God, I miss real tea.' Deborah's whisper took me by surprise.

'Really?'

'Yeah,' she said, 'sometimes I dream about it.'

I wasn't sure how well she could see me in the half-light of the dancing flame, but I smiled anyway.

'Me too,' I said.

'Sometimes the dreams feel so real, it's like I can actually taste it, you know? Do you ever get those?'

I nodded. 'The other night I dreamed I ate a jacket potato covered with melted cheese and baked beans and butter. It was incredible.'

'Oh,' she said, 'what I wouldn't give for some proper cheese right now. Or some crisps. Or pasta. When I was pregnant with Susannah, there was an entire month when I would have sold my soul for one of those huge cookies you get from kiosks in shopping centres. I would wake up in the middle of the night convinced I could smell them.'

'Do you have any cravings this time around?'

'Oh, I don't know,' she said, 'my freedom, maybe?'

She gave a short, awkward laugh and rolled her eyes. I reached out and took her hand from across the table; it was small and warm. I think it must have been the first time I had ever touched her.

'I just keep feeling so *angry*. Do you ever feel like that? Like, all I want to do is scream and throw things. It can't be good for the baby. Although that seems a bit redundant, really, because what part of this is good for the baby? For any of the babies? I mean, I had as shitty a childhood as the next person, shittier probably, but even when I was in care I was allowed to be a kid, you know? I went to school, I went to the park, I could have fun. You know?'

I nodded. I knew I should say something reassuring, but I couldn't think of anything at all, so I gave her hand another squeeze. If I was honest, I never let myself think too much about the children. Constance must have been about twelve. She was my first baby. She was almost seven when we arrived in Halcyon, and old enough to remember what it was like when we lived in the same house. It was hard for her, at first, only seeing me at church. It had been hard for Faith, too, I remembered, although even when we had lived together much of the caring had fallen to Ruth or the other women in Heaven on Earth. I had been busy supporting Elijah and working for the church, and he had been firm, even then, in his beliefs about how families should function, how dangerous it could be for parents to love their children too much. I saw myself as a nurse or a teacher, whose job it was to see them through from one end of the day to the other, and Elijah's preaching helped me to understand that my lack of affection was not a deficiency. Still, I saw the way that other women – and men – behaved with their children. The way their souls slotted together like pieces of a puzzle.

Halcyon and Humility never knew any different – to them, I was always just one of their father's wives, one of three 'mothers' who meant no more to them than any random woman working in the schoolhouse. And then after Humility the babies had just stopped coming, even though I was definitely still young enough to be having them. Elijah and I had seen it as a curse, but perhaps it was a blessing. I pushed the thoughts away and refocussed on Deborah, who had started speaking again.

'But then, if I left, and somehow managed to bring them with me, what would I do then? I don't even have any GCSEs. I've never had a job. We'd be on the street, and then they'd get taken away, and surely it's better to be in here with them, than out there without them?'

We were quiet for a moment. I sipped my tea.

'I don't know.'

It was all I could say.

Chapter Fifteen

Ruth

I didn't have the heart to tell Mim the real reason we needed to move Russell and the pups out of the barn and into one of the outbuildings. Instead, I said it was so the cows weren't disturbed, and so the dogs could have some peace. It wasn't a complete lie, and definitely better than the truth, which would have just upset her. I gathered the pups up into one of the cleaner towels and placed them in Mim's eager arms, and in my own I carried Russell. At first, she squirmed, her small, stocky body twisting in an attempt to get closer to her litter, but I shushed her and stroked her and it didn't take long before she was calm and still. I turned off the torch and tucked it into the pocket of my nightgown.

'I can't see anything!' Mim squeaked.

If she hadn't been holding the puppies, I was sure she would have grabbed hold of me. Instead, she came as close as she could. I could feel her shivering.

'It's okay,' I said, 'walk by me. The outbuilding we need is just outside.'

Together, we inched along the outside wall of the barn towards the nearest lean-to, where we kept the spare tarpaulins. It was the best place I could think of for Russell and her litter to hide out until I decided what to do with them – it would be less draughty than the barn, and there was less chance of someone stumbling across them. The few feet of empty space between the end of the barn and the start of the outhouse seemed to go on for miles, and I was so frightened of tripping over and dropping the dog that instead of lifting my feet, I shuffled forwards so the stony ground scraped the soles of my boots. I let out a sigh of relief when I finally came up against the cold corrugated iron of the outbuilding.

'We made it,' I whispered, more to myself than to Mim, whose breathing had become more irregular and shallow the further we got from the barn.

The night air was freezing cold, and I was reluctant to take one of my hands away from Russell's warm fur in order to reach for the latch. I fumbled, but it didn't take me long to find it. Relieved, I slid the bolt across and tried to pull the door towards me. It didn't budge. I tried again, using as much of my strength as I could without disturbing the dog, and when nothing happened, I tried to push instead. It was stuck fast.

'What's happening?' whispered Mim, her breath hot and clammy against my ear.

'I think it's locked.'

'Locked? Why?'

I could feel myself growing frustrated. I was tempted to ask her to go back to bed and leave me to it, but instead I said: 'I don't know why. We'll have to find someplace else.'

Someplace else. Where else? There were other outbuildings, sure, Halcyon was littered with them, but I didn't know how easy it would be to find them in the dark. Not only that; Halcyon's ground was rocky and slick with mud, and it was hard to tell what was the worn path and what wasn't, so I was worried that I would end up straying off into the night. I closed my eyes and tried to picture the settlement as a whole, running through possible hiding places and mapping out our route. The torch in my pocket banged against my leg, a reminder of how much easier it would be if we could have a little light. I resisted the temptation, and somehow we managed to shuffle our way to the next shed. That one was locked too. By the time we reached the third outbuilding my legs were beginning to shake, and my arms were numb with cold and the effort of carrying the dog. I had no idea how long we'd been out, and though the darkness didn't seem likely to break any time soon, the threat of dawn added a greater sense of urgency to the whole escapade. I was also very conscious that if *I* was cold, the puppies must have been even colder, and there was a very real chance that they would freeze to death while I was trying my best to save their lives.

'Make sure you're keeping the pups warm,' I said to Mim, as my frozen hands fumbled with yet another latch.

'I am.'

The relief I felt when the door swung open seemed to come from my very core; it was the same feeling I got after a tricky delivery ended well. As soon as Mim and our charges and I were safely inside and the door closed behind us, I got down onto my knees and said a prayer of thanks. Russell, who had been quiet and still, must have noticed her sudden proximity to solid ground and twisted herself free of my grasp. The click of her claws against the poured concrete floor pulled me back into reality, and I went into efficiency autopilot, firing instructions at Mim and piling up blankets and towels to build a nest for the dogs. I shone the torch around the rest of the shed in case there was anything else in there that we could use, but the space was almost entirely taken up with empty tins of paint and other prospectively useful odds and ends that had been saved for a rainy day. Nothing which would be any good for keeping dogs warm, but at least it was unlikely that anyone would venture in there any time soon.

'Okay,' I said, turning to face Mim, 'now I need to go and get the rest of the stuff and bring it here. You wait with the dogs, and I'll be as quick as I can.'

As I turned to leave, she grabbed my arm. 'Please can I come with you? They were talking about some man that's been spotted around the compound in evening worship today.'

I ran the possible outcomes through in my head. For the effort it would cost me to convince her to stay there alone, I decided it would be faster to agree. As for the potential intruder, I had no time to think about it.

'Fine,' I said, 'you can help me carry everything.'

I interrupted her eager nod by switching off the torch.

We walked back to the barn in silence, but when we got inside it was as though someone had flipped a switch inside Mim's brain, and suddenly all she could do was talk.

'I think this is the most fun I've ever had in my life.'

'Hmm,' I said. And then, 'Here, please hold the torch so I can see what I'm doing.'

She took it from my hand. From the swaying of the beam, I could tell that she was moving from one foot to the other. If I ever did that growing up, my mom would scold me. *Have you got ants in your pants or something? Stay still – you're making me seasick!* I bit my tongue and concentrated on making up the bundle.

'I don't know how I'm ever going to go back to the schoolhouse after this.' She giggled and then went quiet for a second before adding, 'Of course, I won't be there for much longer. Probably.'

I didn't say anything.

'You know,' she said, 'because I'll probably be getting married soon.'

The silence that fell was a heavy one. I had no interest in encouraging this line of conversation, so even though I knew Mim was holding out for a response I was reluctant to give one. I made another noncommittal *mmm* sound. She continued:

'It'll definitely be good to get out of the schoolhouse. Helen said she's going to be sad to see me go, but I can't wait. It's going to be so nice not to worry about getting woken up in the middle of the night. And I think it must be quite fun being married.'

I'm a quiet person. I like to watch, and I listen pretty well, which means that I've always been good at letting other people speak. Because of this, I seem to be the sort of girl that people enjoy spilling their secrets to. I can imagine there are lots of people in this world who would enjoy having that effect on others, but it's a skill that is wasted on me. I had no idea what to say to Mim. I had no idea what she wanted from me. Did she want me to tell her I was excited for her, happy for her? It was none of my business if she and Elijah married. Silently, I passed her the dish of water and took the torch from her hand.

I was relieved when she didn't say anything more as we walked back to the dogs. It was still pitch dark when we got back outside, but muscle memory guided me back to the outbuilding and I didn't have the worry of dropping Russell this time, so we made much faster progress than before. When we arrived, the dog was lying contentedly on her side with all four pups suckling greedily. Mim seemed antsy, and despite what she had said earlier, seemed keen to return to bed, so I arranged the fresh towels and dish of water quickly. As happy as I was to see Russell so content, I was eager to get back too, so we said a quick goodnight at the door before going our separate ways.

It was good to be back in the farmhouse, and I took great pleasure in closing the door against that strange, long night. My body was achy with tension and frozen from the biting cold, but my hands felt dirty and I knew that I needed to wash up before bed. I don't know what made me go to turn on the electric light in the kitchen – I knew the room well enough to navigate it in the dark – but fate or God guided my hand to the switch. Something in the room seemed out of place. *What's wrong with this picture?* Still in the doorway I cast my eyes around, blinking in the harsh light, trying to figure out what it was. It didn't take me long to notice. On the kitchen counter, by the sink, were two mugs laid out to drain. On the table was a candle, its flame extinguished, burned halfway down.

Chapter Sixteen

Deborah

The morning after our long night, Aoife and I followed our usual routines. Ruth was with us at breakfast so we didn't get the chance to talk about what had happened, although I had been desperate to – 'You hate him too now, right?' I wanted to say over our bowls of porridge and glasses of water. 'How long have you hated him? Do you hate him more than you hate me?'

'Please pass the honey,' I said instead.

I hadn't been addressing either of them in particular, but I was still a bit disappointed when it was Ruth who slid the heavy ceramic pot across the table and into my hand. I'd hoped that Aoife would take it as an opportunity to give me some kind of meaningful sign, and then I felt stupid for hoping.

It would be too much of a risk to go back up to the office during the day, and even if I did go, I knew there was nothing I could really do without being able to look at the laptop files or go onto the internet. The books might have held some clues to Elijah's state of mind, but there were so many and it would take me forever to even read one. It just wasn't worth it. Instead, I wished my sister wives a good morning and went to my work.

The children all seemed bleary-eyed and exhausted that morning as we walked from the schoolhouse to the bunker to work on some preparations for the End. I was carrying my little Susannah, breathing in the scent of her as she rested her head against my shoulder, her skinny legs wrapped around my bump. I wouldn't be able to carry her for much longer. She smelled of fresh air and laundered clothes and milk, her eyelids pink and fluttering, lashes long and dark. She was my reason, along with

Jonah and Noah, for sticking around. I tried to remind myself of that, that it hadn't been for nothing. Still, I'd have to do better for them. I took another deep breath in and Susannah raised a hand to my cheek, resting it on my face just as Helen turned around.

The bunker was a short walk out of the central cluster of Halcyon's barns and outbuildings, so it didn't take our group long to get there. It wasn't much to look at from above ground – heavy corrugated metal covered in turf like a giant Anderson shelter for eighty – but it still made my stomach dip whenever I approached it. Once every couple of weeks we would take the children from the schoolhouse for a day under the ground, getting them used to the space that we were planning to spend the time, either days, weeks, or months, from the onset of total societal breakdown until God was ready to take us. We'd have them rotate the food in the stores, scrub the floors, clean out the vents. It had taken about two years and almost all of our savings from donations and tithes to build, and now, thanks to the children, it waited, gleaming and immaculate for the End.

Helen turned the heavy handle and pulled open the vault door, and we followed her into the cold and clammy darkness. The air in the bunker tasted of damp earth and sat in my lungs like a freezing thing, and it was so thick that I felt as though I should be able to bite down and leave tooth marks in it. The door swung shut and we vanished into the dark. We always spent the first couple of minutes with the electric light off, but it never got easier. I squeezed the sleepy Susannah closer to me, working hard to manage my breathing and keep my heart rate steady. However many times I went in, it never stopped feeling like a tomb.

Helen clicked her wind-up torch on and shone the dim beam to the floor, making the phosphorescent arrows appear. I tried to focus on them, and Susannah and the twins who I knew were nearby. Usually by this point I would be feeling better, not quite so claustrophobic, but the sense of being trapped just got heavier and heavier the further into the bunker that we walked. To either side of me, faintly illuminated by the torchlight, bunk beds and travel cots for eighty lined the walls. When we reached the end of the main space and the door to the storage room, Helen flipped on the electricity and the long florescent light pinged into flickering life overhead.

The main section of the bunker was the largest. As well as beds, it contained a long bench across one wall which doubled as both a seating area and a storage space. The seat of the bench lifted up in various places to reveal carefully packed sleeping bags, boxes of foil blankets, all the stuff you might need for a camping trip or an apocalypse. The bench, like everything else in the bunker, was made to last. The hinges were strong and oiled, so the lids raised without a single creak. The wood was solid pine. Elijah had insisted on the very best of everything. He had even insisted on selecting the colour of the walls himself – a cool, pale blue, which he had chosen after about a month of research into something he called the 'psychology of colour'. Elijah was the father to twelve children, but the bunker was more his baby than any of them. Even the food store in the next room along was organised to the hilt, with labelled shelves of canned goods running in alphabetical order from anchovies to water. He hadn't lowered himself to do the organising, but he had overseen it closely and would sometimes come down when the children were in to supervise their upkeep of his most sacred space. Elijah's attention to the bunker went all the way down the concrete steps to the lower floor, where more strips of fluorescent lighting illuminated our bathroom (three toilets ordered specially from the United States, lots of loo roll, thousands of baby wipes – all exotic luxuries compared to what we had in Halcyon itself), and the panic room. The panic room was closed off behind another heavy metal door, just like the one which opened into the main body of the bunker, with a round handle like the wheel of a ship. If worst came to worst, and the rest of the bunker was infiltrated or compromised, the panic room was built to keep us safe for up to a week, after which point the food down there would run out.

Elijah had spent hours with his Bible, doing complicated-looking sums using numbers which he seemed to choose at random from passages in the Book of Revelation, and when he had finished he announced that God wouldn't make us wait for more than two weeks from the start of the End until he brought us to join Him in Heaven. In that time, though, we could be subject to anything. Crazed sinners descending on our community, determined to steal our food and medical supplies; extreme weather, covering Halcyon in snowdrifts as tall as buildings or intense heat burning anyone outside to a crisp; nuclear war, some pathetic little man with his finger on the button blowing the world into oblivion. Elijah made no promises, other than: 'the End is coming' and 'we will be ready'. We had enough supplies for over two months.

'Well done, everyone,' said Helen, clasping her hands together in delight. 'I know we don't like that very much, do we? But we were all so brave today! And we'll all be so ready if those nasty outsiders break our wind turbines or our generator at the End.'

Jonah and Noah were standing apart, at opposite sides of the group, their dark curls hidden under woolly hats. Jonah was staring up at Helen, listening with the intensity of a three-year-old Elijah. Noah was busily fiddling with the belt loops on his corduroy trousers. Neither of them was looking at me. The sudden brightness stirred Susannah and she lifted her head from my shoulder, squirming to be put down. I held her tighter – it was rare that Helen allowed me to hold her at all.

'We won't be scared, will we?' Helen asked.

'No!'

The sound of all of the children shouting their answer rang in my ears. Even with the lights on, I was still so aware of being under the ground, of how easy it would be to become trapped beneath corrugated metal and tonnes of earth.

'That's right, everyone! We're God's bravest soldiers, because we have our Holy Prophet leading us.' Helen pointed to the mural of Elijah on the storeroom door. It was a good likeness, and showed Elijah in his argyle jumper and ancient jeans leading the population of Halcyon up a golden ladder, away from a flaming city and the grasping hands of sinners and up into a set of heavenly white clouds. There was no depiction of Heaven itself, because that would be sacrilegious, so it looked like the crowd were about to disappear into nothing. All of the church members had haloes, to set them apart from the sinners, but Elijah's was the largest and brightest. It was picked out in gold leaf, which Elijah said he had found lying around somewhere when he had been on a mission trip.

I knew the mural very well, because I'd painted it, but the light was too bright and I couldn't make it out properly. Something about the brightness and my dizziness and how hard

I was suddenly finding it to catch my breath meant that the Elijah in the painting seemed to be looking right at me, smiling. Helen was still talking, but her voice seemed very far away. A grey mist crept across my vision and I felt myself falling slowly backwards as someone grabbed the writhing Susannah from my arms.

Chapter Seventeen

Aoife

I kept going out of my way to walk around the perimeter fence to look for Malcolm, and he kept on being there, waiting for me. Our talks had kept me going in the days Elijah had been away, but my sad little epiphany in the office had made me reluctant to see him again. I imagined myself through his eyes – a deluded, pathetic, lonely woman – and felt even more ashamed than I had been already. He was only there because he was interested in our land, and I was some pitiful sideshow to be laughed at when he got home. I had spent the whole of my silent breakfast running through the situation in my head: how long had I been deluding myself about my position? When had my power started slipping away? And why, after everything we'd been through and everything I'd done, did he not love me any more?

Idiot. Who's to say I ever loved you?

Still, I didn't turn to my accounts that morning at all, or to the community barn or to Deborah (what to say to her, now?). Instead, I wrapped myself up and made my way around the perimeter fence to the spot where Malcolm usually waited for me. Everyone else was already hard at work, but again, nobody seemed to care about where I was going, or at least no one was brave enough to stop me. I had that authority still, which was a mercy. I wasn't like the others, who had to worry about neighbourly eyes catching secret stumbles and turning them over to John.

Halcyon had also been covered by low-lying cloud, which meant it was impossible to see more than a few feet ahead; the mountains which usually guarded our horizon were completely obscured, shrouded by the soupy whiteness. I was far enough away from the centre that nobody would be able to see me, even if they were looking. I could feel little beads of moisture settling on me – my skin, my hair, the fibres of my clothes. The air smelled peaty and damp. I passed the sheep, grazing peacefully by the stream, their fleeces thick and ready for winter, and kept walking until I saw Malcolm's figure emerge from the fog. He must have already spotted me by the time I saw him, as he was waving cheerfully. His smile seemed so pleased, so genuine, that it lifted me and quickened my pace. That wasn't the smile of a man who was just there to talk about buying land. I felt a flutter of pride. I might have been a fool, but *Malcolm* wanted to see me. He was *excited* to see me. He *liked* me, and he didn't need to know about anything that might make him feel differently. *Look at you*, came the voice, familiar and scathing, *how shallow can you get? Your whole life is a lie, and everything is suddenly all right because this man, this stranger, seems to be showing an interest? He'll see right through you.*

I was shaking my head to clear the voice away when I noticed, with a little jolt of panic, that Malcolm's left hand was tucked behind his back. It was obvious from the way he was holding himself that he was hiding something there, a tactic favoured by Elijah when he wanted to catch me out for some apparent wrongdoing in the early days of our marriage. He would come in, all smiles, and then out from behind his back would appear something of mine which he'd found and decided to be a tool of the devil: a tinted lip-balm, a can of diet cola, a box of tampons. Swiftly followed by a lecture, a punishment, or days of silence, depending on his mood.

Elijah would draw it out, waiting for me to notice he was hiding something, letting me sweat, but Malcolm clearly wasn't the sort of man for such games. As soon as he was sure I'd noticed, he revealed a shiny tartan-patterned tin with a delighted flourish.

'Morning, Aoife! Look what my housekeeper made.'

I'd barely arrived at the fence when he opened the tin to reveal rows of shortbread biscuits, neatly nestled side by side.

'I thought you might like one.'

He passed a slender golden slice of shortbread through one of the gaps in the chain link with a leather gloved hand. I took it without thinking; it was still warm.

'How lovely. Thank you, Malcolm, you shouldn't have.'

I hadn't tasted anything so delicious in years.

'These are incredible,' I said, mouth full of crumbs, 'you need to give your housekeeper a pay rise.'

I flinched as soon as the words were out of my mouth. Any such comment made to Elijah, however light-hearted, would be met with rage. *How dare you tell a man what to do?* But Malcolm just smiled again and nodded.

'I'll take that as a solid piece of advice, coming from a church accountant with half a business degree.'

He was being sarcastic, but sweetly so; his gentle laughter was with me, not at me. This kindness, combined with how little I had left to lose, made me bold.

'I suppose that's the reason you're here today, and the other days? To talk accounts, and business?' I raised an eyebrow in what I hoped was a subtly flirtatious way, but my voice turned unintentionally hard as I asked my final question. 'Are you still interested in our land?'

Malcolm's smile vanished, but he didn't seem angry. He closed the lid of the biscuit tin and studied my face, his seriousness unfamiliar and thrilling.

'You're clearly an intelligent woman, Aoife. I have a feeling you know that's not why I've been coming here every day.'

I felt my cheeks redden, and I twisted my wedding ring around my finger. The thin, gold band was as cold as my hand, and loose enough that it spun easily.

'Then, why have you been coming here every day?'

You sound so needy. He knows you're married.

He seemed to be considering his answer, weighing up responses in his head.

'I think,' he said, 'that you're an interesting person. I enjoy talking to you. You're someone I like spending time with.'

I met his gaze for a moment before looking down at my feet. I could still sense the colour in my cheeks, and was ashamed of myself.

He broke the silence that followed with a rough clearing of his throat.

'I actually have a question for you this morning, too. I've been wondering for a little while.'

I must have looked sceptical because he smiled his warm smile again.

'It's okay,' he said, 'you don't have to answer if you don't want to. And I promise it's nothing personal. I just wanted to ask how long you've been here.'

'Do you mean me, or the church?'

'Well, both, I suppose. Did you come to the church, or with the church?'

To the church or with the church? I *was* the church! Was. Everything seemed to be in the past tense.

'With the church,' I said. 'I came with the church. We've been here for five years.'

'Five *years*?' He sounded stunned. '*Here*? But why?'

I sighed, my breath curling in the cold air.

'The city wasn't the right place for us to live the way we wanted to live. There was too much pressure, too much outside influence. It's hard to be a Christian in the truest possible way when you live in a society like that.'

'What do you mean?'

'When you live in the city, working a job, buying food from supermarkets, paying taxes and utility bills, you end up giving your time and your money to places that use it badly. Do you know how much modern slavery is behind so much of the stuff you buy every day? Fruit picked by children in Morocco, and all the little ones trafficked into the cocoa industry?' I could see he was about to interrupt, so I went on, quicker, 'And even if you don't buy the strawberries or the chocolates, even if you just go in to buy a pint of milk, you're still giving money to that supermarket. And when you pay your taxes, the government that takes that money is the same government that sells weapons which wind up blowing up schools and hospitals in Syria. That's just the tip of the iceberg. And it's our children too, the church's children. They were seeing stuff in the streets, hearing things that children shouldn't be seeing or hearing. We did our best but it's impossible to properly protect them out there. The way things are going, we just didn't feel safe. And that's not how God wanted us to live.'

I stopped myself before mentioning the End, the breakdown of society which had felt so inevitable, the arrival of God on Earth to save the righteous and condemn the sinners. I'd spoken to enough people about Heaven on Earth and our work to know how to pace my evangelism. It had been a long time since I'd delivered a speech like that. Remembering why we'd come made me sadder about where we were now. I still believed those things. I still wanted to be the sort of Christian who lived them.

Malcolm nodded again.

'I get it,' he said, 'I can see the appeal of that. And now you're here, and you're all self-sufficient, do you feel closer to God? Excuse me if that's too personal, I'm not really a... man of faith. I don't want you to think I'm being patronising or anything. I suppose I'm just curious.'

I thought about Elijah and his punishments and his secrets. His rages and his games. Did listening to the sound of choking and retching as a room of my friends and neighbours drank what they thought was poison make me feel closer to God? Did watching my husband slide his arm around the shoulders of a teenager make me feel closer to God? I looked up at Malcolm's face, so open and kind and interested. He liked me. He was a good person, and to like me, he must have thought that I was a good person too. I couldn't bear to tell him that I wasn't.

'It's more complicated than that,' I said.

I made my excuses to leave, and had already turned to walk away, when Malcolm spoke again.

'Maybe things don't have to be complicated. Maybe they could be easy. I'm not judging, and I might have got the wrong end of the stick here, but I just want to say it. If you ever want to leave, Aoife, you just have to say the word. I'll be here.'

Chapter Eighteen

Ruth

Some nights, when my soul was heavy, I would lie in bed and think of my early days in Heaven on Earth in the hopes that the happy memories would send me to sleep.

I'd been attending the church for a few months when my relationship with Elijah shifted, and I wondered if the little tug I felt in my heart every time he looked my way might have been reciprocated. Grey city snow was piled in slushy drifts on the sidewalk, and I had been shivering at my bus stop for half an hour after service, my return ticket clutched in my frozen, gloved hand. I was beginning to wonder if I should make my way on foot when Elijah appeared from around the corner, deerstalker hat pulled down over his ears and scarf up to his chin.

He raised his hand to greet me.

'Ruth!' he called, his voice as loud and confident in the street as it was in church.

I waved back, suddenly warm despite the flakes of snow which were melting down the collar of my coat. I had lent my scarf to one of the trainee midwives at work.

'I'm glad I caught you,' he said once he was close enough that he didn't have to shout. 'Let me walk you home.'

'Oh, that's okay, you don't—'

But we were already on our way.

We were about halfway back to my place when Elijah slowed down. On the edge of the sidewalk was a patch of virgin snow, untouched by footprints or grit or mud. He stepped to the side and stamped down purposefully, leaving an imprint of his boot behind.

'I can never resist.' He shrugged, and I laughed.

The action had been so joyful and childish, so out of character, that I hadn't been able to help myself.

He looked at me, a smile playing on his lips. I was reminded of one of my favourite British words – cheeky. His smile looked almost *cheeky*.

'What's so funny?' he asked.

'I guess I just would never have expected you to do that. It seems like such a—' I tried to think of a word other than 'childish', because I didn't want him to think I was being insulting, 'light-hearted thing to do. It made me happy to see it, I guess because I could tell it made you happy to do it.'

'You don't think I'm a light-hearted sort of person?'

'No, not really,' I said.

Something about being side by side made it easier to speak openly to him. We were still walking, but I could feel the sleeve of his winter coat brushing mine. If I had been a different kind of woman, I might have pretended to slip so he would catch me and take me by the arm.

'Care to elaborate?'

'Well, you're just very serious. I didn't think people who were so smart and holy did things like that.'

Then it was Elijah's turn to laugh.

'We're all of us more than we seem, Ruth. Like you. On the outside you're a shy, devout woman. You're charitable and kind, a bit of a rule-follower. But then, you came here from America all by yourself. You do a job that's incredibly physically challenging and emotionally draining. You're tough, and brave, deep down, in a way that lots of people who seem more confident than you just aren't.'

Aoife's name hung in the air between us, unsaid.

'You're being very generous,' I said, 'but I'm not so sure how brave I am. Before I found the church, I was so lonely that I started to feel like I wasn't even a real person.'

'Are you homesick?'

I shook my head.

'Good, I'm glad. I'd hate for you to feel homesick, especially now I hope you've found a family here with us.'

I smiled as demurely as I could, but inside my chest, beneath the layers of my coat and sweater and blouse, my heart thumped hard against my ribs. Emboldened by his words, I allowed myself to look up at Elijah's face. His nose had turned a little red with the cold, and his cheeks were pink. I wanted to rest my hands against them, to warm him.

'I should have done this ages ago,' he said. For a second I was terrified that he might try to kiss me, but instead he unwound the scarf from around his neck and draped it gently over my shoulders.

'There, that's better.'

When we reached the door to my apartment, he waited until I had fished the key from inside my purse. It took me an embarrassingly long time, because I was wearing my gloves, but he didn't sigh or shiver. When I finally got the door open, I went to take off his scarf.

'No,' he said, 'you keep that.'

I brought the scarf with me to Halcyon, when we moved.

'Ruthie?'

I must have drifted off, because the sound of my name being whispered woke me.

'Ruthie?'

I heard my name again and sat up in bed. The voice was coming from outside my bedroom door, and I knew it better than I knew my own. It was Elijah. My heart convulsed with a mixture of relief and fear. He was back, alive and well. But also he was back, alive and well.

The door opened, and he stepped inside.

'Put the lamp on, Ruthie Angel, I want to see your face. I've missed you.'

We had been preparing for our wedding when Elijah learned that my middle name was Angel, and he'd been pleased. 'Suits you', he'd said. He called me his Ruthie Angel sometimes, when he was feeling affectionate, and it embarrassed me although I never told him so. I guess I never said anything because it was nice that he cared enough to give me a pet name, but also because I could never really put my finger on why I disliked it so much.

I leaned across to the electric lamp by the side of my bed and switched it on. The bulb was dim but it still dazzled me, so I could smell Elijah before I saw him. The scent of hard liquor and cigarette smoke, and something else I half recognised but couldn't name, came off him like a vapour. He looked like he hadn't slept in the whole time he'd been away from Halcyon, his eyes red raw and circled with purple. He was still wearing the clothes he'd had on when he'd left, and I noticed that one of the buttons had come off his sheepskin coat. Had he been trying to preach in a bar? That was the only explanation I could find for the smells, so out of place in Halcyon, and the way he looked – as if he'd been in a brawl. Had the Godless outsiders attacked him?

'Elijah.' My voice was hoarse and deep with sleep, and I tried to make it a little higher before continuing. 'Welcome home. We've missed you too.'

He smiled then, the way he did sometimes that didn't make it up to his eyes, and shrugged off his coat. It landed with a heavy thump on the bare floorboards.

'That's what I like to hear,' he said, his words slurring. 'You know, Ruthie, why I came to you tonight?'

I was relieved when he didn't give me the chance to answer.

'You don't ask questions. I can trust you to just shut up and not ask stupid questions. Aoife would be asking me where I'd been, just outright, no respect. She doesn't respect me, is her problem. She thinks she's something. And Deborah, she'd try and be clever, she thinks she's clever. She wouldn't ask but she'd ask, you know? She'd ask, but without asking. Thinking she's clever. You *know* you're not something. You *know* you're not clever. That's what I like about you, Ruthie, that's why you're the Angel. You're the best of them, you are. You're my favourite.'

The whole time he'd been speaking, his words slow and low, sliding into each other, he had been walking towards the bed where I was lying, shedding his sweater and then his plaid shirt, and finally his long thermal vest. Then he was kicking off his boots and working the clasp of his belt with his left hand, steadying himself against the bed with his right.

'You're my favourite,' he said again, this time into my neck. He was lying beside me, and I could feel his mouth, wet and hot against my ear. He was so close now that I could tell the stink of liquor was coming from his skin, from inside his mouth and through his pores. He had been drinking. He was *drunk*. 'Did you hear when I said that? What do you say?'

'Thank you,' I whispered.

My arms and legs had turned heavy. Sometimes that happened, when he was in one of his moods and he still wanted to make love. My body would freeze and I'd have to breathe, in for four and out for eight, like the breathing I did when I birthed my babies, to stop myself getting too tense and making him mad. But this time was different, because I'd never seen him drunk before, never been kissed by a drunk man before, or by a man whose whole mouth tasted of cigarettes. I'd only ever kissed Elijah, and Elijah never drank, never smoked. We didn't even use communion wine any more.

The warmth I'd trapped under my blankets was replaced with cold as Elijah tried to join me under the covers, his jeans still half on. He moved jerkily, getting caught up in my quilt and his pants, and I could sense his frustration growing. It was almost a relief when he finally made it, if only because I knew he wouldn't get madder, but even so that was short-lived. His belt and fly were unbuckled, leaving his hands free to push up my nightdress. It was like being touched by ice.

'You're so warm,' he said, his mouth on mine.

I closed my eyes. *This is normal*, I told myself, *this is all right. He's had a few drinks, because he's stressed, but the rest of it is normal.* He guided my hand to his crotch and held it there. *The only difference is the alcohol. He's still your husband. This is what it means to have a husband.*

With my eyes closed, it was easier to distract myself. The feeling of him moving between my legs, his grunts, the creak of the bed, could almost be drowned out. I could almost imagine it wasn't happening. I thought about my day, and about poor Deborah, who had fainted in the bunker in front of all of the children. Her blood pressure had been low, which was normal for a woman at the start of her third trimester, but still something to keep an eye on. I would have to make sure she was drinking enough water, maybe check our first-aid supplies to see if we had a pair of support stockings that might fit her. She would be recuperating in her bed downstairs, in the room below mine. I hoped that the creak of the bed wasn't disturbing her. I would be so embarrassed if it woke her up. *In for four, out for eight.* Elijah's mouth was no longer covering mine, which made my calming breaths easier. It also meant I could no longer taste him, and that made it easier to pretend that the whole situation was normal. Normal, and soon to be over.

Elijah rolled off me with a shudder, and I turned off the lamp.

He had his back to me, and I thought he was about to fall asleep until he spoke.

'I've been wandering the desert, but now I'm back and I'm here to stay. Now I know what it really feels like to be God.'

I took another deep breath in, counting to four, trying not to let the air catch in my throat. He was quiet for a long time after that. When I was sure he was asleep, I let myself cry.

Chapter Nineteen

Deborah

I was back on my feet less than twenty-four hours after my fainting spell in the bunker, ladling out porridge into bowls when Ruth, who had been sitting at the table for a good while, gave a little cough. Aoife and I looked at her.

'I don't know if you two heard,' she said, speaking into her half-empty mug, 'but Elijah got back last night.'

I dropped my ladle into the saucepan where it sank down into the sticky, bubbling oats. Aoife turned white, and I watched her eyes flicker as she tried to decide what to say. She opened her mouth but seemed to think better of it and closed it again. In the nine years I had known Aoife, I had only seen her lost for words twice: the first time was in Elijah's office, and the second was just then.

'He said he's back for good now,' Ruth went on, still staring into her drink, 'but he won't be coming to breakfast this morning.'

This seemed to knock Aoife back into herself.

'Not coming to breakfast? Really? Is he joking? He goes away to who knows where for days, and then doesn't even have the decency to come to breakfast when he gets back?'

'Did he say why?' I asked, hoping to give Aoife a chance to calm down before she said something she might regret in front of Ruth. I used my best 'Prophet's Wife' voice, light and breezy, with all the rough edges sanded down.

Ruth shook her head, and Aoife snorted. I kicked her under the table, a swift smack to her shin with the side of my boot which she managed to ignore.

'Did you ask him where he'd been?' Aoife was leaning towards

Ruth now, determinedly trying to catch her eye. She looked as though she was ready to take Ruth's face in her hands and turn it towards herself.

'No,' Ruth said, 'he didn't seem like he was in the mood for conversation.'

I wondered if that was supposed to be a euphemism. Clearly Aoife did too, because she let out a sharp, cruel laugh and rolled her eyes. I wanted to shoot her a warning glance, but she was too busy staring at Ruth to notice me, and I wasn't brave enough to kick her again.

'Did he say anything at all, other than the thing about breakfast?' I asked Ruth, as softly as I could.

I had barely got the words out of my mouth when she stood up and whipped around to face me.

'No,' she said, 'I already told you that he didn't want to talk.' She was as close to shouting as I'd ever heard her. 'I don't know what you expect me to do.' Her last words caught in her throat, and she practically choked them out.

Aoife and I turned to look at each other at the exact same moment, and she looked as shocked as I felt.

'Hey, hey, calm down,' she said, raising her hands in mock surrender, 'we were only asking.'

Ruth pushed back her chair. 'And I was just answering you! I don't appreciate you both giving me the third degree.'

She stormed towards the door, shoulders high and tense.

'Wait!' I said, 'You've not even had your breakfast!'

But she was already gone.

Never in a million years would I have imagined seeing Ruth like that. She was always so calm, so nice. She didn't argue with anyone, she gave everyone the benefit of the doubt. She was everything I had been pretending to be, but for real. I was so stunned that I'd half forgotten what the argument had been about in the first place. Aoife broke our silence.

'Well,' she said, folding her arms across her chest, 'I'm getting a bit sick of people storming out of this room in a huff.'

'You shouldn't joke, Aoife,' I said, 'I'm a bit worried. That's not like her at all.'

Aoife arched one wry eyebrow in response. 'Yes it is. She's not said a word to me these past few days.'

I thought back. I couldn't vouch for anything that had

happened during my blackout, but since then I supposed that she hadn't spoken to me either. It wasn't as though she was ordinarily very chatty, but she would usually at least ask how I was feeling, if I'd been sleeping well, that kind of thing. She'd looked after me the day before, after my wobble, helped me back to my bed from the bunker and brought me water to drink, but she hadn't really said anything even then. I felt a little bit bad that I hadn't noticed the change in her mood sooner, but I'd been stressed and distracted, and Helen had been needing my help a lot more in the schoolhouse. This was the first time I'd even had the chance to speak with Aoife since our midnight meeting in Elijah's office.

Aoife must have been able to tell that I was worried, because she came and put her hand on my shoulder. I flinched, still not used to her friendliness and definitely not ready to take it for granted.

'Hey,' she said, 'don't get yourself worked up about it. She's just in a bad mood, okay? Maybe she's on her period or something.'

I shrugged.

'You know I'm right. Now,' she sat herself back down at the table, 'let's eat.'

I looked down into the saucepan full of porridge, which had bubbled over and splattered onto the stove top. I sighed and picked the drowned ladle out with two fingers, trying not to scald myself. Maybe Aoife was right about Ruth just being hormonal. It was nicer to believe that than to imagine something being really wrong. I sat down next to her, and we warmed our hands on our bowls of porridge.

'So,' she said, 'he's back.'

I nodded. It was a relief to have him back, just because it meant that I could finally stop dreading it. *He's here now*, I told myself, *and whatever happens, happens. You'll be okay, Deborah. You always are.*

'I wonder when he plans on showing his face.' Aoife's words were bold, but I noticed that she kept her voice low. We both looked to the door, half expecting him to burst in, ears burning, itching for a fight. When he didn't, she went on: 'The most important thing is just to go on as normal. Don't let him think that we're any different to what we were when he left.'

'That's what I had planned to do anyway,' I said. And then, 'but what about Ruth, though?'

'What about her?'

'Well,' I said, glancing back up at the door, 'what should we tell her?' Even as I asked the question, I wondered what on earth I thought there even was to tell.

Aoife looked up from her breakfast. 'What makes you think that we should tell her anything?'

'Look,' I said, setting down my spoon and turning to face her fully, 'if something comes of this, and if we decide to leave—'

'When we leave,' Aoife interrupted.

'If, when, whatever. We can't go without her. It's not like we can just pack up with our kids and bugger off, and say to her and Eli and Abe and Leah and Moses and Abigail, "oh, sorry, you all just have to stay here, enjoy the rest of your lives".'

She was quiet for a second, and I could tell that she was trying to think of something clever to say.

'Leah and Moses and Abigail were born here, they don't know any better. And it's not like we'd be stopping to say goodbye.'

I shook my head in disbelief.

'That's not the point and you know it,' I said. 'All of my kids were born here, that doesn't mean they're safe here. We can't leave them.'

'We can't take them either.' She lowered her voice even further. 'You saw Ruth just there. She won't want to go anywhere with us, and you know she'd tell Elijah. Plus, she might not see an awful lot of the kids, but I can bet that she would come after us with a machete if we took them away from Halcyon, whether we told her beforehand or not.'

Something in my face must have shown that I agreed with her, because she continued with renewed confidence.

'And anyway, where do we draw the line? Do we take all the kids? What about everyone else?'

I thought of Mim, and wondered what would happen to her if we took off.

'We should take whoever wants to go,' I said.

'And the people who want to stay?'

I sighed.

'Those people should stay, obviously.'

'So, we're agreed.' She looked smug. 'We can't take Ruth.'

We were so deep in conversation that we must have missed the sound of footsteps in the corridor, because we both jumped in our seats when the knock came at the kitchen door.

'May I come in?' I recognised Helen's sweetie-pie voice straight away.

I fixed Aoife with what I hoped was a stern stare and hissed: 'We don't know *what* Ruth wants.'

She didn't respond. Instead, she called out to Helen.

'Of course, come on in, make yourself at home.'

She needn't have bothered; the door was already swinging open.

Helen was always put together. I had never seen her with a hair out of place, even after a long day in the schoolhouse, and although I knew there was no iron in the whole of Halcyon, her clothes always seemed to have been freshly pressed. When I first joined Heaven on Earth I had respected Aoife, but I was scared of her too. Helen was different; gentle and motherly in a way Aoife absolutely wasn't, and in a way my own mother hadn't been. When I was seventeen and new to the church, I'd been stunned that people like Helen existed. She'd been like an advert for Elijah's brand of Christianity, giving off a glow of holiness that I had found weird, then pathetic, then inspiring. Now she just made me tired.

'Oh girls,' she squealed, 'John has just told me the good news!'

Her voice was breathless, as if she'd been running.

'Yes,' said Aoife, 'it's really grand to have him back.'

I managed a smile.

'Thanks be to God and our Holy Prophet!' Helen clasped her hands together. 'This is such an exciting time for us all. A really momentous time.'

Momentous seemed like a strange way to put it. Had she missed Elijah that much?

'Why don't you sit yourself down, Helen, and join us for some tea?' Aoife suggested.

'That's very kind of you, Aoife, but no,' she said, 'I actually came to collect Deborah. It's all hands on deck now, getting the children ready. And we're having a bit of a morning.' She shrugged her shoulders gently but didn't say anything more.

'I'd love to join you, but now that Elijah is back I'll need to go to temple before I can come out and help.'

This time it was Helen's turn to be confused.

'But Elijah isn't going to temple this morning. I just left him, he's with John and a couple of the other men by the bunker. He says he has too much to do.'

I glanced at Aoife, waiting for her response.

'Yes, sorry Deborah, I forgot to mention. He did tell me to let you know.'

Although it was clearly a lie, her tone was so casual and her face so bland that I almost believed her.

'Oh,' I said, 'well, I'll just finish up my breakfast and be straight along?'

I hoped that Helen would take the hint and leave me and Aoife alone again, but she shook her head.

'Actually, Deborah, we really do need you now. Like I said, we've had a bit of a trying morning and we could use your help.'

With as polite a smile as I could manage, I left my porridge half eaten and followed Helen to the door. Before crossing into the hall I turned to glance at Aoife, hoping for some sign of solidarity; instead, she was sipping her tea and looking peacefully out of the window as though nothing out of the ordinary had ever happened to her in her entire life.

I didn't have very long to worry about Aoife's lie or our conversation before we reached the schoolhouse. As soon as the door was opened, I could tell that something was wrong. The younger children were sitting silently in a huddle in the classroom, watched by some of the older ones. They looked cowed and red-eyed. It was with relief that I spotted Jonah, Noah, and Susannah amongst them. Helen took my arm and guided me towards the sleeping quarters, but before we entered she stopped to face me. She looked as though I'd just caught her with her hand in the biscuit tin, her eyes darting from side to side in search of an excuse. Eventually, she placed her hand on my arm and spoke:

'Now, it's not as bad as it looks.'

I shook free of her grasp and ducked through the gap in the tarpaulin. Once I was in, it took me what felt like a long time to make sense of the scene in front of me. It reminded me of a painting I had seen on a school trip to an art gallery years before; bodies in motion, illuminated by firelight, surrounding something I couldn't quite make out. I took another step forward. I recognised Danielle, Annie, and Mim as the figures, but what were they doing, and who were they doing it to? They were speaking, but I couldn't tell what they were saying. My heart was pounding fit to burst through my chest, and I could hear the blood pumping through my body, rising like a red tide into my head. But the noise I was hearing wasn't my own blood – it was water sloshing in a metal tub. I took another step closer, but Danielle and Annie's backs were still blocking my view; as far as I could tell they hadn't even noticed I was there. Eventually Mim glanced up and saw me. She looked distraught, like she'd been crying, and her cheeks were as red as a slap. Water or sweat had plastered her hair to her head. I was searching her face for signs of what was happening, when slowly, she looked down.

I followed Mim's eyes as they landed on the boy in the bath. Oliver. He wasn't one of my children, or Aoife's or Ruth's, but I knew him well from my time in the schoolhouse. I knew them all so well. He was a wispy boy, around seven years old, with a skinny body and a large head of shaggy mouse-coloured hair. Lying there, though, he seemed even smaller than usual, and his hair was slick and wet. I felt my body slacken with relief, and for a brief moment I wondered what all the fuss was about, why I'd been called in to help give someone a bath. It was only then that I realised Oliver was shaking, and the front of Mim's dress was drenched with water from trying to hold him still. He looked like a wild rabbit caught in a trap.

Slowly, I became aware of a wet hand tugging on my skirt. At first I thought it was Oliver's, but his arms were drawn tightly across his chest. The tug came again. It was Danielle.

'Deborah!' she was saying, 'are you listening to me?'

Danielle was the same age as me, and we had been close friends when I had first joined Heaven on Earth. I had taught her how to French plait hair, and later I had helped her dress for her wedding. It was strange to see her kneeling like that, looking up at me as though I would know what to do.

'I said we need to warm him up!' she said, rubbing Oliver's arms.

I lowered myself slowly so I was kneeling by the bath, and reached in with my hand. The water was hot, made hotter by the roaring fire, but Oliver's skin felt like ice.

'What's wrong with him?' I tried to keep the fear out of my voice, because I could see Oliver's eyes growing wider with panic as every second passed.

'I just told you,' said Danielle, 'he's too cold. It's like he's got hypothermia or something.'

'We've made the water as hot as we think he can take,' said

Annie, tucking a sodden strand of hair behind her ear, 'and we put mustard powder in it, from the kitchen.'

'Mustard powder?' I asked.

'Yeah,' she said, 'you know, like a mustard bath?'

I shook my head. I didn't know what she meant, but I wasn't about to waste time by asking for a more detailed explanation. Instead, I turned my attention to Oliver.

'How long have you been this cold, Ollie?' I asked, stroking his head. He was shivering so hard that his body was vibrating, and every nerve in my body was telling me to run away from something which I should not be seeing, which I should have no knowledge of.

He opened his mouth, but no words came out. Danielle answered for him.

'We only just got him in the bath before you came in, but he's been shivering for about an hour.'

'An *hour*?' I turned to look at Helen, who was standing against the gap in the tarp with her arms crossed. 'He's been like this for an *hour*?'

The word *hour* came out in a screech, and Helen winced.

'Keep your voice down,' she said, standing in place. 'We had it under control.'

'Clearly not!' Her calmness made me angrier, and it was all I could do not to get up and shake her.

'Well,' she said, 'you're here now, so help.'

I looked back down at Oliver. I could still feel him shivering, and his breathing was becoming laboured and shallow. I racked my brains for anything I had ever seen in a film or a TV programme that might come in handy, but there was nothing. Years of hospital dramas had vanished from my mind, wiped out by panic or just faded by time. There was only one thing I could possibly think to do:

'We need to get Ruth.'

Annie and Danielle shared a look of concern, but neither spoke against me. It wouldn't have mattered either way, though, because at the sound of Ruth's name Mim nodded, shot to her feet, and sprinted out of the barn.

'I had hoped we could keep this a little bit quieter if I'm perfectly honest, Deborah,' said Helen as we watched Mim disappear through the tarp. 'There are much more important things happening in Halcyon at the moment. We don't want to distract people.'

With Ruth safely en route, and Annie and Danielle continuing to soothe and calm the shaking Oliver, I allowed myself to rise to my feet and face Helen. I stood as close to her as I dared. She had been in Heaven on Earth longer than me, and was older than me, but I was Elijah's wife and ready to pull rank if necessary.

'I know exactly what you mean,' I hissed, 'all of the excitement that you were so thrilled about when you came to collect me from the farmhouse.'

She flushed with embarrassment.

'I can't believe it, Helen,' I went on, 'coming in all chatty and *giddy* and poor Ollie lying here frozen half to death. You didn't even think to mention it.'

He's your son, I wanted to add, suddenly remembering. But I thought better of it. 'You're making a big fuss out of nothing,' she said, gesturing at Oliver, 'he's absolutely fine. We have more pressing things to worry about, and you of all people should know that.'

At any other time I would have stopped to wonder exactly what pressing things Helen was talking about, and who knows, maybe I should have done then, but all I could think about was Ruth, and when she would arrive.

It didn't take long for them to turn up, and they were both panting; Mim must have told Ruth to run.

'What's the emergency?' she said, zeroing in on Oliver and rolling up her sleeves before any of us had the chance to respond.

Annie and I stepped out of her way, but Danielle stayed by Oliver's side. Ruth took one look at his shivering body and snapped into action. Within minutes we had lifted Oliver out of the hot water and dried him off as gently as we could. It was difficult to reconcile this confident, authoritative version of Ruth with the quiet woman I usually knew, but she seemed to shed her shyness like a snake skin, emerging glistening and assertive – a brighter, more powerful version of her normal self. Under her command, we gathered as many blankets as we could from the other beds. With a firm but gentle hand, she took them from us and swaddled Oliver like an enormous baby.

If time had jarred and jolted before, Ruth's arrival set

everything on a smoother course. Before too long Oliver stopped shaking and had warmed up enough that Annie and Helen were able to go next door and tend to the other children. Ruth was perched on the side of Oliver's bed, taking his pulse. All I could do was stand there at the foot of the bed, watching the scene and allowing the adrenaline to drain from my body.

It was during the newly settled calm that it dawned on me. I turned to Danielle, who was mopping up a puddle of spilled water by the tub.

'Are the others okay?' I asked.

She looked up from what she was doing.

'What others?' she asked, wiping sweat from her head with a damp forearm.

'What do you mean "what others"? The other children! If they were all sleeping in here together, and Oliver managed to catch this cold, should we not get Ruth to check that they're all all right?'

The room was dim, but the glow from the fire was enough that I was able to see Danielle's cheeks colour. She touched her hand to the side of her head, as though looking for a strand of hair to play with. When she couldn't find one, she brought her hand back down to her thigh. It must have been wet, because when she moved it again, I saw that it had left a dark print on her skirt.

Eventually she spoke.

'No,' she said, 'no. They're fine.'

'Well, should we just check? Or have Ruth check? Like I said, if it's happened to Oliver…'

I trailed off in disbelief. Danielle had gone back to mopping up the water with the towel.

'Are you listening to me?' I asked, trying to keep my voice from going too loud.

Danielle sighed. 'I already told you, Deb, the others are fine. It was just Ollie. It just happened to Ollie.'

Whether it was the fact that she couldn't meet my gaze, or the shame in her voice, I couldn't be sure. I was winded by the thought that what had happened to Oliver might have been something more than a horrible fluke. My anger was boiling over again and I wanted to shout, or to take her by the shoulders and shake her and make her tell me what had happened. Maybe I would have, if Ruth hadn't called me over when she did.

'Deborah?' she said, her voice no more than a whisper, 'can you come over here for a minute?'

I looked at Danielle, but she was wringing out the towel into the tub and her head was down. Ruth was waiting for me, still perched on the edge of Oliver's bed. She patted a space next to her, and I sat down gently.

'Everything is all right now,' said Ruth, her voice so low that I could barely hear her, 'and Ollie is stable. But I want you to know you called me just in time.'

I nodded, and she went on:

'I don't know whose idea it was to put him in the bath, but that was the dumbest, most dangerous thing that they could have done. He could have died.'

Ruth wasn't looking at me while she was speaking. Instead, she was staring down at Oliver. He was pale, and the delicate skin under his eyes was tinged with a blueish purple. He looked peaceful though, and still.

'I don't know what happened here,' I said, 'because I got here just before you did. But we need to find out.'

It was only then that she looked at me.

'You need to speak to him as soon as he wakes up.'

Chapter Twenty

Aoife

Malcolm's words were echoing around my head as I sat alone in the kitchen after breakfast. Ruth and Deborah were long gone, and I could hear the people of Halcyon at work outside, but I couldn't bring myself to move. I was thinking about how easy he had made everything sound, how confident he had been that I could just leave, that he could help me. I had toyed with the idea of sharing his offer with Deborah, but I wanted to speak to him again first. Now that Elijah was back things would be trickier, and I needed to know Malcolm was serious. Also, I needed to think about what I would say to him, how I would explain myself and Halcyon without driving him away. The last thing I wanted was to find myself speechless again.

I was still in the kitchen, turning the Malcolm situation over in my mind, when the bell rang. The bell at Halcyon was a bit like a fire alarm anywhere else; if you heard it, you were to drop whatever you were doing and head straight to the church. A spirit drill, we called it. I left the dishes I was washing in the sink – not my job, but as a gesture of goodwill to Deborah I'd decided to do them anyway – dried my hands on my dress, and headed for the door. Our front porch was home to an array of boots and coats and I chose some at random, ending up with a pair of poorly repaired wellies that were probably on their way out two winters ago, and a thick navy fleece of Elijah's which smelled of clean sweat and wood-smoke. It was a beautiful sight, stepping outside and seeing the whole of Halcyon converging on the church together. There must have been similar scenes in Biblical times, with people teeming from all directions to hear the word of Christ. It was easy to forget, as I watched the congregation flock into the church, how determined I was to leave.

I managed to make my way through the crowd easily enough and was one of the first to enter the church. Elijah was there already, standing like a statue behind the pulpit. I hurried down the aisle and to my place at the front, secretly glad to notice that neither Ruth nor Deborah were there yet. I looked up at Elijah, hoping that he would have noticed too, but he continued to stare ahead, watching as each person walked through the doors. It was only then that I noticed John was standing at the corner of the raised platform, holding his clipboard. He was also watching the congregation, his eyes darting from person to person. Everyone had been chatting as they walked, but as soon as they entered the church something in the atmosphere turned them quiet. Even as the room filled up, the eerie silence was maintained – the only noise was the sound of footsteps on the concrete, and the scraping and squeaking of chairs as people sat themselves down. Ruth and Deborah were the last to enter, and I couldn't help but feel a pang of jealousy when I saw them walking in together. Deborah looked at me questioningly as they took their seats, but I kept my gaze forward. Now was not the time to appear in cahoots.

Up on stage, Elijah was whispering something to John, who checked his clipboard before beckoning Helen up to the front. She looked around her as she walked self-consciously to where the two men stood. I didn't hear what John asked her, but I saw her cheeks turn red as she replied. I caught the words *not coming* and *ill in bed*. Whatever she'd said had clearly displeased Elijah, who spoke loudly enough that his voice echoed and carried through the silent church.

'I. Don't. Care,' I heard him say to Helen. 'Go and fetch him.'

Helen's face fell, and she looked imploringly to John. Elijah turned to John too.

'I don't have time for this, John, control your wife.'

My throat tightened as I watched John grab Helen's forearm and yank her towards him so hard that her head jerked backwards. He hissed something in her ear before turning to Elijah, who nodded with absent approval when Helen turned and hurried out through the still open doors. Nobody seemed alarmed by what they had just seen, and I felt surprise even though I knew I shouldn't. After all, how many punishments had this barn witnessed? Instead, the congregation waited, soundlessly and for what felt like an age, until she returned.

When she did, even I allowed myself to turn and look. Holding Helen's hand was Oliver, wrapped in a cocoon of blankets which trailed out a little way behind him like a cape. His eyes looked tired, and he was hunched over and shuffling. I remembered when he was born, the April after Ruth and Elijah married and the year before our move. We shared a birthday.

Children were always seated at the back of the church as a rule, so the younger ones could be taken out by the older ones if they became fussy, but Helen walked him all the way down to her place directly behind us. I felt Ruth go to rise, and saw Deborah reach out a hand to keep her in her seat. They were the only ones to move, however – the rest of the congregation remained still and silent, too focused on Elijah to pay attention to the little scene. These weren't heartless people; in usual circumstances, it wouldn't be in anybody's nature to ignore a child who was clearly unwell. They were just captivated. Elijah had been away for days, without having told anyone where he was going, and then there he was, larger than life, back in their midst. Even I was spellbound in spite of myself. Looking up at him sent my heart fluttering in the way it used to when we first met – he buzzed with a familiar pent-up tension which spoke to some deep desire inside me. But it was more than just that. I don't know if I could think of anyone else who could command a room without saying a word. It was an effort to remember that I was no longer supposed to be enthralled by him, that he had made a fool of me, that I wanted to leave him. If he'd looked at me then, if he'd called me to him, I would have been up on my feet without a second thought – a magnet pulling towards its mate.

Eventually, the sermon began. He spoke quietly at first, his voice so low and deep that everyone leaned forward in their seats.

'There are dark times ahead.'

Dark times. Since coming to Halcyon, I'd heard more sermons about 'dark times' than I'd had hot dinners, and the phrase brought me back to my senses somewhat. I forced myself to listen to what he was saying; despite the familiarity of his words, Elijah seemed more tense than usual and I didn't want to miss anything. He paused before speaking again and in the heavy silence I studied his face, searching for a sign of what was to come. I suppose that, with one thing or another, I had not really looked at him properly for a while. Suddenly he seemed old; there were lines on his face that hadn't been there before, and specks of white were showing through the black of his beard. Even his eyes were different – bloodshot and dull, as though he hadn't slept for days. When he started talking again, his words came slowly. At first, I thought he was doing it on purpose, some sort of public-speaking technique to draw us in and hold our interest, but after a while it became very clear – to me at least – that he was trying to keep from slurring his words. Was he really that tired? As he went on, he started to speed up. Words fell from his mouth and tripped over each other, sentences seeping and merging. I wondered, as I sat and listened to him, whether anyone else had noticed the grinding way his lower jaw was moving – surely they must have done?

From what I managed to make out, he was speaking about his recent trip to the outside world. He spoke, in this new, chaotic way, of the downfall of society. 'We must be ready,' he said, over and over again, 'we must be ready.' Every so often he would punctuate his rambling descriptions of rabid locals looking for a safe haven and government officials coming in search of survivors with a strike of the pulpit. I was frightened, but not at the thought of some hypothetical invasion. What scared me was how unhinged Elijah appeared, how detached from reality and his usual self he was. I remembered the night before he disappeared, when he had seemed like that, and I had held him and he had calmed and slept. If we were alone together, I could have taken his face in my hands and looked into his tired eyes and brought him back, but there, with everyone watching, I couldn't have even if I had wanted to. And really, the more he talked, the less I did want to. With every word I felt myself drifting further and further away from him until I no longer cared what he said or what he thought. That glimmer of feeling I'd experienced when I'd seen him again had vanished. The rest of the congregation listened, rapt, apparently unfazed.

It was as though someone had cast a spell over him. Eventually, my husband looked to the side of the stage where John was standing; John's glance must have reminded Elijah where he was, and after a short pause he seemed to pull himself together.

'John,' he said, 'will be supervising bunker checks.' His speech was slow again, but his voice seemed steadier. 'Any stores not in the bunker will need to be moved down there, and we'll need to redouble our work to fill the stockrooms. We're preparing for the worst here everybody, but we've been preparing for a long time.' This time when he paused, I could tell straight away that it was for effect. When he spoke again, he was more coherent. 'When God told me that the time was drawing near, I could never have hoped it would be this near.'

The people of Halcyon, who had been so silent throughout Elijah's sermon, found their voices all at once and the room filled with the rising sounds of fear-tinged excitement. Everyone except for Deborah and Ruth, who sat unmoved and unmoving, staring straight up at Elijah. He, in turn, was surveying the entire room. When he had started his sermon, he had been vacant and hardly there, but the congregation's reaction must have bolstered him, because all of a sudden he seemed more like himself again. He raised a steady hand.

'Quiet.' His voice echoed around the room, and he waited until the final reverberation had faded before continuing. 'We have been preparing for this moment for a long time – some of us for thirteen years. We have nothing to fear. The people who would harm us, now *they* are the ones who should be frightened. *Satan* is the one who should be frightened! We are God's army, and we are ready to fight!'

As soon as the words had left his mouth, I was deafened by a loud roar. For a second, I thought Elijah must have been right, and that something of Biblical proportions was about to happen – a heavenly host descending from the clouds, or a thunderstorm indicating the start of a second flood. None of those possibilities frightened me as much as the reality, though, which was that the entire room had heard Elijah's battle cry and erupted into a wild cheer. It worried me that they could sit through such an incoherent speech and still place their faith so unwaveringly in the person who had given it. But if I was so confused and infuriated by their reaction, why did I feel so sad not to be cheering with them? I felt left out, as though I had missed the punchline of a joke that everyone else had understood, but it was as if that feeling were multiplied by a thousand. I put my hands together and tried to drown out my grief with applause. One of the babies at the back started to cry, but the noise did not stop. Instead it grew louder, and eventually the baby's wail became indistinguishable from the congregation's wild cheer. Someone started to stamp their feet, and soon the whooping and applause was joined by the smack of hard-soled boots against concrete. Someone else gave a loud, high whistle. The barn rattled and shook, and the air was thick with sound.

Elijah watched from above as the congregation whipped itself into a frenzy, and when sufficient time passed, he raised his hand once again. This time he did not even have to speak. The crowd muted instantly at his sign; even the crying baby had given up its tears. He surveyed the panting crowd with pleasure.

'In order to strengthen our army,' he said, his voice clear and strong and familiar, 'I will be taking our sister Jemima as my new wife. God has spoken.'

I felt the room rise around me as the noise erupted again. This time, I couldn't bring myself to join in the cheer. Instead I remained in my seat, numb and dazed, until the congregation fell into an exhausted silence. John took to the stage to give out new orders for the day, but even though I had known this was coming I was too distracted to hear a word. My heart was crashing against my chest, not even beating any more, but clenching like a great raging fist. I could feel it reverberating through my body until even my brain started to throb. When John finally finished and the congregation began to file out, I rose, shaking and sick, to follow behind them. My body was so numb to everything except its own movement that I could barely even feel my feet on the ground. I became vaguely aware of a hand tapping on my shoulder, the sensation permeating my numbness like a figure emerging through the mist. Turning, I was surprised to see John, his arm still outstretched, his mouth half open.

'Can I have a quick word?' he asked.

I scanned the room. Ruth and Deborah were already at the door, and Elijah could have been anywhere. I nodded, confused, and together we walked back to my usual seat. He gestured for me to sit down. When the final person had left the church and the door was pulled closed, he gave an awkward cough. I studied his face. Pale stubble was growing on his chin, and I wondered when he had last shaved. Usually he was so clean-cut, the only similarity I had ever been able to observe between him and Helen, other than their shared devotion to the church. Or in John's case, I supposed, devotion to Elijah. He had helped Elijah start up Heaven on Earth back in the city, when Elijah decided that the preacher at their old Methodist church wasn't a 'true Christian'. When Elijah and I had met, they were still working to convert some members of the old congregation. I had always thought of John as something of a third wheel, an irritating and intense figure hovering on the periphery of mine and Elijah's relationship. And John made no secret of the fact that he felt the same way about me.

'Elijah has asked me to speak to you today about something a little...' he paused, 'sensitive.'

At any other time those words would have drawn out some reaction from me, but as it was I couldn't think of anything that he could say to me that was more shocking, or indeed more sensitive, than Elijah's announcement had been. John was not one to be deterred by a silent conversation partner, though, and he went on.

'I don't intend to be insensitive here, Aoife, but I think that it would be best, given the circumstances, to be as forthright as possible.'

I sighed. I was desperate to get back to my office, where I could sit alone and quietly untangle my thoughts.

'Can you just get on with it, please? I have work to do.'

My voice sounded unfamiliar – flat and quiet. I looked down at my lap, embarrassed to sound so weak in front of John.

'Elijah is worried that you have been putting too much strain on yourself lately.'

'Strain?' I asked.

'That you've been spending too much time doing work that isn't necessarily appropriate for a woman of your station in the community, or, to be quite frank, Aoife, a woman at all. He believes that the pressure on your brain has had an influence on, well... on other things.'

'Excuse me?'

'I'm not sure how to put this delicately, so I'll just say it. Elijah is concerned that your work in the office has led to your current inability to conceive. He wanted me to remind you that he's encouraged you to give up your work in the office before, but he says he wants to do everything he can to get things right. He hopes that it won't be too late.'

I could see John's mouth moving, and hear the words which

were coming out, but my head was filled with a swirling fog and I couldn't decipher his meaning. The confusion must have shown in my face, because he coughed again before clarifying.

'Elijah has decided that it would be best for you if you were to give up your role in the office.'

For the second time that morning, I felt the floor disappear from beneath my feet. I forced myself to look John right in the eye. I had hoped that he would at least have the decency to pretend to feel ashamed or awkward, but there was a barely disguised glee hiding behind his façade of formality.

'Don't worry,' he said, 'you won't be idle. It will be all hands on deck getting things ready for the bunker. I was speaking to Jess earlier, and she's offered to teach you how to use the loom. The deepest circle of hell is ice cold after all; we'll want to be wrapped up warm when it ascends to Earth.'

He smiled.

My head was swimming, but I knew that I had to say something. I pulled myself out of the depths and took a deep breath.

'I appreciate your concern...'

'Elijah's concern.'

'I appreciate Elijah's concern,' I said, 'but my work in the office is very important. I can't just *stop*.'

'Well, Aoife, I'm afraid you have no choice. And I'm sorry to burst your bubble, but the important work at the moment is the work that helps us prepare for the End times. *Not* files and accounts. I'm sure you agree.'

I no longer cared about the accounts or the files. The missing thousands, once an obsession, a charm which I had believed had the ability to bring Elijah back to me if I could recover it, meant nothing. But the removal of my very last ounce of power hit me hard. The final nail had been hammered into the coffin of my life as I'd known it. The room was starting to get chilly in its near emptiness, and I didn't trust myself not to shiver. I hoped that the more amenable I was, the sooner he would let me go. It wasn't usually in my nature to go down without a fight, but I wasn't stupid and knew how to pick my battles when I needed to. Also, I was remembering the way Helen's head had snapped backwards when he had pulled her towards him earlier. I couldn't seem to shake the thought.

'Very good.' He looked surprised, but relieved. 'Very good.

Jess is with the rest of the ladies in the community centre. You can head over there now. *Straight* there mind, Aoife, no detours.'

John clapped his hands together as he rose to stand and looked at me meaningfully. I stood up too, but felt myself wobble as I understood his last words. Had he been watching me take my walks? Did he know I'd been talking to Malcolm? Did *Elijah* know? Oh God. The thought made me feel sick. He gestured for me to walk out ahead, and I made my way outside on shaking legs.

I could see Elijah standing with a small group of men outside one of the outbuildings. John must have seen them too, because as soon as the door was locked he hurried across to them without even a backward glance. I watched until they disappeared into the outbuilding and then I took my chance. If John was on to me, I might not have another opportunity to speak to Malcolm. Elijah's speech had inspired a flurry of activity in the colonists, and they were so preoccupied with their work that nobody seemed to notice as I snuck away from the centre of Halcyon. Still, I quickened my pace as I followed the familiar route around the fence.

To my relief, I saw Malcolm almost straight away. I'd left so unceremoniously the day before that part of me had been worried he might not come back. He gave a languid wave, and I forced myself to smile back. As I got closer, I saw his expression change from one of happiness to one of concern. He gave a big, exaggerated shrug and mouthed *what's wrong?* I shrugged back and hoped that he was still too far away to see the corners of my mouth tremble.

When I reached the fence he asked me again, but this time there was no exaggeration, no hint of humour in his face.

'Aoife! What's the matter? What's happened?'

I couldn't hold it in any longer. He had barely got the words out before I burst into tears; the sort of huge, gulping sobs that you might expect from a toddler who had just finished throwing a tantrum.

Go on then, cry.

'Hey, hey,' he said, pressing his gloved hands against the chain link of the fence, 'take a breath. It's okay. Take a second.'

The way he spoke made me wonder whether he had children. For all of our conversations, I had never even thought to ask him. I couldn't even remember if I had told him about my own children, and the thought made me cry even harder.

'I'm so sorry,' I sobbed, wiping my eyes and nose on the sleeve of my coat, 'I'm so embarrassed. Just ignore me, I'm being ridiculous.'

'You've nothing to be embarrassed about,' he said, 'please don't be sorry. Do you want to talk about it?'

And then I did. I talked and I talked, and I told him everything. I told him about Ruth and Deborah and Elijah, and about Halcyon. I told him about Mim, and losing my job in the office, and the secret computer, and about Jess and her loom, and then about Mim again, and all the time he stood there and listened, his face completely expressionless. *He'll hate you,* came the voice as my words tumbled out, *he'll judge you. He won't understand. Nobody from out there could ever understand you.*

When he was sure that I was finished, he exhaled deeply through his mouth.

'Well then.'

Chapter Twenty-One

Ruth

I had tried not to look at Elijah while he preached, and it was like trying not to look at the sun during an eclipse. I'd managed to keep my eyes off of him, but I could still hear him, his voice slurring and halting like it had been the night before. Instead, I concentrated on my hands, clasped in my lap with my thumbs crossed over each other like I was praying. We'd been taught to sit like that as kids, my sisters and me. I had enjoyed looking down at my neat little hands when I was younger, liking how tidy they looked, folded up like a sweater. When I held my hands like that it made my elbows tuck into my sides, so that all of me felt compact and dainty. And good. Sitting in Halcyon, I was thirty years and thousands of miles away from the little girl I'd been when I was first taught to sit that way, but there I was, still doing it. Still being good. I thought of what Elijah had said the night before, about how I was his favourite. Wasn't that all I'd ever wanted to hear? Not because I was competitive, or because I wanted to be better than my sister wives; I just wanted to know I was pleasing him. So why had it made me feel so awful? As my mind ticked over, Elijah's words dripped into my brain in a slow, steady stream: on, and on, and on. I kept my hands clasped through his announcement, through the cheering, until we were dismissed.

Time had lost all meaning during the spirit drill, as it always did, and when it was time to leave I felt drained and disorientated. The sky above was white, and there was no sun to tell me the time of day. From the grumbling in my stomach I guessed that it might be around lunch-time, although I hadn't eaten breakfast so I couldn't be sure. Either way, I had no interest in returning to the farmhouse where I imagined Aoife and Deborah were now gathered, digesting Elijah's news together over steaming mugs of tea. I decided that the best thing to do would be to return to the cowshed where I could be out of the way, surrounded by creatures who were simple and sweet, and who looked forward to my arrival every day. Russell was there too, and it would give me the chance to check on her. I had decided to remove the pups and Russell from the outbuilding where Mim and I had hidden them. It was too risky for me to sneak in and out of there, and the prospect of getting caught had made me tense and jumpy. The cows seemed to enjoy their company, I reasoned, and it wasn't like anyone other than me spent much time in that barn anyway.

As soon as I was safely inside, I fell to my knees. Prayer had been my comfort and my joy for so many years. My lowest lows and my highest highs had been punctuated by conversations with God, but at that moment there was nothing for me to say. It was God who had told Elijah that he had to marry Mim. And if it wasn't? I opened my eyes. Prayer was pointless either way. I remembered Elijah's words, how lucid they had been after his drunken whispers: 'now I know what it really feels like to be God.' They had shaken me the night before, but kneeling there on the floor of the barn they crushed me like a hand under a steel-capped boot. I had no prayers but was too hopeless to move, so I just stayed there, hunched over on the freezing, hay-strewn floor, hoping against hope that no one would come in.

It was Russell who brought me back to reality. She had left her pups and tapped her way along to where I was kneeling. When she reached me, she stuck her inquisitive face into mine, her nose cold and wet against my cheek. I don't know how long I had spent down there, but when I rose my joints were stiff and achy. It felt self-indulgent to stretch, though, so I didn't. Instead, I shuffled over to check on the pups, who were sleeping peacefully in a nest of towels. A lump formed in my throat at the sight of them. I could only hope that Elijah would be too distracted to remember Russell and his plans for her litter. There was so much else for him to focus on – his wedding, the End. I winced. He had sounded so sure about the End during the spirit drill, and everyone had been so excited about it. I would have been too, if the announcement had come a month or a week, or even a few days before. I had been waiting for the End for years; I had literally dreamed of it on the rare occasions I slept long enough to dream. And now it was apparently just around the corner, and I felt nothing.

A figure appeared silhouetted in the doorway. It stood there a second before it spoke.

'Hi.'

I recognised the voice immediately, although I wished I hadn't. Russell must have recognised it too, because she waddled across to where the figure was standing, her stubby tail wagging in greeting.

'What is it, Mim?'

Even I could hear the dullness in my voice, but it didn't seem to faze her.

'Please may I come in for a minute?'

Mim's voice was so soft that I could hardly hear her from where I was standing. The fact of it annoyed me, and I wanted her to leave. Instead, I nodded.

'Fine,' I said, 'come on in.'

She walked slowly, running her hand along the hard metal edge of the cows' trough, and stopped a little way away from me. In the half-light of the barn she looked paler than normal, drawn and tired.

'Can I talk to you?'

With a sigh, I gestured to my milking stool. Mim perched herself down, but I remained on my feet, arms folded.

'What's the problem?' I asked. 'I'm a bit busy here.'

'Of course. I won't keep you,' she said. After a long pause, during which Mim stared at her hands, she spoke again, 'I suppose I just wanted to speak to someone. I just feel a bit...' she mimed freezing up.

'Oh?' I said.

'Yeah.'

We sat in awkward silence again. I could tell that Mim was waiting for me to say something encouraging but everything about her was frustrating to me, from her simpering voice to the way she was picking at her cuticles, and I didn't feel like making things easier for her. I was done making things easy for people.

'It's just,' she went on, 'you're the only person I feel like I can really talk to.'

This surprised me.

'Really?'

'Yes,' she said, 'well, it's pretty hard to talk in the schoolhouse.

And the other women are always so busy.' She looked worried for a moment before continuing, 'Not that I mean to say that I don't think you're busy or anything, but you always seem to have time to talk to me. And you're always nice.'

I flinched.

'What was it you wanted to talk about?' I asked, even though I was certain that I already knew the answer.

'Well,' she said, 'you were there today, at the spirit drill. You heard what he said.'

I gave a slow nod, guarding myself against what she might say next.

'I've known it was going to happen for a while, I mean, I knew we were getting married soon, but this just seems so sudden. And I just feel like I don't really know anything. About being married.' Mim's face turned pink as she spoke; even the tips of her ears had coloured.

I could feel my body tensing up, and my jaw hurt from clenching. I sensed her staring up at me expectantly, but instead of looking her in the eye I turned around and busied myself with the cows. When I spoke, I spoke to them, not her.

'Look,' I said, 'I get it. But now is just… not a good time. I have a lot to do. I have to take the cows out to pasture.'

I heard her rise to her feet.

'That's all right,' said Mim, 'I can walk with you, I don't mind.'

'Well, I mind,' I said, turning to face her. I was surprised by the anger in my voice. 'I mind. Now is not a good time, Jemima.'

She seemed to crumple right before my eyes, and for a second I thought that she might cry. Instead, she gave a single nod and scurried out the way she had come. When I was sure she had gone, I sat myself down on the newly vacated milking stool. It was still warm, which made me uncomfortable, and I leaned forward and rested my head in my hands. Mim in general made me feel uncomfortable. I couldn't work her out. She seemed to fluctuate between deferential and conspiratorial, which made it difficult to figure out what it was she wanted from me. Flightiness – that's what it was. I wondered what Elijah saw in her. I wasn't so naïve as to believe any of Elijah's marriages, myself included, had been solely love matches. Or else, if they were, it was our usefulness to the cause that had formed part of his attraction to Aoife, Deborah, and me. We each had our strengths. Something we could offer.

I was nothing special as a person, but I had my nurses' training and I was good at pacifying him. Mim, well, there was nothing to her. She was just a teenager. That was it. *Of course* that was it. I don't know why it took me so long to work it out. She was young and pretty and biddable. He wanted someone who he could boss around, and someone to... I winced. I thought of Mim, with her two long plaits and her big doe eyes. She had come to me thinking that I was her friend, and all I'd done was send her away.

I pulled myself up from where I was sitting. The cold was still lingering in my bones and joints, and I ached with every movement. I would have taken the physical discomfort any day, though, over the shame. I caught a glimpse of my reflection in the metallic cladding of the big milk silo which sat in the corner of the barn; it was warped and flat. *Seems about right*, I thought, closing my eyes and screwing up my face in pure distaste at myself. In my head, I ran through every curse word that I knew before putting on my coat and leaving the barn in search of Mim.

Chapter Twenty-Two

Deborah

After the spirit drill, I felt like I had been hit by a bus. My brain was too fried from trying to follow Elijah's manic, rambling sermon to even begin to digest what he'd just said, and all I could think of was how much I needed my bed. The farmhouse, which in reality was just across the yard, felt cruelly distant, and when I finally reached my room I barely managed to pull my boots off before burrowing myself under the covers. The sheets were so stiff with cold that I was frightened to move once I got in, just in case a glimmer of bare skin became exposed to the chill. I could feel my nose running, but I was too frozen and exhausted to raise my hand and stop the flow. Instead, I felt the warm trickle down my cheek and closed my eyes.

I don't know how long I slept for, but it couldn't have been too long because when I woke up I could still see daylight coming through the net curtains in my window and hear the bustle of people outside. It took me a minute to remember exactly where I was, and why, and for a delicious moment I stretched my sore muscles, relishing the warmth now trapped inside my blankets in a state of blissful ignorance. The sound of Helen's voice passing outside my window was what brought me back to my senses again and I swung myself out of bed, my stockinged feet landing softly on the rag rug which covered the hard, chilly floorboards. The room spun, but my mind and purpose were as focused as the point of a knife and I was out of the house faster than it would have usually taken me to get my shoes on.

For the second time that day, I left the farmhouse for the schoolhouse. The cold bit and pinched at my flesh, burrowing through the loose knit of my jumper and slipping shamelessly up my skirt. I regretted not taking my coat the second I was out of the door, but I was only heading across the yard and I didn't plan to be outside for long. With everything that had happened with Ollie that morning, and Elijah's crazed sermon at the spirit drill, I knew that was where I needed to be. Even if all I could do was see my kids.

Annie was standing at the door of the barn, looking nervously around and clutching a heavy shawl about herself. She didn't see me until I was almost on top of her, and when she did she jumped and blushed.

'Oh, hi Deborah,' she said, 'what are you doing here?'

I couldn't tell if she was kidding. Annie had never been much of a joker, but I couldn't think of another explanation. Where else would I be?

'Erm, I'm just here for work,' I said, struggling to keep my tone light, 'you know, like I am every day?'

I heard my voice lift at the end of the sentence, so it sounded like I was asking her a question. Elijah hated it when I did that – he said it made me sound simple.

She shook her head, unable to meet my eye.

'I'm sorry, Deborah,' she said, 'I was sure someone would have told you. John made it sound as though he'd already spoken to you.'

'About what?' I asked, my heart beginning to flutter in my chest.

'They told me not to let you in here any more.'

Annie's voice shook a little, but her face was serious. I knew that I'd have to choose my next move carefully. Talking to people in Halcyon was like playing chess, or at least what I imagined playing chess would be like. Thinking four steps ahead of yourself: *if I say this, they'll think that, so they'll say... but then they'll actually... and I'll end up...* The trick was to always be very sweet to everyone at all times, so they would give you the benefit of the doubt if you ever found yourself in a situation where it would be useful for someone to give you the benefit of the doubt. It was an exhausting way to live, but it usually worked.

'Look, Annie,' I said in my nicest voice, 'I don't know what's going on here, but I think there must have been some kind of misunderstanding. I'm just here to do my job, just like you, just like I always do.'

'I...' she started to speak again, but I reached out my hand and touched her arm – a gentle reminder that I outranked her.

'I know that you're just doing as you're told, which is great, it's what I'm doing too.' I paused for a second, plotting my next move. 'No one has told me not to turn up to work duty. If I wasn't meant to be here today, don't you think Elijah would have said something to me himself?'

Annie's face started to soften, and I could tell she was thinking about what I had said. I clutched my belly and shivered in an attempt to hurry her along. Just as I thought she was about to step to one side and let me in, though, she raised her hand and waved at someone behind me. I turned to see John coming towards us.

'Sorry about this, Sister,' he said to Annie, who looked as relieved as I had ever seen anybody look. 'I'll take it from here.'

Annie nodded her thanks and disappeared into the schoolhouse, leaving me standing in the cold with John. As soon as she was safely inside, John stepped across and blocked the door with his body. He wasn't a tall man, but he was taller than me, and suddenly I was a kid again, standing in front of a teacher and getting ready to be told off. My shoulders squared automatically. It was the wrong move for John, who liked his women timid and submissive, but it was too late to change my tactic. I had committed, so I would just have to hope for the best.

'Can you please tell me what's going on here?' I asked, my voice as calm as I could make it, 'I just want to go to work?'

Another questioning lift at the end, but never mind. John already thought I was an idiot.

He raised his eyebrows; instead of being fazed, he looked mildly entertained. Was he humouring me? He reached out to take my arm, and I jerked away in shock. Men in Halcyon did not touch women who were not their wives. John knew that.

'Deborah!' he said, in exaggerated surprise, 'I'm not going to hurt you. I just think it would be a good idea to talk about this inside. You look half frozen.'

He was right; I was shivering, and the tips of my fingers were turning blue.

'Fine,' I said, 'let's go inside, and you can explain to me why I'm suddenly not allowed to see the children. Or do my job.'

He smiled in the big, wide way Elijah sometimes did when he was preaching. I wondered if he had been taking lessons. This time when he reached for my arm, I let him take it, surprised by just how strange it felt to be held by someone different. His grip was less confident than Elijah's; he seemed to be putting more effort into clinging with his fingers, while Elijah would use his whole hand. His hand was smaller too, and he was shorter. I kept my own arm limp and did my best to avoid touching any more of John than I had to, like a loyal wife, and together we walked back towards the farmhouse. When I had said 'inside', I'd meant the schoolhouse, but I should have known better. I forced myself to take a breath and begin again. I knew that if I was to get anywhere with John, I would have to restart the submissive act. The walk was slower than I would have liked, but it gave me the chance to look around at the people of Halcyon. Hardly anyone was in the courtyard – lots of people seemed to be at the bunker already, their voices carrying on the wind, and the people who were around paid us no attention at all. I watched Alfie hauling a box of crockery from the community barn out in the direction of the bunker, with Lois following closely behind holding a laundry bag. I wanted to wave at them both with my free hand – 'hey, Alfie, Lois, look what this crazy guy is doing! Call Elijah!' They probably wouldn't have looked up even if I had shouted. The people of Halcyon were all very good at ignoring things they weren't meant to be seeing. Myself included.

When we reached the farmhouse, John pushed the door and it swung open with a creak. He waited until I had wiped my boots on the doormat and was safely blocked into the porch before walking in himself and closing the door firmly behind him. I was surprised when we passed the door to the kitchen, and instead continued straight down the hall. We stopped outside Aoife's office. She was protective of the space and I had only ever been in there a couple of times before. John motioned for me to enter. *Aoife's not going to be happy when she hears about this*, I thought. Still, I didn't say anything.

The light in the room was dim, so I didn't notice anything unusual at first. There was electricity set up in there, but either John didn't know about it or he had decided to save on power. I watched as he struck a match. For a moment, his face was illuminated by the raw, yellow glow of the flame. Somehow that made the room seem even darker, and for the first time that day I worried that I might be in danger. My hands slipped down to my belly, and I wondered whether I would be able to get to the door before John if it came down to it. I was busy plotting possible escape routes when the room was suddenly bathed in light. John had used the match to light a paraffin lamp and was looking at me expectantly. I glanced around the room; it didn't take me long to guess what he was waiting for me to notice.

'Where's all Aoife's stuff gone?' I asked.

All evidence that the room had once been an office had vanished. The desk had been replaced by a roughly crafted double bed, and the lamp itself was resting on a bedside cabinet. The Bible scenes which Aoife was so pleased with had been taken down, and the whitewashed walls stood bare and cold, even in the paraffin glow.

'Things are going to start changing around here,' said John as he sat down on the bed. 'For starters, this isn't Aoife's office any more. It's going to be her bedroom from now on, and we're giving Mim Aoife's old one. Seems a shame for that barren witch to get the best room in the house.'

I should have felt enraged on Aoife's behalf, but I was too focussed now on the potential danger of the situation I had let myself into to spare a thought for her potentially hurt feelings. John was breaking one rule after another; he had taken my arm, brought me into a room alone and unchaperoned, and there he was insulting one of the Prophet's wives. What else was he capable of? There was a large space next to him on the bed, and he patted the quilt invitingly. I stepped backwards, so I was as far away from him as I could be while staying in the room. Every fibre of my body was screaming for me to turn and leave, but I fought the urge. *Stay calm. Let's hear what else he has to say.* I think I really believed that if I went along with whatever power-play John was running, we would be able to walk out of the farmhouse and back to the schoolhouse, where everything would miraculously return to normal.

He shrugged, as if to say *fair enough*, and continued.

'Elijah thinks, and I agree, that you wives have been kept on too long a leash. It's time to rein you in.'

'I don't understand.'

John shook his head.

'Don't play dumb please, Deborah. It's embarrassing for us both. You couldn't have thought you would be able to keep your position in the schoolhouse indefinitely. Helen has told me that you favour your own children. All of the other women who work there can maintain the appropriate boundaries but apparently you can't.'

Bloody Helen.

'Where's Elijah?' I asked. 'Why isn't he telling me all of this himself?'

'*Where's Elijah? I want to speak to Elijah,*' he mimicked, his voice a high and whiny copy of my own. 'When will you girls realise that Elijah has more important things to do than worry about you? You're not the centre of his world, Deborah. You're not even a *third*, not even a *quarter* of his world. He's our most Holy Prophet. The end is nigh!' He stood up then, apparently too angry to stay seated. I wondered if he was going to hit me. Instead he sighed a heavy, frustrated sigh and shook his head again. 'You really are irredeemably fucking stupid, aren't you?'

My mouth dropped open in shock. I'd known John since I was a seventeen-year-old convert to the church, and had never heard anything remotely close to a swear word pass his tight little lips. But it had come out so easily, as natural as could be. He was right - I was stupid. Stupid to have ever believed that there wasn't one rule for us and one for the pair of them.

John must have realised that he had crossed a line because he stepped towards me and gave me a gentle pat on the shoulder. I winced, but he didn't laugh.

'Look,' he said, his voice stern but not unkind, 'we are at the very end of times. Not even just the final days. We're in the final hours.'

I nodded, gulping back my urge to scream in his face.

'And you,' he said, placing his hand on my belly, 'are carrying a very precious cargo. We can't have you wearing yourself out with preparations like everyone else. You need to rest. The children are being well taken care of.'

I thought of Ollie, shivering, too cold and frightened to even cry. I still didn't know what exactly had happened to him, but I was familiar enough with the punishments inflicted on rule-breaking adults that I feared I could guess. It was strange to think that I'd been by his side in the schoolhouse just a couple of hours before – it felt like a lifetime ago. I nodded again.

'Good,' he said, 'good. I think it would be best for you to stay in the farmhouse for now, and we can find something nice and stress-free for you to do. Knitting, or something. It'll help you take your mind off things, and I know how keen you are to be of use to everyone.'

I walked with John to the front door and watched from the porch as he locked it behind him. Once he was safely out of sight, I moved as quickly as I could to the other door at the other side of the house – the one that led to the back garden and the outhouse. Aoife would be out there somewhere, and I wanted to find her and talk to her. But even as I was walking, I realised that the whole thing was pointless. I knew that the door would be locked tight, but I tried the handle anyway. Sure enough, it didn't even budge.

When I pushed open the kitchen door, three heads turned to greet me. Aoife, Ruth, and – I did a double take – Mim. A conference of wives. Was that right? Was there even a collective noun for a group of wives, or had no one ever thought to come up with one? Not that Mim was a wife yet, I reminded myself, although it wouldn't be long.

It wasn't until Aoife stood up that I finally snapped back to reality.

'Ah, Deborah! Looks like we've got the full complement.'

I closed the door and took my seat amongst my sisters.

Chapter Twenty-Three

Aoife

I had returned from my walk to find Jemima sitting alone at the kitchen table. She must have been hoping for Deborah, or even Ruth, because when she looked up and saw me standing in the doorway she burst into tears. I didn't know Jemima – Mim – particularly well. For a long time she had just been another one of Halcyon's multitude of young people. But still, part of me was hurt to see her react that way to my presence. Who could blame her, though? She had obviously come looking for sympathy and she had been met by the person she considered to be Elijah's right-hand woman. How strange of me, how out of character, to be so offended by Mim's fear when I had spent years carefully cultivating a persona which inspired just that. And yet I was relieved to feel it. I was embarrassed and resentful and hurt, and I took that to be a good thing – a sign that I might be a nice girl after all.

Since when have you cared about being nice? chimed the voice in my head. It was Elijah's voice, I realised. It always had been. I blocked it out and pulled up a chair next to Mim, whose sobs were slowly becoming less hysterical. I placed a tentative hand on her back, and she turned to face me. She existed in my head as a small, faceless teenager with limp hair and no distinguishing features, so when I pictured her with Elijah, that's what I saw. In reality, she was quite pretty in a bird-like sort of way, like a sharper, more petite version of Deborah. Or maybe even, and my heart skipped a beat when I saw it, a fairer, younger *me*. I wondered if I should be flattered. Her hair was mousy – I'd been right about that – and had been twisted into two long plaits which hung on either side of her face down to her waist. There was a sprinkling of red spots across her chin, something which endeared me to her even more. At her age, I had suffered with the most appalling acne and as an adult was left with pits and scars on my forehead and cheeks. The only blemishes on Mim's cheeks were the heavy red blotches which had come from crying, and a fine dusting of freckles, which I didn't really count as flaws. Grainne had had freckles.

I had thought that Mim would pull away from my attempt to comfort her, but she leaned into me, resting her sodden face in the crevice between my neck and shoulder. With my free hand I touched my own face. The cold Highland air must have dried any tears my sleeve had missed, but I worried that my eyes or cheeks would somehow give me away. I longed more than ever for a mirror. I was ready to be nice, but I wasn't ready to be weak, and the thought of anyone catching me red-eyed like Mim sent my heart into a spasm. On some kind of instinct, I clutched her closer, and the tears picked up again.

'I'm so sorry, Aoife,' she gasped between sobs, 'please don't tell on me.'

I raised my eyebrows in surprise, although Mim's face was still burrowed against my neck and there was no one else around to see. It seemed like such a childish thing to say, although she could have been no older than fifteen or sixteen. I flinched and hoped to God that she was at least sixteen, before shooing the thought into the back of my mind to be dealt with later.

'Shh,' I said, 'it's all right. No one is going to tell on you.'

I tried to mimic the tone that Malcolm had used with me less than half an hour before and hoped that I sounded tender and comforting. We stayed like that long enough for my arm to start aching, but I didn't want to pull away. Instead, I tried to focus my attention on Mim. Looking at the top of her head made me wonder what was going on inside her mind in that moment, a thought experiment which was surprisingly difficult after such a long time devoted to trying not to think too deeply about such things. I had always acted on the assumption that life would be much more difficult if I allowed myself to consider the feelings of others, but it began to dawn on me that life had been pretty difficult anyway.

When I had opened up to Malcolm, I was surprised to find myself embarrassed to tell him certain things. I had known that some parts of my confession would be difficult, but I felt more shame than I'd expected about aspects of our lives that I had considered normal. Actions that had felt appropriate and ordinary became strange and cruel when relayed to someone who was not a part of Heaven on Earth. It was as though I had spent the last twelve years of my life in a parallel world and speaking to Malcolm had broken the spell which had kept me there. Suddenly my universe had shifted, and I was able to look into myself from the outside. I held Mim closer and rested my cheek against her hair.

'It's okay if you don't want to get married.'

I don't know why I said it. I suppose everything was so up in the air, and I still felt slightly lightheaded and vulnerable after my own crying jag. The kitchen had transformed into a sort of liminal space where everything mattered, so nothing mattered, and I could say anything at all. Mim twisted herself out from my embrace and fixed me with a doubtful look. Her eyes were even redder than before, and her pale lashes were wet with tears. With a straight face I met her gaze.

'I have to.'

'But do you *want* to?'

'It doesn't matter what I want. It's what God wants, and I need to do what God wants me to do.'

She was looking down at the tabletop by then, and I moved my head in an attempt to meet her eyes again.

'I didn't ask what you think God wants,' I said, 'I asked what you want.'

When she didn't respond, I worried that my voice had sounded too stern and had frightened her. It wasn't until I heard the uncertainty in her eventual reply that I realised she had merely been thinking, and that she had been quiet for so long because nobody had thought to ask her what she wanted before. I wondered if even Elijah had, or if she had just been informed one day that she would be getting married in the same way that you might tell a child that it was time for bed.

'I suppose I never really thought about it.'

'Well,' I said, 'you can't be all that thrilled about the whole thing if you've come in here crying.'

She gave a damp-sounding snort of laughter before bursting into tears again.

'Oh, hush now,' I rubbed her back gently, 'please don't cry

again. There's been enough crying for one day. I already told you that it's all right if you don't want to get married right now. How old are you, anyway?'

'Sixteen,' she replied, 'so I'm old enough.'

It was my turn to snort then. If you'd asked me earlier that day, I would have agreed that Mim was certainly old enough for marriage, just not to my husband, but after talking to Malcolm the mere thought of it was absurd.

'You know,' I said, lowering my voice, 'when I was your age I was still at school. I had a job at the local shop, stocking shelves.'

She gave a sniff and wiped her red nose on the sleeve of her cardigan. It left a slick line of wetness on the dirty white wool. Usually that sort of thing would have turned my stomach, but instead it just made me feel unbearably sad.

'Really?' she asked.

'Yes,' I said, 'I wasn't ready for marriage then, and I don't think that you're ready for it now.'

She nodded in agreement for the briefest moment before shaking her head again.

'But what am I supposed to do? I don't want to make Elijah or God angry.'

I hated myself then. I had tried to be the kind voice of reason, but all I had done was raise her hopes. What was she supposed to do? She could hardly say no. God was the ultimate authority in Halcyon, and Elijah was His man on the ground, His Holy Prophet. Elijah's word was law, and I couldn't see a refusal of marriage ending well for anyone involved. But at the same time, I couldn't bring myself to look at Mim's sad little face and do nothing, knowing what I did. Only one solution came to mind.

'Deborah and I have been thinking.' I paused then, considering my words. Mim was upset in that moment, but that didn't mean that she wouldn't turn around and grass us up to Elijah before the day was done. Before I could decide whether or not it would be a good idea to continue, Mim spoke.

'I think I know what about,' she said, 'or at least, I can only think of one way out of it. But it's a sin, and anyway I'm too scared.'

I decided to hedge my bets.

'What were you thinking of doing, Mim?'

'Well,' she took a deep breath in, 'there are lots of sharp things in the sheds. And ropes.'

'Good grief, Mim! You were going to kill him?'

Mim's eyes widened in shock, and her face turned pink.

'No! No! I was thinking I could maybe kill me. Like Judas. But I know it's a sin.' She looked at me expectantly. 'Isn't that what you and Deborah were thinking about?'

I gripped her hands tightly in mine while waiting for my words to be returned to me. My throat was tight, a pair of invisible hands around my neck.

'Oh Mim,' I said, 'no, that's not it at all. We were going to leave.'

'Leave?' She seemed genuinely shocked. 'Leave for where? Where would you even go?'

'Well,' I said, 'we hadn't quite decided yet. There are places out there where people can go when they need help. Shelters, things like that. And there are nice, kind people who would want to help us if we left.' *People like Malcolm*, I thought, *and I have a sister, somewhere.* But I couldn't bear to tell her about *him*, nor did I want to lay a jinx on the possibility of Grainne's support. It had been such a long time, and things had ended so horribly between us that the idea of her forgiveness was almost impossible.

'But what about the End?' she asked, frustration bubbling through the sadness in her voice. 'Even if places like that did exist once, they'll be gone now. It's a mess out there, Elijah said.'

I thought of Malcolm again. When I had got to the point in my story about Elijah's sermon at the sprit drill, he had placed his hands against the fence. *I need you to know*, he had said, *that none of that is true. But I think you know it already.* He had sounded almost angry when he said that. Angry and kind.

'No,' I said, 'no, it's not. Don't ask me how I know but I do, I promise. The End isn't coming.'

'But... but why would he say it was?'

She looked dazed, and I squeezed her hand again as kindly as I could.

'I don't know.'

It was then that the front door banged open. Both Mim and I jumped and let go of each other's hands. My heart was still racing when Ruth appeared in the doorway. She stood, motionless, as though she was working out the scene before her. I often forget that people can perceive me in a way that is different from how I perceive myself, so while I believed it was obvious that I must have been comforting the tearful Mim, Ruth clearly saw me as the cause of her distress. She fixed me with a cold glare before turning her attention to Mim.

'I'm really sorry,' she said, 'I was so rude to you earlier. I don't know why I acted the way I did. Well… I guess I do, but it was mean and I'm so embarrassed. I looked for you all over.' Then she turned back to me. 'On my way over here, John stopped me and said not to worry about the animals from now on. That Alfie and Adam would be taking care of them until we have to slaughter them. Do you know anything about that?'

She didn't sound accusatory, which I appreciated, but I was too concerned by the fact that John had also got to her to focus too much on her tone.

'I can't believe it,' I said, 'you too?'

'What do you mean, me too? What's happened?'

I sighed. 'I was also sacked today. It's a theme, apparently.'

Ruth sat down heavily on her usual chair. She covered her eyes with her hands and massaged her temples. I thought I heard her swear under her breath, but I assumed I must have imagined it.

'This is crazy,' she said, 'this doesn't feel real. What are we going to do?'

There was no question any more of whether we should share our intentions to escape with Ruth, but before I could fill her in on the subject the door banged open once again.

'Do you think it's Deborah?' Mim asked.

In perfect synchronisation, Ruth and I raised our fingers to our lips. Out in the hall came the sound of two sets of footsteps, and then two voices. One was unmistakably Deborah's, and the other belonged to a man. John. Ruth opened her eyes wide, and Mim furrowed her brow in confusion. I tried to maintain a calm exterior, but inside my mind was whirring through all the possible reasons for Deborah and John to come into the farmhouse together. None were particularly promising. I heard the familiar creak of my office door as it opened and then closed again. What were they doing in there? The three of us sat in tense silence, waiting for something to happen.

Chapter Twenty-Four

Ruth

Part of me was relieved when it was Deborah who finally appeared in the doorway, but another part was worried. I had the sense that we'd all been backed into a tight corner, and there was no way out. Aoife and Deborah were talking about how things had gone too far and how the only option now was to leave Halcyon, saying stuff like 'it's now or never' and 'we can make a clean break'. But even if we managed to leave Halcyon, which I doubted we could, we'd never escape it. It was in us. There could be no such thing as a clean break.

'What's the use?' I asked, not bothering to wait for a break in the conversation.

Aoife and Deborah fell silent as they turned to face me. They looked shocked, as if they had forgotten that I was there.

'I mean it,' I said, directing my words to the tabletop, 'what is the point? We can't even get out of this building. How do you expect us to leave Halcyon?'

And what the heck are we meant to do with ourselves once we're out? I didn't add.

'Well, we have to try,' said Deborah in the voice I imagined she used to convince the children of Halcyon to wash their hands after visiting the outhouse, 'even if it's just for Mim's sake.'

I sighed.

'This isn't a movie, Deborah. This is real life. We can try as hard as we like but you've already told us that this door is locked and we know the front gates are locked, and also there's a seven-foot-tall fence around the place. Anyway, if Elijah really meant what he said in the sermon, pretty soon we'll all be stuck in the bunker, which has quite literally been built to be impenetrable. So.'

Mim's face crumpled, and for a second I felt a little twinge of guilt even though I knew I was right. It was over. We were all stuck there, at the mercy of whoever had been given the key to the door. By that point the sky outside was pitch black, and the window had become a dark mirror. The thin light coming from the electric bulb was enough to illuminate the scene at the table, and I caught myself unable to tear my eyes away from our reflections. By some strange trick, we all looked more hunched and haggard in the window than we did in real life, and I wondered which was the truer picture. I had no idea how *I* looked in real life, but I certainly felt as beat as my reflection suggested. My daze was interrupted by the sound of someone's stomach growling.

'Sorry,' said Mim, blushing deeply. 'I haven't managed to eat anything today.'

Aoife stood and squeezed Mim's shoulder. It surprised me to see her acting with such tenderness. In all the years I had known her, she had never been one for casual affection. She almost seemed motherly.

'No need to be sorry,' she said, lifting half a loaf out of the bread bin. 'If God wanted us to starve, He wouldn't have let us get locked up in a kitchen. Although...' She paused, her face peering into the cupboard we used as a pantry. 'It appears that we've been looted.'

'What do you mean?' asked Deborah, craning her neck to see where Aoife was standing.

'Well,' she said, 'it looks like someone's been through and taken all of our non-perishables.'

Deborah shook her head and raised her hands in frustration.

'Shit,' she said, 'they must be filling up the bunker already.'

'Never mind,' said Aoife, 'at least they didn't take the bread.'

She turned towards us again, holding the plated-up sliced bread. With two plates in each hand, she reminded me for a second of a waitress in a diner. I half expected her to say *order up!* but of course she didn't. Instead she laid the plates out before us with a hollow smile.

'Eat up,' she said, 'there's no more where that came from.'

I hadn't expected to have any appetite, but as soon as the food was set down my mouth began to water. My hand was already halfway to my plate when Mim piped up again and in her small, nervous voice asked:

'Aren't we going to say a prayer of thanks?'

Aoife, Deborah and I looked at one another in the heavy silence which followed Mim's question. Everyone's face seemed to ask the same thing – *should we?* Both options seemed equally impossible. How could we have even considered eating without blessing our food, but also, who could we pray to now? Thankfully, just as Mim looked ready to either apologise or cry again, Deborah spoke.

'Yes,' she said, 'I think that might do us good. Aoife? Will you lead us?'

Aoife cleared her throat and adjusted herself in her chair.

'Thank you, Deborah,' she said, her eyes closed tight, and her hands clasped in prayer, 'for the bread which you have made. May we be strengthened by it.'

Instead of saying 'amen', the three of us followed Aoife's lead and nodded solemnly. I was ready to reach out once again for my bread when Deborah smacked her hands against the table excitedly:

'Wait!'

We watched in confusion as she rose and disappeared out of the kitchen. She was back again within seconds, holding a half-empty bottle of red wine in one hand and grinning mischievously.

'*Where* did you get *that*?!' I asked, my mouth open wide in astonishment.

'When Elijah decided that we should stop using wine for communion, he told me to pour it away.'

She gave a shrug, as if to say *but then I didn't*, and turned to fetch four mugs from the cupboard. Aoife took hold of the bottle and poured it eagerly so great splashes ended up landing on the table, where they left dark stains on the untreated wood. The pungent smell of alcohol made me wince, and I remembered Elijah the night before, with his hot, reeking breath in my face.

'How many years ago did Elijah ban communion wine?' Aoife asked, swirling the dark, heady liquid around her mug.

'About three,' I said.

Deborah readied herself for a sip, but before the wine touched her lips she stopped and looked at me.

'Will this be okay?' she asked, one hand on her protruding stomach.

I thought back to my training, and the holy trinity of *no*'s for our expectant mothers: no cigarettes, no drugs, no alcohol. Eventually I spoke:

'I think that a couple of units of wine floating around its bloodstream is the last thing that baby needs to worry about.'

Deborah let out a little laugh, and Aoife said, 'I'll drink to that.'

Maybe on some level we all had an idea of what would happen next, and that was why the evening took the turn it did. Even though the wine was terrible and I could hardly bring myself to take more than a mouthful, it gave off the illicit glow of harmless contraband and that alone was enough to make us giddy. For a while we laughed and ate and drank as though the End wasn't right around the corner. And it was around the corner, I was sure, just not in the way we'd prayed for all those years. Even Mim seemed to relax a little, although her own mug of wine lay untouched on the table. The spectre of Elijah's sermon still hung over me, but I had managed to forget that we were locked in the farmhouse until the spirit drill bell rang. The harsh clang reverberated around the room, and the mood changed as suddenly as if a spell had been broken. We had never had two drills in a single day before.

Mim shot to her feet.

'What are we supposed to do?'

As she spoke I heard footsteps in the hall. Aoife must have heard them too, because she grabbed the bottle of wine and thrust it under the table just in time for the door to swing open and John to appear.

'Follow me,' he said.

If he could smell the rancid wine in the air, he gave no sign of it. His face was tired and flushed, and he seemed to be annoyed at the sight of us. I got the feeling that if it was up to him, we'd all just be left in the kitchen forever. He looked at Deborah, and I wondered what had happened between them in Aoife's old office – had she of all people given him trouble? I found it hard to imagine, but then there were a lot of things that I knew for a fact about Deborah that I found difficult to reconcile with the version of her that I saw every day in Halcyon, so it wouldn't have been outside the realms of possibility. We had all heard the stories of her wild youth; she had managed to fit a lot in, if Elijah was to be believed, before she'd joined us at seventeen.

When we got out into the hall, we were met by Niall. He was

standing with his back to the porch door, and in his hand he held one of the big torches we had bought to go in the bunker. The light which came from it was whiter and brighter than any I had seen in years, and I squinted against it.

'Follow me please, ladies,' he said.

One by one we filed out of the farmhouse and into the bitter night, with Niall and his torch leading the way and John bringing up the rear. Everyone must have already been in the church by the time we set off, and Halcyon felt strangely deserted. The path to the church was illuminated by the alien light, and I wondered if maybe I was dreaming. The whole day had been so strange that it didn't feel unlikely, and who knows, maybe I would have passed the whole thing off as some kind of lucid nightmare if it wasn't for the constant reminders of my physical waking body – the freezing cold, the sudden, splitting headache, the rising lump in my throat.

Niall pushed open the door of the church to reveal the entire population of Halcyon, wrapped up in their warmest clothes and staring expectantly up at the stage upon which Elijah was pacing. The air hummed with tension. I'd been to thousands of evening services with the church, but none of them had felt like this. It was familiar and unfamiliar at the same time, like watching a movie with the sound just a little out from the actors' moving mouths, or the slightly distorted reality of a dream. Wrong enough to notice. Evening services had once been my very favourites, back in the old days when we had been city folk, and I tried not to let the strangeness of the situation tarnish the safety and joy wrapped up in those memories.

It was after a session of evening worship, way back when we were still living in England, that Aoife had pulled me aside to talk to me about marrying Elijah. While everyone else was pouring their herbal teas and nibbling homemade biscuits, she took me to the other side of the hall and sat me down on one of the hard plastic chairs which had been lined back up against the wall. She leaned towards me.

'How would you feel about joining our family?'

I looked for some hint in her piercing blue eyes which might indicate the kind of answer she wanted to receive. Did she seem reluctant? Hopeful? Sad? I couldn't tell. Her entire expression was inscrutable, and I wanted to choose my answer carefully.

'I'm not sure I understand, Sister. Am I not already part of the church's family?'

Aoife pulled back slightly, and it almost looked as though she was trying to avoid rolling her eyes.

'I think you might know what I mean, Ruth. Obviously, you're already part of our family in Heaven on Earth, a major part of it. And really, Ruth, that's a big part of the reason that we wanted to ask you this question. Elijah and I would like to invite you to join *our* family. We want you, if you would like, to marry Elijah. That is, to be his wife, his second wife, along with me. To marry him and come and live with us.'

I nodded.

'Right.'

'Are you surprised by my question?' she asked.

I shook my head. Maybe I should have pretended that the thought of marrying Elijah had never crossed my mind, but I couldn't lie to Aoife. For the past few months, Elijah had been keen to spend more time with me than normal: picking me up from work in the church van, helping me close up the soup kitchen when it wasn't his shift. As a church, we had never been against polygamy. Plural marriage was a Biblical phenomenon, and Elijah often preached about Moses and David and Solomon, who had been blessed with more than one wife, so when his interest became so obvious that even I couldn't ignore it, I was only shocked that he seemed to have chosen me.

'You can think about it, you don't have to say anything now.'

'No,' I said. Aoife straightened, and I hurried on. 'No, I mean, no I don't need to think about it. My answer is yes.'

Aoife let out a short sharp exhale and leaned back in her chair, then, after a moment of thought, leaned forward and pulled me into a hug. I could feel the tension in her body, even though she held me at a distance from herself, by the way she gripped the tops of my arms. I placed my own arms around her back, careful not to let my face touch hers, aware of the congregation eating their cookies and drinking their tea at the other end of the hall. They were as much a reason for my 'yes' as Elijah was. I loved them like family – more than my own family, who I had barely spoken to since I had moved to Newcastle – and I wanted to wedge myself in amongst them.

It was strange to think that it was this same group of people I was looking at now, almost exactly, who I had loved so deeply that I'd been willing to give up any semblance of a normal life to be with them. They were so intent on watching Elijah that not a single soul turned to look as we shuffled in, and no eyes followed us as we made our way down the centre aisle to our usual seats. There was Danielle, whose baby I had delivered two years ago, a little boy – breach. Adam, who had put a nail through his hand while making repairs to the community barn after a storm. I'd been so terrified that he'd get an infection that I'd kept changing his dressing every day for a week after I'd needed to. Lois was fiddling with the tassels on her scarf; people were speaking to her again, and the relief glowed off her. I realised I didn't like the gawping, starry-eyed crowd that my friends and neighbours had become, and fought the temptation to go up to each person individually and give them a shake. Had I ever looked at Elijah like that? I shook my head gently. Of course I had. And as I took my seat, and Elijah took his place behind the rostrum, I tried with all my might not to do it again.

Chapter Twenty-Five

Deborah

I couldn't have guessed how long the spirit drill had lasted, but by the time we were finally dismissed the sky had begun to lighten. I had managed to stay awake for the duration of Elijah's sermon, but just barely, and all I could think about once it was over was going to the outhouse and then curling up in my bed. My throat was raw from cheering along with the rest of the congregation, my ears were ringing, and my eyes stung with exhaustion. Ahead of me, I could see the dim outline of Mim leaning sleepily against Ruth's shoulder as they walked. Aoife and I also walked as a pair, which I appreciated; it would be good to have someone to grab onto if my legs finally gave way. The bodies of the other congregants moved around us, slow and silent, heading for the comfort of their caravans to catch a couple of hours' sleep before having to wake up for the day.

In the half-light, I could make out the shapes of the older children carrying the younger ones, although it was still too dark for me to recognise any particular faces. I thought of Jonah and Noah and Susannah, and my heart ached. Being away from them never got easier, but I had got more used to it. I had had forty days with the boys, where they had stayed with me in the farmhouse in my room. There had been some debate about that, apparently – should I get twice as long because I had birthed two? Elijah and John had decided eventually that no, I shouldn't. Ruth and some of the others had looked after me, while I looked after the babies. I could still feel their small, wriggling bodies, the latch of their hungry mouths on my nipples. When the forty days were up and they were moved to the schoolhouse, I had felt a literal tearing in my chest.

'I'm so sorry, honey,' Ruth had said.

I lay back against my pillows, still in my nightdress. I knew that if I didn't force myself to stay lying down, I would have chased after them, those two tiny bundles in Helen's arms. I bit back tears and closed my eyes.

'I need them with me,' I croaked.

It was a risky thing to say, even to Ruth. She could so easily have told Elijah. Instead, she lay down next to me on the bed and put her arm around my shoulders. With her other hand she pushed the hair away from my face.

'I know,' she said, 'I know.'

I remember how grateful I had been that she hadn't given me a speech about how it was our burden as mothers, or how it was for the best, or that I would still get to see them in the schoolhouse every day, and 'really, Deborah, they're just across the courtyard, don't you think you're being a bit dramatic?' which Aoife had said to me the following day at breakfast, once Elijah had left.

When it was time for Ruth to go, I was still lying like a corpse on my bed. My hair was unbrushed and unplaited, fanned out around me, and my eyes were dry and stinging. Milk had soaked through my nightdress, leaving a sodden patch over each breast.

'Don't let him see you like this,' she said.

She was right. Elijah would be there soon, and if he saw me in such a state he would never allow me to keep up my work in the schoolhouse. In a hormone-addled haze, I rose and washed my face, combed my hair, dressed myself. I used the ghostly reflection in my window to practice a smile.

When I'd had Susannah, Elijah had been irritated by the birth of another daughter, but I had been relieved – the Biblical period of purification was longer. With her, I'd been allowed eighty blissful days before the third chamber of my heart was torn out, and it was time to welcome my husband back into my bed.

I must have slowed my pace a little, because Aoife took my arm and propelled me forwards. We walked the rest of the way to the farmhouse door like that – her firm hand gripping me so hard that I could feel it through my layers of coats and jumpers. It wasn't until we came to a stop that I realised Mim was still with us, clinging tightly onto Ruth.

'Please don't make me go back there,' she sobbed. 'I want to stay with you.'

Whether they were tears of fear or exhaustion was anyone's guess, but either way I felt bad for her. I was almost ready to relent when Aoife spoke:

'I know,' she said, 'but they're expecting you at the schoolhouse. If you don't turn up, they're just going to come looking for you.'

She was right, but Mim remained unconvinced.

'But I don't think I want to go back!'

Her voice was choked with emotion and seemed to carry into the hills. By that point I was feeling less sorry for Mim, and more worried that someone would hear her. Somewhere behind us, I was sure John must be watching and listening. To my surprise, before I could say anything, Ruth chimed in.

'Aoife's right,' she said, turning to face Mim, 'but look, it's almost dawn. You'll only be there for a few hours, and then we'll all be up again. Nothing bad is going to happen in a few hours.'

I thought of Ollie, frozen and shivering, and I knew Ruth was thinking of him too. For a second nobody spoke, and I waited for Mim to argue back, to say that both Ruth and I had seen with our own eyes exactly the sort of harm that could be done in a few hours. But she didn't. Maybe she was just too tired to argue, or maybe her upbringing prevented her from talking back any further. Either way, I'm ashamed to say that I was relieved. My brain and body were running on fumes, and there was no energy left in me to think too hard about what might happen if we forced a recently betrothed teenager to return, unsupervised, to a place that clearly terrified her.

Once Mim had disappeared safely into the half-light, Aoife opened the farmhouse door. None of us even bothered to take off our coats and boots before going our separate ways. I guessed that I would get in about three hours of sleep before it would be time to wake up, but ironically I was too exhausted to worry about it. When I reached my room, I just about managed to kick off my boots before curling up under the quilts. My eyes closed before my head even hit the pillow, and I fell into a heavy, dreamless sleep.

When I woke up the following morning, it was to the sound of more bells. I hadn't moved an inch from the spot in which I'd fallen asleep, which made me feel as though I hadn't slept at all. That, combined with the noise, made me feel disorientated, and for a second I couldn't even bring myself to get out of bed. Still dressed from the night before, I pushed back my quilt and felt the trapped heat evaporate into the chilly room. Condensation had built up on the windowpane, and I gave it a half-hearted wipe with the sleeve of my jumper. Little grey fibres stuck to the wet glass and I tried to pick them off with my nail while listening to the bells ring on. My bedroom was at the back of the house, which meant that all I could see were looming, craggy hills, and in the near distance, the heavy metal gate which separated Halcyon from the outside world. Two men, too blurred by the streaks of water for me to be able to make out their faces, stood guard. Strangely, they didn't seem to be moving towards the church at the sound of the bells, which continued to ring. Elijah's paranoia must have reached new heights if he would allow two of his congregation to miss a sermon for guard duty. I stood and watched them for a bit longer, waiting to see if they would move, before I turned with a sigh and walked towards the door. My hand hovered over the handle – usually I aimed to be one of the first to respond to the bells which called us to the church, but such attempts to win Elijah's favour seemed more than redundant at that point, and I had no other reason to want to be there.

Pretty soon, it became clear that I wasn't the only one who didn't want me to join the congregation in church. The handle, when I eventually tried to turn it, moved an inch and then stuck fast. I gave it another try, and then another. I attempted to move it the other way, as though that would do something different. No matter what I did, though, nothing changed. The door was locked, and I was stuck.

Chapter Twenty-Six

Aoife

Bleary-eyed and stifling my yawns, I found myself sitting in my usual seat in church just a few hours after I had last left it. To my left was Ruth, who looked as though she had managed even less sleep than me. She was staring up at the rostrum where Elijah stood, once again, taking in the crowd which had gathered before him. The atmosphere was quiet, as though the congregation had used up all of their fervour the night before and was now struggling against an emotional hangover. For once, I allowed myself to turn and survey the room. It was almost full, but amongst the flock of familiar faces there was no sign of Deborah, Mim, or Helen. That they were all three absent seemed like too much of a coincidence, and I was about to turn and ask Ruth if she knew where they were when John appeared in front of us.

'Excuse me,' he said, gesturing at the slim gap between me and Ruth, 'may I?'

I gave a silent nod and fixed him with a glare as Ruth shuffled along to the neighbouring chair where Deborah usually sat. John was smaller than I was, but his presence between us made it impossible for me to catch Ruth's eye. I wished that I had waited in the farmhouse for Deborah, but my body seemed to have a Pavlovian reaction to the sound of the church bells – the first burst of their familiar clang had me out the door before I even knew what was happening. My clothes were still rumpled from sleep, and I could feel the hair escaping awkwardly from my bun. Not that Elijah would care. He hadn't even looked over since I walked in. If anything, he seemed to be actively avoiding catching my eye. At first, I had thought that he was surveying the entire congregation, but I soon realised that he was actually staring fixedly at the door. I was desperate to speak to Ruth, but every time I moved to look at her John seemed to find a way to block my view.

By that time the atmosphere was tense and heavy. We were all waiting for something to happen when the doors swung open. I turned, expecting to spot Deborah, but she was still nowhere to be seen. Instead, silhouetted in the doorway against the white sky stood two other figures clinging tightly to one another.

Chapter Twenty-Seven

Ruth

I figured it out the second that John came and sat between me and Aoife, but it didn't matter; there was nothing that I could do anyway. It was too late. And by the time the doors opened and Aoife and the rest of them realised what was about to happen too, it was even later, and all we could do was sit there and watch as Mim and Helen walked arm in arm down the centre aisle. The sight of the young bride and her mother seemed to perk up the congregation, and I found myself wishing that Mim would play the part of blushing bride in a way that matched the enthusiasm of everyone else in the room; it would have made it less painful to watch. Instead, she shuffled forwards, her eyes glassy and dazed, her feet catching the hem of her too-large dress on every other step. Someone had taken her hair out of its plaits, and it hung long and crimped down her back. There were no flowers.

It said a lot about the way things worked in Halcyon and Heaven on Earth that I had managed to forget, up until then, that Helen and John were Mim's biological parents. I'd never noticed them paying her any particular attention, and she never talked about them even though they had all lived together before the move to Halcyon in Mim's early childhood. It surprised me that Elijah had allowed Helen to walk her daughter down the aisle. The tradition of a parent giving away their child into marriage suggested that the child had previously belonged to the parent, instead of to God. That was how it was explained to me when Elijah and I became engaged and I had suggested flying my parents and siblings out to attend the wedding. I had barely spoken to them in years – the odd call at Christmas or a birthday, never being sure what to say and so never saying much. They knew I was working, and going to church, and they were happy enough with that. My godmother had cut me off completely long before my engagement, telling me to call her when I was ready to be normal again. In the end I decided not to tell them that I was getting married, so our only guests were the other members of Heaven on Earth. I had worn Aoife's wedding dress, the same dress that Deborah later wore on her wedding day and the dress that Mim wore now. It really was far too big for her, and the white satin bodice hung loose around her skinny waist. The puffs at the top of the sleeves, which I had remembered as being so elegant, looked comically large on Mim. Helen was holding onto her arm with a grip so tight that the fabric of the sleeve was bunched and creased. I winced at the thought of what that grip might be doing to the skin underneath.

The pair reached the front of the church, and Elijah greeted them with a smile. He had lost weight from his face, so when he smiled his skin and lips stretched too thin over his teeth and he looked like a skeleton. Mim turned nervously to look at the crowd; it was the first sign she gave that she had half an idea of what was going on. I wondered if she was searching for me, but she was looking in the opposite direction to where Aoife and I were sitting. That was one small mercy; how could I have looked back at her if she had spotted us? What expression would I have been able to arrange on my face that would have done her any good? Whatever she did see didn't seem to have done her any good either, because she let out a high-pitched squeak. John shifted in his seat when she did that, and Helen tugged her arm hard. Slowly, Mim turned her head back round, but she didn't look up at Elijah. Instead, she kept her eyes fixed firmly on the floor. John relaxed. When it became clear that Mim wasn't about to fall over or run away, Elijah gave a nod and Helen let go of her daughter's arm. As Helen returned to her seat, I managed to glimpse her face. She looked as drawn and tired as everyone else in the room. Her hair was pulled back tightly, but it had escaped in fine wisps which curled out from her scalp like a greying halo. Her jaw, I could see, was tense, and her mouth was set in a tight, thin line.

When Helen had taken her seat, Elijah cleared his throat and reached out a hand to Mim. Hesitantly, she took it and made the small step up to join him on the low stage. As soon as she was by his side, her gaze returned once again to the floor. Elijah didn't seem to notice. His attention was focussed outwards.

'Good morning, everyone.' I could tell that he was trying to sound normal, but his voice had a manic edge to it and his right hand was shaking. 'I am so very happy to see you all gathered here today, to witness this most joyful occasion.'

Chapter Twenty-Eight

Deborah

By the time the bells had stopped, I was lying on my side on top of the covers of my bed, watching a small beetle make its way from one end of the bedside table to the other. My stomach rumbled, and I had already had to use the chamber pot under my bed. Inside me, the baby squirmed and kicked. I placed my hand on the spot where I had felt what I imagined was its foot, and took a deep breath in. If it wasn't for the baby, I might have been worried; after all, finding yourself unexpectedly locked in a room is rarely a good thing. But the baby growing inside me made everything different. When I was pregnant, I was safe by default. I thought back to Elijah's game with the glasses of water, how confident I had been that mine was clean, how quickly I'd gulped it down to keep up my good wife act and impress him. I remembered the sight of the plate flying through the air in the kitchen the night before Elijah left. I had ducked on instinct, but even then I had been certain that he was aiming for the space above my head.

I loved how protected I was when I was pregnant, but I loved my babies too. I had always loved babies. I always thought that if they hadn't been married to Elijah, Aoife and Ruth would never have had so many children, but I'm sure I would have. Even as a child I was desperate to be a parent. I was the kid who insisted on tucking the baby dolls in every night, and if the foster family I was placed with had little children I would be thrilled. Way back when I lived with my mother the first time around, I always hoped that she would have another baby. In hindsight, I'm glad that she didn't, but at the time all I wanted was some small person to fuss over and care about. As I grew older, parenthood became an idealised state. When I was a parent, I thought, everything would be all right. There would always be someone there to love, and always someone to love me back. What a thrilling prospect that was to my affection-starved little self.

The reality of parenthood was different. By the time I gave birth to the twins, we had been in Halcyon for just over a year. The schoolhouse was well established, and Elijah's beliefs about the dangers of the family unit had taken root in the hard Highland ground. In the months that followed Jonah and Noah's removal to the schoolhouse, I spent tearful hours alone in my bedroom, an old-fashioned manual breast pump clamped to my raw, ravaged nipples, trying to drain sufficient milk from myself to fill enough bottles to satisfy the two of them. It was then, with empty arms and empty womb, that I had started to hate him. Until that point, I had convinced myself to believe in the work we were doing and had trusted in Elijah's plan. Everything would be so different for those babies, I had thought, so different to how it had been for me. They would be raised within a community. They would have so many people to love them, and they would be safe, and they would grow up surrounded by God and His wonder. And then I'd gone and lost them, like my mother had lost me, only worse. When I was seventeen, I'd found my mother again, and I got to know her and I got to love her not just because I was half her, but because of who she was. I'd seen her clean and happy. I'd watched her face light up when Elijah preached. I'd heard her voice raised in song. We'd been reunited. I got the feeling that my own children would never get to know me like that.

Not long after giving birth to the twins, I found out that I was expecting again. The first time around there had been hope, and I had stared in wonder at my growing, changing body. My pregnancy with Susannah was very different. Every bout of morning sickness, every stretch mark, every flutter and kick in my belly filled me with dread. Still, at least I knew that for as long as I was pregnant my body was off limits. I was a holy vessel. I no longer had to keep one eye open for minute shifts in Elijah's mood, or fear his strange punishments. After the twins, but before I became pregnant with Susannah, I had taken the Lord's name in vain. A minor sin by most standards, but in Halcyon there was no such thing – a broken rule was a broken rule, and the sinner had to be absolved before they brought the wrath of God down on everyone. I had spent hours pumping, but when Annie came to pick up the bottles, she'd dropped one. Elijah thought that plastic was poison, so the bottles were made of glass, and of course it smashed as soon as it landed on the hard wood floor. I remember being hit with an almighty wave of anger and sorrow, and I had screamed so loudly that Elijah had heard.

'Jesus Christ!'

Pretty tame stuff, especially for me, but as far as Elijah was concerned it couldn't have been much worse. As soon as Annie had left with the surviving bottle, apologising all the way out of the door and almost in tears herself, he crouched down and rummaged around the cupboard under the sink. It was where we kept our cleaning things, and some of the less easily replaceable cooking ingredients. I watched his back as he rose and fetched a mug, into which he poured a mystery liquid. For a second I wondered whether I would allow myself to drink bleach if it turned out that that was what he had served me. As soon as the mug was in my hand, though, one sniff told me exactly what was inside. Cider vinegar. He must have emptied the entire bottle in there; it was full to the brim. He watched coolly, his arms crossed over his broad chest, as I drank the entire thing. By the time I'd finished my mouth and throat were burning, and my stomach was cramping so much that I could barely stand. It was all I could do not to vomit, but something told me that would have been a bad idea, and I forced myself not to. 'It's for your own good,' he had said, as I retched dryly over my wash basin, saliva running from my mouth. He brought me a glass of water, afterwards, and rubbed my back. 'You're forgiven. I love you.'

Lying on my bed, I could still just about see the two guards by the gate. One was facing inwards, towards Halcyon and the house, and the other was looking out into the world beyond. I closed my eyes.

Chapter Twenty-Nine

Aoife

Satellite delay. That's the only way I can think to describe it. I watched the doors open and saw Mim walking down the aisle towards Elijah. I saw that she was wearing my wedding dress. I even heard Elijah begin preaching as he held her limp, white hand. All that, and my brain didn't seem able to comprehend what was going on until the service was well underway. Once I had caught up with my senses, I was met with the urge to stand up, to object, to somehow stop the whole thing. The instinct surprised me, but as soon as I moved to act on it, John's hand touched my thigh.

'I wouldn't,' his whisper was so low I could hardly hear it, 'if I were you.'

His breath was hot, and it made me squirm. I kept my eyes fixed ahead as he continued.

'Jemima has told us everything. She's named Deborah as a traitor. Something about an escape?'

I must have tensed, because he let out a satisfied exhale.

'The three of you can do whatever you like for all I care, but you won't drag my daughter to Hell with you.'

Fear hardened into a lump in my throat. Traitor seemed like such a big, serious word.

'Where's Deborah?' I breathed.

In the periphery of my vision I saw John shake his head and raise a finger to his lips. *Shh.*

For as long as I could remember, being told to be quiet had filled me with a hot rage, but I had other things to worry about. There was Deborah, of course, but in light of her condition I wasn't too worried about her safety – at least her physical safety.

More pressing was Mim, who seemed to be swaying gently, her eyes red from tears, or lack of sleep, or both. She was a sorry sight, up there in an ill-fitting wedding dress which had seen all three of her soon-to-be sister-wives as well as her mother up and down the aisle. I almost felt sorry for that dress. I had been so happy to wear it. It had been the most beautiful thing I had ever worn. It made me feel like a woman. The only sadness I had felt on my wedding day was the knowledge that my sister would never see me in it. Grainne had refused to come to the wedding. She and I had had some disagreements. I told her I disapproved of her lifestyle, and she told me that she disapproved of mine. Now, looking at Mim, I didn't see a bride; I saw a victim. I wondered if that's what Grainne would have seen in me if she had been at my wedding. If she had heard it in my voice when I had called her to tell her that I was getting married to Elijah.

'You're just a silly little girl, Aoife,' she'd said, her voice cold and distant through the phone. 'You'll regret it one day, giving your life to this nutter.'

'His *name*,' I had said, 'is Elijah. And he's not a nutter. He's the best man I've ever known. The best person I've ever known. Better than you, certainly.'

Next to me on John and Helen's sofa, Elijah had squeezed my hand. John and Helen were standing in the kitchen, I remembered the way they were shadowed in the door's frosted glass panel. Mim would have been there too, I supposed, in the kitchen with her parents. Strange to think of it then, as I watched her on the stage. She would have been four years of age when Elijah and I married. I took a deep breath.

'Mammy and Daddy will be turning in their graves, I hope you know that. At what an eejit you're being, cutting yourself off from everyone, leaving your job. To do what? Wait hand and foot on your man who thinks he's some kind of Messiah?'

I remember the feeling of the receiver in my hand – hot, and sticky with sweat. I leaned in to Elijah, as closely as I could. His body felt strong and safe.

'Ha,' I'd said, 'that's rich, coming from you. Are you still shacked up with that woman? It's shameful.' I was almost spitting down the phone. 'I'm ashamed to even know you, I wish you weren't my sister. Elijah was right, I should never have called you. I don't want you at my wedding anyway.'

'Is that right? Then why *did* you call me, Aoife?'

I hung up, then. She didn't call back. It was the last I'd ever heard from her. Elijah drew me into a tight hug as soon as the phone was back on the hook, and stroked my hair as I wept.

'We'll pray for her,' he'd said.

But that was all in the past. In the present, John's clammy hand remained firmly on my leg; my initial burst of adrenaline had faded, and common sense had taken its place. I had no choice but to watch the service. Elijah delivered the exact same words he had spoken when we had married, down to the intonation of his voice. The only difference was that John had officiated our wedding, and this time Elijah was leading it himself. I wondered what that meant. Mim continued to sway, and I doubted she could even hear him. Her part was coming up, the part where she would have to agree to the pledge. The closer it got the tighter John's grip became. I could feel his palm sweating through my skirt. Not so long ago, he would not have dared to touch me.

The unfamiliar sound of the siren surprised us all. Unlike the church bells, the siren was to be used only as a warning for the End. For all of Elijah's warnings about an imminent invasion and the impending End of Days, he seemed more shocked than anyone. For several seconds his mouth continued to move, but no words came out. As panic rose around the room, spreading through the rows from person to person like a virus, the realisation of what was happening dawned on him. His face morphed into a mask of pure elation – the look of a man vindicated – and he raised both of his arms heavenward. No one in the room spoke as Elijah's voice rose up against the sound of the alarm.

'My dear, dear friends! My brothers and sisters! The time we have so eagerly awaited has finally arrived. God is raining down the End of Days upon us. Soon we will all be judged, and we will take our seats beside Him!'

Chairs and benches scraped against the concrete floor as the crowd rose around us. They whooped and cheered with a volume so unholy that it set my flesh and bones reverberating. Elijah, apparently forgetting his almost-bride, stepped forward until he was at the very edge of the stage. He clenched both fists and shot them hard into the air.

'Yes!' he cried, his voice so deep and loud that it fought against the chaos and came out clear and strong over it. 'Yes! Yes! Yes!'

With each call, he pumped his fists into the air again. Briefly, he looked my way. His eyes were wide, but his pupils were so small that it seemed they were all whites and irises. He pulled his lips into a great, manic smile which stopped my heart and made my stomach flip, before turning away and clapping his hands. At that, the crowd fell quiet again. His voice almost shook as he spoke.

'Everyone to the bunker, now! The time has come – it is the last hour! We are vindicated!'

He leapt off the rostrum and into the aisle. John rose next, scurrying to catch up with Elijah before he reached the door. The congregation swarmed out behind them. In the commotion, I reached out to Ruth and pulled her up by her sleeve. She seemed to be frozen in shock, but moved with me easily enough. When she was on her feet, I dragged her into the aisle before turning to Mim, who hadn't moved an inch since she first took to the platform. The wail of the siren combined with the noise from the receding congregation meant that I could shout for her without drawing too much unwanted attention to myself, and that's what I did.

'Mim!' I called, waving in the hopes of catching her eye, 'Mim! Come on!'

Mim slipped back into consciousness, and within seconds had jumped from the rostrum with as much eagerness as Elijah had done just minutes before. She moved as a white blur, and before I knew it she had taken hold of my free hand. Together, the three of us followed the final dregs of colonists out of the church. Once we were outside, we pulled away from the crowd, who were moving en masse towards the newly stocked bunker. Instead, we turned and headed in the opposite direction, towards the farmhouse, and Deborah.

Chapter Thirty

Ruth

My first thought, when that horrible screaming siren first sounded, was that we'd all been wrong. Or, I guess, that we'd all been right at first, right to listen to Elijah and join Heaven on Earth and marry him and move to Halcyon. And then we'd been wrong, oh so horribly wrong, to fall away from him. It was hard to get my head straight, with the noise and the panic, but I suppose that somewhere in my muddled and anxious brain I began to worry that it was disobedience – mine in particular – that had brought about the End of Days. It all started with the puppies, and my duplicity. And then it had been Mim, and then Deborah and Aoife, and all of their talk and all of their sin. Surely the Devil himself must have been sitting with us in the farmhouse that night – last night, or the night before? Time meant nothing to me then. All I could think was *Elijah was right*, and all I could worry about was the fate of our four souls.

When Aoife pulled me up and out of my daze, I assumed that she had had a similar revelation and that we were going to follow everybody into the bunker, but of course I was wrong. My instinct, when I realised where we were actually going, was to let go of Aoife's hand and run away to be with Elijah and the rest of the colony. I'm not ashamed to admit it. The only thing that stopped me was Mim. Keeping pace alongside us, she looked like a kid playing dress-up in her mother's wedding gown. That would have been bad enough, but what shocked me back to my senses wasn't the fact of the wedding itself so much as the sheer relief with which she seemed to feel at running away from it. I'd seen that look before, in the various hospitals I'd trained in, on the faces of patients who had come close to dying but had been saved. I'd seen it on the faces of the mothers who gave birth to silent babies when those babies finally gave their inaugural cry. Relief made even more precious by how close they had come to something unthinkably, unbearably awful.

And so I kept running, away from the promised safety of the bunker and the company of the people I had grown to love so deeply over my years in the church. Away from my children, as they were herded off by women who they knew better and trusted more than me. I was running from Elijah too, I knew. We had been married for eight years, and that thought was like a lasso around my middle, wrenching me backwards, making each step in the other direction a battle against almost a decade of memories. Happy ones, not just from our marriage, but from the two years before when I had been just another member of the Church of Heaven on Earth. The little glances we'd shared across the church hall, the drive to the food bank when we'd just gotten engaged and he placed his hand in mine for the very first time, how filled with joy I'd been then. *You're special, Ruthie*, he would say, if I ever got sad, *God brought you here for a reason. You're not like any of the others, not even Aoife. You've got a goodness in you.* Or, *I'm blessed to have you in my life.* As we lay in bed, he would lean in to me and whisper, *I thank God every day that I get to spend eternity with you.* But I thought again of Mim, and I pushed the memories to one side. It was different now, and it had been for a long time.

And so I gripped Aoife's hand all the harder in the knowledge that God was present in Halcyon that day – just not in the way everyone thought. He wasn't there to usher in the End of Days, but to deliver Mim from evil.

Chapter Thirty-One

Deborah

At the sound of the siren, the two figures who had been watching the gate deserted their post and legged it into the centre of Halcyon. Because of where my bedroom was, I couldn't see exactly what was going on, but I could see my chance, so I took it. As soon as the guards had disappeared around the side of the farmhouse and I could be certain that they weren't keeping an eye on me through the window, I began to shake my pillow out of its case. We had no bags or luggage in our rooms – why would we need those, when we were here until the end? But we did have pillowcases.

The last time I had packed my things into a pillowcase, it was under the watchful eye of the social worker who had come to remove me from the squat I was living in with my mother and her friends. He had been amazed that we had nothing else in the house that could do the job. *Not even bin liners?* he'd asked, and I remember wondering if he was new. I probably had even fewer things to pack in my room at Halcyon than I'd had back then, and that was saying something. I was wearing most of my clothes because of the cold, so I only had a couple of changes of underwear and a vest to pack, and there was little else. I'd only managed to keep hold of a few things from the time before Halcyon – a pristine bar of soap which I had discovered after we moved, a receipt from the first 'date' Elijah had taken me on when we began courting, our wedding photo. The two of us in the centre, me in a white dress with puffy sleeves and a garland of pink flowers in my hair and Elijah in his one grey suit. I was beaming, fresh-faced at twenty-one years old, with

Elijah looking smug and handsome, his arm around my waist. Next to me in the picture was Ruth, smiling, her hands clasped together and resting across her stomach. Aoife was standing next to Elijah, with a face like a smacked arse. Both she and Ruth were pregnant in the photo. Two days after our wedding, we'd all moved to Halcyon. The only other thing I took with me was a picture which had been taken of me and my mother just a couple of months before she died. We were sitting together in the church hall we had used for Heaven on Earth gatherings, and we had our arms around each other. She was frail and thin, her hair wispy and grey even though she was barely into her forties, but she looked happy and so did I. Elijah had been the one to bring her off the street. He'd driven her to and from her AA meetings, given her work in the church's soup kitchen, brought her back to life. He'd even helped her find me again. Because of Elijah, we'd had three happy years together in Heaven on Earth before she died of liver failure. I slipped the photo into my makeshift bag, carefully flattening it against the side to keep it from creasing, and wondered how the Elijah of before could possibly be the same man I had grown to hate. Halcyon had changed him, somehow, for the worse. Just like it had changed the rest of us.

The sound of the siren drowned out the knocking at the door, but when I finally heard it my heart jumped into my throat and stayed there. The pillowcase bag was still in my hands, and I stashed it under the quilt. Then, with shaking legs, I walked around the bed and up to the door.

'Who is it?'

'It's us! Can you open the door?' Aoife's familiar voice sounded through the wood, overwhelming the siren to become the most powerful sound in the room.

I pressed myself as close to the door as I could, and positioned my mouth against the crack between the door and the frame.

'Who's us?' I asked.

'It's Aoife and Mim and me,' said Ruth. Her voice was quieter than Aoife's, but I could just about hear her. 'Are you stuck in there?'

'Yes!' I was surprised to hear the desperation in my voice. 'Yes, I'm stuck. I think someone's locked me in. What's going on out there? Why is the siren going off?'

'We'll explain in a minute,' said Aoife, 'but for now we need to get you out of that room.'

The siren cut off mid wail, and despite the ringing it left behind in my ears I could hear their muffled discussion taking place through the door. When the discussion was over, Aoife's voice once again travelled low and clear into my room.

'We've decided,' she said, 'to keep it simple. We think that the best way to get you out is just to knock the door down. Ruth and Mim are going to grab something heavy for us to use as a sort of… battering ram, I suppose. And then we're going to start bashing. Okay?'

'Okay,' I said.

What I really admired about Aoife was her ability, in spite of the strangeness of our situation, to sound truly excited about the prospect of knocking down a door with a makeshift battering ram. She really was wasted in Halcyon. She should have been a general. I wanted to tell her, but it didn't seem like the right moment for any kind of light-hearted comment. Something big was clearly going on out there, plus I didn't want her to think I was taking the piss. And so we stood in silence, on either side of my bedroom door, until the sound of footsteps echoed along the corridor.

'We're back,' panted Mim.

I'd almost forgotten that she was there.

'Great,' said Aoife, her voice less clear than it had been – she must have been facing away from the door. 'This will be perfect.'

I was just about to ask what they had brought when Ruth spoke directly through the gap between the door and the lintel:

'It's the bench from the hall,' she said, 'it's the only big thing we could carry.'

There was another minute of deliberation out in the corridor before Aoife called out:

'Right, we're in position. Deb, you get as far back as you can – shout when you're ready for us to get going and we'll swing on the count of three.'

I moved back around to the other side of my bed and lowered myself slowly onto my hands and knees.

'I'm ready!'

They wasted no time. The words were barely out of my mouth

before Aoife gave the count, and the first bang rang out. My heart slammed against my chest, and the baby kicked and squirmed. I wanted to place a hand against my stomach to calm it, but I was still kneeling behind the bed and needed both arms to support myself. My wrists and forearms began to shake.

'Okay,' Aoife shouted, 'we're going again.'

There was another crash of wood against wood, followed by an almighty splintering crack. I raised my head up above the side of the bed, but everything was still intact. Before I could duck back down, the door burst open with one final explosion of sound and smacked hard against my bedroom wall. Together, Aoife, Ruth and Mim stumbled into the room amidst a shower of plaster dust, propelled by the momentum of the bench.

All I could do was stare in stunned silence as I took in the scene. My bedroom door was battered and splintered, hanging limply from one hinge, and the wall had a deep crater where the door's heavy brass handle had hit it. The bench where I usually sat to put on my shoes was cracked straight down its middle and lying sadly on its side on the floor. All things considered, I supposed that the damage wasn't really all that bad. What really shocked me, far more than the mess of plaster and wood, was Mim.

'Why is she wearing my wedding dress?' I asked, leaning heavily on the bed for support as I pulled myself up to stand properly.

Her mouth opened and closed silently until Ruth stepped in and took her by the hand.

'The first bell,' said Ruth, using the gentle voice she usually reserved for labouring mothers, 'was to call us to the church. It looks like Elijah wanted to get the wedding done sooner than we'd thought. If it wasn't for the emergency siren, Mim would have been married by now.'

I stepped backwards and leant gratefully against the solid security of the wall as Mim gave a weak nod.

'Yes,' said Aoife, 'it's been a rough morning for everyone. After the siren went off everyone got a bit excited and headed off to the bunker, and we came here to find you.'

A hundred questions fought in my mind, desperate to be raised.

'Do we know why it went off?' I asked. 'I mean, what was the emergency?'

Ruth shrugged her shoulders sadly as Aoife spoke:

'We don't know. Elijah ran off almost as soon as it started.'

Her sharp jaw clenched. 'But that means it could be anything, and I think we should make a move while we can – everyone's so distracted they've probably not even noticed that we're not in the bunker yet.'

I swallowed hard. There were too many things I wanted to say, and the prospect of actually leaving – not thinking about leaving or planning to leave, but actually, really getting away – was so dizzying that I couldn't even begin to comprehend it. I must have paled or wobbled, because Ruth raised a concerned brow.

'Are you all right?'

'Yeah, no, I'm fine. I suppose we'd better get going then. Where are the kids?'

Chapter Thirty-Two

Aoife

My arms were still aching from the effort of breaking into Deborah's room as the four of us made our way down the corridor and towards the front door. The plan had seemed simple enough when we had agreed on it just minutes before, but the closer I came to re-entering Halcyon proper, the faster my heart started to beat. There were too many what-ifs. What if Malcolm didn't show up to see me, even though he promised that he would? What if someone came looking for us? What if Ruth or Deborah or Mim got cold feet? It wasn't unlikely. Mim was only a teenager after all, and Deborah wasn't happy about leaving the children behind, even though we'd assured her it was the only way, and that we would come back for them before the day was over. Various worst-case scenarios played out in my head, but I forced myself to block them out. There was no point in dwelling on the things that could go wrong. I took a long, slow breath in, trying to fill myself up with confidence as well as air before reaching out for the handle. Before I could push it down, I felt Ruth's gentle hand on my arm.

'This person who can help us,' she said, 'it's your sister, right?'

My breath caught in my throat. Part of my argument for leaving now had been to do with Malcolm, although I'd not referred to him by name. All I'd said was that there was someone nearby who had a car big enough to pull down a section of the perimeter fence, and that they'd take us to the police station. I'd assumed that years of learning how not to ask too many questions had been the reason behind their lack of interest in who this person was, but apparently I was wrong.

'No,' I said eventually, my hand still hovering over the door handle. 'No, it's not my sister.'

Deborah stopped in her tracks.

'Wait,' she said, 'if it's not your sister, then who the Hell is it?'

The three of them stared at me expectantly as I fumbled for the answer that would raise the least number of follow-up questions. Eventually, I settled on the truth. After everything, it seemed like the only safe way to go.

'A little while ago...' I spoke slowly, trying to give myself some thinking time between each word. I knew I needed to be honest, but I also had to handle this tactfully. 'I met a person, a man, while I was walking around the perimeter fence. We started talking, and as the time has passed we've spoken more and more. He knows everything. He told me that he'd be back every day, and that if I ever wanted to leave all I had to do was say the word.'

As I spoke, I watched their faces change. Ruth and Mim's eyes widened in sheer surprise – Mim in particular looked as though her entire worldview had been toppled for the second time in twenty-four hours. Deborah's expression betrayed something else. She shook her head slowly, a wry little smile playing on the corners of her lips. I could feel a blush rising from my chest and up to my cheeks, and I placed a cool hand on my neck in what I hoped was a very subtle way.

'Well,' I said, 'there you go. I assume nobody has a problem?'

None of them spoke.

'Grand. Let's get going.'

As I opened the door a gust of wind pushed me back, taking my breath away and almost throwing me off my balance. The farmhouse was far from warm, but it was sheltered, and the sudden icy blast was a shock to my system. I was already wearing as many layers as I had access to, but I pulled them close around me while I waited for Deborah to close the door behind us.

'Okay,' I said, raising my voice above the rising wind. 'Everyone should be in the bunker by now, so all we need to worry about is someone coming out and looking for us. Mim, you stay in the middle. We don't want anyone to spot you. Deborah, keep an eye to the right. Ruth, keep turning back in case someone starts to follow. I'll keep a look out for Malcolm.'

Mim and Deborah nodded quickly and made to start walking, but Ruth brought a slender finger to her lips.

'Listen,' she said, 'do you hear that?'

I strained my ears, trying to hear anything above the whistle and roar of the wind. I shook my head and was about to lead on when Deborah furrowed her brows in concentration.

'Yes,' she said, 'I do hear something. It sounds like voices? I think it's coming from over by the bunker.'

Before I knew it, the three of us were following Deborah around the edge of the farmhouse, inching our way towards the possible source of a sound I still wasn't certain I could hear. Eventually, we broke away from the safety of the farmhouse wall and headed towards the church. From the other side of the barn we should be able to see the small portion of the bunker that existed above ground. Deborah was still leading the way, and she turned the corner around the church barn first. She was barely there for a second when she stepped backwards, raising her arms out to her sides to form a barrier between us and whatever it was she had seen.

'What is it?' I asked, resisting the urge to push myself past and see for myself.

She turned silently and beckoned us forwards. 'Slowly,' she mouthed, 'don't make a sound.'

I had expected Halcyon to appear entirely abandoned – after all, I had watched the entire population head underground as we had left the church. Instead, every member of the Church of Heaven on Earth except for the four of us was standing together, filling the sizable clearing outside the bunker with shivering bodies. Piled up to one side of the cluster of people was a heap of what looked like heavy sacks. I squinted to get a better look, but then wished I hadn't. In reality, the heavy sacks were the lifeless bodies of our three cows, piled up against each other, brown fur soaked with crimson blood. Next to me, Ruth gasped and covered her mouth with her hands. None of the crowd were looking at the cows, though. Instead, they were all staring in the same direction, through the chain-link fence, and out into the wide world beyond Halcyon. I followed their gaze until my eyes landed on the most surprising sight of all. Three police cars, their lights off and their sirens silent, were parked in the near distance. As I watched, they slowly moved closer to the colony, three white vultures with their eyes on the prize.

As one, Ruth, Deborah, Mim and I turned back the way we had come, heading towards the farmhouse as quickly and as noiselessly as we could.

Chapter Thirty-Three

Ruth

Before I moved to England, I didn't have much of an idea of what it would be like. My world was confined to the areas of our town that my father would let me visit, whatever was preached at church, and a short family vacation to Galveston, Texas when I was about eight years old. I'd receive a birthday card once a year in the mail from my godmother in London, but it was too expensive to call her. The rare occasions when she came to visit us, she would spend most of her stay talking with my mother, who she'd gone to high school with, and I would be too nervous to speak to her. That's how we were all raised, my siblings and I: to be seen and not heard around grown-ups who were not our direct blood relations. But also, she scared me a little. She had a loud voice and a big laugh and wore colourful drapey clothes with bright patterns which I thought of as vaguely African. She was nothing like anyone I had seen in my town, but I didn't think of her as English either. Her accent was like ours, although she did mispronounce certain words – water as *woh-ta* – in a way that made my siblings and I giggle behind our napkins at dinner.

So even when I moved to England, my concept of the English was a little hazy. I half imagined England to be full of tall white men in those black suits with long tails and big stovepipe hats, sipping cups of tea with their pinkies sticking up in the air. My funny little fantasy faded about as quickly as I'd expected it to when I arrived, but one thing that did strike me was just how much tea everyone seemed to drink. I remember my first day on the ward at the training hospital, and the ward sister telling me that my tea break would be at four and thinking that she was teasing me.

When our ladies were delivered of their babies, the first thing we would give them was a cup of tea. It was a quirk that never became normal for me in all the years I lived there, so when we returned to the farmhouse and Deborah's first move was to boil the kettle and spoon leaves into the teapot, I could hardly believe my eyes. I felt for sure that Aoife would scold her for not taking the situation seriously enough, but when she passed the mugs around Aoife took hers with more gratitude than I had ever seen her express. I curled my hands around my own mug, allowing the warmth to seep through to my hands and the rising heathery steam to lap at my face. As crazy as it seemed to sit drinking tea while Halcyon was surrounded by police, I had to admit that there was something about it that soothed me. Maybe I'd been there too long.

'So,' said Aoife, 'how are we going to get around the fence without anyone seeing us?'

Deborah, who had been taking a long sip of her drink, returned her mug to the table.

'Well, it's obvious, isn't it? We're not.'

Aoife raised a sceptical eyebrow, and I shrank back into my seat on instinct.

'And why is that?'

'Well, because it's not physically possible. There are too many of us for a start, and *way* too many of them. And we don't know why the police are here. What if they think we're all planning something crazy, like a mass suicide or a – I don't know, what was that thing those religious people did on the metro in Japan? Some kind of bomb thing?'

'Ah, yes,' said Aoife, 'makes sense with all the mass public-transport systems we've got around here, to go with all of our weaponry and bomb-making equipment.'

Deborah let out a frustrated sigh. She was a very pretty woman with very delicate features, but her entire face had hardened.

'A mass suicide then,' she said, 'whatever. It doesn't even matter. What I mean is, if they think we're going to do something dangerous, they'll be willing to use force. I'm not going to leave my kids here alone surrounded by armed police even if I could get out, which as we've already established, is now impossible because of said police.'

'I didn't think police in Scotland were armed.' My fight-or-flight response activated at the thought of it.

All three women turned, looking as surprised as I was that I had spoken.

'Sorry,' I said, noticing the red blotches appearing on Deborah's cheeks, 'it was just a thought.'

Aoife pointed at me in a way that said *see, Ruth knows what she's talking about*, and Deborah ran her hands through her hair.

'You just don't get it,' she said. 'It doesn't matter to me if they have AK-47s or bloody pepper spray or even just a really strong hose. I'm not going to leave my kids here. And I know *we* know we're not going to do anything daft, but they don't know that! What if some pissed-off local from Abercraig has told them we've got a munitions factory in the community barn or something?'

As Deborah spoke, her voice rose higher and higher, her frustration growing with every word. She seemed just about ready to pop, so I was relieved when, after a pause, Aoife nodded her head.

'You're right,' she said, looking Deborah in the eye, 'I'm sorry.'

Deborah bristled, and shuffled uncomfortably in her seat. Clearly, she had been gearing herself up for a lengthier debate.

'Okay, well, good.'

'Good,' said Aoife, 'let's come up with a new plan.'

The wind howled outside like a wild wolf threatening to blow the house down as the four of us huddled together around the table. With every moment that passed I felt my chest tighten a little more.

'Let's try and think about this logically,' said Aoife, clasping her hands together, 'the most important thing is—'

'To get the kids out,' interrupted Deborah.

Aoife faltered. 'Well, yes, obviously long-term the most important thing is getting us and the children out, but before we do that we need to speak to the police. They need to know that we're not dangerous, and that the four of us want to leave.' She paused for a moment. 'And that there are a lot of children here who need to leave too. We need to tell them not to use force.'

Deborah nodded, satisfied. 'And how do we do that?'

'I suppose there's only one way. We can't wait for them to come in, or it'll be too late. One of us will have to go and speak to them. Tell them what we want to do, and get them to pull down the gate or cut a hole in the fence or something.'

My palms grew clammy with sweat at the thought of going

out there, and I prayed silently that I wouldn't be chosen to go. Aoife had just begun to say 'maybe Ruth—' when my prayer was answered in a way that made me wish it hadn't been.

The low chuckle from the doorway made us all jump. I turned to see John standing there, his arms folded across his chest. The whistling wind must have drowned out his approach, and I couldn't bear to think how long he might have been listening to us. He shook his head indulgently before he spoke.

'I don't think that would be a very good idea.'

Deborah rolled her eyes. 'Fuck off, John.'

A sharp laugh bubbled up through my throat and burst from my mouth. I had never heard anyone speak to John that way before. I smacked my palm over my lips but I was too late. John glared in my direction before returning his focus to Deborah.

'Don't get me wrong, Deborah, I was just trying to help. Ruth is apparently half the reason the police are here.'

I felt as if the blood was evaporating in my veins. I wanted to ask what he meant, but the words came out as a dry croak. Nobody else spoke.

'Yes, well apparently,' John continued, 'when someone comes into a country on a student visa, and then they stay on a work visa, the government gets a little… cross, when that person stops working. And when that person starts using the skills they learned while working here to deliver countless unregistered babies, they get even crosser.'

He shrugged his shoulders.

'You're lying.' Aoife's voice was barely a whisper. 'How could they possibly know she was here?'

'That's where it gets even better,' he said. 'You see, it seems like you have a mole in your little coven here. Someone, and I couldn't possibly say who, has been chatting with a very friendly undercover officer who's been visiting all the way from Edinburgh for the past – how long would you say it's been, Aoife?'

I was too busy reeling from the knowledge that the police were here for me to fully comprehend the meaning behind John's final revelation, but Deborah did. She turned with the full force of her body to face Aoife straight on.

'You fucking *idiot*! What were you *thinking* of, talking to some random bloke about all of us? And telling him our names? What else did you tell the police, Aoife? I have a birthmark on my hip and a scar on my foot, did you mention that to your little friend? You seem to have blabbed bloody everything bloody else!'

The louder Deborah grew the broader John's smile became. I wanted to tell her to stop, that he was saying these things because he wanted us to fight, but I couldn't get the words to come. Instead, all I could do was sit and listen and watch as John grew smugger and Deborah grew angrier and Aoife shrunk deeper and deeper into herself.

'And if one traitor wasn't bad enough...'

This time John turned to Mim, who until then had been sitting in stunned silence, and flashed her a smile. Even Deborah stopped yelling at Aoife and refocussed her attention on John.

'We know all about your little plots,' he continued, 'and your secret wine parties, and the treacherous things you gossip about when the decent people of Halcyon are busy working themselves to the *bone* for this community.' A vein had begun to throb in his temple, but he managed to keep his voice level. 'I will say, I was very proud when Mim trotted in and told Elijah and I all about it last night after the spirit drill. But it seems that the glamour of sin is still too much for her little mind to resist, and she's found her way back to your witches' den.'

Chapter Thirty-Four

Deborah

Aoife had turned as white as a sheet, and with all the colour drained from her face she suddenly seemed to be much older than she was. Thin lines ran across the horizon of her forehead and in between her brows, and it was only now that I noticed how deep the purple bags were under her eyes. I don't know whether those features stood out then because of some sudden change in her, or because I had never allowed myself to notice anything so human about Aoife before. It made it worse. I hated seeing her so sad and small and sorry, not because I didn't want her to be all of those things, but because it didn't seem fair that she could do something so awful and then turn herself into a victim. It would have been better if she had shouted back at me, or even if she had apologised to Ruth. But instead she just sat there, shrinking, making me angrier and angrier. My attention was so focussed on Aoife that the rest of the room blurred into nothing and all I could see was her. Somewhere in my periphery I could sense John standing smugly, watching the scene he had caused with pleasure, but I was past caring about giving him the satisfaction. *Let him enjoy it*, I thought, *why the hell not?*

My focus was broken by a stifled cry from across the table. Mim was gripping the sides of her face with her skinny bird hands. She looked almost as awful as Aoife, with huge red splotches spreading over her cheeks.

'I'm so sorry, Deborah,' she choked, 'I'm so ashamed.'

I had been so fixed on Aoife's betrayal that it took me a moment to connect her tears with John's exposure of her own short-lived deflection from our little group. Ordinarily, I would have been hurt, maybe even angry, but the more immediate threat of the police circling Halcyon had done wonders for my perspective. Mim's apology only made me more upset with Aoife than I had been before, and my frustration at her turning the situation towards herself coloured my response.

'Don't worry about it,' I said, itching to turn back to Aoife, 'there are bigger things to focus on right now.'

She shook her head desperately.

'No,' she said, 'it's not just that. I told them it was all you because I trusted you the least, and I was so upset about Ollie and I thought you knew all about it because you spent so much time in the schoolhouse but I was wrong, I can tell now that you didn't know anything about any of it.'

When Mim paused to catch her breath, I took my chance to interrupt. A creeping sickness was spreading over my body, and I needed to know that she didn't mean what I thought she meant.

'What are you talking about? What about Ollie in the schoolhouse? What actually happened to him?'

Mim gave a great sniff and wiped her running eyes and nose on the sleeve of our wedding dress.

'He was being bad so they took him out back with the bucket. They do it all the time.' She worked to hold in a sob. 'I thought you knew! I thought you were in charge!'

Words and images flashed through my mind, but they were too many and passed too quickly for me to stop and focus on one. The room spun around me, and I clung to the tabletop to keep my balance. Ruth's voice, slow and considered, pulled me a little closer back to earth.

'What do they do all the time?' she asked.

'Everything!' Mim practically wailed. 'The buckets, the water, the night drills, the beatings, making you stand outside even if it's cold and dark. I thought she knew!' She turned to me again, her eyes full of shame and sadness, 'I thought you told them to!'

Before I could speak, before I could even look around to see Ruth and Aoife's reactions, John clapped his hands together as if he was distracting a group of unruly children.

'Right,' he said, 'I think I've had just about enough of this ridiculous whinging and crying. If you would all follow me.'

It took me a second to realise that we were all waiting for Aoife to respond. She had become our unofficial spokeswoman, and her silence left us momentarily without a voice.

'We're quite happy here,' I said, shifting my hand over my bulging stomach, 'thank you.'

And that was when he brought out the gun.

I didn't know what it was at first. The idea of there being a gun in our kitchen, or in Halcyon at all, was so alien that even with it right there in front of me, my brain couldn't believe my eyes. There had never been firearms in Halcyon. Elijah had been insistent, even when it was pointed out that lots of people who lived off the land had guns because they needed them to slaughter livestock or shoot pests. He was completely stubborn about it. Jesus Christ had never held a gun, after all, and in Biblical times people had slaughtered their animals with their own hands. Elijah explained to us that this was the most respectful practice, because you had to really appreciate the fact you were taking the life of one of God's creatures – albeit a creature God created for humans to eat – something that could not be achieved with the pull of a trigger.

John had removed the gun from the waistband of his trousers, where it had been concealed under his jumper, in a way that suggested he had been practicing. The situation was obviously dangerous, and far more volatile than any of us could have imagined, but the rehearsed-ness of the move allowed me to relax just slightly. It made everything seem a little less threatening and reassured me that we were all still living in the real world; a world where nobody instinctively knew how to handle a deadly weapon, even if they had somehow managed to gain access to one.

Ruth rose to her feet and raised her hands above her head as soon as the gun was drawn, and the scraping of chair legs against the wooden floor made me jump.

'Where on earth did you get that thing?' I asked, pulled back to my senses by the sound.

John smirked, the tilt of his head suggesting that there were a lot more things we didn't know about. Instead of answering me, he jerked the shaft of the gun towards the door.

'Up you get. Elijah has enough to contend with today without the lot of you making his life even more difficult.'

Mim was the next to stand. She shuffled over to Ruth, then clung to her side like a limpet. Aoife followed, dead-eyed and zombified. I wondered if she had even noticed John was apparently armed, or if she had just moved because that's what everyone else seemed to be doing. The three of them stood, clustered, along the kitchen wall, Mim and Aoife copying Ruth's raised-hands pose. John was still blocking the doorway, clearly not wanting to give up his tactical advantage any sooner than he had to. Once he was satisfied the other wives were not going anywhere, he turned his attention and his gun back to me. Despite the whirlpool of emotions ripping through my body, I was determined to stand my ground and remain in my chair, straight-backed and as defiant as a pregnant Joan of Arc. He seemed less than impressed.

'I won't ask you again,' he said. 'Get up, Deborah.'

I let out an unimpressed *pfft* sound, which came out louder and more sarcastic than I had planned.

'I bet that thing isn't even real,' I said.

Although my heart hammered in my chest, I couldn't help but feel proud of the confidence in my voice. I had always been a versatile actress, and this time I had taken to my new part so well that I almost had myself convinced. Almost, but not quite. John's finger moved slightly towards the trigger and I forced myself not to flinch.

'If you hurt this baby,' I said, 'Elijah will kill you. You know he will, John.'

Up until that moment, John had been pointing the gun towards me, clutching it stiffly and unnaturally in a white-knuckled hand. Once I had finished speaking, though, he lowered his arm and shook his head. There was nothing forced or false about the look of pity and disgust in his featureless face. He stepped towards me and crouched down so we were eye to eye.

'Deborah,' he said, 'this is the End. It's here. We've been waiting for this moment for *years*. Elijah has been tearing himself apart getting ready for this. It's all he cares about now.'

He was so close that I could practically taste his breath, stale and rank. He lowered his voice.

'He's already decided that you're a liability. You're not coming into the bunker, so either way it's a death sentence. You and the baby. Elijah's orders.'

He stood back up, and when he spoke again it was loud enough for the whole room to hear.

'Sorry to break it to you, Deborah. The choice is yours.'

Except, there was no choice. I rose unsteadily to my feet.

Chapter Thirty-Five

Aoife

I expected John to lead us out of the kitchen and shepherd us straight out of the farmhouse door. Instead, he closed the kitchen door then took us to my room. My bed was still unmade from the morning, the tangled quilt and sheets showing everyone what a poor night's sleep I had had. The curtains were closed too, and I was conscious of how strongly the room still smelled of my sleeping body. A pile of dirty clothes sat shamelessly on the floor by my wardrobe. Fortunately, my numbed brain could not bring itself to care about how vulnerable or human my bedroom made me appear. They had already seen the very worst of me, and I already loathed myself more than they ever could. Somewhere in the back of my mind came a whisper of a thought about Malcolm and what he would think, before I remembered that he was the reason for all of this in the first place.

Without a word John left us, the click of the key in the lock his parting remark. I wanted to perch myself on the edge of the bed – according to the little voice straining to be heard through the fog in my brain, this would make the best impression – but as soon as I touched the mattress my body took over and I found myself lying down flat, like a cadaver on an embalming table. And so I waited, tense and ready, for the inevitable onslaught of anger.

Nothing was said at first, but it didn't take long for Deborah to oblige. It was as though she had spent years and years with her lips sewn together, and all of a sudden the threads had been cut and she was free to voice all of the vitriol that had been bubbling in her mind all that time. And in her defence, that was very much what had happened. We were past the point of reality and were all sharing the same lucid dream, where anything could be said or done without fear of consequence. It was fine, though. I could barely hear Deborah at all. I could tell her words were harsh, but they washed over me like water over a rock, smoothing me out, wearing me away. Even if I'd wanted to defend myself, I had no fight left. She might have gone on forever if Ruth hadn't interrupted her.

'Stop it, Deborah, please! I can't take it any more!'

I opened my eyes but didn't dare lift my head, and Deborah's rant stopped.

'I'm absolutely not going to defend Aoife, but don't you think we have more important things to worry about? Elijah wants us to sit here and fight and tear each other apart because it saves him the job. Deborah, I know you're mad at Aoife right now but aren't you even madder at Elijah? We need to remember who the real bad guys are, and I personally don't think that there are any in this room.'

'Are you kidding me?' said Deborah. 'I appreciate what you're trying to do here, Ruth, but don't you get it? They don't care about us any more, they think this is real and they're leaving us here to die! And it's her fault.'

Out of the corner of my eye, I saw Deborah point an accusatory finger in my direction.

'Deborah, please—'

'Oh come off it, Ruth, why are you defending her? She *hates* us.'

I waited for Ruth to speak up again, but instead of coming to my defence, she stayed silent. Did Ruth think I hated her?

'I can trace every single issue in my marriage back to her.'

I pushed myself up so I was resting on my elbows and turned to face Deborah.

'Really, Deb? Every issue?'

'Yes, *Aoife*, every issue. I worked and I worked to make something of this,' she gestured around her, 'and to keep him happy, and there you were, every time, whispering away in his ear – *Deborah's fake, Deborah doesn't really believe in this life, Deborah doesn't deserve you.*'

'I never said that,' I spat. 'You were always the one going on to him about me. He told me all of your nasty little opinions, that I'm past it, and stuck-up, and—'

'I never said that,' Deborah practically screeched.

'I know you—'

'Oh for goodness sake, listen to yourselves!'

I had never once heard Ruth raise her voice, and Deborah, Mim and I all turned at once to look at her, too stunned to do anything but listen. She was sitting cross-legged on the floor with her back to the door, and even in the fading light I could read the exasperation on her face.

'How do you not see what's been happening here? How are you missing this? How did *I* miss it?'

'What are you talking about?' I snapped.

I was itching with annoyance at being interrupted, even by Ruth.

'He was lying, Aoife,' she said, her voice calm and patient, 'he was making it all up.'

Embarrassment hit me as suddenly and overwhelmingly as a wave of nausea. He had been lying. Of course he had. But why did this particular constellation of lies, this messy, petty web, stand out amongst all the others as such a cruel betrayal?

Deborah, too, seemed felled by the realisation. The mattress sank as she sat down heavily at the foot of the bed. It was strange to look at her there, knowing what I did. Even as we had started to get along better in the days since we met in Elijah's office, I had been storing an undercurrent of resentment towards the woman who I had thought had laughed at my vanished fertility, pitied my age, loathed my personality. Now that was gone, or going, at the very least – years of dislike do not fade so easily – she seemed more real. The careful way she cradled her stomach with her arms, even with her head in her hands, no longer seemed like an affectation or a subtle brag. It was just the action of an ordinary woman.

'How could I be so stupid?' Deborah's voice was muffled.

'He said the same to me,' said Ruth, 'but that you'd both thought I was lazy. I guess it makes sense. Divide and conquer. We're easier to manage if we can be kept apart.'

'So,' I said, taking my chance, 'you were right, Ruth. We're not the bad guys.'

Deborah raised her head.

'Oh, you would say that. This doesn't change the fact that you dobbed Ruth in to that policeman.'

I bristled, a familiar flash of anger striking through my chest.

Maybe my thoughts of peace and forgiveness had come too soon. We all looked at Ruth again, waiting for her to speak.

'I think,' she said, eventually, 'that if we're going to get out of here, we need to stop fighting with each other.'

'Thank you,' I replied.

'As for you,' she raised her eyebrows and pulled herself up from the floor, 'you're lucky I'm a very forgiving woman. I'm trying to think of a single other person on God's green earth who would have the grace to react the way I am to you right now.'

Deborah snorted.

'I know, I'm so sorry, Ruth.'

'Apologise to me later, when we're all safely out of here. For now, why don't you worry about helping us decide what we're going to do next?'

I had never known Ruth speak with such confidence outside of a delivery room or some other medical emergency. Something about the authority in her voice caused my body to react to her command, and before my brain even knew what was what I was sitting up and surveying the room. We had no guarantee of how long we could expect to be left alone, which was my first concern. There was no point in spending hours coming up with a foolproof plan only for John to return with his gun before we had a chance to actually do anything, and I said as much. The others nodded. Even Mim, who was doing her very best to disappear into the corner, let out a vague murmur of agreement.

'You're right,' said Ruth, 'and with that in mind, I think our best bet is to get out of this room as quickly as possible. Once we're out, Aoife will have to find a way to speak to her police officer – I guess he's one of the ones out there right now.' She looked down at me, her dark eyes focused and bright. 'Aoife, you'll have to tell him exactly what's going on, and that we all need out, us and all of the kids. Make sure he knows who I am and what I look like and that I'm not going to put up a fight about the deportation or arrest or whatever it might be. Deborah, Mim, you need to give Aoife an exact number of children so the police know how many to look out for.'

All we could do was agree.

'Great,' she said, 'now, how are we going to get out? I mean, the obvious answer is through the window, but I don't think that's going to work for everyone.'

Four sets of eyes turned to my tiny bedroom window. Although my room was on the ground floor, the window was built high enough into the wall that you could only see out of it if you were standing up. Deborah raised her hand.

'There's a key to Elijah's office in the chest of drawers at the top of the stairs,' she said, 'and I'm pretty sure Elijah will have a spare set of keys to all of our rooms in there somewhere. That way only one of us would have to go out of the window. Whoever does that can come back in through the front door, go upstairs and fetch the keys, come back down and let the rest of us out.'

'That sounds good to me,' Ruth said, before casting her eyes around the room again. 'So, who's going to be able to fit through the window?'

'Wait, wait, wait,' I said, 'I know we agreed that we have to move quickly, but don't you think there are a lot of variables here that we haven't considered? Like, what if John locked the farmhouse door, or if Elijah has moved his spare key from the drawers?'

I looked hopefully from face to face, waiting for someone to agree, but nobody did. Ruth shrugged.

'If that happens, then we're back to square one. But at least we've tried something.'

I bit the inside of my cheek.

'Fine. In that case, I suppose I should be the one to go out of the window.'

Again, nobody spoke. I clambered over the bed so I was on the right side, opened the curtains, and peered through the glass and out into Halcyon. From here I couldn't see any of the police cars, or the gathering of colonists – only a cluster of beehives and some outbuildings. Even the hives seemed deserted in the dim light of the late autumn afternoon. I don't suppose I had ever really paid much attention to the window itself before that day. I had not ever felt inclined to open it – even in the summertime, I was never so warm as to need that – and I hadn't thought enough of the view to look out very often. So it wasn't until then that I noticed the frame of the window itself had no handle or hinges by which it could be opened. There were just six small panes of glass, welded together with heavy leaden piping. I pulled my bedside table underneath the window to act as a stepping stool and gave a weak push. Unsurprisingly, it didn't budge.

'Oh, get off there,' said Deborah, raising an arm to help me down from the table.

I took it gratefully, but let go the instant my feet touched the ground. Her feelings about me were clearly still cool, and I didn't want her to think mine had changed too much either.

She bent down as best she could and picked up the bedside table. 'Stand back!'

Ruth, Mim and I moved as far away as the space allowed in the seconds between Deborah's warning and the forceful smash of wood against glass. She dropped the table for a moment and panted, her hands resting on her thighs, before picking it up again and clearing the rest of the frame. Once the window was completely gone, Deborah sat down heavily on the bed.

'Well, I hope no one heard that.'

I doubted it. As empty as Halcyon looked, the sound of police sirens and nervous chatter was enough to block out any noise from the farmhouse.

Before I even got the chance to return to my spot by the window, Ruth shook her head.

'Sorry, Aoife,' she said, inspecting the gap, 'but there's no way you're going to be able to fit through there. I'll have to try.'

We watched in silent awe as Ruth found her balance on the bedside table – still sturdy despite its dealings with the window – and pulled herself up so her forearms were resting against the window ledge.

'Careful,' said Deborah, her hands pressed against her mouth, 'there might still be some shards.'

Ruth nodded and returned to the ground.

'There are going to be shards there whatever we do,' she said, 'I think we'll need to get the whole frame out somehow.'

I nodded, and Deborah stepped forward.

'The plaster around the wood is all crumbly – we should be able to dislodge it if we both push as hard as we can.'

I watched as together they pushed the window frame free from the wall. It seemed to come away easily enough, a testament to the age and decrepit nature of the house, leaving more plaster dust in its wake. By this point we were filthy with it, each of us covered head to toe in a thin grey film.

Once the frame was safely removed, Ruth pulled herself up again, this time thrusting her torso forward and out, until her front half was clear of the room. It soon became apparent, though, that her hips were going to be too wide to make it the full way through. Defeated, she slowly eased herself back down.

'Well, that idea's a bust. Does anyone else have another plan? Maybe we can try and knock this door down too?'

With the window gone the sounds of outside seemed louder than ever, and the cacophony made it almost impossible to think. I was wracking my brain for any other possible escape routes when Mim's reedy voice piped up from the corner.

'It's not a bust. I mean, it might not be yet. I think I could be small enough to squeeze through.'

The idea of Mim, as petite as she was, having the physicality needed to launch herself through a window – wearing a wedding gown of all things – seemed almost funny, but by that point she was our only chance. I could tell from Ruth and Deborah's silence that they, too, were reluctant to give her the job but whatever their reasons were, they were clearly not pressing enough, because within moments Mim was halfway into Halcyon.

Chapter Thirty-Six

Mim

By the time I realised what I was doing I was already perched, knees to my chest, in the empty window frame, looking down at the pile of broken glass below. Getting up there had been a lot easier than I had expected, but I suppose I hadn't really considered the fact that I would also need to get down. The thought of it made me freeze up, all except for my stomach, which churned and growled and made me worry that I might be sick. I tried to remember that I was safe because I was being upheld in God's righteous right hand, but that made me even sicker, because I wasn't sure if God *was* upholding me any more.

I could pinpoint the exact moment that things had started going really wrong. Right in the middle of the second spirit drill, just as Elijah was warning us about the oncoming tide of sin, my bleeding started. I could feel the warm wetness between my legs, and whenever I moved the nasty smell of blood wafted up into my nostrils and made me queasy. It had been Deborah who had first explained things to me the day the first streak of rust appeared in my knickers. She called it my 'monthly cycle', which I found confusing. The name made it sound like it would arrive once a month, which it rarely did, and last a short amount of time, which it never did. Once it lasted straight through from one full moon to another. I became so sick and worried that I confided in Helen, who told me that I must have been doing something very wicked for it to have lasted that long, and that God was clearly very angry with me. Since then I began to see the blood as a punishment or a bad omen. And I must have been right, because look at all of the things that had happened since the blood spilled in church. They were too many and too awful to even think about.

I took a deep breath in, filling my lungs as much as I could in my crouched position. My body must have needed the air, because straight away I began to feel a little bit better. I was still scared of the drop and nervous about my heavy menstrual rag slipping and bleeding into the wedding dress, but at least I could think a little more clearly.

'Please can somebody pass me something that I can throw down to land on,' I called in to Aoife's bedroom, 'so I don't cut myself on the glass?'

I tried not to look down too much, but I could hear the commotion in the room behind me as they looked for something suitable. Aoife's arm reached up and handed me the rag rug. It was the first thing my eyes had landed on when I entered her room because I had made it myself, way back when we had first arrived in Halcyon. The gesture seemed like it might be symbolic, but I couldn't quite figure out how.

There was just enough of a gap between my scrunched-up body and the window frame for me to throw the mat out. I shook it as best I could with my left hand, while my right held tightly onto the inside wall, hoping that it would land flat enough to cover plenty of the glass. Jaw clenched, I watched it fall quickly and heavily to the ground; it managed to fold itself almost clean in half, but at least the biggest patch of shards was covered. I muttered a quick prayer of thanks.

'Are you okay up there? Do you want to change out of the dress before you jump?'

It was Ruth. The concern in her voice warmed my heart, but at the same time I didn't want her to think that I was less capable or brave than the rest of them. I also didn't want to have to climb back down the way I had come to change into something else in case I couldn't bring myself to go back up again. I knew that my voice would shake and give me away if I tried to answer, so I just repositioned myself to let my legs dangle down against the outside wall. I had an idea in my mind that I would be able to use my arms as levers and lower myself slowly enough to avoid a real drop. My muscles – what little of them there were – had other ideas, and I had no sooner attempted to support my own weight when they gave up entirely, leaving me to fall gracelessly in the vague direction of the mat.

The second I landed I forced myself to stand up, knowing that if I waited on the ground for any length of time, I would find it impossible to move. I looked down and surveyed the damage, my body still shaking from the impact. Most of me had managed to find the rug, but my left hand had gone straight down on a thick shard of glass which was now sticking out of the centre of my palm. The back of the wedding dress was another victim of the fall; it had torn badly from scraping against the rough stonework of the outside wall and was hanging in sad, tattered strips. Thanks be to God, the satin had provided enough of a barrier to prevent the backs of my legs from facing the same fate.

'Mim!'

I turned to see Ruth's worried face sticking out of the window.

'Are you hurt?' she asked.

'Not really,' I said. 'Just—'

I raised my left palm up to her, and she winced.

'Before you do anything else,' she said in her nurse's voice, 'I need you to pull that out.'

A lump rose in my throat, and I turned my back to the window. Breathing heavily, I took the glass between the thumb and forefinger of my right hand. The touch alone was enough to make me shudder, but I knew she was right. The longer I left it the worse it would be. If I had learned one thing from my years in the schoolhouse, it was that painful things were best to get over quickly. I had also learned that I could handle more than I thought I could. The first time I was sent outside, soaked from wetting the bed, I had thought I would die from the cold – but I didn't. Every beating I took had felt like the most I could take, but then they would go on and I would realise I could take more. This was just like that. I thought of Christ, and the nails they had driven into his palms, as I tightened my grip and pulled. My skin released the glass with a gentle spurt of blood, and I turned back to Ruth, who was still waiting anxiously in the window. Once she was satisfied that the glass was gone, she allowed herself a small smile of relief.

'Now tear off some of the wedding dress and wrap your hand with it, tight as you can. Then take another strip and wrap it round your wrist, like a tourniquet – do you know what a tourniquet is? To stop the flow of blood.'

I did as I was told. Even with the sound of sirens in the background, the rip of the fabric made me shudder. I hoped Aoife and Deborah would forgive me.

'Good job,' she said. 'Now round you go. We'll be waiting.'

Before she could say anything more, I hurried around the corner of the farmhouse. My lungs struggled to take in the cold air, even though my body was desperate for it. My heart still hadn't slowed at all. I leaned against the wall, not trusting my shaking legs to support me on their own. That was when I heard the voices travelling on the wind. I inched along and peeked around the corner so I could get a better look at the front of the house, where the voices seemed to be coming from. John and Elijah were standing by the door. I ducked straight back around. Could I run back to them, maybe? Fall to my knees at Elijah's feet and beg his forgiveness? But before I could make my mind up, John spoke.

'All I'm saying is, I don't know what we're waiting for,' he said. 'We should grab Mim and get the marriage done. She'll be no bother, once she's away from those—'

'I said no.' Elijah sounded angry. 'Forget about Mim.' The sound of my name made my heart race. 'The police have enough on me already. If they catch me with her, I'm a dead man.' He almost sounded scared when he said that.

'Nobody is going to catch you! We've been preparing for this, that's what the bunker is for. They'll never get in, and by the time we're out of provisions, the Lord will have called us to Him.'

'What a mess,' said Elijah in a low voice that I could only just hear. 'I can't believe I'm risking jail for this lot.'

My head was spinning as I leaned against the wall, listening to the sounds of papers changing hands. If Elijah was frightened, surely we all should be?

'No one is going to jail, mate. The police can't touch you.'

Why was he so worried about the police, I wondered? Didn't he trust the bunker to keep everyone safe? I was still trying to figure out what was going on when I heard their footsteps crossing the courtyard. As they came into view, I pressed myself as close to the wall as I could. They were walking in the direction of the bunker, and Elijah had his hands in his pockets.

'Let's just go back to the bunker for now. You'll feel better when everyone is safely inside. I can always come back up for

Mim later if you change your mind. And I thought I told you to lay off that stuff today? I know you say it helps you focus, but it's got you all on edge.'

Elijah spun round to face John and swung a fist in his direction. My hands rose up to my face as John was knocked to the ground. Elijah looked down at him and said something too quiet for me to hear before walking off, leaving John to pull himself to his feet. I watched him running to catch up, and stayed where I was until they were both out of sight.

Aoife, Ruth, and Deborah would be wondering where I was. I had no idea how long I had been standing there, listening to the men talking. What if they managed to find another way out, and they came looking for me? I knew I was going to have to move, because if they found me there and asked what I'd been doing, I would have to tell the truth. And I wasn't sure that I wanted to tell them. They would have so many questions, and I wouldn't know the answers, and anyway, maybe it hadn't been as bad as it had looked? How could I know for certain what I had seen and heard? It was probably better to pretend it hadn't happened at all.

I inched back around the wall. In the gaps between the farm buildings I could see two figures patrolling the fence. I squinted. It was Niall – I recognised him by his lolloping gait, even though he was obviously trying his best to march – and Mark, his red hair standing bright against the darkening sky. I craned my neck so I could see more, and the first thing I spotted was the cluster of police cars, surrounded by officers dressed in black. I hadn't seen anything or anyone like them since we left the city when I was ten. They looked like crows pecking around, just waiting for Halcyon to die so they could swoop in and pick it to pieces. The thought of it made me feel uneasy. I didn't want to get married to Elijah, or go back to the schoolhouse, but at the same time I didn't want Halcyon to be over, not fully over, its corpse being pulled to bits by hungry police officers who didn't understand us and didn't want to. I remembered Elijah's warnings about the police, and their cruelty, and how even in Biblical times the upholders of the law of man had persecuted Christ and His followers. If he was scared, there was no wonder.

I knew that I needed to keep going, to get to the door and go up to Elijah's office to find a spare key to let everyone out before someone spotted me, but my legs had turned wobbly and weak. I closed my eyes so I could focus on the rough stone against my back and the way the cold was coming out of the wall and into my body. I felt the sting of my scraped skin, and the dull throb of the cut in my palm. My heartbeat slowed, and my legs seemed a little sturdier. I tried to keep concentrating on the little things as I opened my eyes and kept moving towards the front door, blocking out the wail of the sirens and listening instead to the crunch of gravel under my feet.

Just before I reached the door, I allowed myself to turn around. I could see that everyone was still congregated in front of the bunker, the only difference being that now the children were leaning against each other, clearly exhausted. The pile of cow carcasses was still there, and I hoped they weren't frightened of them. Ordinarily, I would have been there with them, holding their hands and keeping them calm. Instead, I was looking over from afar, preparing to bring their whole world crashing down. The thumping of my heart forced me to pull myself together and turn away before I froze up again. The door was locked, but Ruth had mentioned that there was always a spare key under the boot scraper next to the front step. The schoolhouse did not lock, and so I had never actually had to use a key before; I tried it one way, and then another, and then with a heavy click the door opened.

Despite the setting sun outside, the darkness of the farmhouse hallway overwhelmed my eyes. With every door closed and no other source of light, I had to fumble my way to the staircase and climb with my bad hand on the handrail and the other flat against the wall. I had never been upstairs in there before, and I wasn't used to stairs in general – this was the only building in Halcyon with a second storey – so I wanted to be careful. I was very aware that God might no longer be watching over me. The first door I tried swung open with ease, but my relief didn't last long. It wasn't Elijah's office, but Ruth's bedroom. I allowed myself to linger for a moment in the doorway before moving on to the only other door up there. I filled my lungs with the stale indoor air and pressed down on the handle. It was already unlocked.

The curtains were open in the office, and I could just about see all I needed to see with the fading afternoon light from outside. At a glance, everything looked orderly; books lined shelves like rows and rows of Christian soldiers, pens and pencils stood to attention in their pot on Elijah's desk. All as it should be. Gently, I closed the door behind me and stepped further into the room. *If I were a key, where would I be?* As tidy as the room was, there were a host of places things could be hidden. Inside the pages of a book, under a floorboard, inside the desk. I cast my eyes around and decided to start with the obvious. If Elijah never expected anyone to come into his office, I reasoned, why would he go to the lengths of hiding something as innocent as a set of keys? The first drawer I tried was locked, as was the second. *So much for my theory*, I thought. But still – if you were at your desk and needed something from a drawer, you wouldn't want to go far to find the key to unlock it. The only thing on Elijah's desk was an old mug filled with pens and pencils. Not wanting to waste a second, I tipped them out onto the desk. They bounced off the wooden surface and onto the floor, but the small flat key stayed where it landed – right under my nose.

I didn't have any expectations of what I might find inside the drawer, but I was still surprised. Brightly coloured packages caught what little light there was in the room and glistened temptingly. I knelt down so I could see them better, all pain suddenly taking a back seat to my curiosity. The sight of the packets and bags unlocked a pre-Halcyon memory from deep in the recesses of my mind, and a laugh bubbled up from nowhere.

Chapter Thirty-Seven

Ruth

The threat of deportation meant very little to me by then, if it had ever meant much in the first place. All I could think about as I paced back and forth in Aoife's room was getting us all out. The children, of course, but the adults too; good, honest people who just wanted to live better and do better and love one another, who had been taken in and turned into something else entirely. Or, mostly good. Mostly honest. The world outside may not have been perfect, but it was better than what we had here. The little capacity for caring that I had left over was spent on worrying about the animals – the poor cows had already been slaughtered, but Russell and the pups' fate was a mystery to me. Someone would have had to go into the cow shed where the dogs were, and I could only hope that whoever it was had been too focussed on their task to care about a small terrier and her litter.

Nobody spoke; there was nothing to say. The darkness set in around us as we waited. We all jumped when the front door opened, and I prayed that it was her. There was no way to know for sure, though the soft footsteps up the stairs were reassuring, but if it was, it had taken her a long time to get back into the farmhouse. I had become so immune to the sound of the sirens that I couldn't say when they stopped exactly – I only noticed the silence from outside when I realised that I could suddenly hear the small sounds from within the house. Upstairs, Mim – or the person I hoped was Mim – opened and closed two doors in quick succession. *Come on, come on.* Time stretched and warped. It was a race that my life depended on, but I could see none of the runners, and I had no idea how long the track was or how many obstacles would come between them and the finishing line.

Aoife had returned to the bed. She lay flat on her back, and when I passed her on my short loop of the room, I could see her lips moving in silent prayer. Deborah was still standing by the window, staring blankly out of the pane-less frame. They both must have been listening too, straining to hear any sound that might give away Mim's position and tell us how much longer we'd have to wait, because the creak of the top step pulled them out of their freeze frame. Together, we stood and watched the door.

Chapter Thirty-Eight

Deborah

My heart was halfway into my throat as I listened to Mim struggle with the keys on the other side of the door. It took all of my strength not to scream at her to hurry as key after key was pushed into the lock and key after key got jammed and we had to listen as she wriggled it out. When the door did finally swing open, I had to blink to make sure the dark wasn't playing tricks on me. She closed the door with one hand, because with the other she was holding an armful of crisp packets and chocolate bars.

'You'll never believe what I found in Elijah's desk,' she said, dropping her loot on the bed.

'I'm pretty sure I could take a guess,' I said, looking down at the snacks with hungry eyes. Somehow, the sight of the once familiar food calmed me a little. 'Is that what took you so long?'

Mim shook her head as we crowded round the bed.

'The keyring was right at the bottom of the drawer, and the drawer was full of all of this stuff. I thought I might as well pick some up, in case anyone was hungry.'

I was starved, but Ruth and Aoife both shook their heads, so I shook mine too.

'Did you see what was happening outside? Are the police still there? Is it safe for us to make a run for it?' Ruth asked.

Even before Mim spoke, it was obvious that she was not going to give us an answer we wanted to hear. She described the scene outside in stilted detail without looking up from her feet.

'I don't understand why they're making all of the children stand out in the middle of everything? They don't need to be seeing all of this, and they look so tired.'

She sounded sad, as if out of everything, this was what disappointed her the most about Halcyon.

'Surely they just want them where they can see them?' I said.

Aoife stirred from her seat on the bed and shook her head.

'No, I don't think so. They'll want them where the police can see them. They don't want them charging in with hoses or tear gas or whatever riot police do to break up crowds.'

My stomach sank.

'Tear gas?'

Aoife shrugged and lay back down. But the thought of tear gas or anything like it coming anywhere near my children made every cell in my body scream, and I clutched my stomach – at least I had one baby with me.

'Well, what are we going to do now?'

I could feel myself panicking, but I didn't even try to keep the rise from my voice. I was past the point of caring what Mim and Ruth and even Aoife thought of me. Ruth leaned across and took my hand in hers. My skin had been so starved of touch that Ruth's cold fingers sent an electric shock through my nerves and made my heart beat even faster.

'It's okay.' She looked me in the eyes as she spoke. 'I think we need to stick to our original plan; it's the only chance we have of getting out of here by the end of the day. I just think that instead of all of us leaving together, it might be more sensible if only one of us went. That way, we have less chance of getting caught.'

Immediately, Mim raised her hand.

'I'll go,' she said, 'I've done it once already, so I know where everyone is. I think it would be, you know – the sensible choice.'

I shook my head, pulling my hand out of Ruth's.

'Nope, not a chance. You've done enough, Mim. It's Aoife's turn now. She knows which police officer to speak to, anyway. I'm sure she'll be glad to see him.'

The last few words to leave my mouth were coated with an undeniable film of venom, which made Ruth flinch.

'I don't know—' she began, before she was interrupted by Aoife.

'No,' she said, her voice croaky and tired. 'Deborah is right. It wouldn't make sense for anyone else to go.'

Before any of us could say anything more, Aoife rose one last time from her bed and glided as purposefully as a ghost towards the door. Mim put her unbandaged hand up to her mouth, and Ruth began to gnaw on her nails. My heart tugged after her, which I didn't expect or enjoy. I swallowed the lump in my throat and turned my attention to the pile of snack foods on the bed. I unwrapped a bar of Dairy Milk, the purple sheen of its wrapper winking at me as I wolfed down the whole bar in nine swift bites. Once I had finished, I folded the wrapper into a small triangle, laid it on Aoife's pillowcase, and selected two packets of crisps: one cheese and onion and the other prawn cocktail. Even the puff of air which escaped the bags as I popped them open contained more flavour than I had experienced in six years. I could sense Ruth and Mim looking down at me and felt their silent concern, but I was overcome by what I could only describe as a vicious animal hunger. I shovelled the crisps into my mouth in great handfuls, licking the greasy crumbs off my fingers whenever they became too coated for me to easily pick up any more. As the night air whispered through the hole in the wall where the windowpane had once been, and the room became colder and darker, I continued to eat.

Chapter Thirty-Nine

Aoife

Mim's description of the scene outside had been enough to worry me, but it was still not enough to prepare me for what I saw when I left the farmhouse. The police cars had turned their headlights on, and four sets of bright white lights were casting strange shadows from the once-familiar figures and structures of the colony. I secreted myself behind the wall of the church, and from there I could see straight into the cluster of people in the centre of the settlement. Barely twenty feet away, I could hear the muffled whines of exhausted children and the hushed prayers of terrified adults. The whole thing was obscene. Elijah and I had planned for Halcyon to be a utopia, but there it was right before my eyes, transformed into a Jonestown or a Waco; the kind of place you would see on the news and shake your head and wonder at just how people got themselves into such a mess. Thankfully, I didn't have the time or the mental reserves to connect the dots and realise that *I* was now the sort of person people might wonder those things about. Instead, I turned towards the source of the blinding headlights in an attempt to make out the figures of the police officers. One was holding a large white loudspeaker. When she turned it on, the nails-down-a-chalkboard squeal cast a studded silence over the people of Heaven on Earth.

'My name is Courtney Ballantine. I am a Detective Sergeant in the Highlands and Islands police force.'

She spoke with a confidence which I found reassuring, although I worried it wouldn't do her any favours. A confident woman was not something to be appreciated in Halcyon, especially by the man in charge.

'We have spoken to one of you individually, but now we feel that it is time to address you all. I think it's only fair that you all understand what is happening here tonight. None of the officers here want to do you any harm. We have been made aware that there are children here – I can see them all now, and they look cold and scared – and we have a duty to check on their wellbeing.'

I watched as Annie broke away from the huddle of children crowding around her. Illuminated by the headlight beams, she stepped towards Courtney Ballantine and pointed an accusatory finger in her direction. She looked emaciated, her hair coming loose from its braided bun, eyes wild and gleaming. Had she always been so thin?

'Go away! Our children are fine! Go home and worry about your own children, and leave us alone!'

Ironically, Annie's screech set two of the smaller children off crying, but the rest of Halcyon didn't seem to care. Their cheers masked the cries of the babies, and the Detective Sergeant waited for them to stop.

'I understand that this is a very intense situation.' If she was angry, she wasn't showing it. 'We want to make it as stress-free as we can, for all of you, but especially for the little ones. I can see that you love them very much. We need to come in so we can check on them, and we need to speak to your—', she stopped for half a second, '—leader, in person. We ask that you open your front gates and let myself and my colleagues inside. If you do not comply, we will use force to enter your compound and we will arrest anyone who attempts to stop us from doing our job. I don't want that to happen, and I'm sure none of you want that to happen either. It's up to you to decide on the course of action you would like to take.'

The loudspeaker clicked off, and I moved to the other end of the building where I hoped to get a proper look at the detective. She was speaking quietly to another person who I now realised was Malcolm. I held my breath. He didn't seem to be paying very much attention to what she was saying, or at least he wasn't looking at her. He was busy scanning the crowd. I imagined his green eyes straining through the darkness and wondered if he was looking for me. I wasn't sure if I wanted him to see me or not, or what I would say to him if we spoke. I had thought of him as a friend, a person I could trust – someone kind who found me interesting and possibly even attractive. But in the end, he was just another man who had taken me in, the gullible fool that I was. *Prick*. The voice in my head was suddenly my own. I drew my eyes away and snuck back round so I could regain my view on the crowd of colonists. Elijah was nowhere to be seen, but John was there giving instructions to Mark S., a young man who had grown up in the church. Mark nodded and scurried off into one of the surrounding outhouses, returning with his own loudspeaker clutched to his chest. The bright white plastic looked out of place on the Halcyon side of the fence, and I struggled to remember if I had ever seen the loudspeaker before. It didn't seem familiar, but then nothing seemed familiar that night – not even the people.

John signalled for the hum of whispered conversation to stop before he raised the loudspeaker to his lips. There was no ear-splitting screech this time, and even from a distance I could sense his disappointment at the lack of dramatic effect.

'Halcyon is a peaceful community,' he began, 'and we have lived here for almost six years without causing any trouble to anyone. All we want to do is follow the Word of the Lord and of our Holy Prophet without disturbance from the outside world.'

A brief pause was followed by a cheer from the crowd.

'But now the outside world has come to us, you have left us with no choice. In order to move into the next life, we must be here, where we can follow our way of living. We would rather die in Halcyon and meet our Lord in Heaven, than live and burn in hell. And we would rather take our children with us than let them go with you and follow your sure path to damnation.

We will do what it takes to protect ourselves from your heathen ways. We have a stockpile of explosives here which we are ready and willing to use if you leave us no other choice. Either you leave this land now and never return, or we will burn this place to the ground and take ourselves with it!'

At first, I thought the screams and cries were ones of terror, but the more I listened the clearer it became – they were sounds of rejoicing. Choking back the bile which had risen to my mouth, I took the moment of distraction to run out from behind the safety of the church and towards the nearest outbuilding to the perimeter fence. The noise of the crowd and the blood pumping past my ears combined into one deafening roar as I ran, so I felt more like I was running through a nightmare than in real life. The outbuilding – a small tin shack where we stored surplus wool from our sheep – welcomed me like a beacon.

I had not planned to actually go inside; I'd hoped instead to use the cover it provided as a stopping place on my way to the perimeter, a point where I could hopefully attract the attention of someone on the other side of the fence. Once I was there, though, I couldn't resist. The prospect of having somewhere dark and quiet to gather my thoughts and catch my breath was too inviting, and I had barely stopped running before I pulled the heavy door open. Almost instantly, a hand shot through the darkness and grabbed hold of my skirt, pulling me in and knocking me off balance.

'Oh God! I'm so sorry! Please forgive me!'

As panicked and tearful as the voice was, I recognised it immediately.

'Helen? Is that you?'

'Aoife! Thank God! Have you seen Mim?'

Her hands, as frozen and ridged as ice, searched for mine and I almost felt sorry for her, but her desperation made me want to pull away and I shook her off in disgust.

'Well, she's certainly not in here, is she?' I whispered. 'What are you doing, Helen, hiding like a kid?'

'What am I supposed to do? What can any of us do? It's gone absolutely mental out there, Aoife, you must have seen it. There are police outside, and then John—' she broke off in tears before continuing, gasping and gulping, '—saying what he just said – did you hear him? I never thought I'd live to see it, Aoife, it's like a nightmare.'

Even in the darkness I could see her vague shape, curled up and quaking on the floor by my feet. It was unsettling to hear the fear in her voice. Usually Helen seemed incapable of presenting any negative emotions at all, but now her sweet baby-talk voice was gone. Even her words sounded so unfamiliar that I wondered for a moment if she was possessed.

I said the only thing I could think to say:

'Pull yourself together. There's plenty you can do if you actually want to help, instead of hiding out and feeling sorry for yourself.'

With a sniff, she fumbled for my hand once again. I allowed it, but gripped her a little tighter than I needed to as I pulled her from the floor.

'We're going to get everyone who wants to get out, out,' I said, 'but I can't do it alone.'

'We? Who's we?'

I sighed. 'Me, Ruth, Deborah, and Mim.'

'Mim! Mim's helping you? She's all right?'

'Yes, yes, she's fine. Or she's fine for now anyway, as fine as the rest of us. I need to get to the fence to speak to the police, but I can't get there if everyone is looking that way. Can you distract them?'

She sniffed again, wiped her nose with the back of her hand.

'Distract them how?'

Chapter Forty

Ruth

My nails, which had gone unbitten for ten years, had been torn to shreds in the minutes between Aoife leaving the room and the police officer's speech through the loudspeaker. I had been working away at them so distractedly that it was only Deborah's crumb-covered hand gently touching my own that even brought my attention to it. It was getting too dark to see clearly and none of us wanted to turn on the light, so I just sat there, running my fingertips over the ragged ends of my nails, waiting for anything to happen.

When the officer began her address, Deborah, Mim and I moved towards the empty window so we could hear better. We could have left, but although the door was unlocked, an unspoken agreement kept us where we were. We didn't even dare to lean up against it. Since Aoife had disappeared through it, I couldn't escape the feeling that she had been swallowed up, that there was no longer a hallway on the other side but some kind of swirling portal like you might see in a cheesy science-fiction movie – the sort I'd watched with my godmother in the early London days. The unfamiliar voice, tinged with a mechanical echo, did not do much to relieve my mind of that particular fantasy. It occurred to me that I hadn't eaten anything all day and I worried that I might be delirious. That made me feel faint, and I was concentrating so hard on not falling over that I missed almost all of what the officer said.

'Well,' said Deborah, once the speech had been delivered, 'they won't like that one bloody bit.'

I nodded, unsure whether or not she could actually see my head moving, and resumed my nail-biting, frantically searching for an unchewed end with my teeth. I watched as Deborah's shadowy outline shuffled away from the door and back to the bed, where she sat down with a heavy groan.

'Are you okay, Deborah?' I asked, removing my finger from my mouth for as long as it took me to speak, before replacing it.

'Yeah,' she said, 'yeah, I'm just tired. And I feel a bit sick. I think I ate too much crap. How about you, Mim, are you okay?'

Even though we were all stuck in Aoife's pokey bedroom, I kept forgetting about Mim. I mean, I knew she was there – I could hear her breathing and the anxious rumbling of her stomach. It was more that I was starting to forget that she was real in the same way that I knew Deborah and I were. As much as I'd taken to her over the past week, the stress of the last eight hours had eclipsed her personhood in my mind. It was as though my soul couldn't bear to care about another person and had followed a strict 'last one in first one out' policy, expelling Mim to sit alone in Aoife's darkening bedroom, shivering against the cold from the broken window.

She responded to Deborah with a sad squeak and knelt down as if she was planning to pray. I reached out for her shoulder and gave it what I hoped was a reassuring pat, and she lent her head against my hand. I could feel the tendons in her popsicle-stick neck pulling as she moved. That appealed to the nurse in me, and I left my hand there to slowly turn numb under her heavy head. I managed to relax slightly, just in time for John's voice to blare out through his own loudspeaker and send all my nerves on edge again.

This time we stayed where we were. If anything, I wanted to take myself further away from the sound – throw a pillow over my head or cover my ears with my hands and hum or something – but I just stood at Mim's side and listened. Once it was over, it was my turn to speak first.

'I think he's faking,' I said, my quaking voice not doing much to back up my words, 'I don't believe they could even if they wanted to. That gun is one thing, but I think one of us would have noticed if they had started hiding explosives around the place. It's a front, or a test, like Elijah's game with the water at the Feast of the Prophet. For all we know the gun was a fake too. He never fired it.'

Deborah let out a noncommittal *hmm*, but before she could say anything more Mim's shoulders began to shake.

'I believe it,' she said.

She was straining to keep herself from crying, I could tell. I'd worked with enough labouring women to know that.

'But Mim, where would they even keep stuff like that? We're a small community. We keep livestock, we grow vegetables, we pray. We don't blow things up. Someone would have seen something and said something long before now if it was true.'

I was trying to reassure myself more than anything, and I think they could tell.

'I'm not so sure, Ruth,' said Deborah. 'First of all, would you recognise an explosive if you saw one? Would any of us? And if you're looking for a place to hide something, you could do a lot worse than Halcyon.'

My mind turned to the night with Mim and the puppies, and those locked doors.

'Should we get out of here?' I asked.

'And go where? Aoife's already out there, and I think we'd have heard if they'd seen her. For all we know she could be speaking to the police officer right now. We just have to trust her. I trust her.'

It was reassuring to hear Deborah sound so calm, and I believed what she said when she talked about trusting Aoife, but I could not help but worry that after years in Heaven on Earth Deborah just needed desperately to have faith in someone. Even if that person was Aoife.

Chapter Forty-One

Deborah

My back ached and my stomach ached and my head ached. My earthly body felt heavy and worn out. Even the new life which I was supposedly nurturing in my womb felt like a stone. I wished that I had the energy to pray, like Mim was. I could hear her muttering under her breath, words like *saviour* and *peace* and *forgiveness* floating past my ears as they made their way to God's. Or maybe just to the ceiling. It was hard to see God in Halcyon that night.

When I was growing up with my mother, in and out of friends' flats and B&Bs and squats, my knowledge of God came solely from what I'd seen and heard on TV. He was as fictional to me as Dot Cotton or the Fresh Prince of Bel-Air, and a thousand times less interesting. It wasn't until I was taken into care and started going to school that the magnitude of this all-powerful, all-knowing, all-loving being was revealed to me and inevitably I got really into it. I remember coming home from school one day and telling my foster carers about my new discovery.

'Did you know about God?' I asked them, wide-eyed.

They had nodded, tactfully, waiting to hear what I had to say.

'Do you know that God loves *everyone*? And that God made the whole *world*?'

If they had wanted to laugh, they managed to keep it inside. Neither of them was religious; they never took me to church or made me say a prayer before bed, but when my childish fanaticism began they didn't do anything to discourage me. When I asked to bless the food we were about to receive they dutifully said their *amen*s without even the flicker of a smirk, and when I begged to rent *Jesus Christ Superstar* from the video shop they sat and watched it with me. In hindsight, I suppose they were just happy that the skinny little girl who had come to their house covered in fleas and bruises was finding something that made her feel happy and loved. They were nice people, after all, and I like to think that's what I would have felt if I were them. God died when I left that placement and entered my teens, and then He was resurrected when my mother and I reunited and I saw how happy and healthy she had become since joining Heaven on Earth. That evening in Aoife's bedroom it was as though God was comatose, and He would either pull through or disappear from my world forever depending on what happened next.

When the singing began, I wondered if Elijah had been right all along. Had a host of angels descended from heaven to carry the good people of Halcyon to eternal peace at the feet of their Lord? No. Barely two lines into 'Morning Has Broken' it was clear that the singers were too familiar to be celestial. Still, there was something heavenly about the sound of all those little voices, exhausted as they were, joining together in song. 'Morning Has Broken' was one of the songs I had taught the children. It was the first religious song I'd ever heard, the song which had brought God into my life, a fact that allowed me to convince Elijah that it would be suitable to be sung in Halcyon. He had otherwise believed it to be too secular – our other songs were written by him. I tried to remember if I had told Aoife that story.

'Do you think that's something to do with her?' asked Mim, hopefully.

For the first time that day my heart beat with joy instead of terror. My aches and pains were practically forgotten – background noise to the thrill of hope coursing through my veins and playing on the ends of every nerve in my body.

'Yes.' I said, 'Yes, I think so, Mim.'

I felt myself coming back to life.

Chapter Forty-Two

Aoife

Just as I had hoped, the children's song proved to be enough of a distraction that I was able to sprint from behind the shed to the perimeter fence. Courtney Ballantine was the first to see me, and she pointed to a dark patch of fence which the lights from the police cars hadn't reached. By this time my eyes had adjusted to the lack of light, and I was able to get a better idea of her appearance. She looked older than she did when she had been illuminated by the headlights, and shorter too, although she exuded the confidence of a person for whom nothing was new. It must have been an act, considering the location of her constabulary, but I admired her for it nonetheless.

'I need to speak to whoever is in charge,' I said, keeping my voice as low as possible, 'I'm Aoife.'

I imagined that she widened her eyes in recognition, but it was too dark to tell for sure.

'Aoife,' she said, 'DI Andrews, Malcolm, has told me all about you. I'm glad to see that you're all right. Where are—'

'Aoife!'

It was Malcolm; I had been so focussed on Courtney that I hadn't seen him approach the fence. His smooth whisky voice was hushed but relieved. I ignored him.

'Where are…?' I said to Courtney, urging her to continue.

She looked at Malcolm, and then back at me. She seemed ready to speak again, but Malcolm beat her to it.

'Aoife, please. I know they must have told you about me, and who I am. I'm sorry if you feel as though I've misled you. I know you must be angry with me, I understand…'

I was watching Courtney Ballantine as Malcolm spoke, willing her to step in and shut him up. I couldn't bring myself to look at him. With every word that left his mouth, I grew more and more enraged. This man had lied to me. He had seen how vulnerable – as much as it pained me to admit it – I was and he had taken advantage. He had been nice to me and he had *flirted* with me and drawn me in. He had made me like him. He had done everything Elijah had done.

'No,' I said.

'Pardon?'

'No. Stop it, just stop it. You're sorry if I *feel* misled? Bullshit, Malcolm. Bullshit, DI Whoever You Are. What does that even mean? I don't *feel* misled, or if I do, it's because I was. By you.'

'I—'

'Shut up. I am sick,' my voice cracked, 'I am sick of listening to men say the word "I". How dare you make this about you? You have put us all in so much danger here tonight. I came out here to tell you and your colleagues that there are two women and a teenage girl in our farmhouse. One of the women is pregnant. We need you to get us out, and we need you to get our children out. How do you plan on doing that, Mister Policeman? Because that's all I care about right now. Not some half-arsed apology.'

For a brief moment before he regained his composure, his usually open face looked wounded. Had I hurt his feelings? Did I care? I wasn't sure, and I had no time to dwell. He cleared his throat.

'We're doing our best, Aoife,' he said. 'DS Ballantine and her team have found a tunnel which leads into your compound.'

'One of the boys has just come back from investigating,' said Courtney Ballantine, 'but there's a trapdoor at the other end which is locked or jammed from the other side.'

'I don't know about any tunnels,' I said, folding my arms across my chest. 'If I did, I'd be out by now.'

'I understand,' she said, 'I wasn't implying—'

'Where did you say this tunnel leads?'

Malcolm was the one to answer. He pointed in the direction of the schoolhouse, away from the bunker and the crowd.

'It's in that direction, and judging by the distance it opens up in one of your outbuildings.'

Courtney shook her head softly, apparently frustrated by his answer to my question.

'That doesn't matter now,' she said, 'it's a dead end for us because we can't get in. What we'd like to ask you, while you're here, is what you know about these explosives. DI Andrews told us that you'd never mentioned them before. Do you know anything about them?'

'No,' I said, 'that was the first I heard of them too.'

'Thank you. I realise this may be a difficult question for you to answer, Aoife, but can I ask if you believe his threat? We're treating it as real either way, but I would appreciate your insight.'

'I'm sorry,' I said, 'I just have no idea any more.'

No idea at all. About anything. I felt as though I was lost out at sea, no land in sight. The only thing I could see to cling to, the single piece of flotsam, was the tunnel. I had said that I didn't know of any tunnels, and at the time that had been true, but suddenly I remembered the short-lived project of a few years ago. Hadn't some of the men started work digging out a fully underground shelter, one that would eventually connect to the bunker? They had used one of the outbuildings to conceal the trapdoor entrance, although I couldn't remember which one, but they'd had to give it up – something to do with the ground being too hard. Had that been a cover? Had Elijah had them build a tunnel instead, some secret way in and out of Halcyon?

'Here's what's going to happen,' I said, sounding more confident than I felt. 'I am going to find the entrance to the tunnel, and unlock it. Then, I'm going to send my sister-wives and Mim through to you. Once they're safe, you can come in and do what you need to do. Get the kids out first, then whatever you need to do with the rest of them.'

'Aoife, don't be ridiculous,' said Malcolm, coming as close to the fence as he could. 'That's far too dangerous. Anything could happen to you. We'll find another way to get you out, I promise. We have specialists coming in now, professional negotiators, they're twenty minutes away. Please just wait here with us.'

I shook my head. It felt good to say no.

'This will be quicker.'

We had erected some of the sheds and outbuildings ourselves when we first moved to Halcyon, although there had been an abundance of them even before then, remnants of the farm which had been here before us. If some of the members of Heaven on Earth were annoyed that they had to sleep in rusty caravans when our stores got to enjoy the comfort of a real element-proof building they never said, but I imagined a few might have had some private thoughts of complaint to be confessed and repented later. For a relatively small community who had renounced all worldly possessions, we did seem to require a large amount of storage space. Once they were built, I never made it my business to go inside. That was too operational for someone of my status, and anyway, what would I possibly need? Even Ruth, whose job it had been to tend to the animals, didn't have to rummage round for chicken or cow feed herself. Someone was assigned to do that for her and leave whatever she might need in a convenient place. Much like Elijah's office, the outbuildings of Halcyon were a series of closed doors which I had never really cared to look behind. Unlike Elijah's office, though, the thought of exploring the outhouses had never once crossed my mind. I wondered what awful things that might say about me. Did it make me a snob, or just brainwashed? And which was worse?

The first shed I tried was held closed by a great rusted padlock. I had neither the time nor the inclination to go searching for a key, so I scrabbled around on the ground, turning over pebbles and bits of moss until I found a suitably heavy rock. It felt reassuringly solid in my hand. Breath held, I bashed the padlock with all of my strength, but as rusted as it was, it didn't budge. I raised the rock once again, ready to give it a second try, when I was struck with an idea. Feeling carefully around the padlock I located the flimsy hook it was attached to and swung at that instead. It snapped off easily, the closed padlock still swinging, and I pulled open the door. It was far too dark for me to make out any of the shapes, so I pocketed my rock and got to my knees so I could feel around for any trap doors. The floor of the shed was gritty with dust and dirt, and I could feel the undersides of my fingernails growing thick with grime. I found a couple of towels – cold and damp – and other bits of clutter, but no handle or join which might indicate a passage. I gave up and moved on to the next outhouse, a larger one where I knew we stored some of the inherited farming equipment which no one had got around to fixing yet. It seemed a likely enough spot for a trap door, but the floor was poured concrete throughout.

As I searched, I could hear the sounds of rising tension coming from the crowd inside Halcyon. They were obviously anxious for some action to be taken. I thought of my sister-wives waiting in my bedroom and moved on quickly to the next outbuilding. I was running out of options as well as time – there was only one more spot to check after this, and if it wasn't there then I had either missed it, or it had been entirely blocked up. There was a padlock on this door too, but it was already unlocked. I worried that might mean there was somebody inside, but when I pushed the door open I found the building empty except for towering piles of plastic bags filled with raw wool. Wool and grain had spilled out onto the floor and embedded themselves into the palms of my hands as I felt for a hatch or a door. I was getting ready to give in and try the final outbuilding when my finger caught on the sharp edge of a metal hinge. Desperate, I pushed a pile of bags to one side to reveal a thick sheet of plywood with a rope handle. I gripped the rope tightly and pulled but my position on the floor made it difficult to raise the board, which was jammed tightly. I was about to push myself up to stand when I heard the door swing open.

Part Three

Chapter Forty-Three

Mim

'Mim?' said Mel, 'is that right?'

Mel was to be my new carer, and her Scottish accent was so strong I had to strain to understand a single word she said.

I nodded.

'Well, that's not one I've heard before, and I've heard a lot of funny names in my line of work. Is it from your,' she paused, 'church?'

When she said the word 'church' she lifted her hands so they were level with her shoulders, and waggled her fingers. I didn't understand the gesture – it turned out there were a lot of things I didn't understand – and that made me bristle. But my social worker Caro, the lady who had taken me from the hospital to the group home, and then to Mel's house, had told me to be on my best behaviour, and so I smiled nicely.

'It's a Christian name, from the Bible,' I said. 'It's short for Jemima, who was one of the daughters of Job.' I paused before adding, 'From the Book of Job.'

I stopped talking when Mel's eyes began to glaze over, but I didn't mind too much. Everyone who went on mission trips to Abercraig and beyond said people were rarely receptive at first, and that you had to keep trying. I decided then to treat my sojourn from Halcyon as a mission trip. It would be difficult, I knew that, but it would give some purpose to this new season of my life. And it would give me an extra reason to be as nice and pleasant as possible; I was representing Heaven on Earth, after all.

'Well,' said Mel, 'that's very nice, I'm sure. You've a very posh voice you know, Mim. When they said you were all living up by Abercraig, I thought you'd have a nice Highland accent.'

Before I could tell her that we'd moved to Halcyon when I was ten, and that before then we'd lived in England, and that actually I had never been to Abercraig, Mel started speaking again.

'And what's that you've got in your wee bag?'

She pointed at the reinforced shopping bag I was clutching, her finger as pink as the sausages we'd eaten the evening before at the group home.

'Just my toothbrush and toothpaste,' I said, 'and some pyjamas they gave me when I left the hospital.'

Mel sighed and shook her head.

'And is that all? Just those bits and the clothes on your back?'

I nodded.

'You poor lamb. Not to worry, my daughter is about your size, and I've set you aside all of the clothes she doesnae wear any more.'

'Won't your daughter mind?'

'*Won't your daughter mind?*' Mel mimicked, laughing, 'Naw, she's off at the uni now, down Dundee, got a student loan to buy herself all the new clothes she fancies. Now you get yersel up them stairs and have a try of some of those clothes, and you can give me a fashion show. That's what Jodie used to do, when she was wee.'

All this time we had been standing in the centre of Mel's living room. It reminded me a little of the living room John and Helen used to have before we moved to Halcyon, except the sofas at Mel's were made of a shiny white material, and there was a television in the corner. There were some framed photographs on the wall, of Mel and a girl who I presumed was Jodie smiling against a woodland background with their shoes off. I must have been staring a little too long because Mel took me by the shoulders and turned me around until I was facing the door to the hallway, and then gave me a gentle push towards the stairs.

'Off you go then,' she said, 'your room is the first door to the right.'

I took the stairs one at a time, fear of falling keeping me from going any faster. My stomach started to flip when I was barely halfway up, and my heart began to race. I kept going though, up and up, one wool-stockinged foot and then another, until I reached the top. My body, that is my stomach and my heart, had been entirely out of control since the night we all left Halcyon. At first it frightened me, especially because it was accompanied by an overwhelming sense of impending doom, but then I realised what was going on, that it was God giving me a warning, telling me to look out, and that made it less frightening. It's always good to be ready for things, and knowing that God is still looking out for me despite the fact I'm living away from the rest of His True Church is a relief too.

I wondered, as I turned the handle on the door of my new bedroom, what danger lay ahead. The room itself was pretty bare, which was nice; white walls with bobbly paper, thin blue carpet, a wooden bed made up with flowery sheets, a lamp, and a wardrobe. Nothing to worry about yet, but my heart and stomach wouldn't stop fluttering. I wanted desperately to curl up on the bed and lie there until I felt normal again, but if I knew one thing it's that when God gives you a challenge, you have to face it. And so I opened up the wardrobe to see what kind of clothes Jodie had left behind.

It became very clear as soon as I pulled out the first item of clothing what God's warning had been about this time; the denim skirt in my hand looked as though it would barely cover my behind. The fear rising, I lay the skirt on the bed and looked for something longer, but to my horror the only things in there that would reach to my calves were two pairs of trousers. My breath came in jagged gasps as I pulled out immodest garment after immodest garment: tops with straps as thin as pieces of string, or necklines low enough to show my chest. I wanted to cry out, 'there's a problem here', but I had hardly got the first word out when I imagined Mel's mocking voice in my head and stopped myself. The words which were stuck in my throat turned into a hard lump, and before I knew it I was weeping and so loudly and forcefully that I could hardly breathe. I had never cried like that in my life. By the time Mel had made her way upstairs I was practically screaming.

'Jesus Christ, Mim, what's going on up here? Why are all of your lovely new clothes all over the floor?'

I did not answer. I felt Mel standing over me and I knew that I should be ashamed, but the more I cried the harder it became to breathe, and the more terror I felt. When she pulled me up by the arm I allowed myself to rise, but I still could not stop weeping. My neck snapped back as she took me by the shoulders and shook me, the shock of it stopping me mid-wail. I had been shaken like that before, and the familiar jolt and grip returned me to my senses.

'Pull yourself together, woman,' said Mel, her voice quivering, 'and tell me right now what all of this crying is about.'

I swallowed and pointed to the pile of clothes which lay in a creased and tangled mess across the floor and bed.

'The clothes? What's wrong with them?'

'They're not modest,' I said, fighting to keep any more tears away, 'and there are trousers, which aren't appropriate for me, because the Bible says that "a woman shall not wear a man's garment, nor shall a man put on a woman's cloak, for whoever does these things is an abomination to the Lord your God."'

Mel rolled her eyes.

'And what does the Bible say about crying on like a mad woman?'

I didn't answer. Instead, I closed my eyes and silently recounted the verse from the Book of Revelation which Elijah had read to us all so many times, and which had given us all so much comfort. *He will wipe away every tear from their eyes, and death shall be no more, neither shall there be mourning, nor crying, nor pain any more, for the former things have passed away.* I let the words fill my heart.

'Just what I thought. Now go and wash your face and brush your teeth. Then I think it's time for you to go to bed.'

I nodded and took my toothbrush and toothpaste into the bathroom. I hadn't eaten anything since lunch at the group home, and it couldn't have been later than six o'clock, but I was happy to follow Mel's instructions.

When the bathroom door was safely closed, I stood and looked at my reflection in the mirror above the sink. I was pale, and my eyes were red and puffy with tears. I ran the tap and splashed my face with cold water before dabbing it dry with a rough pink towel. When I returned to the mirror my face looked pinker, but I didn't study myself for too long; the last thing I wanted was to end up becoming vain. Instead, I ran the tap again and wet the bristles of my new toothbrush. I left the toothpaste on the side of the sink; we had no toothpaste in Halcyon because of the fluoride turning your brain to mush, and when the nurse at the hospital had insisted I use it my mouth had felt as though it was full of ice. Just to be safe, I squeezed what I thought looked a reasonable amount of paste out of the tube and into the sink, so if Mel were to check it would look like I'd used it. I knew that was both wasteful and deceitful, but my week in the hospital and my day in the group home had taught me how strongly some people felt about the strangest things, including horrible minty toothpaste. And anyway, it's not really wasteful if the thing you're not using is something dangerous like toothpaste, and you can't be deceitful to a sinner.

I didn't sleep at all that first night, but it's been a few weeks since I've been with Mel and sleeping comes a little easier now. I'm still getting used to having a room to myself, but I've started having dreams about Halcyon, so at least I have something to look forward to. I've not told anyone about my dreams; not Mel and especially not Doctor Beck, the therapist they're making me see. I don't tell Doctor Beck anything at all, because of therapists being agents of the Devil, but I do try to be pleasant to her, because I want her to see how well Godly people behave. She talks to me lots about Helen and John, who she calls my mum and dad, and asks if I miss them. I say no, not really, and then she writes something in her little book. Doctor Beck was the one who explained that Helen wasn't allowed to look after me and Ollie at the moment because of everything that went on in the schoolhouse. She says that Helen seems very sorry, and has been helpful to the police, so maybe we'll get to live with her again one day. I know that John is in jail, but I don't know why. Doctor Beck talks to me as though I'm a child, even though I was almost married. Doctor Beck is not married.

In my dreams I return to Halcyon, and everything is how it was before things got bad. People smile and greet me as I walk to the church; they treat me like I've been away on a mission trip. Aoife and Ruth don't speak to me in the dreams, and when Deborah speaks it's to talk about teaching the younger children. Sometimes the dreams feel more real than real life does, and I wish I could think about them during the day. But thinking about Halcyon through the day makes me feel sad, because I know it's not really there any more, and guilty, because I know it's my fault Halcyon is gone. I'm too scared to ask anyone about Deborah or

Ruth or Aoife – I don't really know how to feel about them now – so I don't know if they feel the same way.

When I'm not thinking about Halcyon, I'm thinking about school. Mel wanted me to start straight away, but the social worker said that it's too close to the Christmas break and there's no point, and I should start in January. Mel's house is near to the school, and in the mornings and afternoons I watch the flocks of teenagers as they swarm around the building and its surrounding streets. They jostle and shout and swear, and it makes my heart race, but I can't look away. Mel takes me to the library to look at textbooks and makes me watch documentaries on television, but they make my head spin. She also makes me watch other television programmes with her, because she says I need to learn about the real world if I don't want to get eaten alive by the other kids. I don't like those programmes, and spend a lot of my time covering my eyes and ears to avoid being exposed to sinful things. When I told her I'd never been to school before, even before I came to Halcyon, she said that explained a lot.

I hear her talking about me to Jodie and her other friends on the phone. She has a lot of friends, so sometimes I hear her telling the same story over and over again. *You'll never guess what Mim said today*, she'll say, or *that girl, honestly, it's like she's been dropped from space*, and then she'll relay something I've said or done, usually something I hadn't even thought twice about, and laugh. I try not to let it upset me, because of course I deserve it. I've been praying a lot, and I think God is telling me that this is my punishment for destroying Halcyon and scattering the members of Heaven on Earth to the winds. I lie in bed and imagine going back in time, running up to Elijah and John talking outside the farmhouse and telling them that they need to leave now, and begging them to take me too. I pray that when my punishment is over, I can be the one to bring us back together again.

Chapter Forty-Four

Deborah

Once the police pulled down the fence, things moved quickly, and my memories of the night are jumpy and disjointed. I seem to remember sitting in hospital *before* sitting in the police car, but I don't recall actually being driven anywhere or speaking to anyone until the next morning. The smell of smoke mixes with the smell of bleach. Over the days that followed, countless people – doctors, nurses, detectives – greeted me in a way that suggested we had met before or mentioned previous conversations which I could have sworn had never happened. I've had to piece things together from what I've been told, and what I've read in the papers or seen on television.

Elijah had apparently instructed John to hold the fort before leaving on foot shortly before the police broke in. I remember John, loyal to the end, looking around for Elijah as he was bundled into a police car, the way his voice changed from desperate to angry when he realised he'd been had like the rest of us. It's a fond memory, the only fond memory I have from that night. Of course, Elijah never came back to Halcyon. Instead, he stole a car parked somewhere just outside of Abercraig and was arrested the following day at Glasgow airport after trying to board a flight to Turkey. It turned out that Elijah had been raiding Heaven on Earth's coffers regularly for over a year and using the donated money to buy whatever kind of amphetamine he could get his hands on. Before that, he'd been siphoning money off for a running-away fund – a few hundred here, a couple of thousand there, and it had all added up. The picture they showed of him on the news was a mugshot taken after his arrest, so I suppose I shouldn't have been so shocked by how much he looked like a criminal. He had the start of a black eye, and a puffy gash on his cheek. His dark beard, which had once lent him such an air of respectability and authority, made his face look sunken and cruel. I felt embarrassed that that was the version of him the public was going to see, not for Elijah, but for myself. People would look at him, I thought, and wonder how we could have believed a word he said. How so many people could have trusted a man like that. And, now that I was back in the real world, I wasn't even sure I could have given them an answer. All my reasons for joining the church, then staying there, for marrying him and having his babies and getting up and getting on day after day trapped under his thumb, seemed deficient all of a sudden. Thinking about them was like interrogating a dream, and coming to realise that nothing made any sense.

I wondered if something about Halcyon had stopped us from seeing anything as it really was. When I first looked at myself in the mirror in the hospital, I couldn't believe my eyes. I looked gaunt and pale, and so frail that I could not believe that my body was able to support itself, let alone the baby I was carrying. Back in Halcyon I had thought of myself as plump, glowing, the picture of maternal health. Even my hair, which was easily long enough for me to see without a mirror, was suddenly as dry as straw. I had even pictured its colour wrong. In my head I had hair like spun gold, but in reality it had turned a sort of mousy beige, streaked with fine strands of grey. I looked so much like an old woman that the police officer was visibly stunned when I told him I was twenty-six.

They made me stay in the hospital for almost a week. I lay there quietly on my drip, trying to feel my strength returning. Whenever a kindly nurse suggested I take a little walk up and down the corridor I would shake my head. I only rose on my own to use the toilet, which I allowed myself to do twice a day and where I would stare at my reflection in the full-length mirror on the back of the door as I relieved myself. Sometimes I'd be wheeled off to the maternity unit for scans and blood tests. I'd never had an ultrasound before, or heard one of my babies' heartbeats. I stared at the small stranger on the screen, fascinated by its tiny movements. The midwives were all very nice to me, but I could tell they thought that I was a negligent mother and I was always relieved to be back in my bed.

One of them started talking about folic acid, and when I looked blankly at her she shook her head. Eventually they said I was well enough to leave. I was given two white paper bags bulging with boxes of pills and forced to change into some clothes which I had never seen before. For the first time since I was seventeen years old, I pulled a pair of tracksuit bottoms over my legs and slipped my feet into some canvas plimsolls. There was a T-shirt too, grey and soft and V-necked, which clung too tightly to the sharp edges of my body. I took a deep breath in as I lifted it over my head. It had the anonymous smell of something that had just been washed in an unfamiliar detergent. As exposed as I felt in my new clothes – too pregnant, too many limbs, too much skin – I liked their anonymity. My social worker, Jade, pushed me in a wheelchair to the front doors of the hospital, and then I had to get out and walk. She took me by the arm, and we moved slowly together towards her car.

I watched in awe as the world outside the window whizzed past us. Beige pebbledash homes, children on scooters, big green parks; I couldn't tear my eyes away. Even the River Ness in November, which was as grey and miserable as any stretch of water could be, swelled my heart. I could have sat there quite happily for hours, watching the world go by, but we had barely been driving for ten minutes when Jade flicked on her indicators and pulled into the car park of a modern-looking apartment building.

'Well,' she said, unbuckling her seatbelt, 'this is us.'

I liked Jade. Her hair was dyed an unrealistic looking red, and she wore it short and spiked upwards. She didn't look like a Jade, and I liked that too; I never thought I looked like a Deborah. I wondered how old she was – maybe in her late twenties, so just a little older than me? Or Ruth's age, or Aoife's? My frame of reference was limited. Unlike the social workers I remembered from childhood, she seemed competent, and I trusted her. She opened her door and came around the side of the car to open mine.

It was a women's refuge, the sort of place I might have stayed as a young child with my own mother, with hard-wearing and serviceable furniture and hard-wearing and serviceable staff. Curious faces peered through doorways as I followed Jade and the corridor to my bedroom. The room was set up with a narrow single bed, two camp beds, a cot, and a chest of drawers. Jade must have noticed me staring at them.

'Don't worry, Deb, we'll get you and the kids some bits and bobs to fill those up with. You're not the first lass to come here empty-handed and you won't be the last.'

I nodded.

'When will they get here?'

Jade glanced at her watch, which looked like it was made of red rubber. I fought an almost primal urge to reach out and touch it.

'Not long, an hour or so. The foster carer says they've been asking to see you.'

I smiled. It didn't seem likely that the boys would have been asking for me – Elijah, maybe – but it made me happy to hear it nonetheless. Mainly I was happy that I would get to see them again, and hold them, and play with them, and sleep in the same room as them. All through my time in the hospital I had felt their absence like a physical ache. In all their lives I had never been more than a hundred feet away from them, and then, all of a sudden, I didn't even know where they were. They were playing in rooms I had never seen, being cared for by people I had never met. The thought of it made me feel as though I was being ripped apart from the inside, my heart and gut tearing at the seams, pulled away from me in the unknown direction of my children.

Allegations had been made against the other women who worked in the schoolhouse about the punishments they had apparently been dishing out when I was away. Children telling police about being drenched in cold water and left to stand in the freezing Highland night, beatings with belts and sticks and anything else they could lay their hands on. The police interviewed me at length about that, thinking like Mim had that I must have known, even if I wasn't doing any of the punishing myself. I found myself thinking about it a lot when the lights were off and I was lying on my side in the hospital bed; had I known? I knew Elijah's feelings about sparing the rod and training up. I knew how deeply the women believed in him, how important they felt their task was, how desperate they were to please. I had never seen anything, but how hard had I been looking? Like so many things in Halcyon, maybe it had just been easier not to see it.

I complied with the police in their investigations, telling them that my suspicions had only been raised when I'd been brought in to help look after Ollie just a couple of days before. Once the police were convinced that I was as much of a victim in the whole thing as it was possible to be, I was told that the separation from the children would only be temporary. That knowledge did not make it hurt any less. I had no concept of time. Only of grief, and pain, and shock.

All of Halcyon's children were taken into care, initially anyway. Even Mim, who was of course only sixteen and therefore still a child in the eyes of social services. There was no way of knowing, Jade told me, if or when they would be reunited with their parents. Apparently some people, although no names were named, were still swearing their allegiance to Elijah and Heaven on Earth. The only person I pestered Jade about was Ruth. The last time I had seen her she was being led into a separate police car, wrapped in a foil blanket. Jade said she was looking into it.

I had been in the women's refuge for three days when Shriya, one of the members of staff, called me into the office and handed me the phone. I held the cool plastic against my ear and breathed into the receiver.

'Hello?'

Jade's familiar voice greeted me through the line.

'Hi Deb, how are you? How are the kids?'

Jonah and Noah had barely looked at me since they arrived. They spent their days bouncing off the walls, kicking and biting me and each other and sometimes even the other kids in the shelter the second something didn't go exactly their way. My arms were covered in red welts from their sharp piranha teeth. Serious little Jonah screamed at me so loudly when I asked him to put his new pyjamas on that his face turned purple and the tendons in his neck bulged. Quiet, introverted Noah cried at the drop of a hat, but smacked me away if I came to comfort him. Susannah was the opposite. She clung to me like a limpet, wailing if I put her down, sitting on my knee even when I was on the toilet. I dreaded to think what would happen when my growing bump became too large and I couldn't carry her any more – already I'd developed a chronic back ache and my knees felt ready to explode whenever I stood up.

'We're okay, thanks,' I said, adjusting Susannah on my hip,

'just getting used to everything, you know? Are you still coming down tomorrow?'

'Ah good stuff, Deb, I'm glad to hear it. Yeah, I'll still be down tomorrow but I wanted to call you today because I've just spoken with the police, and they've been able to give me some information about Ruth. I thought you'd want to know as soon as possible.'

I swallowed. Shriya was working at the computer with her back to me and there were no other staff in the office, but I pressed the handset as close as I could to my ear and lowered my voice before speaking again.

'What is it? Where is she? Is she okay?'

'She's all right. She's in police custody. She's going to be extradited to the US – deported. For outstaying her visa. According to the officer I spoke to she has a lot of family over there who have been looking for her, and they're arranging everything with them so she can be released into their care.'

I took a second to digest what Jade had just said.

'And the kids? What happens to them?'

I imagined, briefly, taking them in myself, but I knew they would never allow it.

'They'll be going with her.'

'All five of them?'

'All five of them.'

A sigh of relief left me and I loosened my grip on the phone.

'It really is the best she could have hoped for, Deb, in the circumstances. If you like I can try and arrange for you to talk to her on the phone from the detention centre?'

I didn't know what to say. Earlier that day I would have done anything to speak to Ruth again, but the thought of her being trapped in some dingy detention centre made me want to cry. We'd been apart for less than a week, but already our lives had diverged so rapidly that I couldn't imagine what I would possibly say to her.

Jade must have sensed the uncertainty in my silence, because she spoke again.

'Don't worry, I know how strange this all is for you. Have a think and you can let me know tomorrow when I come to see you, all right? Oh, and before I leave you to your day, there's something else. Aoife's kids are out of care.'

My attention had already drifted away from the call, but the sound of Aoife's name brought it back. Aoife. I couldn't think about her without feeling angry and sad.

'And? Who are they with?'

I knew they couldn't be with her. For a wild moment I wondered if Elijah had somehow managed to get custody, before remembering that he was currently behind bars himself.

'As soon as the story broke about Heaven on Earth and Halcyon, Aoife's sister apparently came forward. She and her wife have taken them all in. She seemed pretty keen to speak to you – Grainne I mean, the sister. But like I said about Ruth, don't worry too much about it right now. There's no pressure there.'

The phone call didn't last long after that. Once it was over, I returned to my bedroom, ignoring Shriya's concerned look and passing the open door of the lounge where Jonah and Noah were playing with some of the other women in a rare moment of peace. It was a good news call, I knew, but my heart felt heavy somehow. We were all scattered. As overjoyed as I was to have Jonah and Noah and Susannah there with me, there was still a gaping hole in my heart where the rest of Heaven on Earth had once lived.

The weeks that followed now seem blurred and lazy. I was supposed to be preparing to apply for work but my CV was almost ten years out of date and, to the disbelief of everyone around me, I have no paperwork whatsoever. Before we moved to Halcyon, we had all burned our passports and birth certificates and cut our national insurance cards in two – except for Elijah, apparently. While others work hard to make me a real person in the eyes of the government, I spend my days in and around the refuge. I have become a minor celebrity amongst the women here, a status which bestows several privileges, namely: everyone is generous with their snacks, and no one makes me share the remote control. Because of this, I am able to spend many hours munching my way through bags of crisps, inhaling their heady saltiness, cleansing my palate every so often with a knock-off brand biscuit bar or a packet of sweets, and staring at the TV. Susannah curled up at my side, I watch as our story is hashed out on daytime television, and then the news, and then on late-night talk shows. Panels of women start sentences with: 'I just feel like, as a mother…'; reporters talk over footage of Halcyon with cold, emotionless voices, focussing on the botched police response; groups of well-spoken men analyse Elijah and the concept of 'new religious movements', or sometimes in relation to male mental health. I don't know which is worse, but still I consume it all, growing frustrated every time the topic changes. I have been asked to appear on one of the programmes, a big one that I remember from before I joined Heaven on Earth, and have decided to say yes.

Chapter Forty-Five

Ruth

During the six years I spent in Halcyon, I was just a woman, and my trials and troubles were the same as my sisters'. As soon as the police broke down Halcyon's fence, I became Black again – with a capital B. Bundled into a police car and taken straight to the station, it wasn't until I spoke to Deborah's social worker much later that I learned Deborah and Mim had been driven directly to the hospital. And after that it was the little things. The young female officer looking uncertain as she handed me a toiletry bag before my first shower, and then snatching it back from my hands and removing the small bottle of shampoo before returning it to me. The new officer who drove me to the airport asking where I was being sent back to, and the surprised look on his face when I said the US. 'Oh, is that right?' he had said. 'I thought it might be somewhere a bit more… exotic.' And suddenly, I had to worry about my children too. Eli and Abraham had been so tiny when we had moved to Halcyon that I had never had to let them out of my sight, and then before I knew it, they were gone. The others had never left Halcyon at all before this. Who were they with? How were they being treated? I hadn't ever needed to speak to them about those kinds of things, and now they were suddenly going to be mixed race in a place where that meant something, without me or even the other Halcyon children who looked like them by their side.

Things have been better since I arrived back home. I try not to think too much about the lost time between leaving Halcyon and landing back in the States. The only good thing to happen in that period, the only part worth remembering, was the look of confusion on the officers' faces when it became clear that I thought the raid on Halcyon was because of me and my outstayed visa. My visa, it turned out, was low down on the long list of infractions – both minor and major – of which Halcyon was guilty. Most of them related to Elijah. He had never insured the car, he paid no taxes on the land, and had recently got himself into a whole lot of trouble with some drug dealers in Aberdeen. My mom and my siblings and their husbands and wives and children met me at the airport. The kids were holding a banner, dotted with love hearts and hand-prints, which read 'Welcome Home Auntie Ruth'. I collapsed at the sight of them, my legs weakening and giving way; I was knocked out by the tidal wave of their love. The only person missing was my father, who had died after a series of heart attacks three years before, and my own kids, who were arriving later. That night we stayed at my little brother's apartment in Des Plaines, because it was close to the airport. My mother and I shared a futon, and lying there in the darkness of my brother's living room, I tried to explain myself.

'Mom,' I said, turning to face her, 'I just wanted to say—'

She untangled her fingers from mine, and pressed them against my lips.

'I don't want to hear it.'

'But Mom, please, I need to explain—'

I felt her shake her head.

'That's all over now, Ruth. We need to forget that it happened.'

Her fingers were still resting on my lips when I woke up the next morning.

The arrival of the kids was tougher than I had expected. They landed a few weeks after me, once the lawyers my family found to take my case managed to convince Elijah that things would go better for him in the courts if he showed some decency by waiving his parental rights. I was surprised that he agreed, but also not so much – any lingering power it might have given him was not as attractive as potential time off his sentence, and I knew that self-preservation was his main priority. For the first few nights none of them slept, and Eli, the oldest at seven, started to wet the bed. It bothered my sisters and my mom that the children didn't call me mommy or momma or even mum, and that in fact, they didn't seem to know what to call me. Mom and I had stayed those weeks with my brother; I wanted to stay as close to the airport as possible, and they indulged me. The day they arrived we made the long journey to my childhood home together. All the siblings had moved out, so it was just me and Mom and the five kids. Nothing much had changed there, except for the way it felt. When my mother pushed open the front door, I'd expected to experience the same suffocating feeling which used to grip me as a teen whenever I stepped into the house, a feeling I'd been remembering and dreading since I got on the plane. I waited for the familiar rush of anxiety to strike, ready to bat it away, but it never came. The sense of something or someone watching over my shoulder, waiting for me to slip up, which had haunted the house when I last lived there, was gone.

The TV has played a big part in the kids' transition to their new lives. The first words three-year-old Moses spoke to his granny were: 'Excuse me, do you have Peppa Pig in this country?' Which drew a big laugh from everyone but me.

'What on earth is a pepper pig?' I asked him.

He blinked up at me with his big, serious brown eyes.

'She lives in the TV with her family.'

'And how do you know that?' I asked, incredulous. There had been no television sets in Halcyon.

'From Alan and Gemma's house.'

'Oh,' I said. My sister squeezed my hand as the room swayed.

Abigail, who is barely one, hardly seems to notice that anything new is going on. She babbles happily on whoever's knee she is placed, and grasps for her bright new toys with sweet starfish hands. Moses stares, fascinated, as the world continues to reveal itself to him. He clings to his older cousins, who must remind him of the other children at Halcyon. My sister Anthea has promised to take him to the amusement park at Bloomington before Christmas, if the snow holds off.

It's been twelve days now since the kids arrived in Illinois. Eli's bedwetting is less frequent, and all five children have started calling me Momma, a transition which came much quicker than I'd expected. Abraham and Leah still won't sleep in their own beds, but I don't mind that one bit.

Abigail is napping and I'm sitting on the vinyl couch watching Leah and the boys play marble run with their big cousins. The clatter of plastic and the sound of children's laughter is slowly becoming the soundtrack to my new life, and Halcyon is already starting to feel like it happened a very long time ago, to someone very different. There has been no word from anyone back in the UK, which helps Halcyon fade into memory. Mom must have gotten to everybody already, because none of my family mention it at all. They looked for me, they found me, and in their eyes it's all over. My oldest sister, Candice, whispered something about finding a therapist, but the thought of talking about that part of my life to someone who wasn't there feels sacrilegious. How could I explain to someone what it feels like to wake in the night in your childhood bed, only to cry when you realise you're not in a crumbling farmhouse in Scotland? How Halcyon haunts my nightmares, but also colours my dreams?

My mother sends the kids to play in the kitchen, places a cushion on the floor, and turns on the TV. She sits on the couch, comb and scissors in hand, and I settle myself between her knees, adjusting my position on the cushion until I'm comfortable. There are no soap operas on the TV this afternoon, so we watch a home makeover show as she combs out my damp, freshly conditioned hair. By the time it's combed through, we've watched three episodes. In Halcyon I would comb my hair with my fingers, before winding it into a bun.

'I'll just snip those dry ends off, baby,' she says, 'then we can braid it.'

But it's clear to both of us that my hair is too dry, too damaged from years of washing only in water and homemade soap, to be rescued now. She snips and snips, dark coils falling heavily to the floor until I'm sitting in a nest of curls. I hear my mother sigh.

'There's just so much of it. What do you say we just cut it short?'

I nod.

More hair falls, and I can feel the air as it caresses my scalp.

'I'm just going to get Daddy's old razor, to tidy you up.'

I shift in my spot as Mom squeezes past, and then again as she returns with a battery-operated razor in her hand. The buzz of the razor feels strangely pleasant against my scalp, and when she's done my mother passes me her enamel hand mirror so I can look at my reflection. Behind me in the glass I can see her face. She looks anxious, which is unusual.

Elijah hated short hair on women. It occurs to me that the half centimetre of growth on my head is likely the product of the past month, which means that there's not a hair on my head that Elijah has touched. The thought makes me feel weightless, as though I could float away. A silent stream of tears falls down my cheeks.

'Oh baby, it'll grow back,' Mom says, taking the mirror from me. 'I can call Candice and ask her to bring some wigs over when she comes for Mimi and Tyler.'

I nod and wipe away the tears with the backs of my hands. Together we sweep my shorn hair, a relic of another time, into a garbage bag.

The reverence of the moment – even my mother seems to feel it, and is quiet – is interrupted by a squeal of delight from the kitchen.

'Mailman!' shrieks Moses.

His accent is still so British that it's weird to hear him use the American words which have entered his vocabulary since our arrival. Garbage, refrigerator ('fridator'), and of course, mailman. Moses has become entranced by the mailman, and his greatest pleasure is reaching up and unlatching the front of the mailbox in Mom's yard to retrieve the letters. I hear someone open the door for him so he can run out and fetch whatever mail has been delivered.

'Here, Granny,' he says, passing her a handful of flyers before turning his attention to me.

He's only been outside for a minute, but his hands are cold as he rubs them over my buzz cut.

'I want my hair like this!'

'Oh don't you worry, baby,' says Mom as she flicks through the pile of letters, 'I'll keep my clippers out and you'll be—'

I think she is going to say 'next', but instead she trails off into silence. I look away from Moses and up to her. Amongst the colourful fliers and take-out menus there is a fat, white envelope. She's holding it between her thumb and forefinger, as though it's dirty.

'This one is for you, Ruth. It's got an airmail sticker.'

I disentangle myself from Moses and stand to take the letter from her. It feels heavy and thick.

'I'll open it for you,' she says, reaching to take the letter back, but I pull it to my chest.

At that moment, Abigail wakes from her nap and starts to cry. There's a short stand-off before Mom takes Moses by the hand and goes to soothe the baby, and then I am left alone with the letter.

The handwriting on the envelope is messy and unfamiliar. I tear it open to reveal sheets of lined paper, folded and thick with the same large, untidy writing. The edges are ragged where the pages have been torn from a ring-bound notebook.

Dear Ruth, I read, *I hope you don't mind me writing to you.*

I leaf through the rest of the letter, my eyes skimming over words and phrases: *miss you... been tough... prison... not what I expected* until I reach the final page, desperate to see the name, to know for sure who it's from.

I have put my address on the back of the onvilope, in case you want to write back. Or if you like you can call me at the womens shelter, the office number is online. I really hope I get to hear from you again.

Lots and lots of love from Deborah (and Jonah and Noah and Susannah)

XOXOXOXOXOXOXXO

With shaking hands I retrieve the discarded envelope from the floor and turn it round to see the name of the shelter where Deborah is staying. I type the name slowly into the browser of my new cell phone, which is actually my niece Mimi's old one. It all seems too easy, once the webpage loads, to hit the blue call button under the shelter's name.

Chapter Forty-Six

Aoife

'Good to see you on your knees, Aoife.'

I stopped pulling at the rope handle and turned to face my husband. He was holding a lantern in his left hand, and it illuminated the small shed with an eerie yellow light. Looking up at him from my position on the floor, he seemed taller, more imposing than ever.

'I hope you're praying for forgiveness?'

His voice was hard with anger.

'Forgiveness?' I asked.

'Don't play dumb, please,' he said, hanging the lantern on a hook on the wall. 'You're many things, Aoife, but you're not stupid. You know what you've done. We all know what you've done.'

I waited for him to continue. I knew him well enough to be sure that he would.

'John told me that you were sneaking around the whole time I was away, talking to that outsider man. That's a commandment broken, Aoife.'

My cheeks burned with indignation. Had John told Elijah that I'd been having an affair? Why else would he think I was an adulteress, as he was clearly insinuating? Unless he'd come to the conclusion himself.

'Elijah, I—'

'It's commandment number one! How *dare* you?!'

Number one? I knew my commandments off by heart, and the commandment to not commit adultery was number seven. Number one was—

'THOU SHALT HAVE NO OTHER GODS BEFORE ME!'

My ears rang and I fell backwards onto the cold, hard floor. Elijah raised his fist, but instead of landing on me it met with the wooden wall, shaking the outbuilding so much that I feared it would tumble like a house of cards.

'Am I a joke to you?'

His voice was a hoarse whisper, but it still dripped with loathing.

I shook my head. The bravado that had allowed me to stand up to Malcolm had melted to nothing in the face of Elijah's white-hot rage.

'You think you can disrespect me like that and get away with it? You think you can bring the Devil to our door and get away with it? I built this place from nothing and you have single-handedly *destroyed* it. I told you they were going to come for me, and now they're here, because of *you*.'

He stepped towards me and bent down so his face was almost touching mine. His eyes glinted in the light cast by the lantern's dancing flame.

'You have ruined *everything*,' he spat.

I held his gaze and lifted myself up onto my elbows. He was so close that I could almost taste him.

'*We* built this place,' I said, my lips moving within millimetres of his, 'together. And we've ruined it separately.'

He lingered for a moment, and rested his hands on my shoulders. He tilted his head slightly, as if he wanted to get a better look at me – for half a second, I even wondered if he was going to try to kiss me.

'You can believe that if you want to,' he said, 'it doesn't matter any more. Halcyon is dead. Heaven on Earth is dead. If I end up in jail, it will be all your fault.'

Did he remember that our daughter, as well as our home, was called Halcyon? I was about to ask him when he tightened his grip on my shoulders and threw me down to the straw-strewn ground. I heard my head crack against the concrete before I felt it. Through the haze of purple spots which clouded my vision, I watched as he moved towards the door.

'Where are you going?' I asked, instead.

Without looking back at me, Elijah lifted the lantern from its hook, the swinging light casting strange shadows on his face so I could barely recognise him. Purposefully, he lifted the glass shield from the lantern and the naked flame flared. He dropped the lantern into one of the bags of wool and retreated out of the door without a backwards glace.

Stupidly, I felt hurt that he left without saying goodbye.

By the time I have realised what is happening, I have also realised it's too late. The door is closed and bolted, and the fire has spread so that it seems to be coming in from all sides, growing faster than I would have thought possible. Time slows as I try to claw at the trapdoor with desperate, blistering hands, and it still won't budge.

Is this it, then? I wonder, heat rising, smoke rising, fear rising. *Am I about to meet my maker?*

I am surprised to find my mind spinning back, all the way back to the day I met Elijah in the café. He wasn't even called Elijah then; he was still going by his birth name, Ed. My thoughts continue to spool out filling the smoke around me with visions of the past, but in no particular order; memories of my childhood with Grainne lap up against the building of Halcyon, my work promoting Heaven on Earth curls gently around the birth of my children. Constance, Faith, Halcyon, Humility. I wonder if this is what people mean when they talk about your life flashing before your eyes. It's like it's all there, dancing amongst the smoke and the flames.

Is this what martyrdom is? Am I a saint who will arrive in heaven, flesh mortified, ready to take my place at the side of the Father? Or is this just the start of my eternal punishment?

I am coughing now, and breathing is too difficult for me to waste any more energy on the trapdoor. I lie back and close my eyes to pray for salvation but all I can see is him, imprinted on the inside of my eyelids as clear as if he was standing right in front of me. *Was it worth it?* I can't tell if the voice is his or mine, but I see his hand reach out to me. I know he's not there any more, not really, but I still try and raise my arms towards him. They don't seem to move. The other memories have faded away like smoke, and he is all I have left.

Epilogue

Genesis

'That bloke you fancy is in again,' said Sarah, 'if you hurry up you can catch him. His weird mate is already putting his jacket on.'

I looked away so Sarah didn't see me blush, and fumbled with my apron strings while facing the wall. She was younger than me, still at school, and I resented the way she talked as if we were equals.

'I don't know who you're talking about,' I said, tucking a notepad and pencil into my front pocket, 'I don't fancy anyone.'

I turned back around just in time to see Sarah roll her eyes. They were ringed heavily with liner, and her mascara had clumped together so her lashes looked like spider legs.

'Spare me,' she said, 'I don't know why I bother.'

As soon as she left the cramped little stockroom, I flipped open my compact and dabbed some powder on my nose. Then, I took my clip out and shook my hair so it fell about my shoulders in thick black waves. My lips were another matter entirely. I had no lipstick with me, so instead I bit down hard, first on my lower lip and then on the upper one, until they turned red. Then I ran my tongue over them, adding what I hoped looked like a delicate sheen of gloss. It was a Sunday, and he never usually came in on a Sunday.

When I left the stockroom, I was relieved to see that he was still there, sitting at one of the Formica tables with a Rizla in one hand and a packet of tobacco laid out in front of him. His friend hadn't left yet – he was standing there with his jacket on, even though it was July and nowhere near cool enough for a jacket. The friend had a reputation in the café for clicking his fingers to get our attention, and Sarah refused to serve him after his hand lingered on her backside one evening when they were both in alone.

'Anyway, good service today, Ed,' he said, sticking his hands in his jacket pockets. 'I think everything is really starting to come together. Couple of familiar faces from Trinity Methodist, word is obviously spreading.'

Ed moved his head to nod, catching my eye as he did so. He winked.

'Yeah, see you, John,' he said, his eyes still on mine, 'give Helen my best.'

As soon as John was safely out of the door, I collected myself and walked around the counter to his table.

'You know you can't smoke that in here any more,' I pointed to the cigarette he was rolling between his fingers, 'they're really enforcing the new ban, we could get in trouble from the owner.'

My voice shook a little, but Ed smiled.

'I'd hate to get you in trouble,' he said. His own voice was steady and deep. He had no accent – he could have been raised in any upper-middle-class household from Berwick to Brighton.

He ran the tip of his tongue along the paper to seal it, before putting the finished cigarette in his shirt pocket.

'Anyway,' I said, 'can I get you anything?'

The sight of his tongue had felt too intimate, and my pencil shook as I held it poised above my notepad.

'No,' he said, 'I was actually just about to leave.'

'Oh.'

'But I was wondering, what time do you finish today?'

'Me?' I squeaked.

Ed laughed gently, his eyes sparkling.

'Yes, you,' he said, 'what time do you finish? Six?'

I nodded.

Ed dropped a handful of coins into his saucer and headed to the door.

'Great,' he said, 'I'll see you at six.'

I didn't even bother trying to keep the smile from my face as I walked back to the counter. Sarah shook her head.

'Shame you don't fancy him,' she said.

'You smoke?' he asked.

He had been waiting outside the café at six on the dot, the sleeves of his checked shirt rolled up to reveal his forearms. I wanted desperately to say yes, just so I could take the cigarette from his hand and put it between my lips. I imagined him leaning forward to light it for me, cupping his hand around the flame, but I had never smoked in my life and the thought of coughing and spluttering in front of him was unbearable. I shook my head.

'Good,' he said, 'women shouldn't smoke.'

I started to object when Ed laughed, furrowing his brow in what I took to be an impression of myself.

'You're very pretty when you're cross.'

No man had ever called me pretty before, and I laughed along with him. I wanted him to think I was pretty when I laughed, too.

'I'm actually giving it up,' he said, 'too much tax. This'll be my last one.'

'Good for you.' I was unsure how he wanted me to respond. He was fixing me with a thoughtful stare, as though he expected me to do or say something remarkable.

'Do you ever get bored, Aoife?'

My name seemed at home in his mouth, even though I had never introduced myself to him directly. He must have heard it from the girls in the café.

'I work in a café, of course I get bored. Sometimes I feel like I'm bored every day of my life.'

He looked down at me, that same thoughtful look on his face. I hoped that he wouldn't be disappointed by my admission. Didn't only boring people get bored?

'I think,' he said, suddenly very serious, 'that you're made for bigger things. I think that's why you're bored.' He pointed to the thin gold crucifix which hung around my neck. 'You should come to my church some time.'

I nodded, and we began to walk. Ed moved purposefully and I followed, taking two quick steps for each one of his long strides in order to keep up.

'Where are we going?' I asked.

Acknowledgements

Thanks to Lisa Highton, my incredible agent, for her direction and insight. Thank you for championing me and my work, as well as for your wise words and good humour. I think we make a great team.

I am also so grateful to Cari Rosen, my wonderful editor, for sharing her knowledge and for her unwavering support and belief in this book. The editing process shaped *The Wives of Halcyon* into the best version of itself and has made me a better writer.

I firmly believe that I could not have reached this point without the immense support which I have received from New Writing North and the team there, particularly Will Mackie. Winning a Northern Writers Award put me on the trajectory to publication and the team's ongoing support has been life changing. I can't thank you enough for the time and energy you put into developing and championing writers from backgrounds whose voices are so seldom heard in the literary world. You made me believe that there was room for me in this space. Thanks also to The Literary Consultancy for offering the 'Free Reads' prize, and for the generous and constructive feedback which I received from my assigned reader Sally OJ.

To my very earliest readers, Sarah Rowe, Eleanor Bradford, Ellen Mackenzie and Emily Caulton, for your encouragement, feedback, and kind words. Thanks also to my copy editor Lusana Taylor-Khan, whose eagle eyed reading helped to make this a better book.

To Lucy and Olivia and all the fabulous team at Legend Press who have worked so hard to bring this book to the world – thank you for answering my questions and for your ongoing support, expertise, and friendliness.

Thank you to Rose Cooper for creating the most beautiful cover design; I could not have imagined anything more perfect.

To the wonderful North East Novelists community; how lucky am I to get to spend time with such a talented, supportive group of people? Thank you to Grace and Heather for bringing this group together, and for allowing me to be a part of it.

To my lovely colleagues, past and present, at Newcastle University for your endless encouragement and support. Thanks in particular to my managers Hilary and Lucy, and to Charlotte.

I am lucky to be surrounded by wonderful family and friends, too many to name individually, who have been with me throughout the process of writing and publishing this book – I could not have done this without your support and love. Special thanks to my Mam, for being by my side every step of the way, and for raising me to believe I could do anything I put my mind to.

To my husband Aidan, for being this book's biggest cheerleader. Your confidence in me and my abilities has been unwavering and I am grateful beyond words.

To Nell, the sunshine of my life – you are the reason I do everything, and I'm sorry that this book has no pictures.

Follow Legend Press on X
@legend_times_

Follow Legend Press on Instagram
@legend_times